MAGILL'S
LITERARY ANNUAL

1981

MAGILL'S
LITERARY ANNUAL
1981

*Essay-Reviews of 200 Outstanding Books
Published in the United States during 1980*

―――――――――――

With an Annotated Categories Index

Volume Two
Ke-Z

Edited by
FRANK N. MAGILL

SALEM PRESS
Englewood Cliffs

LIBRARY OF CONGRESS CATALOG CARD NO. 77-99209

ISBN 0-89356-281-5

First Printing

PRINTED IN THE UNITED STATES OF AMERICA

KENNEDY AND ROOSEVELT
The Uneasy Alliance

Author: Michael R. Beschloss (1955-   )
Foreword by James MacGregor Burns
Publisher: W. W. Norton and Company (New York). Illustrated. 318 pp. $14.95
Type of work: Biography
Time: 1900-1960, with a concentration on the period 1917-1945
Locale: The United States and London

A dual biography describing the lives and times of Franklin D. Roosevelt and his millionaire friend and adviser, Joseph P. Kennedy

> *Principal personages:*
> FRANKLIN D. ROOSEVELT, thirty-second President of the United States, 1933-1945
> JOSEPH PATRICK KENNEDY, millionaire Wall Street speculator, first chairman of the Securities and Exchange Commission, and Ambassador to the Court of St. James
> WILLIAM RANDOLPH HEARST, newspaper publisher and political manipulator
> FATHER CHARLES COUGHLIN, Detroit parish priest and well-known radio personality during the 1930's
> ARTHUR KROCK, Chief of *The New York Times* Washington bureau, political columnist, and friend of Kennedy

Michael R. Beschloss has written a somewhat unusual double biography. he looks at two very powerful and very different men who lived through the same time period (late -nineteenth to mid-twentieth centuries) and whose lives intersected at some points, widely diverged at others. The presupposition of the work is that these two men, Franklin D. Roosevelt (FDR) and Joseph P. Kennedy influenced each others' lives and the nation's future in significant ways and also reflected certain salient tendencies of their age. Beschloss is most successful in dealing with the two individuals, and Roosevelt's impact on Kennedy's life, somewhat less so in viewing them as representatives of their times, and least successful when he attempts to show Kennedy's influence on the policies of FDR.

The contrasts between the men are clearly described and interesting. Roosevelt was outstandingly successful as a politician but far less fortunate as a businessman. Kennedy saw his political hopes fail repeatedly but had a Midas touch with things financial. It certainly was not inevitable that they would meet, but since they did, their lives make a fascinating contrast which illuminates the interplay of moneyed men and political power in American government.

The author sees two distinct definitions of public and private leadership in America: the visionary tradition of Jean Jacques Rousseau which posited the subordination of individual interests to a broader public interest; the other, a more pragmatic tradition growing from John Locke and Adam Smith in which individuals would follow their own private interests and the common good would naturally be enhanced. FDR, Beschloss argues, represents the former view, if imperfectly, and Kennedy the latter. Since neither man carried forward his views with absolute consistency (American business and politics do not lend themselves to ideological purity) they frequently do not fit the author's Procrustian bed. Nevertheless, it is a useful device.

Both men were from families which combined political and business interests, but in rather different ways. FDR came from the Hyde Park background of old money and *noblesse oblige*. Kennedy, with far smaller financial resources, grew up with the rough and tumble of Irish ward politics in Boston and its creed of personal loyalty and gratitude. They both had attended preparatory schools, Groton for Roosevelt and Boston Latin for Kennedy, who then followed FDR to Harvard eight years later. One senses early in the work the differences between the two men brought about by class and background. Roosevelt "belonged" at Harvard. He "fit in" and Kennedy did not. The reader can infer that it was early insecurities that caused Kennedy's driving need to succeed in business. Financial security for his family became, for him, the ultimate test. FDR did not have to succeed in business and when he attempted it, his failures were frequent but did not seem to be particularly important to him. At the same time, his political successes, emotionally more necessary, were more quickly forthcoming.

The two men met for the first time when Roosevelt was Assistant Secretary of the Navy and Kennedy was managing the United States Steel shipyard at Fore River, Massachusetts. It was, or should have been, an instructive meeting for Kennedy. A dispute between the Argentine government and U.S. Steel over payment for ships had held up delivery and FDR smilingly warned Kennedy that the Navy would not stand for any more delays. Kennedy, thinking that he was dealing with "just another rich man's son, . . . a smiling four-flusher," flatly refused to deliver without payment. He returned to the yard to see Navy tugs with armed marines cast off the lines and tow the Argentine warships out to sea. Roosevelt in power was a hard man to push.

Both men used the 1920's, as many did, to try to get rich or richer. FDR's schemes, some of which the author believes ran fairly close to the legal line, frequently came to naught. Kennedy succeeded in banking, motion pictures, and the stock market, pulling out of the market prior to the 1929 crash, and ended the decade a millionaire with friends in politics, journalism, business, and finance. FDR had returned to his first love, politics, winning the governorship of New York in 1928 and becoming the leading contender for the Democratic presidential nomination in 1932.

It was during the 1932 campaign that Roosevelt and Kennedy became friends. Kennedy, fearing a Depression-caused revolutionary upheaval which would threaten the financial security of his family, saw FDR as the one man who could save the country. He contributed money, traveled with the presidential campaign train, and was useful in pressing Roosevelt's case with William Randolph Hearst. Friendly with Raymond Moley, he joined that group of business-oriented advisers who would be important, especially during the first two years of the New Deal.

One receives the distinct impression from Beschloss that FDR was the "user" in this and other relationships, setting people aside when his need for them had passed. The author's sympathy seems to be with Kennedy who had to wait a year for his first real reward, the chairmanship of the newly formed Securities and Exchange Commission (SEC), rather than an immediate appointment as Secretary of the Treasury which he coveted.

The controversy over Kennedy's appointment to head the SEC was stormy. To appoint one of the sharks of Wall Street to supervise it was the height of folly to many 1930's liberals. His behavior while chairman disarmed his critics, convinced business of the need of some kind of regulation, and, according to the author, set the SEC on an intelligent regulatory course. With his success came more frequent visits to the White House for social / political meetings and strategy sessions. These were presided over by FDR with his biting wit, often at Kennedy's expense, and frank, often loud exchanges of opinion. One senses that it was personal rather than programmatic approval that kept Kennedy loyal to FDR through disagreements over the Second New Deal, and, increasingly as the decade concluded, over foreign policy. He was used by the president as an ambassador to independent power barons such as Hearst and Father Charles Coughlin. In neither case could he keep these men from ultimately opposing the New Deal and its leader, but he delayed the fractures and kept them as muted as possible.

After substantial maneuvering by himself and his friends and a lengthy period after the 1936 election when he was virtually ignored by the White House, Kennedy was appointed as Ambassador to the Court of St. James in early 1938. The naming of an East Boston Irish Catholic to be Ambassador to England was partly FDR's "great joke," and partly shrewd politics. It marked for Kennedy a kind of culmination in his drive for respectability and acceptance and also got him out of the country in case he might develop political ambitions toward the presidency in 1940, which was very likely.

The two men were probably furthest apart on issues during this period. Kennedy was accused, with some justice, of being overly supportive of the appeasement policies of British Prime Minister Neville Chamberlain and, after 1938, of being excessively friendly to the Nazi German leadership. He believed, from early 1940 on, that England would probably lose the war and certainly could never win it. He urged on the administration any form of accommodation with Germany. Roosevelt himself was increasingly convinced that all-out aid to Britain would enable her to survive and as time went on, that the United States would probably have to join the war against the Axis. His ambassador feared this for his country and for his family and made no secret, in private, of his opposition to the President's policies. He would not, however, satisfy his friends in the America First movement and elsewhere by going public with his criticisms. He was increasingly ignored by the State Department and Roosevelt, who carried on personal diplomacy with the new Prime Minister, Sir Winston Churchill, while consulting only rarely with his ambassador. Kennedy, however, supported FDR for a third term and, although occasionally critical of Roosevelt in ways that came to public attention, led no crusade for the isolationists against aid to Britain, Lend Lease, and increasing involvement in England's cause. His continuing loyalty to a man whose policies he had come to despise grew either out of a general political and personal loyalty or the knowledge that the political hopes which he had for his boys would be shattered by an open break with the President.

With Pearl Harbor, Kennedy again wanted a significant government post, but his entreaties were turned down. His sons went to a more violent battle. His eldest was killed in action in 1944, a son-in-law died in battle a month later, and another son was seriously injured. The war that he had so feared had cost him deeply.

Also mortally wounded was his relationship with FDR. For reasons that the author can never make completely clear, those in the White House and others close to FDR who disliked or distrusted Kennedy had apparently gained the upper hand. Kennedy had been too friendly to those in and out of the country who hated Roosevelt, had opposed him too often, and now his earnest pleas for some important task to help win the war vanished without a response. The men met only rarely during the war and Kennedy began the investments in real estate and oil that would make him one of the wealthiest men in the world. Unable to make a continuing impression in politics, he returned to the thing that he did best. There was, however, a frustration there to which he gave voice some years later. He had wanted power, he said, and thought that money would give it to him. After making money, however, he discovered that it was really politics that gave power. He could never reach the rung on the political ladder that would give him what he sought.

The author worked extensively in manuscript collections and interviewed approximately twenty public figures. His citations, however, are frequently too general to be helpful and there are none of the usual numbered footnotes. It is well that Beschloss does not have to deal more deeply with military and naval matters. The book began as a senior honors paper at Williams College and has been gracefully expanded. It tells readers in some detail of the lives of two important men, one much more important to history than the other. It is not, however, particularly illuminating in bringing new material to bear on what is already known about them as individuals and about their times.

Charles Johnson

LABORS OF LOVE

Author: R. V. Cassill (1919-   )
Publisher: Arbor House (New York). 275 pp. $10.95
Type of work: Novel
Time: Summer, 1975
Locale: Cape Cod

A summer's events, including the terrorist murder of a woman he hardly knows, shock Troy Slater out of his complacent adultery and into writing his long-delayed novel, the events and characters of which are strikingly similar to Cassill's

> *Principal characters:*
> TROY SLATER, a successful editor and stalled writer
> NANCY SLATER, a former dancer and shrewd wife
> MARGARET GILL, Troy's whimsical younger lover
> W. T. BOWMAN, a wealthy, successful novelist
> JAN SAVERY AND GENEVIEVE GEORGE, Troy's aging colleagues
> JOKAANEN OBER, Bowman's beautiful mistress whose death affects everyone

In a *New York Times Book Review* column in 1967, R. V. Cassill wrote that "Of all the arts, fiction is the one which most broadly connects the homely, private, errant, ridiculous and immature phases of our lives with the ripened abstractions of philosophy." In his most recent novel, *Labors of Love*, Cassill makes just such a "broad connection," but the reader may not be convinced that the "homely, private, errant, ridiculous and immature phases" of Cassill's protagonist are convincingly connected with the "ripened abstractions of philosophy."

At the end of *Labors of Love*, Troy Slater has what one must judge as an epiphany. Cassill writes,

> . . . in the change that had come over him, past and present tense had no useful distinction. Now he loved everyone he had ever loved, back to his eighth grade crush on one Pamela Stone. But love had ceased to be an appetite. He wanted to possess nothing that would stand in the way of his duty.

Unfortunately, Cassill has not made very clear what Slater's *duty* is, and it remains unclear whether Slater has achieved selflessness or is merely rationalizing his old habit of doing what he wants to do.

A page earlier, Cassill writes that Slater could not save his children "by love or caution." To save the children, himself, or his wife, he must do "something more radical." Then, "To be faithful to his little family, he had first to be faithful to the decision that would dissolve it." Again, the reader looks for necessary—and logical—connections. What are the forces at work which justify this paradox? Has Cassill demonstrated this necessity, or merely asserted it?

The question is not whether Cassill, or his fictional character, believes what Cassill writes, but whether the novel embodies these meanings. Gratuitous realizations, no matter how high-minded, can neither delight nor instruct. An epiphany must contain realization inherent in the stuff of the fictional experience.

The fault with *Labors of Love* is not with the writer's craft but with his grasp. What this fine writer has achieved in twenty chapters of good, often delightful, writing is essentially trivial, and no amount of philosophic "realization" can save the book from that triviality. The plot involves Troy Slater's rekindled desire, or need, to write. Ostensibly, the violent death of a beautiful, mysterious woman he scarcely knows has something to do with his return to the typewriter. His relationships with two women—his wife and his mistress— also appear to be catalysts, but the reader may have trouble in discerning anything like necessary connections between these several story threads.

The opening page of the novel establishes Slater's paralysis. Slater's daughter Ursula accuses him of *not reading*. He is on the deck of his Truro summer home "with his eyes fixed on the great blue emptiness of the Cape Cod sky." His wife, Nancy, is off at Harvard taking a business course, and, although Troy Slater regularly hides behind the excuse of work, he is reading not manuscripts but "the signs of the times." He is, Cassill tells the reader, looking "for an exception in the small print," and Slater's imagination has provided an angel in the sky signaling appropriate warnings. Even here, however, Cassill goes further than the situation warrants. Slater thinks of writing his story and can think only of "a fictional ending with decisive violence . . . as a resolution to the grim absurdity about to stifle him."

The grim absurdity turns out to be no more real than the angel in the sky. Troy's mistress, a younger woman named Margaret Gill, has indicated her intention to abandon their love nest in Cincinnati and return to New York "to be near you until you have settled with Nancy." Margaret's decision threatens to disrupt Troy's idyllic situation, but he is in no danger from "the grim absurdity" Cassill speaks of. Nothing is "about to stifle him." Cassill's first chapter engages the reader's affection and sympathy for Troy Slater, who, like most people, wants to have his cake and eat it too—and unlike most, admits as much. The chapter neatly sets up conflicts, establishes the identity (if not character) of important people, and provides several important continuity devices. For example, on the first page, Cassill describes Slater's daughter as "furtive as a chipmunk," and the incursions of the neighbors' cat to chase chipmunks recur regularly. Late in the book, while Slater's wife and mistress talk about their situation, the Bronstein's cat passes the deck "with something dangling helpless from its mouth." The neighbor, a psychiatrist, finds his way into Troy Slater's dreams, and so does the cat.

Cassill's first chapter foreshadows several events important to the novel's conclusion. Cassill suggests similarities between Nancy Slater and the cat and between Margaret Gill and the chipmunk, for Nancy kidnaps Margaret— physically subduing and binding her—to bring her home, helpless, to Troy.

A letter (Chapter 1) from the seemingly guileless but admittedly "strange" Margaret Gill mentions the possibility of her being "mugged by junkies in this ratty neighborhood." Later, Margaret suffers that very fate in her New York neighborhood, and the violent rape begins a new phase of her life in which she disassociates herself from Troy and, as Nancy puts it, "goes public," first with her rapists and later with homosexual occupants of a Cape Cod lodging known as the Deep Six.

The fictional ending "with decisive violence" which Slater imagines in the novel's opening chapter comes to pass with the terrorist murder of a lovely German woman named Jokaanen Ober whom the Slaters have known briefly in the company of a wealthy and successful novelist W. T. Bowman. Nancy Slater makes Bowman's acquaintance on the beach and brings him, his son Vachel, his wife, and his mistress Jokaanen home to meet her husband. Slater and Bowman are both writers, and both have been Marines and both are involved with more than one woman. Bowman, however, is more successful in all three areas than Troy Slater; he was a behind-the-lines fighter during World War II, has written many books, and has a large following, and lives amicably with wife and mistress—in the kind of arrangement Slater would like for himself.

Bowman invites Slater to go target shooting with him, and apparently wishes to help Nancy in her effort to make Troy begin writing again. In the meantime, Nancy, although originally convinced Bowman is a phony because he claims to be a Christian despite his multiple marriages and love affairs, has a sexual encounter with him and, consequently, feels freed from physical dependence upon, or loyalty to, Troy. With Bowman, she does not hold back as she has with Troy, and her orgasmic experience effects a change in her apparently as great as the change in Troy.

Too often the reader must accept events and subsequent changes on Cassill's word alone. The turning point for Troy Slater appears unworthy of him—and of Cassill. Slater goes looking for Margaret at the nudist beach frequented by homosexuals. He remains fully clothed and attracts the attention of a woman whom he had threatened with violence at a riding stable the day before. At the woman's urging, a group of naked young men move in on Slater with threats of sexual violence.

Apparently, Cassill wants the reader to regard Slater's reaction to this threat as his "finest moment." Earlier, on the firing range with Bowman, Slater fell ill; now, he proves himself a real Marine. As he prepares for battle, Slater recalls someone's telling him to trust God and play. Cassill writes: "In the spirit of the Marines, the most playful branch of the services, he was going to take out an eye, rip off an ear, he thought happily." He assaults the enemy shouting a battle cry which sounds like his own name "shrieked in the night by a transported girl. TROH-EE! TROH-EE!" For every man, Cassill writes, "there is a perfect war cry and a time to use it." When Margaret spies blood on Troy's shirt, he claims it is a wine stain. "How precious the blood was," Cassill writes, "she would never know."

At the book's end, Troy Slater has lost Margaret who continues, now as at the beginning of the novel, to do what she does for no very good reason, and what she intends to do is to live and travel with an aging homosexual and continue a life of promiscuity. Slater is determined to be faithful to his "little family" by dissolving it—all in the name of that duty he suddenly feels. As Slater's wife and mistress hold their conversation and as the Bronstein's cat plays with the chipmunk, Slater is busy pounding out the pages of his novel—ostensibly the one Cassill has published.

The book lacks a center, and although the reader may be titillated at times, amused at times, and told that the events make some kind of sense, the fact is that changes occur largely because Cassill says so. R. V. Cassill's strengths as a writer probably suit him best for the short story, not the novel; for, despite his skills in dealing with the parts, he has failed in *Labors of Love* to produce a totality which connects human failings with significant ideas about contemporary life. Neither Cape Cod nor the atmosphere of Watergate become real in the book, although Cassill defines his setting by allusions to the events of the summer of 1975.

Leon V. Driskell

THE LADY FROM DUBUQUE

Author: Edward Albee (1928-   )
Publisher: Atheneum (New York). 161 pp. $9.95
Type of work: Drama
Time: The present
Locale: The living room of a house in a prosperous American suburb

An enigmatic play about a visit by a mysterious "Lady from Dubuque" and her black companion to a dying suburban wife, her husband, and their friends

> *Principal characters:*
> SAM, a middle-aged suburban male
> JO, his terminally ill wife
> ELIZABETH, the stylish, handsome "Lady from Dubuque," a mysterious intruder
> OSCAR, her elegant middle-aged black male companion
> FRED,
> CAROL,
> EDGAR, and
> LUCINDA, friends and party guests

After being the dominant American playwright of the 1960's, Edward Albee's production in the following decade consisted of only two full-length dramas, *All Over* (1971) and *Seascape* (1975), and two one act plays, *Counting the Ways* and *Listening* (both 1977), none of which is really comparable, either artistically or commercially, with his earlier successes (although Albee did receive his second Pulitzer Prize for *Seascape*). To begin the decade of the 1980's, Albee has offered a new full-length play, *The Lady from Dubuque*. Given his sparse recent efforts and the thematic experimentation evident in those works, one might expect it to indicate new directions, concerns, techniques, and insights.

This experimentation, however, is not evident. For better or for worse— rather, for better *and* for worse—*The Lady from Dubuque* is a thoroughly typical Albee play, almost a synthesis of his earlier methods and themes. On the positive side, it is theatrically exciting, the timing and pacing are adroit, the characters are vivid and animated, if not complex or always convincing, the dialogue is sharp, potent, biting, clever, and occasionally beautiful, and the emotional climaxes are explosive. On the negative side, however, like so much of Albee's post-*Who's Afraid of Virginia Woolf?* work, *The Lady from Dubuque* is never quite in focus, either intellectually or emotionally. The relationship between the action of the play and the intellectual substructure that supports it seems needlessly ambiguous, perhaps even duplicitous.

Like *All Over*, *The Lady from Dubuque* explores the meanings and effects that a dying character has on those surrounding him / her. Yet, unlike the earlier play, the focal character in this essay on mortality is not hidden behind a hospital screen to expire out of sight, but is kept in the midst of things. Early in the play, during a game of "Twenty Questions," Jo, a dark, slight suburban wife, tells her husband, the other partiers, and the audience, that "Your name is Sam, and this is your house, and I am your wife, and I am dying. . . ." Die she does throughout the play, a little bit at a time, painfully, bitterly, sarcastically, and, finally, gently.

This juxtaposition of the party game with the dying throes of the play's heroine establishes the very uneasy, ambiguous context of the play. The group activity is reminiscent of *Who's Afraid of Virginia Woolf?* Two couples visit Sam and Jo to drink, talk, and play party games. They seem to be old friends who have done this sort of thing for years, yet they treat one another with unrelieved disdain. "Where else," says Fred, the most unpleasant of the unpleasant crew, "can you come in this cold world, week after week, as regular as patchwork, and be guaranteed ridicule and contempt?" The dynamics of the group are puzzling and unnerving. Is the steady stream of bitter vituperation that Jo heaps on her guests a reaction to her illness or was she always a bitch? Is the constant barrage of sophisticated hostility among the guests likewise a defensive reaction to Jo's pending demise or has this been the group's style from the beginning? There is no way the reader or audience member can know.

In *Who's Afraid of Virginia Woolf?* the brutal, manipulative games played by the two couples had a purpose and direction that was gradually revealed in the course of the play. Although undeniably unorthodox and neurotic, George, Martha, Nick, and Honey do eventually emerge as believable, understandable human beings. No such design is evident in *The Lady from Dubuque*; it is extremely unlikely that anyone would actually behave in real life the way the characters do in this play. The guests are at best types: Fred is the crude, bigoted, loudmouth lush; Carol, his girl friend, the "dumb floozie"; Edgar, the painfully "niceguy" that nobody can stand; Lucinda, his pitifully mediocre, ordinary wife. Jo and Sam are perhaps more real, yet their personalities are fixed by her illness: she is the bitter, dying wife, he the sympathetic, but increasingly helpless husband. Thus, if we must accept the characters and action of *The Lady from Dubuque* exclusively as "realistic melodrama," we must judge it a somewhat disjointed and unconvincing failure.

Such a facile judgment, however, slights at least half of the play. Despite its realistic surface, there are numerous clues planted throughout the first act to warn us against taking the action too literally. Most importantly, the characters not only talk to one another, but also directly to the audience. Albee states very precisely how this is to be done in a long "Performance Note" that precedes the text: "*It is of utmost importance that the actors make it clear that it is not they, but the characters, who are aware of the presence of the audience.*"

At first, this direct contact with the audience seems like a quirky device, a bit of theatricality inserted into the play for its own sake, with little relation to the action. Nothing that is said to the audience is important in terms of plot, characterization, or theme. For the most part, the asides simply repeat, directly to the audience, what the character has already said to the cast. By the end of the first act, however, Albee's strategy becomes clear. The asides have been necessary to undermine the play's realism and prepare the audience for the thoroughly unrealistic element that will dominate the remainder of the work, the appearance of the "Lady from Dubuque."

The inspiration for the character, as well as the title of the play, comes from the famous facetious remark made by Harold Ross, editor of *The New Yorker*, that he did not edit his magazine for "the lady from Dubuque." Albee's lady— called Elizabeth in the text for reasons never made clear—is, of course, the antithesis of Ross's archetypal mid-Western matron. She is beautiful, elegant, sophisticated, and extremely articulate; she arrives in the company of an equally elegant, handsome, worldly black man named Oscar. When they confront Sam in Act Two, the morning after the party, Elizabeth insists that she is Jo's mother, come to her daughter in her hour of need. Sam denies this vehemently and it does seem most unlikely, especially since Jo's mother had been described in the first act as an "old lady with pink hair" who lived in New Jersey. Almost a fourth of the act is devoted to Sam's insistent, progressively distraught questioning of Elizabeth and her evasive, ironic, provocative responses, fortified by Oscar's jocular, increasingly menacing asides. Sam is further frustrated when his previous night's guests return and, except for the "dumb brunette" Carol, accept Elizabeth's claims. When Sam's frustrations provoke him to physical action, Oscar subdues him easily and Fred ties him up. Sam's final puzzlement / humiliation comes when Jo enters, extremely disoriented, and not only accepts Elizabeth as "mother," but also ignores Sam and is finally carried to bed, presumably to finish dying, by Oscar.

Thus, although Jo's death is the focal event of the play and Elizabeth's visit is ostensibly to her, it is Sam who emerges as the primary character in the play. His reactions to the mysterious visitors give the drama both its movement and its meaning. Whatever is to be learned in the play is learned by Sam and, through him, by the audience.

Sam's development in the second act roughly corresponds to the "typical" behavior pattern exhibited by those facing terminal illness, either their own or that of an extremely close loved one. He begins with puzzlement and simple denial of the "reality" of Elizabeth and Oscar. He demands that they go away and, when that fails, he pleads. This leads to an attempt at "bribery" ("Take whatever you want. Take the stereo; take the television; there are *three* of them, take 'em all"), followed by active hostility, anger, loss of control, and violence. When these fail, helplessness, deflation, and quiet despair set in.

Bye-bye; bye-bye.
   (*A silence. Finally,* SAM *rushes from his chair, over to* JO. ELIZABETH *gestures* OSCAR *not to interrupt.* SAM *kneels by* JO, *grabs her by the shoulders, shakes her. We see that* SHE *is rubber.* OSCAR *watches from his position on the stairs.* ELIZABETH *stays where* SHE *was standing with* CAROL).

                         SAM (*Tears; choking; loss; fury; tenderness*)
Do you want this? Hunh?
   (*Shakes her*)
Is this what you want!? Yes!?

                         ELIZABETH (*Level; gentle*)
Of course she wants it. Just . . . let her go.

                         SAM (*Shakes her*)
Because if this is what you want, I'm not any part of it; you've locked me out. I . . . I
don't exist. I . . . I don't exist. Just . . . *tell* me.
   (JO *manages to look at him, puts her hands to his face, cups it*)

                         JO (*Explaining; gently*)
Please . . . just let me die?
   (SAM *pulls away, stares at her, wracked with sobs. To the audience; explaining*)
Just let me die . . . please?

Through all of his denial and hostility, we get the feeling that Sam really knows who Elizabeth and Oscar are and why they have come to the house. At the end, after Oscar has taken Jo away, there is a kind of reconciliation to the inevitable. Elizabeth ministers to Sam by telling a story about the end of the world. He listens like a little boy before a mother figure (as Jo had earlier). The final vision of death is as a gentle release: "No time to be afraid?" "No! No time! Everything done before you know it."

Elizabeth—or Elizabeth and Oscar together—would seem, then, to be symbolic of death. Perhaps she represents the "gentle" side of death—cessation of pain, peace, resolution, return to the "bosom" of nature—while Oscar, a "dark angel," suggests its violence, harshness, and finality. Both Albee and Alan Schneider, director of the Broadway production, however, have denied such an interpretation, while refusing to confirm an alternate view. Yet, if Elizabeth and Oscar are not symbols, what could they possibly be? Jo's real mother and her paramour? A kooky couple that travels around spooking terminal patients and their families?

This is the kind of apparently contrived ambiguity that has plagued Albee's work since *Who's Afraid of Virginia Woolf?* When Samuel Beckett denies that he knows who Godot is, we believe him, because the play is clearly about "waiting," not Godot, and the identity of Godot is all the more provocative for being unknowable. We feel that Albee knows who Elizabeth and Oscar are, however, and is simply not telling. It seem like willful cleverness rather than metaphysical ambiguity.

This criticism may be too harsh: the problem may be less a matter of duplicity than of artistic indecision. Perhaps the difficulties in *The Lady from Dubuque* lie in the conflict between Albee's desire to present a realistic view of people caught in a tragic situation and his inclination to dramatize abstract ideas about Death, Reconciliation, and Meaning. These two objectives are not necessarily antithetical, but in *The Lady from Dubuque* they clash, as they have clashed in a number of Albee's later plays. All of Albee's successful plays have either been straightforwardly realistic (*Zoo Story, Who's Afraid of Virginia Woolf?, A Delicate Balance*), or honestly symbolic (*The American Dream, The Sandbox, Seascape*). When he has tried to mix the two approaches in a single play, as in *Tiny Alice* or *All Over*, the results have been, at best, provocative confusion, and at worst, pretentious mannerism. *The Lady from Dubuque* escapes the excesses of these previous plays, but the realistic / symbolic split still prevents the play from achieving its dramatic or thematic potential. What could have been Albee's most potent work in two decades is, rather, an intermittently powerful, occasionally provocative, ultimately disappointing play. In this theatrically barren time, however, even flawed Albee stands out.

Keith Neilson

THE LAST DECADE
Essays and Reviews, 1965-75

Author: Lionel Trilling (1905-1975)
Edited by Diana Trilling
Publisher: Harcourt Brace Jovanovich (New York). 241 pp. $9.95
Type of work: Essays

A collection of eleven essays, lectures, and reviews from the last ten years of the life of a respected American literary critic

Since 1950, with the publication of his first collection of essays, the influential *The Liberal Imagination*, Lionel Trilling has sustained, at least in conservative critical quarters, his reputation as being a man of letters in the grand old nineteenth century tradition. As a broad literary and cultural critic, Trilling has expressed his opinion on a variety of literary individuals and cultural issues for the past forty years. To the delight of those who agree with him, and to the chagrin of those who do not, his opinion has almost always been the same one.

In 1955, when his collection *The Opposing Self* was published, that rather placid era applauded Trilling's concern with social reality and shared his distaste for those who wished to escape what he perceived as the conditioned nature of reality by attempting to impose their own conditions. Trilling's old-fashioned Victorian reaction against the perennial romantic preference for artifice over social reality, however, settles dustily on the sensibilities of the 1980's. It is only because Trilling defines "mind" so narrowly that he can in this current collection of essays decry what he calls the contemporary "ideology of irrationalism" which celebrates the "attainment of an immediacy of experience and perception which is beyond the power of rational mind." In a well-known 1956 attack on Trilling, Joseph Frank says the weakness of the conservative imagination "lies in imposing its sense of the ultimate conditioned nature of life on areas where the will may fruitfully intervene." An even less generous critic might suggest that Trilling's limitation lies in the fact that he did his doctoral dissertation on Matthew Arnold and never really got over it.

Such a statement is not intended to underestimate Lionel Trilling, or to undervalue his contribution to American critical thought; rather, it is simply to suggest that the essays in *The Last Decade* not only offer nothing new, but they are also seriously out of step with current critical thought. In *The Liberal Imagination*, Trilling convincingly argued that ideology oversimplified human experience, that only literature was complex enough to do life justice. He also powerfully argued for the artist's intensity in confronting the "recalcitrant stuff of life," and he influentially defined culture as the "locus of the meeting of literature with social actions and attitudes" and as a "continuous bargaining with life." Trilling's essays in *The Liberal Imagination* on Sigmund Freud and Literature, on William Wordsworth's Immortality Ode, on *Huckleberry Finn*, and on Henry James's *The Princess Casamassima* were concrete, individual-ized, and specific; they were evidence of an energetic and tough-minded young critic. The current collection, edited posthumously by his wife, Diana Trilling, is an uneven collection of mostly occasional pieces, which are primarily polemical, generalized, derivative, and meandering.

The heart of the book are the essays, "Mind in the Modern World," deliv-ered as the first Thomas Jefferson Lecture in the Humanities of the National Endowment for the Humanities; "Art, Will, and Necessity," a lecture deliv-ered at Cambridge University; "The Uncertain Future of the Humanistic Educational Ideal," a paper delivered at a conference at the Aspen Institute for Humanistic Studies; and "What Is Criticism?" which is the Introduction to Trilling's edited collection, *Literary Criticism: An Introductory Reader*. The first three are important because they reiterate Trilling's basic themes of will, effort, and intention; the latter essay is the longest in the book and summarizes Trilling's view of literary criticism.

The remaining essays are extremely heterogeneous, although the same basic themes arise again and again, and often the same examples of literary figures and works are evoked. "A Novel of the Thirties" is a reprint of an Afterword that Trilling wrote for the republication of Tess Slesinger's novel *The Unpos-sessed*. The essay is an informal piece that relates the book to Slesinger's relationship to the Jewish intellectual community of the 1930's, especially those associated with the *Menorah Journal*; Trilling discusses the book as a reflection of the radical movement of the 1930's. His criticism of the book, however, is that it does not encompass the "political particularities" of that time and place firmly enough. The real subject of the book, says Trilling, is that dialectic between "life and the desire to make life as good as it might be"—what Thomas Mann has called the dialectic between nature and spirit. Because the book does not develop the actuality of politics of its time, how-ever, its real theme has been misunderstood and it is currently being read simply as a book of "feminist protest." Trilling therefore criticizes Slesinger for writing a book that is susceptible to being misunderstood as a feminist book which celebrates nature over the tyranny of spirit rather than, as Trilling would have it, as a dialectical novel in which the work of spiritual intellect should have been more emphasized.

Trilling launches a similar criticism against James Joyce in his review of Richard Ellmann and Stuart Gilbert's three-volume edition of the *Letters of James Joyce*. Trilling's focus is on the ambivalence of Joyce reflected in his love/hate relationship with Ireland, his admiration/scorn for social status, and the simultaneous innocence/perversity of his sexual desires. Trilling is himself ambivalent about his own claim that Joyce was largely responsible for destroy-ing nineteenth century fiction's emphasis on the confrontation of the moral and spiritual life with the values of the world. Trilling reveals his own nostalgia for such an emphasis and his impatience that the modern reader prefers that literature have a metaphysical rather than a moral aspect. Trilling's delight in the letters is that what Joyce denied in his fiction, he once affirmed with a great deal of intensity—a delight sparked by Trilling's disapproval of what he considers essential to Joyce's genius—his desire "to move through the fullest realization of the human, the all-too-human, to that which transcends and denies the human."

Trilling's review of *The Correspondence Between Sigmund Freud and C. G. Jung* and his introduction to the republication of his own novel *The Middle of the Journey* are of limited interest and one wonders why they were included here; there seems to be no reason except that they were there. The first simply summarizes the Moses-Joshua relationship between Freud and Jung recounted in the letters, and the latter is a personal apologetic account of Trilling's use of Whittaker Chambers as the model for his character Gifford Maxim in his 1947 novel.

"Aggression and Utopia," a paper on William Morris' *News from Nowhere* and "Why We Read Jane Austen," a paper prepared for the Jane Austen conference in Canada, but incomplete at Trilling's death, are similarly limited and of narrow interest. Trilling's attitude toward Morris' utopian romance and Austen's more mimetic novels, however, does reveal a common concern for Trilling—his preference for Austen's actuality (which involves frustration, effort, work) over Morris' regressive ideal of childlike hedonism. Trilling affirms the humanistic tradition that effort and aggressive energies constitute the ground of our dream of transcendence, value, and worth. It is, for Trilling, this aggressive energy that marks personhood—a personhood that although is lacking in the fiction of today, is amply evident in the novels of Jane Austen. In fact, Trilling attributes the enthusiasm that his own students have for Jane Austen to their need to see persons represented by an author with a strong moral imagination, rather than persons (as in the Morris romance) as projections of ideal desires. The most interesting ideas in these essays are Trilling's points about the relationship between actuality and fictionality. Even as Morris' works suggest that characters in his ideal, regenerate society are not fit subjects for art, in Jane Austen's work, says Trilling, readers are made aware of a continual dialect between the awareness of life being the subject of art (or being made into an aesthetic experience) and life remaining earnest and literal, the essence of what Western culture feels life to be. It is unfortunate that Trilling was not able to complete his discussion of this dialectic in Jane Austen, nor able to develop these ideas further, for they perhaps would have led him to a more balanced consideration of the self-reflexive aspects of modern fiction that he seems to abhor.

Trilling was, however, at the time of these essays much too old a dog to be taught the new tricks of post-modernist criticism. In his long essay, "What Is Criticism?," he adds little or nothing new or significant, being content to follow the outline of the four-part division of literary criticism established in the first chapter of M. H. Abrams' *The Mirror and the Lamp*. Throughout his summary of the critical focus on the maker of the work, the work itself, the universe, and the audience, Trilling emphasizes the importance of judgment in criticism. The motive of all literary criticism, says Trilling, is to say what literary excellence is and to indicate how to discriminate the degrees of excellence. To read Trilling here is to believe that nothing has happened in literary criticism since the turn of the century. He even continues to beat the dead horse of New Critical formalism in his warnings about the chimera of objectivity and the inadequacy of genre and art-object description. His focus here, as it was thirty years ago, although with more cogency then, is on the cultural conditions under which the literary work comes into being, and with the moral sensibilities of the author and his or her time. Current students of literature might just as well read Trilling of three decades ago as Trilling of his last decade.

In his "Mind in the Modern World" lecture, taking H. G. Wells's 1946 *Mind at the End of Its Tether* as his text, Trilling laments that in recent decades the study of literature has proceeded on the assumption "that literary works are not so readily accessible to the understanding as at first they might look to be." Moreover, he turns up his nose at, although he does not seem to deign to understand them, the many theories and elaborate, sophisticated methods for the comprehension of literary works which he says have "tended to make literature seem an esoteric subject available only to expert knowledge." As a result, Trilling says, literature has lost its profession—"We can therefore say that in our time the mind of a significant part of a once proud profession has come to the end of its tether."

Indeed, the time when the profession of literature was the province of genial talkers and "well-educated" humanists and generalists like Trilling has come to an end. Edmund Husserl, not Matthew Arnold, is now the precedent to seek; and Jacques Derrida, not Edmund Wilson, is now the voice that commands respect in the literary academic marketplace. In all fairness to those critics who have developed elaborate and sophisticated theories, it must be said that they will never supplant the well-read amateur, the old-fashioned Arnoldian man of letters; such a critic will continue to be read by the general lay reader. They do hope to redeem the study of literature, however, from its dilettantish status and give to it the rigor and significance now given to the sciences.

In "Art, Will, and Necessity," Trilling uses Harold Rosenberg's book *The De-Definition of Art* and a recent essay in *New Literary History* by literary critic Robert Scholes as an excuse once again to lament, as does Rosenberg, the loss of the importance of will and necessity in contemporary art. Rosenberg says that art is being deprived of its redemptive power because the will has so far neutralized itself and that art is moving toward extinction. Scholes, one of the leading American proponents of French structuralism, admires the modern novel precisely because it has moved beyond the nineteenth century focus on individualism toward typification. Scholes admires such novelists as John Barth, Thomas Pynchon, John Fowles, and Robert Coover for their presentation of human life as a structure and pattern of events; Trilling laments the popularity of such writers because they indicate the loss of the nineteenth century sense of individual destiny.

Trilling's criticism in this last collection seems an anachronism in the 1980's atmosphere of structuralism and poststructuralism. The antagonism between Trilling and contemporary critics, however, stems from the basic difference between their view of art. Trilling, in the fragment of an autobiographical lecture that concludes *The Last Decade*, admits that his work in criticism comes from his initial interest in the novel and his desire to be a novelist; for he says he has always been less concerned with aesthetic questions and more concerned with moral questions, with questions of culture and history. Critical claims at least since Cleanth Brooks and Robert Penn Warren for the autonomy of literature, Trilling still feels are the result of a failure of sensibility.

Trilling was one of the last of the old-fashioned culture critics. This collection of final essays marks not only his final nostalgic look backward at the more spacious and tough-minded values of the nineteenth century, but perhaps also signals the swan song of such genial Arnoldian criticism in American letters, which is now so enamoured of the siren song of structuralism from France.

Charles May

LECTURES ON LITERATURE

Author: Vladimir Nabokov (1899-1977)
Edited by Fredson Bowers, with an Introduction by John Updike
Publisher: Harcourt Brace Jovanovich (New York). 385 pp. $19.95
Type of work: Literary criticism
Time: 1948-1958
Locale: Cornell University and Wellesley College

Lectures on prominent European and British writers of the nineteenth and twentieth centuries by the most outstanding international novelist of his own time

Complete with an appreciation by John Updike, this handsomely printed volume is an impressive tribute to an intriguing decade in the colorful life of one of this century's most brilliant and inventive authors. There he was, an urbane and liberal émigré-aristocrat from Russia (with Berlin and Cambridge in his background), teaching a general education requirement in literature to a crowded hall of Cornell undergraduates, who had great difficulty in piercing the thickness of his accent. When they could, however, reach across his rolled "r's," what they heard, over and over again, was (as conveyed by John Updike in the words of a student who attended the lectures) "Caress the details . . . the divine details." For Vladimir Nabokov, a great work of literature was a triumph over abstraction and therefore a blow against tyranny and common sense which he thought were allies dedicated to the vulgarizing of the mind. The infinitely suggestive details of great art, which asserts the supremacy of felt detail over foolish generalizations, contribute to rendering the goodness of man a plausible thing in which to believe. By disciplining the subjective imagination, the detailed realizations of art make credible the worlds of hope that art brings to life.

It is true that Nabokov balked at the suggestion that great books had a moral or instructive purpose; they were simply beyond the crudities of any pragmatic function or intention. Nevertheless, he would end the semester by insisting that despite the fact that great literature could teach little of practical value, the close study of its structure and style might help readers

> feel the pure satisfaction . . . [that] goes to build up a sense of more genuine mental comfort, the kind of comfort one feels when one realizes that for all its blunders and boners the inner texture of life is also a matter of inspiration and precision.

To alert his students to the brilliant "textures" great writers were capable of weaving, he would spend a great deal of time quoting at length from the books themselves. These creative readings, however, were constantly inter-rupted with remarks on style, meaning, and literary influence. The "divine details" were evoked by the enchanter's wand. One of his most effective tricks was to stress the distortions of mistranslation of Gustave Flaubert and Marcel Proust; this dramatized the full power of "detail" by showing how the slightest errors in translation could do terrible violence to the writer's intended meaning. The vulnerability of a text to translation was only added proof of the power behind the delicacy of texture. Readers of *Lectures on Literature* have one distinct advantage over the students who originally attended the lectures: the editors have reproduced pages from Nabokov's teaching copies of the English translations of Flaubert and Proust assigned to the students, and his outraged pencilings and corrections bring his illuminations of the text to startling life. One gets a strong impression of the indignation with which Nabokov must have called these violations to the literary bench *and* the gusto with which he condemned them to everlasting perdition.

Nabokov's insistence that students master the details of a literary text went far beyond the New Critical attention to diction and imagery that dominated the literary pedagogy of his time. He delighted in drawing maps that forced students to appreciate the intricate nature of setting. For example, he blocked out the rooms at Mansfield Park and measured, almost to the metre, the exact proportions of Sotherton Court. This was his way of stressing Jane Austen's capacities for "precision" (good novels, insisted Nabokov, "merge the precision of poetry and the intuition of the sciences"), her gift for design and structure that he ultimately locates in her style itself: "Prominent among the elements of Austen's style is what I like to call the 'special dimple' achieved by furtively introducing into the sentence a bit of delicate irony between the components of a plain informative statement."

In his analysis of *Bleak House*, Nabokov catalogues the great variety of devices that Charles Dickens perfected to throw out the great net that his "considerable constellation of characters and themes" required: impersonations and disguises, false clues and true, vivid evocation, abrupt listing of descriptive details, figures of speech, repetition, oratorical question and answer, the Carlylean apostrophic manner, epithets, evocative names, alliteration and assonance, play on words, oblique description of speech, and so on. All these fictive and stylistic strategies, in their very variety, sustain the "magic democracy" of Dickens' worlds. Flaubert's design in *Madame Bovary* is less democratic in its variety of techniques than that of Dickens, but more suggestive through the subtleties of syntax and imagistic structure. It is less a novel than a prose poem. Nabokov demonstrates this not only by going over the novel's language but also its symbolic texture. There is a highly detailed survey of what Nabokov calls "the Equine theme": "To pick out the appearances of the horse theme amounts to giving a synopsis of the whole of *Madame Bovary*." There seems no end to Nabokov's fascination with the mimetic precision of great writers; in addition to the maps he extracted from *Mansfield Park*, he pulled others out of all the novels he presented to his students.

Perhaps Nabokov is at his best when discussing Proust. He lingers lovingly over Proust's images. After Proust's description of Combray's horizon of strips of forest topped by the "finger-nail" of Saint Hilaire's steeple, Nabokov writes "There is an intense vibration of poetry about the whole passage, about the purple spire rising above the jumbled roofs, a kind of pointer to a series of recollections, the exclamation mark of tender memory." Nabokov is captivated by Proust's fascination with memory. Proust's heavy reliance on musical phrases, colors, and intricate metaphors for the constant fueling of his memory strikes Nabokov as a kind of aesthetic, an aesthetic of memory. Art becomes for Proust, says Nabokov, the only means of recapturing the past. What was true for Proust became true of Nabokov himself whose own fiction is a lyrical cry of memory in pain and rapture.

When Nabokov approaches twentieth century writers, he dismisses the reliability of Sigmund Freud's theories as interpretive approaches to Franz Kafka and James Joyce and insists that they are continuing in the "objective" and memory-haunted aesthetic of Flaubert and Proust. Their precision is scientific, but they are essentially humanist writers glorifying the human imagination. Kafka's Gregor Samsa in *The Metamorphosis* is not a cockroach (as popular opinion has it) but a beetle, a "fantastic insect." Samsa's transformation into an insect is a symbol of the absurdity of modern experience, but it does not dehumanize Samsa or reduce him to a psychological abstraction. a sign of Oedipal guilt and worthlessness. On the contrary, insists Nabokov, "the Samsa family around the fantastic insect is nothing else than mediocrity surrounding genius."

The compact detail of Joyce's *Ulysses*, the events of a single day (June 16, 1904) in one city (Dublin) involving the most private thoughts of three distinctly different characters (Stephen, Bloom, and Molly), provides Nabokov with an embarrassment of riches for "caressing." The charged detailing of Joyce's style becomes for Nabokov a vindication of the kind of artistry he has been insisting all along is at the heart of the best nineteenth and twentieth century writers.

Underlying all of Nabokov's literary criticism in these lectures is the paradoxical insight that by deeply immersing himself in the empirical realities of time, space, and memory, the creative literary genius becomes a transforming magician: "Finally, and above all, a great writer is always a great enchanter." The Cinderella transformation in *Mansfield Park*, the supernatural transformations in *Bleak House* and *Dr. Jekyll and Mr. Hyde*, the fantastic transformation in *The Metamorphosis*, all spoke directly to Nabokov's own literary genius. One cannot help but muse over the fact that as Nabokov was elaborating his ideas of literary art in these undergraduate lectures, he was putting them to the test creatively at the same time. Out there in his student audience, year after year, were hundreds of freshman coeds whose composite traits, studied with passionate objective detail, were eventually sifted and transformed by Nabokov's creative memory into the supremely comic fiction *Lolita* (1956)—the world of the "nymphet," that transformation of the pubescent American child-woman that proved at least as fantastic as Kafka's beetle, and no less human.

Peter Brier

THE LETTERS OF EVELYN WAUGH

Author: Evelyn Waugh (1903-1966)
Edited by Mark Amory
Publisher: Ticknor & Fields (New Haven, Connecticut). 664 pp. $25.00
Type of work: Letters

A heavily annotated selection of Evelyn Waugh's letters, entertaining in their portraits of social and family life and useful as background to many of the novels

The overwhelming impression of the world of Evelyn Waugh which emerges from these letters is of names: Pamela and Penelope and Pansy; Diana and Daphne and Cyril and Robin; Bloggs and Honks and Bobo and Pug. They are all here as well as hundreds more. Fortunately for the reader of Evelyn Waugh's letters, they are almost all identified. The zeal of the editor, Mark Amory, in pinning down Dig and Decca, Boots and Poll, Violet and Elspeth, can only be admired and commended, for without some idea of who is who these letters would be almost unreadable.

Amory has selected 840 of about forty-five hundred available letters, those which seemed to him most interesting or funny. Amory has divided these letters into the period of Waugh's education (1903-1924); of his schoolmastering, his first literary successes, and the break-up of his first marriage (1924-1929); of his continued accomplishments in letters, his travels, his conversion to Roman Catholicism, and his second marriage (1929-1939); of the war years (1939-1945); of his family years at Piers Court in Gloucestershire (1945-1956); and of his final years at Combe Florey in Somersetshire (1956-1966). The selection is a bit unbalanced, with almost three-fourths of the letters coming from Waugh's last twenty years, while fewer than fifty letters cover his first twenty-six years.

The editor has supplied a general introduction to the work, a brief biographical sketch of Waugh at the beginning of each section of the letters, capsule biographies of the more important subjects and correspondents, a useful index, and extensive annotation. The most startling example of this last is a letter, of no more than a page and a half in the printed text, which requires thirty-one separate footnotes. This is not to be construed, however, as a fault of the editor but as a reflection of Waugh's practice of cramming his letters with notes and reflections on all sorts of persons, many trivial and thoroughly forgettable. Indeed, sometimes Waugh's letters read like the gossip columns so beloved of the Bright Young Things of the 1920's. The letters are generally sprightly and interesting, often amusing and entertaining but rarely deep or intellectually challenging. Despite the editor's suggestion, Waugh is probably not one of the great letter writers in the manner of Horace Walpole or Lord Byron.

If one seeks here fresh information on those events or periods of Waugh's life which might be supposed to have had some watershed importance in his career—his Oxford years, his attempted suicide in 1925, his first marriage and its breakdown, his conversion to Roman Catholicism, his second marriage, World War II, the deaths of his father and mother—one will be disappointed. With the exception of the war, these events leave little or no record in the letters here collected. This can be all the more disappointing because the recently published diaries are also silent or nonexistent for almost exactly the same events. By reading between the lines of the letters and the diary, one can guess a good deal about Waugh, but he is in fact surprisingly reticent about many of the more personal and intimate parts of his life and emotional experience.

As might be expected, Waugh corresponds with a wide variety of people, from close friends to casual fans; it is noteworthy, however, that other than groups of letters to Sir Harold Acton, Graham Greene, Randolph Churchill, and A. D. Peters, his literary agent, his main correspondents were women: Lady Acton, Katharine Asquith, Lady Penelope Betjeman, Lady Diana Cooper, Ann Fleming (wife of Ian), the Ladies Dorothy and Mary Lygon, Nancy Mitford, and his wife Laura. Waugh simply seems to have been more comfortable with the ladies, and the great majority of his letters to them are friendly, witty, chatty, often scandalous, and occasionally risqué. His letters to Nancy Mitford are the most extensive, and those to his second wife are sometimes moving in their expression of a mature and secure love.

For a writer, Waugh speaks little of writing. His letters are blessedly free of theorizing on the nature of his art and of any sort of philosophizing on the function or future of the novel. Such remarks as he does make are those of the thoroughly professional craftsman, dealing with the specifics of his or someone else's work. One has the distinct feeling that Waugh would have made an excellent editor, a practical man who could give great aid to young, talented writers who needed a sense of economy and discipline. Perhaps this skill in some way derives from the example of his father who was for many years the Managing Director of the publishing firm of Chapman and Hall.

Above all else, the letters are social. They are full of alliances and misalliances, marriages and divorces, parties and country houses, "who gave the ball or paid the visit last." This is, of course, preeminently the world readers associate with Waugh's novels and the world, the portrayal of which made his reputation. With due allowance for the exaggeration and farce of the novels, the reader can clearly see from the letters (and the diary) precisely how actual this world really was. If it is an axiom that writers write best about that which they know best, then Waugh proves the axiom. In his letters Waugh frequently begs for the latest gossip, bemoaning the fact that he is out of touch, that he never sees anyone anymore. In return, however, he always seems to have his fair share of scandal, rumor, and tidbits to relay. It is an oversimplification but one which still contains a good deal of truth that Waugh wrote about the people he knew best from Oxford and the 1920's, and as they grew older he remained with them, chronicling their doings through the Depression, the war, and after. His is a clear record of what became of at least a part of his generation. When accused (in 1945) of not writing about real people, he responded, in a letter to Ronald Knox, that "'Metroland' is my world that I have grown up in & I don't know any other except at second hand or at a great distance." Perhaps this partly explains why Waugh's travel books, interesting and occasionally amusing as they are and furnishing plentiful material for many of the novels, are not to be numbered among the classics of travel literature.

As with the people he wrote about, Waugh reveals himself in these letters as frequently self-centered, concerned for his ease and comfort. He was a man with a great need to be entertained, to have something to take him out of himself. All too often, as with his characters, it was another trip to London, another drinking bout, and another regretful morning-after. After the war, he strove to create for himself the life of a country gentleman, but he could never resist the attractions of London or Oxford. As with drink itself, he deplored the waste but could not resist the itch to imbibe again and again. The parallels with his disillusioned characters, who, bored with their daily rounds of party and drink, can nevertheless find nothing to do but continue, are sometimes painful to observe.

There is more than simple disillusionment in many of Waugh's characters, however; there is often the note of desperation, a note also to be found in these letters. Waugh's characters may not attain tragic stature in their desperation, for they rarely come to the sort of self-realization or self-knowledge needed for tragedy; but they do occasionally have inklings that somehow all is not well with their lives, blank misgivings that perhaps there is something that might be done to change things, a desperation of futility.

This is certainly the tone of Waugh's novels of the 1920's and 1930's, and it continues on into the war novels. His war letters reflect his own experience with the absurdity, the cross-purposes, and the frustrations of the military life which he chronicles in the fictions of *Sword of Honor*. On one level, the lack of communication, the lack of meaningful response, can be, and often is, hilarious; but on a deeper level the muddles and discomfitures bespeak a soul-destroying emptiness.

The emptiness and aimlessness of almost all of the characters of his novels are clearly, in Waugh's eyes, the result of the decline or loss of standards, from standards of personal honor to standards of cuisine. In Waugh's fiction, there are almost no heroes. Those with whom the reader would like to identify (Guy Crouchback, Adam Fenwick-Symes, Paul Pennyfeather) are all passive, more acted upon than involved in determining their own destinies. They reflect the fate of the man and the society without any coherent value system. This is the central meaning of virtually all of Waugh's works. Waugh was probably always taken with the theme of the loss of standards and values, and it became more explicit and probably more personal in the novels after World War II.

Clearly, his attachment to Roman Catholicism, an attachment that never wavered after his conversion in 1930 in spite of what he saw as the destructive changes wrought by Vatican II, was his personal anchor in a drifting world. Even if one could not tell from the novels, these letters make clear that Waugh took his religion with deadly seriousness. For him it was less a religion of joy and love than a religion of duty and principle. Despite his own lapses, he was a bit of a puritan. His letters reflect a fondness for the traditions and minutiae of the life of his adopted Church, a desire to attach himself to something with rules and customs, and to something not a common property.

With such views about the decay of Western civilization, exaggerated though they may have been, it is hardly any wonder that Waugh came to be seen by most as a cantankerous curmudgeon. The image of a testy, middle-aged Waugh, writing peevish letters to *The Times*, polishing biting remarks on all aspects of the modern world, is one that dominates the literature on Waugh. It is usually explained as a pose he adopted, perhaps partly out of self-protection, perhaps partly out of his own sense of frustration. It was, perhaps, less of a pose than usually is assumed, for it can be seen clearly even in the young Waugh. He was regarded, even by his close friends, as a quarrelsome and waspish fellow; and the list of people with whom he managed to quarrel, often permanently, would cover several pages.

Waugh did not depend on his religion for his only anchor, but put out a second one in his family. After the breakup of his first marriage in 1929, a series of events which wounded him greatly and probably occasioned some of the shell which he built around himself, he eventually found safe haven in a second marriage to Laura Herbert in 1937. it was a good marriage and good for Waugh, for it gave him some stability. Although there were the inevitable strains occasioned by his travels and his war service, the letters speak of a trusted and growing love. Waugh also gloried in his children, taking great interest in their doings and their education, even if from a distance at times. Of all the letters in this volume, the forty or so to his children are the most touching and engaging. He can be tender without sentimentality and whimsical without silliness; he was not blind to his children's faults, but he can correct with firmness and without hectoring. He can do brilliantly that most difficult thing: to write to a child without being childish. These letters could indeed be taken as models of their sort, of how to write to children, whether youngsters or young adults.

This collection of Waugh's letters, then, shows a Waugh whom the reader has come to know from his novels, a Waugh who can be both participant and disinterested and disenchanted observer. At the same time, the letters soften some of the exaggerations and reveal aspects of his life and character that help to make him, in the eyes of the reader, a more human and rounded figure than the stereotyped figure often presented. Now that these letters have been published (and with the unpublished ones available for examination), now that the diaries have been published (1976), and now that Waugh's friend Christopher Sykes has published an authorized and anecdotal biography (1975), interested readers probably have available, along with the works themselves, as much basic information as they are likely to get. The time is therefore ripe for someone to undertake the much-needed full-scale critical and biographical study which an artist of Waugh's accomplishment deserves.

Gordon N. Bergquist

THE LETTERS OF GUSTAVE FLAUBERT 1830-1857

Author: Gustave Flaubert (1821-1880)
Edited, selected, and translated by Francis Steegmuller
Publisher: Belknap/Harvard University Press (Cambridge, Massachusetts). 250 pp.
$12.50
Type of work: Letters
Locale: France, Egypt, Palestine, Turkey, and Greece

The first of two volumes selecting representative correspondence by one of the world's greatest novelists and letter writers

> *Principal personages:*
> GUSTAVE FLAUBERT, a most fastidious and deliberate major novelist
> LOUIS BOUILHET, his closest friend
> ALFRED LE POITTEVIN, an early friend of Flaubert who died of tuberculosis
> MAXIME DUCAMP, a lifelong friend of Flaubert who was one year his junior
> LOUISE COLET, eleven years Flaubert's senior and his occasional mistress from 1846 to 1855
> MME. FLAUBERT, his mother, in whose house he lived for much of his life
> DOCTOR ACHILLE-CLÉOPHAS FLAUBERT, his father, an eminent surgeon who died in 1846
> CAROLINE (FLAUBERT) HAMARD, his three-years-younger sister who also died in 1846

Not all great writers are also great correspondents—witness the preoccupation with trivia by William Butler Yeats and James Joyce, and the pomposity of Thomas Mann as he sends resonant messages to the Muse of Posterity. Gustave Flaubert, however, is a magnificent letter writer—perhaps the finest of that small group of literary men who also excelled as correspondents; only John Keats, Lord Byron, Stendhal, Henry James, and Anton Chekhov belong in his company. This volume is therefore of first-rate importance, particularly since it admits the reader into Flaubert's creative laboratory during the years, 1851-1856, that he was sweating out the tortured progress of the novel that would forever alter the form of its genre: *Madame Bovary*.

Francis Steegmuller, the editor-translator, is an old Flaubertian. His translation of *Madame Bovary* has long been admired; it remains available in a Modern Library edition. In 1939, he published a double biography, *Flaubert and Madame Bovary*, analyzing both the genesis of the novel and the accompanying course of its creator's difficult liaison with Louise Colet. In 1953, he edited a selection of Flaubert's letters for the Great Letters series. And, in 1972, he edited *Flaubert in Egypt*, a narrative of Flaubert's travels of 1849-1851 as drawn from both his letters and journals and the writings of this trip companion, Maxime DuCamp.

The present volume is announced as the first of two that will draw from the new Pléiade edition of Jean Bruneau (volume 1, 1973). The previous standard edition, Conard's of 1902, had been supervised by Flaubert's niece Caroline, who had brutally bowdlerized a great deal of bawdry from Flaubert's letters. Moreover, Steegmuller's 1953 selection includes about one third fewer letters from the 1830-1857 period, and has a far scantier apparatus of summaries, bridging passages, introductions, and footnotes. To be sure, Steegmuller's edition is still a stringent one compared to its source: it includes 160 letters, while the Pléiade edition, so far published to the year 1851, has 389, plus more than one hundred replies to Flaubert's correspondence. Since Steegmuller is himself a fine stylist, his new edition reads naturally. It convincingly captures Flaubert's tone and content.

Gustave Flaubert was born in Rouen's municipal hospital, second son of its distinguished chief surgeon. He was slow to learn the alphabet and to write, causing his demanding family premature concern (and Jean-Paul Sartre to title his study of Flaubert *L'Idiot de la Famille*). Once started, however, the boy became a brilliantly profuse writer, with his early notebooks and letters exhibiting a fine flow of adolescent rhetoric; Steegmuller includes ten precocious letters written between the ages of nine and eighteen.

When he was almost fifteen, Gustave fell into his first infatuation with a married woman of twenty-six, Elise Schlesinger, who gave him the nourishing love his own rigid and frigid mother had denied him. As with other people, he cherished the memory of her over many years, finally portraying her as Mme. Arnoux in *A Sentimental Education*, published when he was almost fifty. Yet, Flaubert resisted love far oftener than he admitted it to his morose, caustic, pessimistic temperament. From age eighteen on, his erotic preference was for whores and brothels, the seamier and sleazier the better. "For me," he wrote when he was twenty-five, "love is not and should not be in the foreground of life; it should remain in the back room."

What consistently did remain in the foreground of Flaubert's life was his devotion to his dour mother, in whose Croisset house he lived out much of his adulthood, and to several male friends. He wrote effusive letters to a trio of them: Alfred Le Poittevin, Maxime DuCamp, and Louis Bouilhet. These epistles manifest a marked homosexual streak—or, perhaps more precisely, femininity. Le Poittevin played elder brother to Gustave. Their parents were close friends; both became reluctant law students; both cultivated romantic languor, extensive whoring, and pervasive cynicism. In his letters to Alfred, Gustave often opened his heart and pen to intimate declarations of his disgust with ordinary life. Here is a good example, written in 1845:

> Do as I do. *Break with the outside world*, live like a bear—a polar bear—let everything else go to hell—everything, yourself included, except your intelligence. There is now such a great gap between me and the rest of the world that I am sometimes surprised to hear people say the most natural and simple things. It's strange how the most banal utterance sometimes makes me marvel. There are gestures, sounds of people's voices, that I cannot

get over, silly remarks that almost give me vertigo. Have you sometimes listened closely to people speaking a foreign language you didn't understand?

When Le Poittevin decided to marry in 1846, Flaubert felt betrayed and devastated. He turned for intimacy to Maxime DuCamp, also a law student, whose worldliness and efficiency contrasted with Flaubert's reclusiveness and aversion to practical affairs. DuCamp lent himself to the office of go-between when Gustave began his liaison with the married Louise Colet, but was jealous of her, soon finding her vapid and exasperating. From 1849 to 1851, Gustave interrupted his affair with Louise and traveled to the Middle East with Maxime. The route included Egypt, Palestine, Greece, and Turkey. Everywhere the two made a triumphal tour of not only aesthetic antiquities and ruins but also verminous brothels catering to both sexes and polymorphous sensations from buggery to bestiality. Flaubert writes here of sexual couplings involving not only whores but transvestites, bardashes, monkeys, donkeys, even ostriches. One day, he proclaims, he "fired five times and sucked three." What added exotic excitement to this performance, achieved with a locally famous courtesan, was a regiment of bedbugs on the wall which he amused himself killing without changing his position with the woman. When Louise Colet was later to assert her disgust with Flaubert's description of the bedbugs, he wrote her in 1853:

> . . . You tell me that Kuchuk's bedbugs degrade her in your eyes; for me they were the most enchanting touch of all. Their nauseating odor mingled with the scent of her skin, which was dripping with sandalwood oil. I want a bitter undertaste in everything—always a jeer in the midst of our triumphs, desolation in the very midst of enthusiasm. . . .

Most of Flaubert's Oriental correspondence is addressed to Louis Bouilhet (1822-1869), whose friendship with Gustave was to be termed a "liaison" by Louis. The two, Steegmuller informs the reader, "grew to look strikingly alike." Bouilhet's affection and admiration for Flaubert consoled him for Le Poittevin's "defection" to marriage and death of tuberculosis in 1847, but also created an adversarial situation between not only Bouilhet and Louise Colet, but also Bouilhet and DuCamp. Yet, both friends agreed in advising Flaubert not to publish the bloated version of *The Temptation of Saint Anthony* that he read to them for no less than thirty-two hours in 1849.

Bouilhet became not only Flaubert's erotic but also chief literary confident, the "midwife" (Flaubert's word) in the creation of *Madame Bovary*. Flaubert abandoned several other writing projects when, in July 1851, he heard (either from his mother or Bouilhet, Steegmuller is uncertain):

> . . . of the death, during his absence, of a Norman country doctor whom the Flauberts had known, named Eugène Delamare, and that this brought to mind certain country gossip. Delamare had been an impecunious and mediocre medical student under Dr. Flaubert at the Hôtel-Dieu. He never passed all his examinations, and became not an

M.D. but an *officier de santé*—a licensed "health officer," practising in a small town near Rouen. His second wife, Delphine, who had died before him, had been the subject of scandalous local talk: the details, unknown today, were apparently such as to make both DuCamp and Bouilhet urge Flaubert to make use of them.

Bouilhet was a gifted, discriminating reader, listener, and editor. He and Flaubert had endless (and, of course, unrecorded) conversations about the novel during the five-year course of its creation. Bouilhet would visit Croisset virtually every Saturday or Sunday during those years, hearing Flaubert read what he had fastidiously labored over during the week, suggesting revisions, rendering priceless assistance, comforting his friend in his never-ending struggle with what Gustave often called "the agonies of Art." When Flaubert's relationship with Louise reached a particularly dangerous crisis—with her in Paris and him, as usual, in Croisset—he enlisted Bouilhet's aid as mediator. Steegmuller prints an 1853 letter from Bouilhet which describes in outraged terms Louise's demands:

> Do you want me to tell you what I feel? Do you want me to say straight out what she is after, with her visits to your mother, with the comedy in verse, her cries, her tears, her invitations and her dinners?
> She wants, and expects, to become your wife!

The only sensible comment of this epistle is the editor's: "Bouilhet, in the present letter, speaks of Louise's wish to marry Flaubert as though it were a crime, rather than the normal ardor of such a woman to possess the man she loved in her way—as he had possessed her in his."

Flaubert's greatest letters during this period—perhaps the greatest letters ever written by an artist—are those nominally addressed to Louise Colet but actually dedicated to his Muse, his Art, whom he adored above all human relationships.

Flaubert first met Louise Colet in 1846 at the salon of a Parisian sculptor. She was a minor poet and actress eleven years his senior, had married a music professor, but had been for years the mistress of the philosopher Victor Cousin—possibly the father of her daughter. When Gustave and Louise met, she had been quarreling with her lover and was plagued with debts; he had long been ill and celibate, and had lost his father, sister, and Le Poittevin's friendship within the past year. They became lovers at their second meeting, but he left her for Croisset two days later—a pattern he was to repeat for years, to her increasing mortification and frustration.

To be sure, Flaubert did, during the first weeks of the connection, write her passionate love letters—the only rhapsodic celebration of eros in his life. The content of his correspondence, however, soon became primarily literary, a contrapuntal accompaniment to the composition of his great novel. As early as the second week of their affair he felt obliged to warn her of his morbidity, his self-disgust, his bookishness:

Ever since we said we loved each other, you have wondered why I have never added the words "for ever." Why? Because I always sense the future, the antithesis of everything is always before my eyes. I have never seen a child without thinking that it would grow old, nor a cradle without thinking of a grave. The sight of a naked woman makes me imagine her skeleton. As a result, joyful spectacles sadden me and sad ones affect me but little. I do too much inward weeping to shed outward tears—something read in a book moves me more than a real misfortune.

At the start of their relationship Gustave is not yet twenty-five. Yet, his bearing is that of a weary valetudinarian sealing himself up against the world, pursuing the making of perfect sentences:

My deplorable mania for analysis exhausts me. I doubt everything, even my doubt. You thought me young, and I am old. I have often spoken with old people about the pleasures of this earth, and I have always been astonished by the brightness that comes into their lackluster eyes; just as they could never get over their amazement at my way of life, and kept saying "At your age! At your age! You! You!" Take away my nervous exaltation, my fantasy of mind, the emotion of the moment, and I have little left. That's what I am underneath. *I was not made to enjoy life.*
You speak of work. Yes, you must work; love art. Of all lies, art is the least untrue. Try to love it with a love that is exclusive, ardent, devoted. It will not fail you. Only the Idea is eternal and necessary.

Louise, naturally, wanted him to visit her frequently in Paris. Gustave, true to his nature, preferred to live and work in Croisset, increasingly shutting her out of his life with icy determination and self-discipline. Even during the first month of their affair he managed to wait almost three weeks between brief visits to Paris. During the eighteen months of the pre-Oriental phase of their liaison, 1846-1848, he saw her only six times, but wrote her one hundred superb letters. No matter that she would grow increasingly irritated: he would simply reprove her in his condescending, austere fashion.

You tell me, my angel, that I have not initiated you into my inner life, into my most secret thoughts. Do you know what is most intimate, most hidden, in my heart, and what is most authentically myself? Two or three modest ideas about art, lovingly brooded over; that is all. The greatest events of my life have been a few thoughts, a few books, certain sunsets on the beach at Trouville, and talks five or six hours long with a friend now married and lost to me. [Alfred Le Poittevin]. I have always seen life differently from others, and the result has been that I've always isolated myself (but not sufficiently, alas!) in a state of harsh unsociability, with no exit. I suffered so many humiliations, I so shocked people and made them indignant, that I long ago came to realize that in order to live in peace one must live alone and seal one's windows lest the air of the world seep in.

Louise suffered during these years. What good did she derive from having Flaubert inform her that "The three finest things God ever made are the sea, *Hamlet*, and Mozart's *Don Giovanni*"; or, that "When two persons love, they can go ten years without seeing each other and without suffering from it"?

Her marginal comment on the last statement was poignant: "What a sentence!"

Flaubert's Eastern trip interrupted their stormy romance for almost two years, during which her husband died. When Flaubert returned to Paris in June, 1851, he refused to see her in the city—he was in his mother's company. He left for Rouen; she followed him; she rang the bell of his house; Flaubert appeared at the front gate, denied her admittance, agreed to visit her at her hotel in Rouen, and there told her to marry Victor Cousin. She fled to England. In September of that year, however, Gustave went to Paris and they reconciled for what proved to be three and a half more troubled years.

The second phase of the affair directly coincided with Flaubert's work on *Madame Bovary*, although its inevitable dissolution in March, 1855, came at an unfortunate time for literary history: he still had a third of the novel to write, and the travail of that last compositional period remains unrecorded.

The reader of these letters can hardly help forming a strongly disagreeable impression of the man: dogmatic, cold, self-important, cruel, somehow feeling himself too deeply scarred for life's common joys of love, marriage, and children. In October, 1851, he sadly tells Louise:

> . . . I wish there were nothing in my heart that reached out to others, and nothing in the hearts of others that reached out to me. The more one lives, the more one suffers. To make existence bearable, haven't there been inventions ever since the world began— imaginary worlds, opium, tobacco, strong drink, ether? Blessed be he who invented chloroform. The doctors object that one can die of it. But that is the very point! You lack sufficient hatred of life and of everything connected with it.

Louise had chronic financial difficulties, but Gustave, although in comfortable circumstances, usually managed to ignore them. "Oh woman!" he berates her in September, 1852, "Woman, be less so! Be so only in bed!" When barely thirty-one, he is horrified by the possibility of paternity: "May my flesh perish utterly! May I never transmit to anyone the boredom and the ignominies of existence!" He manages sometimes to mask his disgust with the world (and himself) as disappointed idealism: "Let us always have a vast condom within us to protect the health of our soul amid the filth into which it is plunged." By early 1855, his sadism to Louise is lashing: "I have always tried (but I think I have always failed) to turn you into a sublime hermaphrodite. I want you to be a man down to the navel; below that, you get in my way, you disturb me—your female element ruins everything." No wonder that the long, largely *non*liaison ended bitterly in March, 1855.

Why bother to read the correspondence of such a repellent man? The answer can only be the obvious one: he was a literary genius, not only in his carefully contrived fiction but also in his carelessly written but supremely revealing letters. They contain many passages that have become sacred texts of modernism. They celebrate the religion of art, the ascetic devotion and devoutness of the artist, the supremacy of style, the autonomy of the artistic view of the world. They ring with dedication, integrity, fervor, and eloquence. They preach the justification of art in a fragmented, materialistic, money-mad, bourgeois society. They sustain and console their author for the pains of his unhappy temperament. They have exerted an incalculable influence on Flaubert's innumerable disciples, of whom Ivan Turgenev, Henry James, James Joyce, Virginia Woolf, Joseph Conrad, Marcel Proust, André Gide, Vladimir Nabokov, Jorge Luis Borges, and Samuel Beckett are but the most illustrious.

Gerhard Brand

THE LETTERS OF MARY WOLLSTONECRAFT SHELLEY
Volume I: "A Part of the Elect"

Author: Mary Wollstonecraft Godwin Shelley (1797-1851)
Edited by Betty T. Bennett
Publisher: The Johns Hopkins University Press (Baltimore, Maryland). 591 pp. $30.00
Type of work: Letters
Time: 1814-1827

A superbly edited and annotated collection of letters describing the author's life as the wife of Percy Bysshe Shelley and as professional writer

One of the most positive results of the women's movement of the past two decades has been the rediscovery of talented women writers whose works have been largely ignored. Mary Shelley is one of these. Her name has never, of course, vanished altogether from the literary scene; her position as the wife of one of England's greatest Romantic poets has provided her with at least vicarious immortality, and her own best-known creation, Frankenstein's monster, has become a part of popular folklore, although it is rarely associated with the name of its creator. Betty T. Bennett's new, definitive edition of Mary Shelley's letters, however, and its excellent and appreciative introductory essay should do much to establish her as a writer worthy of much greater recognition for her own accomplishments than she has heretofore received.

This volume, the first of a projected three-volume edition, contains 396 letters, approximately eighty of them previously unpublished. They were written between 1814, the year in which Mary Wollstonecraft Godwin, seventeen, eloped with the twenty-three-year-old married poet Percy Bysshe Shelley, and August, 1827, the month of her thirtieth birthday. The letters, fully but unobtrusively annotated by the editor, record the Shelley's trip to the Continent in 1816, their debt-plagued months in England, Harriet Shelley's suicide and their subsequent marriage, their move to Italy, the births of four children and the deaths of three of them, Mary's near-fatal miscarriage, Shelley's drowning in a boating accident, and, finally, Mary's struggle to make a life for herself and procure an income to raise her one surviving child, Percy Florence.

Considerable interest naturally falls on what she has to say about her circle of friends, the "Elect" referred to in the subtitle. This group included many of the best-known figures of the Romantic period: Lord Byron and his mistresses Claire Clairmont (Mary's stepsister) and Countess Teresa Guiccioli, Leigh and Marianne Hunt, Charles and Mary Lamb, William Hazlitt, Greek patriot Alexander Mavrocordato, and American writers Washington Irving and John Howard Payne. The letters are, indeed, filled with fascinating literary gossip, but, more important, they show Mary herself in a much more sympathetic way than she has generally been seen in biographies of her husband. Especially important to a fuller understanding of her are the newly published letters to Jane Williams Hogg. Jane and her husband Edward Williams shared a house near Pisa with the Shelleys for several months in 1822, and the two men died together in a storm at sea in July of that year. The young widows remained intimate friends until almost the end of the period covered by this volume, and Mary poured out her deepest feelings in her letters to Jane.

There will be some disappointment that Mary's letters do not reveal more about Shelley. Although he is mentioned in most of them, he remains a rather shadowy figure. Several factors may account for this vagueness. First, Mary completely idealized him after his death, writing of "my Lost One," a creature of "wondrous excellencies" pursued by a "strange fate." She berated herself, although not as severely as some Shelley partisans have criticized her, for "not making my S.—so happy as he deserved to be." Second, the couple were rarely separated after 1817, and the twenty-five surviving letters from her to him date chiefly from the years 1814-1817, when her attention was focused principally on domestic details, their precarious finances, the health of Shelley and their babies, and the tangled affairs of Claire Clairmont and Allegra, her child by Lord Byron. Third, perhaps anticipating the attention that was to be paid to her husband in the future, Mary was guarded about their relationship in both her letters and her journals. It is, however, refreshing to see glimpses of the famous poet as husband and father, not too ethereal to be instructed at the beginning of a letter to purchase a new hat for his small son and then to be told two pages later, "Perhaps you had better not get William's hat as it may not fit him or please me."

The letters show clearly the intellectual ties that bound Mary and Shelley. She shared his passionate involvement in English political issues, and they undertook formidable studies in Latin, Greek, Spanish, and Italian literature together. While there are no extended discussions of their creative pursuits, scattered brief references to the progress of his work and hers make it clear that they were closely in touch with each other's writing. There is little in her letters to suggest the estrangement between them that others have reported. If her depression over the loss of two children within a year and her understandable preoccupation with the baby born shortly afterwards left her unable to meet Shelley's emotional needs, she was apparently unaware of the problem at the time. The depth of her grief at his death, extravagantly expressed in letters to a number of friends, suggests that for her, if not for him, their relationship was still an unbroken one.

If Mary's loyalty and reserve kept her from discussing Shelley's feelings and actions as candidly as a modern reader would like, they did not prevent her from being frank about her own emotions, and she herself comes vividly to life and grows from page to page. Her earliest extant letters introduce her as a coquettish passionate adolescent. She plaintively lamented Shelley's absence when he was hiding from his creditors in 1814 and wrote flirtatiously to her lover's friend, Thomas Jefferson Hogg, with whom Shelley apparently suggested she share her favors. She matured rapidly under the stress of parental disapproval, social ostracism, constant debt, and the death of her first daughter, born prematurely in February, 1815. At twenty she wrote a friend, "I, you know, am an old woman," and she does by this time sound like a settled matron. The years with Shelley were undoubtedly the richest and most exciting of her life, but they were never free from anxiety. Only toward the end of the period covered here, when she was resettled in England regularly writing for publication and receiving (after long and painful negotiations) a modest allowance from her father-in-law, do her letters show fully the warm, intelligent, witty individual she was always capable of becoming.

Many of the problems that beset Mary Shelley—poverty, illness, death—were beyond her control, but much of the unhappiness described in her letters arose out of her relationships. Although she often appeared cold, reserved, and detached, her correspondence suggests that she was an intensely emotional person who craved uncritical affection and acceptance. Her friends and relatives had great power to hurt her, and they frequently did. Her father, William Godwin, whom she almost worshiped during her childhood, caused her continual pain during her marriage with his endless peremptory demands for money. It was Shelley's admiration for Godwin that had brought about his meeting with Mary, and the young poet was already providing Godwin with money before their elopement. Godwin strongly opposed their union but continued to act as if Shelley had a moral obligation to support him. His demands were so distressing to Mary that in the period following the children's deaths Shelley would not even show her Godwin's letters if he felt they would upset her. The relationship between father and daughter was not fully restored until Mary returned to England after Shelley's death.

Relations were also strained between Mary and other members of the loosely connected Godwin family. Her own mother, the distinguished feminist Mary Wollstonecraft, had died when Mary was born, and she detested her father's second wife, who had introduced into the household her own two children, Charles and Mary Jane, later Claire Clairmont. Charles occasionally asked the Shelleys for money but otherwise interfered little in their lives; Claire, however, was a vexatious but inextricable part of Mary's existence from the time their parents married. Mary frequently complained of Claire to Shelley and their mutual acquaintances, yet she permitted her to live with them for much of their married life, she saw her through the many crises of Allegra's brief life, and she continued to worry about her welfare even after Claire had gone to Moscow as a governess in 1823. There has been gossip through the years that Claire was Shelley's mistress as well as Byron's, but this is one of the few complaints Mary did not make against her.

Mary looked to friends for the affection she did not find in her family, but even the closest friendships recorded in this volume were tarnished from time to time. Maria Gisborne, a friend of Mary Wollstonecraft, became a surrogate mother for the Shelleys when they moved to Italy; almost a quarter of the letters printed here were addressed to her and her husband John. Mary wrote her about her domestic concerns, her children's progress, and Shelley's health, as well as about their reading and English politics. Maria Gisborne undertook endless commissions at Mary's request, forwarding letters and packages, purchasing clothing, and making inquires about servants, without ever suggesting that she felt burdened by the Shelley's demands. Yet, when the Gisbornes returned from a trip to England in 1820, Mary felt that they insulted her by refusing to visit right away, and she kept a hostile distance between the two families for several months. The causes of the quarrel are not entirely clear in the letters or in Bennett's usually informative notes; the disagreement seems to have been connected in some way with the Gisbornes' meeting with the Godwins in London.

Mary's friendships with Lord Byron, Jane Williams, and Leigh and Marianne Hunt followed the same pattern of intimacy and disillusionment. She may simply have been unlucky in her choice of confidants, but the letters show that she made considerable demands, both practical and emotional, on them, and she required absolute loyalty to herself and her husband. She wrote gratefully and respectfully to Byron, who provided considerable assistance to her in the months immediately following Shelley's death, but after he rescinded, or threatened to rescind, his offer to provide funds for her return to England with her son, she wrote Jane of his "unconquerable avarice" and recoiled in a fit of hurt pride that temporarily blotted out any memory of his former services to her. She was, however, able to put aside personal resentment to pay tribute to him after his death in Greece in 1824.

The most painful betrayal was that of Jane Williams, who committed the unpardonable sin of speaking disparagingly to others of Mary's treatment of Shelley during the time the two couples lived together in Italy. There is no such clear reason for the loosening of ties with the Hunts, to whom she wrote a number of the most delightful of her letters in 1823. Perhaps the pressures of supporting their large family simply left them little time for the kind of intense friendship Mary seems to have needed in the early years of her widowhood. Her efforts to improve their financial situation through negotiations with Hunt's brother John, reported at some length in her letters, may also have exacerbated existing tensions.

Mary did manage to sustain one comfortable friendship over a number of years; her relationship with American playwright John Howard Payne, whom she met in 1824, was distant enough to prevent the emotional upheavals of earlier connections but close enough to permit her to enjoy his company and write easily and often of her activities and her work, providing readers with an excellent picture of her life in London and its environs.

She made new friends among musicians and writers, indulged her interest in the opera and the theater, and dedicated her energies to preserving her husband's literary reputation and establishing a minor one of her own. As she wrote on many occasions, she found her greatest consolation in her studies, and she was justifiably confident in her ability to support herself and young Percy at least modestly by her pen. She did not discuss her literary efforts at length with her correspondents, but her letters indicate both the care with which she researched the background for her novels and essays and the competence with which she handled their publication. Her attitude toward her work was pragmatic and modest, quite different from the reverence with which she regarded Shelley's achievements. She wrote to Payne of *The Last Man*, generally considered one of the most interesting of her novels,

> If I had at the commencement fore seen the excessive trouble & then (much worse) the state of imperfection in which partly for want of time I was obliged to leave it—I should never have had the courage to begin. Here and there you will find some things to like, but your critical taste will be hurt by it as an whole.

Viewed together, Mary Shelley's letters demonstrate the range of her concerns and the versatility of her prose style. One letter might include a description of the customs in an Italian town, a critical comment on the poetry of Ariosto, a report of Shelley's progress with *The Cenci*, a paragraph of gossip, and a list of half a dozen household items to be purchased for her. She could be kittenish with her youthful admirers, quintessentially romantic in her description of remote mountain passes, businesslike in her dealings with publishers and lawyers, maudlin in her grief for Shelley, imperious in her demands for favors from friends, playful in her interchanges with the Hunts and Payne. The same talent for drawing people and places that made her a successful novelist enlivens her correspondence with the result that the letters, skillfully linked by Bennett's commentary, form a connected narrative that is as fascinating as a good novel.

Elizabeth Johnston Lipscomb

THE LETTERS OF VIRGINIA WOOLF
Volume VI: 1936-1941

Author: Virginia Woolf (1882-1941)
Edited by Nigel Nicolson and Joanne Trautmann
Publisher: Harcourt Brace Jovanovich (New York). 556 pp. $19.95
Type of work: Letters

This final volume of Woolf's letters covers the last five years of her life, which saw publication of The Years, Three Guineas, *and* Roger Fry: A Biography

"Without someone warm and breathing on the other side of the page, letters are worthless." So Virginia Woolf begins *Three Guineas* (1938), a book which many of her friends disliked and which she herself called, in a letter to Vita Sackville-West, "a piece of donkey-drudgery." *Three Guineas* is in many ways the least typical of Woolf's novels and literary essays. Factual, argumentative, sober, it was written, its author tells the Viscountess Rhondda, "because I could not write anything else." All the same, Woolf clearly visualizes its audience: a middle-class man; a lawyer, graying at the temples; a respectable man with a family and a little property and the best education England could provide. In rhetorical form, *Three Guineas* is a letter, and the grave tone of its writer is only one of the voices she could command simply by imagining different interlocutors. Nothing lets the reader hear her voices more clearly than the six volumes of her letters, the last of which covers the years 1936-1941. In this final volume, edited like the others by Nigel Nicolson and Joanne Trautmann, one meets again the most intimate of Virginia's friends and relations—her sister Vanessa Bell, her niece Angelica Bell, her friends Vita Sackville-West and Ethel Smyth—as well as many other literary, artistic, and social figures of her day.

Volume VI of Woolf's letters displays the grace and brilliance and wit of her voices just as the other volumes have done, but it certainly has its sober moments, moving as it does toward Woolf's suicide in March of 1941. Nicolson argues in his Introduction that Woolf's decision to take her life was a rational, premeditated act, that she made the decision because she feared she was losing her power over words. This fear seems directly related to her belief that she no longer had an audience. To her friends she occasionally suggested that it was the war which had taken readers away and thus made writing impossible. In the middle of a letter to Ethel Smyth, in September of 1940, Woolf was interrupted by the noise of a plane being shot down on a nearby hill; when she resumed, she commented that "its so difficult to write a coherent letter. . . . Its odd to feel one's writing in a vacuum—no-one will read it." Shortly before her death, she observed to Elizabeth Robins that "Its difficult . . . to write. No audience. No private stimulus, only this outer roar." The "outer roar" created by the war damaged one of the Woolfs' London houses and destroyed the other, forced the removal of the Hogarth Press from London to Letchworth, and brought the business of book publishing to a virtual halt. It is no wonder that as the war intensified Virginia Woolf felt she was writing in a vacuum; neither is there any doubt that this lack of connectedness with an audience contributed to her growing conviction that she was permanently losing her mastery of language.

There were other elements, however, in her sense of a loss of mastery. Volume VI of the letters covers the period when Woolf produced the books generally considered to be the least successful among her mature works. Just as *The Voyage Out* (1915) and *Night and Day* (1919) represent her apprenticeship, the books after *The Waves* (1931)—*The Years* (1937), *Three Guineas*, and *Roger Fry: A Biography* (1940)—represent to most critics if not a falling-off of Woolf's aesthetic power, at least a period when she was casting about for new forms in which to shape her prodigious gifts. Although she became profoundly discouraged at times about all of her books, and although completing a book always produced in her a despair which could be life-threatening, these last three works gave her particular trouble, both in the writing and afterward. Correcting manuscript, typescript, and proofs for *The Years* proceeded at an agonizingly slow rate, interrupted by headaches and days in bed. When Leonard Woolf read the novel in proof, he committed what Quentin Bell's biography calls a "calculated falsehood," telling his wife that the book was "extraordinarily good," because he thought that if he were any more critical, she would kill herself. The book was a popular success in England and the United States, but its author wrote to Ethel Smyth, "I loathe it and see a sweat stain, a tear stain, a gash—200 pages cut—on every existing page." Her opinion of *Three Guineas* was not much higher: ". . . it only repeats The Years, with facts to prove it, not fiction; and is a hurried piece of work. . . ." The biography of her friend Roger Fry she described as "only a piece of cabinet making, and . . . of no interest that I can see, except to his half dozen devotees." Even after one has allowed for Woolf's famous tendency to exaggerate and for her long-standing and pervasive feelings about the inadequacy of language in general and of her words in particular, one cannot avoid concluding that Woolf's sense that her power as a writer was failing and that her audience was gone was a major factor in her decision to take her life. "I begin to hear voices and cant concentrate. . . . I cant read," she wrote to Leonard; "you see I cant even write this properly."

In spite of the fact that Nicolson tries in his Introduction to reconstruct Woolf's mental state in the days just preceding her suicide, and in spite of the fact that the problem of dating the three suicide notes, two of them to Leonard and the third to Vanessa, is the subject of an Appendix, Volume VI as a whole is not a gloomy book. Even Woolf's last letters are straightforward rather than grim, although one can catch in them glimpses of the despair which was rapidly overwhelming their writer. "I cant . . . make my hand cease to tremble," she says to her friend and doctor, Octavia Wilberforce, in December, 1940, attributing the infirmity to having moved books all day. To Ethel she writes, in January of 1941, that her hand is "a mere claw," but explains that its condition is a result of the unusually cold weather. Her comment to Vita, in early March, that her orchard is "beginning to dapple" is "One of the sights I shall see on my death bed" seems ominous only to the reader who knows that the end of the volume, and of Virginia's life, is near. Except for such glimpses, Woolf's desire to entertain her correspondents and herself animates the entire volume, infuses even the most obligatory of letters with grace and often also with comedy. A note which has the mundane function of confirming Sybil Colefax's plans to visit the Woolfs in Sussex warns Sybil of the discomforts of Monk's House and ends with the postscript, "No clothes but nightgowns worn here." Vita is the recipient of two of what must be the most splendid thank-you notes in the language, one for a gift of paté— "what immortal geese must have gone to make it"— and the other, during wartime, for a pat of butter. This second letter begins with a hilariously effusive parody of the style of Queen Victoria and continues with a rhapsodic description of the novelist eating bread and butter; "It would have been a desecration to add jam."

Parody is also a technique Woolf uses when writing to her niece, Angelica; the letters enclosing Angelica's quarterly allowance are often enlivened by Aunt Virginia's wicked mimicry of her own aunt, Mary Fisher. It is Angelica, too, who inspires some of the most fantastic of Woolf's imaginative flights, as well as some of her most amusing gossip: "Quentin has just been to tea: practically naked; had to borrow Leonard's shirt which looked like a hand-kerchief on a hippopotamus." Even Woolf's description of her own bombed houses, written for her niece's eyes, seems hyperbolically fanciful rather than despairing. Woolf recognizes Angelica's effect on her imagination—"You see when I write to you, I'm almost mistress of the other art of poetry"—and the humorous, almost childlike intimacy between aunt and niece reveals the unadulterated affection in which the two held each other.

The tone of Woolf's letters to Angelica ironically illuminates a number of almost diffident passages in her letters to Vanessa. One imagines Virginia longing that her undemonstrative sister, whom she adored, could be more abandoned in her professions of love. Virginia tells Vanessa of her "rapacity" for Vanessa's company, and when Vanessa and the children are in France, Virginia says, "I feel a lost old crone without you all . . . when you're not there the colour goes out of life, as water from a sponge; and I merely exist, dry, and dusty." Then, commenting on her own metaphor, Woolf adds, "not a very beautiful illustration of my complete adoration of you; and longing to sit, even saying nothing, and look at you." If Virginia in Vanessa's absence is a dry and dusty crone, Vanessa is a butterfly, "my own darling creature," a dolphin whose children swim in her blue wake. Especially in the letters written just after the death of Vanessa's oldest child, Julian, in the Spanish

Civil War, Virginia's love for her older sister emerges as one of the strongest feelings of her life. As for returning Virginia's love, Vanessa could only tell Vita, and not Virginia herself, that after Julian's death Virginia's love was what kept her alive, but that "when she [Virginia] is demonstrative, I always shrink away."

Virginia's hunger for Vanessa's affection remained intense throughout her life. By contrast, the passion of her friendship with Vita Sackville-West eventually cooled, but the friendship itself remained satisfying, a "warm slipper relation," as Virginia described it to Ethel Smyth. Ethel herself was another matter entirely. An energetic, determined, vital woman more than twenty years older than Virginia, Ethel had initiated their friendship in 1930, and a vigorous correspondence ensued. The vigor of the correspondence, at least on Virginia's side, seems to have been in part a means of keeping the indomitable and very deaf Ethel at bay. As Virginia wrote to Vita, "I find these strenuous interviews, and she [Ethel] can't help it, the very devil." Perhaps because Virginia knew that Ethel's affection for her was far greater than hers for Ethel, Virginia wrote to her friend effortlessly, "as I scribble in my diary." Despite this apparent carelessness, Virginia appreciated Ethel's acceptance and admiration enough to tolerate her literal-mindedness, her lapses in literary taste, and even her bad table manners. After a disagreement between them, Virginia wrote, "how I adore your broad human bottom—how it kindles me to think of you."

One of Woolf's most interesting devices for amusing Ethel, Vita, and Vanessa, as well as her other friends, is her sensory descriptions of landscapes. Especially when she and Leonard are traveling, her letters glow with color. Duncan Grant receives the following postcard from Scotland: "Skye is often raining, but also fine: hardly embodied; semi-transparent; like living in a jelly fish lit up with green light." Describing the French towns of Vannes and Auray to Vanessa, Woolf observes, "How I love reflections in water—fishing boats dripping blue, the green so green it seems to make every other colour either black or purple. . . ." Woolf might as well have labeled herself an impressionist, so great is her sensitivity to water, light, and color; the beauty of landscape for her is, she says, "almost entirely colour, very subtle, very changeable, running over my pen, as if you poured a large jug of champagne over a hairpin." As much as Woolf delights in visual beauty and in describing it, however, she is sensitive to the predilections of her audience. To Ethel from Skye, Woolf writes, "Do you like descriptions of nature? or do you skip?" Ethel apparently is not overly fond of such flights, but even in friendship Virginia is not always able to resist them. "Every other second I take my eyes off the page to look at the elms outside—burning orange against a deep blue," she writes to Ethel from Monk's House; "Then theres the little cross of the Church against the snow. . . . But I must add the smoke convoluting out of Asheham Cement Works is a ruffled pink that absolutely defies description—

you'll be glad to hear."

Woolf's visual pleasure in the natural landscape, both foreign and domestic, is rivaled in these letters only by her pleasure in the city of London, which she calls "the passion of my life." Seeing the city "all blasted" by the war "raked my heart," she tells Ethel; and a few days later she observes that "London looked merry and hopeful, wearing her wounds like stars. . . ." The city itself—its buildings and squares—is admirable even in ruins; so, too, are its people, who, as the war wears on, evoke Woolf's respect and awaken her democratic sympathies. London and its people come to represent for her the England of Geoffrey Chaucer, William Shakespeare, and Charles Dickens, and she calls her love for the city "my only patriotism." This literary patriotism serves also to mark the passage of time during the blitz; telling Ethel in February of 1941 that she is rereading English literature, Woolf calculates that "By the time I've reached Shakespeare the bombs will be falling. . . . Instead of thinking, by May we shall be—whatever it may be: I think, only 3 months to read Ben Jonson, Milton, Donne, and all the rest!"

The rereading of English literature was part of a project Woolf had been considering since September of 1940, a book on the relation between social history and literature. To be called *Anon*, this "Common History Book" or "new Common Reader" occupied her during the intervals when she was not working on *Pointz Hall*, later titled *Between the Acts*. Although she mentions such undertakings in her letters to her friends, she rarely dwells on the details of constructing her books, and she adamantly refuses to comment, even informally, on the work of her literary contemporaries. When her good friend T. S. Eliot sends her a copy of his most recent poem, *East Coker* (1940), Woolf responds, "through diabolic shyness I swerve from your poem; isn't it odd, how difficult it is to talk of writing—I mean one's own; or t'other persons?" May Sarton, not such an intimate friend, receives a tart refusal to discuss *The Single Hound* (1938): "I have lost all belief in written criticism— anyhow my own," Woolf writes to her; "But if you're in London later and still want wild and random impressions verbally probably we could arrange it." Woolf is much more ready to discuss what she is reading if it is not the work of a contemporary. The habit formed in her father's library, of reading, "in a casual way, masses of books," accounts for her voracious appetite for literature: William Wordsworth's *The Prelude*, for example, is "so good, so succulent, so suggestive, that I have to hoard it, as a child keeps a crumb of cake." Except for such comments, literary criticism is less common in this volume than one might expect. In fact, Woolf emerges here not as a critic, not as a snob, not as a manic-depressive—although she certainly was all these—but, instead, as an extravagantly affectionate and wonderfully witty woman whose chief delights were books, nature, and people.

The most beloved of all these people is undoubtedly the one to whom she wrote least often, because they were so rarely separated. Leonard Woolf is everywhere in these letters, giving advice, paying his respects, sending his love. His involvement in politics and in his own writing goes on unabated in the background. Leonard is "entirely submerged" in politics, Virginia observes at one point; "I might be the charwoman of a Prime Minister." And there is intimacy, too. Describing to Vanessa a day of "divine loneliness," Virginia writes, "I said to L. as we strolled through the mushroom fields, Thank the Lord, we shall be alone; well play bowls; then I shall read Sévigné; then have grilled ham and mushrooms for dinner; then Mozart—and why not stay here for ever and ever, enjoying this immortal rhythm . . .?" Later, after making tea, she goes to "call in L from the ladder on the high tree—where he looked so beautiful that my heart stood still with pride that he ever married me. . . ." Although Volume VI ends with a suicide note to this same devoted man—"you have given me complete happiness," she writes—the total effect, even of these last years' worth of Woolf's letters, is not at all depressing, but buoyant, light-filled, and hauntingly beautiful. Perhaps that is because, for all her reputed snobbery and aestheticism, Virginia Woolf fully understood the complex vitality of the human personality. She never forgot that there, on the other side of her page, was someone warm and breathing.

Carolyn Wilkerson Bell

LIFE BEFORE MAN

Author: Margaret Atwood (1939-   )
Publisher: Simon and Schuster (New York). 317 pp. $11.95
Type of work: Novel
Time: 1976-1978
Locale: Toronto

An often grim, occasionally satirical, portrayal of human relationships in modern Canada

> *Principal characters:*
> ELIZABETH SCHOENHOF, an unhappy woman in her mid-thirties
> NATE SCHOENHOF, her husband
> LESJE GREEN, a young paleontologist, half-Ukrainian and half-Jewish
> WILLIAM, her lover, an environmental engineer, and an Anglo-Saxon

Life Before Man is another chapter in Canadian author Margaret Atwood's bleak commentary on the modern world, one that develops and expands the visions of absurdity, madness, and death of her earlier novels, *The Edible Woman, Surfacing,* and *Lady Oracle,* and of her highly acclaimed poetry. The feminist emphasis of much of her earlier fiction here gives way to a wider perspective; her male characters are as trapped by society, as powerless against encroaching oblivion, as her females. There is a good deal of sardonic humor in her depiction of marriage and adultery in contemporary middle-class Toronto, but the dominant tone is a darker one, set by recurrent images of extinction and oblivion that are linked to the dinosaur exhibits at the Royal Ontario Museum, where two of the main characters work, and to a planetarium presentation called "Cosmic Disasters" that one of them attends.

The structure of the novel contributes to the impression that modern life is mechanical and doomed. There are five parts of the book and each contains a number of brief sections, headed by a date and the name of the character (Elizabeth, Nate, or Lesje) whose thoughts are being examined. The third-person narrator reports these thoughts in a voice as detached as that of an anthropologist making reports on a foreign culture. Mores, settings, clothing, and conversations are depicted objectively and accurately, and the feelings of the characters are studied in great detail, but the reader is kept at a distance, prevented from sympathetic emotional involvement in spite of the unhappiness being portrayed.

The plot might come from any soap opera or drugstore paperback that features interlocking triangles. It begins with Elizabeth Schoenhof emotionally paralyzed by the suicide of her lover, Chris, who has blown off his head with a shotgun. Her husband, Nate, is in the process of breaking off a relationship with a secretary in the law firm where he once worked and making tentative advances to Lesje Green, a young paleontologist employed at the museum where Elizabeth is also a staff member. Lesje leaves her lover, William, to live with Nate, and Elizabeth has a brief affair with William to soothe her ego. She makes life generally difficult for Nate and Lesje by sending her two daughters to visit them regularly, demanding substantial child support payments, and delaying divorce proceedings. To get even with Nate for not being able to stand up to Elizabeth, Lesje throws away her birth control pills. The book ends with nothing resolved, the two women pulling at Nate but neither of them much interested in his well-being, and all three feeling isolated and misunderstood.

What lifts this material above the level of popular trash is Atwood's handling of it. The three main characters are presented with considerable insight, and the shifting point of view and the skillful use of imagery underline their dissatisfaction with themselves, their isolation from one another, their inability to communicate, and the intrinsic hopelessness of their condition.

The novel begins and ends with Elizabeth, who is in many ways both the most unpleasant and most pitiable of the three. Described by one of her colleagues as "haute Wasp," she appears to others to be an intimidating figure with the assurance that comes from being reared in Toronto's dominant Anglo-Saxon society. She exerts considerable control over those around her; Nate's cast-off mistress accuses her of trying to supervise even her husband's love affairs. The reader, however, sees her as a basically vulnerable, insecure person who strives for control only to stave off chaos.

Her veneer of self-assurance covers the scars of a trauma-filled childhood. Her mother was an alcoholic; her father deserted the family when she was a small child. Elizabeth was frequently the only one capable even of buying food for herself and her younger sister, Caroline. At ten and seven, the children were rescued—stolen, Elizabeth later concluded—by their mother's sister, "Auntie Muriel," who provided a loveless but respectable home with "advantages" the girls were expected to be grateful for. Caroline showed signs of mental illness all through her childhood, eventually becoming catatonic and finally drowning in a bathtub in a mental hospital. The stronger Elizabeth responded by becoming a fighter. She learned how to manage money, to manipulate people for her own advantage, to struggle to preserve what was hers—husband, home, children—and she drew strength from her hatred of her aunt, who remained in her mind the terrifying "wicked witch of the west" of her childhood fantasy.

Chris's death severely shakes her composure, and Nate's departure further assaults her ego, although she is able to convince him and others that she is still the one in control. Auntie Muriel dies, wasting away from cancer, "melting, like the witch in *The Wizard of Oz*, and seeing it Elizabeth remembers: Dorothy was not jubilant when the witch turned into a puddle of brown sugar. She was terrified." The last section of the book presents Elizabeth alone, looking tearfully at an exhibition of contemporary Chinese peasant art, pro-

paganda depicting a never-never land of bright colors and cooperative enter-
prises. Atwood leaves her with the comment, "China does not exist.
Nevertheless she longs to be there."

It is not difficult for Elizabeth to dominate Nate, who seems to have no
capacity to enforce his will on others; he hardly seems to *have* a will of his
own. He is an intrinsically gentle, caring man, more sensitive to the needs
of their two daughters than Elizabeth is. He has left the practice of law for
a more congenial occupation, making expensive hand-crafted toys, but he is
dogged by failure. In the recessionary economy of the late 1970's, no one can
afford eighty-dollar hobby horses, and as his life becomes increasingly frustrating his animals have blank expressions instead of the joyful ones he has
aimed for. He sometimes thinks of himself as "a lump of putty, helplessly
molded by the relentless demands and flinty disapprovals of the women he
can't help being involved with": Elizabeth; his rejected mistress, who tries
to avenge herself on him with a faked suicide attempt; his widowed mother,
who devotes her energies to what he sees as a totally futile effort to right
international injustice and expects him to do the same.

He is drawn to Lesje for her apparent passivity, her quiet, exotic foreign
beauty, which seems to offer him a chance to be the protector for once in his
life. He hopes to become with her a different self, to transform his white
rootlike feet into healthy brown ones running on a tropical island where she
will stand waiting for him wearing hibiscus blossoms in her hair (and where
Elizabeth and the children will also be, tucked away somewhere in a grass
hut). What he actually achieves through the affair, however, is boredom and
business suits. He cannot break free of Elizabeth and his sense of obligation
to her and the children, and so he returns to his old law firm to earn enough
for the child support payments Elizabeth really does not need. Inevitably, his
work there is the legal aid cases, the hopeless ones no one else wants to
handle. In trying to hold on to both of his lives, to possess the Lesje of his
dreams without giving up his family, he succeeds only in turning Lesje into
a second Elizabeth and leaves himself trapped once again.

Lesje has only the vaguest idea of what Nate wants of her. She yields at
first partially because of his almost pathetic longing for her, or for what she
represents to him, but more because of his connection with Elizabeth and
Chris, whose affair and its violent conclusion seem to show "an adult world
where choices had consequences, significant, irreversible." Her life to that
point seems to her static, incapable of change—even her relationship with
William, who talks incessantly of sewage disposal and will never, she knows,
marry her because she is too foreign to bear his children.

Lesje is at heart an observer of life rather than a participant in it. She
escapes by creating fantasies of herself crouching in the top of a tree fern,
watching stegosaurs through binoculars. Until she becomes involved with
Nate, she is essentially still the child who has dreamed of discovering another

Lost World, a lush, beautiful Lesjeland where she will be safe from the squabbling of her now-dead grandmothers, one Ukrainian, the other Jewish, who fought over her and tried to fit her into their own cultures. She is at first no match for Elizabeth, who cuts her to shreds at a dinner party to which she has invited Lesje and William—to look over the opposition and establish her own territorial rights. Eventually, however, the younger woman learns to stand up for herself. If it takes children to hold Nate, she decides, she will have a child, whether he likes it or not. She arrives at the maturity she has sought and finds it to be the time when "you get to the point where you think you've blown your life." She loses something in the process; she can no longer call up her visions of prehistoric worlds. She does not fear Elizabeth any more, however, and she learns some of the tricks of survival in her environment—she reflects at one point that she would have been better off if she had studied primate behavior rather than fossils. She, too, is almost without hope at the end of the book. To be happy, she and Nate would have to be different, only a little different, but the necessary change would require a miracle, and this is a world in which miracles do not take place.

The characters' feelings about themselves and one another are brilliantly conveyed through the imagery that Atwood uses with her poet's skill. Elizabeth thinks of herself as an hourglass with sand flowing through it; as the slowly dwindling candle of a familiar nursery rhyme; as the planetarium ceiling—the night sky—with "small holes glow[ing] red in her stomach, eating their way into her flesh." Her favorite objects are the beautiful pottery bowls "of nothing" in her living room. When her aunt comes to remonstrate with her about the breakup of her marriage, it is one of these bowls that she hurls at the older woman in her rage, an appropriate symbol of the hollow, brittle life she represents.

Nate, too, sees himself in nonhuman terms. Visiting the museum with Lesje, he "feels his bones eroding, stone filling the cavities," and tries not to recognize the mummies and suits of armor as images of his own lifeless existence. He is merely "patchwork, a tin man, his heart stuffed with sawdust." To Elizabeth, he seems remote, like a "star that moved on thousands of light years before," and to himself, "the solitary wanderer under the cold red stars."

Extinction and death also haunt Lesje, whose work keeps her constantly aware of transience and death. She thinks of her feisty grandmothers as the last of their species, the end of an era. In a hotel room with Nate, as he prepares to leave her to go to his children, she imagines herself a lungfish and feels her heart "gulping for oxygen in the blackness of this outer space." At times these bleak visions offer her consolation; in a hostile encounter with Elizabeth she takes some satisfaction in the thought that they are both conglomerations of molecules and ions destined for dissolution.

Nate's imagined tropical island and Lesje's Jurassic paradises give fleeting glimpses of hope, but almost all the rest of the imagery supports Atwood's conception of her society as moribund, perched over the edge of the abyss, frozen in space like the man in the planetarium show, who is sucked into a black hole and "hangs spread-eagled against the blackness while the voice explains that he has actually disappeared. He's an optical illusion."

Life Before Man is a devastating portrait of a hollow society in which people are doomed to suffer alone, completely incapable of making the connections with one another that might ease the pain that seems inescapable. Atwood is an enormously gifted artist, and this novel is in many ways her best, most mature, work of fiction. Its haunting images lift it above the level of social criticism and give it universal significance. Its view of the world is such a dark one that readers may not return to this book for pleasure, but they are not likely to forget it.

Elizabeth Johnston Lipscomb

A LITTLE ORDER
A Selection from His Journalism

Author: Evelyn Waugh (1903-1966)
Edited by Donat Gallagher
Publisher: Little, Brown and Company (Boston). 192 pp. $12.95
Type of work: Essays, reviews, and commentaries
Time: 1921-1962
Locale: England and the United States

A collection of occasional essays, book reviews, and commentaries drawn from all stages of Waugh's career as a writer, this collection illustrates the full range of interests and passions of a man better known as a novelist

As American literature came of age in the twentieth century, the United States produced a great number of major artists who captured the attention of most American readers of fiction. As a result, many English writers who might in an earlier age have interested the American reading public passed most of their careers unnoticed except for the occasional work which achieved some attention on this side of the Atlantic. One such writer is Evelyn Waugh, whose sixteen novels, assorted biographies and travel works, and collections of short stories passed in and out of print attracting little notice among Americans except for those few specially attuned to the state of the English literary scene. In fact, Waugh is best known in America primarily as the author of the novel *The Loved One* because it was used as the basis for the satiric movie of the same name, a movie remembered for its viciously black-humored attack on what Jessica Mitford called the American way of death.

Lately, however, Waugh has been undergoing a revival of interest in America not so much because of his fictional output but because of his distinctive personality. The recent publication of his *Diaries* (1976) and his *Letters* (1980) makes clear that what is now interesting about Waugh is not the work of a literary career but the occasional and private writings which, one hopes, will reveal the man behind the works. The present volume, *A Little Order*, is much in this vein. It brings together a selection of Waugh's journalistic output from the full range of his adult career, grouped conveniently under topical headings—pieces devoted to discussions of himself, pieces of art criticism and commentary on culture, discussions of books and writers, pieces on contemporary political circumstances, and, finally, essays and reviews related to religion, especially Catholicism.

Several things must be said at the outset. In the first place, the editor of this volume, Donat Gallagher, has exercised great selectivity. Many pieces are only excerpts of longer works. Many of Waugh's more famous pieces, the more acid ones, are not included. Even so, the overall quality of the work is uneven. Many of these essays and reviews reflect the haste that is part of the world of daily journalism. Others require an understanding of issues and controversies long-dead if readers are to grasp the significance of what Waugh is getting at in them. For these pieces, their appearance here will be chiefly of interest to fans of Waugh who want to read everything he wrote or to scholars of the English literary and cultural scene since World War I. Occasionally, however, the pieces gathered here reveal that mastery of language and style which sets Waugh apart from many of his contemporaries, or that penetrating insight into the foibles and failures of modern life which makes his novels of continuing interest. To have these works conveniently arranged and printed in this volume makes this book of more than passing significance.

Perhaps the current interest in Waugh the man is a reflection of the current conservative mood in American life. Certainly, his personal combination of conservatism in political matters, his defense of the English class system, and his devotion to Catholicism make him more at home with a relatively small segment of American society. For example, his persistence in arguing that the English monarchy was the source of all political authority in England, and his refusal to vote for members of parliament because that might suggest that sovereignty was vested in the people, are attitudes with which few Americans would feel comfortable. What is intriguing about Waugh is the shock of discovering a man who is so totally opposed to most of what happened in culture, art, and politics in the past fifty years. Waugh adopted that attitude early in his adult life, this collection reveals, and he cultivated that image with meticulous care and diligence until the end of his life.

For, clearly, Waugh found in his public persona a marketable pose, one that attracted attention precisely because of its outrageousness. As Samuel Johnson once said about women preaching in the eighteenth century, the thing that attracts attention is not how well it is done, but that it is done at all. In Waugh's comments on contemporary culture, there is precisely that combination of pointing out over-blown claims and human foibles and advocating alternatives blatantly impossible and unworkable that at once delights and infuriates. People know that there is a good measure of human fallibility and pretension in all that is done; it is delightful to find that pointed out, for it makes people more honest with themselves and others. The extent to which Waugh delights the reader is a measure of the degree to which people enjoy seeing the other man's ox gored; the extent to which he enrages readers is a good measure of their own pretentiousness. These are the qualities that make Waugh's novels entertaining; when they appear in these occasional pieces, they lend a more universal appeal to controversies long-forgotten.

There remain aspects of Waugh's public mask, however, that continue to annoy. For many writers of any political or cultural stripe, their career in writing is a high and noble calling, demanding the profoundest learning and wisdom. For Waugh to claim that he backed into his writing career because "it was the only way a lazy and ill-educated man could make a decent living" may appear as genteel self-effacement; it also demeans the character of those who take writing more seriously. Waugh's own career also gives the lie to his comment; a "lazy and ill-educated man" could not have produced either the volume or the erudition of his *oeuvre*.

In the same mode, Waugh's depth of Christian faith is not open to question. The snideness of his attitude toward others of equal faith who do not happen to share his devotion to the more arcane aspects of some theological explanations of Christian belief is distressing, however, precisely because it goes against the profound biblical injunctions to charity and acceptance and reconciliation. Even as Waugh was aristocratic in temperament, so he was an aristocrat of the faith. He was unable to reach out in love to those who did not share the particular collection of doctrines he found attractive. He actively sought the role of Christian apologist, yet in a profound sense he failed because of the narrowness of the tradition to which he responded, and his haughty treatment of those who did not respond in just that way to the same narrow tradition.

The leaven in all this, however, is the generosity with which he did respond to those people, including a good number of writers, who met with his approval. This volume is filled with essays of appreciation which are lyrical and deeply moving. They reveal depths of the man unaccounted for in his conventional presentation of his persona. As Paul Fussell has pointed out in his recent study of English travel literature between the wars (*Abroad*, 1980), when Waugh was working outside the narrow confines of the English social setting in which he set up his public mask, he was capable of a responsiveness and openness that he denied to himself in his more conventional setting. Some of the pieces collected here reveal this, more human, side of the man.

In short, this volume has all the strengths and weaknesses of such anthologies of occasional work, in that it reveals both the richness of an attitude toward life and the limitations of the man who held it. Fans of Waugh will like it, for they will find in it more of what to look for in his longer, major work. Students of his age will appreciate it because it offers work that gives the flavor of that age, work echoing the immediate social situation in ways that longer, more considered pieces cannot provide. The rest of us will respond as we might to the man himself, alternately delighted and enraged, as perhaps he would want us to respond. As we become more aware of and interested in the middle years of the twentieth century as a period now open to historical study, we will find Waugh a convenient guide to some of its complexities, and this volume a helpful guidebook.

John N. Wall, Jr.

LIVES OF THE MODERN POETS

Author: William H. Pritchard
Publisher: Oxford University Press (New York). 316 pp. $14.95
Type of work: Literary criticism and history
Time: 1900-1940

A collection of writings which serve as introductions to nine important modern poets

What may turn out to be the most interesting feature of William H. Pritchard's *Lives of the Modern Poets* is not his lucid, amiable, occasionally original, ultimately unnecessary collection of prefaces to the lives of the nine most "interesting and important poets writing in English in the first part of this century," but his Introduction which amounts to a polemic on the state of contemporary literary criticism and Pritchard's explicit discontent with it. It is this section which has drawn the most response from reviewers and one worth investigating.

Pritchard begins on a Leavis-like note of self-confidence. His aim is to provide "introductions to, reevaluations of" the life and poetry of the nine poets whom he feels constitute the great tradition of modern poetry—Thomas Hardy, William Butler Yeats, Edwin Arlington Robinson, Robert Frost, Ezra Pound, T. S. Eliot, Wallace Stevens, Hart Crane, and William Carlos Williams. He presumes that his "ideal" reader will be literate, "at ease with a complicated novel, less so with poetry perhaps; but who in any case is curious about, if relatively unfamiliar with, at least some of the figures treated here." Who, after all, would not want such an audience? The days, however, when poetry has enjoyed general acclaim ended with the death of Robert Frost, the last great publicly loved poet. Since then reading, appreciating, and wanting to know about poetry has increasingly become an academic pastime and even within English Departments few professors read contemporary poetry for pleasure.

Pritchard's emphasis, therefore, should be toward a more general, uninformed, only slightly interested reader. This, despite his stated wish, he at first seems to promise in his rejection of "certain tendencies and attitudes in contemporary literary studies." Pritchard rightfully is not at ease with the structuralists of France (Derrida, Barthes) nor with the deconstructionists of the Yale English Department (Geoffrey Hartman), both of whom seem to view a poem as a verbal coda whose message and meaning are uncovered through precise, impersonal critical methodologies. Nor does he agree with those like Gustave Flaubert in the nineteenth century and Foucault in the twentieth who talk about the "disappearance of the author" in a work, particularly when one has in mind lyric poetry. For Pritchard "the push of the whole man" can be found in the lyric, and he sets as his principal aim the task of uncovering that presence and amplifying the voice speaking to readers. To do so, like the old-fashioned critic he is, Pritchard provides both a biographical sketch of the poets' lives and a recapitulation of the literary criticism which helped to explicate the poems as they were written.

The aim and approach are good, but the results are far from satisfactory. In presenting the background of his nine poets' lives, for instance, he states that he has relied on details from letters, revealing anecdotes, and bits of gossip. What he actually presents, however, are bare-boned biographical accounts which leave the general reader without any substantive biographical background to relate to the poet's work and the more "literate" reader with a rehash of facts with which he is already familiar.

Similarly, Pritchard acknowledges that in this "age of criticism" by which everyone has been influenced, even burdened, an overwhelming amount of commentary has become part of the atmosphere in which the poet or poem now live. He is to be commended for giving credit to these sources. Much of this criticism has shaped the reading and conception of modern poetry, and any reader, literate or not, should know about them. Yet, when it comes to discussing these critical works, Pritchard fails to probe fully the standard interpretations associated with each poet and focuses instead on more idiosyncratic or specialized issues. In his Preface to Yeats, for example, Pritchard never mentions Richard Ellman's name. Or, in discussing *The Waste Land*, he gives the reader only passing reference to those such as F. O. Matthiessen and Helen Gardner who helped to unravel the erudition of the poem and turns his attention instead to three current, tangential views of the poem which may be of interest to Eliot scholars but hardly serve to open the meaning of the poem or to reveal how its importance in present cultural life came into being. These oversights, compounded by a lack of a good critical bibliography, occur throughout the book, and are one of its principal failings.

Another point on which Pritchard seems to miss the mark is his adamant denial that his book has any similarity to Samuel Johnson's *Lives of the English Poets*, the title of which Pritchard acknowledges he had in mind. He correctly states that Johnson divided his fifty-two prefaces into a tripartite structure, consisting of a biography, a character sketch of his subject, and, finally, a criticism of the work in chronological order. Although Johnson's memory and his scholarship were not always accurate, one generally puts down Johnson's book knowing what the character of the poet was about. Pritchard, too, admires Johnson's *Lives of the English Poets*, but he argues that this three-point approach to analyzing a man and his work is neither possible nor relevant today. "We no longer see the facts of a man's life, his character, and his works as existing in separate compartments." Yet, in looking at the Yeats Preface, as an example, Pritchard does exactly what he suggests can no longer be done: he begins with a brief biographical outline of Yeats's life; he proceeds with a section on Yeats's development as a poet from the early romantic poems rooted in nineteenth century sensibility to the late modern poems; and finally he gives the reader lengthy discussion on the "Yeats Problem"—his egotism and how it affects the universality of his work. If Pritchard weaves these elements into a more general essay than Johnson had done, the fundamental structure remains essentially Johnsonian.

Also in the Johnsonian vein, fortunately, is the most refreshing aspect of Pritchard's work: the way in which he successfully conveys his own personal, firsthand response to years of reading, rereading, teaching, and writing about modern poetry. In his Introduction, Pritchard writes:

> Temperamentally I am less interested in the practice—too often a grim one—of interpretation by an extended prose exegesis, than in suggesting what the experience is like of reading a poet on the basis of his best or mostly typical poem. Here my classroom bias is apparent. . . .

Like the wonderful teacher he must be, Pritchard conveys this firsthand quality in many ways. With tongue-in-cheek, he tells the reader that next to Hugh Kenner and Harold Bloom he must be regarded as a "weak" critic for indiscriminately liking so many poets and not canonizing any one of them. Or, in his conclusion, he plays a game with the reader and reveals his own favorites by ranking those who will last—Eliot, Stevens, Yeats, and Frost—with those who will have less good fortune. Curiously, those whom Pritchard clearly admires, Frost and Eliot, are those whom many would regard as the least modern. Throughout the prefaces, he also throws in a remark, such as the following on Eliot's "The Love Song of J. Alfred Prufrock," which helps to hold the readers interest and causes him to pay attention:

> Eliot wrote the poem just after entering his twenties; I remember memorizing it at age twenty on a bus bound for Albany, New York. It was an extremely useful poem with which to convert late-adolescent feelings of inadequacy into satisfying romantic posturings. . . .

Like John Barrell's *The Idea of Landscape & the Sense of Place*, a superb analysis of the poetry of John Clare, Pritchard's work is best in moments such as this. It is a shame that he did not choose to reveal more of his own self.

Finally, in the Introduction, Pritchard states that the unity of his collection rests on the supposition that these nine poets all flourished in and around 1914, the year in which

> Yeats . . . published *Responsibilities* with its proud declarations and dedications of new purposes in a style which Pound . . . praised for its "hardness." Pound himself was to bring forth *Cathay* in the next year with its significant experiments. . . . Frost's *North of Boston* was published in 1914 and also reviewed by Pound. . . . Hardy's *Satires of Circumstance*, dated 1914. . . . D. H. Lawrence's first book of verse, *Love Poems and Others*, appeared in 1913; E. A. Robinson's best one, *The Man Against the Sky*, in 1916. Eliot published "Prufrock" and Stevens "Sunday Morning" in 1915. . . .

Pritchard here is clearly stretching his argument to make a point which serves little real purpose.

It is often unfair to criticize a work for what it does not do, but in this case it is perhaps justified because Pritchard leaves out that which most general readers might expect to find in a book of this kind. Rather than arguing a year around which to group these nine poets' lives, would it not have been more useful to discuss why these poets are modern, certainly the key word in Pritchard's title, or what principles they held in common, what poetic aims they shared, or how their sense of language was affected by the modern movement? Pritchard addresses this point, yet shies away from coming to terms with it:

> Operating at a high enough level of abstraction, a critic with sufficient ingenuity could probably take these nine poets and show that they hold certain principles and practices in common; but I am not this critic nor do I have the intention of arguing that the nine really do belong together in ways more profound than is indicated by the chronological continuity of work that converges around 1914.

So too might one expect Pritchard to discuss why so many of these poets whose lives were touched by alcoholism, madness, suicide, and egomania suffered from these problems. Taking a cue, say, from A. Alvarez's *The Savage God*, Pritchard could at least have offered the general reader some personal speculations on these modern biographical issues. Instead, what is given is simply a citing of these problems and a chronological presentation of nine seemingly separate lives whose only connection is the rather thin thread of 1914.

In sum, admittedly, each Preface is a lucid, generally enjoyable, always erudite recapitulation of a poet's life, but nothing a reader could not already obtain from a good introduction to an edition of the poet's work. Further, as a collection, the book has little unity or critical theme except Pritchard's *annus mirabilis*. What is useful, however, is Pritchard's Introduction because in it he raises issues which not only concern academicians, but also how each individual has come to respond to art. Pritchard has set out to challenge the more fashionable literary attitudes of the day by viewing art not as an isolated, autonomous, impersonal construct, but as something that has to do with an artist's life, with the common life of each person, and with the supposition that art is needed because it helps people to live their own lives. In other words, art is personal. By focusing on biography, the issue of an artist's character, historical issues, and his own personal responses, Pritchard has sought to redirect critical attitudes to the safer, more comfortable, familiar shores of a bygone era. He should be applauded for being so boldly old-fashioned, yet, regrettably, the results are not as illuminating as they might have been.

Bryan Fuermann

LOON LAKE

Author: E. L. Doctorow (1931-   )
Publisher: Random House (New York). 258 pp. $11.95
Type of work: Novel
Time: Primarily between World War I and World War II
Locale: The United States

Using the time between World War I and World War II as metaphor for our past and future history, Doctorow attempts to show by means of the juxtaposition of mirrored reflections that all our times are one, all our people replicas of one another

Principal characters:
> JOE OF PATERSON, born Joseph Korzeniowski in Paterson, New Jersey, who becomes in metaphoric rebirth Joseph Paterson Bennett son of F. W. Bennett
> WARREN PENFIELD, a poet, whose search is similar to Joe's and whose death in an airplane crash is simultaneous with Joe's rebirth
> CLARA LUKÁĆS, Joe's girl, Warren's girl, Bennett's girl, a replica of everybody's girl
> F. W. BENNETT, an American capitalist and financier
> LUCINDA BENNETT, his wife, an aviatrix, who dies in an airplane crash with Warren Penfield
> TOMMY CRAPO, an American gangster, in Bennett's employ
> RED JAMES, an industrial spy, in Crapo's employ
> SANDY JAMES, his wife, a fifteen-year-old mother

In *Loon Lake*, Doctorow uses just about every device that has come to be associated with the contemporary mode in prose fiction: a shifting point of view, a metafictional frame, doublings and layerings with the mirror as major metaphor, use of the dream or dream structure, elements of what has been called "magic realism." The whole purpose being somehow to communicate the nonlinear, the synchronistic through a form (the novel) which by its nature is linear, because, try as we might, we read words one after another while seconds tick away. When the effort is successful, as it is in such masters of the contemporary mode as Vladimir Nabokov, Gabriel García Márquez, Jorge Luis Borges, Thomas Pynchon, and even the Joseph Heller of *Catch-22*, the effect is stunning; readers are caught in new dimensions. Doctorow, however, is no Nabokov, at least not yet. In *Loon Lake* the mechanism is there, but it creaks; the parts need oiling; still Doctorow's effort is mighty, and the result praiseworthy.

Although the major focal characters of the novel are Joe Paterson and Warren Penfield, the point of view shifts from first person to third and occasionally to second as an apparent author speaks directly to the reader. Chapters primarily in first person are juxtaposed with chapters in third person and all of this is juxtaposed with poems (some annotated), and what appears to be computer based data. Part one of Chapter One, for example, begins in first person with the voice of Joe. On page eleven the first-person voice shifts to third person for the space of a paragraph and then moves back to first person. In Chapter Two, the poem that was started in Chapter One becomes longer and merges with computer data composing Warren Penfield. Chapter Three begins in the third person and then shifts to the first-person voice of Joe. Chapter Four gives the reader more computer information about Warren. Chapter Five is a dramatic scene focusing on Warren but told in the third person. This kind of juxtaposition of point of view continues throughout the novel. The final chapter of the novel is a composite of all points of view used, with the last page being a sheet of computer data.

The shifting point of view, used to make the point that no one view is totally authoritative, is undercut by the fact that all the voices actually turn out to be the same voice, thus the metafictional frame. Metafiction is fiction about fiction, and in this novel narrative merges with poems which merge with computer data, all three modes telling the same story. That Warren Penfield is a poet is, of course, no accident, but a strategy, as is the fact that he is the seeker of the *koan* whose answer would involve him in an unspeakable paradox. The unspeakable paradox is what Doctorow seeks in the novel, so that, in a sense, author is character and character, author; a mirroring that reflects the major structural patterns in the novel.

Although Joe Paterson and Warren Penfield are a generation apart in years, and Warren a poet and Joe a young roughneck, they are set up as symbolic doubles. Joe, born in Paterson, New Jersey, of Polish parents whose name is unpronounceable, is an isolate. His mother and father work in a factory, and they live on Mechanic Street. For the first years of his life he is lonely and sick, but at the age of fifteen, he takes to the streets and becomes adept at thieving. The end of the first chapter finds Joe in the symbolic act of stealing money from the poorbox in a Catholic church. Caught by the priest who is doubled with God, the Father; Joe, in an act of rebellion, kicks the priest in the groin and flings the money in the air as he runs away.

Warren is born in Ludlow, Colorado, and his father works in the mines. A gifted child, Warren, like Joe, is detached from his parents; and although not himself violent, he finds that watching violence thrills him. Both Warren and Joe are from "company" families and bound up with the capitalist F. W. Bennett. Warren's family is forced away from their company home after a strike. This is one of the reasons that Warren seeks Bennett in his private retreat at Loon Lake and attempts to kill him, although he fails.

Warren is in Seattle in 1918 for the first general strike in United States history; this is the year of Joe's birth, and one year after the United States entered the first great war. It is the result of a threatened strike in Atlanta that Red James is murdered and Joe arrested, as a consequence of which Joe goes back to Loon Lake, not actually but symbolically, to kill Bennett. Warren thinks of Joe as the son he might have had, and Joe, in taking Clara away from Warren and lying to him about it, metaphorically castrates him, repeating his act with the Catholic priest.

Warren serves in World War I and Joe in World War II and both are decorated for their actions. Warren's death with Lucinda, Bennett's wife, in an airplane crash, makes it possible for Joe to assume his role as Bennett's son, and finally to accomplish the act of castrating and killing the father. Toward the end of the novel Joe says that he will kill Bennett by testifying that he is not sub or superhuman but simply human and he will do this by extending his reign, by becoming his son. Joe, also, like Warren and Bennett, is without issue, although he marries twice. Warren, the poet, makes the point in a letter to Joe, written just before the airplane crash. Warren sends to Joe all his papers, chapbooks, letters, *pensées*, journals, all, he says, that is left of him. He tells Joe that he knows that Joe will reappear at Loon Lake, because "perhaps we all reappear, perhaps all our lives are impositions one on another."

Loon Lake is, of course, the major metaphor in the novel. Hidden inside Bennett's retreat in the Adirondacks, the lake is the essential mirror in which we see ourselves. Again, the poet makes the point in the poem "Loon Lake." The image is of loons diving into cold, black water and coming back out again. Their cries are in protest against falling, against having to fall and having to struggle up again and again "the water kissing and pawing and whispering/the most horrible promises." The act of falling and the return extrudes the organs and "turns the birds inside out." This, then, is death: "the environment exchanging itself for the being," an act mirrored in the black holès of the universe. This same image of falling is repeated in the opening lines of the final chapter of the novel, here extended to motifs of falling through space, through skies, through dreams, "through floor downstairs down well down hole downpour."

There are at least three meanings for the word "loon." A loon is a bird, a grebe; "loon" is also, in Scottish dialect, a lout, a rascal, a lad, and a harlot; and, adding a "y" and coming from the word "lunatic," the word means crazy or daft. All meanings fit the novel, Warren even having spent some time in Nutley Sanitorium. The act of falling or diving into water is also highly suggestive of the sexual act, a point that Doctorow underscores inside Warren's poem when he speaks of water kissing, pawing, and whispering, and later when the falling is down wells and holes.

Except for Lucinda, who herself falls through the air, the women in this novel exist simply as sexual beings. From Fanny the Fat Lady to Sandy, the child mother, they exist as fatal attraction. Joe's sex life is an exemplum. When he is a young boy he is admitted into the bedroom of a maid, Hilda, who puts a pillow over her head when they make love. She is for Joe both repository and play toy, an object of manipulation. Fanny the Fat Lady is repository for the sperm of all the men who gang up on her, and her death agonies double with copulation and climax. Joe, still young, is horrified by what happens to Fanny; so he takes out his anger and his frustration on Mrs. Hearn, attacking her sexually in a way he considers similar to the gang attack on Fanny and flinging her money into the heavens in a way similar to his actions after he attacked the priest. Immediately after the attack on Mrs. Hearn, Joe sees the railroad car with Clara in it, and, besmitten by her, follows it. Clara is lover to them all—to Warren, to Bennett, to Crapo, to Joe. At one and the same time she is dispassionate love goddess and the infant girl of Warren's recollections, hanging naked and exposed, crying and urinating. Joe uses Sandy, the fifteen-year-old mother in a similar manner. After Clara leaves him, Joe uses Sandy's money to get him back to California. Recently widowed, Sandy is vulnerable, and she believes Joe when he says he will marry her. He leaves her asleep in a railroad car, however, her baby in her arms.

Doctorow uses an actual dream only once in the novel, in the final chapter where all the motifs come together. There Joe recounts a dream of his. He envisions himself a country lord traveling with a servant boy who is a girl in disguise. They book rooms in an inn. In order to disguise the fact that his boy is a girl he calls for a woman, himself responding to her with ordinary lasciviousness, the girl with the affection of a child for her mother. In order to keep the woman from finding out that the boy is a girl in disguise, Joe must use on the woman all of his sexual arts which quickly move to the violent; and he beheads her. Their journey continues, the fairy-tale motif becoming more apparent, for soon his young love becomes a giantess. He trips her, felling her, and runs into her vulva, searching, he says, for the godhead; but his way becomes narrower; he is flattened, becoming sperm searching for the light. Then he feels himself enlarging. He becomes his own size again and breaks her open, like an egg.

Doctorow or Joe (it makes no difference by this time) comments directly to the reader. "You are thinking it is a dream. It is no dream. It is the account in helpless linear translation of the unending love of our simultaneous but disynchronous lives."

Although there is only one actual dream in the novel, Doctorow makes use of dream structure involving archetypal patterns throughout the book. Joe of Paterson is obviously a knight in search of the grail as he crisscrosses the country by means of one conveyance or another. Warren, too, is seeker; the poet trying to understand the paradox both here and in Japan. The search for the father is also a search for the godhead, and the best option is F. W. Bennett, American "king," who bestows his favors as if by chance and as if by chance withholds them. His power and wealth trickle down to the people as do the poisoning of the air, the wastes, the ruins, and the wars that keep his power intact. His retreat is a magic land surrounding the miraculous and shimmering Loon Lake on which, in a speedboat, he points out to gangster, poet, and love goddess the extent of his beneficence. His power, like the railroad that grew to immense proportions between the two World Wars, extending to all the places of the western world and even to Japan whose people learned from Warren the customs of Americans, is finally passed to his knighted son, who in fairy-tale splendor when "the whole spring of the earth has come forth and Loon Lake is a bowl of light" accepts the mantle of power and wealth, whose symbol is Loon Lake.

Mary Rohrberger

LOUIS-FERDINAND CÉLINE

Author: Merlin Thomas
Publisher: New Directions (New York) 249 pp. $16.50
Type of work: Literary biography
Time: 1894-1961
Locale: Primarily France, Germany, and Denmark

A critical biography of the twentieth century French novelist, Louis-Ferdinand Céline

> *Principal personage:*
> LOUIS-FERDINAND CÉLINE (DESTOUCHES), a medical doctor, pamphleteer, and novelist

Louis-Ferdinand Céline, by Merlin Thomas, was first published in 1979 by Faber and Faber in England. The American edition, published by New Directions, reflects the book's British origins. Conventions of punctuation adhere to British custom; the period, for example, follows the closing quotation marks, instead of being enclosed—American style—within the marks. Also, British orthographical rules obtain; hence, *honor* and *splendor*, for example, are spelled *honour* and *splendour*. Further, Thomas is somewhat given to trendy tautologies such as "plot-wise" and "at that point in time." Yet, these are but minor stylistic irritants. The substance of the book is the ultimate determinant in evaluating its worth.

In this critical biography, Thomas undertakes a formidable task. The publishing world commonly assumes that biographies are highly popular with the reading public, since such readers seem to be voyeuristically captivated by intimate details about the famous as well as the infamous. Thomas, however, faced a problem of a different sort; his subject, Céline, suffered from neglect. To be sure, Thomas explicitly acknowledges that his first priority is an assessment of Céline's art; yet, he concedes with equal candor that Céline had been ignored for political reasons rather than for reasons of legitimate literary criticism. Thomas thus sets for himself a delicate matrix: a balance between art and politics.

Moreover, it is axiomatic that best-selling works do not threaten the reading public by being challenging or innovative. Here, Thomas is on shaky ground in two respects. First, his subject was unpopular among the reading public for generally unacceptable political views. Second, Céline was certifiably an original, unique stylist; he crafted language to suit his purpose as very few of his predecessors in French literature were capable of doing. In fact, Thomas enumerates fifteen writers whom he considers equals of Céline and nine potential equals—a mere twenty-four writers from the Renaissance to the present—to underscore Céline's unusual talents. Hence, Thomas is dealing with a novelist who is a political pariah as well as a gifted artist who defies convention to challenge the reader's intelligence. As a consequence, Thomas' work also will not have popular appeal.

Nevertheless, Thomas brings impressive credentials to bear on this task. He is a Fellow of New College, Oxford (England), in French. Further, he obtained access to Jean-Pierre Dauphin's collection of Céline's manuscripts and memorabilia, a source not readily available to earlier Céline biographers. In addition, Thomas' fluent French enabled him to translate into English extensive passages from Céline's novels and pamphlets. In a prefatory note, Thomas points out that his translations are deliberately literal, rather than idiomatic, in order to emphasize Céline's innovative use of language—an important point in defending Thomas' thesis that Céline's artistry transcends his unpopular political views.

Also, Thomas states his critical biases explicitly. He views twentieth century French prose as something of a wasteland, with Céline a stellar exception in prose style. Céline's uniqueness thus captures Thomas' interest. Hence, between Thomas and Céline, there is a symbiotic match of biographer and subject.

Limning his study, Thomas explains his purpose on the basis of the paucity of material in English on Céline. Without cavil, Thomas' point is well taken. Most critical works on Céline are in French. English-language studies on Céline are, indeed, scarce. In fact, Thomas cites in his annotated bibliography of works on Céline only one book published in the United States and another published in England, even though other English-language works on Céline are available. For example, Erika Ostrovsky's *Céline and His Vision* (New York University Press) was published in 1967, with extensive notes and bibliography. The reasons for such omissions and for the brevity of Thomas' annotated bibliography—no journal articles are cited—are not apparent. Still, interest in Céline has increased in France, and several recent studies of a serious nature have been published. Yet, Thomas rightly calls attention to two notable lacunae in Céline scholarship: some aspects of biography have been overlooked, and Céline's later works have received short shrift. Nevertheless, Thomas does not set out to fill these lacunae. He does, however go a long way, despite protestations to the contrary, to overcome these gaps.

The basic facts of Céline's life are clear cut. He was born Louis-Ferdinand Destouches on May 27, 1894. His father, Ferdinand Destouches, was an insurance man in Courbevoie, a suburb of Paris; his mother, Louise-Céline Guillou, owned a lace shop. Céline grew up and was educated in Paris. He joined the army in 1912, was wounded in World War I in 1914, and was discharged in 1915 for disability. During a brief sojourn in London, he married Suzanne Germaine Nebout and then spent about a year in West Africa. In 1919, he returned to France, began to study medicine at Rennes, and—now divorced—married Edith Follet, daughter of the head of the medical school. A year later, they produced a daughter, Colette. In 1924, Céline qualified as a medical doctor, whereupon he traveled extensively through Europe, Africa, and America. Edith divorced him in 1928, and he returned to medical practice in France.

Shortly thereafter, in 1932, Céline launched a second and parallel career as a novelist. For that career, he adopted his mother's Christian middle-name as a surname and pen name. Dr. Louis-Ferdinand Destouches became Louis-Ferdinand Céline in 1932 with the publication of *Voyage au bout de la nuit* (*Journey to the End of the Night*). Céline had published before—medical treatises under the name Destouches. His parallel careers, however—doctor and novelist—converged in the late 1930's: the thesis (medical doctor) and the antithesis (novelist) forged a Hegelian dialectic into synthesis: Destouches-Céline became a political figure and a pamphleteer.

Continuing his medical practice as well as his writing and his political involvement, Céline married again (to Lucette Almanzor) in 1943. In the meanwhile, his public anti-Semitic pronouncements prior to and during World War II made him anathema in many circles. Although he traveled widely, he incurred the wrath of many Allied authorities and fled across several countries in the waning days of World War II to escape prosecution for collaboration with the Nazis. He spent two years in Denmark (1945-1947) under nominal house-arrest, remaining there until 1951, after a French court in 1950 condemned him *in absentia* for collaboration with the Nazis and confiscated his property. A 1951 amnesty allowed him to return to France and resume his practice of medicine and continue his novelist's craft until his death on July 1, 1961.

Thomas meticulously details Céline's work: both polemical and fictional. The format of the book makes it especially valuable for researchers. All sources are carefully acknowledged, as are the biases and the approaches. A two-page biographical note affords handy reference. The bibliographical listing of Céline's works, however—even though it is conveniently arranged in chronological order—mixes medical treatises with novels; further, it omits shorter works (articles, letters, and pamphlets) with a reference to *Cahiers de l'Herne* (Paris, 1972) on Céline, where such works are reprinted. The accessibility of that material is limited, thus restricting first-hand assessment of Céline's complete works. While Thomas disclaims a definitive approach to Céline's biography, he nevertheless asks a great deal of trust from his readers, for his source materials are not readily verifiable, although Céline's novels have been widely translated.

The format of Thomas' book is, however, a strong point in its favor. Tabular and introductory information is presented at the outset so that the reader may easily extract data and just as easily discern critical biases in order to determine the value of the volume for the reader's immediate purposes. In addition, the chapters are logically arranged, with assessments of major works intercalated with critical analyses at appropriate points. The volume concludes with a bibliography of translations of Céline's works and a thorough and accurate index, essential to the serious scholar.

One of Thomas' major points, rightfully, is that Céline's use of language in his novels places him in a special category of French authors who are truly creative. In this respect, Thomas defends his point adeptly, for his definitions of terms include Céline's creative use of vulgarity. The French language is particularly rich in such terms, nearly matching Yiddish in its imaginativeness. Céline, as Thomas clearly points out, certainly took advantage of every nuance, including eccentricities in punctuation, to produce a rich—if somewhat offensive to English readers—vocabulary, the better to vividly etch in his readers' minds the images which he wished to create.

Such language is admittedly obscene; however, it is not—as is sometimes charged—pornographic. The serious reader must recall that, etymologically, pornography is the depiction of acts of harlots, whereas obscenity is merely a description of acts not normally delineated or performed in public. Céline thus has merely made private acts public. He has written somewhat obscene novels, but he is neither erotic nor pornographic. First Amendment issues and case law need not be delved into extensively; and, as Thomas points out, medical treatises are exempt from such considerations. Yet, Céline's novels are, within the strictest definitions of terms, obscene. Céline denotes ordinary human functions in ways which would offend the ordinary reader. Consequently, the ordinary reader—or reading public—would find Céline's novels too challenging to be acceptable as popular fare. Still, sophisticated readers would be able to accept such material without prejudice, on its own merits as those merits stem from the organic presence of such language in the novel as a whole.

Even more serious is the matter of racial and ethnic prejudice. This theme permeates Céline's work and presents Thomas his most difficult problem. In Céline's nonfiction and nonmedical prose, the author presented a skewed view of human nature. Thomas has down-played Céline's bias in favor of a literary evaluation. Céline's political-ethnic-racial views, however, cannot be down-played as Thomas would do, since the novels are strongly autobiographical. Céline's images, as Thomas properly acknowledges, present a rather dismal perspective on human behavior. In fact, Céline's vision may, with some justification, be likened to Thomas Hobbes' depiction of man's life as "solitary, poor, nasty, brutish, and short." Céline was an avowed anti-Semite, and his focus informed all of his work: medical treatises, pamphlets, and novels.

It was thus Céline's political and racial position that presented Thomas with a thorny dilemma in writing Céline's biography. For Céline's political and racial views made him an essentially unpopular figure. When Alex Haley published *Roots* in 1976, the American reading public became sensitized to biography through genealogy. Such an alert reading public is thus likely to approach Thomas' biography of Céline more critically than earlier reading publics approached biographical accounts. While Thomas is British and not entirely subject to American sensitivities, these circumstances must be taken into account, for the book is published for the American reader. Consequently, this book must stand or fall on its own merits for the American reading public.

First, Thomas has done a thorough job of research and documentation. He has gone to original sources—all of Céline's works in French—read them, and translated germane passages literally into English (a valuable service in itself). Further, Thomas has interviewed many of the principals in Céline's life to collect even more information. Thomas' scholarship cannot be faulted. Yet, everyone must acknowledge that biography is history—to be sure, history of a personal sort—and that no man lives in a vacuum. Personal history is affected by political history. As a result, it is necessary to call attention to a current conflict among historians, since that conflict has bearing on the accurate reporting about the life of Céline.

Traditional historians have laid claim not only to authenticity but also to objectivity. They have avowed that they report only the facts. These so-called facts, however, have recently been challenged as misperceptions by a group of historians who characterize themselves as "revisionists." The "revisionist" historians propose to correct the misperceptions of the traditionalists. The heart of the matter is that traditional history has always been written by "winners"; the revisionists want to present other points of view. This brief summary does disservice to both historical factions in oversimplifying a highly complex issue. Such a summary, however, lends insight into the manifold difficulties of trying to present an account of Céline's life and fortunes.

During World War II, passions ran high. Both the Allies and the Axis peddled propaganda with reckless abandon in order to elicit support for their respective causes. Céline—for reasons of personality as well as political convention—chose to accept the propaganda of the Axis. Accordingly, he was chastised, after the war, by literary critics who aligned themselves with the postwar nations who comprised the World War II Allies. Thus, Céline's novels—genuine monuments in the canon of Western literature—were ignored or demeaned because of his political position. Rightly or wrongly, Céline was made a straw man by the traditional historians, literary critics, and others who accepted such assumptions. Consequently, Thomas is placed in the position of a "revisionist."

Under these circumstances, Thomas approaches Céline as a novelist primarily and as a political figure secondarily. Such an approach is Thomas' weakness. By attempting to defend Céline on artistic grounds, Thomas equivocates on Céline's politics and appears to try to rehabilitate Céline. In effect, Thomas sets up an artificial controversy by side-stepping political issues.

In the final analysis, Thomas argues his case proficiently—given the unstated premise of his argument: that a novelist should be forgiven his political errors so long as his novels are artistically and esthetically satisfactory. Most sophisticated readers in America, however, have been attuned to the importance of politics—if not by the propaganda of World War II or the subsequent McCarthy era, at least by the Vietnam War or the Watergate scandal or some other incident. Therefore, Thomas' claim to separating art from politics does not obtain in his biography of Céline, at least in America, for Americans see through the simplistic black-and-white dichotomy between art and politics quite clearly. Unlike Thomas' original British readers, American readers are clearly able to discern that a man's politics affect his view of life as presented in novelistic form. Hence, Céline's pessimistic view of human nature has little appeal to American readers, and Thomas' scrupulously researched biography will attract a few scholars but not the general reading public.

Joanne Kashdan

LUTHER
An Experiment in Biography

Author: H. G. Haile (1931-   )
Publisher: Doubleday & Company (Garden City, New York). Illustrated. 422 pp.
$14.95
Type of work: Biography
Time: The early sixteenth century, primarily 1535-1546
Locale: Saxony

An analysis of the great German Protestant reformer, concentrating on the previously largely ignored last decade of his life

> *Principal personages:*
> MARTIN LUTHER, the father of the Protestant Reformation and the most prolific writer in German history
> PHILIPP MELANCHTHON, a humanist, Greek and Hebrew scholar, theologian, and Luther's closest friend and coworker at the University of Wittenberg

Martin Luther, the father of the Protestant Reformation, has been the subject of an enormous literature, either as the exclusive subject of biographies or as a central figure in general studies of the Reformation. It has been estimated that more books have been written about the Doctor of Wittenberg than any other figure with the exception of Jesus Christ, especially in very recent times. Indeed, British historian Gordon Rupp contended over twenty years ago that more books had appeared in Britain alone on Luther since the end of World War II than in the four centuries before. This does not even include the renaissance in Luther studies that has taken place in Germany and the United States. Luther's popularity as a biographical subject is certainly understandable. He was, himself, the most prolific writer Germany has ever produced, and long before he died, he contributed to his own legendary stature by his writings and by his observations on every conceivable topic to his disciples, who dutifully transcribed them and collected them into what became the now-famous *Table Talks*. His popularity as the subject of historical analysis, especially since World War II, is closely related to the conviction held by some that Luther played a paramount role in the development of the peculiar collective German psyche that was receptive to the extremist tenets of National Socialism. Luther's idiosyncracies, health problems, and penchant for making controversial statements also led to the production of the first attempt at psychohistory, Erik Erikson's *Young Man Luther: A Study in Psychoanalysis and History* (1958), and a moderately popular play and film, John Osborne's *Luther*.

With this knowledge, then, the reader initially questions the need for still another biography of Doctor Martin. H. G. Haile, the author of *Luther: An Experiment in Biography*, however, quickly overcomes this skepticism by immediately noting the incompleteness and inadequacy of earlier Luther studies. Virtually all earlier biographies of Luther, Haile asserts, have concentrated upon Luther's life before 1530, the year of the production of the traditional Lutheran confession of faith, the Augsburg Confession, by Luther's lieutenant Philipp Melanchthon while Luther remained in hiding as an outlaw. These biographies have emphasized the topics that have now become part of the Luther legend, and many of them have come to form the corpus of a Luther hagiography. The high points of the traditional Luther biography are summarized in Haile's opening paragraph: the excessively strict upbringing as a child by hardworking parents; the thunderstorm crisis when a lightning bolt led to Luther's terrified vow to become a monk; the unhappy, questioning years in the Augustinian monastery when Luther sought assurance of his salvation; the turning point when Luther discovered the doctrine of justification by faith alone; the nailing of the Ninety-five Theses on the door of the castle church in Wittenberg; and the appearance before the Diet of Worms and Luther's affirmation of his convictions in the face of overwhelming opposition. Haile questions the veracity of some or all these events, noting that none can be proved or disproved by contemporary documents. They are in fact the boasts of Luther in his later years. They represent Luther's creation of his own heroic legend and are thus suspect.

Haile is also concerned by the "rigid denominationalism" that has long dominated Reformation and Luther historiography. Only a brief summary of these approaches confirms Haile's concern. Early students of the Reformation had to content themselves with the bitterly critical biography of Luther by John Cochlaeus and the excessively laudatory appraisal by Melanchthon. This partisan tradition has continued into the present century with the polemical biography of Heinrich Denifle, O.P., which was criticized by Protestants and Catholics alike for its negative excessiveness. Recent Protestant biographies have been more evenhanded than that of Melanchthon, but they have almost without exception restated the elements of the legend Luther worked to create. During the nineteenth century another ingredient was also added: the economic-materialist interpretation of history which was stimulated by the writings of Karl Marx and Friedrich Engels, by the industrial revolution, and by the spread of materialism. Engels in his *The Peasant War in Germany* and Karl Kautsky in his *Communism in Central Europe in the Time of the Reformation*, by identifying economic and material motives for individual and group identification with the Protestant cause, led historians to deemphasize the religious and spiritual features which were of much greater importance in the sixteenth than in the nineteenth and twentieth centuries.

Haile contends that the rigidity of these three schools of historical writing— Catholic, Protestant, and economic-materialist—has failed to produce the total picture of Luther, and as a result has distorted the contemporary image of the man and his age. His objective is to produce a new type of biography, "an experiment in biography," that concentrates not on the subject's entire life, but only on the last decade of his existence, from 1535 to 1546. While regretting Erik Erikson's uncritical use of documents because of his lack of training as a historian or philologist, Haile does express his indebtedness to Erickson and his pupils for "calling attention to the phases of adult life," and emphasizing the many different roles men assume during their lifetimes. By so doing "they have shown that we must approach the unique character and problems of each time of life on its own terms." Instead of concentrating on the earlier, more dramatic years of Luther's career, Haile believes that a truer picture of the man can be obtained by viewing him in his years of fullest maturity. The Luther that Haile chooses to examine is the settled family man. Married to his beloved "Lord Kate" (née Catherine von Bora) in 1525, Luther was by the mid-1530's the father of a large family, including not only his natural children but numerous students and disciples who enjoyed his hospitality at the Black Cloister in Wittenberg, a former monastery which had been donated to him by the town and which had, under the tutelage of himself and his wife, developed into a large farm. It should be noted, however, that Haile does not fail to refer to earlier events in order to make his post-1535 account more understandable.

Haile is Professor of German at the University of Illinois and the author of several books on the Faust theme. He comes, therefore, well-equipped to analyze the subtleties and crudities of Luther's writings and remarks. All too often in the past historians have lacked the philological training that is necessary to penetrate Luther's complex, often nearly impenetrable, thought processes. Haile possesses this ability and also has a sense of humor, characteristic of Luther as well, that is often absent in the rigid, theologically centered bulk of Luther literature. As a result his book, based almost exclusively on heretofore inadequately used primary sources, is a joy to read and at the same time enlightening about an often little understood major personality in the history of the Western world.

As noted previously, Luther was the most prolific writer Germany has produced. While theological debate remained an abiding interest it was by no means an exclusive one. He wrote continuously on a large variety of subjects and in a wide variety of forms. Haile is absolutely correct when he notes that Luther's "literary output is mountainous not only in sheer volume, but also in the baffling variety of faces it presents to an explorer." The author devotes a significant part of his study to chapters on these various facets of Luther's expression.

Luther was the author of at least thirty-six songs, several of which have become standard hymns in Protestant denominations. These songs, which range from a Christmas tune written for his children to the Protestant anthem, "A Mighty Fortress Is Our God," were often the products of immediate need, sometimes a personal one, thus reflecting Luther's desire to play a pastoral role. He produced glosses, characterized by his often intemperate attacks on theological foes. Although they were the least important of his writings to himself, they are important because they give the student insight into Luther's evolution from an academic debater to a publicist and molder of opinion.

Always the adoring father and a man who enjoyed the company of young people, Luther also produced several animal stories which he regarded as a most effective means of communication. "Not only children," he said, "but also great lords are best beguiled into truth, in their own best interest, by conveying it to them through foolishness. Fools are tolerated and listened to by those who cannot suffer the truth from a wise man." Luther's biting wit also made him adept at the art of satire which he often directed against the papacy and its official pronouncements. He also produced political tracts, adages, moral exhortations against such practices as monasticism and usury, a never-ending stream of letters, and tomes of ponderous scholarship. Added to this, of course, were his daily observations recorded by his students in his *Table Talks*. Haile devotes considerable attention to analyses of all the above with the exception of the *Table Talks*. These casual remarks by Luther are used as sources throughout the book.

Undoubtedly, Luther's greatest literary achievement was his translation of the Bible into German. This was an endeavor that occupied him throughout his later years. He participated in its final revisions in the 1540's and lived to see two editions published, in 1545 and 1546. The translation's significance is that it served as an inspiration and model for other vernacular translations, especially the English, and encouraged the growth of literacy which contributed to the dispersement of "the dank fogs of barbarism." Haile provides an informative analysis of Luther's work, emphasizing Luther's personal identification with certain Old Testament figures and his belief in the merit of brevity as a most effective means of conveying ideas.

One of the most interesting but darker sections of Haile's book deals with Luther's last years of illness and pain, particularly following his near fatal attack of kidney stones at the conference at Schmalkalden in 1537. After this his writings become fewer in number but more vitriolic in tone. This change is clearly seen in his scatalogical diatribes against the papacy, the Anabaptists, and especially the Jews. To his credit Haile does not apologize for Luther's statements on the basis of senility or mental instability. Indeed, he affirms that Luther remained rational and quick-witted until his death. Haile simply portrays Luther as a sixteenth century man, untutored in the liberal and tolerant sentiments of a later age. Haile also does not attempt to draw long-term historical consequences from Luther's anti-Semitism. He does not hold Luther responsible, as some have, for the Jewish Holocaust of the twentieth century. Haile is to be commended for not reaching conclusions that cannot be historically demonstrated. Indeed, it would be insulting to Luther's protean intelligence to associate him with the intellectual barrenness of National Socialism.

Perhaps the most distinctive feature of this book is that the author portrays Luther as much as possible in his totality and emphasizes his humanness. The reader sees Luther in the many roles that came to occupy his mature years: father, husband, teacher, celebrity, adviser to and castigator of princes, generous friend, implacable foe, polemicist, and scholar. Haile portrays Luther as a man much like all men: fearful, sentimental, filled with doubt about his own abilities and about the hereafter, boastful, vain, rude, and kind. He is neither the cardboard saint as portrayed by some Protestants nor the *bête noir* of some Catholics. Most of all, Haile portrays Luther as a man of his times, and it is only by placing oneself in the value structure of the period one is studying that the student can hope to understand the people of that age. Haile never attempts to encumber Luther with the values of a later age and thus is not judgmental about him or his views. Although there are other good biographies of Luther which emphasize his earlier years and the dramatic break with Rome, of which Roland H. Bainton's *Here I Stand: A Life of Martin Luther* (1950) is perhaps the most balanced and readable, H. G. Haile's work is a major and unique contribution to Luther scholarship. It does not, as probably no book can, portray the Protestant leader in all his complexity, but it provides the reader with an analysis of a period in Luther's life heretofore largely ignored and thus rounds out and transforms earlier pictures of him. In all, it must be agreed that Haile's "experiment" has been successful.

J. Stewart Alverson

LYNDON
An Oral Biography

Author: Merle Miller (1918-   )
Publisher: G. P. Putnam's Sons (New York). 645 pp. $17.95
Type of work: Political biography

The often funny, sometimes tragic story of the political career of Lyndon Baines Johnson, America's thirty-sixth President, as told through the memories of family, friends, and enemies

Principal personages:
LYNDON BAINES JOHNSON, the powerful Senate Majority Leader who became president upon the assassination of President Kennedy in 1963
HUBERT H. HUMPHREY, Democratic Senator from Minnesota, Vice-President to Johnson, 1965-1969; and a presidential candidate in 1968
FRANKLIN DELANO ROOSEVELT, thirty-second President of the United States, 1933-1945
SAM RAYBURN, a three-time Speaker of the House of Representatives
LADY BIRD JOHNSON, Lyndon's wife, formerly Claudia Taylor
JOHN FITZGERALD KENNEDY, thirty-fifth President of the United States, 1961-1963

Lyndon Baines Johnson (LBJ) is frequently associated with two important occurrences in American history: civil rights and Vietnam. In these two areas, the thirty-sixth President of the United States had his greatest achievements and greatest failures, making him a man both revered and detested. In *Lyndon*, popular biographer Merle Miller brings LBJ to life with a candor that helps the general public understand contradictions in the former president's character and the reasons behind the most crucial decisions of his presidency.

Miller is a veteran writer whose last book, *Plain Speaking: An Oral Biography of Harry S. Truman*, was a number-one best-seller. He has written other acclaimed novels and nonfiction exposés, many of which draw upon his experiences as a combat correspondent during World War II. His biography of LBJ, which is heavily researched and documented, took him five years to write and is a reliable, well-written political history.

The term "oral biography" means the story of a person's life told in large part by the people who knew him. It is a writing style rich in anecdote, metaphor, and quotation which must be skillfully arranged into narrative. Miller accomplishes this task well in a lengthy biography that covers LBJ's life from birth to death. Many colorful, intimate details abound, especially since LBJ himself never stopped talking and was a larger than life public figure whom interviewers could not ignore.

Miller captures LBJ's physical exuberance by describing the former president's zest for work, coarse manners, and overpowering manipulation of others, particularly Hubert H. Humphrey, whom he destroyed as a presidential candidate. Many voices recall Johnson's escapades as an iron fisted wheeler-dealer politician who would go to extremes to control others. One common manipulation was paying excessive attention to detail; for example, noticing the hairstyle of his secretaries, and then demanding improvement.

Johnson frequently assessed those around him, subjecting new and old acquaintances to the famous "Johnson treatment." He would probe and question, looking hard for weaknesses and character flaws, then he would preach nonstop about some important matter until he had motivated the person to do his will. Often he would yell and be excessively dramatic as he destroyed all defenses. He was a performer and an operator whose Rabelaisian behavior, while it frequently offended others, made him a master legislator. Miller describes how, as Democratic Majority Leader, Johnson exhibited unusual skill in marshaling support for President Eisenhower's programs.

Although Miller concentrates on LBJ's political career, he also delves into Johnson's family history and early life in "Young Lyndon," the first of six sections of his book. Born in 1908 near Stonewall, Texas, into a farming family, LBJ was graduated from Southwest Texas State Teachers College in San Marcos in 1930 and taught in a Texas high school before entering politics.

The story begins with accounts of Lyndon's birth and his devotion to his mother, Rebeckah Baines, who had a lasting influence on his character. Lyndon experienced poverty in his childhood, but, as a former colleague recalls, he exaggerated that poverty to attract sympathy. There was always something dishonest in his character that made him distrust others and bend the truth for personal advantage. Yet, there was also a strong moral streak instilled by his mother and a sympathy for the underdog. While a teacher and principal at Cotulla High School in Texas, he became deeply moved by the plight of the Mexican-Americans, a concern that blossomed later into his war on poverty. The experience profoundly changed him from a narrow conservative into an expansive New Dealer.

Then as later, LBJ had enormous physical energy that made him a human dynamo and an ambitious problem solver. In his first political job as secretary to Congressman Dick Kleberg, he demonstrated his later acclaimed ability to get things done through personal contact. He even persuaded Western Union boys to leak him telegrams announcing federal projects and then released the news first under his own name. Resourceful and devoted to basics, he attended to his job in his own as well as his employer's best interest.

Lyndon once told a friend ". . . the way you get ahead in this world, you get close to those who are the heads of things." True to his extremist nature, he would go to considerable lengths to ingratiate himself with influential leaders. A favorite story concerns his arranging a surprise birthday party for senior congressman, Sam Rayburn. President Roosevelt allegedly gave the party but Johnson, then a freshman congressman, did all the work, arranging everything to the last detail. He delighted the President by presenting him with a Texas stetson, then made sure that he was photographed along with Rayburn and Roosevelt. He made himself important in such ways and a recipient of favors from senior politicians who could best guide his career.

Lady Bird Johnson recalls her first impressions of her future husband as a whirlwind. He proposed on their first or second date which seemed like sheer lunacy until she realized he was serious. Johnson's intensity and exuberance often aroused this reaction in people, even during his presidency. Miller documents many meetings in which such notables as former Secretary of State Henry Kissinger wondered if LBJ were crazy. George Reedy, Special Consultant to the President, said that Johnson would enjoy leaving a visitor wondering if he were a king or a lunatic. This exuberance was his way of challenging limitations, keeping ahead of others, and forcing others to accomplish beyond their own expectations.

Miller shows where LBJ's will to succeed and commitment to causes were so strong that he mowed down the opposition long before he attained a powerful stature as Senate Majority Leader. In 1935, as Director of the National Youth Administration in Texas, Lyndon allocated federal funds to put black youths through college and find them jobs, a brave decision that defied deep-seated Southern prejudice. In the summer of 1941, Congressman Johnson gave major speeches and pressured colleagues to approve an extension of the public draft against great public and political opposition. Johnson's hard-sell pressure tactics worked well even though he was not a member of the House leadership. Lyndon simply knew how to engineer victory and enjoyed confrontations when he could champion unpopular issues.

Known to others as "Roosevelt's Boy" because he wholeheartedly supported New Deal programs, LBJ was always a New Dealer in practice. Miller's sources describe how Johnson's bias blinded him to reality. When, as president, he toured South Vietnam, he saw that country's problems through the eyes of a New Dealer. He saw rural electrification and the construction of dams as solutions to the problems faced by Vietnamese farmers. He failed to see where his answers were uniquely American and that other cultures may not be ready to accept progressive ideas. What comes through very strongly in such accounts is that LBJ was not a team player. He made the rules and the decisions as he saw best and forced others to comply.

This character trait served him well as Senate Majority Leader but undermined his success as president. He hobbled the Vietnamese Peace Negotiations by refusing to make such logical concessions to Ho Chi Minh as halting the bombing of North Vietnam. He ignored the advice of key advisers and the constant public outcry against the continuance of the war. As a result, when he retired from the presidency in January, 1969, he left the country bitterly divided by the war and caught in an imperial presidency that would topple his successor, Richard Nixon.

Miller does not dwell on LBJ's political failures; in particular, he fails to assess sufficiently the extent of the damage done by LBJ's Vietnam policy. Brief explanations and comments cannot explain away hard truths; the Vietnamese War was unnecessarily destructive and prolonged, and it was so costly that to defray costs, Congress had to scuttle much-needed domestic programs. Praise of Johnson's successes far outstrip criticism of his failures. Perhaps it is the nature of oral biography to stress achievement and underplay tragedy since the memories of others become embellished with time and border on legend.

To remember only Vietnam however, leads the reader to view Johnson unfairly. Johnson played so many roles in his remarkable career and accomplished so much before Vietnam that he earned the title of the Great Conciliator. To his credit, he was the first man to champion the black farmer and the first president to get a sweeping Civil Rights Act (in 1964) through Congress. He pushed hard for a medicare bill which provided free medical care to the aged under Social Security, for an expansion of federal aid to education, and for a more ambitious antipoverty program. Miller shows how Johnson pushed the eighty-ninth Congress (1964-1965) to enact the most economic and social welfare legislation since the New Deal. Of course, many of these programs were proposed by Johnson's predecessor, John F. Kennedy, but Johnson got them through Congress where they were stalled under Kennedy.

An accidental president, LBJ became chief executive upon the tragic death of Kennedy, and, according to Miller, he filled the role naturally. He was used to wielding great power. His vice-presidency was a humbling experience during which LBJ's ties to the White House were strained. There is evidence that Kennedy liked and respected him but Bobby Kennedy referrerd to him as Uncle Corn Pone and severely limited his voice in government. To keep Johnson busy, Kennedy sent him on fact-finding trips through Asia and India where Johnson made a big hit with impoverished masses. He genuinely cared for the poor and the downtrodden and felt at home in their company. He may no longer have been Mr. Democrat in the nation, but he was a most uncommon vice-president in his enthusiasm for impoverished people and in their enthusiasm for him. From these trips emerge a portrait of Johnson as a great humanitarian and a great liberal because he never lost touch with ordinary people and their problems.

Johnson often bragged about his homespun, down-to-earth background in speeches filled with country similies, rhythms, and metaphors. The memories of others are filled with his plain folks anecdotes. On the campaign trail, Johnson always addressed key political issues after entertaining an audience with country yarns that proved to them he understood their needs. From 1937 to 1946, Johnson was consistently reelected to the House despite some formidable opposition because he was such a popular campaigner.

Some of the most amusing sections of this book cover Johnson's colorful speeches and shenanigans in his various political campaigns. The chapter covering his first bid for the Senate in 1941 reads like comic relief as Johnson courts the hillbilly vote against a Texas flour salesman, Pappy O'Daniel, with no talent for politics. Observers recall the 1941 campaign as a combination of circus and carnival as both men employed country bands and dramatic props and were willing to put on any kind of ostentatious show to win the election. Pappy proved himself a better showman and manipulator of the ballot box. He marginally defeated LBJ even though Johnson had Roosevelt's support. Johnson, however, had the satisfaction of seeing Pappy perform ineptly in Washington, and went on to gain the Senate seat in his next bid. Unlike Pappy, LBJ proved himself to be an exemplary senator because the Johnson hyperbole was never only an act.

Miller portrays Johnson as immersed in politics; but the former president was also an adept businessman. In his wife's name, they bought a radio station, KTBC in Austin, which grew into a lucrative radio and television business. Miller superficially covers the Johnsons' broadcasting enterprise and the FCC investigation of it. A possible explanation for this lack of emphasis may be that the major thrust of the biography is on LBJ the politician, not LBJ the private citizen.

Miller also glosses over the Bobby Baker scandal. Baker, as Secretary to the Democratic Senate Majority from 1955 to 1963, was indicted and convicted by a federal grand jury on nine counts including misappropriating $100,000 in campaign funds. Lyndon Johnson was implicated in the crooked deals, an allegation he and Baker denied. This was a major scandal which should identify Johnson's weakest traits even though he was exonerated. Again, the oral biography format may be responsible for the superficiality since it relies on reminiscences rather than on documented testimony.

The life Johnson led may not have been totally ideal or honest, but Miller shows it to be a life that on the whole satisfied Johnson and contributed to the betterment of society. Compassion was practiced in national policy as the former president improved the lives of blacks, the poor, and uneducated through his comprehensive social legislation. Impatient to get things done, he risked the anger of others, even that of his southern constituency to move a bill through Congress. He identified with the common man, but was a most uncommon man in public life. Miller may make him more of a hero and celebrity than his record deserves, but LBJ would not be a fitting subject for oral biography if his career was not larger than life.

Anne C. Raymer

MAN IN THE HOLOCENE

Author: Max Frisch (1911-   )
Translated from the German by Geoffrey Skelton
Publisher: Harcourt Brace Jovanovich (New York). 111 pp. $7.95
Type of work: Novel
Time: The present
Locale: A small village in the Swiss mountains

An elderly man, in his final days, helplessly feels his mind fragmenting and disintegrating and fears that the world about him is doing the same

Principal character:
HERR GEISER, an elderly widower living alone

Thumbing quickly for the first time through the pages of *Man in the Holocene*, one is immediately struck by the fact that this is a curious book, a book which—even in its appearance on the printed page—is unlike the novels to which one is accustomed. Where the reader expects to find neatly arranged, orderly paragraphs following one after the other, he finds instead paragraphs of radically varying lengths separated by gaps of empty white page. Stranger still, sections set off by a gray background are found, and these sections contain such diverse materials as biblical quotations, lists, sketches of prehistoric animals, and dictionary definitions. Returning to the beginning and reading slowly—for this is a book to be read slowly and savored—through these odd-appearing pages, the initial impression of strangeness is confirmed. The realization is made, however, that this is strangeness for a purpose, strangeness which is integral to the very subject matter of the book. *Man in the Holocene* portrays with devastating accuracy and effect the vain effort of an elderly man to stay the disintegration of his mind and to find for himself a stable and enduring place in the universe. Lest this description make the book sound like a weighty philosophical tome, let it quickly be said that this is a book of unusual clarity and directness, a book which is, in short, a small literary masterpiece which brilliantly weds subject and form while remaining entirely free of literary artiness.

Herr Geiser, age seventy-three, is a widower who lives alone in his house in a small Swiss village. For several days the village has been deluged by rain. The power has intermittently been off, and the mail truck has been unable to get through. There may have been landslides along the roads, but the news is conflicting. Herr Geiser first appears at night with thunder clapping and rain pouring down outside while inside he tries to build a structure of crispbread. To no avail, however, for as the fourth floor is being constructed, the whole edifice wobbles and then collapses into ruins. This is the first image of collapse and disintegration, but others appear throughout the book: a collapsed wall in the lower garden, the sound of rushing water signifying new streams channeling changes into the earth, a television screen on which figures appear and then flicker and disappear, an apparent fissure in the ground outside Herr Geiser's window. Geiser perceives these images and fears the collapse and disintegration of his world. Further, precisely when Geiser perceives these external images, he—and the reader—also perceive the lapses in memory and the fragmentation which signal the collapse and disintegration of his mind.

"What would be bad would be losing one's memory," Geiser thinks. "No knowledge without memory." Knowledge becomes Geiser's obsession. He feels the necessity to organize and to categorize, to put all meaningful information into orderly arrangement and to have it available for instant recall. This, in fact, becomes Geiser's mission. Elsbeth, his deceased wife, read novels. This retreat, however, is not for Geiser because novels deal with the relationships among people "as if the place for these things were assured, the earth for all time earth, the sea level fixed for all time." Facts are what Geiser is after. Facts about creation, about the geological changes the earth has undergone, about prehistoric animals, about emerging man—thus, Geiser seeks facts. He listens to the thunder and isolates sixteen or more different types. He plunges into his encyclopedia, his dictionary, and his other books that provide facts. Shortly, however, he realizes that the facts slip from his mind soon after he has acquired them. So, he begins to write them out in longhand and to attach his writings to the wall; however, this process is too slow. So, he finds scissors and begins to cut out articles and append them to the wall. Always, he is threatened by time, which he knows is running out; by his memory, which he knows is failing him; and by the uncertainty of what he is after. Distractions come between Geiser and his task. A salamander in the house must be removed. Age-old cobwebs in an inaccessible location gnaw at his mind and must be cleared away, so Geiser tears out the handrail of the bannister to use as an extension rod for his broom and then is unable to affix the handrail back in place.

At dawn one day Geiser sets out on foot with his rucksack, his hat, his raincoat, and his umbrella. The path, however, is not as he remembered it, age has taken his agility and stamina, and the rain continues to fall. This is his escape, but, to where? Then it is night, and Geiser is heading back home barely aware that he has decided to turn back. Home again, Geiser continues his work of accumulating information, but his perceptions become more disjointed and his memory falters further. He awakens to find himself on the floor, spectacles lying unbroken nearby, and hat still on his head. The telephone rings, but Geiser does not answer. Men enter his house and look about, but Geiser throws a cup at them and drives them away. Numbness sets in on the left side of his body. An old memory of climbing the Matterhorn with his brother comes into his mind in lucid detail. His daughter arrives, but by now Geiser has slipped far away. Why, he wonders, does she talk to him as if he were a child?

Geiser's mind dwells quickly on the broken bannister, then on the snipped pages of his books. Geiser sees that "all the papers, whether on the wall or on the carpet, can go. . . . Nature needs no names. Geiser knows that. The rocks do not need his memory." The reader is told that an article about apoplexy occupies a place on the wall; it seems to describe much of what is happening to Geiser. Finally, the reader is told that life goes on, business as usual, in the village—with, it must be assumed, Geiser gone, dust to dust, to take his place in the timeless story of the earth which evaded his mind but received his remains.

Herr Geiser, this elderly man about whom one learns very little factually and for whom one has no particular reason to feel anything except pity, somehow exerts such power upon the imagination that he continues to live and grow in the mind long after the final page has been turned. This, one must feel, is because of the awesome economy and clarity which Geiser's creator, Max Frisch, used in telling Geiser's story. It is interesting to consider how different this book might have been if the materials had been in the hands of someone like James Joyce or William Faulkner. One thinks of the great soliloquys of Molly Bloom and Quentin Compson, and one can easily imagine a book two or three times the length of Frisch's with great convoluted sentences piled upon one another—a book, in other words, of great artistry but one which, because of the artistry, inevitably calls attention to the artist.

Not so with Frisch. His method is that of understatement. He disciplines himself against the temptation to record all of the workings of Geiser's mind and all the external experiences with which Geiser comes into contact. Rather, Frisch simply and directly draws the reader's attention to the shifting points of focus in Geiser's mind and then steps aside to allow the imagination to add the details and the colors. The result is a reading experience of far more complexity, depth, and richness than one would expect from a short book filled with straightforward declarative sentences. Indeed, time and time again while reading the book, one is drawn to close the eyes and to project oneself into the consciousness of Herr Geiser and to linger while Frisch's images grow and expand. So doing, one can feel in a palpable and visceral way the loneliness, the fear, the obsessiveness, and the frustration felt by Herr Geiser.

Man in the Holocene, in addition to its considerable inherent quality, might be hoped to achieve the further distinction of introducing its author to a wider audience in the United States. Max Frisch is widely known and admired in Europe but is relatively little known in this country despite the availability of English translations of a number of his works as well as occasional performances of his plays. He deserves the same sort of widespread audience that such European writers as Jean-Paul Sartre and Albert Camus have found. He is a writer of tremendous diversity who, in addition to fiction and drama, has written philosophical essays, travel articles, political commentary, personal reminiscences, and other types of nonfiction. Two volumes of sketchbooks as well as several plays and novels, including *Man in the Holocene*, are available in English translation. They are the work of a man who has spent a lifetime examining closely, critically, and unflinchingly the human condition of his time, and they merit Frisch a place among the serious and important writers who are alive today.

L. W. Payne

MAO
A Biography

Author: Ross Terrill (1938-   )
Publisher: Harper & Row Publishers (New York). 481 pp. $17.50
Type of work: Biography
Time: 1893-1976
Locale: China

A lively and well-researched narrative account of the life and impact of Mao Zedong, relating both his achievements and faults to the history of modern China

> *Principal personages:*
> MAO ZEDONG, Chinese Communist Party leader and unifier of China
> CHIANG KAI-SHEK, Chinese Nationalist leader
> ZHU DE, Red Army leader and collaborator of Mao
> ZHOU ENLAI, Premier of People's Republic of China
> JIANG QING, Mao's third wife and ultraleftist

Ross Terrill, a prolific author/editor of six books on China and numerous magazine and newspaper articles, brings together numerous sources, some only recently available, to create a study of the life of Mao Zedong (1893-1976). His approach falls between two earlier classics on Mao: Stuart Schram's *Mao Tse-tung*, which developed an analytical structure of Mao's thought, and Edgar Snow's *Red Star over China*, the exciting personal-interest story of the military struggles of the Chinese Communist Party (CCP).

Terrill uses personal and psychological aspects of Mao's life with political and cultural analysis to show that Mao was a complex man who was often inconsistent in his intellectual development. Mao is described as China's greatest figure in this century, a "Marx-Lenin-Stalin rolled into one" with all the variety that view implies. As a young iconoclast, an adapter of Marxist doctrine in the Chinese context, and a military strategist, Mao led the CCP to victory over the forces of imperialism (Japan) and Chiang Kai-shek's Nationalists. Once the revolution had been achieved in 1949, however, he was much less effective as a manager and builder of the new China.

Mao was born into a fairly well-off peasant family in Hunan province, a mountainous region with a history of rebellions. His mother was a considerate and devoted Buddhist, while Mao's father was a disciplinarian. The young Mao revolted early against his father's commands, but when he himself was in power, some of the same personality traits emerged. As a young man, he preferred tales of war and banditry to the Confucian classics, although he learned the lessons of both. Terrill suggests that these early experiences and the traumas of growing up help to explain Mao in later years.

In 1911, Mao left his village for middle school at Changsha, but his academic training was marked with starts and stops. Largely self-taught, Mao always held a jaundiced view of education and intellectuals. There was greater excitement in the changes occurring beyond the school walls. In 1912, the archaic Ch'ing dynasty finally fell and China began a long period of division and chaos.

In 1918, Mao went to Peking, where he worked in the periodical room of the library of Peking University. On the fringes of academic life, he found himself snubbed by many students and teachers. Nevertheless, Mao read widely and came into contact with Marxist philosophy, given new weight by the successful Bolshevik Revolution in Russia. In April 1919, he returned to Changsha as a political activist. He was a patriot but not yet a Marxist. Terrill claims that Mao's sense of social injustice actually dated from his early youth and was given shape later by Marxism.

In 1920, Mao traveled back to Peking and then to Shanghai where he and twelve other young men (the average age was twenty-six) secretly met to form the CCP. At that time there were only fifty-seven members in all China, but political chaos and social injustice were fertile soil. Mao spent most of the next six years organizing peasants in his native Hunan, while the CCP followed an urban policy dictated by Moscow. Cooperation with Chiang Kai-shek in 1927 proved disastrous to the CCP as Chiang's troops slaughtered the Communists, including thirty-thousand in Hunan alone. Under orders, Mao led an abortive urban uprising, but its failure only proved the weakness of following Russian policy. He retreated, with a small band, to a rugged area of eastern Hunan.

From 1927 to 1935, Mao was in no way the leader of the CCP, but those years were critical for his later success. He advocated a rural strategy of mobilizing the peasant masses and training an army. Terrill argues that this was Mao's unique contribution: the union of the gun, peasant power, and Marxism. These ideas individually were not new, but the combination was; and it was based on a pragmatic assessment of the realities of Chinese society, not Marxist theory. With Zhu De, who arrived in April, 1928, Mao built a force of ten thousand men, the nucleus of the Red Army that would carry him to power over all of China in 1949.

The army that Mao and Zhu built was quite different from the warlord bands Chinese peasants had come to dread. The Red Army was infused with a spirit of democracy and political training. Instead of victimizing the peasants, the Red Army helped them and always paid for food. In time, the Army won the support of the peasantry, which was essential for guerrilla warfare. A policy of modest land reform was aimed at building support while antagonizing as few as possible. These tactics were attacked by Moscow-trained members of the CCP who controlled the party. Meanwhile, from 1930 to 1933, Mao had to survive encirclement campaigns launched by Chiang Kai-shek. By 1934, aided by German advisers, Nationalist troops had greatly reduced the Red Army base. Survival required an escape further into China's interior.

The Long March, as it came to be called, began as a retreat, but it proved to be the test that brought Mao leadership of the CCP. In 1932, Mao respectfully urged the CCP to declare war on Japan, a brilliant political stroke as it gave him the mantle of a patriot. To fight Japan, it was essential to break out of Jiangxi and join with other Communist groups in the north. Using the slogan, "March north in order to fight Japan," Mao transformed a military retreat into a symbol of national and revolutionary effort. He developed, according to the author, "flexible, nativistic, and mind-over-matter military tactics." The crossing of twenty-four rivers and eighteen mountain ranges cost Mao ninety percent of his followers, but the remainder formed a disciplined corps.

Once established in Yanan, Mao began the fight with Japanese troops occupying North China. This phase, from 1937 to 1945, proved the viability of his guerrilla tactics and revealed his nationalism. The people's war reversed Chinese military tradition, taking it out of the hands of specialists. As the guerrilla leader, Mao became the "high priest of anti-Japanism." Like earlier studies, Terrill shows that Chiang wanted to appear a patriot, but his lack of peasant roots led him to depend more and more on foreign backing.

During the Yenan years, Mao put on weight, took as his third wife a former actress from Shanghai, Jiang Qing, and began to build his image. He further revealed the pragmatic Chinese nature of his Communism: "Marxism-Leninism has no beauty, nor has it any mystical value. It is only extremely useful." Terrill sees the Yenan years as a golden period for Mao in that he both taught and ruled over a growing movement.

Japanese defeat in 1945 brought with it a renewed struggle for China with Chiang Kai-shek. Terrill reveals that Mao asked to come to Washington in January, 1945, to discuss a postwar coalition, but Major General Patrick Hurley did not transmit his message. Terrill thinks that if Mao had made a trip to the United States in 1945 years of bitter relations between the two countries might have been avoided. Negotiations between Chiang and Mao failed, however, as the United States and Stalin leaned toward the Nationalists. Mao had one-third the men and one-fifth the arms of Chiang's armies in 1945, but the success of his peasant-based political and military tactics soon undermined the urban and foreign supported forces of Chiang. Chiang controlled territory, but the Communists had won the populace. The three billion dollars in United States aid to Chiang was of no help: most of the military equipment landed in CCP hands. When the Red Army entered Peking in late 1948, many of their tanks, jeeps, and heavy artillery were American.

By 1949, the Nationalists had retreated from the mainland, and Mao proclaimed the People's Republic of China on October 1. He suggested that this event was the culmination of the struggle against imperialism since the Opium War (1839-1842). His task was now far different from the road to power. Power had to be consolidated and 550 million people politically mobilized. Organizations were established for almost every activity: women's federations, youth leagues, labor congress, Young Pioneers. In addition, economic development was a pressing need. China received a paltry three hundred million dollars from Stalin, to be repaid with goods and materials. Stalin's lack of generosity was noted by Mao: he was the only Soviet bloc leader not to attend Stalin's funeral in 1954.

Success was paradoxical for Mao, for as the CCP gained control of China, he found it harder to control the CCP. To some degree, all of his subsequent shifts in policy in the 1950's and 1960's were attempts to control events and maintain a revolutionary purity that he saw as essential. Terrill analyzes the various campaigns against corruption and bureaucracy, economic inefficiency, and intellectual heterodoxy. Mao's methods were traditional: he wanted China to be like a family, and he saw the ideal Communist state as one of complete harmony in thought and values. At the same time, he preferred enthusiastic participation to coercion and administrative fiat, grass roots initiative as a balance to central control.

Others in the CCP hierarchy did not share Mao's enthusiasm for continual revolution and renewal. Disagreements over policy and Mao's unwillingness to stick with a political successor dragged China into a labyrinth of political intrigue, the policy disasters of the 1958 Great Leap Forward, and the Cultural Revolution of the 1960's. The Great Leap was partly a challenge to Russian economic development policy, and it marked a lasting split between the two Communist superpowers.

Mao's concern about the revolutionary purity of the party and the lack of revolutionary experience of three hundred million young people born since 1949 led to the excesses of the Cultural Revolution. In a misguided attempt to "crystallize a moral consensus," Mao set young Red Guards against the Party itself. "It was," argues Terrill, "a mindless theory and it issued in mindless practice." Zhu De and other old comrades were attacked for their lack of devotion to the Mao cult. It is still unclear—estimates range from tens of thousands to as high as twenty million—how many lost their lives as political disorder challenged the bureaucracy of socialism that Mao detested. He was not prepared, however, for the degree of anarchy and factionalism that emerged, and, by 1967, Mao turned to factions within the army to control the ultraleft.

In Mao's last years, only Zhou Enlai remained in Mao's favor. Chinese politics after 1969 were "built on Chinese feudal intrigue and mystification." Mao came to hold an almost obsessive fear of what he called Russian "hegemony," and this was one of the factors which made him receptive to the Kissinger-Nixon *rapprochement*. When Nixon arrived in Peking in February, 1972, twenty-four years of hostility were replaced by a new guarded dialogue. The situation was delicate for both Nixon and Mao, since both had domestic critics of closer relations with the former *bête noir*. Nevertheless, China gained a seat in the United Nations and Russia could no longer count on China-United States hostility.

In late 1975 and early 1976, Mao, now frequently ill, once again favored a political swing to the left. An acerbic debate arose over the issue of "red" versus "expert" as a mini-Cultural Revolution was launched in the realm of education and culture, presided over by Jiang Qing. Proximity to Mao became very important as Jiang's faction maneuvered with the followers of Zhou Enlai. When Mao died in September 1976, he left a bitterly divided country because of his periodic assaults on bureaucracy. The triumph of revolution in 1949 had created a new social reality that threatened revolutionary ideology. Terrill thinks that "China might have been better off if he had died twenty years earlier than he did."

Whatever faults Mao had, the author clearly shows his importance in restoring the unity and position of the world's most populous country. His ideology was based on Chinese tradition and practical experience as well as Marxism, and he tried to create not simply a new socialist state but a new altruistic citizen. Under his rule, China made great progress toward social modernization and some progress toward economic development. His faults were many, however, and his abrupt shifts in policy alienated the masses. Today many Chinese resent or hate Mao.

Terrill's fascinating study of Mao should become a standard to judge such works, especially in his skillful and culturally sensitive analysis of Mao's ideological development. Terrill guides the reader through the Byzantine labyrinth of Chinese politics in the 1960's and 1970's. Marxists will not like this book for the author stresses the indigenous Chinese origins and personality quirks of Mao more than doctrinaire theories of Marxism. Mao was not a consistent thinker. His departures from Marxist canon, his use of traditional Chinese revolutionary symbols and peasant tactics set him apart as a true nationalist.

Terrill writes in a lively journalistic style that gives his account interest, especially in the pre-1949 period, but his use of short paragraphs makes for choppy reading. The book is laced with metaphors that often provide a provocative and vivid image, but occasionally they are glib *bon mots* rather than solid analysis. Terrill makes some sweeping statements that call for support: for example, a theme that reappears is his view that "all through history the semi-intellectual has been the most potent person in an inchoate political situation." The example of Lenin, an intellectual par excellence, immediately springs to mind.

The book would be more useful if it contained a chronological chart of the major events in Mao's life as a quick reference. It would also be enriched by a section of photography. These are minor faults, however, in what is a solid biography. It is the most up-to-date book on Mao available and suitable for the average reader. Those with scholarly interests will find Terrill's book provocative but will want to use it in conjunction with studies of Mao by

Stuart Schram, Edgar Snow, Doak Barnett, Jerome Ch'en, and Richard Solomon.

Richard Rice

THE MARRIAGES BETWEEN
ZONES THREE, FOUR, AND FIVE
(As Narrated by the Chroniclers of Zone Three)

Author: Doris Lessing (1919-   )
Publisher: Alfred A. Knopf (New York). 245 pp. $10.00
Type of work: Novel
Time: The unspecified time of fantasy
Locale: Zones Three and Four, mythical kingdoms of the planet Shikasta

The Providers, mysterious rulers of earth, unite the gentle Queen of Zone Three and the warrior King of Zone Four in marriage; after they learn to love each other and have a son, the Providers dissolve their marriage and order the King to marry the savage queen of Zone Five

> *Principal characters:*
> AL·ITH, Queen of Zone Three
> BEN ATA, King of Zone Four
> JARNTI, Ben Ata's chief of staff, friend of Al·Ith
> DABEEB, Jarnti's wife

The Marriages Between Zones, Three, Four, and Five is the second work in Doris Lessing's series entitled *Canopus in Argos: Archives.* The first and third works of the series to appear so far are cast in the form of reports, letters, and journal entries about the history and development of the planet Shikasta (earth). Shikasta has had a violent past and faces a questionable future. In the author's fiction, Shikasta is settled as an experiment by scientists from three space empires: Canopus, Sirius, and Puttiora. The Canopans espouse goodness and kindness in their dealings with the settlers with whom they people the earth. The Sirians likewise experiment with different sorts of hominids in the continents in the southern half of the planet. The Puttiorans, however, especially those who come from the planet Shammat, send no settlers, only troublemakers who teach the Canopan and Sirian settlers brutal habits such as human sacrifice and cannibalism. *Shikasta* and *The Sirian Experiments* (the third work in the series) are reports from Canopan and Sirian experimenters respectively, but this second work, *The Marriages*, is about the subjects of the experiments, a fable of those who have been selected as the guinea pigs of the alien plans.

The novel begins with a chronicler of Zone Three, a country of an unspecified region of earth, explaining that for unknown reasons the Providers (who must be either Canopans or Sirians) have commanded a marriage between the Queen of Zone Three, Al·Ith, and the King of the neighboring Zone Four, Ben Ata. The chroniclers, poets, and songwriters, although keepers of tradition, are not sure exactly what a marriage is. They know what sex is, and they know that children can result from marriage, but the authorities and the Queen herself are in doubt about the meaning of the command. Al·Ith, however, allows herself to be escorted to the border of Zone Four.

As the procession moves through Zone Three, glimpses of the rich and beautiful countryside are given. Zone Three is set in foothills, with a high range of mountains on one hand and fertile, grain-filled golden meadows on the other. In the grasslands of Zone Three live many small animals, who greet the Queen without fear as she journeys toward the frontier. A small deer steps up to Al·Ith's horse and rubs its muzzle in greeting. The beauty of the land contrasts with rumors of worry that Al·Ith hears for the first time: some evil is falling on the land, bringing with it feelings of heaviness and discontent. The animals are not mating as they did, and even the people feel no urge to procreate.

Zone Four, which Al·Ith's party reaches, differs sharply from Zone Three: not only are there no hills, but also its people fear hills. They build little, isolated villages far from one another on the dark plain. Just as the villages are isolated, so too are the people alone and afraid. The first citizen of Zone Four that Al·Ith meets is the young soldier Jarnti, who commands the troop sent to bring her to the King. Jarnti fears the possibility of war, and guards Al·Ith closely through their trip. Al·Ith, however, laughs at him. Zone Three needs no soldiers or armies for they have no enemies, and have never experienced war. Jarnti is astonished, because he has been brought up to believe that preparation for war is the norm of existence, and nothing that Al·Ith can say reassures him.

At last, Al·Ith comes to the marriage pavilion prepared for her and Ben Ata. The setting is a pleasant surprise, composed of a bridal chamber fronting on a garden filled with sparkling pools and jetting fountains. Her husband-to-be is not as charming as the surroundings. Ben Ata is rough, blond, and muscular, and he takes an instant dislike to the dark-haired queen. He is insulted at her dress, a simple one regal neither in material nor cut. To show his scorn, he throws Al·Ith to a couch and rapes her without his feet even leaving the floor. He expects an emotional reaction of outrage, but is astonished to find that Al·Ith is only puzzled and trying to learn, if she can, the meaning of his action. Neither of them knows what the Providers want of them or of their union.

As days pass in the pavilion, Al·Ith and Ben Ata try to discover their mission, their purpose. The evil influence that had been noted in Zone Three has spread to Zone Four: their birthrate too is down. The two come to the realization that the saving of their peoples is in their hands.

Besides the puzzle of the purpose of their marriage, another question is raised. Early in the journey to Zone Four, Al·Ith asks Jarnti to look back with her toward her homeland in the hills just as the sun is setting. Jarnti obviously wants to look—Al·Ith sees his eyes flicker toward the hills—but he cannot raise his head. On questioning, he tells Al·Ith that he had been accused as a child of daydreaming, of cloud-gathering, of looking up to the hills. As a punishment he had been made to wear a heavy metal helmet that prevented him from looking up. He had worn it for such a long time that he was no longer able to raise his head.

Ben Ata refers to this fear of his people when he sees Al·Ith sitting in the pavilion gazing toward her country. She, for her part, cannot understand why the inhabitants of Zone Four should be so fearful of this simple and natural action. Yet, when she returns to her own country for a short visit, she notices that her people themselves do not look toward Zone Two, which lies even farther up the slopes of the high mountains. Like the people of Zone Four, those of Zone Three are complacent, accepting life as it is, never dreaming or hoping for better.

When Al·Ith returns to Zone Four, she makes friends with a native woman in hopes of understanding what the Providers want her to learn. The woman is Dabeeb, Jarnti's wife, and she is willing to teach Al·Ith what she can. When Al·Ith is taken to a secret rite of the women of Zone Four, she is shocked to witness a moment in the ritual when the women turn their faces toward the hills. Some have to hold their heads between their hands because their necks are too weak to lift their heads. Then in tears the women put the heavy metal helmets on their heads. When Al·Ith asks the meaning of the strange rite, Dabeeb tells her that the women do so because the men have forgotten to look at the mountains. The men only prepare for wars that never come, or attack Zone Five in border skirmishes. They have forgotten the hills, and in sorrow the women must look in their place.

In the meantime, Al·Ith and Ben Ata have come to love each other, and as their relationship deepens, they hear a drum softly beating in the garden, but they are never able to discover the source of the sound. Al·Ith bears Ben Ata a son, but as time passes and they disagree about the care of the child, their union becomes strained, and the drum falls silent. At this point, Dabeeb tells Al·Ith that her marriage has been dissolved, and the Providers have ruled that Ben Ata must marry the savage Queen of Zone Five, the desert country that lies even lower than Zone Four.

The saddened Al·Ith leaves her husband and son and returns to the land that she had left not long before. The purpose in all that had happened was still a mystery to her, and moreover, she now feels an exile from her own people, having been changed by her stay among the people of Zone Four. She looks about her in Zone Three, and is appalled, because her own folk now seem fat and self-satisfied. She then flees higher up the mountains to Zone Two, where she experiences a mystical state, in which the spirit-like inhabitants of Zone Two speak to her in whispers. Surrounded by these hazy flame-like visions, time passes as in a dream. When she returns from the mountains she finds that months have passed.

Longing for her son prompts a visit to Zone Four, where she finds that changes for the better have taken place. Much of the poverty has been wiped out, and people are happy and joyful. When Ben Ata tells her about his new wife, she finds that Vahshi, Queen of Zone Five, is even more spoiled than Ben Ata had been when Al·Ith had married him. Ben Ata, however, has become a capable and beloved ruler, and his healthy, strong son promises to be his father's equal one day. Al·Ith is satisfied, and she returns to Zone Three, where she joins a band of youngsters going up the mountain to a country retreat. One day she walks up into the mountains and does not return.

The Chronicler reveals that where there had been distrust and unhappiness, there was now joy. Sterility has been replaced by fecundity. Where the frontiers had been closed, there is now free passage between the zones. War has been replaced by universal peace, and all this was in the minds of the Providers when they commanded the marriage, and through the union of Al·Ith and Ben Ata, a universal benediction has fallen on the entire planet.

The Marriages invites being read as an allegory of men and women in the relationship of marriage. Why is it that a certain man and a woman will be drawn to each other, and how is it that having loved they are never the same as they were before, even if the union is dissolved by divorce or death? In her Introduction to *The Sirian Experiments*, Lessing writes that she is interested in the nature of the "group mind," that collective intelligence people share with all other humans. She states her conviction that certain ideas must flow like tides through all humanity. In the same way, the narrator of *The Marriages* says that mankind is the visible aspect of the whole all share. In this reading, Al·Ith and her people are the gentle and humanitarian aspects of men and women, while the people of Zone Four are the strife-filled parts of human nature, embodying lust to conquer or hurt people. The marriage of these two aspects of the human personality can only be accomplished by the working of a will—personified by the Providers who, like the intellect, rule both the passions and the higher emotions. The completely integrated personality, however, must add to these the ability to dream, to hope, in a symbolic sense to look toward the hills. In other words, to yearn for something better than the present state. Whether the two sorts are individuals or merely parts of the same personality, the object is the same: a unified and wholesome totality that combines the gentle kindness of Al·Ith and the striving for achievement of Ben Ata.

Walter E. Meyers

MAUGHAM
A Biography

Author: Ted Morgan (1932-   )
Publisher: Simon and Schuster (New York). 711 pp. $17.95
Type of work: Literary biography
Time: 1874-1965
Locale: France, England (much of Europe), parts of Asia, and North and South America

A literary biography of W. Somerset Maugham and more generally a literary history of the late Victorian, Edwardian-Georgian, and Modern periods in British literature

> *Principal personages:*
> W. SOMERSET MAUGHAM, cynical British playwright, novelist, and writer of short stories
> SYRIE BARNARDO MAUGHAM, his wife
> LIZA, their daughter
> GERALD HAXTON, Secretary-companion to Maugham
> ALAN SEARLE, followed Haxton as companion to Maugham
> BERTRAM ALANSON, San Francisco stockbroker who made Maugham rich

W. Somerset Maugham was one of the most secretive, wealthy, and—so it might seem, given this biography—most dislikable authors of the twentieth century. Maugham's personal wish was that a biography about him never be written. He requested that friends destroy all his correspondence, and quite formally, he asked his literary executor, Spencer Curtis Browne, to resist any requests for cooperation in any attempts at writing Maugham's life story. In spite of all of these obstacles, and after numerous less informed biographical attempts, Ted Morgan has succeeded in writing a major and probably the definitive account of the mystery that was W. Somerset Maugham.

Not only does Morgan outline the important events and people in Maugham's life, but he also presents them as ingredients, as experiential subject matter for Maugham's plays, novels, and short stories. He also places Maugham's life fully (some might say too fully) in the context of his times so that the literary biography of Maugham becomes a literary history of the several eras through which Maugham lived: Victorian, Edwardian, and Modern. As one might expect, given the wars and social disruptions of the late nineteenth and twentieth centuries, Morgan's account of Maugham's life and times is not a pretty one. Yet, in spite of Maugham's many flaws as a man and, to a lesser extent as an artist, the overall result is somehow inspiring because Maugham's perserverance and accomplishments are notable.

Morgan takes the attitude that his role as biographer is not so much either to glorify or condemn Maugham as man and artist; rather, his stance as a biographer is one of utmost objectivity. Maugham is a famous author, was an inscrutable character, and posterity deserves to know the details of the

Maugham story—without excessive editorializing and passing of judgment. Maugham himself said about the biographer's "problem" of presentation, that it is wisest to know both the failings and the successes of an individual for both can be inspirational to others' lives. (He did not, however, feel this way about his own biography, and his autobiography is maliciously distorted against his wife and daughter.)

It is something of the attitude of objectivity too that led Maugham's literary executor to assist Morgan in presenting the version of Maugham that is this book. Of course, Maugham's enemies would cast his failings in an even worse light; his friends (and he did have true friends, one of whom was Winston Churchill) would place him, doubtlessly, in a better light. Maugham, like anyone, might be analyzed and thus portrayed in many ways. Morgan's approach, by no means psychoanalytical as is often the modern biographer's tendency, is to discuss Maugham's friends—in what becomes at times a tedious chain of mini-biographies—to examine the wider social-political-cultural milieu, and to place Maugham in it. Evaluative judgments and the attribution of motive, as enjoyable as they might be, are few and far between in Morgan's presentation. Rather than criticize him for the choices he did not make in this portrait sketch of Maugham, it is best to comment on the choices Morgan does make in his objective, plodding, and most comprehensive telling of a life in its times.

Without getting at the "figure beneath the carpet" in any detail, as is the wont of the master of modern biography, Leon Edel, suffice it to say by way of summary that Maugham's salvation as a person and his talent as an artist were enmeshed in his ability to convert his experiences, his feelings of loneliness and alienation into the narrative stance of a detached but inquiring observer. As a very young boy, he developed a stammer, a handicap that prevented him from following in his father's law profession with its requirements of ability at oration. The death of his mother when he was eight years old and an unhappy childhood in the home of his uncle, Henry Maugham, gave him the materials for his early autobiographical novels, *Of Human Bondage* (1915) and *Cakes and Ale* (1930).

Plagued by a dual nature and pulled in opposite directions, his life became a paradox which nourished an inquisitive, searching view of things. He was reared in France for the first ten years of his life and learned first to speak French; and yet he was to spend much of his life in England as an "Englishman" never really sympathetic to things English. He loved and revered his mother more than anyone in his life, and yet he developed into a thoroughgoing misogynist who disliked most of the women he knew and especially his wife, Sarah Louise (Syrie) Barnardo, and eventually their daughter, Liza Maugham Hope (Lady Glendevon). Although married and a father, he was by preference homosexual and had two obsessive male loves of his life—his secretary-companions Gerald Haxton, and after Haxton's death,

Alan Searle. (Maugham was also from time to time a pederast, going to bed with young boys solicited by Haxton.) He was a physically small man, five foot six, and much embarrassed by his height, of generally frail constitution and a sufferer of tuberculosis, but one who took good care of himself through cellular therapy and survived as a rather robust traveler-adventurer. He was a cynic, a misanthrope and a pessimist, but still tolerated human frailty. He was a medical student, a sedate writer, and a fop but was courageously and loyally involved in espionage and spy work for the British government. He was an ambulance driver in Flanders, was lionized as a West End dramatist, the most widely read novelist since Charles Dickens, much in demand socially in London, knew many influential people—and ended his life in senility trying to disinherit his daughter and adopt his manipulating secretary-lover, Searle. He earned over four million dollars from his writings and through well-placed investments by his broker, Bertram Alanson, was the owner of an extensive collection of modern paintings, and was as much a businessman concerned with marketing a product as he was a literary artist.

Maugham was in his personal and in his literary life both a great and a petty man. Morgan presents them both, reflected in the panoramic mirror of Maugham's twenty novels, thirty plays, eight volumes of short stories, four volumes of essays and miscellaneous travelogs, reminiscences, and jottings.

The organization of *Maugham* is straightforward, a chronological rendering of Maugham's life. There is no beginning at the middle or end of his life and circling back. Morgan structures his book (and Maugham's life) in seven parts as follows: 1874-1897, childhood, early schooling, medical school and first attempts at serious writing; 1897-1907, ten hard years establishing himself as a writer of several plays and five novels—a professional; 1907-1917, the years of first success at the end of the Edwardian era, his service with the Red Cross in World War I, his travels to Hawaii and Samoa, and the writing of his masterpieces, *Of Human Bondage* and "Rain," and his marriage to Syrie (already mother to Liza) in 1917; 1917-1926, travels for material to China, Malaya, Southeast Asia, and Mexico, and his arrival at middle age in the modernist 1920's; 1927-1940, years of continuing love for Haxton, divorce from Syrie and the beginning of the Maugham legend with his residence at the Villa Mauresque—his Moorish fortress at Cap Ferrat on the Riviera which became his home for the rest of his life; 1940-1953, his pleas in New York for American support of British war efforts, followed by the completion of *The Razor's Edge* (1944)—the same year of Haxton's death from tuberculosis—and later his liaison with Alan Searle who took care of Maugham for twenty years; 1954-1965, the final pathetic years of demise into querulousness and senility. From birth to death, Morgan blocks out Maugham's life in clear, scrupulously detailed segments.

For most readers, this chronological portrayal of Maugham will reveal a progression of responses from favorable and sympathetic, at the early end of the spectrum, to some modicum of respect during the middle years, to an unfavorable, unsympathetic, perhaps outright dislike of Maugham in his later years. If ever a biography proved that an author's life inevitably finds its way into his writing, this is it. It might also follow, although somewhat speciously, that readers generally prefer Maugham's early writings to his later ones, his novels and short stories to his plays. The more one knows about Maugham's personal life, chances are that the common reader might understand Maugham's writings better but like them less, or if liking them better, then begrudgingly so. At any event, the most "enjoyable" parts of *Maugham* are the early parts. For further insights into the making of such famous works as *Of Human Bondage*, *The Moon and Sixpence* (1919), *Cakes and Ale*, *The Razor's Edge*, and short stories such as "Rain" and "The Letter," Morgan's exposition and explications are indispensable.

One must respect Maugham in that he struggled and lived much beyond his friends and his own best times. He began life alone, orphaned, and he ended life an old man at ninety-one, with all of his friends dead before him. Thus, it seems that throughout most of his life he was bored—with living and with dying—but nevertheless made the best of it he could. When he was born, a staid Queen Victoria was still on the throne. When he died, the atom bomb and the Cold War were commonplace horrors. When Maugham began, Robert Browning, Lord Tennyson, Thomas Carlyle, and John Ruskin were the giants. By the time of his death the heroic age of British fiction had passed: James Joyce, D. H. Lawrence, Virginia Woolf, E. M. Forster—all had advanced the frontiers of fiction.

Nowhere is Maugham anymore appealing or Morgan any more enlightening than in his account of how the early years of Maugham's life converged into the successful telling of his own maturation. His *Bildungsroman* (really *Künstlerroman*), *Of Human Bondage*, a work that like Samuel Butler's *The Way of All Flesh*, Joyce's *Portrait of the Artist as a Young Man*, or Lawrence's *Sons and Lovers*, captured the anguish of growth into consciousness. Maugham's first draft carried the title, "The Artistic Temperament of Stephen Carey" and was rejected. With more experiences lived and worked into the book, Maugham—fifteen years later—revised Stephen Carey's story, now Philip Carey's story, Maugham's own story, into *Of Human Bondage*.

Taking his title from one of the books in Benedictus de Spinoza's *Ethics*, Maugham wrote the novel in an attempt to free himself from the trauma of his youth. Into the novel, he placed all of his obsessions: the death of his beloved mother, his wretched school years, his year in Paris, and his training in medical school. In keeping with the form of the autobiographical novel, he mixed fact with fiction, but the emotional center was Maugham's own. There was no posing as an Edwardian gentleman as he had done in very early works—no cuteness. Here was the world of a cripple (Maugham transposed his handicap of stammering into a club foot). It was not the world of frivolity but of bondage—the bondage of Maugham's analog, Philip Carey, to his deformity, his heritage, and the woman who misuses him. What Maugham and Carey seek is freedom and the struggle is intense. A *roman à clef* like much of Maugham's fiction, his real-life friends such as the writer Violet Hunt, make their cameo appearances. A confessional novel leading to a naturalistic conclusion that one must struggle against ever-defeating odds, Theodore Dreiser called Maugham's novel a work of genius. For nearly seventy years it has been representative of Maugham's life and his best work.

As in his treatment of this representative Maugham novel, Morgan is very thorough in his discussions of each of Maugham's works, minor and major. Since Maugham was a prolific writer, Morgan's biography is a lengthy book; and, although he seems to digress a bit too far into explaining the lives of almost everyone Maugham meets, Morgan's account of W. Somerset Maugham is biography at its best, about the literary artist at his best—and his worst.

Robert Gish

THE MIDDLE GROUND

Author: Margaret Drabble (1939-   )
Publisher: Alfred A. Knopf (New York). 277 pp. $10.95
Type of work: Novel
Time: The present
Locale: England

A fictional exploration of the joys and pains of entering middle age in contemporary England

> *Principal characters:*
> KATE ARMSTRONG, a journalist, divorcée, and mother of three
> EVELYN STENNETT, her friend, a social worker
> TED STENNETT, a doctor, Evelyn's husband, and Kate's former lover
> HUGO MAINWARING, an author, Evelyn's cousin, and Kate's confidant
> MUJIB, an Iraqi student in his late twenties

The reader who likes a novel to be tightly constructed with a clearly defined beginning, middle, and end will be thoroughly frustrated with Margaret Drabble's latest book. It has very little plot, enough characters to people a volume three times its length, and a narrator who periodically pauses to discuss the proper handling of the story. Those willing, however, to allow the author to take them where she will—from East London sewers to surrealistic plays to suburban dining rooms and into the minds and lives of dozens of individuals—will find themselves richly rewarded. Since 1962, when she published her first novel, *A Summer Bird-Cage*, Drabble has been analyzing contemporary English society, particularly as it affects the women of her generation. As she has passed from her twenties to her forties, so have her central characters, the young mothers and career women of *Jerusalem the Golden*, *The Garrick Year*, and *The Waterfall* giving way to the more mature and established Frances Wingate of *The Realms of Gold*.

Like *The Realms of Gold* and Drabble's most recent novel, *The Ice Age*, *The Middle Ground* probes the dilemmas of characters in "the middle years, caught between children and parents, free of neither: the past stretches back too densely, it is too thickly populated, the future has not yet thinned out." The book focuses on the lives of four men and women who are struggling to make sense of this difficult period—Kate Armstrong, Evelyn and Ted Stennett, and Hugo Mainwaring. Kate's story is the central one, but her problems with her parents, her children, her work, and her sense of self are universalized as they are mirrored in the experiences of her friends.

All four grew up in an era when life seemed to hold order, meaning, and the possibility of progress. They threw themselves into causes that provided salvation of one kind or another and achieved affluence in the process. Kate escaped the confines of her East London background as a journalist writing about women's issues. Evelyn became a social worker, fulfilling the expectations of public service handed to her by her prosperous, well-established parents. Ted elected to be a doctor, an expert on world health problems. Hugo embarked upon a career as an anthropologist, but after three months as a prisoner of the Kurds in Iraq, he found a more promising future as a writer on Middle Eastern affairs.

Facing middle age, all four question in one way or another the value of what they are doing. Kate confesses to Hugo early in the book that the women's issues that have been her bread and butter now profoundly bore her: "I used to enjoy the smell of battle, but I've got sick of it, I'm really sick of it. I'm worn out." Evelyn, too, comes to doubt her sense of vocation as she faces her instinctive distaste for the helpless elderly people she encounters and wonders why she goes on pushing herself to the point of exhaustion when she could so easily settle down in her comfortable home. The restlessness of the two men is less tied to their work but no less real. Ted, who has broken off his relationship with Kate, his mistress for several years, and with the Cambridge woman who succeeded her, feels, as he flies to one in an endless series of international medical conferences, "a black cavern of growing dislike, largely for himself." Hugo has recently lost an arm in an encounter with a grenade in Ethiopia. He refuses to have an artifical limb, preferring, Drabble suggests, to appear helpless. He feels a sense of relief that he no longer has to prove his manhood; "nobody expected him to play at being a limbless war hero." He is in a kind of limbo, however, marking time by acting as confidant to Kate and worrying over his once beautiful and still possessive mother who is suffering from severe arthritis.

As Drabble moves back and forth between past and present events in the histories of these characters, she interweaves fragments of the lives of their children, their parents, their brothers and sisters, acquaintances, colleagues— even characters from at least two of her earlier novels. In so doing, she gives the reader a sense of the density of "real" life, of the multiple, multi-generational ties that bind most people during their middle years.

These minor characters, almost Dickensian in their eccentricities, provide much of the vitality that makes this novel such a delight. Among the most memorable of Kate's companions are her father, a retired sewer worker fanatically committed to the value of his work; her agoraphobic, obese mother, imprisoned in front of her television set by her passion for respectability; the drunken, aging bohemian, Hunt, who helped Kate escape her East Romley origins and periodically appears on her doorstep intoxicated; Mujib, her serious, inquisitive Iraqi boarder, a student she has taken in at the request of an old friend, his Lebanese fiancée's mother; little Rubia Subhan, an eight-year-old Pakistani girl, streetwise and mature beyond her years, who summons help for Evelyn when she is injured by a client.

Drabble's descriptive powers are demonstrated not only in her characters but also in the details of their physical environment. She deftly delineates whole ways of life in a few well-chosen words: the "dangling strings of onions and vegetables arranged like fruit in wooden bowls" in the kitchen of Kate's artistic ex-mother-in-law; the "water jugs, the canteen glasses, the wooden napkin rings, the white bowl containing stewed fruit" on her parents' dining room table; the "vast off-white, gold-tasselled, slubbed-silk settee" and the "fluted rose-painted gold-rimmed thin-stemmed porcelain cup" of movie actress Marylou (née Shirley) Scott, who attended the East Romley secondary modern school with her. London restaurants, theaters, day-care centers, and housing developments are equally concisely described to heighten the reader's experience of contemporary England.

At the heart of the book, and its message, is Kate herself, as complex and as vital as the world in which she lives. Her comfortable, chaotic, cluttered home is a reclaimed fish-and-chips shop. She dresses in rummage-sale shirts and eighty-pound boots from Liberty's, unable to live in the lower-middle-class environment of her childhood but unable to abandon it for neat, well-polished suburbia either. Drabble devotes most of the first quarter of the novel to an account of Kate's life to the point at which the story begins, tracing her progress through a miserble childhood and an unexpectedly suc-cessful adolescence, when she learned "that one of the ways to avoid being a butt or laughingstock yourself is to make people laugh," a talent she cul-tivated into a profession. She married an impecunious artist, bore two sons and a daughter, and at one point helped support them by assembling can openers on her kitchen table. Her husband's failures and her successes even-tually brought them to divorce, although like almost everyone else who entered her life, he continued to rely on her for motherly concern. Kate then entered into a no-strings affair with Ted Stennett, a relationship that appar-ently did not impair either his marriage or her friendship with his wife.

At that point she believed she embodied the ideal liberated woman of the 1970's, energetic, independent, competent. Then there intervened one of those random blows of fate that Drabble frequently inflicts upon her char-acters. Kate unexpectedly found herself pregnant with Ted's child. After deciding she would have the baby and cope with the problems it would present, she underwent tests and found that the fetus was suffering from spina bifida. Reluctantly, she chose to terminate the pregnancy, convinced on one level that she had made the right decision, but on another seeing her deep maternal instincts betrayed and herself a murderer. To compensate for her pain, she threw herself into a series of affairs with unsuitable men who bored and irritated her—and brought her their laundry to do.

Finally, on the advice of her eighteen-year-old son, Mark, she threw them all out of her life and arrived at the impasse, the "mid-life crisis" (a cliché both Kate and the narrator ridicule) that is central to the novel. Kate thinks,

The whole thing had . . . depended on a natural flow of good spirits, a natural cheerfulness.

Now they had abandoned her, these kindly spirits, and left her in an empty plain. What
on earth should one do next? She had tried fun, but it hadn't been much fun. What was
left? Work? Living for others? Just carrying on, from day to day, enjoying as much of it
as one could? Responding to demands as they came, for come they would?

Gradually, as Drabble takes Kate through a series of experiences that make
up the meager plot of the novel, the heroine begins to regain the *joie de vivre*
that makes such an appealing character. A new assignment, to make a television film on "Women at the Crossroads," sends her back into her past to
visit her old school and interview women who had remained in the world of
her youth. She hikes up the sewage bank she climbed as a girl and smells its
familiar odor, which acts on her like Marcel Proust's *madeleine*, forcing her
to recall and come to terms with hidden memories of her family—the brother
she had looked up to, defended, and pitied, and the strange parents, "two
terrible people, [whom] in the dark before dawn, in the underground she had
loved." Slowly, she begins again to appreciate the courage of all those willing
to carry on in whatever circumstances they find themselves.

It is, paradoxically, another unexpected blow of fate that provides the final
step toward renewed wholeness for Kate. The victim this time is Evelyn, who
is nearly blinded when she walks into a bottle-throwing domestic dispute at
the home of a client. Helping Evelyn, consoling her children, able at last to
converse with Ted in a voice that is not brittle and artificial, Kate concludes,
"Enough of patterns, she'd get nowhere if she spent the rest of her life forcing
things into articles and programmes when they didn't want to be forced.
Shapeless diversity, what was wrong with that?" Visiting Evelyn's hospital
room, she looks out the window onto the "higgledy-piggledy" roofs of London
and sees "its old intensity restored, shining with invitation." Nothing has
really changed. The two women still have aging parents, difficult children,
frustrating work, and complicated relationships to contend with, but both of
them face the future with renewed enthusiasm, feeling an overwhelming sense
of wonder and tenderness for the people whose lives touch theirs.

Like Virginia Woolf, Drabble chooses a social occasion as a satisfying
symbol for the restoration of community among her characters. The book
concludes with Kate's preparations for a party to celebrate Evelyn's recovery,
and Mark's birthday, and to bid farewell to Mujib, his fiancée, and Hugo,
who has taken his own steps back into life and is returning to the Middle East
to work on a new book. As Drabble describes Kate and her family clearing
away the debris of years and preparing to welcome more guests than the fish-
and-chips shop can possibly hold, she attests to her own belief in the redemptive power of friendship and the value of living, even in an unpredictable,
violence-filled world. A story that begins as a portrait of disillusion and despair
is transformed into a joyful affirmation of life.

The Middle Ground is not a book without weaknesses. Even those who
most enjoy Drabble's style may find her narrative techniques maddening when

she begins to summarize the events of the month of November in the lives of a dozen characters, or when she debates with the reader whether she should discuss Ted's parents as well as Hugo's, Kate's, and Evelyn's. Too, her male characters, especially Hugo and Ted, fail to become as convincingly alive as Kate and Evelyn. The very topicality of the novel, its grounding in the easily recognizable places and problems of the present, may ultimately limit its appeal. In the "shapeless diversity" of plot and character she exuberantly presents here, however, Drabble has provided a lively, moving account of what it can mean to face middle age in comtemporary western society.

Elizabeth Johnston Lipscomb

MOORTOWN

Author: Ted Hughes (1930-   )
Publisher: Harper & Row Publishers (New York). 182 pp. $10.95
Type of work: Poetry

A record of the unmediated energies of nature and the paradoxical energies of man within it

Ted Hughes's work is like Gerard Manley Hopkins' without the Christian focus but with the thick pictures and thumping energy. His poems are not about looking out windows but about being outdoors where the work is hard and life is physical and instinctual and calls for strong feelings, not drawing-room irony or mental finesse. Even when he makes a fool of himself, Hughes makes his work seem as though he had to write it.

Especially in the title section of the book—the first—Hughes takes nature for his theme and shows as much of it as he knows as a sheep and cattle rancher on his father-in-law's farm in Devon. The violence of nature is in storms, where "Cows roar/Then hang their noses to the mud" ("Rain"). In "Orts," Hughes partly describes a heat wave like this: "The desert has entered the flea's belly." Winter comes in "New Year Exhilaration" with the "Rolling of air weights" and while "The river/Thunders like a factory." There is violence in the cattle grinding into each other in "Dehorning," and shortly before the storm breaks in "Feeding Out-Wintering Cattle at Twilight." In a windy snow, "The field smokes and writhes/Burning like a moor . . ." ("Bringing in New Couples"). Another kind of violence in nature occurs in "February 17th," where a strangled lamb is stuck in the birth canal and the speaker has to cut its head off and reach inside the ewe and pull the rest out. Everything in nature, including man, pummels and is pummeled ("Prometheus on His Crag," 14), and even in myth the hero is "torn to pieces" ("Actaeon"). There is also the violence of the hunt in "Fox Hunt" and of the kill in "Orts" in which a fly is trapped and mashed backside-first by a spider.

There seems to be no thought in nature, only action, which sometimes immobilizes man's world ("Tractor") or threatens to ruin it ("Last Load"). In animals, nature moves without thought but instinct as the calves rush about and end back at their mothers' udders ("Turning Out"). Even when a calf sleeps, its "ears stay awake" ("Happy Calf"), and it instinctively keeps trying to feed until it learns how ("Teaching a Dumb Calf"). Machines themselves are like animals, as when the tractor is "Shuddering itself into full heat," and animals like machines, as when a predatory fish on the ocean floor is seen as a "Gadget of spectrum hunger frenzy" ("Photostomias"), and when hounds are called "A machine with only two products—/Dog shit and dead foxes" ("Fox Hunt").

If action without thought is a basic feature of nature, so is struggle and endurance. In "Feeding Out-Wintering Cattle at Twilight," the cattle are thrown around as they battle to feed, and in "Fox Hunt" the fox runs for its life from the hounds until either "his lungs tatter" or he makes the wrong turn. The struggle is man's too as he labors to get the hay in before the storm breaks ("Last Load"), and forces a calf and its mother together for feeding ("Teaching a Dumb Calf"), and strains to get a barbed wire fence up ("A Monument").

Similar to the fox, birds struggle to stay alive searching "everywhere/For . . . safety" ("Poor Birds"). The calf in "Little Red Twin" is sick and gets wedged in a harrow in murderously hot weather, but survives. The sheep are in chaos after shearing, but gradually "fit themselves to what has happened" ("Sheep"). In the human world, even old age tries to stay alive, and every morning "Pulls its pieces together" ("Old Age Gets Up").

Life seems to be a kind of glorious tragedy in three acts to Hughes. Act I is birth, and there are hardly any easy ones in Hughes's poems. The calf in "Struggle" has to be all but yanked out, and although the one in "Surprise" slides out almost unnoticed, the lambs in "Last Night" are stillborn and one is left with its frantic mother and eaten by predators, as is one of the lambs born in "Ravens." Again and again, Hughes presents a bloody afterbirth to point out the indelicacy of birth, even in its beauty, which he acknowledges when he describes the calf "Collapsed wet-fresh from the womb, blinking his eyes/In the low morning dazzling washed sun" ("Birth of Rainbow").

Part of Act II is eating, as the calves and lambs are often shown doing, and as the ewe finally does in "Last Night," having gone without food while she mourned her stillborn twins. The other part of Act II is sex. Two rams fight to mount the ewe in "Last Night" at the same time, and the reader is given a detailed picture of a frustrated bull in "While She Chews Sideways." In "Nefertiti" a female clerk in a slaughterhouse is a "Gorgeous, delicate,/Sipping insect." In "Orts" (13), the sex in nature is described: "Foxglove rearing her open belly . . .//. . . Lobworms coupling in saliva. . . ."

Nature's third act is death, and Hughes often takes it up in his poems. Besides the sheep and cattle, which are born dead or die soon after birth or have to be shot, there are the heaps of human dead unearthed in "Here Is the Cathedral," where the authorities eject a bum from the ruins, as though the living dead were a threat to the real dead. The spirits of the English soldiers who fought in World War II die in peacetime, while a young man dies violently on a motorbike, a ruined image of prewar vitality in "A Motorbike." Hughes also says of death that it "only wants to be life. It cannot quite manage" ("Life Is Trying to Be Life"). In "The Stone," he explains how hard it is for him to forget the death of someone close to him, and in "A God" he uses Christ to describe the helplessness of those who are dying.

Hughes allows no illusion between himself and nature or being. He defines this view in "Roe Deer," where the power he would like nature to give him is a dream which nature itself dissipates. There is "No God—only wind on the flower," he says in "Prometheus on His Crag" (17), taking this human dream about nature away, too. If there is ease in nature, it comes after a brutal and painful creation of living things, he says in the same poem (21). The remote shapes of nature are "a calculus/Woven by atoms on a lost warp of sunlight" ("Photostomias"), and what is "hatched" in nature is a "No . . ./Wet with Yes." Finally, the stars, an image of existence itself, are not "good, or friendly, or corruptible" ("Four Tales Told by an Idiot," 4).

Against the dense background of nature, man is sick, a killer and a paradox. In spite of all his strength, he still helps himself to death, as in "Hands." Like Prometheus, he is "disabled" in the very means he uses to survive. In "Deaf School," however, although his identity is remote, his affliction attains a kind of grotesque facility. He is the bum who comes to the door in "A Knock at the Door," and "Unmanageable parcel of baggy pain." He is also a butcher as in "Nefertiti," and, unlike the tiger, he kills indiscriminately and mechanically his own kind and anything else that gets in his way in "Tiger Psalm." When he loves and has a partner, he puts together and is put together by the other, until the result is "two gods of mud/Sprawling in the dirt."

Man is also unique in nature because there is something in him that cannot be pinned down: "What it is/. . ./That stares through a face" ("Seven Dungeon Songs"). In the same poem, Hughes touches on this elusiveness when he says about a woman that it is not her body that defines her link with men, but the mysterious "what" for which she uses her body. Moreover, it is uncanny how adulthood is a ruin our early life left behind.

Besides the nature of man, Hughes—like most modern poets—writes about the nature of the poet. In "Adam and the Sacred Nine" (11), the phoenix seems to be his image for the poet, "Its voice . . . flaming and dripping flame." It dies by creating and is created by dying. Words themselves "are the birds of everything" to Hughes—"Everything . . . on the wing and gone" ("Prometheus on His Crag," 19). The poet would like to fuse words with the shapes of nature ("If skin of grass could take messages"), so that "The speech that works air/Might speak me" ("Seven Dungeon Songs"). Words are one thing in the mouths of dainty poets, another in the mouths of loud ones, but the words of the poets who want to get to the bottom of things belong to the time "When the first word lumped out of the flint" ("Orts," 6). Finally, the poem is that "song" which came "Pouring out over the empty grave/Of what was not yet born" ("Adam and the Sacred Nine," 1).

Weather, landscape, animals and machines are Hughes's most powerful images when he takes them as they are. When he puts them in the framework of old myths such as Prometheus or in the guise of the Muses, they seem made up; at these times he philosophizes, and becomes confusing and overbearing. Sometimes, as well, he overuses participles, so that poems otherwise strong start to sag.

Hughes's prosody, though, is full of spondees and muscular syllables, which has not appeared much in English poetry since Hopkins and Dylan Thomas. A good example of this and of Hughes's direct syntax is in "Four Tales Told by an Idiot" (3): "Nightwind, a freedom/That wanted me, took me/Shook doors . . ./Twitched gates. . . ."

All in all, the poems in Hughes's book, especially in the Moortown section, push and corner the reader, and even when they huff and puff like bullies and make one angry, they are never boring, which is unusual in today's poetry. If Hughes indulges in a sort of reverse romanticism, it is not to flood it with human projections but to show its physical presence—mindless and absolute. As for the man himself, if Hughes's view is sometimes stupidly bitter, it is also masculine and concerned, without sly contempt or intricate self-pity.

Mark McCloskey

MORGAN'S PASSING

Author: Anne Tyler (1941-   )
Publisher: Alfred A. Knopf (New York). 311 pp. $9.95
Type of work: Novel
Time: 1967-1979
Locale: Baltimore

Anne Tyler's seventh novel is the comic story of the fascination of a middle-aged, drama-loving hardware store manager with two young puppeteers and their life, until, at length, their life gradually becomes his life

> *Principal characters:*
> MORGAN GOWER, a hardware store manager and father of seven daughters
> BONNY GOWER, his exuberant wife
> EMILY MEREDITH, a young puppet maker
> LEON MEREDITH, her husband
> GINA, their small daughter

Anne Tyler seems to be playing on the word "passing" in the title of her latest novel. Near the end of the book Morgan Gower's obituary is published in the newspaper, suggesting that he has indeed "passed on." Actually, though, Morgan is not dead; he reads the obituary and is seized with fury, knowing that his wife Bonny, from whom he is separated, has inserted the death notice as a trick or sign. As it turns out, the sign is that she has a new boyfriend and will now give Morgan a divorce. He has, therefore, passed out of Bonny's life, his own former life, and into a new one in which he hardly has an identity. He cannot protest to the newspaper about the false obituary because he now goes by someone else's name. His own mother does not know him when she sees him (a nice ironic touch). His life is not settled yet, and, as the novel ends, Morgan is looking to a future rich in possibilities. He seems, however, to have passed into a life in which he can be more fully himself.

Morgan has thus made a "passage" in another familiar, in fact, trendy sense, one that is rather a cliché: a middle-aged man leaves wife and family for a much younger woman. There is otherwise nothing overfamiliar about Morgan or his story. He is a vital, original comic hero, the product of a generous and richly inventive imagination.

In his first life Morgan hardly knows who he is, but he works at being a number of people. Romantically black-eyed and black-bearded, he gets up each day and chooses not clothes but a costume. His closet is jammed with outfits—soldier, sailor, Mexican, Klondike, African safari—and hats of all kinds. On his way to work at the hardware store or on his lunch hour he may become several different characters. One person knows him as Father Morgan, the street priest of Baltimore, who works with drug addicts. Another knows him as a poor immigrant, speaking a language that sounds something like Russian (but is actually gibberish) and sadly longing to hear from his far-off family.

By assuming different identities, Morgan thus preserves a sense that he is not settled in any dreary, mundane existence, but that the world has infinite possibilities. In this way he wards off his father's fate. When Morgan was in high school, his father, for no discernible reason, committed suicide. Forced to speculate on why a man should do such a thing, poring over what he has left from his father (a sheaf of technical instructions), Morgan thinks perhaps his father ended his life because he did not really know what else to do. He was just bored. There is, thus, a dark side to Morgan's desire to invent and reinvent his life. He has become a person who makes things look more interesting than they really are.

In a way, Morgan's life is interesting, and in a way it is not. He lives in a house bulging with female relatives: his senile mother, his spinsterish sister, his wife, and seven daughters. Luckily they have a nice, big house, given to them by Bonny's wealthy father. Luckily, also, Bonny is a blowsy, easy-going, spontaneous sort of person, who can cope good-humoredly with the endless demands, quarrels, and stresses of her life. Her house is so full of a kind of energy and endless entertainment that even after they have left home, the daughters when ill come home to recuperate. Yet, Morgan is not fully a part of this life; he stays on the edge. Himself a person with many interests and hobbies, most unrelated to any of the others, he lives in a house of related people with unrelated worlds.

Needless to say, Morgan does not find managing a hardware store very interesting. The store is owned by his wife's family, who have given him the job. Now forty-two, Morgan has been looking for a better job for nineteen years. Most of the work is handled by the clerk Butkins. Once Morgan had had a female clerk, and Morgan came to think of her and himself as Ma and Pa Hardware. He began to live in the scenario he was creating until one day he called her Ma, and alarmed her so much that she quit. The store is now a dreary place for him, although he gives it little of his attention.

At an Easter fair at a Presbyterian church, Morgan enters the lives of Emily and Leon Meredith. He does so rather dramatically, under the identity of Dr. Morgan, by delivering their baby. Suddenly the puppet show stops, just when Cinderella is dancing with the prince, the audience is dismissed, and a gangly young man steps outside the curtain and asks if there is a doctor in the house. Morgan rises to the occasion with aplomb, announces himself as doctor, starts out to drive the young couple to the hospital, and on the way helps Baby Gina into the world. He is untroubled by his deception—after seven daughters, he has a good idea of delivery procedures—and behaves with great confidence. Then he simply disappears, leaving Leon and Emily to wonder whether this curly bearded man, dressed in a coat that seemed to be made out of blankets and a pointed red ski hat, might not have been a gnome.

Morgan, however, does not disappear for good. For the next four years sometimes when the Merediths turn quickly or perhaps look down the block into a doorway, they may spy Morgan out of the corners of their eyes. Later, they come to know him, and eventually, at the age of fifty-three, he becomes Emily's lover and the father of a baby boy, Joshua. By this time Morgan has, of course, displaced Leon who has moved to Richmond, become a banker, and assumed custody of Gina. Now Morgan, known as Mr. Meredith, is the Prince in the Cinderella puppet show; and he is living the settled, stripped-down life that the Merediths always led, not bohemian, not romantic at all. At the book's end, Morgan and Emily are living drably in a trailer in a little town in Maryland some distance from Baltimore, and Morgan has a cold. He is still ready, however, to pose as someone else for his own amusement, and he is still writing letters loaded with instructions (some kind of heritage from his father), and he is happy.

At the heart of *Morgan's Passing* is the contrast between Morgan and Emily. A shy, quiet Quaker girl with a penchant for the clear and exact, she expected to be a mathematics major at college, but she got married instead. Leon was the dramatic one, wanting to be an actor, but too abrasive and angry to be successful in any theater group around Baltimore. Emily seems undramatic to the bone. Yet, she has the idea of giving puppet shows, she remembers the fairy tales, and she makes the puppets, sitting on a ladder in a bare room. Emily's skill and imagination are behind the puppeteering. Yet, she is otherwise timid and passive, more of a victim than an independent person. Her daughter, Gina, provides the color for her life. In contrast to Morgan and his costumes, the Merediths wear always the same clothes: Leon a corduroy jacket, white shirt, and khaki pants; Emily one of three leotards with a matching wraparound skirt. She can move her things anytime in half a suitcase, but she and Leon stay in the dark, narrow-roomed Baltimore apartment for a dozen years.

What draws Morgan to the Merediths is their occupation: he conceives of their life as richly dramatic at the same time that he sees that it has no drama at all. What cements him to Emily, makes him fall in love with her, is her steady clear-sightedness, made evident to him from some pictures she has taken.

At this point in the book, photographs have already been established as a motif. For example, Brindle, Morgan's sister, at last married to Robert Roberts, her girlhood love who has stepped out of the past to claim her, soon finds that he pays no attention to her but instead spends hours gazing at her graduation photo. After two years, Brindle leaves him. "I tell you, there's nothing worse than two people with the same daydream getting together, finally," she tells Morgan. Then there is the Gower family album with family pictures widely spaced, mostly from vacations at the beach, giving a sense not only that life was an endless vacation but also that years and generations collapsed on one another in a swiftly moving stream of time.

Emily's pictures, probably underexposed and at any rate bathed in thoroughly unreal amber light, show each person alone, glowing, idealized, gazing out with trust. Emily, who always seems the same herself, absolutely steady, simple, quiet, and clear, somehow photographs others so that they exist as if in that same direct, clear-eyed vision. Morgan, with his shifting view of himself and his desire to see the world as it is not, is irresistibly drawn to Emily as a calm, plain, lucid center. Morgan, on the other hand, brings to Emily an assurance of love (which she certainly did not get from the self-centered Leon) and a free-wheeling energy, which her life normally lacks.

One can understand, more or less, then, why Morgan and Emily end up together. The relationship, however, is left rather vague. It is simply fact, as matter-of-fact as everything else about Emily's life except her puppets. Nevertheless, the reader may be left feeling a bit at sea. There is something missing from this novel (as from Anne Tyler's previous works). She somehow fails to come to grips with her material. Her characters are often out of the ordinary, but they are odd, not grand, and she does not take her reader all the way into them to get a sense of depth and significance.

The novel is, however, a delight to read. The author's Southernness emerges in her eye for detail, and her ability to sketch odd characters vividly and sympathetically. She is the Eudora Welty of Baltimore; its houses, stores, signs, citizens, and sights come to life on the page. In a few pages, too, she calls up a warped tarpaper beach house at Bethany Beach, Delaware, furnishes it with thinning rugs, metallic mirrors, and cracked furniture, and then plays off vacation-frayed tempers and harassments against each other with a realism, humor, and irony that are simply splendid.

Tyler has a direct, informal style and a quirky imagination. Frequently, she addresses the reader as "you": "You could say he was a man who had gone to pieces," she will tell you; "Or look at his house," she will say, taking you by the elbow and steering you inside to describe the glorious clutter created by a household of eleven people, all messy and some eccentric. She has a Southern fondness for eccentrics and their place in the community so that even transplanted to Baltimore and writing about life in a huge city, she gives a sense of neighborhood community life and friendliness, rather than strangeness and alienation.

One may wonder how much Anne Tyler, also a Quaker, sees herself in Emily, the pupper maker. The novel's characters and scenes are vibrant with wit and imaginative detail like Emily's puppets and plays, yet the characters' relationships are essentially low-key and undeveloped, as if the author could not fully commit herself to them. If the characters are more puppet-like than one might prefer to have them, however, they are presented with a cheerfulness and optimism, tempered with a biting humor, that makes the comic world of *Morgan's Passing* extraordinarily pleasurable for the reader who enters it.

Mary C. Williams

THE MORNING OF THE POEM

Author: James Schuyler (1923-   )
Publisher: Farrar, Straus and Giroux (New York). 117 pp. $10.95
Type of work: Poetry
Time: 1927 to the present
Locale: New York, New England, and Italy

The life of a homosexual aesthete is presented as unabashed, self-conscious, self-effacing autobiography

> *Principal personages:*
> JAMES SCHUYLER, "Jimmy," poet, aesthete, and homosexual
> DARRAGH PARK, his closest friend, but not his lover
> ANNE DUNN, a friend
> FRANK POLACH, a friend, poet, and botanical librarian at Rutgers
> DOUGLAS CRASE, a friend of Jimmy and Frank, a poet, and an
>   industrial speech writer
> BILL AALTO, Jimmy's first adult lover
> WYSTAN AUDEN, Jimmy's friend and patron
> MOTHER
> BERNIE, a friend and lover of his early youth
> PAUL, a friend and lover of his later youth

It is equally easy to be attracted by this book or repulsed by this book, for the wrong reasons. Without question, those who collect "gay literature" for professional or personal reasons will find it unavoidable, worthier for inclusion on their shelves than Quentin Crisp's memoirs, less worthy than Ronald Firbank's novels. James Schuyler does not mind shocking and titillating, but any summary of the "good parts" would leave a false impression. Measured by expectations of the risqué, much of the book is dull and harmless.

Readers with contemporary common knowledge of the portrayal of homosexuals in literature, film and nonfiction and who have unabashed homosexuals among their acquaintances, may find nothing new or interesting in the most explicit passages of these poems. Further, the point must be made that the poems in this collection which have nothing to do with homosexuality have a consistently aesthetic voice, which *intimates* homosexuality to many readers, but does not automatically so hint to careful students of the aesthetic movement, as Martin Green makes clear in his admirable book *Children of the Sun* (1976).

This collection of poems is at an awkward crossroads in literary history and in its own self-conscious backtracking. This is not a book for those offended by homosexuality or its "intimations," nor for those offended by homosexual self-caricature, nor for those who find the homosexual life-style a shop-worn, jaded subject. For those interested by these considerations, rather than offended or bored, the large issue remains: are these poems interesting in themselves, as poems? At least two views are possible.

The case can be made that Schuyler's poems are simple, thin, lightweight, devoid of richness of any sort. He deplores poets who write "reams of shit" but he takes delight in product brand names and dated slang. His daily doings and reminiscences are self-indulgent and dull. It makes a difference to him what soft drinks he consumes and who starred in the television series "Mod Squad," but such drivel can only interest readers who do not understand the purposes of poetry, who think that a poetic equivalent of the visual art of Andy Warhol is a worthy notion. With the economy of the Imagists and the richness of Theodore Roethke, Robert Frost, Dylan Thomas, Robert Lowell, and W. D. Snodgrass available, however, a "happy medium" is not sought or needed. One who buries his deepest fears under caustic wit has not earned the right to call himself a poet.

That is one view. The opposite, positive case can be made from the same poems as data. Schuyler is spare, terse, direct, economical, devoid of allusion or obscurity. He writes as one who says "Creative writing has never been my trip." The poems depict his daily doings and reminiscences of his childhood and youth. Apart from homosexual equivalents of heterosexual "crushes," flirtations, affairs, and heartbreaks, his life emerges as extraordinarily ordinary. He strikes a nice balance: his poems are more fleshed-out than those of pure Imagism but without the painful ruminative self-consciousness of Robert Lowell or W. D. Snodgrass. Like Lowell and Snodgrass, he has depression and institutionalization to draw on. These are mentioned in passing, in black-humored medical memoirs such as those of Oscar Levant. All in all, Schuyler is as jolly a poet as America has produced, altogether too jolly to be lionized by academics and highbrows.

For the average readers, those two views will shift in and out of dominance, poem to poem and line to line, like an optical illusion which is either a black square with a white frame or a white square with a black hole in the middle.

Metrically, the poems are of two kinds: short poems with short lines, six syllables or less, and longer poems with longer lines. "A Name Day" has some lines of more than ten syllables. "Dining Out with Doug and Frank" has seven- and eight-syllable lines and covers nine pages. The title poem has alternating long and short lines which are really lines tucked-in because they are too wide for the page: "Mostly because Bernie was Catholic and worried about confession/and such: me, in those days I was randy most." This poem covers sixty-one pages; the other poems total less than that. Again, the reader can choose to view the poem from two perspectives: Schuyler is uninterested in meter and dully and duly goes through the motions; or, Schuyler is a craftsman who keeps the music muted and comfortably varied.

Three levels of organization are at work in the arrangement of the poems. First, the "New Poems" show where the poet is. "The Payne Whitney Poems" show where he has been. "The Morning of the Poem" allows the reader to apply the shorter lessons on the life and times of the poet to the poet writ large. Some readers will not find that a pleasant task; some readers will.

Second, the poet is very literally at the center of the universe. He can look outside or inside himself. If inside himself, he can move backward in time, predict his future, ruminate on his present. If outside himself, he can look ahead, to the right, to the left, behind himself. He can walk, shifting all these relative directions. The inside and outside can interplay. The house on the left, which he has never been inside reminds him of a house from his past. Bored with that house, he can turn to the house on his right and remember actually going inside it.

Third, Darragh Park, to whom the book is dedicated, appears as a shadowy figure, just off-stage in the short poems, a Godot for whom the poet waits. Surely, the unnamed painter in the mammoth title poem whom the poet addresses and heckles throughout a large part of the poem is the long-awaited Park.

Two short poems, "The Dark Apartment" and "I Sit Down to Type," the longer "A Name Day," and "Dining Out with Doug and Frank," along with a portion of the title poem, will serve to illustrate the range of the collection.

"The Dark Apartment" is the first poem in the collection. It is an often-told story for contemporary readers. A homosexual loses his married bisexual lover to a petty crook. Its importance is clearly in Schuyler's desire not to be coy with the reader, to reveal "the worst" at the outset.

"I Sit Down to Type" is somewhat uncharacteristically detailed in self-disclosure. The poet is drinking a 'Tab. God, in the form of a sunbeam, reminds the poet of his atheism. He notes his respect for two believers (who will be mentioned again in the collection). He recalls that he lost his faith when he read *Of Human Bondage*. His atheism, however, has roots in his childhood. When he came home from a Mass, at age four, his father made fun of him. Now, quite seriously, he hopes he can find Grace and die a Catholic.

"A Name Day" is the most conventional poem of the collection. Thinking of his friend Anne Dunn's birthday, he thinks of all the shades of green in nature, of expensive brand-name gifts, of greenery and other living things that make rich symbolic gifts.

"Dining Out with Doug and Frank" pushes the issue of violence in the world of the New York City artistic homosexual. The poet has a friend who was beaten in Central Park, who died a year later from his injuries. Another friend threw himself under a train. Bill Aalto, his first adult lover, chased him with a knife and they were never reconciled, even when Aalto was dying of cancer.

The middle of "The Morning of the Poem" is characteristic in its modified stream-of-consciousness structure and thematic interplay. Homosexuality is not a neurosis; a friend died, the poet has injured himself and limps to the grocery store with a list, oatmeal is hard to get in New York, life is tough (compared to the softness of oatmeal), people are killed by lightning, men lie about having sex with famous men (as irrationally as lightning strikes), men poison themselves, a young man died from swallowing crushed castor beans, the poet remembers castor oil from his childhood, he remembers his grandmother.

At the very least, this collection of Schuyler's poems presents a standard against which readers can put their philosophies of poetry to the test. If he asks too much tolerance for self-indulgence and gives too little voice to be heard through the casual idiosyncracies, how far does he fall short of being worthy of serious attention? It is not altogether fair to demand of Schuyler that he be a more interesting homosexual or be so interesting that he does not need homosexuality as subject matter. The most positive cumulative effect of these poems is to present a personality trebly courageous, in its own way. As a homosexual, Schuyler is never really safe from the threat of internal and external violence. As a man dedicated to contemplation and comfort, he is never safe from the jeers of workaday America. As a fascinated observer of his own daily doings, he is never safe from charges of self-indulgence. Such a personality is worth sampling. Yet, some readers may have or acquire a taste for it.

T. G. Shults

MORTAL ACTS, MORTAL WORDS

Author: Galway Kinnell (1927-   )
Publisher: Houghton Mifflin Company (Boston). 72 pp. $8.95
Type of work: Poetry

A collection of poems, divided into four parts, which reflects a personal, imagistic, spiritual, and cosmic vision of the progression toward mortal truth

Galway Kinnell's *Mortal Acts, Mortal Words* affirms the claim sometimes made that poetry's three eternal themes remain beauty, love, and death. Whatever seeming innovations and bizarre topics contemporary poetry may present, unless it deals in depth with these themes, it somehow fails to sustain our interest or make us feel that something substantive has been said. Kinnell's success in *Mortal Acts, Mortal Words* derives from his varied handling of these themes, which he discovers in fleeting instants defined by human acts and accompanying words. Taking an epigraph from Plutarch—"mortal beauty, acts and words have put all their burden on my soul"—Kinnell gathers behind it particulars of experience that invest life with meaning, that lead speculative minds to organize consciousness into a desperate wisdom.

Kinnell's poems are rich, emotional experiences, producing a current of despair. Real pain shows through but is balanced by real joy at knowing life and the beauties that can fill it. Ultimately, a philosophical strain born of fatal knowledge ties these poems together in a sort of search after wisdom, a search after serenity.

Structurally, *Mortal Acts, Mortal Words* might be likened to a sort of four-fold vision, a hierarchy that progresses toward awareness grounded in elemental mortal truths. Section by section, the poems seem to move along toward a place of wisdom, along a path that burdens the soul. Generally, Part I contains personal glimpses, intimate familial images, a sense of personal sensitivity and bared feeling. This part culminates in "Wait," a meditative poem about discovery's ephemeral nature. It accentuates the need to observe particulars, thus introducing Part II's poems in more imagistic modes. Here nature images, verbal fun, and fantasy combine to display beauty perceived in a miscellany of voices and subjects reflecting diverse human interests. The observer steps outside himself. The somber, chastening tones of Part III's poems signal a move toward spirituality, close encounters with the dead, and the definite constraints of mortality. All five poems in Part III return to the personal point of view, self examination gathering impetus from the truncated lives of kindred souls. In response, it seems, Part IV presents a more cosmic point of view, injecting philosophical tones and discourse, the reflective light that sheds enlightenment grounded in personal attachment and commitment.

The last stanza of the book's last poem, "Flying Home," seems to base that enlightenment on a realization about love:

that once the lover
recognizes the other, knows for the first time
what is most to be valued in another,
from then on, love is very much like courage,
perhaps it *is* courage, and even
perhaps
only courage.

Thereafter, the large jet touches down, landing "all of us little thinkers," and "with sudden, tiny, white puffs and long black rubberish smears/all its tires *know* the home ground." The idea of a home ground—a place secured by love, the place where acts prove most telling on the words and feelings exchanged—runs through the whole of *Mortal Acts, Mortal Words* anchoring the poems to realities of space and time, but giving them a timelessness that comes with love's endurance.

Explorations of different kinds of love constitute a major part of this volume, defining in part what it means to be mortal, to touch and hold others literally and figuratively. Carnal love gets its due, but more striking are the measures of familial love—parent toward child, child toward parent, brother toward siblings. Always these loves engender insights. For example, "After Making Love We Hear Footsteps" describes a feeling familiar enough to parents whose children crawl into bed between them, sharing the warmth and peace. Fergus, the poet's son, awakes in the night while his parents lie together after making love, and he patters in to ask, "Are you loving and snuggling? May I join?" Then, he flops down, hugs his parents, and "snuggles himself to sleep." At other points, only memories can provide the cherished love, the serene feeling brought on by knowing that love has been granted, as when the poet remembers his mother after her death and recalls:

I have always felt
anointed by her love, its light
like sunlight
falling through broken panes
onto the floor
of a deserted house: we may go, it remains,
telling of goodness of being, of permanence.

Love's permanence defies mortality, encumbers the living with memories and regrets, such as the lament by the poet that he was not at his mother's bedside when she died, not holding her hand "to hand her, with more steadiness, into the future." He knows, as a result, that "there are regrets/we can never be rid of." At another point, Kinnell comes to the final realization that "It is written in our hearts, the emptiness is all. That is how we have learned, the embrace is all." Out of despondency, a fitful wakening to mortality's finite character, comes an affirmation, a decision to make the most of every real, fleshed encounter with the world's beauty and the beauty of people who love. Love and the closeness generated by love are their own rewards in this gratuitous universe.

So, Kinnell's vision is essentially tragic, a lonely searching after fulfillment, isolation that comes from being sensitive to beauties that others often do not perceive and from articulating feelings derived from those perceptions. After all, honest feeling admits to pain, admits to hopelessness and despair, admits to those recognitions that humans choose to ignore in order to remain complacently content with their illusions. Close attachment implies hurt, it seems, implies eventual loss, and only the strong are likely to survive close attachments all too soon severed by death or disillusionment. *Mortal Acts, Mortal Words* asserts that these feelings of loss are humanizing, in fact, help define mortal being.

Recognizing the negative liberates the soul and opens it to the grander possibilities that delight the senses. Thus, Kinnell responds to simple natural beauties and takes true delight in detail, providing a real sense of energetic mind bending images by imaginative force. Starfishes burying in mud at dawn become stars crossing heaven to fade. A gray heron approached across a salt marsh becomes a stony lizard questioning the intruder's reality. Ripe blackberries eaten from the vine transform to words, "certain peculiar words/like *strengths* or *squinched*,/many-lettered one-syllabled lumps." The poems from which these images come affirm the fact that beauty resides in simple observations, in passing flickers of insight that lodge in the mind and come unbidden to the receptive soul. The key, of course, is receptivity, a quality to be cultivated by patience, by waiting, by trusting the hours as Kinnell says in "Wait." Kinnell would have us "wait a little and listen," hours if necessary, "to hear . . . the flute of [our] whole existence,/rehearsed by the sorrows, play itself into total exhaustion." The words recall William Wordsworth's "still, sad music" and remind us that meditation—deliberate confrontation with eternity—reveals the essence of being.

The philosophic touches that appear throughout *Mortal Acts, Mortal Words* anticipate the philosophic concentration in the last section's poems. Part III's poems all deal with death in some way, as has been noted, but the somber tone shifts significantly with the first lines of "Rainbow," the first poem of Part IV:

> The rainbow appears above us
> for its minute, then vanishes, as though
> we had wished it, making us
> turn more carefully to what we can
> touch and feel, things and creatures
> we know we haven't dreamed.

Significantly, the philosophical discourses that follow find their origins in commonplaces, in particulars of experience encountered randomly in the course of living. Because the rainbow's ephemeral nature renders it a part of the dreamlike portion of experience, where hopes and aspirations reside in a pristine splendor, turning from it signals people to look at "flutings on a match stick," or "the pelvic bones of a woman lying on her back" and the birth that everyone knew there. That birth initiated one to pain and a reality that can "put terrified grooves/permanently into the throat,/which can't relax ever again,/until the day the carcass expels/defeated desire." The death gasp comes "in one final curve of groaning breath." It leads to the infinite, in what Kinnell calls the "misery-arc farewelling hands have polished before each face." It approaches "the other, unfulfilled galaxies,/to win them over, too, into time and ruin."

Again, the note of tragedy sounds, the mournful tone generated by all too true realizations about the eventual finality everyone faces. In this last section's poems, however, the tragic vision is balanced, even outweighed by a central buoyancy of spirit. The assertion that love *is* courage, coming as it does at the end of the book's last poem, defines mortality in a seemingly positive way, in a way that moderates the essential pessimism of Kinnell's tragic vision. The effect is to release the burden to an extent, to unfetter chains of memory and pain with the actualization of love's embrace, the embrace that is all.

That the release remains personal and passionate is not surprising, for Kinnell's poetry has always had these characteristics. *Mortal Acts, Mortal Words*, however, seems an affirmation of those parts of experience that are not necessarily part of the tragic view. It seems more of an affirmation because of the variety of voices, the multiplicity of poetic forms displayed in spontaneous lines and rhythms. Certainly Kinnell shows in *Mortal Acts, Mortal Words* that he is capable of numerous effects with voice, most notably the rich personal statements derived from personal tragedy. The short lines and terseness in the shorter poems in Part II, however, capture a mood worth noting for its variance from the solemnity of the longer-lined poems. Playfulness in those poems reflects in the play with lines, the changes in rhythm that can produce the delightful effect of laughter in the poem "Crying," or the blatant wordplay that occurs in "Lava," which incorporates several Hawaiian words in a zany collection of alliterative and assonant sounds.

In general, *Mortal Acts, Mortal Words* articulates a hopeful vision, one that recognizes pain brought by mortality, but that refuses to be daunted by that pain and instead strains after some solidity tangible in the world's wealth of images. Those images, perhaps illusory, perhaps temporary, nevertheless come from experience that binds mortals together, that encompasses them in mutual understandings; and that bond is real when held to desperately, when cherished and fostered out of courage. To act at all, to reach out and touch at all when aware that "emptiness is all" takes courage. To utter words in explanation hoping they will touch some other beings in some truthful way also takes courage, and that courage sinks its roots into some hope for survival, some link with the eternal, some bond beyond mortality's limit.

Gary B. Blank

NAPOLEON III AND EUGÉNIE

Author: Jasper Ridley (1920-   )
Publisher: The Viking Press (New York). 768 pp. $25.00
Type of work: Biography
Time: 1808-1920
Locale: France, Western Europe, and the United States

A comprehensive biography of both Napoleon III and his wife Eugénie, concentrating primarily on Napoleon III and the major historical events in which he was involved in the turbulent era of the French Second Empire

> *Principal personages:*
> CHARLES LOUIS NAPOLEON BONAPARTE, nephew of Napoleon I and Emperor of France, 1852-1870
> MARIA EUGENIA IGNACIA AUGUSTINA BONAPARTE, a Spanish countess and wife of Napoleon III
> JEAN GILBERT VICTOR FIALIN, COMTE DE PERSIGNY, a loyal and ruthless adventurer who aided and influenced Napoleon III in his rise to power
> NAPOLEON EUGÈNE LOUIS JEAN JOSEPH BONAPARTE, the Prince Imperial and son to Napoleon III and Eugénie

In his Foreword to this mammoth study of two important figures of the French Second Empire, Jasper Ridley states, "This is not a history of the Second Empire, but a biography of Louis Napoleon and a biography of Eugénie." He further points out that he has included much historical background merely to "show the significance of Louis Napoleon's and Eugénie's reaction to them," and has omitted others on the basis that they were of little importance to the biographies with which he is concerned. The reader of the book may question this judgment because, for the most part, the book does read like a history. Such an approach is necessary, however, in that the Second Empire is a time filled with complex and relatively little-known events, negotiations, and conflicts, and any writer dealing with the period must fill in massive gaps existing in our twentieth century understanding of the minutiae of the political situation in nineteenth century Europe. As expected, those portions of the book devoted to Eugénie, who was not involved in politics except through her husband, concentrate instead on accounts culled from gossip and recollections of her contemporaries. The result is a book in which Napoleon III emerges as the central character despite the several early chapters devoted entirely to Eugénie. It is not until Louis Napoleon's death that she takes on much of a life of her own in these pages.

Ridley informs the reader that his interest in Napoleon III derived from his earlier 1976 biography of Garibaldi, although he must certainly have become intrigued with Eugénie from stories his grandfather told, who had met her when he was resident engineer of the newly constructed railway at Durban. Indeed, this feeling of closeness to the past gives the book one of its pleasures as Ridley recounts Eugénie's relationships with such twentieth century figures as Clemenceau, King George V, and Kenneth Clark. One can almost feel the closeness of Napoleon himself.

Although he is sketchily known to all but professional historians, Charles Louis Napoleon Bonaparte, known as Louis Napoleon, was born on April 20, 1808. Doubly related to his namesake, the future emperor was nephew on his father's side to Napoleon I as well as son to Napoleon's stepdaughter and sister-in-law. His parents' marriage was arranged by Napoleon himself as a means of establishing a dynasty. Ridley exhaustively but inconclusively tracks down the rumors that Napoleon fathered two of his brother's sons. Despite such credentials, Louis Napoleon's rise to prominence was as difficult as it was unlikely due to his being the youngest son. Yet, Napoleon Charles, his eldest sibling, died in 1807 and, upon the death of his second brother, Napoleon Louis, in 1831, the way was prepared for Louis's political aspirations. Ridley claims that Napoleon's one hundred day successful return to France in 1815 was the most formative event in the life of the young Louis Napoleon; it was from this experience that he gained his lifelong belief that the French people would always welcome a Napoleon in favor of imposed rulers. Although it was not until the death of Napoleon's own son, Napoleon II, in 1832, that Louis Napoleon became more or less undisputed heir of his uncle, Ridley states that upon the death of his elder brother the year earlier he changed overnight, becoming conscious of being "nothing but a Bonaparte."

The rigid educational regime imposed upon him by his mother, Queen Hortense de Beauharnais, when he was twelve years old, helped to reverse his earlier apparent laziness and lack of mental concentration. Beginning shortly after his brother's death in his role as heir apparent, he frequently authored pamphlets and books outlining his political doctrines, a combination of Republicanism and Bonapartism. As early as 1836, he was involved in an attempted coup at Strasbourg which lasted two and a half hours. Ridley indicates that at this time Louis had come under the influence of the man "who was to have the greatest influence on his life," the totally loyal Jean Gilbert Victor Fialin, a man described by Ridley as a "ruthless and unscrupulous adventurer."

Subsequent to and as a result of the abortive coup, Napoleon spent some time in New York where he met major American figures including the writers Washington Irving and Fenimore Cooper. The following year, having moved to London after being convicted of sedition for writing his account of the Strasbourg coup, Louis met most of the important political leaders of England whom he easily charmed. These social contacts led to his long and cordial relationship with that country.

For his 1840 attempted coup at Boulogne, Louis was sentenced to life imprisonment in the Castle at Ham, near St. Quentin, eighty miles from Paris. This imprisonment Ridley refers to as the "university" of Ham because of the many amenities accorded to Louis and his opportunities for study and the writing of articles. He was granted a handsome per diem allowance along with almost unlimited visitation privileges from his friends. An indication of his freedom is that during this period he fathered two sons, Eugène and Louis, by his laundress.

While Ridley does catalog Louis Napoleon's rather prodigious sexual escapades, he suggests that Louis's comment that, rather than attack as other men do, he spent most of his energies in defending himself against women's advances, sometimes surrendering, is not to be taken as seriously as other biographers have insisted. Yet, it is in these affairs that Ridley's book leaves most questions unanswered. His accounts show that, indeed, Louis Napoleon frequently did "surrender," but his explanation of Eugénie's tolerance of his behavior and her apparent frigidity as "Her refusal to take a lover, even after she knew that Louis Napoleon had several mistresses, was due to her principles, and also perhaps to a lack of enjoyment of the sexual act, but not to a natural coldness or hardness of character," is less than satisfactory. He suggests that after giving birth to a son, Eugénie was warned against future pregnancies and that sexual relations were difficult for her. He also states that Louis's passion for her began cooling at this time. The intimate part of their life together remains elusive.

After the abdication of Louis Philippe in February of 1848, the "year of revolutions," Louis Napoleon's chances looked very meager. They seemed worse after he gave a poor speech in the Assembly prior to the presidential election upon the establishment of the Second Republic; however, in the subsequent election, primarily because of the magic of his name, he polled seventy-five percent of the votes to become president.

During his years as France's leading political figure Napoleon III was almost constantly at odds with the various political factions—radicals, socialists, moderate republicans—and Ridley details both his open fights and his secret and public negotiations with the different groups. It is difficult to reconcile these official actions with the apparently leisurely days described by Ridley which included rising at ten in the morning, driving about with his then mistress Miss Howard, and attending the many balls and receptions scheduled, without realizing there had to be much more to the man than appeared superficially to his contemporaries. In addition to all this activity, Louis Napoleon also found time to complete two volumes of a biography of Julius Caesar, which Ridley claims to be a sufficient memorial to its author even if he had never entered public life.

Ridley describes Louis Napoleon's methods of dealing with his political enemies within France as the granting of "every possible concession to his enemies immediately before destroying them." When he failed in his attempt to change the constitution to enable himself to run for reelection, Louis Napoleon simply arrested deputies, officials, radical and socialist leaders, and took over the presses, issuing a proclamation setting up a referendum for a new constitution. He then dissolved the Assembly. When the remaining members of the Assembly met and voted a resolution deposing him, he had them arrested too. Although the Constitutional Court ruled him guilty of treason and declared him no longer president they had no power to enforce their edict and the referendum was duly held in December of 1851. Louis Napoleon's winning margin was overwhelming; only one electoral district voted against him. In the following year, the Second Empire was established by a vote of more than seven million; Louis Napoleon became Emperor Napoleon III.

Louis Napoleon's love for Eugénie is described as contrasting with that of his more rational usual affairs. He allegedly "fell madly and overwhelmingly" in love with her. Her initial reaction is not as clear. Ridley tries to sort out the rumors of Eugénie leading a loose life and of her attempted suicide over Pepe Alcañices, Duke of Sesto, concluding that any definite evidence is lacking. Nevertheless, Ridley says, her attraction to him was not as strong as his. Their marriage, in January of 1853, over the objections of his ministers proved initially injurious to his career. That she was unpopular with the French is attested by the many rumors and insulting epithets aimed at her. Even the Pope was concerned about the scandals associated with her resulting in his refusal to come for the coronation of her husband. Napoleon III was never formally crowned.

Remembered mainly for his failures, Napoleon III was involved in most of the intrigues on the international political scene if not in all the wars. Ridley claims that it is a "grotesque exaggeration" to suggest, as historians have, that Napoleon III "deliberately schemed" to engage Britain and Russia in the Crimean War. In Ridley's view, he was engaging in his usual tactic of scheming with both sides to his own advantage. His success in this case was not matched in the 1859 Franco-Austrian War in Italy where he surreptitiously negotiated a personal treaty but gained political enemies at home and abroad instead of the hoped for peace. His fiasco in Mexico, Ridley says, is again entirely due to his usual tactics and not to his being misled by his advisers, as is often cited by historians. Ridley claims that he was acting with his usual motives of defending French honor, promoting self-interest, and striking against republicanism in his usual deceitful way. In this case, he was suffering from two false assumptions: that the Mexican radicals had no support in the country and that the South would win the Civil War in the United States. On the more successful side, French involvement in Cochin China and West Africa began at this time.

Louis Napoleon also attempted to emulate his great namesake by leading the French on the battlefield, although he had no military training. When he was forced to surrender to the Germans at Sedan in September of 1870, the immediate result was the proclamation of a new French Republic and his imprisonment. He was deposed and spent the rest of his days in England. On his death following an operation for kidney stones in January of 1873, a controversy again arose over the cause of his death. Although Ridley does not dwell on Louis Napoleon's health at any great length, he does point out that he had had intervals of being prostrated by ill health from the stone in his bladder as well as rheumatism contracted while imprisoned at Ham. The post mortem indicated the cause of death was kidney disease, but Ridley suggests there was a possibility of an overdose of chloral. Again, the evidence available today is inconclusive.

After Louis Napoleon's death, the Empress Eugénie lived for fifty more years until her death at age ninety-four in 1920. The most significant crisis in her life was the death of their son, the Prince Imperial, Napoleon Eugène Louis Jean Joseph, on June 1, 1879, in Zululand, where he apparently was deserted by the English with whom he was a "distinguished visitor attached to the general staff." Ridley says it took Eugénie twenty years to recover. Because of her personal friendship with Queen Victoria (Ridley points out that Queen Victoria asked her to write in the informal style) a monument was built to the Prince Imperial at Windsor. Ultimately, Eugénie did recover despite her later comment that she had died in 1870. She learned to ride a bicycle in her seventies and she traveled widely despite frequent ill health, which was due to rheumatism, gout, neuralgia, and headaches. She died shortly after a cataract operation undergone in Spain without anesthetic.

Throughout this double biography, Ridley is thorough in his coverage of those events he feels of importance to the principals. There are, however, some areas omitted in which the reader may question his judgment, such as the industrial revolution and its impact, and such civic works as the railroad building, establishment of hospitals, reorganization of the banks, and the reconstruction of Paris. These are briefly noted by Ridley, but it is a matter of debate how much these influenced Louis Napoleon personally, as well as in the minds of his public who had relinquished their liberty for him. Nevertheless, to have included as detailed an analysis of these as is contained in the rest of the book would certainly have made the length formidable, and as it is, many would question whether Napoleon III is important enough to warrant the present sized book. Despite Ridley's attempt to give Eugénie equal treatment, most of the interest is focused on Napoleon III; and despite the author's disclaimer, the book does read more as history than as biography. Had Ridley included those few domestic works during the Emperor's rule instead of including so much about Eugénie, this book would certainly be in contention as the definitive study of the Second Empire.

Considering his scope, Ridley's organization is clear and adequate. He devotes separate chapters to Louis Napoleon and to Eugénie detailing their lives before their marriage. Because of the information available on each, as well as Louis Napoleon's greater historical importance, most of the chapters are devoted to him, and the reader's understanding of the inner workings of the man is much more thorough than that of his wife. Nevertheless, this book presents as much information as one could expect concerning this relatively obscure couple who played a major role in nineteenth century Europe.

Roger A. Geimer

NATHANIEL HAWTHORNE IN HIS TIMES

Author: James R. Mellow (1926-   )
Publisher: Houghton Mifflin Company (Boston). 684 pp. $19.95
Type of work: Literary biography
Time: 1804-1880
Locale: New England

An expansive and luxuriant treatment of the life of an American literary brahmin

> Principal personages:
> NATHANIEL HAWTHORNE, author of *The Scarlet Letter* and *The House of the Seven Gables*
> SOPHIA PEABODY HAWTHORNE, his friend, companion, and loving wife
> HENRY WADSWORTH LONGFELLOW, the celebrated poet who wrote "The Song of Hiawatha" and "Evangeline," and friend to Hawthorne
> RALPH WALDO EMERSON, a poet, essayist, philosopher, and friend to Hawthorne
> HERMAN MELVILLE, author of the classic novel *Moby Dick* and friend to Hawthorne
> HENRY DAVID THOREAU, author of *Walden* and friend to Hawthorne
> FRANKLIN PIERCE, a boyhood friend of Hawthorne who became President of the United States, 1853-1857
> CHARLES SUMNER, a friend to Hawthorne and a United States Senator

The author of *Nathaniel Hawthorne in His Times*, James R. Mellow, comes well suited to the task of interpreting a major American writer's life, not only having had considerable experience as a literary critic for *The New York Times*, *The Chicago Tribune*, *The New Republic*, *Commonweal*, and other publications, but also having written the acclaimed biography, *Charmed Circle: Gertrude Stein and Company*, published in 1974. At present, he is writing a life of Hawthorne's friend, Margaret Fuller.

With this study of Hawthorne, Mellow focuses on things other than the growth and development of his subject's mind, demonstrating how the writer struggled with his art and finally gained the enviable reputation he continues to enjoy. What Mellow brings forth is a vivid sense of the age in which Hawthorne wrote, a time of growth for the young Republic. He sets out to show that unlike Henry David Thoreau, with whom he is often compared, Hawthorne was a person consciously and voluntarily immersed in events of his day. No idle bystander, he helped his old friend, Franklin Pierce, run for the office of President.

Hawthorne is best known as the political appointee musing over ancient Salem, Massachusetts, docks portrayed in his novel, *The Scarlet Letter*. His self-portrait in the novel is that of a dissatisfied Custom House keeper at once haunted by ghosts of his ancestors and anxious to escape his dull duties. If

Hawthorne became restless as Custom House director, he was happier when he took the Consul's position in Liverpool, England. There he became an active American representative, personally intervening in disputes and rescueing hapless Americans caught in British red tape or in trouble with British authorities.

The writer's early days were lived in the midst of increasing stress between Northern and Southern states and he, like many intellectuals of the day, was deeply bothered by the coming storm over states' rights and slavery. In Salem and Concord, it was easier to escape the tensions of the times than it was in New York and Boston, but still news of the outside penetrated his enclosed world and that news, especially in the 1850's, became very bad indeed.

The Northern ports were in varying states of repair, Salem being numbered among those that were in decline. Its sleepy and decaying docks allowed him a place to dream of the past and write *The Scarlet Letter*. Concord too, although not a port city, was quiet and, for the most part, rather dull. Its advantages were that Thoreau and Henry Wadsworth Longfellow lived there and that books could be written there. Elsewhere, America was stirring, which intrigued Hawthorne. Canals and railroads were being constructed and towns were going up quickly across the Northeast and into the newly opening lands to the West. Yet, as fascinated as Hawthorne was by all the hurly-burly taking place outside of his home cities, it was not proper grist for his literary mill.

For inspiration, Hawthorne turned to reading ancient chronicles and records and to intense dreaming of days gone by. All the while, he was lovingly cared for by wife Sophia, herself a gentle intellectual who enjoyed walks in the country and long talks with her husband. Mellow does a fine job of describing the close relationship that grew between husband and wife. From him, one discovers that Sophia was not only an inspiration for some of Hawthorne's books, but also that she alone guided him through difficult times and kept him writing. Her insistence that he keep developing as a writer paid off after *The Scarlet Letter* became a decent selling book. That Sophia and her husband were unusually close is very apparent. They would write diaries for each other and discuss things carefully for hours on end.

If Sophia was important, so were other people who passed in and out of Hawthorne's life: Margaret Fuller, editor of the important journal *The Dial*; George Ripley, founder of the utopian colony called Brook Farm of which Hawthorne was briefly a member; Edgar Allan Poe, who was violently jealous of his fellow writer's talent; Herman Melville, a good friend and confidant; Franklin Pierce, fourteenth President of the United States who was Hawthorne's friend in high places; and Charles Sumner, another friend in high places, to name but a few. All of the people he came in contact with seemed to enjoy Hawthorne's company, thus dispelling his traditional image of an ivory-tower writer.

What comes through strongest in this book is Hawthorne's happiness. He seems happy and fulfilled and has everything worth having: a loving family, friends, a fine avocation, leisure time, travel, and enough money to live decently if not luxuriously. Mellow, like any good biographer, makes the reader aware of the humanity of his subject. One sees Hawthorne in the round, as it were: fully human, fully believable.

Also what comes through is Hawthorne's decency and tact. He is shown doing all he can to help unfortunate friends such as Melville and tension-wracked Franklin Pierce. Friends, however, were not the only people he assisted; he aided strangers as well, especially those he helped in England. If ever a person deserved literary fame and the admiration of his fellow man, it was Hawthorne.

Somehow or other, it is difficult to reconcile Hawthorne the open, loving father, husband, and friend with the haunted creator of "Young Goodman Brown" or *The House of the Seven Gables*, and yet he is often caught up in visions of evil and madness. He is able to disassociate himself from his happy world and withdraw into the strange twilit world found so often in his writing. One thing Mellow does not do is explain why Hawthorne wrote about what he did. Was he really possessed by a kind of demonic spirit?

That Hawthorne turned to the past so often in his work rather than to present-day America has bothered certain critics, some of whom have felt that he neglected to capture his own time, while instead focusing on a time long gone and unknowable. From what Mellow says, he was unable to write about America in the early nineteenth century because it was simply too new, too raw, without real traditions or picturesque ruins or the requisite tragic feelings of romance. Only the earliest colonial times could furnish him with the proper setting for his tales and the appropriate far-away world of sun and blackest shadow. Witch trials were dramatic things and so were pillories and scarlet letters.

Hawthorne seems to be in love not only with family and career but also with the history of his native turf. One sees him constantly investigating his surroundings, noting leaves on the trees and their configurations as well as the contours of hills and the colors of native wild flowers. Certainly, it would be difficult to imagine Hawthorne outside of New England, for he fits so perfectly there. One sees, for instance, how deeply and profoundly his ancestors have affected him. They live again in his teeming imagination. Their sins are his sins. He feels the pain of guilt over their past deeds as well as his inability to match their more heroic exploits. His Puritan past is his stalking horse, its moral code, his to contend with, its narrow vision of earthly life, his ultimately to forsake.

For anyone interested in literary analysis, this is the wrong book, for what is discussed is the man *in his times*, not the kind of symbolism or theme he employed in what he wrote. Also, there is no real attempt on Mellow's part to say that this or that person became this or that character in this or that story. One is given the chance to make one's own decisions. Perhaps the closest the author gets to this kind of approach is when he speaks of Una, Hawthorne's daughter, as a very close likeness of the little sprite, Pearl, in *The Scarlet Letter* and there are hints that Hester may be patterned after his wife.

The best reason on earth to read *Nathaniel Hawthorne in His Times* is to get to know Hawthorne as someone other than simply a famous writer. He was, after all, a splendid human being living in an exciting time of national expansion and tension.

John D. Raymer

NATIVE REALM
A Search for Self-Definition

Author: Czeslaw Milosz (1911-   )
Translated from the Polish by Catherine S. Leach
Publisher: Doubleday & Company (Garden City, New York). 300 pp. $12.95
Type of work: Autobiography
Time: 1911-1960
Locale: Lithuania, Poland, East Prussia, France, Switzerland, and the United States

An impersonal autobiography, emphasizing the ideological and social currents of his time, by Poland's foremost contemporary poet

Until he received the Nobel Prize for Literature in late 1980, Czeslaw Milosz was a relatively obscure poet-scholar, born in Lithuania, writing in Polish, fleeing a Stalinized Poland in 1951, and settling into a professorship at the University of California, Berkeley, in 1960. After his departure for the West the Polish Communist regime had proscribed publication of all his writings except a volume of poetry written in 1945, *Salvation.* For thirty years, the Party censors insisted on his official nonexistence, while his legend as a great poet grew in Poland through private recitations, tapes circulated in nonconformist circles, even illegal publication.

In 1981, the publicity of the Nobel award coincided with the liberalization of Poland's cultural as well as political life. In June of that year, Milosz returned as a poet-hero to the land he had left in despair more than a generation ago. He became an instant symbol of Polish national pride, joining the small club of native-born immortals that includes Nicolaus Copernicus, Frédéric Chopin, Joseph Conrad, Marie Curie, and Ignace Paderewski. Hundreds of flower-offering countrymen mobbed him at Warsaw's airport; thousands attended his speeches; twenty-two of his titles are now in sanctioned print in his homeland. Remarkably, this moving illustration of the Lazarus myth is paralleled by Milosz's most recent literary venture: he has devoted his creative energy the past several years to translating the Scriptures into Polish.

Milosz's literary career is unusually eclectic. In addition to his autobiography, he has written two novels, *The Seizure of Power* (1955) and *The Issa Valley* (1955, reissued 1981); an eloquent tractate against Soviet anti-intellectualism, *The Captive Mind* (1953, reissued 1981); and a collection of critical essays ranging from Emanuel Swedenborg to modern Russian authors to Simone Weil, *Modes of Eccentric Vision* (1977). His verse includes such titles as *The Light of Day* (1953), *Treatise on Poetry* (1957), *The Land of Ulro* (1977), and *Bells of Winter* (1978). The poet Joseph Brodsky, a fellow exile from Russia, has called him "one of the greatest poets of our time, perhaps the greatest."

Native Realm is a highly unusual autobiography in its deemphasis of its subject's personality, its preference instead for choreographing the grim dialectic of power struggles between Poland, Russia, and Germany in the 1930's and 1940's. It traces Milosz's intellectual and emotional education from his roots in Wilno, Lithuania, to his maturation in Poland, travels to Western Europe, underground survival in German-occupied Warsaw during World War II, unhappy service as a minor diplomat from 1945-1950, and agonized decision, in 1951, to exile himself from his East European heritage. The dominant perspective is that of a reflective, long-range lens focusing on theological and ideological debates, historic changes, philosophical observations, psychological nuances, above all the shaping of the author's complex, profoundly reflective mind. Hardly ever does Milosz permit himself intimately personal revelations, so that the reader is only informed by way of casual parentheses that "my parents had long ago moved away, and I had been doing as I pleased since I was sixteen." One learns little about his relationships with women, and nothing about his wife and two sons. "This is not a book of feelings," Milosz explains:

> . . . if I were to present a personal history with a purely subjective slant, I would solve nothing because I would be leaving out the most interesting part . . . this is not a diary; I am not telling what happened to me from day to day or from month to month. . . . The frames I cut should be intelligible to a wider audience, not just to framers of Expressionism.

Whether a "wider audience" will welcome republication of *Native Realm* remains to be seen; the original text sold sparsely, addressed as it was to an intellectual, historically informed audience by a virtually unknown émigré artist-scholar. Yet, the book rewards close attention: it is subtly argued, intensely if quietly felt, powerful in its loyalty to the traditional humanistic values of enlightenment and fraternal understanding, sad in its recall of romantic loyalties to ideologies that have now proved bankrupt.

Milosz stresses his East European roots throughout the book, alluding to himself as no more than "a sociological phenomenon." His native Lithuania has an old history of being pressed on its Western flank by Roman Catholic Poles, on its Eastern by the Greek Orthodox princes of Moscow and Kiev. In William Shakespeare's time, the country's dense forests supplied England with live bears. In the nineteenth century, German universities introduced courses in Lithuanian since it turned out to be the oldest Indo-European language, akin to Sanskrit. By 1911, when Milosz was born and baptized into Roman Catholicism, he was "a child of defeat," with the Russians dominating all public institutions while Polish and Yiddish were the everyday tongues of the streets and marketplaces.

Shy about describing his own life, Milosz draws vivid portraits of several relatives. One was a libertine, adventurous uncle who tamed bears into becoming his bodyguards and fell in love with the portrait of a beautiful young woman placed in a shop window. She turned out to be a Jewish schoolteacher's daughter; he married her anyway, despite the strong disapproval of his gentry-Catholic family; their son, Oscar Milosz, became a brilliant linguist and writer who emigrated to France and generously befriended his younger cousin Czeslaw in later years, treating him as an honorary "nephew" by virtue of their mutual profession of poetry.

Milosz's earliest memory dates to 1914, when the Germans beat the czarist occupiers of Lithuania into retreat. A young Cossack, whom the boy had considered his friend, helped ambush and slaughter a little white lamb of which Czeslaw was fond. This was his first encounter with "irrevocable unhappiness," his first "protest against necessity." He began his childish play in cemeteries, with the graves of Germans covered with blackberry and raspberry thickets, while no one tended the Russian dead.

Milosz waxes sentimental in his description of his native city Wilno, called Wilna by Germans and Byelorussians. Its 200,000 inhabitants were largely Catholic, making it one of the most powerful Jesuit centers in Europe, and attaching it emotionally to Poland. Yet, only the Lithuanian landed gentry accepted Polish culture: the peasantry, stubborn in retaining its Flemish heaviness, mistrusted it. Then there was a large Jewish population, which considered Wilno a Northern Jerusalem; most of them spoke Yiddish, with an emancipated minority—the Litvaks—preferring Russian, almost none Polish. Hence, Wilno had many sectarian schools; even at the university level student organizations separated themselves into Polish, Jewish, Lithuanian, and Byelorussian entities.

Milosz devotes a number of pages to the complex phenomenon of anti-Semitism, insisting upon its subtle occupational, political, religious, and geographic variations. The Polish bias was mainly racial-religious.

> Yet if ever the object of [the Gentile Poles'] oddly ambivalent feelings were somehow missing, they would be overcome by melancholy: 'Without the Jews it's *boring*.' . . . No cabaret could get by without Jewish jokes, and the pungent gallows humor peculiar to cities like Warsaw bears the clear stamp of Jewish popular humor. This symbiosis prevented indifference. At the opposite pole it produced specimens of philo-Semites for whom . . . non-Jewish women had no appeal because they were regarded as intellectually inferior.

At the Catholic high school he attended in Wilno, Milosz's mind was divided between real-life counterparts to the Jesuitical Naphta and humanistic Settembrini of Thomas Mann's *The Magic Mountain*. The former was inquisitorial, ugly, and sexually disturbed. His adversary was an elegantly ironic classicist who inculcated in Milosz a love for the rhythms of poetry. A simpler student would have sided with the benign Latinist, scorned the despotic religionist; not Milosz. His mind disdained shallow affirmations or denials: ". . . My relationship to [the humanist] could be described as sympathy corroded by mockery, and my relationship to [the Jesuit] as mockery corroded by sympathy." His propensity was for an uneasy Manichaeanism, misunderstood by most teachers and fellow-students, who regarded him as "a Jew among the *goyim*." Milosz's philosophical and theological position was formed in this struggle to understand conflicting doctrines and mind-sets. He has difficulty elucidating it; perhaps the vague label of "Catholic humanist" would best describe it.

As for Milosz's political position, it was easier to define by its negations than assertions. He was a consistent opponent of the anti-Semitic, fanatically nationalistic far Right, which dominated the Lithuanian Home Army and both Lithuania's and Poland's military forces. He was also contemptuous of the bourgeoisie, while at the same time mocking his contempt as immature self-righteousness. His resistance to reactionary obscurantism drove him toward a rather fluid Leftist allegiance by the time he attended the University of Wilno. He began to publish liberal poems and articles, and associated with arts-loving fellow students most of whom were Polish Jews. By an easy process of osmosis, he even became a Marxist at the University: ". . . the Marxists not without reason valued the doctrine as the inevitable outcome of a nineteenth-century scientific world view carried to its logical conclusion." Milosz stresses the significance of the years he attended the University—1930-1935: the worldwide depression's mass unemployment; Hitler's seizure of power; and the consequent hardening of ideologies—". . . the Right became more and more Fascist, and the Left more and more Stalinist."

Milosz comments on his position during that time: "My mind worked . . . like the mind of an artist. . . . It advanced from negation to negation and actually delighted in the contradictions it attempted to resolve. . . . Long years of theological skirmishes . . . had left me with a fondness for fencing with myself." He was too much the Catholic to accept Russian atheism-materialism; too much the humanist to embrace easily a Popular Front that included Soviet apologists; yet consistently felt nauseated by the rabid patrioteering of the Polish Right. "Happy are they who can avoid radical choices," he sighs. "My state of mind in those days could be described as the same dream over and over: we want to run, but cannot because our legs are made of lead."

Milosz devotes a long, thoughtful chapter to a discussion of the traditional differences and dislikes between Poles and Russians. He agrees with Conrad in regarding their tempers as incompatible. Poland's dominant force is that of the landed gentry, who adopted the ideas, literature, architecture, and craftsmanship of humanist Western Europe, receiving their permanent cultural imprint during the sixteenth and seventeenth centuries. Russia did not get its cultural imprint until the nineteenth century, when it came from the Asiatic East's absolutism as much as from the West. Milosz endorses the great Polish poet Adam Mickiewicz's aversion to Russia's "savagery in human relationships, the passivity and apathy of the people in their bondage." He recalls that Karl Marx favored the Poles, Hungarians, and Serbs as "creative and freedom-loving," while expressing violent antipathy to the tyranny of Pan-Slavic Russia. Above all, Milosz mistrusts the Russian inclination toward eschatology.

By 1936, Milosz had received his law degree but, disdaining the legal profession, instead obtained a cultural-activities position with a Wilno radio station that was a subsidiary of a Polish network resembling the B.B.C. when the Spanish Civil War erupted, its repercussions cost him his job: a Catholic newspaper accused him of belonging to a Jew-loving, Communist cell; county authorities consequently demanded his dismissal; the local station director fired him. The network's Warsaw Head Office quickly hired him for its literary section, however, accounting for his presence in the capital when World War II began in 1939.

The agreement that led to virtually immediate hostilities was the Molotov-Ribbentrop Pact, signed August 23, 1939, in which Hitler's Germany and Stalin's Soviet Union promised each other nonaggression, and carved Poland's territory into respective zones of influence. This event shocked millions of left-wingers by its cynical betrayal of their opposition to Nazism. While the German blitzkrieg conquered Poland, Milosz experienced a "mixture of fury and relief. . . . The nonsense was over at last. That long-dreaded fulfillment had freed us from the self-reassuring lies, illusions, subterfuges." Later he adds, ". . . in my heart I could not regard National Socialism as a durable phenomenon . . . it was too pure an evil."

The war years in Warsaw liberated his thought and poetry. He made close studies of Western poets such as Arthur Rimbaud, Stéphane Mallarmé, and T. S. Eliot, received small sums from the underground resistance, and filled a typewritten literary journal with anti-Nazi articles. Milosz managed to publish his own poetry in volumes printed on ditto sheets, sewn together by hand, and circulated through the underground structure. He tried to obey the advice given by Martin Luther when asked what he would do if he knew the world would end tomorrow: "I would plant apple trees."

Milosz's "apple trees" included a number of essays on novelists and philosophers. "They filled more than a private need," he assures the reader: "They were read at clandestine gatherings where they provoked serious discussion." He also compiled an anthology of resistance poetry, prepared a new translation of Shakespeare's *As You Like It*, and generally led an active intellectual life.

Toward the end of the war, he became an intimate friend of a remarkable personality, the philosopher-poet Boleslaw Micinski, nicknamed "Tiger" because of his aggressive skills in debate. "Tiger" was a subtle, Hegelian dialectician who masochistically and sardonically allied himself with Soviet policy as the locomotive heading for an irrevocable future. He taught philosophy in both Paris and Warsaw, but, after a journey to Moscow in 1950, he returned "livid with fear," yet afraid to remove his mask of Stalinist apologist, playing "with the absurdities of official doctrine like a juggler tossing balls into the air." Thereafter, he retreated into reading Marcel Proust and Friedrich Hegel. "Tiger" died of a heart attack in 1958.

Milosz was caught in the tragic Warsaw Uprising of August, 1944, saved from transportation to a concentration camp by the ministry of a "majestic nun," unknown to him, who persuaded German soldiers to release him to her custody as her "nephew." He never saw her again. From then on, as he reflects on the ashes of Treblinka, Maidanek, and Auschwitz, his pages grow increasingly mournful with news of, and meditations on, torture and corruption, death and apocalypse.

From 1945 to 1950, he served in Washington, D.C., as a cultural second secretary of the Soviet-dominated "Embassy of People's Poland." The post sickened him: he wondered why he, a poet who refused to join the Communist Party, "warranted the privilege of being sent to America." On his desk lay a letter from Polish relatives of a Siberian prisoner in a labor camp, asking for a food package; in Manhattan he encountered a former Warsaw actress who giggled when she told him of her husband's horrible death when he had run up to a German tank loaded with dynamite. It is no wonder that he felt guilty outrage in the land of orange juice, milk shakes, and new shirts; that he "walked the streets of Chicago and Los Angeles as if I were an anthropologist privileged to visit the civilizations of Incas or Aztecs." He identifies only with the blacks—they, like Europeans, "were alive, tragic, and spontaneous."

Milosz felt he had to try once more to live in Eastern Europe. He returned there in the fall of 1950, "because for my despair to come to a head I needed to see for myself Poland's Stalinist nightmare." He does not relate the details of his final disillusionment; it is enough that he quickly broke with the Communist regime and moved to France. There he exposed Stalinist doublethink in *The Captive Mind*, only to wince with embarrassment when this work was misinterpreted as knee-jerk anti-Communism by right-wing United States reviewers. As usual, the scrupulous and subtle mind of a poet-historian had been inadequately apprehended.

> Many of my contemporaries may regard such thrashing about as the neurotic unhinging of a modern Hamlet. Their jobs and their amusements prevent them from seeing what is really at stake. I was not a philosopher. Events themselves threw me into my century's towering philosophical pressures, into the vortex of its hardest and most essential questions. Perhaps these exceeded my grasp, but they mobilized all my energies.

In this concluding paragraph, Milosz resigns himself to being misunderstood.

Gerhard Brand

THE NEED TO HOLD STILL

Author: Lisel Mueller (1924-   )
Publisher: Louisiana State University Press (Baton Rouge). 63 pp. $9.95
Type of work: Poetry

A collection of poems which build toward the notion of the child and the adult finding common ground in the art of storytelling

Lisel Mueller's division of her poems into four groups is a compliment to the reader's intelligence without overtaxing the reader's ingenuity. The first section contains relatively personal poems dealing with relatively ordinary experiences. The second section presents conceits and fantasies. The third section's one long poem is a fantasy, but with a reference point in ordinary experience. The final section's poems interweave all three motifs: the art of the bard or storyteller is to make the fantastic part of everyday life.

The first poem, "For a Thirteenth Birthday" addresses a child who has mastered the noble world of Count Leo Tolstoy and is ready for the more common world of Theodore Dreiser. In "Another Version," however, the adult speaker clings to the "Russianness" of life in the American countryside. "Drawings by Children" depicts the crude nobility of the world children draw. "Talking with Helen" implies that Helen Keller's breakthrough into the world of words was a breakthrough into the world of childlike notions of nobility, while her multiple handicaps made her immune to the dreary adult world. In contrast, the speaker of "Beginning with 1914," with full use of senses, can imagine a documentary film of her family's sufferings in the midst of a World War.

Having proven that she understands the difference between child and adult, nobility and dreariness, Mueller takes a holiday in the world of fantasy, whimsy, and downright silliness. An observer of frantic dancers in a college gymnasium prefers to watch the birds dancing outside. Snow is anatomized: "rabbinical snow, a permanent skullcap," the "snow" of poor television reception, and Elinor Wylie's snow. Eggs are eaten with gusto because humans were once eggs themselves and cabbage is anthropomorphized so that its enthusiastic human devourer becomes a cruel cannibal.

The title poem concludes the second section more seriously. Ugly winter weeds are gathered by an equally ugly woman and brought into her home. They have "freedom from either/or" which she lacks. The dignity and significance of their spare, dry forms suggest, however, that she, too, has been through enough adversity to rest in a similar still and aesthetic patience.

Having employed adult and childlike voices in the first two sections, Mueller presents the eight-part "Voices from the Forest" in which either a precocious child or a childlike adult reduces an array of German fairy tales into typologies. Some of the most interesting of these reductions are the all-purpose shapeshifter who warns virgins to beware of enchanted bears, frogs, dwarves, and beasts;

the all-purpose beauty who warns that old age and reduction in status come to her kind, after the happy endings; and the sister of all enchanted ravens, swans, and fawns who confesses that she prefers her brothers in that form, under her control.

In the fourth section, adult, child, and storyteller combine to produce "The Triumph of Life: Mary Shelley." The poem does not succeed, but its failure provides some hindsight for problems in the earlier poems and foreshadows difficulties in the remaining poems. Mueller has some excellent conceits in which there are no ideas and some excellent ideas which she cannot flesh out. This poem is one of the latter. It does not give insight into Mary Shelley nor does it develop Mueller's theme of adult-child-storyteller, but such a figure *could be* personified in Mary Shelley.

"Testimony," "The Artist's Model, ca. 1912," and "The End of Science Fiction," are more successful presentations of the adult-child as storyteller. "Testimony" is the vague but nevertheless vivid complaint of the first sea creature to walk on land. The Artist's Model has seen her body mutilated by the history of modern art from its "real" beauty to its fragmentation, conversion into blocks, addition of extra eyes and a horn, reduction to giant lips or nipples, and finally evaporated into an absence, a space. The speaker in "The End of Science Fiction" laments that the science fiction world is already here and so, for variety and freshness, storytelling should return to the Greco-Roman myths.

The long-range view of history undergirding these three poems is beyond a child's grasp, but the views expressed by the speakers are also not from an adults perspective. It is perhaps not too farfetched to suggest that the relationship between researching poet and unreliable speaker is comparable to Robert Browning's historical character monologues. "What Will You Do" and "Why We Tell Stories" have exactly the right rhetoric for the end of the book but, as with "The Triumph of Life: Mary Shelley," the ideas do not flesh out. If the world has gone wrong, as the trio of lamenting Browning-like poems indicate, what will humankind do? The answer is direct enough; start over. Why do humans tell stories? To help humankind start over. The child is the father and mother of the storyteller and the storyteller has the past and future in his grasp. That theme does more than justice to the collection of poems. All the poems, however, do not always rise to the theme.

In "For a Thirteenth Birthday" the point of taking a child from Tolstoy to Dreiser was adequately made in the first two stanzas. The stanzas sketching the nature of reality and praising Dreiser are superfluous. "Drawings by Children" is wonderful on the starkness of child-drawn skies, but the stanzas on self-portraits and houses are weak.

"Postcards from All Over" is lovely in its conceit of an array of friends abroad sending back picture postcards, but the cards literally and figuratively pile up with no idea to pull the poem together. "Talking to Helen" and "The

Triumph of Life: Mary Shelley" do not add much imagination to the research. These poems present metrical exegesis on the known biographical facts.

Finally, "Picking Raspberries" will serve to illustrate the problem of these lesser poems and something of the problems of the major ones. The childhood experience of being so greedily involved in picking berries that painful scratches are not noticed until later is a wonderful idea for a poem. Only the poem is lacking. Mueller reaches for a notion of otherworldliness and loss of memory. The motifs of greed as an anesthetic, the moment of pleasure-pain balance, and the confusion over the strangeness of the experience are not referred to in the poem at all.

The weakest of Mueller's poems are abstract commonplaces—a middle range of profound treatment of the trivial and trivial treatment of the profound. Even her best poems have some dead spots, lines rendered anticlimactic and dull by both form and substance, all the more irritating because she can clearly write wonderful lines and fine poems. "Nefertiti's head/and Mozart's piano float to the top/side by side, like contemporaries" shows her all-too-common mannerism of dropped voice and anticlimax.

Mueller is impatient with form. The mainstream metrical voice is a couplet of 6-8 syllables in the first line and fewer in the second, resulting in anticlimax, afterthought, amplification, repetition. The three most notable attempts to break out of this pattern are hardly experimental, with three-syllable lines and single words as lines.

Mueller clearly is not quite sure of her readers. She assumes everyone knows who "Kitty and Levin" are and what Elinor Wylie has to do with snow but not that readers know the life of Mary Shelley, for which she provides a prose headnote. Lisel Mueller is clearly a delightful, well-read person, given to both profound thinking about the human condition and forays into whimsy and fantasy. The attempt to do both at once presents difficulties for her. One does not so much await Mueller's next new volume as wish for this one to be pored over and revised as Mueller's own good taste could dictate.

T. G. Shults

NEIGHBORS

Author: Thomas Berger (1924-   )
Publisher: Delacorte Press/Seymour Lawrence (New York). 275 pp. $9.95
Type of work: Novel
Time: The present, a twenty-four-hour period
Locale: Rural suburbia

New neighbors arrive in smug rural suburbia and precipitate a series of wild, manic, slapstick events

Principal characters:
EARL KEESE, forty-nine-year-old homeowner
ENID KEESE, his wife
ELAINE KEESE, his daughter
RAMONA, the new female neighbor
HARRY, the new male neighbor

It is hard to imagine an odder book than *Neighbors*. When one is imagined, however, it will probably be imagined—and written—by Thomas Berger. In a career spanning some twenty years, this underrated writer has produced ten novels of remarkable diversity. Whether consciously or not, Berger has written in several distinctive literary genres, and to each new genre he has brought a level of imagination and creativity which seems to expand the boundaries of the genre while at the same time gently satirizing the formulas into which the genre has slipped.

Berger himself has provided an explanation for this. In an interview in *The New York Times Book Review* he said, "I write for the purpose of providing myself with an alternative to reality." In his career, Berger has availed himself of such fictional alternatives as the Old West, the days of King Arthur and the hard-boiled detective milieu. Berger is probably best known as the author of a book (*Little Big Man*) which was made into a film starring Dustin Hoffman. Arguably, *Little Big Man* is his best book. His other works, however, also merit reading; indeed it may be said that the totality of his literary output to date is as impressive, both quantitatively and qualitatively, as that of almost any active American writer.

Berger brings a strange but acute sensibility to his material. He is a master of the small observation, the subtle nuance, the careful shade of meaning. One must always guard against accepting things at face value, for things are often not what they seem in Berger's work. His books abound in unexpected shifts of plot and surprising revelations of character; and, so it is with *Neighbors*.

What an evocative word "neighbors" is: a friendly wave of the hand while mowing the grass, a bit of casual gossip across the back hedge, a borrowed cup of sugar, a trusted watchdog and mail collector during vacations. Yet Thomas Berger has a somewhat different view. Suppose, he must have thought before writing *Neighbors*, all the amenities, all the polite little dishonesties that lubricate the friction in social relationships were stripped away. Suppose that all of the latent mistrust, aggression, and hostility were allowed to mingle freely and unrestrainedly with the higher impulses that usually direct our actions—thus, *Neighbors*.

Earl Keese, forty-nine, and his wife Enid live in the country within commuting distance of the city. Their daughter Elaine, who is away at college, is the perfect child who honors her parents and achieves high marks and popularity at school. Earl and Enid have settled into a rather dull and smug middle-class routine. As the book opens they are making small talk about the need to invite the new neighbors over for a drink; and this is where the commonplace ends. The Keeses are soon abruptly introduced to the new neighbors, Harry and Ramona, and for the next twenty-four hours are plunged into the sort of situation comedy that might come from the pen of a "Father Knows Best" scriptwriter while in the grips of a prolonged and very bad acid trip. Events move at such a rapid-fire pace that a plot summary would be nearly the length of the book. A few random occurrences will serve as examples: Earl pushes Harry's car over an embankment into a creek, Earl and Harry exchange punches and harsh words, Earl and Harry exchange handshakes and warm words, Ramona accuses Earl of rape, Elaine returns home accused of stealing, Harry makes sexual overtures to Elaine, Ramona seduces Enid and Elaine, Harry fires a shotgun at Earl, a garage owner punches Earl in the stomach, Harry's house burns to the ground, and on, and on. The madness ends only when Earl suffers a stroke and dies while Ramona says to him, "Earl, it could happen to anybody."

Most of this strange narrative is concerned with physical action, much of it of the slapstick variety, and Berger chooses a style of writing which is appropriate. In his earlier books, Berger has displayed a variety of styles. *Little Big Man* purports to be the more or less verbatim transcript of a series of recorded reminiscences by Jack Crabb, an 111-year-old survivor of Wild West days, and Berger there uses an appropriately slangy approach. In *Arthur Rex*, Berger's treatment of the King Arthur legend, the storytelling is in the old manner, as in "And so it came to pass in the kingdom of. . . ." When Berger ventured into the hard-boiled detective genre in *Who Is Teddy Villanova?* he chose a style which the book's dust jacket describes, accurately if a bit rhetorically, as "rococo" and "reminiscent by turns of Thomas DeQuincy, Thomas Babington Macauley and Sir Thomas Malory." Berger, then, is a writer who knows his craft and who is consistently able to fit his style to his material. *Neighbors* is no exception. Here, he puts aside stylistic eccentricity in favor of a low-keyed, straightforward narration. As usual his choice is correct. The direct style contributes to the rapid flow of events and avoids the slowdowns of action which authorial excess might have caused.

Despite the apparent directness of the style, however, a caveat is in order. Early in the book the reader is told that Keese, since adolescence, has been unable to "accept the literal witness of his eyes" because "outlandish illusions" appear to him from time to time. "Perhaps a half-dozen times a year he thought he saw such phenomena as George Washington urinating against the wheel of a parked car (actually an old lady bent over a cane) . . . a rat of record proportions (an abandoned football). . ." and so on. Berger thus sows seeds of doubt which makes the reader leery of what is told. For example, was Ramona really staring avidly at Earl's crotch? Or, was this an outlandish illusion? So, in addition to the dizzying flow of strange happenings, one must also try to ascertain what, if anything, is real.

For those who relish the exercise of puzzling out the "hidden meanings" in literary works, *Neighbors* is worth a bit of rumination. What is this book all about anyway? Or, is it simply the work of a skillful and highly imaginative author kicking up his heels a bit? Several possibilities come to mind. At one level the book seems to comment on the ambivalence that is experienced when newcomers move into the neighborhood. Naturally, an effort is made to help them feel welcome and to convey the sort of pride and attachment that people feel for their surroundings. Yet, on the other hand, who are these people? Can they be trusted? Will they let the yard go to seed and the house paint chip away? Are they thieves?

Perhaps the book can be said to be something of an epic test to which the hero, Earl Keese, is subjected. Who are Harry and Ramona? From whence did they come? These questions are not answered for the reader; but it is known that because of Harry and Ramona, Earl sees things as he has not seen them before and does things of which he would not have thought himself capable. Indeed, at the close of the book, Earl has thrown his lot with Harry and Ramona; he has joined them in the car and is prepared to sally forth with them. To where? Earl will not know that because he is felled by a stroke. He died a different man, however, from the Earl who lived in respectable boredom a mere twenty-four hours earlier.

Berger himself has said that the book is a tribute to Franz Kafka "who taught me that at any moment banality might turn sinister, for existence was not meant to be unfailingly genial." Further, he has described the book as "a bizarre celebration of whatever gift I have, the strangest of all my narratives." The latter may be the most satisfying explanation. For after all, there is no immutable law that requires every interesting work of fiction to bear its weight in meaning and relevance. Coming from a master of escape genres, *Neighbors* perhaps is best viewed simply as an escape, a titillating diversion to an imaginative world of experience that some will never know.

L. W. Payne

NEW CRITICAL ESSAYS

Author: Roland Barthes (1915-1980)
Translated from the French by Richard Howard
Publisher: Hill and Wang (New York). 121 pp. $10.95
Type of work: Essays

Eight essays on various aspects of French literature, examined from the point of view of semiology by one of its leading practitioners

This small collection of essays is the most recent text to have been published in English by the man who was probably the most adventurous and original literary critic of the third quarter of this century. Tragically, Roland Barthes died in March, 1980, following an automobile accident. This provoked an inevitable feeling of *deéjà vu*, since, exactly twenty years earlier, France lost another of its greatest writers, Albert Camus, in just this way. Other similarities exist as well: at his death, each man was at the height of his powers as a writer (and, in the case of Barthes, as a teacher), each occupied a position of enormous prominence within the world of French letters, and each had relatively recently received a prestigious award—Camus the 1960 Nobel Prize for Literature, and Barthes, in 1977, elevation to *La Chaire de la Sémiologie Littéraire* at the Collège de France, a post created expressly for him.

Nevertheless, the appearance of this book in English not long after the death of its author is nothing more than a coincidence. While events compel the reader to scrutinize the text as one would a "last will and testament," it is hardly that. For that matter, the French text appeared in 1972 in conjunction with his reissued first book (1953), *Le degré zéro de l'écriture* (*Writing Degree Zero*), published by Editions du Seuil as *Le degré de l'écriture suivi de nouveaux essais critiques*. Yet, despite the fact that this volume lacks the significance of such works of Barthes as *Sur Racine* (*On Racine*, 1963), *Système de la mode* (1967), *S/Z* (1970), it is nevertheless representative of the catholicity of Barthes's interests. This is also demonstrated by the fact that the most recent of his texts to have been published in France is *La chambre claire: note sur la photographie* (1980). Certainly, *New Critical Essays* provides an opportunity to comment on the significance of Roland Barthes and the important implications of some of his ideas.

An important result of the career of Roland Barthes was an expanded definition of "critic." Barthes regarded a given text as being capable of yielding a multiplicity of meanings—as a cultural "sign" pointing to nonliterary domains as well as to the enterprise of literature. Accordingly, his own studies and investigations carried him into a number of different fields. If one endorses Barthes's critical practice, it becomes impossible to say "just a critic," for criticism ceases to be the appendage of "creative writing." In fact, the task of the Barthesian critic at least equals, if not surpasses, the creative challenge facing the novelist, poet, or dramatist. For, like Gustave Flaubert's Bouvard and Pécuchet, he must be prepared to investigate everything; albeit, one would hope, in a less ludicrous fashion. The boundaries between "critic" and "anthropologist," "linguist," "psychologist," and so on dissolve in the effort. For Barthes, the interpretation of literary texts is subsumed under a more broadly defined "semiology," a science of signs in society. These signs, which inhabit works of literature but which are to be found as well in popular entertainment, sports, advertising, public ceremonies, and the leisure activities of the bourgeoisie lead one to nothing less than the understanding of man and society.

This is not to say that Barthes lost sight of literature. During his career, he commented on the works of many of France's greatest writers, such as Jean Baptiste Racine, Honoré de Balzac, Jules Michelet, and Marcel Proust, and on *enfants terribles* such as Alain Robbe-Grillet and Raymond Queneau. Moreover, his observations on literature as a vocation and as a way of life constitute perhaps the most eloquent example of such testimony since the writings of Proust, as in the latter's passages on Bergotte. In addition, one must not forget that, for Barthes, literature is more, even, than writing and criticism. There is the crucial act of reading, wherein the richness and fecundity of a given text are made manifest. Reading equals pleasure: intense pleasure, many kinds of pleasures. It is true that, without reading, there could be no literature, yet, when reading Barthes, one senses that reading is everything. Indeed, in *Le Plaisir de texte* (*The Pleasure of the Text*, 1973), the work in which Barthes gives the greatest primacy to reading, one is left with the conclusion that, precisely because of the intensity of the individual reading experience, there exists no one "text" of which one may speak. For the text itself is transformed and undergoes some degree of metamorphosis each time it is read.

Does this mean that Barthes sends conflicting signals? On the one hand his radical approach to reading rejects the possibility of "definitive" exegesis. Yet, this is the same Barthes whose name is associated with "the science of signs." Semiology, to many of those who oppose its aims, seems to be about superimposing a forbidding hermeneutic system on the humanistic study and appreciation of literature. Once Barthes has been read, however, the tentative nature of his assertions becomes clear. Barthes was not one to make the kinds of grandiose claims for the efficacy of his methods for which some structuralists are known. The word *"essai"* ("essay") should remind one of a test, a trial, something tentative. Readers should remember its kinship to the verb *essayer*. It was Michel de Montaigne who introduced the *essai* as a literary genre, and he made it clear that, just as he avoided taking himself too seriously, so should we. These *essais critiques* of Barthes, informed as they are by an erudite consciousness, are trial balloons and should be regarded as suggestions— catalysts to further thought and investigation. Thus, there is no real conflict within the ideas of Barthes. Suffice it to say that he is a complex thinker who presents many different aspects of his thought to a reader. Clearly, the critical endeavor is forever unfinished, continually evolving.

Even in such a formidable work as *S/Z*, the text of Barthes which seems most to intimidate those who are wary of his method, the spirit of trial and experiment is evident. In this book, Balzac's *Sarrasine* could be likened to a building that Barthes dismantles brick by brick, in order to demonstrate that it can be reconstructed differently. *S/Z* is an astonishing display of semiological activity, and quite a feat of reading. The point, however, in this controversial book, is not that Balzac's text must necessarily be approached in this way to the exclusion of other methods of interpretation. Instead, Barthes offers this as an example of the kind of reading that might be done. In other words, if one's role as reader is expanded along the lines suggested by Barthes, the text is radically transformed, revealing new treasures. Ostensibly, each subsequent reading opens the door to a new text, understood to be the product of the combined creative efforts of the author and the reader. Barthes's "criticism," then, is open-minded.

Since he is always eager to suggest, to provoke, to spur other readers onward, Barthes often does little more than to offer a brief sketch of an idea. Many of his writings convey this sense of play, of a restlessness to go on to the next topic or the next little revelation. Many would argue that these *New Critical Essays*, without the sustained concentration and intellectual rigor of texts such as *S/Z* or *Sade, Fourier, Loyola* (1971), are more typical products of Barthes's imagination. Admittedly, they are fragments. Some originally appeared as prefaces to other books. There is a certain Leonardo da Vinci quality to these meditations, as if, like that great but troubled genius, Barthes seizes with wonder and fascination upon a new idea, only to lose interest after a brief span. For this reason, as well as because of the timing of their publication, Hill and Wang has not really served Barthes well by publishing *New Critical Essays* by themselves.

Le Seuil, the French publisher, must have understood this when it combined the *Nouveaux essais critiques* with the seminal text *Le degré zéro de l'écriture*. Why was the decision not made to publish *New Critical Essays* along with another text? True, *Writing Degree Zero* remains in print in this country, and might not, therefore, have been an ideal choice, but a precedent does exist, since a Beacon Press combined volume of *Writing Degree Zero* and *Elements of Semiology* (1967) was available a few years ago. A number of Barthes's texts, however, have never been translated into English, and one might have been selected for the occasion. For example, it would be desirable to have in English another of the texts in which Barthes gives some kind of account of himself or outlines his credo for an audience of students and colleagues. Two such examples come to mind: his "Réponses" in *Tel Quel* 47 (1971, a special issue of that journal devoted to Barthes) to questions submitted to him concerning details of his life and career, and his *Leçon inaugurale*, presented at the Collège de France on January 7, 1977. As things stand, the isolation of the *New Critical Essays* unfortunately invites comparison with the much more substantial *Essais critiques* (*Critical Essays*, 1972). In this light, they make for a somewhat lackluster sequel.

This collection nevertheless has its moments, although the imperfectly realized essay on Jules Verne ("Where to Begin?") is not one of them. One most certainly gains a sense of Barthes's vast familiarity with French literature. At times, as in the essays on Eugène Fromentin or Pierre Loti, he calls attention to forgotten or neglected writers whose texts he feels would move a reader imbued with the modern critical consciousness. Or, his quarry might be a little-read text of a major writer, as is the case with François René de Chateaubriand's *Life of Rancé*. In the essay that he devotes to this example, Barthes asks rhetorically whether it is even possible for such an impassioned text, radiant with a would-be medieval religious aura, to speak to the heirs of "Marx, Nietzsche, Freud, Sartre, Genet, or Blanchot." Naturally, he thinks it can, if readers pay the right kind of critical attention to it. To be sure, Barthes is interested in more than written language. In probably the most original of the essays, "The Plates of the *Encyclopedia*," he focuses not on Denis Diderot or the *philosophe* movement, but on the signifying aspects of the machines and man-made objects depicted in the plates of this great achievement of the eighteenth century *savants*.

Barthes is at his best, however, when he comes to terms with a truly major writer, as he does in the essays on François La Rochefoucauld, Proust, and Flaubert. As for La Rochefoucauld, whose *The Maxims* has usually been approached as barbed commentary on court life at Versailles or as a source of *bons mots*, Barthes in "La Rochefoucauld: 'Reflections or Sentences and Maxims,'" succeeds in considering *The Maxims* on several levels. By turns analyzing the structure of a typical maxim, "The maxim is a hard, shiny—and fragile—object, like an insect's thorax . . ." and considering the cumulative effect of reading all the maxims straight through, Barthes tries to map for us the moral universe of La Rochefoucauld. He asserts that the ultimate endeavor of the writer was to arrive at self-knowledge, and to pass through self-understanding to an understanding of human nature in general.

In "Proust and Names," Barthes takes up the subject of Proust's use of proper names in *Remembrance of Things Past* and tries to show how these onomastic devices enable Proust to write a book that is, on one level, the story of the acquisition of the ability to write. Readers of Proust, who cannot help but be aware of the seductive power names like Guermantes, Bergotte, Balbec, or Combray have for the narrator/protagonist Marcel, would probably find "Proust and Names" the most convincing of these essays. Barthes's success with this essay may be attributable to his obvious aesthetic affinities with Proust. Both are intoxicated with literature, and preoccupied with the writer's vocation: the writer as the person who lives in and through his writings, and whose life outside his literary activity, if he has time for such a life, is of little or no importance compared to his *oeuvre*.

In letters to Louise Colet and others, Gustave Flaubert often complained that he had forfeited *his* right to any kind of life beyond the solitary toil of writing. Flaubert is often cited as an example of a writer who suffered, at times, excruciating labor pains in the act of literary creation, and in "Flaubert and the Sentence" Barthes writes approvingly of the hours Flaubert apparently spent in crafting a single sentence. Barthes approves because he recognizes in this his own aesthetic: that "style," a word for which one ought not to apologize, is everything. Style is not a means to an end (communication of the literary message, or whatever), but an end in itself. The modern writer writes in order to experience the pleasure of writing, just as a modern canvas celebrates the materials and techniques employed by the painter.

This brings one back to a reason why the criticism of Barthes developed in the way that it did. Many of the major texts of French literature since Stéphane Mallarmé have been complex and baffling, defying traditional strategies of interpretation. Barthes's criticism constitutes, to some extent, an attempt to satisfy the need for a new criticism to accompany and amplify a new kind of writing: writing that refers less to "the real world" than to itself and other texts—in a phrase, writing about writing. Such texts are not meant to be "understood" in the traditional sense of a text that contains messages about a world that lies beyond its boundaries. These kinds of texts can be extremely difficult to read, and the same holds true for certain texts of Barthes. This makes Richard Howard's English rendering of the *essais* all the more admirable, since he has had to come to grips with Barthes's at times eccentric and mystifying terminology.

Reading Barthes can produce both pleasure and exasperation in the reader. The realization that Barthes has willingly abandoned any attempt to provide the "correct" reading of a text brings the reader up short. In his works, one passes from moments of luminous brilliance to veritable eclipses of obscured meaning. The effect of adjusting to his unusual use of language can be dizzying. Indeed, one of the major critical studies of Barthes, the title of which suggests such an effect, is Stephen Heath's *Vertige du déplacement: lecture de Barthes* (1974). Yet, just as in the case of many of the writers Barthes admires, it is not always necessary to understand him to appreciate the strength and elegance of his writing. Often profound, he is nearly always engaging. Even when his ideas and phrases are only sketchily developed, as is the case with the book at hand, they reverberate in the mind.

James A. Winders

NIKOLAI BUKHARIN
The Last Years

Author: Roy A. Medvedev (1925-   )
Translated from the Russian by A. D. P. Briggs
Publisher: W. W. Norton and Company (New York). 148 pp. $10.95
Type of work: Biography
Time: 1929-1938
Locale: Russia

A sensitive but partisan study of the last decade of one of the most prominent early founders of the Soviet state

Principal personages:
NIKOLAI IVANOVICH BUKHARIN
MAXIM GORKY, pen name of Aleksei Maksimovich Peshkov, a close friend and most prominent writer in the Soviet Union
ANNA MIKHAYLOVNA LARINA, Bukharin's third wife
VLADIMIR VLADIMIROVICH MAYAKOVSKI, leading Russian poet of the Bolshevik Revolution and the early Soviet state
ALEKSEI IVANOVICH RYKOV, a close friend and along with Bukharin a leader of the "Rightist Opposition" in 1928-1929
JOSEPH STALIN, former friend and eventual destroyer of Bukharin
MIKHAIL PAVLOVICH TOMSKY, the third leader of the "Rightist Opposition" in 1928-1929 and close friend of Bukharin

Roy A. Medvedev, a Soviet dissident historian who has become famous during the past decade, has added a new and valuable volume from the "underground press" emanating out of the Soviet Union in his biographical study of the last decade of the life of Nikolai Bukharin. In his Foreword Medvedev notes that even today the public name, reputation, and career of Nikolai Ivanovich Bukharin (1888-1938), who was one of the foremost members of the "Old Bolsheviks" and a pioneer founder of the Soviet state, is taboo in the Soviet Union. This the author finds is an absurd case of gross historical injustice. Nikolai Bukharin was, after all, one of the leaders of the Bolshevik (Communist) Revolution of November, 1917, was a member for twenty years of the Central Committee of the Bolshevik Party and a member of the Politburo for a decade, was the managing editor of the chief Soviet newspaper *Pravda* from 1917 until 1929 (and editor of the only slightly less influential newspaper *Izsvestiya* from 1934 until 1937), and was a world-renowned Marxist economist during the 1920's. In his Last Testament, V. I. Lenin, the founding father of the U.S.S.R., referred to Bukharin as "the greatest and most valuable theoretician in the Party . . . deservedly the favorite of the Party." Yet contemporary Soviet citizens either regard Bukharin as a counterrevolutionary or are totally ignorant of his importance in early Soviet history. This condition exists because the Stalinist regime destroyed Bukharin personally and obliterated his memory. Under the destalinization program of Nikita Khrushchev, some attempt was made to rehabilitate Bukharin's name and reputation which, however, ceased with Khrushchev's fall from power in 1964.

In his unceasing struggle against the legacy of Stalin and his regime, Roy Medvedev believes that the memory of Nikolai Bukharin must be restored to its proper place in Soviet history. Medvedev is aware of recent biographical studies of Bukharin by Westerners, of which the most detailed one is the biography done by the American professor Stephen F. Cohen which appeared in 1973. Yet great obscurity still exists in the West about the last decade of Bukharin's life.

From unpublished memoirs, newspaper articles, and speeches in existence within the Soviet Union, Medvedev carefully reconstructs Bukharin's twilight years. Briefly, the author describes the earlier successes that Bukharin enjoyed in pre-Stalinist Russia as economist, theorist, academician. His position as one of the leaders of the Soviet Union terminated in 1929, however, when Joseph Stalin emerged as the unquestioned master of the Soviet state. The hostility between Joseph Stalin and Nikolai Bukharin was caused by the debate over the future socio-politico-economic development of Communism within Russia. Bukharin, together with his close friends of the later 1920's, Aleksei Rykov and Mikhail Tomsky, were labeled by Stalin the "Rightist Opposition" since they believed in the continuation of the New Economic Policy (NEP) introduced in 1921 by Lenin. This policy permitted a semi-capitalist economic structure (especially vis-à-vis agriculture) to exist within the Soviet Union. Stalin and his associates were determined to end NEP by force in order to collectivize agriculture and institute massive industrialization. Stalin, a master at political maneuver and intrigue, cleverly gained the support of the Politburo to his program by a five-month campaign of innuendo and vilification against his opponents in the spring of 1929. By the end of April, Bukharin, the "Rightist Opposition," and NEP were defeated.

As did all other "Old Bolsheviks," Bukharin believed that the Communist Party and its leaders were the sole vehicle of Marxism, socialism, and history. Although ideological and political disputes could and did occur between individual members of the Party's power elite (the Central Committee), open opposition was not permitted once the Central Committee had formulated official Party policy. The belief in the unquestioned authority of the Party and its leadership is a central theme of this book for it explains Bukharin's willingness to admit openly his "errors" and join in fulsome praise of the new leader of the Party, Joseph Stalin. Both at the end of 1929 and in 1930 at the Sixteenth Communist Party Congress, Bukharin, Rykov, and Tomsky were forced by Party pressure to denounce publicly their former "Rightist Opposition." These pronouncements allowed them to remain as members of the Central Committee but virtually ended their roles as major political figures within the Soviet Union.

From 1930 until the end of 1933, Bukharin made no attempt to become involved in any major aspect of Soviet political life. He was convinced that the NEP years were gone forever and that any real opposition to Stalin was out of the question. Stalin, in turn, recognized Bukharin's reputation within the international Communist movement. Therefore, in 1930, Bukharin was appointed to head the research and planning section of the U.S.S.R. All-Union Council of National Economy. He spent the following three years as an editor of journals (the most famous of which was *Socialist Reconstruction and Science* or *Sorena*) devoted to the presentation of the most recent scientific and technological research being done in the Soviet Union.

Bukharin was a leading advocate of the superiority of Soviet-Marxist technology over that of capitalism both in his journals and in a rare visit to England in 1931 when he presented a paper at the 2nd International Congress on the History of Science and Technology. He became a full member of the Soviet Academy of Science and was one of the founders of the first All-Union Conference on the Planning of Scientific Research Work in Soviet history. Throughout the early 1930's Bukharin was a brilliant polemicist who in many articles and pamphlets extolled the virtues of Socialism and Socialist Technology. He also undertook the massive task of editing the second and third editions of the complete works of Lenin and wrote a book entitled *Studies* (1932) which dealt with Soviet art, aesthetics, and poetry. In January, 1933, at a plenary session of the Central Committee of the Party, he once again recanted his former "errors" and ended his speech with a prophetic statement: "It's a simple question. . . . You are either for the Party or against the Party and there can be no in-between position."

Bukharin's pioneering work in the field of scientific planning and research and his continued obeisance to Stalin was rewarded in February, 1934. Bukharin was given the editorship of the second most influential Soviet newspaper, *Izsvestiya*, which he held until January, 1937. This post marked the partial reentry of Bukharin into the mainstream of Soviet politics. As the editor of *Izsvestiya*, he became one of the leaders of Soviet official propaganda which included the creation of the cult of Stalin as the true heir of Lenin. Bukharin made *Izsvestiya* the major Soviet newspaper which dealt with international affairs and he consistently warned his audience about the dangers of Fascism and Hitlerism. He also improved the quality of his paper because of his ability to obtain contributions from those individuals who comprised the "Who's Who" of Soviet literature.

In addition to the editorship, Bukharin also became one of the founders of the first (and most important) Congress of Soviet Writers, where he exhorted Soviet poets to "be venturesome" in their attempts to create a new and vital proletarian poetry. Finally, 1934, the same year which saw him become the editor of *Izsvestiya* and a founder of the first Congress of Soviet Writers, marked an important turning point in his personal life. He married his third wife, the beautiful nineteen-year-old Anna Mikhaylovna Larina who became the mother of his only son Iuri and who remained devoted to her husband in the terrible crisis of his last years.

From 1934 until the summer of 1936, Bukharin appeared to be a firm prop of the Stalinist regime. Most of his newspaper editorials were part and parcel of Stalinist hagiography. He was appointed one of the thirty-one men who composed the Soviet constitution of 1936 which remains today the legal basis of the Soviet state. In the spring of 1936, he was also appointed the head of a Soviet delegation which was sent to Paris in order to purchase part of the original archives of Marx and Engels which were being sold by the German Social Democrats. Two Russian émigrés living in Paris, Fyodor Dan and Boris I. Nicolaevsky, were the principal "go-betweens" in this transaction. The price for the rare documents, however, was considered exorbitant by Stalin, who refused to purchase the documents and ordered his delegation to return to Moscow.

The trip to Germany was the last Bukharin made outside of Russia, and many stories have circulated about how Bukharin told foreign observers about the true conditions of Stalinist Russia. Several commentators on Bukharin, in fact, believe that he was the originator of the famous "Letter of an Old Bolshevik" which appeared in the Paris socialist paper *Socialist Herald* in late 1936 and early 1937 which condemned many aspects of Stalin's treatment of members of the Communist Party. Medvedev is convinced that the stories of Bukharin's complaining about Stalin to these foreign socialists are not grounded in fact. He also conclusively proves that the "Letter of an Old Bolshevik" was written by Boris Nicolaevsky, as it contained data on events which occurred after May, 1936, when Bukharin returned to Moscow.

One of the still unexplained mysteries of Bukharin's life is the sudden and complete collapse of his career in the late summer of 1936. In August of that year at the first great public or "show" trials staged by Stalin in his purge of the "Old Bolsheviks," Bukharin, Rykov, and Tomsky were alleged by the two chief defendants, L. B. Kamenev and G. E. Zinoviev, to be guilty of "criminal political activities." These allegations were simply fabrications which did not spare the defendants lives but did provide the basis for the destruction of the three former leaders of the "Rightist Opposition." Tomsky, in fact, committed suicide before the trial ended, and Bukharin was taking a holiday in Soviet Central Asia while the trial was in progress. When he heard of the allegations uttered against him, Bukharin wrote a long letter to Stalin begging him to permit an open confrontation between Kamenev, Zinoviev, and himself. Bukharin's letter went unanswered and Kamenev and Zinoviev were executed.

Bukharin returned to Moscow a broken man and both he and Rykov, Medvedev points out, contemplated suicide during the autumn of 1936. The secret state police, the NKVD under the direction of Stalin's protégé, N. Yezhov, began a thorough investigation of all activities of Bukharin over the preceeding two decades. Oddly enough, both Bukharin and Rykov, still members of the Central Committee, received copies of the evidence compiled against them since all members of the Central Committee had to be informed about any proceedings against any of its members. In December, 1936, at a plenary session of the Central Committee, the expulsion of Bukharin and Rykov from both the committee and the Party was discussed at length. Stalin persuaded the Central Committee to allow the NKVD to continue its investigation of the pair.

Stalinist "justice" soon followed its inexorable course. In mid-January, 1937, Bukharin and Rykov were summarily dismissed from all their political posts. One month later they were expelled from both the Communist Party and the Central Committee by unanimous vote of the latter body and spent the following year as prisoners of the state. Nothing is known of their imprisonment or of the continued investigation which the NKVD conducted against them. In Moscow, on March 2, 1938, the trial of Bukharin, Rykov, and fifteen other Communists began; it was the last great "show" trial of the "Old Bolsheviks." The verdict was never in doubt. Bukharin and Rykov confessed to all their "crimes" against the Soviet state (which included espionage activity for Nazi Germany). All foreign observers commented on the fact that although Bukharin admitted to his crimes in general, in specific answers to the prosecution he consistently denied his guilt. In the early hours of March 13, 1938, the verdict of "guilty" and the sentence "to be shot" were handed down against Bukharin and his codefendants. Two days later the sentence was carried out. Shortly before he died, Bukharin wrote a brief note to Stalin demanding to know why his death was necessary; Stalin kept this note in his personal papers for the rest of his life.

This biography of Bukharin's last years is undoubtedly the definitive work on this subject to date. Roy Medvedev shows himself to be a champion of Bukharin, who is portrayed as a valiant "Old Bolshevik" ruthlessly destroyed by the evil Stalin. This appraisal is true but there is another aspect to Bukharin; he was a man who frequently publicly admitted his earlier errors, who helped in the creation of the cult of Stalin, and who undeviatingly supported the Stalinist regime until his own death. Bukharin once wrote an obituary of another "Old Bolshevik" in which he remarked: "He lacked the iron character, the strength, the will, the stamina essential to a true leader of . . . men." Bukharin's comments about one of his old comrades could equally be applied to himself.

Michael G. R. Kelley

1943
The Victory That Never Was

Author: John Grigg (1924-   )
Publisher: Hill and Wang (New York). Illustrated. 254 pp. $12.50
Type of work: Military history
Time: 1941-1945, with a concentration on the year 1943
Locale: Primarily North African and European theaters of war

A study of the question of when the Allies should have opened the Second Front

Principal personages:
> WINSTON LEONARD SPENCER CHURCHILL, Prime Minister of Great
> Britain, 1940-1945
> FRANKLIN DELANO ROOSEVELT, thirty-second President of the
> United States, 1933-1945
> JOSEPH STALIN (IOSIF VISSARINOVICH DZHUGASHVILI), Soviet Dic-
> tator, 1924-1953
> GENERAL GEORGE CATLETT MARSHALL, United States Army
> Chief of Staff
> FIELD MARSHAL SIR ALAN BROOKE, Chief of the Imperial General
> Staff
> GENERAL DWIGHT D. EISENHOWER, Commander of the TORCH
> and OVERLORD Operations
> GENERAL CHARLES DE GAULLE, leader of the Free French

John Grigg, an English political journalist, is presently working on a four-volume biography of David Lloyd George, two volumes of which have already appeared. In his latest book, *1943: The Victory That Never Was*, Grigg deals with high politics and grand strategy of World War II. He advances the thesis that had the Allied invasion of northwestern Europe taken place in 1943, instead of 1944, the war would have ended that much sooner, many lives would have been saved, and the nature of the ultimate victory would have placed the Allies in a much stronger position relative to the Soviet Union in the postwar era. In discussing the wartime cooperation of the Allied powers, Grigg necessarily gives special attention to their leaders—Winston Churchill, British prime minister; Franklin D. Roosevelt, President of the United States; and Joseph Stalin, the Soviet dictator.

In its overall scope, the book is divided into three parts. Part One covers the period to 1943—the course of the war from America's entry at Pearl Harbor in late 1941 to the Allied landings in French North Africa in late 1942. In Part Two, the author analyzes those aspects of 1943 which relate to his central thesis. Part Three is devoted to a discussion of how the war actually ended; a summary of Chester Wilmot's view of the war's last stages as set forth in his early Cold War study, *The Struggle for Europe*; a refutation of the major arguments against a cross-Channel invasion in 1943; and finally some reflections on the victory that might have been if the Western Allies had decided to invade in that year.

Once the United States entered World War II, Winston Churchill immediately sought to influence President Roosevelt as to what the American role in the conflict should be. Accordingly, he presented three major arguments to Roosevelt in their meeting at the White House in December, 1941. First of all, Churchill believed that in 1942 the war in the Western Theater should comprise as its main offensive effort the occupation, by Great Britain and the United States, of the North and West African possessions of France, and the further control by Britain of the whole North African coast from Tunisia to Egypt, so as to secure Allied passage through the Mediterranean and the Suez Canal. Second, Churchill wanted Great Britain and the United States to reassert their naval supremacy over Japan by mid-1942. The Far Eastern War, however, should not unduly absorb a large proportion of United States forces. Finally, by 1943, he hoped that British and American armies could support uprisings in those Nazi-occupied countries that bordered the sea.

Both Roosevelt and his principal military adviser, United States Army Chief of Staff General George C. Marshall, were in agreement with Churchill that Hitler must be defeated first. Disagreement, however, emerged on the nature of the grand strategy by which this goal was to be accomplished. Marshall, disturbed by Churchill's call for piecemeal landings in support of local revolts, called for a possible Anglo-American assault across the Channel in the fall of 1942 to shore up the Soviet Union if it seemed in danger of collapsing. The decisive cross-Channel invasion would take place in 1943. Sir Alan Brooke, the British Chief of Army Staff and Churchill's principal military adviser, emerged as Marshall's most relentless antagonist on a cross-Channel attack of any kind in 1942 and 1943. As for Roosevelt, he showed an interest in Churchill's ideas for action in North Africa. He viewed an American landing in North Africa as the best way to counter the inevitable public demand for greater involvement in the Pacific. In addition, he regarded the opening of a front in North Africa as providing some help to the beleaguered Russians. Grigg feels that it was unfortunate that the whole question of a Second Front became entangled with the issue of aid to Russia instead of being judged on its own merits as the strategy for defeating Nazi forces in Western Europe.

The views of Churchill, Brooke, and Roosevelt prevailed, thus setting the stage for Operation TORCH, the Anglo-American invasion of French North Africa late in 1942. Churchill's opposition, Grigg observes, to any large-scale landing in northern France during 1942 was reinforced by his doubts about the fighting quality of the British Army following its disastrous defeat by the Japanese at Singapore in February, 1942. In May, he dispatched Lord Louis Mountbatten, the Chief of Combined Operations, to Washington to convince Roosevelt that a cross-Channel invasion would certainly fail in 1942 and perhaps even in 1943. In yielding to Mountbatten's arguments, Roosevelt suggested that American troops might, instead, be sent to North Africa. This fitted in perfectly with Churchill's plans, especially after the fall of Tobruk to General Rommel's Africa Korps in June, 1942. Nevertheless, Churchill continued to press the British Chiefs of Staff, in late 1942, to prepare for a cross-Channel assault in 1943.

In brief, the Allies, under the command of General Dwight D. Eisenhower, successfully landed and secured positions in French North Africa in November, 1942. By January, they had linked up with the British Eighth Army driving west from its triumphant victory over Rommel at El Alamein. The Germans were now reduced to a bridgehead in Tunisia which they held until May, 1943.

Early in January, 1943, Churchill and Roosevelt met in Casablanca to discuss the future of the war. Grigg decries what he regards as a series of blunders that were made at Casablanca. Overall, Churchill and Roosevelt accepted Brooke's scheme for the adoption of a succession of operations in the Mediterranean, including the elimination of the Tunisian bridgehead, the conquest of Sicily, and the invasion of Italy with the hope of knocking that country out of the war. This plan was tantamount to postponing the cross-Channel invasion until 1944. Grigg takes Churchill and Roosevelt to task for giving in too easily to Brooke's scheme. Roosevelt, according to the author, had no coherent plan for winning the war in Europe that would match his stated policy of defeating Hitler first. Instead, he insisted on Germany's unconditional surrender. Grigg condemns Roosevelt for advancing this idea and Churchill for accepting it. Finally, the author deplores the failure of both leaders to support General Charles de Gaulle, leader of the Free French, and thus take advantage of the Free French movement that was growing inside France and in large parts of the French Empire. Casablanca, thus, set the tone for military operations in 1943 which altered the entire course of the war.

Grigg offers some views on the scope of the ultimate victory in 1945 and the victory that might have been, had the Allies undertaken a cross-Channel invasion during 1943. As events turned out, the invasion, Operation OVER-LOAD, under the command of General Eisenhower, took place on June 6, 1944. Germany surrendered in May, 1945, followed by Japan four months later. In surveying the fighting in Western Europe during 1944, Grigg joins a large number of writers who have criticized the failure of the Allies to drive into Germany in September when Nazi defenses were in such disarray. Operation ANVIL, the landing in the south of France in mid-August, only had the effect, in Grigg's view, of pushing a German Army, that might have been trapped in France, back into Germany. Japan's defeat, he writes, was assured once the United States recovered its naval supremacy in the Western Pacific. Great Britain and France emerged from the war weaker than when they had entered it, the United States and the Soviet Union stronger.

In speculating on the victory that might have been, Grigg of course begins with the Allies agreeing in 1942 that their big operation in 1943 would be the cross-Channel invasion of Europe. The adoption of such a strategy meant that the Allies also agreed that it was far more important to bring France back into the war than to knock Italy out of it, and that de Gaulle was the French leader who deserved their greatest support. The TORCH operation would have been undertaken only on the strict understanding that it would lead to no further commitments in the Mediterranean prejudicial to the main plan in 1943. At Casablanca, Roosevelt and Churchill would have developed plans that would keep the enemy guessing about Allied intentions in the Mediterranean area. One guarantee for the success of the invasion in 1943, in Grigg's opinion, was that the two fronts on which Germany would be obliged to fight were much further apart than in 1944. The summer of 1943 found the Eastern Front well inside Russia; thus German east-west communications would have been overtaxed. Final victory, Grigg speculates would have found the Russians still approaching the main centers of Eastern Europe. The Western Allies would thus have been in a much stronger position to deal with Russia than as events actually turned out. Finally, an invasion in 1943 would have spared literally hundreds of thousands of European Jews from being exterminated by the Nazis.

Grigg compares his ideas on the grand strategy of World War II with the position advanced by Chester Wilmot in his book *The Struggle for the Mastery of Europe* published in 1952. Wilmot wrote his book against the backdrop of the Cold War when critics were condemning the failure of the Western Allies to capture Berlin in 1945 instead of leaving it to the Russians. According to Grigg, the fundamental flaw in the Wilmot thesis is that it deals with criticism of Allied strategy in the last year of the war, when the Russians had already pushed so far into Eastern Europe that the Western Allies' chances of meeting them at some point east of Berlin were rather slim. Given Wilmot's concern about the position of the Allies at war's end, Grigg states that he should have addressed himself to the question of a landing in France in 1943. Wilmot, however, the author notes, like other writers, takes the case against 1943 for granted.

In order to strengthen his case for a cross-Channel invasion in 1943, Grigg seeks to refute the three standard arguments against such an attempt in that year. These arguments stated that in 1943 Hitler's Atlantic Wall was too strong, the Allies lacked sufficient numbers of landing craft, and technical resources were inadequate. Grigg rejects the first argument by observing that the defensive fortifications that comprised the Atlantic Wall were much weaker in 1943 than after they were strengthened early in 1944. German manpower in the West was about the same in both years. As to the alleged shortage of landing craft, Grigg points to the large number available for the invasion of Sicily and for the Pacific Theater. Once the Allies decided to postpone the landing in France from 1943 to 1944, more landing craft were sent to the Pacific and their production was even scaled back in the United States. Finally, Grigg dismisses the argument about the inadequacy of technical resources, such as the artificial "Mulberry" harbor, by stating that, if necessary devices did not exist in 1943, it was because there was no pressure to produce them at that time.

Grigg summarizes his rejection of the view, that it was impossible to land in France in 1943, by asserting that there were four vital preconditions for invasion. These preconditions, all of which existed or could have been made to exist in 1943, included overwhelming Allied air superiority, sufficient numbers of Allied troops, adequate means to transport them, and preventing the enemy from concentrating its forces against the Allied bridgehead before it could be secured. The Allies, according to Grigg, had the ability to establish air control over northern France in 1943. By that year there was no shortage of Allied troops ready and trained for combat. The bulk of the German Army was pinned down on the Russian Front. Had the Allies decided to launch the invasion in 1943, the technical aids for landing and supplying men would have been rushed into production just as rapidly as they were in 1944. In Grigg's opinion, then, there was no genuine excuse, where men and matériel were concerned, for postponing the invasion from 1943 to 1944.

John Grigg's central thesis that the Allies should have launched the cross-Channel invasion in 1943 will always remain controversial. Wars, more than any other events in history, lend themselves to much soul-searching and speculation after the fact. Where World War II is concerned, Grigg acknowledges and refutes to his own satisfaction the arguments, advanced during and after the war, that appalling risks would have confronted any cross-Channel invasion attempted before 1944. Grigg stresses that little consideration, then or since, has been given to the equally appalling risks of delaying the invasion. These risks lay in allowing Hitler to perpetuate his tyranny and genocidal policies any longer than necessary. There was, in Grigg's opinion, not a moment to lose.

Readers will find Grigg's *1943: The Victory That Never Was* a stimulating account that provides some good insights on grand strategy in World War II. In addition, his study sheds light on the increasing friction between the Western Allies and the Soviet Union that was perpetuated in the Cold War.

Edward P. Keleher

NO MAN'S LAND
1918: The Last Year of the Great War

Author: John Toland (1912-   )
Publisher: Doubleday & Company (Garden City, New York). Illustrated. 651 pp.
  $17.95
Type of work: History
Time: 1918
Locale: The Western Front, Russia, and the capitals of Europe

A dramatized version of the military and political events of 1918 in Europe

By habit historians have become fond of (or, perhaps, obsessed by) talking about turning points or watershed epochs in history. Often a reader encounters the aggressive attempt to find that moment in the past that somehow encapsulates the elements of what had come before it, and which simultaneously laid the ground for what was to come. John Toland has chosen, in this his tenth book on an aspect of twentieth century history, the year 1918 as just such a moment of conclusions and beginnings. Certainly, there is nothing original in focusing on the year World War I ended as closing an age that would not be seen again. As to whether the year 1918 holds, in its historical tracings, the root secrets of the world that was to come into shape is a more problematic proposition.

A decade ago, Geoffrey Barraclough, in a short volume entitled *Introduction to Contemporary History*, argued that the year 1917 was the pivotal point for the subsequent course of history—marked as it was by the two-stage revolution in Russia and by the intervention of the United States into World War I. He maintains that those two events foreshadowed the eventual "eclipse" of Europe and the emergence of the United States and the Soviet Union as the two global superpowers. Toland's argument, by contrast, is neither as broadly gauged nor as compelling as Barraclough's. Moreover, by framing his book within the strict chronology of the year 1918, Toland foregoes any treatment of the Versailles Conference in 1919 that sought to remake the map of Europe, and which—in the minds of some—wrote a peace treaty that was bound to end in war.

A reader may question Toland's claims for the significance of the year 1918 in a broader context. No one can argue that, once having chosen the year, he fails to stick with his choice. The book's action begins on New Year's Day of 1918 and proceeds painstakingly through the armistice on November 11. Within the chronological framework of those eleven months, the Pulitzer Prize-winning author manages to bring on stage a panorama of figures. A few such Toland summonings seem a bit contrived—not the least among them are passages describing the fretting young lance corporal Adolf Hitler in the trenches.

Militarily the strategies of 1918 differed little, if any, from what had come before. Whatever else might have reached its turning point in 1918, it was hardly the mentality of the commanding officers. Their thinking still followed the notion of marshaling men and munitions for a concentrated assault that would produce a breakthrough in the enemy lines, which, in turn, would cause a shift in the Front, which had barely shifted since late 1914. Neither had there been a great change in the weapons used, save for the fact that mustard gas was more readily available and more likely to be deployed. The use of mustard gas, however, was problematic in itself since a shift in the winds could send it right back in the direction from which it was fired. A sophisticated knowledge of meteorology was more important to its successful use than any other single factor.

The situation, however, had altered, and, one might say, it had shifted primarily because of the events of 1917. Russia was out of the war, and the Bolsheviks left no question about their intentions to be out of it by pursuing peace with Germany and sealing that peace in March, 1918. This, in itself, gave Germany a victory in half the war, accompanied by tremendous gains geographically and in matériel at the cost of the new leaders in Russia. Ostensibly, the victory in the east gave the Germans every reason to hope that a transfer of troops no longer needed there to the west would swing the war in her favor against Britain and France. The counterweight, or obstacle, to this action was the intervention of the Americans. Only in 1918, as Toland is at pains to argue, did the Americans arrive, full of vim and vigor and a good measure of that same enthusiasm and apparent blood lust that the Europeans themselves had had back in 1914.

Toland organized the book chronologically which is, however, not strictly binding and is open to imaginative leaps. Throughout, Toland attempts to personalize every incident and to filter especially the military and strategic situations through the perceptions of individual characters whom he tries to "bring to life."

The spring thaw saw a massive German offensive. In the war officially for almost a year, the Americans were only beginning to trickle to the Front. The French armies were still shaken by the aftermath of the 1917 mutinies in the ranks, and the British were worn thin and ragged, having skimmed the cream of their youth long before. Nevertheless, the Allies held, even though seriously challenged. The psychological effects of the Allied stand must have been devastating to the Germans. Toland manages only to scratch the surface of this issue, leaving the speculation of an in-depth perspective to others.

To many readers, Toland's most interesting chapter may be the one he devotes to Allied attempts to keep the Bolsheviks in the war in the first months of 1918. It is entitled "Red Dawn in the East," and in it Toland is at his best. Here the integration of the personal with the historic and of the temperamental with the ideological succeeds. These negotiations, conducted on the Allied side by the American emissary Lieutenant Colonel Raymond

Robins and the British envoy R. H. Bruce Lockhart, reveal valiant commitment, chicanery, and the meeting of two entirely different world views. Right up to the eleventh hour, Robins and Lockhart sought to convince the Bolsheviks, mainly through Trotsky, not to come to terms with the Germans. Five days before the peace was signed, President Wilson even wired Trotsky directly, advancing what—in retrospect—seem to be quite startling claims of friendship and rapport with the Bolsheviks. The peace, however, was duly signed. The intrigues and the lobbying of the previous months served only to deepen the antagonism of the Allies toward the Bolsheviks, and the distrust of the Bolsheviks toward the Allies.

By June/July, Wilson would be persuaded to give the appearances of picking up the gauntlet militarily in Russia to aid the anti-Bolsheviks. Toland's account of this decision implies that the Allies were already at ease in counting on victory in the west, and genuinely ready to commit significant arms, men, and matériel in Russia. At this juncture, however, such a decision would have been premature. The Germans, in fact, pushed the front closer to Paris by the second half of July. Toland displays the kind of dramatic and imaginative writing that he does best by leading the reader into the streets and cafés of the French capital and recording the reactions of average Frenchmen to the nearness of the "Boches."

With that final advance of the Germans, however, came a Franco-American response. This counterattack caught the German General Staff unprepared; why this was so goes unexplained. The German military did rise to the moment well enough to proceed with an orderly withdrawal, taking new positions farther back from the approaches to Paris by August 1. At the same time, however, the American ambassador in Russia was interpreting a communiqué from Wilson as endorsing an all-out military effort by American troops against the Bolsheviks. The interpretation was incorrect, and once more the prospect of Allied action against the Reds fizzled in confusion.

The retreat of the Germans and their taking what appeared to be a quite tenable defensive position could have led an observer to conclude that the seemingly endless war was about to bog down again, as it had in 1914. The turning point came with the breakthrough of British troops along the Drou-court line in early September. Hearing this, the Kaiser jumped to an emotional conclusion and proclaimed: "Now we have lost the war, poor Fatherland." In the wake of this news the Kaiser's mental state deteriorated rapidly over the next few days. In many quarters of Germany, his immediate abdication was feared, and his son, the Crown Prince, did little to calm matters when he issued a rambling public declaration. In it, he asserted continuing German hopes for victory, but allowed that now "victory" would mean saving Germany from "annihilation" only.

In the Toland account, the action and perspective shifts to Germany from this point forward. This shift is pronounced, but it hardly excludes the attempts to balance out the other events occurring elsewhere. Toland's final chapter, "The End of the Beginning," attempts to tie together a number of loose ends—the Kaiser's abdication, rebellion in Germany, victory for the Allies on the Western Front (although their military forces had not yet penetrated Germany's boundaries), and the Allies continuing vacillation and lack of cohesion vis-à-vis the Bolsheviks. Coming through all of this is the personality of Woodrow Wilson, whose liabilities Toland implies while overtly emphasizing the positive about him.

No Man's Land is quick-paced, and characterized by all the recognizable Toland techniques—easy, clear language and emphasis on the pithy comment placed imaginatively into the mouth of one or another of the historical personages. In sum, however, this book is not equal to Toland at his best. His accounts of vacillation, confusion, and missed cues on the Allies' part in Russia during the year are original and lively. His accounts of the Western Front, by contrast, seem turgid and flat.

Paul Monaco

NUNS AND SOLDIERS

Author: Iris Murdoch (1919-   )
Publisher: The Viking Press (New York). 505 pp. $14.95
Type of work: Novel
Time: The present
Locale: London and rural France

A novel of obsessive relationships and compulsive searching for meaning in a world that seems to have denied both meaning and love

> Principal characters:
> GERTRUDE OPENSHAW, a well-to-do London matron
> GUY OPENSHAW, her dying husband
> TIM REEDE, a rather seedy, bohemian artist
> DAISY BARRETT, Tim's mistress, also an artist
> ANNE CAVIDGE, Gertrude's friend, a former nun
> PETER SZCZEPANSKI (THE COUNT), a friend of Gertrude

Iris Murdoch is one of the foremost novelists in the English-speaking world today. She also is popular with a wide range of readers. Originally achieving prominence in 1954 with *Under the Net*, she was one of two female writers to be grouped at that time with several male writers under the collective banner of Great Britain's "Angry Young Men," the other was Doris Lessing. While most of the writers in that group—including John Osborne, Kingsley Amis, John Wain, and John Brain—have continued to produce important works of literature, perhaps none of them has so consistently maintained both output and quality as these two women. At this point, it would be difficult to determine whether Lessing or Murdoch has achieved the preeminent position in the literary world today, but there can be no question that Iris Murdoch's body of work is of a size and a stature which invites comparison with the great Victorian novelists. She may well loom in twentieth century literary history as George Eliot and William Makepeace Thackeray stand among the peaks in the landscape of nineteenth century literature.

The popularity of Iris Murdoch's long and often intricately plotted novels remains all the more significant when their intellectually demanding philosophical framework is considered. Although Murdoch is a gifted stylist and a creator of vividly realized characters, it must not be forgotten that she began her career as a philosopher, writing about Jean-Paul Sartre and the French existential movement. Choice, which is the basis of all freedom, is one of the sacred precepts of the existential point of view. In her novels, Murdoch repeatedly confronts her characters with existential choices, exposing not only their own weaknesses and fears in the process, but also revealing the central existential crises of our society. The aware moral life is the basis of all of Murdoch's fiction.

Fiction which has such a strong philosophical underpinning can emerge as ponderous and boring if not in the hands of a master—even the novels of

Sartre and Simone de Beauvoir are at times heavy going—but readers have been turning the pages of Murdoch's novels, which now number more than a dozen, for nearly three decades because they *care* about her characters and want to know what eventually happens to them. Iris Murdoch is an artist as well as a philosopher.

Nuns and Soldiers is one of Murdoch's most successful and enjoyable novels. On one level, it is an elegant comedy of manners involving the intricate movements of a large cast of characters; it is also a vivid portrayal of a society that, if not precisely declining, certainly is experiencing the painful spasms of dramatic change. The well-drawn characters linger in the reader's mind, as if they are individuals that one has met and gradually become acquainted with in one's own life. The episodes which compose the story, arresting in themselves, follow a relentless inner logic of development. Yet, underlying all of the very real art in *Nuns and Soldiers* is an intellectual framework which gives the novel that resonance and depth which must stand as the basis of any first rate work of literature.

In a fiction scene which tends to be dominated by academic writers who produce small, finely wrought explorations of their own inner-psyches and pop writers who compulsively analyze their own sensational success, Iris Murdoch's solid, architecturally structured novels stand tall. With an objectivity rare today, as well as with a deep sense of compassion, she allows her characters to move, grow, and develop as human beings, recording their progress in precise, graceful, and vigorous prose. In *Nuns and Soldiers*, the struggle between individual will and destiny is highlighted by an honest and sympathetic awareness of the pain the individual suffers when battling against unyielding fate. The question which has been at the center of most of Murdoch's fictional works—how much free will does a human being actually possess?—never has been put to the test as vividly, or as touchingly, as in *Nuns and Soldiers*.

The book begins with a death, a death which propels the large cast of characters into a complex sequence of events. In a sense, the death of Guy Openshaw represents an awakening for his wife Gertrude and a number of his friends. In death, the intellectual and noble Guy becomes a catalyst, freeing the others from the conventions and fears which have been holding them back from exploring their own human possibilities. In *Nuns and Soldiers*, Murdoch analyzes more completely than ever before the quest of human beings to discover their own capacities and to achieve their human potential. Gertrude Openshaw, Guy's widow, had lived in his shadow, secure and content, and until his death never had dared to take risks with her life. Her good friend, Anne Cavidge, returning to Gertrude after years in the security of a nunnery and struggling with her own belief and doubt, also discovers in the sequence of events which follow Guy's death a new sense of her own personality and individual worth. Each of them finds, in the conflicts inherent in human relationships such as theirs, the values which mean the most to her, the rock upon which, ultimately, her reason for living must stand or fall. Only when free of husband or church doctrine was either able to acquire this knowledge.

For the characters in *Nuns and Soldiers*—as for most people in actual life— self-knowledge does not come painlessly. The Count, a lonely Pole who is not a count, but a young civil servant who obsessively relives his émigré father's patriotic anguish, suffers silently, waiting for the moment to offer his love to Gertrude, while she blindly accepts his devotion and loves another. Tim Reede and his mistress Daisy are so accustomed to the squalor of their poverty-stricken would-be artists' lives that any other kind of existence is nearly beyond their comprehension; yet, they move into Gertrude's world with an almost voracious hunger, looking for a way to survive (Tim steals food out of Gertrude's refrigerator) but coming to discover surprising truths— some of them ugly—about themselves. All of these characters are torn between the various forms of desire and inbred obsessions with guilt and obligation. The characters wonder why should they feel so much guilt if they have acted in good faith. Yet, they also are aware that no one ever is able to act totally with pure motivation. It is this ambiguity of purpose and action that fascinates Murdoch and which gives her characters and her books their unique texture and psychological resonance. As in all of Murdoch's novels, the complicated plot and intricate interactions of the characters can be graphed in an almost schematic way; yet, the narrative power and the vivid details save the story from being sacrificed to theoretical intentions. The scenes of London, both upper-middle class and pennyless bohemian, are sketched with great economy and powerful and gritty realism. Murdoch's impressive powers are called into play with equal success when she describes the French countryside. Perhaps her narrative skills are demonstrated best in the action sequences, however, in which characters are forced to confront both the harshness of the world and their own resources or lack of resources. The scene in which Tim nearly drowns in the swiftly moving farm canal, for example, unites thematic purpose with suspense and realistic detail. It is possible to read *Nuns and Soldiers* on several levels, not the least of which is that of an entertaining and well-drawn realistic novel of contemporary life.

While symbols play an important part in Murdoch's fiction, they are not allowed to intrude. They rise organically out of the story, rather than being tacked on as an afterthought. From the submerged bell in *The Bell* to the Japanese sword in *A Severed Head* to the flood in *Bruno's Dream* to the sea, itself, in *The Sea, The Sea*, the symbols in Murdoch's novels have helped to explain character, to move plot, and to make clear meaning. This is also true in *Nuns and Soldiers*. Guy Openshaw, reading the *Odyssey* as he lies dying, sees himself as Odysseus setting sail on his last journey. In fact all of the characters in this book are sailing on undetermined and often frightening journeys, journeys which are symbolized by the farm canal in France, the Thames in London, and the English Channel across which they travel so many times. And, as Leopold Bloom is a modern-day Ulysses in Dublin, so Tim, Daisy, Anne, and the others transform London into a whole world, a strange and fearful place in which they wander aimlessly while searching for security and a place of rest. For some, such as the Count and Anne, there can be no home, and they will wander until they die; others, such as Gertrude, are allowed a brief rest by the gods; however, the threat always remains that they may be turned out again, forced to wander once more, searching for peace.

The symbols of the Christian church, and most particularly the Catholic Church, are also important in this novel. The cloistered life appeals not only to the former nun, Anne Cavidge, but also to several of the other characters in the book. In separating oneself from the hustle and turmoil of the larger world, one may be able to find a form of tranquillity, but the peace thus acquired is tenuous, at best, and often disappointing. Iris Murdoch seems to feel deeply that only in the active life can human beings achieve any degree of true self-understanding and contentment. Although a man or woman may try to deceive himself or herself, there are no easy victories. Peace must be hard-won if it is to be true and enduring.

This is not to say that *Nuns and Soldiers* is in any way heavy or ponderous as it deals with these questions. Quite the contrary, it is an often funny and always dramatic story of human relationships. Humor is an important aspect of the Murdoch fictional technique. Since her first novel, *Under the Net*, in which a movie star dog is kidnaped and held for ransom, Murdoch has demonstrated in her writing a gift for comedy. Her characters often have a very biting and witty way with words, mercilessly focusing on one another's faults and weaknesses. With equal precision, Murdoch captures the little traits and gestures by which individuals expose themselves. No bit of phoniness, no whisper of fake grandeur, is allowed to escape her eye. In her own manner, Murdoch is quite as accurate in portraying and satirizing the social customs and mores of today's society as Jane Austen was of capturing those of her day.

Nowhere are Murdoch's descriptions as accurate as when they are exposing the would-be artists, Tim and Daisy, and their pathetic efforts to rationalize their failures. Yet, there is sympathy, too, in her portrayal of their comical little struggles for survival, and their need to preserve some form of self-respect. Each individual must come to terms with his own limitations, if he ever is to achieve any peace. At the same time, a certain nobility can be seen in the stubborn efforts of people such as Tim and Daisy to attempt, year after year, to realize their early dreams of greatness.

Murdoch clearly relishes the designs formed by the lives of her characters, the abstract patterns which are formed by the interconnection of individual lives. Further, she is fascinated by the role of the unexpected in human life.

632   *Magill's Literary Annual 1981*

Perhaps she sees this part of the conflict between existential free will and fate. One's existence seldom, if ever, turns out as one anticipated; and if this is true for oneself, it is even more true regarding the lives of the people one knows only through observation. Nothing in the world can provoke amazement as consistently as the lives of other people.

Nobody, including themselves, would have expected Tim and Gertrude to fall in love or to marry. Peter, the lovesick Count, like a character from a Chekhov play, certainly never intended to become so obsessed with Gertrude, or to have his life take the turn which it did because of his love. Anne's life, perhaps more than any of the others in the book, broke all of the bounds of expectation. When she was young, nobody expected her to become a nun; then, after years in the nunnery, she again surprised herself and her friends by turning her back on convent life and again seeking an existence in the active world. Her dedication to service finds an unexpected outlet in her relationship with Gertrude, just as her obsessive need to love (a need which had been satisfied by her love of Christ) finds an even more unexpected outlet in her passion for the Count. Yet, this love does not preempt a continuing religious fixation which culminates in erotic-religious visions of Christ visiting her in her bed. In the same way, it is not logical that Tim, who loves Gertrude so fervently, should compulsively return to his former mistress, Daisy; yet, he does this repeatedly. Human beings in Murdoch's novel—as in life—are not logical animals. They are subject to whims and impulses, to contrary pressures of existence, and to the powers of the unexpected. This ability to see the authentic patterns in life makes the fiction of Iris Murdoch both satisfying and true.

Bruce D. Reeves

OF KENNEDYS AND KINGS
Making Sense of the Sixties

Author: Harris Wofford (1926-   )
Publisher: Farrar, Straus and Giroux (New York). 485 pp. $17.50
Type of work: History
Time: The 1960's
Locale: The United States

A remembrance of the turbulent decade of the 1960's in terms of the ideals and legacies of John Kennedy, Robert Kennedy, and Martin Luther King, Jr.

> *Principal personages:*
> JOHN F. KENNEDY, thirty-fifth President of the United States, 1961-1963
> ROBERT F. KENNEDY, Attorney General of the United States and candidate for the Democratic Party presidential nomination in 1968
> MARTIN LUTHER KING, JR., Head of the Southern Christian Leadership Conference
> LYNDON B. JOHNSON, thirty-sixth President of the United States, 1963-1969

With the possible exception of the rambunctious 1920's, no decade in twentieth century American life has been as celebrated and as scorned as the 1960's. While every decade can claim to have had its moments of high drama and low comedy, the 1960's seemed to produce more than its quota of such episodes. Like the 1920's, the 1960's often appear to defy adequate description or convenient summarization and may prove to be immune to the clarifying perspectives of time and hindsight.

Harris Wofford was not exactly a child of the 1960's, but he was certainly a figure who moved through the period alongside some of its most notable personalities. A lawyer acquaintance of Martin Luther King, Jr., a campaign aide to John F. Kennedy in 1960, a White House staffer and Peace Corps organizer, and a noted educator, Wofford did more than merely brush against the human vanguard of American leadership during the decade. Unlike the typical historical commentator on the period, or even the casual citizen who struggled through it, Wofford was in a position to observe the idealism in its formative terms. Paradoxically, this vantage point is both the strength and the weakness of his book.

Of Kennedys and Kings offers a veritable avalanche of personal remembrances of the Kennedy years suggesting that Wofford may have drawn extensively on personal diaries. Unlike others, however, who enjoyed even more intimate contact with the Kennedys and King and who have written about their experience, Wofford is not simply attempting to reminisce. *Of Kennedys and Kings* strives through numerous vignettes of both a social and political sort to rekindle a genuine appreciation for the dream. It is a credit to Wofford's fine writing style that he largely succeeds, but a clear prerequisite to enjoying *Of Kennedys and Kings* is a fondness for the policies being espoused at the time.

Wofford admits, in his Prologue, that he did not intend to conceal his own sympathies which are, perhaps understandably, highly favorable to the policy directions of the Kennedys and Martin Luther King, Jr. Additionally, however, there runs a current of awareness on Wofford's part that the attractiveness associated with these views has not worn well. As such, Wofford attempts not only to retrace some of the memorable episodes of the Kennedy and King eras, but also to expound on the relationship between progressive liberal agenda and the personalities themselves.

The result from such an approach is a book which has among its most appealing features a gradually emerging series of portraits. In his various depictions of the Kennedys and King deeply emersed in the issues of the day, Wofford also produces an evaluation, however indirect, of their personalities. Because all three figures share the common denominator of tragedy, the author seeks out the classic drama in each of their lives. Through each man's personal tragedy, what began as an inspiring reach for an almost secular utopia was transformed into an unfulfilled reality. By weaving together his assorted recollections, Wofford suggests that the stories themselves are the best explanation as to how this could have happened.

Through the various stories and personality-revealing quotations that Wofford offers on the three men, there results a conscious deflating of the almost mythical image that has come to surround them as historical figures. Wofford appears anxious to remind the reader that the Kennedys and King were, after all, human beings who touched and were touched by human events. In stripping away a measure of the transcendental quality that often surrounds heroic personalities from the past, Wofford intends to make their respective crusades all the more genuine. As an active participant in those policies and programs, Wofford is very conscious of the realities of the political process, and also of the need to equate ideals with the bluntness of the system itself. Regardless of the particulars of the outcome when pitting such idealism against these barriers, Wofford suggests that a measure of success lies in the effort alone.

In purely historical terms, *Of Kennedys and Kings* has much to offer. Wofford was personally involved in the Civil Rights Movement with King and, in a governmental sense, served during 1961 and 1962 as Special Assistant to the President for Civil Rights. In addition, Wofford was intimately involved with the formation of the Peace Corps as both its Special Representative for Africa (and director of its Ethiopian program) and eventually as Associate Director of the Peace Corps as a whole. Extensive portions of this book draw upon Wofford's firsthand knowledge of these efforts during the Kennedy Administration and the subsequent Lyndon Johnson presidency. It is enlightening at times to have the Kennedy and Johnson administrations viewed from the unusual vantage point of the social legislation bureaucracy, but Wofford offers no radical redefinition of the two presidents or their styles of governing. Left intact is the more or less common public assumption that Lyndon Johnson's expansive desires for a Great Society program of legislative gains gradually fell victim to the expense of and commitment to the Vietnam War. Much the same can be said for the inability of the Kennedy Administration to shepherd its civil rights legislation through Congress successfully, dominated as it was by conservative interests on key committees. Wofford is well aware of the forces standing in opposition to such policies, but sheds little unique insight on the matter.

Perhaps because of Wofford's own personal commitment to the causes in which he was associated, *Of Kennedys and Kings* often seems to produce a tone of melancholy as it recounts the events of the time. Ironically, this was almost certainly not Wofford's intention. Instead, Wofford strives to chart the course of well-meaning and humanitarian policies during the decade when such aspirations not only seemed attainable but also were personified in the dynamic leadership of vibrant individuals. Yet the tragic deaths of the two Kennedys and Martin Luther King, Jr., and the still rather contemporary nature of those incidents, cannot help but interject at least a modicum of remorse. Because the subsequent years have not been kind to the notion of liberal reform, Wofford's effort to reawaken the dream manages to blend admirable devotion to principle with the pathetic state of its condition.

In a curious way, *Of Kennedys and Kings* seems more dated than many of the less detailed and less well informed memoirs of 1960's figures connected in some fashion with the Kennedy saga. Because Wofford's book aims at more than the status of a mere recollection, it cannot be read casually in the spirit of the times. Instead, *Of Kennedys and Kings* seems intent upon reminding the reader of the value of those ideals and aspirations and virtually calls out for a rededication to the kind of public service Wofford personally displayed.

If a weakness exists in Wofford's book, it does not stem from his beliefs, commitment, or command of historical knowledge. The work offers a collection of mementoes charting the progress of a goal from one who intimately participated in its promotion. As such, the book's emotional appeal for the unfulfilled aspects of the policies of the 1960's appears stronger than its ability to outline a new rationale for their continuation.

Terry Alan Baney

PACKAGES

Author: Richard Stern (1928-   )
Publisher: Coward, McCann & Geoghegan (New York). 151 pp. $10.95
Type of work: Short stories

A collection of eleven stories by Richard Stern, whose novels—mostly out of print and unnoticed by academic critics—are among the finest in contemporary American fiction

Packages is the title of Richard Stern's new, very slim, elegantly produced book of short stories. It is also the title of the most powerful story in the collection, and it provides the governing metaphor of the book.

The literal package—around which the story "Packages" revolves—is a silvery can containing the ashes of the narrator's mother; the story begins as he picks up the package at the "funeral factory" which has handled the cremation. In a story which is mostly reverie and recollection, the principal action is the narrator's disposal of the package: he strips off its label, rewraps it, covers it with newspaper in the trash, and covers the newspaper with "a plasticine sack of rinds and fishbones." Later, he watches while the garbage collectors throw the can into the maw of their truck.

Thus the title, "Packages," becomes a necessarily brutal metaphor, intended to force acknowledgment that people are merely packages, finally: packages of chemicals. "But this way is better than a slot in that Westchester mausoleum. Foolish, garish anteroom to no house. Egyptian stupidity."

There is, however, another reading of the metaphor. After disposing of the package, the narrator lies down, listens to a "cello suite of Poppa Bach." Overwhelmed, he reflects that vastness is accessible to him because it has been reduced to a "portable" form: "A package." From the bookshelf above his head he pulls *The Mind of Matter*, and reads about Planck's constant, "that stubby transmitter of universal radiance . . . Nature's own package." He makes a connection—deeply felt, no details worked out—between Planck's "package" and Bach's and "the one which held what was left of what had once held me."

This connection does not cancel out the brutal reality, as Stern sees it, of the human condition, but it turns the mind elsewhere, to reflect on wonderful incongruities. Stern's story—all stories—are only packages, incommensurate with what they contain yet indispensable to understanding. A story is not real; yet without it, people would never know the real.

In the title essay of his forthcoming book, *The Invention of the Real*, Stern considers story-making not as the prerogative of fiction-writers like himself, professional falsifiers, but as a habitual human activity—indeed, not merely habitual, but incessant. He goes further: "Is it even possible to say that this 'storification' is itself the means of humanization?" Yes, for

stories convert the data of event into a coherence which doesn't just transform actuality,

but creates it. That is, it makes sense out of sensation. Consciousness depends on storied notions. . . .
We're all story-makers, constant inventors of the realities we call *our life.*

From his first book (the novel *Golk*, 1960, which took off from "Candid Camera," renamed "You're On Camera" in the novel) to his latest work, Stern has been preoccupied with the "invention of the real."

The stories in *Packages* do not show Stern at his best, although several (including the title piece) are first-rate. Stern's best is very good indeed. *Packages* is dedicated to his friends Saul Bellow and Philip Roth, and Stern belongs in their league, although he has not had (except from fellow writers) a tenth of the recognition they have enjoyed. It is hard to say why. One reason, perhaps, is that Stern the novelist is not particularly interested in himself. He lacks entirely the intense self-absorption which Bellow and Roth project onto their various fictional personae.

Stern's novels are a gallery of interesting, successful, energetic, creative people. He has written the best novel about Ezra Pound (*Stitch*, in which the poet is metamorphosized into a sculptor, Thaddeus Stitch, and the *Cantos* into a fantastic stone garden on an island off Venice). He has chosen for protagonists a composer (the novella "Veni, Vidi . . . Wendt," in *1968*), a biologist (*Other Men's Daughters*), and a high-powered journalist (*Natural Shocks*). His minor characters are wonderfully knowledgeable: a typical Stern novel includes tidbits on current sleep research, the poetry of the troubadours, and a dozen other unpredictable subjects, laced with gossip about the celebrated.

His immense "appetite for experience" (noted by Bellow as early as *Golk*), his connoisseurship of grotesque incongruities, have a cumulative effect on the reader. Without ever preaching, Stern seems determined to break down any dogmatic certainties about human life and human nature with a barrage, a bizarre catalogue of human variety and inconsistency. In *Natural Shocks*, journalist Fred Wursup recalls a lunch with a Belgian colonel, "a red-haired Apollo," who quotes Euripedes "to dramatize his thesis that motives for belligerence only masked 'life's essential motif: self-purgation.'" A reader of contemporary poetry ("For him, Char, Jacottet, Larkin, Hughes, and Berryman were antiques"), the colonel talks about war while a younger soldier, "Apollo Junior," serves their lunch. "One way or another, missiles will purge our superfluity."

Like many memorable Sternian characters, the colonel is a walk-on: in a page and a half, he has come and gone, as Stern prepares to bombard the reader with fresh, irreducible particles of experience. The colonel exists; this spirit of almost belligerent wonder informs Stern's journal as well, raw material for fiction, extracts from which recently appeared in *Triquarterly* (Winter, 1981). The last entry, dated August 23, 1973—Calcutta—concludes thus: "Back at the hotel, four men work their way froglike across the lawn.

What are they doing? Picking up uneven blades of grass." What Explainer can explain even a fraction of the world's myriad worlds?

Stern's fiction is not impressionistic, diaristic, random and shapeless, like many a prose poem. On the contrary, he is a master of complex novelistic plotting. A novel's plot, however, gives him room to maneuver, and every page is richly textured with bits like the lunch with the Belgian colonel. The short-story form seems to cramp him. He is not at his best, either, when he chooses for a story's central consciousness a mind much simpler than his own. In *Packages*, for instance, there is "Riordan's Fiftieth," a story about a bus-driver coming home after work on his birthday. His wife is harsh and mean-spirited. He feels estranged from his older children; of the twins still at home, only one is affectionate. He wonders, quite simply, "What was it all about?" This is a good story, not false and sentimental, but it lacks the distinctive quality of Stern's best work.

Of the eleven stories in *Packages*, three or four (in addition to the title story) are quite good, worth rereading. (Oddly, the best stories are all clustered at the beginning of the book.) "Wissler Remembers" is a professor reminiscing about his years of teaching, reflecting on the special poetry, the "humanscape" of a class—together for thirty hours, and then off to the ends of the earth. Wissler's *vita* is identical with Stern's and there's much personal feeling here although distanced by Wissler's slightly pedantic tone—a far cry from Stern's own antic blend of street talk and high diction. Anyone who has taught for a few years will value this story.

In "Mail," the narrator's pedantry is more extreme, and he bears the absurd name of Marcus Firetuck (a private joke of Stern's?). Here, Stern's own experience as a writer—who is bound to receive many crank letters, and a few wonderful, probably unanswerable ones—is transmuted to the case of a cartographer who is good at his profession, and who has also, over the years, published a few poems. The story meanders delightfully among various letters written to him, gems of letters, ranging from bashful, awkward kindness to bizarre monomania. Firetuck's pedantry is a bit grating by story's end.

"Troubles" is, after "Packages," the strongest story in the collection. Dense, economical, wonderfully paced and plotted yet with no neat resolution, this story has the intelligent, almost impatient speed of his best prose, Stern's trademark: speed of insight, of metaphor, of wit; shifting levels of diction and allusion:

> Vanessa couldn't look a dog in the eye, but in class she scorched inferior analysis, and leaped from language to language as if Babel had never been. The intellectual blaze burned connectives from her speech; she spoke a code it took months getting used to.

With no forcing, "Troubles" illustrates Stern's thesis that we are all story-makers, constant inventors. His protagonist, Hanna—beautifully realized—is troubled, troubled first in her marriage, "home" now in Chicago after a

Peace Corps match in Indonesia. She begins keeping a diary, inspired by Franz Kafka, "a pillar of her marooned dissertation." What does she finally learn? She learns that she is in trouble, "down there with the others."

John Wilson

THE PANDA'S THUMB
Further Reflections in Natural History

Author: Stephen Jay Gould (1941-   )
Publisher: W. W. Norton and Company (New York). 343 pp. $12.95
Type of work: Essays

A collection of popular biological essays which pursues the principles of biological evolution

Stephen Jay Gould possesses the rare ability to write competently and interestingly about science for intelligent laymen. In this he is a national treasure and must be placed in the ranks of those possessing a similar ability such as Isaac Asimov, Lewis Thomas, and Carl Sagan. Gould's latest collection of essays was originally published as columns in *Natural History*. *The Panda's Thumb* follows on the heels of his equally readable *Ever Since Darwin* (1977), a collection drawn from the same journal.

The book is arranged in eight sections, but there is a single unifying theme running throughout: the principle of biological evolution. Gould is by profession a paleontologist but is obviously well read in other fields to which he relates the evolutionary idea. One finds, then, the following subthemes in his book: the major ideas of evolution, evidences for that principle, human evolution, science in cultural context, and debunking both of pseudoscience and of uncritically accepted scientific "orthodoxy." In regard to the last, he is as gentle as possible in pointing out that Arthur Koestler's notions about evolution are simply wrong; but he can also come down rather hard as he does in discussing the scientifically useless practice of measuring human skulls in attempting to establish differences of intelligence among races and between men and women.

Gould's approach, although taking evolution as its central theme, is a blend of paleontology, anatomy, morphology, physiology, ecology, genetics, and borrowed ideas from other disciplines such as mathematics and physical science. He makes use of mathematics and physics, for example, in discussing "scaling theory" which deals with size and form as they change over time. The geometry of the organism has everything to do with the relation between, say, brain weight and body weight. There is a ratio that applies from the smallest to the largest animals. The percentage of the body weight taken up by the brain remains essentially the same. Interestingly, humans are the exception—the human brain takes up a greater percentage of body weight than in any other animal, and this is one, although not the only, reason why humans are preeminent among living things. It was not, by the way, the attainment of a large brain in proportion to body weight which marked the start of human evolution (the earlier orthodoxy) but rather the emergence of an upright stance. There is empirical evidence for this with the fossil

"Lucy"—a small protohominid with upright posture and a small brain recently discovered in Africa.

Gould unabashedly advocates his own interpretation of the nature of evolution. The prevailing orthodoxy dating from the time of Darwin maintains that evolution is a slow gradual process involving the slow accumulation of "variations" (now termed "micromutations") and then the eventual selection of those species able to obtain the environmental factors necessary for survival to reproductive age and the elimination of those less capable. This evolutionary interpretation fits neatly with the orthodoxy prevailing in geology— uniformitarianism—the theory that geological changes of the past were just like those of today, such as the gradual wearing down of a mountain by erosion over geological time. This uniformitarian perspective has been challenged now in both geology and the biological sciences. That it has been challenged does not mean that it is totally false and certainly does not mean, as some "scientific" creationists seem to think, that the old catastrophist view of the world is vindicated. It means, simply, that geological or biological catastrophic events could have occurred and, further, that they could have been significant in determining future states. Witness the recent hypothesis of Louis Alvarez which attributes the massive extinctions of organisms sixty-five to seventy million years ago to a catastrophic encounter between the earth and an asteroid perhaps five or six miles in extent.

Gould holds for an evolutionary theory of "punctuated equilibria" in opposition to "gradualism." Evolution does not *require* gradual change as Darwin had supposed. The absence of transitional forms in the fossil record which would bear out gradualism is described by Gould as the "trade secret of paleontology." Such transitional forms (missing links) are rare, Gould believes, because evolutionary change was so rapid that the chance of such forms being preserved as fossils is statistically very low. As he reads the fossil record (and this is the paleontologist's job), Gould finds that most species exhibit no change over their lifetimes in geological time and that new species appear very quickly from the standpoint, once again, of geological time. So evolution takes place not simply in the gradual change of one species into another but rather in two ways: the first, termed "phyletic," involves the change of an entire population of organisms from one state to another; the second, termed "speciation," sees the branching off of a species from a main stock. For Gould, speciation is rapid splitting in small populations which for geographical, behavioral, or other causes are isolated from the parent stock. (For behavioral reasons a small group may still be geographically associated with the parent stock but no longer breeds with it. A recent report in *Science*, in July, 1981, suggests precisely such a phenomenon involving hamsters.) Thus, the means by which speciation takes place involve not the gradual accumulation of minute variations but rather some sort of macromutation (large mutation).

The geneticist Richard Goldschmidt had urged such a hypothesis from the 1940's onward. Gould believes that Goldschmidt was wrong about details and mechanisms but right in concept. As people learn more and more about the processes of individual development (ontogeny), they understand that small changes arising from mutation could produce small changes in early developmental stages. These small changes can translate into large differences in adults, hence, a possible means of accounting for rapid origins. Gould, in the very best scientific spirit, admits that this is his opinion. He does feel that his hypothesis evades the earlier criticisms of Goldschmidt's hypothesis of macromutations. Goldschmidt had held that macromutations resulted from wholesale rearrangement of genetic material. Such mutations as these are almost invariably lethal to the organism in which they occur.

Although he does not use the word, Gould would have to be classified as an "emergentist" in philosophical biology. He continually stresses hierarchy in biological structure and function and is critical of reductionism—the attempt to explain wholes solely in terms of their parts and the denial of the existence of emergent or global properties found on higher levels of organization. As he puts it: "Different forces work at different levels." He is critical of those who would, like Sir John William Dawson, attempt to reduce the external characteristics of an organism to explanation in molecular terms and who would thus claim to have explained the most complex structures, functions, and behaviors in terms of gene action alone.

There is a hazard in writing the type of biological essay that Gould writes so well. Readers possessing some familiarity with the biological sciences might find themselves wincing as they come across the occasional teleological statement, that the attribution of purpose to biological processes or to evolution. Leaving to one side the question of human motivation, apparently purposive biological phenomena can always be explained in functional language. The problem is that it takes more words to do so; but this is perhaps a minor quibble. Despite these minor lapses, Gould is clearly no vitalist. He rejects both the reductionist and vitalist alternatives in favor of the hierarchical view. Gould is no believer in vital forces as was Henri Bergson nor is he a believer in directed evolution as was the early evolutionary pioneer Chevalier de Lamarck.

Gould in his discussion of evolution could have tackled the question of whether there could be natural selection at the molecular level—whether there could be some sort of internal selection. It might well be that selection takes place *inside* the organism at the level of chromosome or gene. This would be consistent with Gould's hierarchical approach and might be the source of his mutation producing the change early in embryological development that would culminate in great adult differences.

A fascinating story unfolds in Gould's chapter on the Piltdown hoax. It will be remembered that the Piltdown affair was one of the most celebrated scientific hoaxes of this century. In Piltdown, England, a skull was planted so that it could be found. Without tracing tediously the entire story (which has been told many times before) Gould turns up what may be a new angle on the hoax—the possible involvement of the famous Jesuit paleontologist Teilhard de Chardin in the deception. Chardin was probably not involved in the manufacture of a skull from human and ape parts but may have participated in the planting of the pseudofossil. Gould draws some morals from the largely uncritical acceptance by eminent scientists of the genuineness of the fossil. Scientists are human and practice science in a social context. Piltdown man *had* to be genuine because England *had* to have had an early form of man. After all, had not the French found myriad prehistoric human remains and great abundances of prehistoric material culture? Species bias figured in as well. Humans are on top of the evolutionary heap because of large brains; ergo, Piltdown must be genuine for it had a large cranium. It was widely believed at the time of the "discovery" of Piltdown that the missing link would be discovered eventually and that a large brain case would be a prominent feature of such a fossil. Thus, Piltdown confirmed the prejudice of the theory dominant during the first three decades of this century.

Gould also deals with the science and politics of human differences. Scientists, even such famous scientists of the past as Baron Cuvier, have been guilty of asserting differences among races and between men and women and of using such alleged differences (of intelligence) as justification for racial and sexual discrimination and eugenics. Gould points out that it is not that there are no differences but that they are not of the kind that *make* any difference. In this area, Gould's analysis is devastating. Time and again he shows that such science is done in a social and cultural context. Hence, it is not surprising that some so-called science was really an attempt to justify a belief in European or male superiority. Such science is, of course, circular (in the sense of a logical fallacy). The earlier scientific racists and sexists through the selective choice and selective interpretation of evidence found exactly what they were looking for. This same sort of pseudoscience goes on yet in the IQ controversy which has been fueled in our time by the evangelism of William Shockley.

Gould's examples throughout are fascinating. He apparently loves those oddball characters in the living world, and their life-styles intrigue him. In fact, in the books' first essay, "The Panda's Thumb," Gould makes the case for evolution through oddity. The panda's thumb (not really a true thumb) is an adaptation to food supply. Other strange organisms with strange habits, structures, and functions with which he deals are turtles, anglerfish, bacteria, dinosaurs, and Mickey Mouse. The lesson to be drawn from oddity in the biological world is that people should not look for perfection there. It is not perfection that should be sought in the evolutionary process either, but rather the odd arrangements which are the "senseless signs of history" indicating evolutionary change.

Occasionally one will encounter some technical biological terms in the text but this should not put the reader off since, in almost all cases, Gould explains what they mean in ordinary language. So the reader should not despair the encounter with phyletic, allpatric, and the like. There is one minor slip. It was Francis Crick, not James Watson, who coined the phrase "Central Dogma of molecular biology." The book has a bibliography and an excellent index.

Robert L. Hoffman

THE PEOPLE'S EMPEROR: MAO
A Biography of Mao Tse-tung

Author: Dick Wilson (1928-   )
Publisher: Doubleday & Company (Garden City, New York). 530 pp. $17.50
Type of work: Biography
Time: 1893-1976
Locale: China

A popular introduction to the life of Mao Tse-tung stressing the importance of his problematic relationship with his father

Both Chinese and world opinion of Mao Tse-tung has undergone a sometimes startling revision since his death in 1976. In the West, his image had begun to change even before his death from that of the devil incarnate to a rather lovable old Buddha. In China, his successors—men of his own generation who knew Mao during his long rise to power—are attempting to demystify his reputation, to dismantle the cult that had been built up around him and which stifles their freedom of action. Many of the statues of Mao have been torn down, posters bearing his portrait have been removed from public places, and his words are now criticized openly, although still apologetically, by the nation's new leaders.

Although tome after tome has been written about this peasant who became one of a handful of truly great leaders produced in our century, much about the man remains a mystery. What forces motivated him in his struggle for leadership of the Chinese Communist Party and of China itself? Why, when already well-advanced in age and his country at peace, did he initiate the Cultural Revolution that brought government, education, and commerce to a standstill? Why, finally, did he make peace with one of the world's best-known anti-Communists, Richard Nixon, and even show public support for him after his disgrace?

The People's Emperor: Mao addresses such questions as these in an easily accessible manner, and, in the process, tells the reader much about the modern history of this land of nine hundred million people. In the sense that it imputes rather neurotic underlying motives to Mao's political involvement and views him as a continuer, *mutatis mutandis*, of the Chinese Imperial tradition, this work joins those that have attempted to demystify Mao's image. Its author, Dick Wilson, currently an editor of the respected *China Quarterly*, tells surprisingly little about the personal life of Mao. The sources on his childhood and youth are few, the main one being the autobiographical account he dictated to the American journalist, Edgar Snow, who published it in his well-known book, *Red Star over China*, still one of the best sources on communism in China. Without corroborating evidence, however, the accuracy of this information is difficult to assess. Moreover, Mao apparently remained aloof from even his most intimate friends, so we lack the light they might have shed on his inner life. No doubt much of this mystery is due to the fact that Mao was primarily a man of action, not given to constant and deep introspection, like his Indian counterpart, Mahatma Gandhi. His personal life was, from a very early age, subordinated to his political life and ambitions. What warmth and sensitivity he had seems to have been expressed primarily in his classical poetry, which he composed throughout his life.

The personal picture that emerges in Wilson's book is that of a man of modest habits, the most likely among the world's leaders to appear in patched trousers and sagging socks, as the author puts it. Beyond these superficial characteristics, however, the few glimpses the reader gets are of a man driven by a profound resentment of authority stemming from his difficult relationship with his father. Born into a moderately well-off peasant family in the southern province of Hunan in 1893, Mao chafed under the rigid control of his father, who was unwilling to give his head-strong son the freedom and recognition he desired. In a society that valued so highly respect for one's elders, and particularly for one's father, Mao was a rebel from the start, arguing often and violently with his father, and trying on several occasions to run away from home.

On the scant evidence available on his early life, Wilson builds his interpretation of Mao's personality. He believes that Mao's enormous drive to succeed was a compensation for a "personal sense of rejection," originating in his stormy relationship with his father. This feeling was in later life reinforced by his rejection by a whole series of father-figures—classmates from a better background than his, teachers, fellow Communists, and foreigners. This sense of being an outsider, Wilson maintains, is what led to Mao's identification with the peasant masses of China, who were rejected by their society. Like many attempts by biographers to theorize about their subject's psychology, this one leaves the impression of being overly neat or simplistic. The dearth of evidence from Mao's youth makes any speculation of this sort haphazard at best. Even if valid, the hypothesis begs the question of why Mao's effort to compensate for low self-esteem took precisely the form it did, the answer to which requires a larger framework than that provided by Wilson. Interestingly, another recent biographer of Mao, Ross Terrill, specifically denies that he was a neurotic and claims that his rebellion was not personal, but rather against what his father stood for. Even the evidence presented by Wilson leaves one with the impression that his rebelliousness was of a very self-conscious variety, not an irrational lashing-out.

Mao had many obstacles to overcome in his rise to the leadership of his nation. He had to fight hard for an education and was unable to enter secondary school until he was eighteen. He was basically self-educated, consuming volume after volume of books on subjects that interested him, but neglecting his classwork in areas he disliked. At the provincial capital where he went to secondary school, he had to overcome the prejudices of the other students, generally sons of landlords, who chided him for his rural background and lowly status. He quickly managed to win these students over through his strong leadership abilities and rhetorical skills.

Soon after completing his schooling in 1918, Mao went to live in Peking. He was confronted there with the choice of whether or not to join a group of Chinese students who were leaving to study in France. He chose not to go, apparently because he feared that living in France might render him an "internationalist," unable to enjoy the full trust of the common people of his country. He feared too, perhaps, that he would not stand out among his peers abroad. This desire to remain fully Chinese and, by extension, to maintain Chinese cultural integrity, was later manifested in the independent line he followed toward the Soviet Union and its proffered advice.

Through an acquaintance, Mao was able to acquire a job at Peking University Library, whose Director was Li Ta-chao, the man who effectively introduced Marxism into China. More than Li Ta-chao, however, it was the example of successful revolution under the Bolshevik banner in Russia that led Mao to Marxism-Leninism during his late twenties. One might question Wilson's claim that Mao chose Marxism because "it came into fashion at the time when he needed a weapon." Mao was certainly impressed by the radical ideology's successful application in Russia and said that "Communism is a hammer which we use to destroy the enemy." Wilson's own evidence, however, contradicts the implication that Mao was attracted to communism merely out of faddishness. It expressed more forcefully than any available ideology Mao's concern for the impoverished masses of his country and focused attention on the issue of imperialism which, in the form of Japanese and Western designs on Chinese rights and territory, was of major interest to Mao's generation of nationalists.

Mao shortly returned to his provincial capital, Changsha, where he began in earnest his propagandist and organizational efforts. He started a radical publication, which was quickly suppressed by the local governor, and helped organize a successful strike by coal miners in Anyuan. He served as a Communist liaison to the Kuomintang which, under Sun Yat-sen's leadership, was then leaning to the left and friendship with the Soviet Union. Mao supported his Party's alliance with the Nationalists against more purest elements in the Party which favored a more independent role in the labor movement for the Communists. He continued to support periodically cooperation with the Kuomintang, even under the more conservative Chiang Kai-shek, when the interests of the two coincided. In fact, throughout his life, Mao displayed a flexibility in the choice of allies and strategies in the pursuit of his goals that seems to contradict Wilson's portrait of a rigid personality, one that was unable to accept positions that diverged from his own.

Very early in his career as a Communist, Mao developed an unorthodox position which initially was rejected by most of his comrades. Orthodox Marxism, in its Euro-centric form, insisted that the proletarian class of the advanced industrial nations would lead the struggle toward Communist revolution. This presented the nationalist leaders of predominantly agricultural colonial or semicolonial nations like China with a dilemma. Were they simply to wait for their countries to develop to the point when the working class was large and strong enough to carry out a successful revolution? Or, should they look for nonworking-class allies with whom to pursue this end? Many in the Chinese Party insisted that China's small urban proletariat be the focus of their attention. These Party members generally maintained close ties with Soviet Russia and the Comintern, which advocated this strategy. Mao broke with this tradition, maintaining his strong allegiance to the peasant masses, and insisting on their primacy in carrying out revolution in a backward country such as China. Although Mao's early identification with China's rural poor might be explained psychologically, as Wilson wishes, it is difficult to imagine what strategy other than his peasant-oriented one could realistically be chosen under these circumstances.

Mao began to build an armed base, the first of the Chinese "soviets," in the remote Chingkangshan Mountains of his home province during the late 1920's. Wilson follows closely the vicissitudes of Mao's fortunes as he rose from the leadership of this small encampment to become the dominant figure in the Party and the country. He continued to enter into disputes with fellow Party leaders over doctrinal and strategic questions and often found himself displaced from the governing committees and offices of his party, only to fight his way to the top again. Wilson implies that these conflicts were often the result of a fundamental flaw in Mao's personality which prevented him from accepting reasonable and principled opposition, seeing all opposition as a threat to the interests of the peasants and, subconsciously, seeing it as personal rejection like that suffered at the hands of his father. To Mao's credit, he was not as vindictive toward those Party leaders who disagreed with him as was Joseph Stalin, and believed that "re-education" was generally sufficient to mend one's ways. Although an interesting interpretation of the disputatious aspect of Mao's personality, it leaves one wondering how Wilson would explain the similar factionalism which has characterized most radical political movements in modern history. Is this quality inherent in the nature of political movements, or in the nature of the personality types which are drawn to such movements?

A further consequence of this personality trait was that—with the sole exception of Chou En-lai—Mao surrounded himself with sycophantic second-raters. The most abject of these was Lin Piao, who was primarily responsible for the editing and publishing of the *Quotations of Chairman Mao*, the bible of the Red Guards during the Cultural Revolution. The collective leadership of the Party no doubt suffered from Mao's inability to work for long with men of talent and self-confidence. This trait did not bode well for China's future governance, although remarkable reversals have occurred since Mao's death in the fortunes of many of the more outspoken critics who had been disgraced during his lifetime—including the currently dominant figure of Teng Hsiao-ping.

Mao consolidated his leadership over the Party following the epic 6000-mile Long March, which saw fewer than half his original forces arrive safely at their destination in Shensi province, at Yenan, which was to be their base for several years. This period in Yenan was to be one of the most productive in Mao's career, when he read extensively in politics and philosophy, gradually elaborating that distinctive body of ideas that the world has come to call "Maoism." It was also during this time that the outside world began to take note of Mao, as Western journalists and activists such as Edgar Snow and Agnes Smedley made the difficult pilgrimage to his mountain hideaway.

In 1937, Mao received a boost in the form of tacit recognition from Stalin of his position as senior Party leader, although the Soviet dictator urged that Mao abate his struggles with other Party leaders and accept the help of his Russian-trained comrades in overcoming his theoretical deficiencies and uncertain grasp of Marxism. In the same year, Mao met the woman who was to be his companion for the rest of his life, a twenty-three-year-old film actress known as "The Blue Apple," better known to posterity as Chiang Ching.

The Communist effort prospered in the years following Yenan, especially after the conflict between China and Japan grew into a full-fledged war. Chiang Kai-shek was forced to wage a two-front war against the Japanese on the coast and the Communists at his rear. Wilson attributes Mao's final victory to this situation and to the Kuomintang's general corruption, although this view underestimates the extent to which the Communists had succeeded in winning the allegiance of the Chinese masses away from the Nationalists.

The Red Army finally captured Peking in 1949. Mao proceeded to proclaim the founding of the People's Republic, and the nation's new leadership set about putting their ideology into practice. As Wilson makes clear, however, the intra-party conflicts in which Mao had been embroiled throughout his career continued after the consolidation of the Party's power. Disputes over economic policy led the list, but the root of the problem again lay in Mao's inability to accept criticism or differing viewpoints from other Party leaders.

Wilson likens Mao's personality and situation as China's ruler to that of a traditional Chinese emperor—an analogy that runs throughout the book and provides it with its title. To be sure, Mao explicitly compared himself to the founder of the Chin dynasty, which first unified China. Then, too, one wonders how seriously to take the question he is reported to have asked as the traditional Chinese capital fell to his forces: ". . . as soon as we enter Peking, I'll be an emperor, won't I?" The struggle for control of the Party which Mao participated in, likewise, has a certain similarity to the dynastic conflicts of the past. One can easily imagine Chiang Ching as the Dragon Lady and Chou

En-lai as the honest court mandarin, in the midst of a coterie of sycophants who tell the Emperor he can do no wrong. Finally, Wilson goes so far as to suggest that the natural disasters which befell China in the year of Mao's death were portents of this event, just as an emperor's reign was believed to end in the midst of such natural events. At this point, Wilson stretches his analogy to its limits, and forces readers to consider whether it has been merely a literary device rather than a seriously thought-out comparison. It is up to the reader to judge how useful this analogy is. Does it really tell much about Mao the man or about Chinese politics? The personality traits he points to are not, after all, entirely uncharacteristic of non-Chinese political leaders, whether democratic or totalitarian.

Wilson judges Mao's career a failure, ultimately, in terms of the high goals he set for himself and his country. In the Great Leap Forward, he sought to make over the Chinese economic system totally, as in the Cultural Revolution he tried to reform human nature. In both these efforts he failed, in part because he lacked the practical and administrative skills to see his ideals put into effect. His romanticism, perhaps, lay at the root of these abortive efforts, for his ideals and style of leadership, Wilson argues, were derived as much from the romantic egalitarianism of the stories he read as a youth as they were from the theoretical works of Marxism. To judge Mao's career a failure, however, is only to say that his goals were too high, for by any standard Mao's impact on China and even the Chinese personality has been significant and likely to last for some time to come.

The People's Emperor: Mao provides a readable and entertaining summary of the main events of the life of a great twentieth century figure. Yet, Wilson's meager attempt at psychoanalyzing his subject and his suggestion of an imperial model for the life of Mao—neither very original in themselves— offer little justification for yet another biography of Mao. In the years to come, there are likely to be many more literary efforts like Wilson's which try to profit from the Western public's fascination with Mao's life. For those who want a simple introduction to the subject, these books will probably suffice. The more sophisticated reader would do well to consult more substantial works, or classics such as Edgar Snow's account.

Rand Edwards

PETER THE GREAT
His Life and World

Author: Robert K. Massie (1929-   )
Publisher: Alfred A. Knopf (New York). Illustrated. 909 pp. $19.95
Type of work: Biography
Time: 1672-1725
Locale: Russia, with sidelights on Western Europe, Sweden, and the Ottoman Empire

A comprehensive popular biography of Peter I that discusses in detail the characters and context, European and Russian, of the Czar's life and work

> *Principal personages:*
> PETER I, the Great, Czar of Russia, 1689-1725
> PATRICK GORDON, general of Scottish origins in the Muscovite armed forces
> FRANZ LEFORT, general of Swiss origins in the armed forces
> CHARLES XII, King of Sweden, 1700-1718
> IVAN MAZEPPA, hetman of the Cossacks of the Russian Ukraine, 1687-1709
> LOUIS XV, King of France, 1715-1774, in minority to 1723
> ALEKSEI, son and heir apparent of Peter I
> ALEKSANDR MENSHIKOV, Russian general and statesman
> IAKOV DOLGORUKII, Russian statesman, First Senator
> CATHERINE I, wife of Peter I and Empress of Russia, 1725-1727

During the reign of Peter I, 1689-1725, the gathering forces of change, modernism, and the movement to European ways in culture and technology were given direction and impetus under the great Czar. The clash of the traditional and the Western factors in Russia's political and social life left a lasting imprint on its development as a nation; that many of the innovations introduced under Peter's rule were promoted under conditions often of civil unrest and of almost continuous war further underscored the elements of upheaval during this period that signaled overall a change in the course of Russian history. As portrayed by Robert K. Massie, the life and times of Peter the Great are unfolded as a vast and panoramic narrative, an evocation of the man and his world within the many spheres of activity by which Peter and his associates effected the transformation of Russia. In a work of history on a direct human level, many of the leading personalities, soldiers, administrators, and heads of state are portrayed within the encompassing perspective of the great Czar. As befits the outsized, larger-than-life figure of Peter himself, Massie's work is very long, yet inspired by the relentless energy and attention, both to the Russian land and people, and to European capitals and battlefields, that were characteristic of the Russian ruler himself.

The beauty and also the brutality of old Russia are presented at the outset: the Kremlin and the splendid churches of Moscow take their place beside Massie's description of the seclusion of women and the punishment of civil and criminal offenders. As yet, Russia remained a distant outpost on the borders of the Western world. From his early years, Peter had chafed at the rigid, tradition-bound ways of old Muscovy; while still young, he had witnessed the violence and horror of a revolt of the *strel'tsy* (old guard musketeers). Quite unabashedly, he had sought the company of craftsmen and soldiers in the foreign suburb outside the capital. There he found some of his earliest friends, among such older, hardened military men as Patrick Gordon, a Scotsman, and the Swiss Franz LeFort. With their assistance, he proceeded with the formation of army units in the European style; in their company he indulged in those epic drunken entertainments that so frequently were to provide diversion from his labors. He had a characteristic penchant for personal initiative and for work with his own hands; he cut timber for ships and in person led his troops under enemy fire during the first of his campaigns, against the Turks at Azov in 1695-1696.

The first Czar to travel outside his own country, Peter's great embassy of 1697-1698 furnished the opportunity for first-hand study of shipyards and laboratories. Notwithstanding some destructive excesses, when their hosts were appalled by the antics of the exuberant Russians, Peter was able to converse with churchmen and heads of state. In Holland and England, skilled workers were recruited for service in Russia. His return to Moscow rendered the more urgent by a revolt of the *strel'tsy*, Peter exacted a fearful retribution; the interrogations, torture, and public executions are described by Massie in grim detail. His authority within Russia unchallenged, Peter embarked on that series of military ventures that incontrovertibly were to establish Russia's status as a great power, during the Great Northern War of 1700-1721.

One of the features that adds a certain depth to Massie's work—which in some places, however, amounts to digression—is the extent to which other lands and rulers are portrayed. Here, after a brief disquisition on eighteenth century methods of warfare, Sweden and its young ruler are depicted in some detail. Charles XII, the brilliant, impulsive, headstrong King who was to be the leading rival of Peter the Great, at first was able to defeat the Russians with ease. As the war continued Russian forces gained in training combat experience. Undeterred, Charles allowed himself to be lured deep into his opponent's territory; even with the defection of his trusted hetman, Ivan Mazeppa, Peter subdued rebellious Cossacks and left a trail of scorched earth before the oncoming Swedes. Particularly sharply drawn is the climactic Battle of Poltava (1709), where Massie succeeds in evoking something of the dust and weariness, the hardships of long, forced marches, the smoke and blood, and the gallantry and suffering of this epic struggle and crowning victory of Peter's career.

Thenceforth, with Russia's military fortunes in the ascendant, the scope of Russia's operations was dramatically expanded. Although an impetuous foray into the Balkans, against the Ottoman Turks, was turned back in 1711, Peter turned again to the Northern War. Here Massie, in continuing his narrative of this conflict, discusses at some length engagements often reviewed in outline elsewhere. In pursuit of the Swedes, Russian forces were deployed across the Baltic coast of Germany, and against Finland; for the first time the fleet built under Peter's supervision successfully engaged the Swedish navy. As a result Peter and his Russia had become the more highly regarded in Europe; a second round of visits to the Western countries, to Copenhagen, Amsterdam, across Germany, and to Paris, afforded a grand view of the European capitals. For a sojourn of some time at the French court during the regency of Louis XV, Massie provides a number of glimpses of the social and cultural life of France. In the process, Peter's conviction of the utility of Western art and learning was upheld.

On his return, Peter had to deal with the errant ways of his son Aleksei, to whom he feared to entrust the throne lest the reforms of his reign, and the military strength he had brought Russia, be abandoned. The contrast between the violent, indomitable energy and will of the great Czar, and the timid, reflective demeanor of Aleksei, sharply drawn and at some length by Massie, culminated in the most tragic—and frightful—episode of Peter's reign. Aleksei fled across Europe, was captured by Peter's agents, and was brought back to St. Petersburg to be interrogated by his father. When he ordered Aleksei beaten, and the young man collapsed and died, Peter felt little remorse for having sacrificed his son for reasons of state.

When on another front, Charles XII, ever in quest of new danger and conflict, was killed while on a campaign against Denmark (1718), a successful conclusion to the Northern War was in sight. During the later years of his reign, indeed until his death early in 1725, Peter often turned to questions of administration and finance, as well as matters of science and education, where his initial efforts previously had been distracted by wartime exigencies. On issues of this sort, however, Massie is inclined to consider the personal factor in Russian government, to relate some of the anecdotes associated with the great Czar and his colorful, if sometimes less public-spirited officials. Some of the figures sketched in this regard do command interest. The man closest to Peter, who from humble origins attained great wealth and influence, was Prince Aleksandr Menshikov; overbearing and self-interested, he adroitly managed somehow never to lose the Czar's favor. Prince Iakov Dolgorukii, the firm and upright First Senator, attended to legislative consultation within the government. In a domestic context Peter's wife, Catherine, an unlettered peasant girl possessing a certain shrewdness regarding her own concerns, but also a unique ability to instill calm in his tempestuous nature, frequently provided some comfort and solicitude for the Czar.

As for Peter himself, Massie does capture much of the essence of the man. Many episodes illustrate the inner drive which determined that he be ever active, and his zest for physical labor, as well as that practical bent by which Peter measured the utility of any new device or proposal he encountered. In a lighter vein, Peter was also fond of good company, and he could yield himself to revelry and strong drink as readily and as tirelessly as he could work on his lathe or on his ships. State business he took seriously enough, composing decrees on every concern that involved him, military or civil, and reordering the form of Russian administration as he went along. Whenever possible, he applied his personal attention to the conduct of his officials; sometimes tolerant and sometimes threatening, he insisted that they were answerable to him, and more than that to the state. From what can be gathered, he was at times moved by religious feeling, notwithstanding his distrust of the church and his pointedly irreverent mockery of the religious authorities.

On the whole, Massie is inclined to be sympathetic to his subject: the dark, violent impulses that came to the surface during times of political stress, and the more raucous and crude elements in his play seem merely the all too human features of a great man otherwise dedicated to his own monumental and constructive endeavors. The human costs of Peter's reign, whether expressed in terms of the disruption of the social fabric, or more directly by the numbers killed by war or forced labor, are not really brought to account, as has been done by more critical historians. For that matter, Massie does not attempt to assess—or even to delineate in systematic form—the two leading themes of Peter's period of Russian history, changes in military and civil administration, and the impact of Western culture and technology. To be sure such concerns are discussed here and again, but largely where they are revealing of the character and interests of the man.

Massie concludes that Peter's life and work resembled nothing so much as a force of nature, and in this wise suspends judgment on the great Czar. This biography is clear, well written, and, in its treatment of the events of Peter's life, remarkably thorough. There is little in the way of background, whether on the Russian past or from the European setting, that is lacking; some readers, however, may be daunted by the very length of the work. Illustrations have been particularly well chosen, and maps provide clarification of the geographical context. The documentation to be found here, however, is relatively thin, and for the most part consists of rather well-known works; essentially all of the primary sources are familiar to historians. More to the point, however, is the lack of focus, of a basic thread of research and writing that distinguishes the essential from the ephemeral. It is for this reason that the reader will find little exposition of the significance of Peter the Great, or of the meaning of his work. In this regard Massie's work, while genuinely rewarding for those in quest of the vast human drama of history and great men, will be received with reservations on the part of historians or indeed those of a more critical turn of mind.

John R. Broadus

PLAINS SONG
For Female Voices

Author: Wright Morris (1910-   )
Publisher: Harper & Row Publishers (New York). 229 pp. $9.95
Type of work: Novel
Time: The early 1900's to the present
Locale: Madison County, Nebraska, and Chicago

A lyrical and compassionate portrait of Nebraska women and their efforts to understand life, love, and their changing times

Principal characters:
CORA ATKINS, a Nebraska farm wife
EMERSON ATKINS, her husband
ORION ATKINS, his brother
BELLE ROONEY ATKINS, his wife
MADGE ATKINS KIBBEE, daughter of Cora and Emerson
SHARON ROSE ATKINS, daughter of Belle and Orion
FAYRENE ATKINS DICKEL, her sister
BLANCHE KIBBEE, Madge's daughter
CAROLINE KIBBEE, her sister
NED KIBBEE, Madge's husband
AVERY DICKEL, Fayrene's husband

Plains Song: For Female Voices, Wright Morris' twentieth novel, redresses an imbalance in his previous fiction in which the women characters are almost always in the background, either quietly supporting their men, trying to ignite them into action, or tormenting them for their sins, real or imagined. In the end, it is usually his men's problems or triumphs, their visions of the world, which matter. The end of his previous novel, *The Fork River Space Project* (1977), may have subtly signaled a change in Morris' perspective as the protagonist's wife, another shadowy female, leaves him. Neither the reader nor the husband is surprised or upset by her departure since she is presented as clearly having a right to a choice, a right to choose escape, even escape from a comfortable, trouble-free marriage. Most of Morris' previous women would have been unlikely to have even considered such a drastic change.

In *Plains Song*, Morris carries this idea of the woman's right to choose what kind of life she wants, her need to escape to a more fulfilling environment, much further. Morris' men and women usually have unsatisfying relationships, and those in *Plains Song* are typical. The only happy wife is Madge Atkins Kibbee who is completely fulfilled being a domestic drudge and childbearer. Sharon Rose Atkins, her cousin, avoids the problems inherent in heterosexual entanglements by shunning men altogether. Sharon's goal in life is to establish and maintain her independence, and she becomes something of a heroic figure for her success.

Morris is also reexamining some of his traditional concerns in *Plains Song*. Nine of his prior novels take place mostly in Nebraska, depicting how the frequently harsh life on the plains has affected the inhabitants, turning them inward but not toward introspection. His Nebraskans are usually good people who do little good because they are passive, uncommunicative, unanalytical Westerners whose vision of the dream they or their ancestors pursued west has become cloudy. Morris condemns them for their unthinking lives yet sympathizes with them because of the potential goodness of their natures. This ambiguity toward the people of the plains underscores Morris' efforts, in the words of critic Leslie A. Fiedler, "to convince his readers that Nebraska is the absurd hell we all inhabit."

Morris' ambiguity about the plains is embodied by the two most prominent characters: Cora Atkins, who stays and endures, and Sharon Atkins, who leaves and blossoms. Cora is living in Ohio with an uncle who operates a hotel and stable when she meets Emerson Atkins who has come east to buy supplies for the farm he and his brother Orion have started just north of the Elkhorn River in Madison County, Nebraska. Emerson proposes because a man beginning a homestead on the plains needs a wife, and the six-foot, solemnfaced, sober-gazed Cora, although clearly no prize, is the sort of level-headed woman a commonsensical farmer needs, and she accepts simply because she is expected to. The possibility of eventual affection is not important for these oh-so-practical pioneers.

A cliché of life and fiction is that such couples will grow to love each other, but Morris knows better. Cora, thrust into a situation she has not been prepared for, one she understands only on the most superficial levels, bites through her hand on her wedding night, a reaction which, like everything emotional, baffles her husband. Emerson's inability to understand this incident foreshadows his failure to try to comprehend Cora for the remainder of their long marriage. For him, she is as much an employee, a servant, as a wife. Cora's scarred hand comes to represent a fear of or indifference toward sex on the part of many Atkins women, to suggest an almost insurmountable barrier between Morris' plainswomen and their men.

Cora more easily reconciles herself to farm life than to marriage, growing to enjoy her endless chores, and when she realizes she is pregnant, she sees having the child as simply another job she is expected to perform. Beulah Madge, however, turns out to be Cora's only child because of her abhorrence of the sexual act. Unable to overcome this barrier between them, Emerson implies that Cora has failed him: "What a farm needed was sons. She had borne a daughter, to be fed and clothed, then offered on the marriage market. Who would be there to run the farm as they grew old?" Morris calmly criticizes the way Nebraska, the American West, and most of civilization have failed to see more in women than Emerson sees. Morris, as he so often does, softens the blow by turning his criticism into comedy as generations of Atkinses are "cursed" by producing nothing but daughters.

Orion marries Belle Rooney, an Ozark hillbilly whose constant chattering is her only weapon against the suffocating silence of her environment and its inhabitants. Belle seems lost amid the taciturnity which Morris convinces the reader is indigenous to the plains. Her daughter Sharon Rose and Cora's Madge are mirrors of their mothers; Sharon babbles and demands attention while Madge quietly follows and watches her cousin. The girls develop a friendship and interdependence whose eventual weakening helps Sharon to sever herself from her home. They become even more like sisters after Belle dies giving birth to Fayrene Dee, whom everyone ignores and whom Orion blames for his wife's death. As the Atkins girls grow up, Sharon discovers an innate talent for the piano while Madge's "special talent" is watching Sharon.

During these years Cora becomes reconciled to her life, having "little desire to see more than she had already seen, or feel more than she had already felt." Her life totally defined by her daily routine of looking after her chickens and their eggs, Cora has peace of mind if little else, especially when it comes to the emotional life some choose to have. She is not even particularly affectionate toward her daughter and nieces. Orion allows himself to be so close to Belle that he is shattered by her death, eventually running away to join the Canadian Army to fight in World War I. The change in Orion is proof for Cora that her insularity is the best approach to life.

Less than halfway through *Plains Song*, the focus shifts to Sharon who, even as a teenager, sees what those around her are missing: "She pitied Cora, who seemed to lack the sense to pity herself." Sharon feels betrayed when Madge, who has seemingly existed all their lives only to witness Sharon's accomplishments, marries Ned Kibbee. Sharon leaves soon afterward when she receives a scholarship to the Schurz Academy of Music in Chicago.

Away from home, Sharon begins making judgments about it which have always been there beneath the surface of her consciousness: "*They* were intolerable, all of them, their otherwise decent lives more like that of livestock than aspiring human beings. It both shamed and elated her to have such unthinkable thoughts." Sharon becomes aware that "this partially conscious life" she is fleeing offers some comforts she will never know, although these comforts demand sacrifices she finds unreasonable. The example of Cora has always been there as well as that of the mother she cannot remember, and now there is Madge, plunging submissively into the unvarying routine of domesticity and childbearing. Still, Sharon has needs which go unfulfilled: "It startled Sharon to realize that she would like the city better if Madge lived in it." Sharon's awareness of "the contradictory needs in her nature" does not make matters any better. The tragedy in Morris' fictional world is often that the half-conscious characters cannot realize their limitations and that the others can make this realization without being any better off for doing so. For Morris, however, missing out is better than giving in.

Although Sharon has suitors, she does not intend to marry. Madge wants her to get married so that they can discuss sex, which she has found different from what she expected. The dangers of male-female relationships, the traps set for the weak, become even clearer when Fayrene gets pregnant and has to marry Avery Dickel, the most "repugnant" young person Sharon has ever seen. Fayrene's marriage sets yet another obstacle between Sharon and her old life, because of the way the family is so accepting of it. If they can readily accept an Avery Dickel as one of their own, how do they perceive the attractive, talented, intelligent Sharon?

As Sharon boards the train back to Chicago after this visit,

> The clang of the last crossing bell rang down the curtain on ceaseless humiliations, inadmissible longings, the perpetual chores and smoldering furies, the rites and kinships with half-conscious people so friendly and decent it shamed her to dislike them.

People such as Sharon need to break away from their roots to come fully alive, but such a Morris character is always aware that the break, in order to be complete, must be a painful one. A major theme throughout Morris' work is how the past haunts Americans, often forcing them to try to exorcise it as if it were a demon. Sharon, however, recognizes that she can never truly be free of her past and tries to understand it: why are these people as they are; why are they happy to settle for so little? Neither Sharon nor Morris has the answer, but the question must be asked. Even Cora intuitively senses the differences between her view of the world and her niece's. In Chicago for the 1933 World's Fair, she cannot bring herself to visit Sharon who, on her own ground, would more clearly be a creature beyond the child Cora once controlled with the whack of a hairbrush.

Sharon tries to rescue Madge's oldest daughter Blanche from farm life when the girl comes to live with her while attending a girls' school. Blanche's "unusual nature and remarkable beauty" make it imperative that she be saved from the life into which her mother has settled. Blanche is not a Sharon, however, but is even more silent, passive, and sluggish than Madge. Sending Blanche back to Nebraska, Sharon has to be satisfied with saving herself.

Meanwhile, Cora and Emerson survive the Depression without any help from the government, whose representatives Emerson, a simplistic version of his namesake's self-reliant man, chases away with a shotgun. Cora's feelings for her husband remain as distant as ever: "It shamed her to look at him with his eyes closed, feeling in her soul he was a stranger to her, and she to him." After Emerson has a stroke and slowly dies, Cora descends into madness, becoming a vegetable whenever taken from the farm she loves. In the 1960's, Madge also becomes an invalid after a stroke and is cared for by Blanche who, like Cora has been all these years, is happy simply to be busy.

When Cora dies, Sharon, now a teacher at Wellesley, returns to Nebraska for the first time since World War II. She learns that she is considered a pioneer in women's independence; Madge's daughter Caroline tells her, "we

don't get married anymore unless we want to. We all had your example."
She also sees that some of her past has disappeared: Cora's farm is nothing
but a field of tree stumps. The bleak emptiness reminds her of Cora and
frightens her, her memories of her aunt being among "the many things she
preferred not to face." She sees that the past is very much a part of her.
Leaving "home" again,

> A sweet sadness, a longing touched with dread, filled her with a tender, pleasurable self-
> pity. Whatever life held in the future for her, it would prove to reside in this rimless past,
> approaching and then fading like the gong of a crossing bell.

Cora and Sharon are among Morris' most vivid and moving creations, male
or female. He induces the reader to admire Cora, for all her alienation, her
inability to love and be loved, because of the dignity she maintains in the
face of failure. Like William Faulkner's Dilsey, she endures. Sharon is a more
positive portrait. She gives up some of the emotional attachments humans
are supposed to need, but unlike the other characters, she is aware of what
she has sacrificed. She is a Huck Finn in reverse, fleeing the territory and its
lovelessness to seek her independence in her own way, gaining—as do all of
Morris' best characters—self-knowledge along the way. Americans can save
themselves, Morris suggests, through the strength of their imaginations and
their individuality.

The reader's awareness of Morris' intentions with his observations about
the relationship between a place and the character of its inhabitants, the
pervasive absence of love in so many American lives, the horror of the banal,
failed and compromised American dreams, and the hold Americans allow the
past to have over them may depend somewhat on how familiar he is with the
rest of the writer's work. Morris has frequently said that his novels grow out
of each other, and *Plains Song* is clearly the product of forty years of acute
analysis and reexamination of aspects of the American character which most
other contemporary novelists bypass as being too prosaic.

Morris continues to amaze his loyal readers with how much freshness he
is able to discover in his traditional subjects, delving here where he has not
been before, treating the American woman with a sympathy and depth new
to him while avoiding the pitfalls of sexual politics. Readers who demand that
their literary encounters with the past be infused with nostalgia will be disappointed with Morris' distinctively tough-minded approach. Morris has
always seen nostalgia as a major obstacle in America's development. Other
readers may object to the novel's plotlessness, although Morris has always
emphasized character, theme, and style at the expense of the story. Perhaps
the most notable aspect of *Plains Song* is its style. Morris, unlike most writers
who fade quickly after passing middle age, writes as succinctly and poetically
as he ever did, choosing precisely the right image to unite character and

theme. His elliptical treatment of time gives this short novel an almost epic scope, convincing the reader that he has seen many complete lives in depth.

Many reviewers called *Plains Song* Morris' highest achievement since *Ceremony in Lone Tree* (1960), and this redoubtable master of evoking time and place and delineating the American character is near the height of his powers here. The praise the novel has received together with its winning the American Book Award may signal that this literary maverick, who has always eschewed the fashionable subjects and self-promoting gestures, may finally be receiving the recognition he has long deserved.

Michael Adams

POLITICS AND IDEOLOGY IN THE AGE OF THE CIVIL WAR

Author: Eric Foner (1943-   )
Publisher: Oxford University Press (New York). 250 pp. $13.95
Type of work: Essays
Time: 1830-1877
Locale: The United States

The interplay of race, class, and political ideology with respect to the causes and consequences of the American Civil War

Eric Foner's collection of essays *Politics and Ideology in the Age of the Civil War* is a refreshing departure from the direction the historiography of this field has taken in the past decade. The study of the Civil War and Reconstruction era needs the challenge of new approaches and ideas which the author provides. In the 1970's, political historians became somewhat beleaguered by charges from a generation of "new social" historians that scholarship must shift from the traditional emphasis on institutions, politics, and ideas to subfields of social investigation in which quantifiable data can be utilized. Many historians who continued to research and write in the field of political history began to ignore pointedly ideology as well as national issues and explain voter behavior in terms of ethnocultural affiliations and other social factors. Thus, historical scholarship became increasingly fragmented as researchers sought the social roots of ideas. Rather than taking ideas seriously in their own right, many historians attempted to study them either as direct reflections of underlying social processes or as inferences from statistically ascertainable data about human behavior. Customs, values, and psychological motivations began to take the place of ideas.

Foner's collection of essays, most of which were previously published, address major concerns ignored in recent years: politics and ideology. Written between 1965 and 1980, they offer interpretations with respect to the causes and consequences of the Civil War and reflect the author's ongoing desire to reintegrate the political, social, and intellectual history of the period. The major theme running through many of the essays is "the interplay in a society undergoing both a sectional confrontation and an economic revolution." He describes the conflict which occurred between the American tradition of republican government and the complex, interrelated issues of race, class, and ethnicity. In addition, Foner documents the dichotomy of maintaining a society based on freedoms derived from natural law constantly being fractured by slavery, sectionalism, and other devisive forces.

Fundamentally, Foner reasserts the centrality of the Civil War to the people of this period. The first section of the book deals with the causes of the sectional conflict, the second discusses the antislavery movement, and a final group of essays treats land and labor after the war, especially the way in which the complex issues of race, class, and ethnicity affected Reconstruction and the evolution of radical movements. A consistent pattern discerned by the author is the contradiction between republican ideology (a lasting legacy of the American Revolution) and the expansion of capitalism. This tension between "virtue and commerce" posed ideological problems for the anti-slavery movement, shaped the debates of the Reconstruction era, and affected virtually every subsequent effort to recast American society. A second theme is the development of an American radicalism based on economic independence as the key to personal freedom.

Foner is at his best in dealing with the causes of the Civil War. In the essay entitled "Politics, Ideology, and the Origins of the American Civil War," he carefully chronicles how the American political system became increasingly ineffective as a mechanism for relieving social tensions, ordering group conflict, and integrating the society. National political parties attempted to forge alliances between political elites in various sections of the country. As the North and South took different paths of economic and social development, however, and as contrasting value systems and ideologies emerged with respect to the question of slavery, the political system came under chronic disruptive pressures. This intrusion of sectional ideology into the political system served to exacerbate social and sectional conflicts.

Foner brings the question of causation back to the central issue of viewing the entire sectional conflict as a battle to determine the character of the nation's future. He points out that the Republicans succeeded in developing a coherent ideology which, despite some internal ambiguities and contradictions, incorporated the fundamental values and expectations of a majority of Northerners. The party rested on a fundamental commitment to the Northern social order and espoused the virtues of social mobility, enterprise, materialism, and the ascendence of the self-made man. It also fused older antislavery arguments with the idea that "Slave Power" posed a threat to Northern free labor and democratic values, tapping the egalitarian outlook which lay at the heart of Northern society. The South—characterized as a backward, stagnant, aristocratic society, totally alien to the Nothern social order—was faced with deciding whether to remain loyal to the nation or loyal to itself and the social order created by its "peculiar institution." In this lucid and brilliant analysis, the author correctly concludes that the onset of civil war illustrated that "the Constitution and national political system had failed in the difficult task of creating a nation—only the Civil War itself would accomplish it."

In "Abolitionism and the Labor Movement in Ante-bellum America," Foner discusses the tensions that existed between the labor movement and evangelical abolitionism. Abolitionists viewed slavery not as a class relationship, but as a system of arbitrary and illegitimate power exercised by one individual over another. The intense individualism of the abolitionists cut them off from laborers who viewed "the Lords of the Loom and Lords of the

Lash," the factory owner and slaveowner, as nonproducers who fattened on the fruits of the labor of others. To the abolitionists, the industrialists were objectionable because of their proslavery political stance rather than their treatment of employees.

Foner traces the interplay of ideologies and political processes, through which the free soil movement became the meeting ground for the two strands of antislavery thought which had remained estranged in the 1830's and 1840's. The ideological debate between labor and abolition was solved by the early Republican Party, for which the difference between Northern and Southern labor became a potent political rallying cry. Republicans absorbed much of the abolitionist moral fervor while making it politically respectable and abandoning the abolitionist demand for equal rights for free blacks. They also promoted a conception of labor and freedom that had much in common with the themes articulated by the labor movement. Therefore, the party identified itself with the aspirations of Northern labor in a way abolitionists never did, but it helped turn those aspirations into a critique of the South, not an attack on the Northern social order.

In a challenging essay entitled "Reconstruction and the Crisis of Free Labor," Foner asserts that central to the process of Reconstruction, both Northern and Southern, was the transformation of labor relations and the emergence of widespread tension between capital and labor as the principal economic and political problem of the period. In the South, planters had to adjust to their new status as employers, and freemen faced the difficult transition from slave to laborer. While the Southern situation involved a revolution in social and racial relations in the North the process of change was more subtle. The antebellum system of labor was not overthrown, but the Civil War ushered in new forms of industrial organization and labor discipline. Furthermore, the prewar free labor ideology of harmony between diverse economic groups seemed increasingly less plausible.

The author offers a brilliant analysis of the evolution of the South's labor system during Reconstruction. Planters, believing that freemen could never achieve the internal self-discipline necessary for self-directed labor, contended that only legal and physical compulsion would make the black work. Foner suggests that while complaints about black laziness in reality reflected a desire by the freedmen for autonomy and freedom from the impersonal marketplace. Blacks rejected the meretricious charms of capitalism and "King Cotton"; and turned to food crops as a first priority, much as did the antebellum white yeomen. Ultimately, a system of tenancy and cotton production was fastened on the region by the "Redeemers" who mobilized the various state legislative, executive, and judicial institutions toward the goal of labor control. With great perception, Foner notes that by 1877 both the North and the South were having to face the question of preserving social order in the face of a large, propertyless class of laborers. Thus,

Reconstruction came full circle. It began with southerners trying to adjust to the northern system of free labor. It ended with northerners having to accept the reality of conflict between capital and labor—a reality that southerners, white and black alike, had understood all along.

Foner's social and economic cosmology sometimes gets in the way of his scholarship. Too much emphasis is perhaps placed on viewing this period in terms of class considerations. Collectively, some of Foner's essays emphasize the aspirations and ideology of the labor movement at the expense of larger economic, social, and sectional factors. Perhaps he gives organized labor an undeserved central place and influence in American life during this period. Nevertheless, his broad and deep analysis is too sophisticated to be described as "Marxist" or in terms of some other simplistic interpretive model. Simply put, Foner's essays collectively offer a refreshing new synthesis of the Civil War and Reconstruction era that will profoundly influence scholarship in this field for decades to come.

Michael C. Robinson

THE PROGRESSIVE PRESIDENTS
Roosevelt, Wilson, Roosevelt, Johnson

Author: John Morton Blum (1921-   )
Publisher: W. W. Norton and Company (New York). 221 pp. $11.95
Type of work: History and political science
Time: 1901-1969
Locale: The United States

A survey and analysis of the presidential administrations of Theodore Roosevelt, Woodrow Wilson, Franklin D. Roosevelt, and Lyndon Johnson highlighting their respective contributions and failings in the name of progressive liberalism

> *Principal personages:*
> THEODORE ROOSEVELT, twenty-sixth President of the United States, 1901-1909
> WOODROW WILSON, twenty-eighth President of the United States, 1913-1921
> FRANKLIN D. ROOSEVELT, thirty-second President of the United States, 1933-1945
> LYNDON B. JOHNSON, thirty-sixth President of the United States, 1963-1969

John Morton Blum clearly ranks among the foremost American historians on the political course of twentieth century United States domestic affairs. Through such earlier works as *The Republican Roosevelt, Woodrow Wilson and the Politics of Morality*, and *Roosevelt and Morgenthau*, John Blum has established a respected view of the presidency in contemporary American history and a cohesive portrait of the potential of that office. While profiles on American presidents are not rare, Blum has repeatedly written on the subject from the perspective of presidential leadership in relation to national policy and the American political culture.

The Progressive Presidents is essentially a continuation of this approach modified by contemporary events. On the one hand, the author extends his analysis of presidential leadership to include Lyndon B. Johnson; something of a deviation from his traditional emphasis upon the first half of the twentieth century. On the other hand, he presents a strong undercurrent of reexamination of the liberal political faith—an ideological belief that has fallen upon hard times in recent years.

Blum's work in no way attempts to disguise the fact that he personally retains an unshaken belief in the merits of progressive liberalism. Nevertheless he is well aware of the current malaise that hangs over left-of-center political values as a result of such events as the Vietnam War, the increased size and cost of governmental activities, and the disappointments associated with White House leadership. To a certain extent, then, *The Progressive Presidents* is an attempt to rejuvenate the tattered liberal philosophy by examining its twentieth century foundations in the hopes of uncovering both its more problematic areas and the continuing strength of its vision.

The focus of this volume represents a conscious effort to survey liberalism's twentieth century patterns in relation to a hallmark of that ideology's faith: an unswerving commitment to presidential policy direction. In selecting the presidential administrations of the two Roosevelts, Wilson, and Johnson, Blum is directing his attention toward the four chief executives most commonly associated with a strong and expansive interpretation of the role of the presidency in Federalism. Despite the fact that each of these presidential leaders experienced varying foreign and domestic challenges, the common denominator that runs through their administrations is the vision of an almost messianic chief executive positioned to direct the course of events. Beginning with the Theodore Roosevelt years, the office of the president has consistently been the most visible symbol of American policy and the processes which help to produce it. For traditional liberals in American political thought, such an expansive presidential role has been the vanguard of progressive growth in the realization of the American Dream. The absence of an emphasis upon such presidents as William Howard Taft, Warren G. Harding, and even Dwight D. Eisenhower is, at least indirectly, a critical evaluation of their unwillingness to grasp a similar vision.

Ironically the liberal faith in an enlarged presidential leadership became subject to increasingly vehement criticism not only from the more conservative circles, but also from those further to the left. While the conservative view of the presidency can be traced as far back as the formation of the Republic and the legacy of arbitrary British colonial authorities, the more radical left is essentially a twentieth century phenomenon. In reaction to the almost inevitable shortcomings which the rising expectations of forceful executive reform leadership produced, serious questions emerged concerning the relative merits and value of so potent a presidency. Arthur M. Schlesinger, Jr.'s *The Imperial Presidency* in 1973 was one such reaction directed, in part, to the excesses perceived in the Johnson-Nixon era so clouded by the war in Southeast Asia. In a deeper sense, however, the critical reaction from the left was also a commentary upon the frustrations inherent in the political process which seemed structured to convert almost utopian progressive goals into a compromised gradualism. The failure of an enlarged presidential role to bulldoze a dream into reality produced a growing disenchantment with both liberalism and its inherent beliefs.

Blum is well aware of these trends and the nature of the criticisms being expressed. *The Progressive Presidents*, thus, does not apologize for the liberal philosophy but attempts to discover its roots, the courses it has taken in twentieth century American life, and the misdirection which has occasionally dampened its image.

Beginning with Theodore Roosevelt, the president traditionally most associated with initiating the marriage between progressive reform and presidential leadership, the author examines his personal view of the office and his efforts to alter its role. Perhaps more than any other president, Theodore Roosevelt was responsible for creating the image of the office of the president as being accountable for the direction of governmental policy. By spurring the nation into both the international arena and the commitment to domestic reform, Roosevelt established a precedent of aggressive executive leadership which eventually came to be the yardstick by which future presidents, and even governors and mayors, would be judged.

Yet in spite of his larger-than-life leadership style, Theodore Roosevelt remained fully cognizant of the realities of the political process. Despite the enlargement of the presidential role in that process, many of the particulars of his policies were, in retrospect, rather moderate. In terms of the progressive dream, much remained yet to be done, and the subsequent Taft Administration did little to enlarge upon the progressive Roosevelt foundations.

After Theodore Roosevelt, the mantel of reform leadership passed into the hands of the Democratic Party where it has remained, with few exceptions, to the present. Except for two distinct administrations under Grover Cleveland, the Democratic Party had been out of national power since the 1850's. As a result of the 1912 presidential election, however, the party roared into the forefront of progressivism under the leadership of Woodrow Wilson. Wilson shared with Roosevelt a positive belief in the power of the presidency as a forum for policy coordination. Yet Wilson added to this vision a sense of moral righteousness which transcended the Roosevelt hard-line approach. The son of a Protestant minister and a political scientist at Princeton before entering public politics, Wilson transformed the presidency into a pulpit dedicated to reform in the public interest. Under Wilson, the role of president was one of public educator and spokesman for the public interest and worked as a counterbalance to the established and more limited interests in Congress. The moral crusade of the Wilson years came close to fulfilling the brash beginnings set under Theodore Roosevelt in both domestic and foreign policy.

Yet in spite of the high idealism reached during Wilson's presidency, the limitations again became apparent through the unexpected disillusionment of World War I and the Versailles Treaty failure. Woodrow Wilson's commitment to the ideal increasingly lost touch with the political process which was capable of bringing that vision to reality. Once separated from the process, either consciously or unconsciously, the presidential leadership so essential to progressive reform lost its value. Worse still, misguided efforts in the presidency could become a genuine liability to a cause if perceived as being divorced from the mainstream.

The perceived excesses of Wilsonian idealism resulted in a sudden dissatisfaction with the reformist impulse and the decade during which the presidency reined. While Herbert Hoover may not have been the classic conservative president as commonly assumed, the sweeping disaster of the

Great Depression's onslaught forever exempted him from an association with progressive reform. It was not until the election of Franklin D. Roosevelt that meaningful alterations and adjustments in the American system returned the presidency to the mainstream of political culture.

Arguably Franklin D. Roosevelt (FDR) was one of the most loved and hated of twentieth century American presidents. To the present, Roosevelt has become a scale by which many Americans, both in and out of active politics, measure their political leanings. Blum, who has written extensively on Franklin Roosevelt, clearly places the Democratic Roosevelt within the tradition of presidential leadership previously established. While both Theodore Roosevelt and Woodrow Wilson certainly faced assorted crises, neither experienced the sheer magnitude of the challenges related to the Depression and World War II.

In certain respects FDR was the beneficiary of the enlarged presidency. Perhaps even indirectly, the spread of authoritarian leadership styles in Europe could be viewed as creating a social and political climate receptive to executive dominance in national affairs. Yet despite the incredible flood of New Deal legislation and executive orders, Roosevelt's reformist urge largely remained within the mainstream of the political culture. As Blum emphasizes, the New Deal was radical but only in its scope, not in its structural intent. In a manner similar to both Theodore Roosevelt and Woodrow Wilson, FDR's reform efforts aimed at revitalizing the traditional American Dream— not attacking it. FDR was determined, like the earlier presidents, to foster executive leadership within both the government and the political culture of the nation. It would not be difficult, as the author implies, to imagine FDR as a kind of synthesis of Theodore Roosevelt's boldness, but without the rougher edges, and Woodrow Wilson's highminded idealism, but without the excessive moralism. Most importantly, however, FDR was in a position to benefit from the failings of the previous reform eras.

The result was a progressive presidency that forged an atmosphere of reform well within the confines of mainstream opinion and structure. Although capable of failings, perhaps most graphically with the so-called "Court Packing" episode, FDR's unprecedented twelve years in the White House rarely fell victim to the leadership crises that marred the final days of Theodore Roosevelt and Woodrow Wilson. This accomplishment was in large part due to FDR's ability to discipline his own vision of what was possible. Blum repeatedly stresses the realization by FDR that, in both domestic and foreign affairs, all that perhaps should be done was not always compatible with all that could be achieved. The acceptance of the limitations of presidential leadership, as well as the dynamics of that role, formed the central component of FDR's political longevity.

To quote Blum, Lyndon B. Johnson lacked "the animal energy of Theodore Roosevelt, the eloquence of Woodrow Wilson, the wit and charm of FDR."

Yet the absence of these traits did not deter Johnson from positioning himself in the progressive presidential tradition. As Blum suggests, Lyndon Johnson was perhaps less comfortable in the presidency than the two Roosevelts and Wilson, but his determination to expand upon the liberal agenda was nevertheless genuine. In addition, few chief executives of the past could match the political credentials of congressional experience that Johnson possessed.

Curiously, Blum is of the opinion that Johnson's compelling desire to promote a progressive agenda through the sheer forcefulness of executive will clashed uncomfortably with Johnson's own presidential manner. Superficially, Johnson appeared to be operating well within the established parameters of presidential leadership, it was the often crude and unrelenting nature of that style which undermined his appeal. Insisting upon an almost militaristic loyalty from his staff, Johnson's approach to the American public carried similar overtones. Despite his frequent capacity for securing congressional support for his domestic and foreign initiatives, rarely did there emerge a sense that Johnson's policies were the product of a national consensus. The initial admiration which surrounded his ability to get his programs accepted in Congress later translated into an uncomfortable sense that Johnson was not leading the national will but ordering it.

Although more critical of Johnson than the other presidents surveyed here, Blum nevertheless accepts him as an integral component of the liberal progressive tradition he personally admires. In an attempt to clarify that tradition, Blum's analysis in *The Progressive Presidents* may appear less than objective. A truer appreciation, however, may rest with the fact that this work serves as a reminder of a rich tradition which, despite its current lack of direction, continues to be an integral feature of the American Dream.

Terry Alan Baney

PUFFBALL

Author: Fay Weldon (1933-   )
Publisher: Summit Books (New York). 248 pp. $10.95
Type of work: Novel
Time: The present
Locale: Somerset and London

A pregnant child-wife is beset by the evils of contemporary London and the evils of ancient rural witchcraft

> *Principal characters:*
> LIFFEY LEE-FOX, a pregnant and immature wife
> RICHARD LEE-FOX, her husband, a junior assistant brand manager for soups
> MABS PIERCE, a Somerset witch
> TUCKER PIERCE, her husband
> AUDREY PIERCE, her oldest daughter
> MRS. TREE, Mabs's mother
> RAY NASH, a professional gourmet and friend of the Lee-Foxes
> BELLA NASH, his wife and colleague, also a friend of the Lee-Foxes

The title of Fay Weldon's novel refers to the fungus which resembles a pregnant swelling, has an evil reputation as a potion ingredient among herbalist witches and, for the gourmet, is delicious and cheeselike when grilled with meat. This symbol provides only a mild hint of the complexity of the novel.

Other writers have packed more into shorter novels, but Weldon does not pack, in the sense of creating something dense in the manner of Stella Gibbons or Evelyn Waugh. The word "economical" has been used to describe her work. Her prose style is indeed economical: short sentences, paragraphs, and chapters. It would be absurd, however, to call a novel "economical" which has twenty-six noteworthy characters creating a tangle of plots and subplots.

What Weldon attempts to depict is a massive web of plots and characters. The novel contains a technical, clinical view of motherhood and a metaphorical view of motherhood; an omniscient authorial voice which deals even-handedly with science and witchcraft; a witchcraft comedy of errors with misapplied potions; a guilty sex-farce comedy of errors; a town-and-country conflict with incidental urban scenes involving hippie squatters, open-marriage gourmets, disapproving in-laws, sex-starved secretaries, and wise children, as well as rustic types sillier than those of Thomas Hardy but nobler than those of Evelyn Waugh.

The series of "Inside Liffey" interchapters explain what happens in Liffey Lee-Fox's body when she is on the pill, when she is first off the pill, why she gets pregnant at one time and not some other times, and what is happening to her husband Richard Lee-Fox's sperm. Thorough research is diluted with dashes of whimsy. At first, these interchapters may strike the reader as "public service" padding: good information, bad literature.

It becomes increasingly apparent, however, that something new and odd is being perpetrated. If Liffey and Richard, and Mabs and Tucker Pierce knew any of this "inside" information, all their fears, jealousy, and guilt would vanish. It is not Liffey's fault that she does not get pregnant sooner; it is not Tucker who fathers her child. The authorial voice, and the reader, know things that the characters can never know.

Clearly, women, and men, must act in massive ignorance about the minute-to-minute activities inside their bodies. The reader, however, is told more than the most expert, continuously monitoring medical team could know, more than readers will want to know, given that this information does not connect to any developed notion of fate or providence. The omniscient narrator does not control, sympathize, laugh, judge, or marvel.

On another level, the readers are asked to forget what they omnisciently know, and sympathize with Liffey as the potential victim of everything evil in the past and present that hates motherhood. Liffey is a woman of no distinction, except as a mother, and it is only through motherhood, exemplified in her unborn child mystically speaking words of comfort, that she has a chance for survival.

Liffey as a mother is trapped between the inscrutable workings of her body and witchcraft, which Weldon has researched as thoroughly as she has gynecology. The herbalism of witchcraft interacts with gynecology when the "Inside Liffey" interchapters explain what effect the potions are having on Liffey and her baby. The less rationally explainable aspects of witchcraft are given weight in the novel by the simple fact that they work. Mabs's most notable failures are amply foreshadowed by her mother Mrs. Tree's cautions that witchcraft directed against an innocent rebounds on the witch.

Mabs's miscalculations create a comedy of potion errors. Richard and his homely secretary, Miss Martin, share a love potion. A drug that will cause Liffey to abort is given in too small a dose and prevents a natural miscarriage. Mabs knowingly takes a temper-unleashing drug and is surprised at how much control she loses of the situation as a result.

Richard's loss of control of his sex drive and loss of his sense of loyalty to Liffey generate the most detailed and uninteresting comedy of errors: a tedious sex farce in the manner of John Wain's lesser novels. Nothing Richard thinks or does as a result of looking for sexual gratification while Liffey is pregnant is new or interesting to readers of contemporary British fiction. He beds his and Liffey's friend Bella Nash, Bella's *au pair*, two secretaries, an actress, and a young prostitute. Bella's husband, Ray Nash, has an affair of his own, and he and Richard and Bella come to blows and communal soul-searching. Weldon presents a quick flatly drawn sketch of the hippies who occupy Richard and Liffey's London flat and their affairs which end in tragedy as one of the women has a stillborn infant. The freshest, most interesting characters in the London scenes are Tony and Tina Nash, Ray and Bella's children. They are clearly more decent and sensitive than their parents. The same is true of Mabs and Tucker's children.

Mabs and Tucker and their children seem researched rather than observed and are, therefore, flat in every sense. Weldon attempts to invest them with ordinariness, to show that the local witch is accepted, yet feared, as a necessary evil in the rural community. Her peers know about her "crushing spells" that have left her rivals and enemies maimed for life. The medical establishment sees her as an abusive parent whose home remedies are part of the abuse she gives her children.

It is suggested that Mabs's mother and Mabs's daughter, Audrey Pierce, possess sensitivity and intelligence and lack the desire to hurt with witchcraft that Mabs and her sister possess. The novel suggests that witchcraft can become a channel for thwarted opportunity and neglected education, for good or ill.

Readers will be intrigued and dazzled by the sheer audacity of attempting so much, but the most impressive juggler of diverse objects must have a finish and risks disappointment and anticlimax. Liffey, in labor, is deserted by the contemporary hardness and meanness of her friends and husband at Mabs's home. She can be saved only by the strength her baby gives her and the slight chance that Audrey, the young witch, will bring a doctor. This scene is very well done, full of suspense, but the suspense has nowhere to go. If Liffey dies, or if the baby dies, the power of goodness and normality has been defeated and the overall lightness and liveliness of the novel cannot justify such grimness. If she lives and prospers, with her baby, the novel must dredge up some superhuman role for Liffey, surrounded by enemies, or, in the few remaining pages, reform and redeem husband, friends, witch, and all so that normality triumphs in a rather smug way. *Puffball* is an interesting failure. Like Kingsley Amis in *The Green Man*, Weldon seeks to rejuvenate the novel with lashings of the occult, but the occult does not lend itself to "lashings." It has various workable forms from *Wuthering Heights* to *Rosemary's Baby*, but all the workable forms involve dominance of the occult itself. The light novel of the occult has not yet found an audience.

It is only fair to add that in spite of gynecological lore and a pregnant heroine and the general ripeness of *Puffball* for praise and attack in Women's Studies seminars, Weldon's attempt deserves a different sort of label. Weldon has been called "the new Margaret Drabble," which is just as nonsensical as calling Drabble "the new Jane Austen." It is not clear what happened to the Brontës, George Eliot, Virginia Woolf, and Dorothy Richardson in this apostolic line.

Austen, Drabble, and Weldon are not any more comparable than Sara K. Knight, Edgar Allan Poe, and Sinclair Lewis. "Sinclair Lewis" is not a random comparison. Like Lewis, Weldon rushes introductory information and anything that smacks of epilogue; and, like Lewis, what Weldon hurries is some-times more promising than what is developed more fully. With more of the interesting children and less of the dull philandering Richard, *Puffball* would have a quality of wise innocence which would make the witchcraft believable without making it ordinary.

For better or worse, the American sense of economy has invaded the home of the well-made and impressionistic novels. Weldon even essays the Amer-ican style of "one-liner" wit. That flat wit, however, needs audacity to make its very flatness part of the joke. When Richard's parents grudgingly concede that Liffey is improving, wearing thicker shirts so that her nipples do not show, that is flat enough wit, but not audacious enough wit.

The interplay of American, Australian, New Zealand, and English tradi-tions and manners may beget solidity without tediousness and lightness with purpose. Weldon may become an important figure in that process, but much difficult labor remains.

T. G. Shults

RAY

Author: Barry Hannah (1942-   )
Publisher: Alfred A. Knopf (New York). 113 pp. $7.95
Type of work: Novel
Time: The present
Locale: Tuscaloosa, Alabama

An eloquent soliloquy in which Ray, a thirty-three-year-old doctor, examines himself and his world

> *Principal characters:*
> RAY, a doctor, husband, lover, drinker, liar, talker, and more
> WESTY, his second wife
> SISTER, a teenage rock and roll singer and lover of Ray
> MR. HOOCH, a friend to Ray, father of Sister, and a poet

Ray is a superbly written, compelling little book which must be ranked among the finest recent works of fiction and which—along with two earlier novels and a collection of short stories—merits Barry Hannah a place in the highest rank of young American writers. At the risk of unfairly and improperly consigning Hannah to the status of "regional writer," it is nevertheless true that many of the themes and attitudes in his work have a distinctly Southern flavor. Like the work of any good writer, however, Hannah's work transcends geographic labels and speaks to matters of common concern. From beginning to end, *Ray* contains a consistently high level of writing—not simply a journalistic narration of facts in the manner of most best-sellers, but rather a masterful manipulation of the language which results in a truly artistic treatment of materials which, in less sure hands, could become vulgar and commonplace.

An image which appears more than once in the work of Barry Hannah and which contains much of what is unique about Southern literature is "the end of the pier where the old liars are still snapping and wheezing at one another." Other similar images come to mind: wizened old-timers squatting and spitting on the porch of a country store; weather-worn dirt farmers with leathery skin and squinting eyes sitting around a warm wood stove while the chilly winds of winter blow outside. These are people who have known or heard or read or imagined the fall of the homeland to the enemy, people who have tried to wrest crops from unyielding soil, people to whom death and loss and violence and cruel caprices of nature are daily affairs. Yet, they are also people who have taken from their suffering and defeat a certain black and laconic humor which allows them to grin wryly about the monstrous jokes of which they are the victims and to emerge with a stubborn and implacable optimism which demonstrates that, as William Faulkner said, man will not merely endure, he will prevail.

If it is true that the poor, rural, war-torn Old South of Faulkner has now become the New South of shopping centers, cloverleaf highways, and modern industry, then it is also true that something still remains of the attitudes engendered by the Old South. In *Ray*, Hannah deftly presents a contemporary man through lenses which have been indelibly colored by hues from the Old South. Or, more accurately stated, Hannah allows his hero to present his own story; and from the words Hannah puts in Ray's mouth it is clear that— contemporary though he is in many ways—Ray also shares much with the old liars at the end of the pier.

The biographical facts about Ray are rather mundane. He is a thirty-three-year-old doctor who practices medicine in Tuscaloosa. He is a former jet pilot who saw death and inflicted death in Vietnam. He is working on his second marriage, this one to a somewhat older woman named Westy. In his medical practice, he attends mostly to common folks, and he has seen his share of shot, cut, and beaten victims. He is an alcoholic capable of debilitating binges and thoughts of suicide. Yet, he is a respected author of medical papers as well as a popular lecturer on American civilization at the local university.

Ray, however, has little to do with biographical facts. Indeed, they are but a skeleton to support a complex, intriguing, enigmatic man who has the sensitivity, imagination, and voice of a poet. Perhaps "voice" is the word which most nearly summarizes Hannah's achievement. For Ray is a talker, an inveterate lover of words, whether his own or Shakespeare's or those of his friend Mr. Hooch. So convincing is Hannah's performance that after a few pages one forgets that Ray is a fictional character being presented through the intermediary of an author, and one hears only the voice of Ray, a voice that by turns is buoyant, profane, angry, bitter, frustrated, gay—but a voice that is always honest. Ray is aware of the paradoxical yearnings and feelings which war within him, of the lust, love, gentleness, and violence which compete for his soul. His voice gives eloquent expression to every warring impulse as he searches to understand and reconcile all of the varied and contradictory elements of his nature and of his world. At one point Ray states,

> The land is full of crashing jets, carbon monoxide, violent wives, and murderous men. There is a great deal of metal and hardness. . . . Why in the hell is there so much cancer today, anyway? Ray's humble opinion is that it serves us . . . right.

Then he can also say,

> I'm dreaming of the day when the Big C will be blown away. I'm dreaming of a world where men and women will have stopped the war and where we will stroll as naked excellent couples under the eye of the sweet Lord again.

Ray is fascinated and mystified by his sexuality, by the incomprehensible nature of women, and by his own inconsistent feelings and relationships with women, including both his wives. "One of the great bad strokes I did was marry the prettiest girl on campus," he says of his first wife. "We got married stupid and frantic, Millicent and me." Then Westy comes into his life: "Westy has an uncommon adventurous warmth to her, a crazy hope in her blue eyes, and a body that will keep a lover occupied. I was gone for her about first sight." When things are good Ray rhapsodizes, "Sweet God, there is nothing like being married to the right woman." Things, however, are not always fresh and new and romantically alive, and Ray despairs: "Yet she's tired. The Westy of the encouraging eyes is tired. At forty-two, she looks as if she's throwing in the towel," and again: ". . . and Westy is colding off like the planet, except I can't believe it in either case." When Westy is not enough, Ray seeks out other women and then wallows in guilt:

> But this lousy barnacle of unfaithfulness would not leave my mind. It is enough to be married to a good woman. It is plenty. Ray, the filthy call of random sex is a killer. It kills all you know of the benevolent order of your new life.

Large- and small-scale violence weigh heavily in Ray's life. He considers jet flying in Vietnam the closest he will ever come to glory, and yet he reproaches himself because his reflexes were too slow to allow him to save a fellow pilot from an enemy missile. Ray daydreams often of the Civil War and sees himself riding into battle, saber held high, under the command of General Jeb Stuart. Further, violence is a legitimate technique of medical practice for Ray. Into the emergency room comes an eighty-year-old-man "who had abused three wives, beaten his youngest son, twelve, with a tire tool, and had borrowed from everybody in Gordo." Asked what he will do when he is well again, the man says, "Kill the sons of bitches." So Ray "yanked out the connections and shut down the monitors and let him pass over the light into hell." In other episodes Ray's sense of justice prompts him to render kicks to the gonads, break ribs, and inflict gunshot wounds.

Like many other Southern writers such as Faulkner and Flannery O'Connor, Hannah has a fertile imagination for creating eccentric characters. Several of these appear in *Ray*, and two in particular deserve mention. Mr. Hooch is an old fellow with more than his share of troubles who talks in phrases of bold imagery and writes poetry that Ray admires and envies. Of his foreman at work, Mr. Hooch says, "He's a big man with the makeup of a warhorse and the mind of a shrieking little woman. I told him little certificates come out his mouth and he ain't got the wings of a bee." Sister is the teenage daughter of Mr. Hooch, lover of Ray, rock and roll singer, and victim of a violent death at the hands of a deranged fundamentalist preacher. "Women are . . . awful. Sister was the one exception," Ray cries.

This propensity for creating eccentric characters is the cause of the only serious flaw in *Ray*. Early in the book, Ray occupies ten pages or so with a rather pointless and rambling story about one Charlie DeSoto and some curious characters with whom DeSoto became involved. This section does little to develop the novel and has about it the distinct scent of a young writer doing a bit of showing off. Let it quickly be noted, however, that minor flaws are forgivable in a work with the quality of *Ray*.

Ray, then, is a work dominated by the themes of lust and violence and peopled by characters of startling originality. No themes are more common than lust and violence, however, and original characters appear in many fictional works. Why, then, is *Ray* different from and better than its brethren? The answer is in the skillful way the material is organized and the brilliance of the language. Hannah does not use traditional chronological development to tell his story but rather divides his book into sixty-two sections ranging in length from a couple of lines to several pages. In these sections Ray, mostly speaks in the first person, but occasionally he speaks to himself in the second person or about himself in the third person. Dividing his material into brief sections allows Hannah to make quick changes in mood and subject matter. One moment Ray is sadly bemoaning the impenetrable mysteries of females, the next he is with Sister sharing a bliss of sex and music, the next he is in a reverie in the sky over Vietnam or on a battlefield with Jeb Stuart. Always there lurks close by the Southern sensibility, the black and laconic humor, the wry grin at the hand fortune has dealt. Always there is the language— strong, clear, colloquial, profane but most of all true. Ray lives. He must, because his voice rises truly and surely from every page of this remarkable book.

L. W. Payne

REICH AND NATION
The Holy Roman Empire as Idea and Reality, 1763-1806

Author: John G. Gagliardo (1933-   )
Publisher: Indiana University Press (Bloomington). 380 pp. $25.00
Type of work: Political and literary history
Time: 1763-1806
Locale: Germany and Austria

A study of the proposals of reform and literary defenses of the Holy Roman Empire

> *Principal personages:*
> NAPOLEON BONAPARTE, military genius and Emperor of France
> KARL VON DALBERG, elector of Cologne and imperial archchancellor
> JOSEPH II, Holy Roman Emperor and head of the House of Habsburg
> FRIEDRICH KARL VON MOSER, political publicist

"The Holy Roman Empire was neither holy, nor Roman, nor an empire." These words of Voltaire have for so long been used to describe the Holy Roman Empire that they almost immediately come to mind whenever that erstwhile institution appears in print or speech. The implication is that by Voltaire's own time—the mid-eighteenth century—the Empire had not only ceased to be what it was intended to be but also no longer served any purpose whatsoever. Consequently, it deserved to expire, and, when it did so in 1806, no one mourned its passing.

As John G. Gagliardo himself points out in his Introduction, historians have recently taken a fresh look at the Holy Roman Empire, and, while not finding that it was indeed holy, Roman, and an empire, they have displayed convincingly that it was more than an anachronism in the minds of many Germans. There are two recent and impressive studies of the Empire in its last days; one is the two-volume work of Karl Otmar von Aretin entitled *Heiliges Römisches Reich, 1776-1806* and the other is this book. Each has a focus that complements the other. Whereas Aretin shows that the officials of large and small German states regarded being part of the Empire a fact of considerable importance, Gagliardo asserts that among popular writers as well there was not only an interest in the fate of the Empire but also substantial desire that it continue.

Before beginning his central thesis, Gagliardo offers three chapters on the nature of the Empire since 1648, including explanations of its constitution, the kinds of territories belonging to it, the major bodies involved in political affairs, and the purposes the Empire was supposed to serve. Nowhere can one find a clearer, more succinct discussion of these complex and often confusing institutions. For those in need of a brief, lucid description of the Empire's structure after 1648, this is indeed the place to look.

The main body of the work is not, however, concerned with institutional history but with the Holy Roman Empire in popular literature. Gagliardo implies that German popular writers gave the Empire little serious thought until after the Seven Years' War, when events confirmed what had begun in 1740: the Holy Roman Empire was entering a period of serious crisis. Gagliardo cites the writings of Friedrich Karl von Moser, a Pietist who had supported Prussia in the Seven Years' War, but who afterward began to wonder if Germany needed to be divided into warring factions or if there were instead a true, uniting "German spirit." Moser believed that at one time there had been such a spirit, but that it had slowly and surely dissolved in the religious strife of the Reformation, the provincialism encouraged by the Treaty of Westphalia (1648), and the Austro-Prussian rivalry. There was but one institution left that reflected that spirit, Moser concluded, and that was the Holy Roman Empire. He proposed no changes in the Empire, because a revival of spirit could not take place through institutional reform. His idea of revival was spiritual, and so he focused his ideas of reform on changing attitudes through education and law.

Moser's works touched off spirited debate in German literary circles, and from then on the Empire remained a favorite topic of discussion, not only because many realized that it was of importance, but also because in the last two decades of the eighteenth century events vital to the future of both it and Germany came tumbling one after another. The first of these events was the formation in 1784 of the League of German Princes. It grew out of a proposal by Joseph II, Holy Roman Emperor and head of the House of Habsburg, to trade the Austrian Netherlands (today's Belgium and Luxembourg) and a title of King to Karl Theodore of Bavaria for Bavaria itself. To prevent this exchange, which would add considerably to Habsburg power in Germany, Frederick the Great of Prussia organized the League of German Princes, which eventually included many of the large, medium, and small princes of the Empire. The two primary antagonists, Joseph and Frederick, viewed the League as a purely Prussian device to stop the Belgian-Bavarian exchange, but the lesser princes who joined and many writers who discussed it looked upon it as a means of injecting new life into the Empire's moribund Diet and courts.

The interest in and amount of literature debating reforms in the Empire did not diminish with the League's dissolution in 1790, because the onset of the French Revolution in 1789 and the shattering events that followed accelerated discussions of the Empire's nature and purpose. In 1797, these discussions took on a new urgency when the very existence of the Empire became a question. The Treaty of Campo Formio, signed that year between Austria and France, called for French annexation of most of the left bank of the Rhine River. Since some larger German states had possessions west of the Rhine, the Treaty provided for their compensation with lands belonging to

Roman Catholic ecclesiastical states. This Treaty represented the first time that the Emperor had agreed to the wholesale destruction of one group of states within the Empire. The secularization of clerical lands not only eliminated one body within the Empire but also destroyed its staunchest and most persistent defenders. Each time thereafter that Austria rose against France and was defeated by Napoleon Bonaparte, the antagonists signed peace treaties that eliminated more and more of the members of the Holy Roman Empire. The Treaty of Lunéville, concluded in 1801, eliminated all of the imperial cities but six; the Final Recess of 1803 confirmed the confiscation of the ecclesiastical lands and the imperial cities; the Treaty of Pressburg in 1805 recognized the Kingdoms of Bavaria and Württemberg and set the stage for the expropriation of the lands of the imperial knights and some counts. By 1806, the Holy Roman Empire was dead indeed, and its formal dissolution in August of that year was simply the recognition of an established fact.

The enormous body of literature that flowed from the pens of political writers from the formation of the League of German Princes to the end of the Empire focused primarily on two issues: the value of the Empire and how it could be reformed. Of those who discussed the Empire's value, the main arguments were that it represented freedom and justice, freedom from both internal and external domination and justice for political systems and individual citizens alike. Those who criticized the Empire for its weakness missed the point, these defenders argued, for the weakness was in terms of political power only, and that was not at all what the Empire represented. It stood not for power but for law, liberty, and an openness to ideas. It was the antithesis of *raison d'état*, and in that it was good.

The reformers, while appreciating the arguments of the defenders, pointed out that the Empire could not stand for any of these virtues if it could not protect itself, and it could not protect itself without significant changes. It is to the reformers that Gagliardo devotes most of his attention and for good reason. The defenders were restricted in their arguments; the reformers' imaginations knew no bounds. The range of suggestions was enormous, many of them forecasting events to come in the nineteenth century. For some, the principal weakness of the Empire was its domination by the two great members, Austria and Prussia, who subordinated the needs and interests of the Empire to their own dynastic policies. Instead of depending upon these two states, these reformers argued, a "third Germany" should be created, a Germany which would have not necessarily its own government but its own means of defense without Austria and Prussia.

For other reformers, the most needed changes were economic. In terms prophesying the *Zollverein* of the nineteenth century, they suggested the abolition of excessive custom duties within the Empire and improved cooperation in the development of roads and canals. While not opposing efforts to protect German manufacturing as a whole, they proposed that free trade within the Empire would enrich all of the German states and many of the German people.

Form of government also became an issue. The particularism and provincialism of the German states seemed inseparable from the existence of the petty German princes; so, some reformers, again influenced by the French Revolution, advocated the creation of a German republic. Only by allowing German citizens to choose their government officials could they regenerate their pride in and devotion to Germany. Moreover, a German republic would inspire its soldiers in the defense of the fatherland, an inspiration sorely lacking in the meek efforts to withstand Napoleon.

Finally, for the young G. W. F. Hegel, the most important reform was to create a state with power. Education, economics, and national spirit were important to the state, Hegel declared, but none could be improved without power. Forecasting, perhaps, the events surrounding the unification of Germany by Prussia in 1871, Hegel advocated that the first step toward reestablishing Germany would have to be military, led if necessary by an imperial dictator.

Gagliardo explains in exemplary fashion these and other reform ideas and literary defenses of the Empire, but, when he is finished, the reader is still left with a few nagging questions. Do these writers, not as a group but as individuals or in some cases schools, reflect any particular European intellectual movements? Gagliardo is careful to avoid using the words "Enlightened," "nationalist," "reactionary," and "modernist," and it is probably right that he does so. Nevertheless, so many ideas appear that fit into intellectual movements before and after the Revolutionary period that the reader's mind churns with thoughts of who influenced whom. Probably the ideas were so intertwined with the times that it would be dangerous to speculate about such matters; it is, however, tantalizing to do so.

Finally, one wonders if these thinkers had any significant influence in their own day. The powerful men of the time apparently ignored them, for Gagliardo emphasizes that they made no impact on the course of events. Yet did they have any influence on the intelligent Germans of the time? Did many read their suggestions? Again, these are probably intriguing but in the end unanswerable questions. In any case, Professor Gagliardo has written a marvelous discussion of the demise of the venerable old Empire and of the men who cared for its passing.

Karl A. Roider, Jr.

RESHAPING THE GERMAN RIGHT
Radical Nationalism and Political Change After Bismarck

Author: Geoff Eley (1949-   )
Publisher: Yale University Press (New Haven, Connecticut). 387 pp. $30.00
Type of work: History
Time: 1890-1920
Locale: Germany

A major work of basic research and historiographical criticism on the nature and substance of the right-wing pressure groups in Germany before World War I

Academic historians, like other scholars, spend much of their time and effort writing for one another. A great deal of their work is basically competent, but generally perfunctory and unexciting. They demonstrate their mastery of their craft, but their work is little noted nor long remembered. They receive their recognition from their peers, including tenure and promotions, and after a while their expensive university press books are remaindered out at cut-rate prices. Occasionally, however, a work appears which is head and shoulders above the generally competent. It not only demonstrates that some historian has mastered the secondary literature and has turned up a few interesting new materials from primary sources, but that he or she has developed a challenging thesis which will cause other historians to turn again and again to the work in order to test their own hypotheses and conclusions.

Geoff Eley's book has come very close to this model of excellence. The author, a product of the University of Sussex (England), completed his Ph.D. dissertation on the German Navy League in 1974 under Hartmut Pogge von Strandmann. Although this book is clearly an outgrowth of that dissertation, it has advanced well beyond it in both depth and scope, dealing with significant interpretive matters on the course of German history and with general theoretical questions of political and social history, as well as filling significant gaps in our knowledge of right-wing nationalistic organizations in the Germany of Bismarck and William II.

A work of such excellence is deserving of vigorous critiques, and one hopes that it will be duly acknowledged and debated in the professional journals. The general reader may also perceive apparent shortcomings, some of which should be indicated here. The book sometimes uses an unnecessarily esoteric style and vocabulary. Even allowing for the Anglo-German training of Professor Eley, and the highly scholarly nature of his discourse, it might be suggested that he could have broadened the impact of his work by some judicious copy editing. For example, terms such as "conflate" and "salariat" may obscure where they are intended to enlighten. In addition, many readers will find the leading personalities in Eley's work, men such as Heinrich Class of the Pan-German League, August Keim and J. E. Strochein of the Navy League, and Gustav Stresemann of the National Liberal Party, portrayed as rather lifeless figures instead of the intense, opinionated, and even exciting individuals which they must have been. Aside from the dust cover, there are no visuals in the book. Not only are readers left in the dark about how these people looked, but they are also limited to only verbal descriptions of the visual propaganda which these men developed in profusion to encourage pride in Germandom, a bigger and better fleet, and so on. Yale University Press, which has done a very professional job of producing this volume, would surely have been capable of adding some reproductions of naval posters and other such materials. They were designed to be eye-catchers at the turn of the century. They would doubtless still be so, making the book more attractive and intelligible for the general reader and providing more depth of understanding for the professional scholar. These criticisms aside, however, one must reiterate that Eley, given his scholarly goals, has written a very fine book indeed.

Its theme is the gradual disintegration of the patrician political forms of German conservatism during the period from 1890 to 1914, and the rise of populist agitation on the right wing of the political spectrum. During Bismarck's time, the conservative and the Free Conservative Parties were formed of a "natural" elite, consisting of *Junkers* and other landowning aristocrats, army officers, and high civil servants. Similarly, the bourgeois liberal parties were led by self-appointed notables: well-to-do businessmen, able lawyers and journalists, and a sprinkling of more liberal aristocrats and civil servants. This "politics of notables," so admirably described by Thomas Nipperdey, involved very few people and virtually no political apparatus. Election campaigns were leisurely and gentlemanly, if indeed there was much campaigning at all. The "better people" of any given district simply formed a committee, named their choice, and (depending on the demographics of the district) either won or lost the election.

By the 1880's, and in increasing measure thereafter, the Social Democratic Party and the Catholic Center Party set out to mobilize the masses of voters and thus enlarge their share of the vote. Traditionalist liberals and conservatives at first rejected mobilization of the masses, partly because they did not know how to go about it, and partly because they saw mass politics as crude and beneath their dignity. By the 1890's, however, conservatives and liberals alike saw that they would have to do something to match the electoral appeals of their clerical and socialist opposition. Nationalism, in its various forms, seemed to be the banner around which the masses could be mobilized without undermining the interests of persons of education and property, whether of conservative-agrarian or of liberal-bourgeois orientation. The notables of both of these two groups had been brought together as an alliance of "rye and iron" during the Bismarck years. If the rural and urban masses could be mobilized along nationalistic lines, then the traditional rye and iron elites of the German Empire could retain their power.

Many West German, British, and American historians have quite properly used this theme to emphasize elements of continuity between the nationalism of the Wilhelmian Reich and that of Adolf Hitler's Third Reich. Eckart Kehr, an outcast during the Weimar Republic who has recently become a candidate for historiographical sainthood, argued that the naval policy was the lodestar of the protectionist, anti-Socialist, promonarchical manipulation of the masses to keep the old elites in power. Numerous postwar historians have enlarged upon this argument and stressed the similarities in the nationalistic manipulation of the masses. In an earnest and sometimes angry search for the roots of Nazism, the various right-wing groups became "prefascist" with the old power-elites as the "stirrup holders" for Adolf Hitler.

This general interpretation, which has passed into the "common vocabulary of German historiography" has, according to Eley, "hardened by usage into a dogma." Eley's thesis is that such a dogmatic view explains very little about the reality of German history. On theoretical grounds, he rejects the "functionalist notion of political integration" and the note of "structural determinism" in such an interpretation. On more empirical grounds, he argues that the detailed study of the complexity of the various nationalistic groups shows that they were not simply establishment organizations by which the masses were manipulated by traditional elites. Organizations such as the Agrarian League, the Navy League, the Pan-German League, and the Society for the Eastern Marches were organized and populated by a new breed of right-wing activist, better described as populist than establishment. This new breed was tired of the notables who based their power on social deference and had little interest in mixing with their grass-roots constituents.

These men were convinced that the government of the Kaiser was not patriotic enough, and they brought pressure upon it to change its policies, whether through activities of the electoral process or through a direct political agitation. To be sure, the old elites sought to make use of these organizations when they needed them, as during the Reichstag battles over the naval expansion bills of 1898 and 1906. The groups, however, were not easily or continuously controlled from the top down; instead, Eley finds they were the result of "the widespread self-activation of the subordinate classes."

Small businessmen, minor officials, school teachers, farmers, and even artisans, had been largely ignored by the traditional politics of notables of the conservative and liberal parties. At most they had been the objects of propaganda campaigns. Now these were the local and even the national leaders of the extraparliamentary organizations of the right wing; they changed the nature of German politics. Other historians have recently brought their skills to the study of this question for the English language world, including Abraham J. Peck and William W. Hagen. Eley's book, however, is clearly the most significant treatment of this phenomenon.

Doubtless the scholars who stress continuities between the Second and

Third Reichs, and whom Eley attacks with such skill and vigor, will object that they are not as dogmatic as he presumes. They are well aware of the complexities of Bismarckian and Wilhelmian Germany, and the best of them go out of their way to reject simplistic cause and effect relationships between traditional German nationalism and Nazism. Thus, they may well remain unconvinced by Eley's arguments.

They might also raise some objections to Eley's own emphases and interpretations. For example, Eley has little to say about anti-Semitism within the radical nationalism of the Wilhelmian period. If the pre-1914 populist (*völkisch*) movement was very different from the *völkisch* movements which coalesced into Nazism, as Eley implies, then an explicit contrasting of the roles of anti-Semitism within the movements of the two periods would be useful. Contrariwise, if Jewish Germans could be shown to have been active in the various nationalist leagues, as they were in the national movements of 1848 and 1866-1871, one might be able to pin down important differences between the *völkisch* nationalism of the two periods.

From another viewpoint, one might inquire into the nature of the self-activation versus manipulation dichotomy which Eley develops. Surely the growth of Nazism between 1928 and 1933 shows a combination of the two phenomena. Hitler and many of the Nazi rank and file were surely self-activated populists (*Völkische*) of a particularly malevolent kind: yet, many from the traditional power elites, such as Franz von Papen and Fritz Thyssen, thought the Austrian Corporal and his movement could be manipulated to save the traditional elites from the "ravages" of the republic. They were wrong, of course, but they found out too late. Thus, one could suggest that even *if* Eley is wholly correct in arguing that the commonly accepted generalizations about political manipulation in pre-1914 German politics are in error, there is still significant continuity between the radical nationalisms of the Second and Third Reichs.

Eley's book will doubtless not settle these issues. One volume by an assistant professor at the University of Michigan, no matter how well done, could hardly be expected to do so. Yet, it should raise the questions anew and force all serious historians to refrain from dogmatizing their pet explanations of why German history developed the way it did. As one who has never been convinced that Hitler and Nazism were inevitable for Germany, this reviewer applauds Eley's work; for those who have the professional interest or the stamina to read and absorb it, this book should contribute mightily to the sophistication of their understanding of modern German history.

Gordon R. Mork

THE RETURN OF EVA PERÓN
With The Killings in Trinidad

Author: V. S. Naipaul (1932-   )
Publisher: Alfred A. Knopf (New York). 228 pp. $10.00
Type of work: Essays

Essays on recent social problems in Trinidad, Argentina, and Zaire, concluding with an essay on Conrad's insights into backward and colonial cultures

A pervading sense of despair over mankind's inability to rise above self-interest and its penchant for stupidly destructive acts links the four essays which make up V. S. (Vidiadhar Surajprasad) Naipaul's *The Return of Eva Perón*. Three of the essays focus on particular situations in widely separated countries of the third world—Trinidad, Argentina, and Zaire—which stand as historical exempla of the heart of darkness taking in all; and the fourth is an analysis of Joseph Conrad's somber understanding that most men go mad when denied a clear vision of the world. Naipaul searches for some sign of human excellence struggling to assert itself in these countries, but finds none. It is a depressing book, but so well argued and researched that its melancholy message cannot be dismissed, however unpalatable it may be.

"Michael X and the Black Power Killings in Trinidad" chronicles the aberrant rise and ignominious fall of Michael de Freitas, or Michael X, as he called himself. In brief, Michael X had left Trinidad in 1957, spent fourteen years in England where he was a pimp and drug dealer, had been caught in the spirit of Black Power, achieved newspaper notoriety as a black spokesman, established a commune called Black House in Islington which existed more in words than reality, got in trouble with the law, and, in 1971, returned to Trinidad. There, his megalomania nourished by a very few followers, he began another commune, advertised himself as the best-known black man in the world, and within a year, participated in the murder of three of his followers.

Michael X was a man of limited intellectual ability, but street wise and cunning. If he lacked any moral vision, he did not lack the language of political and social revolution characteristic of the time. He tried to exploit the situation, as exploitation was the only means of growth he understood. He is of interest to Naipaul because he illustrates not simply lack of virtue and common sense, but the near hysteric attempt of a person oppressed in an oppressive system to use for his own the very means which have been used on him. He, however, is unequal to the task. The energies he would take from the system and turn back on it have already worked their distorting power on him, and he is caught in the illusion they present.

Displaying considerable investigative skill, Naipaul reveals a man tormented since childhood by the shame of thwarted expectations, deluded by his own rhetoric and the happy pandering of English newspapers to it, and deceived by the support of secure, self-indulgent, middle-class whites playing at revolution. Michael de Freitas was a fool and a villain, but a victim as well, caught in a historical trap beyond his comprehension. Black Power for him turned out to be a sentimental hoax, a deep corruption. Instead of freedom and power, all it brought him was illusion, madness, and the gallows.

If the story of Michael X provides Naipaul with the text for a meditation on the foolishness of a man, his inquiry into the soul of Argentina illuminates the malaise of a whole society. His operative image is that Argentinian history is best likened to a story by Jorge Luis Borges—unbelievable, yet horribly real. How did a country as big as India, but with a population of only twenty-three million, rich in land, cattle, grain, and oil fall into such social, economic, and moral chaos? What lack of insight precipitated so calamitous a decline from the rich days of the early twentieth century? Argentina has become known for its absurd inflation, its institutionalized torture, terrorism of the right and the left, and a mindless stagnation. Naipaul compares the life of Argentina, full of events, full of crises and deaths, with the mindless life of an ant community. Everything happens, nothing is accomplished. Each year ends as it began.

One Argentinian answer to the perplexities besetting the country has been Perónism. More a political cult than a political party, it gathers and keeps its adherents by enthusiasm and slogans and not by rational civic vision, or plain practicality. Perónism is a species of debased religion with its own unholy family of Juan and Eva Perón. Perón was a sterile god unable to rouse his country to growth, and Eva was a conniving tart. Tart and thief, yet a saint to the shirtless masses, her *descamisados*. She levied tribute from everyone, and dispensed money to the poor who came to her and told her their needs, their miseries. Garish portraits of her in the oil-slick pastels of popular hagiography are everywhere, and when she died she was embalmed by Dr. Ara, the renowed Spanish master, in a process that lasted six months and cost a quarter million dollars.

Whichever aspect of Argentinian culture Naipaul turns to, he finds ruin, illusion, and despair. Argentinian history keeps being erased, peoples' memories fluctuate with the inflation rate, and the Ford Falcons without license plates charge through Buenos Aires carrying the official killers on their rounds. People watch them fearfully and then ignore them. Anyone can be picked up, by accident or design. All who are picked up, however, are beaten, often tortured, sometimes killed, sometimes released. Many simply disappear. The patterns of Argentinian life are mean, repetitive, and meaningless. In eighty pages, Naipaul delineates the curse afflicting the land: Perónism, a debased intellectual life, inflation, a degenerate machismo which seeks to sodomize its women, or place them in a brothel, and the never-ending terror.

It is difficult to ascertain the causes of such disorder in a society, but Naipaul looks back into Argentinian history to find a pervasive thrust of exploitation.

The Indian problem was solved in the nineteenth century by the simple expedient of slaughtering all the Indians. It took thirty years, and then the pampas were free. Argentina was a colony whose great wealth was to be plundered, and the loot taken to Europe. It was a place to come to turn a profit, and nothing more, even to those who became Argentinians. In the early part of this century, Paris supported a population of more than one hundred thousand Argentinians living well on the strength of the peso and the endless supply of beef from the pampas. Time and again Naipaul reports Argentinian sentiments decrying Buenos Aires as a "small town" in spite of its eight million inhabitants, or cynically asserting that there are no professionals in the country, no one who really knows his job. It is a country which has never demanded excellence of its citizens, and as a consequence has never developed character, or this discipline of mind which makes for civilization. It is a land which does not offer a country to its citizens.

Argentina's society is materialistic; it is a simple colonial society created in the most rapacious and decadent phase of imperialism. For men in a society so diminished, machismo, or the humiliation of women, is an easy expression of dominance over a weaker group that compensates in some way for the inescapable inadequacies of a bastard culture. Naipual writes brilliantly and savagely of machismo and the toll it takes. If much of this book is tinged with despair at the sight of so many societies failing their members, the pages describing the debasement of women by machismo are fierce with contempt.

In January of 1975, Naipaul went to Zaire, formerly the Congo, and spent three months investigating the realm of Joseph Mobutu, formerly sergeant in the Force Publique, later General, and now Mobutu Sese Seko Kuku Ngbendu Wa Za Banga, chief of chiefs, absolute ruler. Zaire is ruled according to his vision, his dreams, his whims. The vision, however, is not working, and Zaire is drifting slowly toward the nihilism of the bush. It is a huge country precariously held together by the great river which runs slowly through it. Yet, just beyond the scattered river-bank settlements, just outside the decaying, artifical cities devised long ago by Belgian colonists, there is the jungle, the forest, the bush. The legacy of hateful semi-order left by the Belgians is rapidly disappearing, but no new African order is taking its place. There is reaction against colonial ways and symbols, against the west and the white man, but nothing vital and sustaining is taking their place except the old rhythms of the bush. Every attempt at change has been short-sighted, wrong. Naipaul sums it up in four words: "It is lunacy, despair."

Had a white citizen of one of the developed nations written as melancholy an account as this of the ineffectiveness of the efforts these nations of the third world are making in their attempt to enter the community of nations, he would likely be accused of racism and imperialism. Naipaul, however, born in Trinidad to an Indian family, cannot be so dismissed. His sympathies are clearly with the citizens of these societies who are being so cruelly misled and deceived, even while he remains a severe, austere critic contemptuous of those who, given the opportunity to learn, are not able to develop either the clarity or discipline of mind to rise above the stagnation which surrounds them. It has become too easy to blame the colonial past for ills which are of present making and reflect slovenly habits, egoism, and prejudice.

Naipaul's concluding essay on Conrad reveals a long personal struggle to come to terms with this writer who wrote so acutely of the Colonial experience and of the encounter of the Western mind with the dark gods of the forest, and with the easy illusions the West made itself comfortable with during the Colonial era. Conrad pursued an understanding of the effect living in dark and remote places and dealing with the workings of alien psychologies had on ordinarily clear-headed representatives of Western culture. He found the experience usually brought them low; but as it did so, as in the final turning of a tragedy, a rich, if bleak, insight about the human soul came clear.

Naipaul has written an honest, beautiful, and desperate book. He sees much of the world settling toward chaos and degradation, and life steadily becoming more hopeless for millions. There is no brave old wisdom in the bush, no primitive harmony with nature, no instinctive sense of ecological and social balance. Life is a struggle, and ignorance the great burden carried everywhere.

Howard McCord

RITES OF PASSAGE

Author: William Golding (1911-   )
Publisher: Farrar, Straus and Giroux (New York). 278 pp. $10.95
Type of work: Novel
Time: Post-Napoleonic era
Locale: Atlantic Ocean, from England to the Antipodes

In this fiction concerning a troubled sea voyage during the post-Napoleonic era, Golding treats on several levels of meaning the coming-of-age of a young, well-born English gentleman

Principal characters:
> EDMUND TALBOT, a young Englishman with important political connections who, during the voyage, undergoes a significant "rite of passage" to maturity and moral responsibility
> THE REVEREND ROBERT JAMES COLLEY, a timid young English clergyman who precipitates the tragic events of the novel
> CAPTAIN ANDERSON, chief officer of the vessel and Colley's main persecutor; a cunning despot
> ZENOBIA BROCKLEBANK, a once attractive but aging flirtatious passenger, object of the amorous attentions of Talbot, Colley, Rogers, and several officers of the deck
> LIEUTENANT SUMMERS, an officer born of the lower class who has risen through the ranks because of his competence and integrity
> LIEUTENANT DEVEREL, born a "gentleman," whose civil manner conceals a corrupt, cynical nature
> BILLY ROGERS, the attractive and charming, yet vain and evil Foretopman who is Talbot's chief rival for Zenobia's attentions

Rites of Passage, like most of William Golding's novels, is an extended parable that treats aspects of the great Christian themes of sin and redemption. *Darkness Visible* (1979) examined the impact of revelation, personified by the mystic Matty Windrave, upon both ordinary people and those tainted by supernatural evil. In his parable of apocalypse, Golding intended to show how symbols of Christian redemption continue to break fitfully upon the consciousness of the modern world. The author's most recent novel, presenting this same theme from a different point of view, centers around ordinary people who are tested by evil. *Rites of Passage* reduces the spiritual conflict to a smaller scale, to the parable of a ship's voyage to represent the soul's passage either to sin or redemption.

Golding's title serves as a complex metaphor for at least three different but harmonizing rites of passage. The most obvious one concerns Edmund Talbot's coming-of-age. Through his memoirs, written in the form of a ship's log while he is aboard a decrepit post-Napoleonic vessel-of-the-line, Talbot discloses to the reader, at least initially, the image of a priggish young English aristocrat, patronizing to the lower classes, vain, and politically ambitious. Near the end of the ship's voyage, however, he has changed decidedly for the better. He is now a man, with a man's sense of conscience and responsibility.

The changes that signal Talbot's maturing consciousness are partly internal and partly in response to the conditions of his voyage. He experiences a variety of circumstances that test the strength of his character: he suffers illness at sea; is sexually aroused but is later repulsed by a flirtatious woman of indifferent virtue; is embroiled in the politics of a vessel commanded by a despot; and he is captivated—both his sympathies and moral passions—by a young, feckless English clergyman, the Reverend Robert James Colley, whose ordeal unifies the separate actions of the novel. Through these experiences, Talbot is educated, not by any sudden enlightenment or revelation but gradually, to a proper understanding of the conditions of men and the moral order of things. Basically a decent, conscientious, sensitive young man, he grows in wisdom by casting off his weaknesses—pride, lust, vanity, and indifference. By the end of the book, he has come fully of age. His pride is broken, his lust exposed and chastened, his vanity shamed, and his indifference turned about to moral action.

Just as Talbot undergoes a symbolic initiation, so the crew and passengers change at the point where the vessel "crosses the line" from the Temperate Zone to the Tropical Zone. In Golding's metaphor, the Equatorial Line is a demarcation zone between reason and passion, moral sense and viciousness. Most of the characters aboard the vessel—a "ship of fools" recalling both the older and modern versions of Sebastian Brant's classic *Das Narrenschiff*—are moral simpletons, people not specifically evil but foolishly indifferent to the presence of supernatural evil. The passengers represent a microcosm of ordinary humanity. A lower-class woman gives birth to a child; a servant falls (or is pushed) overboard to his death; a betrothal is announced; a funeral takes place at sea. During the course of the voyage many actions, some significant but most petty, occur as parts of a symbolic drama concerning rituals of human experience: friendships formed and betrayed, justice temporized, life and death played out as rites with some ambiguous meaning.

Similarly, as in Joseph Conrad's *The Nigger of the "Narcissus"*, the ship's crew represent a variety of types. The officers are not simply characters with specific psychological qualities; they symbolize a range of moral attributes, from the devilish Captain Anderson, to the complaisant officers Cumbershum and Deverel, to the honorable Lieutenant Summers. As Talbot comes to understand these people more judiciously, testing them on the basis of reason rather than prejudice, he discovers their true natures. The smug Deverel, he learns, is not a gentleman, although educated as a privileged member of the upper class; and the sensible Summers, although self-educated from his lower-class background, is really a man of integrity and virtue. From Captain Anderson, a menacing figure resembling two of Herman Melville's tormented seamen—Ahab for his monomania and Claggart for his animosity—he learns that overt wickedness, no matter how base, is not the ultimate evil. The evil of sin, he learns, conceals itself within a pleasing disguise.

As the ship approaches the Equator, the passengers and crew, driven to violence by the sun's heat and their various passions, undergo a primitive rite of savagery. The object of their senseless fury is Colley, a devout young clergyman, feckless but well meaning, who, for ambiguous reasons, rouses Anderson's ire. On one level, Anderson reviles Colley's pious sentimentality as pretentious humbug. On another, more deeply psychological level, he hates the clergyman as a symbol of simple virtue, of the kindliness that Anderson has lacked in his life. Darkly vengeful, the Captain persecutes Colley and encourages his officers to bait him. Surrogates for their master's hatred, they force Colley to become intoxicated, strip him naked, and, as he is exhibited to the passengers, ridicule him as he urinates on the deck.

Following his ordeal, an initiation rite that resembles a childish prank, Colley changes from an absurd figure, amusing but insignificant, to one of tragic dimension. He becomes strangely ill, in fact drifts toward death, without uttering a complaint. In some terrible way, he has suffered a spiritual wound. As a kindness, Talbot tries to succor the wretched man and, by accident, comes upon his diary; from fragments of the diary, Talbot pieces together a story of the clergyman's agony.

To understand this story, presented in Golding's usual eliptical fashion, the reader must become involved in a climactic rite of passage, from moral ignorance to enlightenment. Until this point in the novel, one supposes that Captain Anderson, with his virulent and quite insane hatred of Colley, represents evil in the moral scheme of the fable. The reader, however, comes to understand that a more terrible figure than Anderson precipitates the tragic events of Colley's humiliation and death. That figure, unlike the crudely sinister officer, is a physically attractive character, the charming young Foretopman, Billy Rogers. With his handsome face and muscular form, Rogers seduces, more for the sake of vanity than passion, both men and women. He is Talbot's rival—and rival as well of most of the officers—for the attentions of Zenobia Brocklebank. In a parody of Melville's *Billy Budd, Foretopman*, Rogers can be understood as the barely articulate lower-class sailor for whom evil, not good, is the guiding principle. It is Rogers who ignites in Colley a homosexual passion that drives the clergyman to sexual abuse. Exposed as a sinner, Colley cannot face his shame, and he dies. The rest of the characters fit much less securely into the pattern of Melville's novella: Anderson resembles Claggart, and, to a slighter extent Talbot resembles Captain Vere, a man of honor who perceives justice but cannot act.

As the reader comprehends the message of Golding's parable—that an innocent and beautiful appearance may conceal inner corruption—he also passes through a rite that leads to moral knowledge. To experience this ritual fully, however, he must discover the tricky revelation, hidden in ambiguity as Golding customarily hides the moral of his parables, during the course of the action. In this novel, the author presents his clue first indirectly, then directly, lest the casual reader miss the subtle point. Through a vulgar remark of sexual innuendo that Rogers passes off, the reader perceives that the Foretopman has tempted Colley to commit an act of oral sex—a slight enough offense measured by modern standards, but to the clergyman a damnable sin. To the reader, Colley's act appears at worst disgraceful, but not wicked; on the other hand, the motives of the tempter, Rogers, show the mark of sin.

Rites of Passage, a complex, well constructed novel that demonstrates once more Golding's important place among contemporary English novelists, engages the moral imagination. The flaws of the book, however, are quite as obvious as the virtues. By setting the novel in the first half of the nineteenth century and allowing his major character to tell the story as a memoir in the typical effusive style of the Romantics, Golding is bound to put off many readers who prefer a simpler prose style. Worse, the offensive mannerisms of young Talbot—his mean prejudices and snobbery—are certain to distance other readers. Quite as grave a flaw as Talbot's stilted diction or his only partly sympathetic character is the brief role played out by Billy Rogers, whose actions complete Talbot's rites of passage. Although his actions are crucial to an understanding of the parable, Rogers appears late in the novel and his character remains sketchy. As for the parable itself, Golding overloads a fairly simple moral anecdote—that the rites of passage from innocence to experience involve a true perception of evil—into a much heavier theme than is appropriate. By alluding to other voyagers pursuing a great quest—Noah, Coleridge's Ancient Mariner, Melville's Billy Budd—Golding merely shows the pretentiousness of his own fable. Nevertheless, through his art Golding is able to involve the reader's curiosity in working out the fable. In spite of its flaws, *Rites of Passage* is difficult to put aside—or to put out of mind.

Leslie Mittleman

ROBERT LOUIS STEVENSON
A Life Study

Author: Jenni Calder (1941-   )
Publisher: Oxford University Press (New York). Illustrated. 362 pp. $19.95
Type of work: Literary biography
Time: 1850-1894
Locale: Scotland, France, Switzerland, the United States, and the South Pacific

*A life study of Robert Louis Stevenson, exploring and explaining a man and a writer,
with greater emphasis on the man and his personality*

> *Principal personages:*
> ROBERT LOUIS STEVENSON, a novelist, poet,and essayist
> MARGARET STEVENSON (NÉE BALFOUR), his mother
> THOMAS STEVENSON, his father
> FANNY OSBOURNE STEVENSON (NÉE VANDEGRIFT), his wife
> LLOYD OSBOURNE, his step-son

It may come as a surprise to the casual reader to discover that a collected
edition of the works of Robert Louis Stevenson runs to thirty-two volumes,
for that same casual reader probably knows of Stevenson as an author of no
more than three or four adventure novels, mainly for children, a slim volume
of children's verse, and perhaps a few essays. The casual reader is almost sure
to have some remembrance of Stevenson as a gallant young man who struggled
cheerfully against a life-long illness and roamed and died in the most romantic
circumstances. The lack of awareness of the thirty-two volumes is probably
accounted for by the over-awareness of the romantic life.

The life is the main subject of Jenni Calder's book, although she claims it
is not a biography but a life study—an attempt to explore and explain a man
and a writer. The main thrust is made clear early in the work, where Calder
asserts that the most important thing to emerge from a study of Stevenson's
life is that "his genius lay in who and what he was, rather than in the products
of his pen." This may seem to be a startling admission to be found in the life
of a literary figure, but in the case of Stevenson it is clearly correct. Virtually
every page gives testimony to the attractiveness of Stevenson's personality.
The reactions of his English literary friends to the news of his death were
almost entirely in terms of the loss of a beloved, generous, and vivid personality, rather than of the loss of a talented writer and the products of his
genius. That the author herself has fallen under the spell of the man is clear
from the closing pages where she says that "to get to know the man is an
exciting and moving experience."

This dichotomy between man and writer, between what he was and what
he did, raises a fundamental question in biography: whether the life of any
writer has any importance for the outside world other than it *is* the life of a
writer. In the broad, human sense, the life of any man, known in its well-
springs and hidden places, can or even should be of interest to other men.

The proper study of mankind is, after all, man. In a practical sense, however, the life of writers such as Thomas Hardy, Charles Dickens, and Bernard Shaw is of interest or significance precisely because of their works, which can be better understood or appreciated if more is known about their lives. From the critical or scholarly point of view, if not from the theological or philosophical, the life exists for the works, which come first.

Although it may be difficult to re-create at this distance, there can be no denying the attractiveness of Stevenson the man. What he seemed to be was almost what he was. He had virtually no enemies, and he seldom quarreled with anyone. Close friends and casual acquaintances give testimony to their delight in his company. He was physically striking, with a lank frame, dark, deep-set eyes, a full brow, and a face that was mobile and lively. People from Sidney Colvin and Henry James, pillars of the literary establishment, to sea captains and Samoan natives were drawn to him. Wherever he settled, however briefly, friends and admirers would begin to arrive. By every evidence, he was, from his school days in Edinburgh on, something much more than simply a likable chap, a Scottish Dale Carnegie. He was gay and witty in conversation, charming and fun-loving in company. Both men and women fell equally under his spell; he could drink with the boys and talk with the ladies. His eccentricities of dress and manner and his mild iconoclasm were not such as to evoke fear or distrust, but only served to make him more attractive to many. Above all, he was cheerful, and sincerity shone from his striking eyes.

To all of this must be added his openness to experience, his frank delight in other people and in new adventures. Surely it is this quality that explains why he was so good with children; he shared their games, took them at their own valuation, and did not talk down to them. Calder details well this openness, and it is certainly one of the things which makes most of Stevenson's work a pleasure to read. All who knew him commented on the life and vitality, which, while it often must have been simply Stevenson having a good time, was certainly infectious. He gloried in good talk, good wine, and exciting fellowship. Calder shows clearly, however, that there were occasional dark patches in his optimistic cheerfulness; when beset by bouts of illness and drained psychically by the demands of those about him, he could be testy and wounding. It rarely lasted long, however, nor did it happen often, and the reader is more likely to feel "Who can blame him!"

To the portrait of Stevenson must be added the coloring of his physical debility (tuberculosis or something like it) and his renowned cheerfulness and optimism in the face of such adversity. Other romantic elements in the picture would be a reputation like John Keats' for dying young of a wasting disease (though forty-four is not very young and the disease which dogged him all his life was not what killed him), a reputation like Lord Byron's for selflessly taking the part of a native race (although Stevenson's actual efforts for the

Samoans were of no more effect than Byron's for the Greeks), and a reputation like Ernest Hemingway's for testing himself with robust adventuring
(although Stevenson is blessedly free of the rather manic *machismo* of Hemingway).

Finally, the picture is capped by the fact that he was a writer of some talent,
although it is stretching the term to call him a genius. It is astonishing how
everyone insisted that he *was* a writer of genius, even before he had produced
more than a few essays and short stories. There is always this curious distance
between what everyone was sure he was, not merely what he would become,
and what he actually produced. It is simply that people were so taken with
the personality of Stevenson that they could not conceive of him to be other
than a genius.

The personality, then, of Louis Stevenson, as he was always known, dominates this book; and with that as the explicit subject, this is probably the
definitive work. As with many biographies, this work is full of "he probably
felt" and "he would have thought" and "he might have said," but unlike many
biographies it is almost always justified, as far as such things can be, by
reference to actions, letters, and events. Calder has left very few loose ends.
Nor, though under the spell of Stevenson she may be, does the author in any
way idealize or idolize. This book shows Stevenson with all his warts—despite
how amazingly few there are.

His works get relatively brief treatment in this volume, with much generalization and little detail or analysis. Calder rightly emphasizes Stevenson's
power of work (thus the thirty-two volumes) which along with illness is one
of the main themes of the book. The most common picture of Stevenson is
of the man at work, propped up in bed, writing on drawn-up knees. He was
concerned to make money, for money was the sign of his independence. He
was in fact dependent for most of his life upon his parents' largesse, which
they seem to have fairly freely given in spite of their distress at his agnosticism
and bohemian ways. His father, beginning in 1880, provided him with a yearly
payment of £250 and in 1884 gave Stevenson and his wife a house in Bourne-
mouth as a wedding present. After his father's death and Stevenson's removal
to the South Seas, although he was by then making some money on his own,
he still took upon himself the necessity of supporting not only the estate of
Vailima, but also his wife, his step-son, his step-daughter and her husband,
his mother, and assorted Samoans. It is no wonder that Stevenson occasionally
grew fretful about finding the time to proceed with his writing.

Calder frequently touches upon the moral ambiguity of much of Stevenson's
work, the mixed motives, the uncertain allegiances, the morally dubious but
strongly attractive characters. In an essay of 1883, "A Gossip on Romance,"
Stevenson maintains that "drama is the poetry of conduct, romance the poetry
of circumstance." He equates the first with the active and the second with the
passive. He admits to the power of the first, but clearly finds the second the

more attractive, claiming that there is a great deal in both life and literature that is simply amoral; he prefers to concentrate not upon what a man shall choose to do but upon how he manages to do it. Such ideas give the reader an insight not only into why Stevenson was such a poor writer of dramas (he tried four in collaboration with W. E. Henley), but also into his fondness for romance and tale-spinning. There is a certain passivity in some of Stevenson's central characters, such as David Balfour and Jim Hawkins, which results in their being lifted by the wave of circumstance, moved in directions which they might not choose but which are chosen for them.

Calder also deals well with Stevenson's rejection of the harsh morality represented by cold and stony Edinburgh. His goal was, as she says, to articulate a "genuine, unhackneyed, unrestrictive, and above all positive, morality." He was never able actually to pin this down and define it; as a result, he was unjudgmental about other people and their actions, although he was continually bedeviled by his urge to morality, an inescapable legacy of his Scottish upbringing. Calder defines the ultimate problem of Stevenson the man and the writer as the inability, of which he was painfully aware, to organize into a coherent vision his parents, his love for his friends, his marriage, and his art.

It is Calder's contention that in his final years in the South Seas Stevenson was finding challenging and important subjects that were related to contemporary life; she further implies that in the South Sea tales, he was beginning to find his true metier as an explorer of alienation and isolation, much like Joseph Conrad. Scotland would seem to have been his true subject, but because of his ambivalent feelings about it, its past, and his place in it, he was unable to handle Scottish topics with complete ease and satisfaction. There is also in the book a tendency to make Stevenson more of a thinker and a rebel than he actually was. It is true that Stevenson's letters and conversation were much more outspoken about his opinions on those subjects not uncommon to many young men of the late nineteenth century: the loss of faith, the dislike of the bourgeois, the longing to escape, the concern with art. Again, however, most of this is in the person of Stevenson; very little really gets into his published work. It is a disservice to Stevenson, or to any other, to try to make him into something he is not.

What Stevenson is above all else is a writer of romance, indeed one of the best writers of romance in the language; and to be this is no mean thing. As Calder shows and as other critics have noted, Stevenson's romances, at their best, are marked not only by vivid scenes, striking characters, and an attractive style, but also by an attempt, generally successful, to give psychological depth to the characters of romance. This should not lead us to think of Stevenson as a precursor of the modern psychological novel. The difference is in quality, not in kind; it simply means that Stevenson's romances are better romances than almost anyone else's. One has only to compare his writing with that of

Anthony Hope or Rider Haggard to see this. One would like to think that with his cheerful and open personality, Stevenson would have been content to rest with the knowledge that his reputation is secure as the author of *Treasure Island, Kidnapped, The Black Arrow, Dr. Jekyll and Mr. Hyde*, and *A Child's Garden of Verses*, stories and poems that are today as successful as when they were written. Whatever may have been the appeal of the man, and the man is dead but the books live, as a writer his true epitaph is the name the Samoans gave him, Tusitala—the teller of tales. It is a title of no small honor.

Gordon N. Bergquist

ROGER FRY
Art and Life

Author: Frances Spalding (1929-   )
Publisher: University of California Press (Berkeley). 304 pp. $19.50
Type of work: Biography
Time: 1866-1934

The first complete biography of Roger Fry, the prime mover in the famous 1910 exhibition of post-impressionist art in London, author of numerous books and articles explaining modern art to the public, an important member and stimulus of the Bloomsbury group of artists, writers, and thinkers

As a critic and historian who interpreted contemporary trends in art for an entire generation of Englishmen, as an organizer of important and sometimes notorious avant-garde exhibitions, and as a member of the Bloomsbury Group of artists and writers, Roger Fry was a powerful freshet, or series of freshets, amid the swirling cultural tides of early twentieth century Britain, and a full-dress biography of this many-sided man is long overdue. To spice the life, there is considerable sexual interest as well in Fry's extended and often painful courtship of Virginia Woolf's sister, Vanessa, in his affair with an Amazonian Polish Communist, and in his relationship with Helen Anrep, who, when Fry met her, was one of two women living with her Russian husband. There is, in fact, a Frenchwoman who, in love with Fry but assuming, incorrectly, that he failed to return her passion, shot herself on the cliff at Le Havre, her face toward England and Fry.

Frances Spalding has explored and provided new funds of data in a number of areas of Fry's life, and yet, oddly enough, her detailed effort to reconstruct a hitherto neglected aspect of Fry's career—his work as a painter—creates a curious imbalance in her biography, for she almost necessarily is led to make larger claims for the paintings than they can possibly support. Although he took his painting seriously and wanted the world to take it seriously, Fry never could bring himself to commit himself to a career as an artist; nor does he seem to have understood what such commitment necessitated. Thus, he remained a glorified Sunday painter, working away on vacations and during visits to friends. Necessarily, there is good deal of discontinuity in the work, and changes in style and theme often seem to be dictated, not by inner necessity, but by stray and accidental associations. Working alongside Jean Marchand, Fry "developed his use of close-toned subdued hues and an interest in a consistent texture." When the Royal Academy opened an exhibition of Dutch art, Fry entered a Dutch period of his own. Later, visiting the Pissaro Centenary Exhibition and a show of Sisley's work, Fry changed his approach to light and shade and employed a looser brushstroke. If few took him seriously as an artist in his own day, and if almost no one does today, his work as a painter clearly sharpened his perceptions as a critic. Indeed, as Spalding makes clear, what was weakness in one area was strength in another; for, as he regularly translated the techniques of others into his own paintings, so he made room for them, as much as possible, in his critical structures, structures that continued to grow and provide for new responses and fresh insights.

Spalding is particularly useful in tracing the development of Fry's critical attitudes and areas of interest, and she indicates clearly what changed in Fry's perceptions and what remained steady. Married at age thirty but still supported by an allowance from his father, Fry turned increasingly from canvas to criticism. His first efforts were, intriguingly, made at a considerable remove from the region of the avant-garde of which he ultimately made himself a leading citizen; he drew instead upon his knowledge of the Italian Renaissance for a series of books, articles, and lectures, and, in fact, tended to compare the moderns—or the French Impressionists who were the moderns for Fry at the time—quite unfavorably with the Italians. As one might expect, Fry was still the child of the nineteenth century in these early critical ventures and frequently enough revealed an embarrassingly subjective or associative approach to the work (thus a portrait of St. Francis by Giovanni Bellini is "the most human conception of the man in Venetian Art, and the most convincing in the rendering of spiritual passion"). Nevertheless, impelled by his reading, by his association with Bernard Berenson, and by his own insights, Fry increasingly concerned himself with matters of form and design that he ultimately saw at the center of Italian Renaissance art, concerns which became the locus of his evaluation of contemporary art, and which were finally embodied in the famous phrase "significant form."

From Spalding's account, however, it is apparent that Fry might well have become and remained a fixture in the world of old-master scholarship, for it was in this phase of his career that he achieved a series of triumphs—being made art editor of the influential *Athenaeum*, becoming a founding member of the inner circle of the *Burlington Magazine*, and, finally, being appointed curator of the Metropolitan Museum of Art, whose board of trustees was headed by the man who was seen by many as the economic sovereign of the United States, J. P. Morgan. The museum's first effort to hire Fry foundered when Fry sought to negotiate his salary and ran afoul of Morgan's autocratic refusal to negotiate. A second effort succeeded—at a time when Fry was also being offered the directorship of the National Gallery in London. Anyone familiar with the holdings of the Metropolitan will recognize at least some of the paintings that Spalding lists as being bought at Fry's recommendation and will therefore also recognize the importance of Fry's brief association with the institution. It was almost necessarily brief. Fry himself was blind to the virtues of the American landscape artists that the trustees urged upon him. On the other hand, as late as 1906, he could not persuade Morgan to support the purchase of a Degas because it might offend the more conservative element among the trustees and the public, and it was with some difficulty that he did manage to have the museum acquire the Renoir painting *La Famille Charpentier*. Despite it all, Fry might have continued to work for the Metropolitan had he managed to get along with—or, more likely, to toady to— J. P. Morgan, who expected museum employees to act as part of his private court, and it was inevitable that the independent Fry and the captive museum go their own ways, as they did in 1910.

It was only now that, at the age of forty-four, Fry entered the phase of his career that made him a public figure. A chance meeting with the Bloomsburyite Clive Bell gave substance to a plan already lodged in Fry's mind for an exhibition of recent French art, and, with the help of another member of the Bloomsbury circle, Desmond MacCarthy, they fashioned the famous exhibition "Manet and the Post-Impressionists" toward the end of the year Fry left his museum post. Apparently, it was Fry who, unable to find a clearer and more logical designation for the variety of styles gathered at the exhibition, devised the unfortunately broad and unfortunately lasting term "Postimpressionist." Categories and explanations did nothing, of course, to lessen the fury and hostility aroused by the show, which has become a standard symbol of the eternal conflict between creative artist and philistine public, and the story of the British reaction has been told often enough, most recently by Ian Dunlop in *The Shock of the New: Seven Historic Exhibitions of Modern Art*.

Trapped by their island in an artistic backwater, the English were reacting to work that had, in many cases, become old hat on the Continent. A few years later there was a similar reaction to a similar show in the United States. It is part of the merit of Spalding's treatment of Fry, however, that readers come to realize how slowly and painfully Fry had himself awakened to the merits of the avant-garde. Gradually in the course of his criticism and suddenly in an epiphanic moment, he acquired the critical means and approach by which he could come to terms with painters such as Paul Gauguin and Paul Cézanne. The epiphany, as Fry told it, came in front of a still life by Jean-Baptiste Chardin, whose formal means, Fry discovered, could arouse feelings as deep as any awakened in him by the frescoes of the Sistine Chapel. Even the merits of Cézanne, that keystone of the Postimpressionist movement, were not recognized by Fry before 1906, the year of Cézanne's death, and not fully understood until the year of the exhibition itself, when Fry was able to examine a large number of the Frenchman's paintings. He failed utterly to cotton to Henri Matisse when he visited that painter's studio in 1909; in fact, in the best style of the philistines of all nations, he likened Matisse's work to the products of his own seven-year-old daughter. Working, however, with a few attitudes of his own and a good many derived from others he managed, around 1909, to articulate a set of doctrines that, as in the case of his response to the Chardin still life, linked emotional responses in the viewer to the formal elements of the painting. Reprinted in *Vision and Design* in

1920 these doctrines reached and directed the thinking of a large audience. By World War II, *Vision and Design* had acquired something of the standing of a classic, and copies of the book were circulating through American campuses in the familiar Penguin format.

In and out of these events, Spalding weaves the tale of Fry's personal life which, from 1898 on, was colored by the despairing fact of Helen Fry's mental illness. In 1910, the year of disaster at the Metropolitan and of triumph at the Postimpressionist exhibition, he finally had to certify his wife and commit her permanently to a mental institution. Thereafter, he was free for a series of affairs, most importantly with Vanessa Bell, sister of Virginia Woolf, wife of Clive, and one of Fry's portals of entree into the Bloomsbury Group. Indeed, he suffered intensely and at length when Vanessa turned her affection and attention to the painter Duncan Grant, with whom she lived and whose child she bore despite his homosexual inclinations. It was a bitter pill to swallow, but as usual, Fry was capable of throwing himself into furies of work to overcome or compensate for his bitterness.

By the 1920's, Fry was a grand old man of British art, sought for reviews, for books, for help in organizing exhibitions. For a time he grew increasingly formalist, but gradually managed to reconcile his own emphasis on formal matters with the fact that representation can, after all, affect one's emotional responses to a painting. There remained entire realms of modern art he could not accept—expressionism and surrealism, for example. He often seemed distinctly limited in his own circle, and he was frequently denounced as a result. Ultimately, however, with the exhibition of 1910, he redirected the course of British painting, and with *Vision and Design*, he affected the course of British perception. For all of this, Spalding provides a thorough grounding.

Max Halperen

SAINT AUGUSTINE'S PIGEON
The Selected Stories of Evan S. Connell

Author: Evan S. Connell (1924-   )
Edited by Gus Blaisdell
Publisher: North Point Press (San Francisco, California). 291 pp. $12.50
Type of work: Short fiction

A collection of short fiction that deals with a variety of realistically presented characters and situations

Short fiction is a difficult medium, perhaps the most demanding of the literary art forms. Within a relatively brief space, the successful short-story writer must make believers of us. Through the spell cast by compelling psychological delineation, the creation of an evocative atmosphere or sense of place, or a thematically resonant pattern of events, dialogue, and descriptive detail, through all or some combination of these elements, the writer of a short story must bring readers into the world as he sees it and stir their hearts and minds in such a way as to make them feel that they have observed or been made a part of something that is or could be true. There is no disguising a weak short story; neither cleverness of craftsmanship nor a way with words can validate a story with a facile, artificial heart.

All of the short stories in Evan S. Connell's collection *Saint Augustine's Pigeon* are well written and well structured; and most of them deal significantly and compellingly with some aspect of the human situation. Five long stories comprise the core of the collection. Although they are not equal in merit, they are among the most interesting because, when considered together, they reflect a good deal of the range of Connell's vision as well as his artistic strengths and limitations.

Two of the longer stories focus on a highly romantic protagonist who has turned his back on the conventional patterns of society while three treat a middle-aged insurance expert who has outwardly conformed to these conventions but, at the same time, kept his mind and spirit free.

The character of J. D., the protagonist of "The Walls of Avila" and "The Palace of the Moorish Kings," is seen through the point of view of one of his boyhood friends. All of the friends with whom J. D. has corresponded over the years have, like him, dreamed of escaping in one way or another from the humdrum patterns of small-town life. Only J. D., however, has had the courage, enterprise, and initiative to live out the dreams of his youth. He has wandered the face of the earth, living by his wits and savoring the variety and fascination of life, while his friends have hardened into middle age and, in various ways, followed conventional tracks of experience. In "The Walls of Avila," J. D. has returned for a brief visit after ten years of roaming over, and sojourning in, exotic places to meet mingled feelings of fascination, envy, disapproval, and resentment. J. D. discovers that it is impossible to make his friends aware of how the perspective of distance may remove the film of familiarity that hides natural beauty and leads to a recognition of the essential poignance of life. Their minds remain as closed and impenetrable as Avila, an ancient town in Spain whose walls become a symbol of what is absolute, unchanging, and indestructible on its own terms.

"The Palace of the Moorish Kings" focuses on the reaction of J. D.'s friends to his decision to give up his glamorous, free-spirited life and settle down to a career and marriage. Precisely what J. D. is returning to is made evident in the banal conversation which his friends carry on with him when he calls long distance to announce his plans. The final act of humiliation for J. D. lies in the necessity of his turning for help in finding a job to the most successful and the most prosaic of all his friends, who cannot resist the opportunity to chastise him, with grasshopper-and-ant triteness, for having the audacity to live out a boyhood dream. Ironically enough, however, the dominant feeling of his friends is not that of smug self-righteous gratification but of a sense of loss. The end of J. D.'s unconventional career signals the end of their youth.

The three long stories "Arcturus," "Otto and the Magi," and the titular "Saint Augustine's Pigeon" concern themselves with the mind and experiences of a protagonist who is outwardly the opposite of J. D. This set of stories contains the most powerful and ambitious efforts in the collection, although they are not all equally successful. The masterpiece of the set, and indeed of the collection, is "Arcturus," which brilliantly celebrates the virtues of intelligence and strength of character. This powerful story presents us with a variety of vividly drawn characters: a small boy, crafty in his encroachments upon the conventions and good will of the adult world; two hunters who bring the chill of death briefly to the drawing room; an artificially exotic ballerina who lacks soul; a beautiful dying wife and mother who reaches out desperately in an attempt to recapture something glamorous from her past; and a minor diplomat whose charm and sophistication mask a superficial heart and spirit. At the center of all these characters is Muhlbach, the rock-solid husband and father who is suffering his wife's physical decline, understanding without acquiescing servilely or bitterly to her desire to recall momentarily another love, and gradually asserting firmly and unequivocally his superiority as a man to his wife's former lover. At the conclusion of the story, the reader views Muhlbach under the stars through the eyes of his charming obstreperous son. He is the man who can assure his son that the stars will not fall. He is also, in symbolic terms, Arcturus, the warder of the bear.

"Otto and the Magi" is thematically more ambitious but less successful than "Arcturus." The story is more interesting for what it attempts to do than for what it actually accomplishes. It sets out to explore the irrationality of contemporary civilization. The rational or wise man, Muhlbach, still grieving the loss of his wife, has built a bomb shelter in his backyard to protect the future of his children; and, during the course of a social evening, shows it off to two other wise contemporary men, a doctor and a chemist. The essential irrationality of the bomb-shelter cast of mind is exposed through an irrational action of Muhlbach's young son, Otto, which nearly costs his father his life. The force of the story, as the title suggests, is meant to come through the ironic juxtaposition of Christian story with a contemporary situation. There are, however, two flaws in the story—one minor and one major. Although Muhlbach's sardonic reactions to the ludicrously inane illustrations which accompany the government specifications for the bomb shelter are amusing and pertinent to the story's theme, this section of the story is so extended that it interferes with the development of the action. The major flaw lies in the puzzling climactic action of Otto, which is obviously designed to illuminate the central point of the story. Here in a story firmly grounded in realism, psychological plausibility is sacrificed on the altar of symbolic action. Otto's irrational action is meant to reflect a child's intuitive rejection of the quasi-rational bomb-shelter mentality of the contemporary world and to allude obliquely and ironically to the sublime unreasoning wisdom associated with Christian story. Uncharacteristically, however, Connell has stretched our willing suspension of belief to the breaking point for the sake of his theme. It is interesting to compare the quiet, understated, psychologically compelling symbolic ending of "Arcturus" with the high-pitched tone of uncertainty on which "Otto and the Magi" concludes.

"Saint Augustine's Pigeon" is less successful than "Arcturus" but more impressive than "Otto and the Magi." The story deals with the manner in which even the most rational of men, such as Muhlbach the widower, may become the ludicrous victim of the desires of the flesh. The virtues of the story lie in the believability of Muhlbach's thought processes and the blend of the predominantly comic tone with an underlying current of pathos. The weakness of the story is somewhat similar to that of "Otto and the Magi" although not as pronounced. The concluding symbolic action, in which Muhlbach after a night of indignities plays statue for a pigeon, is thematically perfect; but the accumulation of coincidence at the end of the story almost suggests the influence of O. Henry. It is not the chance action of the pigeon that one questions but the fact that it should take place precisely at the point when characters earlier encountered in the story—one of whom has played Columbine to Muhlbach's Harlequin—reappear at a place they have no good reason to be. At this point in this basically realistic story, the brush strokes are too heavy. Nevertheless, the story is redeemed by its comic exuberance. In various ways, harem dancers, a dwarf, a pickpocket, a Bohemian teenager, an overripe cocktail waitress, and a hamster contribute to the decline of Muhlbach from rational man to clown, and to the resonance of the insight he receives into himself and his lot in life.

Of the shorter pieces in the collection, five are particularly noteworthy. Although the situation in "At the Crossroads" is somewhat implausible, it is justified by the evocative symbolic atmosphere of the desert setting; and the story ends on firm psychological ground. Through the juxtaposition of a youthful tramp, whose mind is turned eagerly toward the future, and a dying, half-demented old woman, whose mind travels into the past for sustenance, the reader is presented with a powerful commentary on the nature of life.

"The Fisherman from Chihuahua" is concerned with the impact of a remote and mysterious passion on a prosaic mind. Its success is due to a masterful blend of diverse effects: the psychological action of the story involves several realistically drawn characters and takes place in a dilapidated restaurant which is surrounded by a mysterious symbolic fog.

"The Yellow Raft" is a *tour de force* in which the protagonist, an unnamed navy war pilot in World War II, is scarcely mentioned. Although the main point of the story lies in the downed pilot's struggle to survive the onslaught of the ocean, the reader is not even made aware of the point at which the struggle is lost. Such a narrational strategy intensifies our awareness of the plight of humanity in an alien, chance-ridden universe. "The Yellow Raft" might well be described as a bleaker, more obliquely presented version of Stephen Crane's "The Open Boat." Everything is implicit; there are no philosophical passages extrapolated from the mind of the protagonist; and he is seen briefly and then only from outside. There is also within the brief compass of this story no human force to compensate for the indifference of nature to the plight of man.

"The Caribbean Provedor" and "The Scriptwriter" are hard-edged, skillfully crafted stories which follow the thought processes and experiences of Koerner, a cosmopolitan, somewhat cynical observer of human nature. In the first of these stories, Koerner, an avid chess player, finds himself, as a result of a misunderstanding, caught in a psychological chess game that threatens his life. The second story, which is thematically more provocative, explores the manner in which the death of a brilliant scriptwriter is mocked and robbed of feeling by the qualities of mind which had brought him success.

Three of the remaining four pieces in the collection are competent but undistinguished. "The Marine" makes its point about the dehumanizing effect of war flatly. It lacks the richness of irony and the effectiveness of narrational angle that account for the success of "The Yellow Raft." "The Short Happy Life of Henrietta," "The Corset," and "Promotion" are all stories which rely on too easy an irony for their effects. The final piece, "A Brief Essay on the Subject of Celebrity," is interesting, but it does not contribute significantly to the collection.

William B. Toole III

THE SCAPEGOAT

Author: Mary Lee Settle (1918-   )
Publisher: Random House (New York). 278 pp. $11.95
Type of work: Novel
Time: 1912
Locale: West Virginia

A novel of "The Beulah Quintet" that relates characters and their personal involvements to the beginning crises of major mine strikes and the impending violence

Principal characters:
BEVERLEY AND ANN ELDRIDGE LACEY
MARY ROSE LACEY
ALTHEA LACEY
LILY LACEY
JAKE AND ESSIE CATLETT
EDUARDO PAGANO
CARLO MICHELE
MOONEY MCKARKLE
MOTHER JONES

Despite praise from Granville Hicks, Malcolm Cowley, George Garrett, and other major critics, Mary Lee Settle is a novelist whose career has been marked by neglect and confusion. Many newspaper and television critics who were angered by the selection of *Blood Tie* as the winner of the 1978 National Book Award for Fiction, confessed they had not read the novel nor did they bother to find out what Settle had written previously. Since 1954, Settle has published ten novels.

Settle's latest novel, *The Scapegoat*, is the fourth in "The Beulah Quintet." Perhaps the confusion that surrounds these five novels is due in part to the conflict between Settle's changing conception of the whole and the order in which each was published. When the first three books, *O Beulah Land* (1956), *Know Nothing* (1960) and *Fight Night on a Sweet Saturday* (1964) were ready, Settle wanted them published as a trilogy, but Viking, then her publisher, refused. They were later published as a trilogy in paperback by Ballantine Books. Settle also claims that her editor cut *Fight Night on a Sweet Saturday* so drastically as to disturb its relation to the other novels, and she is now rewriting it to make it connect with them. That it was originally entitled *The Killing Ground* further complicates the pure picture she wishes to see emerge from the five books.

If "The Beulah Quintet" is to be read in the related order Settle now intends, the physical order of publication must be discounted. The novels should be read chronologically as follows: *Prisons* (1973), set in England in 1634; *O Beulah Land*, the region that is now West Virginia, from 1755-1774; *Know Nothing*, West Virginia between 1847 and 1861, leading to the Civil War; *The Scapegoat*, West Virginia in 1912; and *Fight Night on a Sweet*

Saturday, West Virginia in 1960. Although any one of the books may be read without any of the other four, the delineation of families and characters and the changing land is enhanced by the proper order.

Settle was born in and spent a major portion of her life in and around Charleston, West Virginia. Although the four books growing out of this geographical area are not autobiographical, she combines personal elements in her life with intensely researched material and imagination to allow the reader to perceive events of history from within a personal structure. The ancestral tree, its branches extending from Johnny Church in *Prisons* to Hannah McKarkle in *Fight Night on a Sweet Saturday*, provides the characters for each of the novels. Johnny Lacey, Johnny Church's descendant in *O Beulah Land*, establishes an estate in the valley west of the Endless Mountains before the area became West Virginia; in *Know Nothing*, Peregrene Catlett is descended from Johnny Church and Johnny Lacey; *The Scapegoat* includes several offspring from the Beulah dynasty—Jake Catlett, Beverley Lacey, Mooney McKarkle; and Hannah McKarkle in *Fight Night on a Sweet Saturday*, named after the first Hannah in *O Beulah Land*, becomes the chronicler of the collective history of Beulah land.

The events around which Settle shapes her narratives are sometimes ritual (marriages, feasts, funerals) sometimes broader historical crises (the English Revolution, the Civil War). In *The Scapegoat*, the characters gravitate around and converge in major strikes in the coal mining area of West Virginia that eventually led to the Matewan Massacre in Mingo County in 1920.

The axis of *The Scapegoat* is a seventeen hour period from 3:00 P.M. on Friday, June 7 until 8:00 A.M. on Saturday, June 8, 1912. Although Settle uses fictional names for the creeks and towns, the location is very probably the sharp, jagged mountains between Paint Creek and Cabin Creek in Logan County, West Virginia. This sparsely settled mountain region expanded because of the increased demand for coal. Many of the natives thought it was bad luck to work underground and so the coal mine operators turned to two sources for their manpower supply: the cotton-growing states of the South and the over-crowded slums of central and southern Europe. People from those two areas were tempted by agents of the mine operators with offers of free transportation, steady work, good wages, and company houses. Once these men, with their families in many cases, were transported to the foreign soil, they had no choice but to work under intolerable conditions and often for unscrupulous mine owners.

Union organizers in 1912, moved into the territory and in April, seventy-five hundred miners went on strike. Others chose to continue working. They had families to support. As the threat of violence grew greater, the county sheriffs were unable to police all the mining camps. To cope with this situation, each coal company deputized one of its employees to serve as the keeper of the peace in the camp. Mine guards came in from outside, mostly supplied by the Baldwin-Felts Detective Agency and were called "Baldwin Thugs." The mine guards, in their black coats and hats, and the company sheriff became the chief law enforcement agency in the coal counties. The mine guards loaded the striking miners' household goods into freight cars, hauled them across the lines of the company property, and dumped them along the railroad tracks. Homeless and hungry, the strikers and their families were forced to find shelter in caves, tents, and improvised shacks on privately owned lands. "God is everywhere, on land and sea, but He has not visited Paint Creek and Cabin Creek recently." This crucial time and place is the setting of *The Scapegoat*.

The large number of characters grows from the two established families, the Lacey's and the Catlett's, and includes numerous townspeople, several of the Baldwin detectives, women and children of the miners, and even Mother (Mary) Jones, the "Miners' Angel" who did not bring trouble, but appeared where trouble was. Paralleling the conflict between the striking miners and Mother Jones and the Baldwin detectives (the strike breakers) is the conflict between Beverley Lacey, owner of Seven Stars mine that is not on strike, and Jake Catlett, who feels a strong loyalty to Beverley, but is now on the side of the Union, and who allows the striking miners who have been dispossessed of their homes to erect a tent city on his property.

The three Lacey girls, Mary Rose, Lily, and Althea are central to the novel; they are the stabilizers, the shoring that keeps personal disaster from occurring because of respect for the Lacey family and the protective attitudes of the other characters. These three girls live on the edge of the impending violence, are involved in complex relationships with other characters, and are engaged in competition with one another, yet they are curiously untouched as they continue their lives in different directions, each wishing to escape in some way their narrow environment. Whether they have accomplished escape in the end is ambiguous and depends upon the angle by which each perceives her final destiny.

The novel itself seems to hang over a precipice as its characters experience premonitions about the future. Mother Jones, meeting with the miners, suddenly feeling her eighty-two years, "had a flick of a vision, like a glimpse of her death or the intrusion of a dream." Eduardo, the intended "scapegoat," kept "listening for something down the mountain. He didn't know what it was. Something worried his peace he didn't want to recognize." The women felt "Their ears were cocked listening for something to happen, they didn't know what. They knew it with their skin."

Like Carlo Michele, the unintended "scapegoat," who planned when he came to this country to travel in a circle, Settle's characters travel in an unplanned circle; after many missed opportunities, they come to the realization of an event that is genuinely significant to them and to those with whom they interact. These convergences tighten the novel and enforce its power.

Because the characters are not fully aware of the significance of their actions and thoughts, they are held in suspense and somehow barely miss participating fully in those suspenseful developments. The subtle, complex relationships among the characters of *The Scapegoat* and their already built-in more complex relationships set in motion in earlier books of the quintet form a network that links them all together in a spiderweb design. As the five novels have evolved from one, in *The Scapegoat*, one event breeds another, and the characters circle around these events in confusion, apprehension, memory, and speculation. In this sense, Settle may be compared to William Faulkner, although her digressions from the main focus of the story are not as complex as Faulkner's. The complex shifts in point of view, with their consequent changes in style, and the shifts in time and place demand a great deal of attention and flexibility of the reader.

From the beginning of her career, Settle, not only in this quintet, but also in other novels and in her autobiographical account of her service in World War II, *All the Brave Promises* (1966), has used a variety of point of view techniques. In *Prisons*, Johnny Church tells his story in the first person, and in *Fight Night on a Sweet Saturday* Hannah McKarkle speaks. In *Know Nothing*, Settle projects the action through the third-person central intelligence point of view of Jonathan Catlett. In *O Beulah Land*, she employs the omniscient point of view. In *The Scapegoat*, she combines all of these techniques, moving back and forth from first- to third-person central intelligence to omniscient points of view. Settle's shifting point of view techniques produce a structure that corresponds to the structure of the mines of West Virginia. Sometimes Settle's vantage point is the top of the mountain, looking down at the fragmented relationships among her characters; then she enters the mind of one character after another, exactly as one might explore the separate subterranean compartments. Suddenly, she shifts to the illuminating first person, as though turning on the light on the miner's cap. Occasionally, it is difficult to follow what appears to be an omniscient beginning to a paragraph, but is actually third-person central intelligence point of view. Here the shift occurs in a single sentence. "Francesco had changed in all their eyes, but not in his own." Settle seems in such instances to lack control of point of view.

While the actual events occur in a single day, Settle diverges from chronology. In three of the novel's four parts, Settle plays with the time factor. Although the first part is labeled "3:00 P.M. to 5:30 P.M., Friday, June 7, 1912," Mary Rose projects almost a year later, as she talks about appearing before the Senate Committee headed by Senator William H. Borah of Idaho, formed to look into the mining situation in Logan County. In this same section, however, Settle returns to the immediate events of June 7. In Part II, she advances fourteen years into the future, as Althea looks back to June 7, 1912; within this same section, not only does Settle shift the time again, this time to 1921, but she also sets part of the narration in France as Lily participates in World War I as a nurse. Despite transitory confusion, all these shifts seem to work. There is an underlying compulsive thread that must be fully unwound; although the thread loops in its unwinding, it finally reaches the present, where the action is immediate and coincides with the characters' experience and consciousness. Events in *The Scapegoat* sometimes proceed at a very fast pace, sometimes come to a standstill, but eventually converge at some predestined point.

As the coal mine and its extensive effects on the characters and on the land underlie the novel, the mine also becomes symbolic. Lily, who has been away at Vassar and who has come home afire with new liberal ideas and the stubborn wish to help the miners despite her father's opposition, begs Eduardo to take her into the mines so she can know what the miners experience; when he refuses, she enters the mine alone one night. As she stumbles along in the dark and the silence, she "had never felt so lonesome in her whole life until now as she stood on the balustrade, watching the trees along the Ancre gradually defined in halos of mist." She knew with a startling clarity that "she was trying to get a thrill by sticking her nose in where she had no business."

Contrasting the black coal dust, the white dresses the Lacey girls always wear, and the colorlessness of the bleak mountains, Settle develops a symbolic color motif. She sets it up in the first few pages, as Mary Rose speaks.

> That was the year I was finding colors for everything, like when you say you're blue—or they're blue in the face, or a black look, or a purple passion, or you see red. You know. Well, a pink revenge is slow and light and bedroomy and interminable and almost undetectable and absolutely killing. Althea is the queen of the pink revenge. She inherited thin hair.

This motif is repeated throughout the novel, even when the omniscient narrator speaks or through the voice of other characters.

Mary Lee Settle, with her passion for historical events and her almost obsessive dedication to the research of those events, and her vision of character situations that develop within these monumental crises, has created in *The Scapegoat* characters who will certainly go on to form their own story. Wherever Settle goes next, in whatever complex manner, she is certainly worthy of following.

Peggy Bach

THE SEARCH FOR ALEXANDER

Author: Robin Lane Fox (1946-   )
Publisher: Little, Brown and Company (Boston). 453 pp. $24.95
Type of work: Biography
Time: 500 B.C. to the present
Locale: Greece, Egypt, and Asia Minor

An archaeological, political, and military history of the greatest conqueror of antiquity

Principal personages:
ALEXANDER THE GREAT
CALLISTHENES, a historian and friend of Alexander
DARIUS III, Persian king
HEPHAISTION, Alexander's greatest friend
OLYMPIAS, Alexander's mother
PHILIP II, King of Macedonia and Alexander's father

Do the times make the man, or does the man make the times? This question is the major one to be faced in a "search for Alexander." The question is as old, perhaps, as the legends surrounding Alexander, who had all of, part of, or none of the following attributes: son of a god, supreme tactician and besieger, murderer of friend and of foe, avenger of the Greeks, successor to and heir of Darius III as ruler of the largest empire of antiquity. It is the problem of dealing with antiquity which impels Robin Lane Fox to state repeatedly: "Alexander is the subject of a search, not a certain narrative. . . ."

Lane Fox begins his work with a summary of the place Alexander holds in history and legend. Most certainly, whatever the Macedonian king's other claims may have been, his story holds the record for transmission throughout the world, from China to Iceland, as the most "cosmopolitan tale in world history to have spread without a religious message."

The tale, itself, has often been shaped to fit the needs of the tellers. In the Hindu Kush regions of ancient India, the area where Alexander reached his easternmost penetration, contemporary tribal leaders trace their ancestry to Alexander and the invading Greeks. When Alexander burned Persepolis as part of his sweep through the Persian empire, he burned the holy books of the prophet Zoroaster; hence Alexander is the "force of evil" cited by the Zoroastrians. Such an explanation is a fabrication according to Lane Fox, for "the priests had then been illiterate," but Alexander provided a convenient *post hoc* rationalization for a lack of early writings by the prophet.

Just as the historian must sift through the stories and histories and artifacts which came after Alexander in the "search," so must the time before Alexander be scrutinized for facts and legends.

Socrates once said to his friends: "We sit like frogs around a frog-pond." Such a comment seems at first glance to belittle the accomplishments of the Greeks of the time, Greeks who had ventured to the east to serve powerful Persian kings, had sailed north on the Black Sea, and had traveled west on the Mediterranean to Spain. Thus, although the "frog-pond" may have been largely limited to the Mediterranean, the "frogs" had produced artistic ideas and political solutions which still fascinate and awe our greatly expanded "frog-ponds" of today. Although the Greeks of Socrates' time knew nothing of the Jews and Jerusalem and little of northwest India, they still had "the liveliest culture in the world," a culture which had already produced drama and the theater, athletics, and democracy.

The city-states of Athens, Sparta, and Thebes developed sporting games, with the results based upon athletic prowess, not military strength, and political expedience based upon "conflict and a widened social self-confidence." The city-states had a long and glorious history well before Alexander became a political-military force. In fact, it was the city-states which first felt the extended power of the Persians through invasions led by Darius I and Xerxes I, whose forces captured Athens and burned the Acropolis about 480 B.C. Ironically, that destruction was to provide a rallying cry and justification for Alexander's invasion of Asia, for he said he sought to avenge the barbarian atrocities upon the glories of Greece.

Certainly the Athenians were willing to be avenged, but another irony of history is that when the Acropolis was burned, Macedonia—Alexander's power base—was not considered part of the civilized Greek world, only a loose federation of tribes far to the north. As the city-states consolidated power and treaties and cultured refinements, they became less powerful militarily. They could and did raise troops when necessary, but military excursions were no longer the prime activity of most of the cities by the middle of the third century B.C. In addition, although there was a feeling of common culture, there was no Greek nationalism in the contemporary sense. This guarded, *laissez-faire* approach actually allowed the rise of King Philip II of Macedonia to a position of power.

In regard to Philip, Alexander's father, the answer to the question about the man and the times is more easily answered. Certainly he was a powerful ruler, a shrewd politician, and a brilliant creator of military power. In fact, he was "the greatest builder of a kingdom and army in the ancient world." In twenty years he doubled the size of Macedonia and made the former upstart kingdom the "protector" of all Greece. Philip required the sons of leading men to be sent to Pella, the ancient capital of Macedonia, for their education. Thus, he began the inculcation of his viewpoints early in the lives of future leaders, and he also acquired handy hostages should any of the fathers of the young men decide to revolt against Macedonia. Yet, for all his power and cunning, Philip was a product of his times, whose "early rise owed most to historical coincidence, the fatigue and preoccupation of almost every neighbor."

In 336 B.C., Philip was murdered, and Alexander became king, although not without the usual struggle within the group of potential successors.

Alexander, himself, never doubted his right to rule and to conquer. From childhood he had kept a copy of Homer's *Iliad* under his pillow each night. He wanted to be judged in terms of the Homeric heroes, most especially in terms of the achievements of Achilles, who, in fact, was a maternal ancestor.

Alexander immediately established himself as the rightful ruler by having himself elected by the league of city-states as the leader of an Asian expedition, but before he could leave, a quick excursion against rebels on the shores of the Danube was necessary. A rumor of Alexander's death in the north led Thebes to revolt against the Macedonian rule. Alexander marched back—two hundred forty miles in two weeks; when the citizens of Thebes refused to settle the conflict diplomatically, Alexander's army destroyed the city, killed six thousand inhabitants, and enslaved all survivors. The rest of Greece was aghast at the force of Alexander, but he seems to have made his point. Never again during his reign was there a revolt by the Greek cities serious enough to demand his undivided attention.

At the age of twenty-two, in 334 B.C., Alexander crossed the Dardanelles into Asia to "punish the barbarians for their wrongs against Greek temples a century and a half in the past." In the next eleven years, Alexander conquered all the land from the Aegean Sea on the northwest to the Hindu Kush Mountains on the northeast to the Indian Ocean on the southeast to Egypt on the southwest. Much has been written about Alexander's victories and his strategic brilliance, including works by Lane Fox. So much has appeared, in fact, that specifics do not bear repeating here. What is worth considering is what the battles, and the events surrounding those battles, can reveal about the man who led them, the seeming contradictions and anomalies which controlled his efforts.

As a besieger, Alexander "has never been surpassed," the author states repeatedly. What began with Thebes was continued throughout Asia Minor whenever necessary, including Tyre, Gaza, Halicarnassus, and a host of lesser cities. If the people would not surrender, Alexander's siege machinery and well-stocked army could bring down any city. Yet, if the satrap—the local Persian-appointed ruler—surrendered before a battle or siege was necessary, he often found himself reappointed to his former position by Alexander, who recognized the value of persons trained in the complex procedures of the local government. Thus Alexander did not try to supplant every satraphy with a Greek-oriented city-state. For those cities which had a history of exposure to Greece, Alexander was quick to provide—in fact, to require—a Greek democracy, but for most cities in Persia and India and Egypt, a democracy would have destroyed the local structure; so, expedience found Alexander supporting the established system. Of course, the satraps now owed allegiance to Alexander, and their troops were under Macedonian command.

With the capture of Darius' body in July, 330 B.C., another oddity bears consideration. With the Persian capital of Persepolis captured and burned and with the Persian ruler slain by his own followers, Alexander could have stopped; the Greeks had been avenged. Yet, seven years of Alexander's life remained, and those seven years contained many more battles, battles of conquest and expansion, not just the fights necessary to consolidate and hold power already gained. In the view of many observers, not the least of them Alexander's own Macedonian troops and commanders, Alexander moved from avenger to heir. The former Persian ruler was gone, certainly, but now Alexander seemed to be more concerned that he be viewed as the new and rightful ruler of that empire, the heir of Darius, who would now carry the boundaries of his new kingdom even farther. For some of his original troops, the change was almost too much.

Here the answer to the original question about Alexander begins to assume its final shape, for it was by sheer strength of personality that Alexander persuaded his troops to follow him on to India, to fulfill his plan to conquer all the known world. He exerted his strength because he knew his plan was correct, in fact, was favored by the gods.

When Alexander had visited the desert temple of Ammon—the Egyptian equivalent of Zeus—in 331, the priest had greeted him as "the son of Zeus." Lane Fox and others point out such a greeting might have been only a formality based upon the priest's assumption Alexander was by then Pharaoh, and all pharaohs automatically were given status as the son of Ammon. In addition, shortly after his accession to Philip's throne, Alexander had been called "invincible" by the oracle at Delphi, and Alexander had cut the famed Gordian knot, a feat which could be accomplished only by one destined to "rule all Asia."

From 330 B.C. until the summer of 326 B.C., Alexander led the men on what was his own campaign, a campaign he felt was preordained to complete success, a campaign to rule all the land east of Greece right to the Outer Ocean, the line which determined the end of the earth.

The favor of the gods must have changed, however, because by the time the monsoons, the elephants, and the jungles took their toll of the Greek invaders into India, Alexander's troops would go no farther.

> The rains and the snakes, in the end, had broken morale. The men had marched more than 11,000 miles in seven years. There were above all common hardships. But they had been drenched in the monsoons. Weapons had corroded. The food was stale, their uniforms were sodden and steaming. . . . A dream was gone. He would never master all of Asia unless Asia were differently defined. He would never reach the Outer Ocean. . . . The men had let him down when the end was all but in his grasp.

It is to Alexander's credit that this retreat, this defeat by natural forces, could later be seen as victory. Alexander did make sacrifices and give thanks when he reached the Indian Ocean, which could be seen as part of the Outer Ocean, that long-sought border of the world, and, as the author points out, "it was a grand moment, although a second-best." Later, after a nearly disastrous desert march along the Persian Gulf, Alexander said his victory over the desert pleased him as much as the conquest of India. "There had been a time when Asia had included the whole of India. The concept had shrunk, perforce, to fit his own achievement."

Much of this story of Alexander—and many other stories—is found in Lane Fox's magnificently illustrated volume, commissioned to accompany the exhibition by the same name, yet existing easily on its own merits. Because he has written extensively on Alexander elsewhere and because much of the traveling exhibition was archaeological in nature, with artifacts only recently discovered, Lane Fox includes one chapter devoted to what may be Philip's tomb as well as extensive data about the many cities established by Alexander during his marches.

These far-flung cities, all of which were called Alexandria, give the final answer to the opening question. Alexander the Great made the times to fit his own image, according to his own desires. That he died on June 10, 323 B.C., aged 32 years, 10 months; without accomplishing much he set out to accomplish is a puzzle left for the fates to answer.

The final anomaly attests to the appropriateness of "the Great" as part of the way history remembers Alexander. Although known in popular legend and romance for his military conquests, for his admitted personal strength as a leader, that very strength proved to be a weakness. Once Alexander died, his empire began to fall apart almost immediately. The satraps and Macedonian regional rulers began to proclaim themselves kings. Greece as a military power would never be the same again, but Greece in the form of art and architecture, law and bloodlines, had been permanently established in the far-flung Alexandrias, from Egypt to Afghanistan, in almost all the known world beyond the Aegean Sea. Alexander's conquest is greater than even he could have imagined.

John C. Carlisle

THE SECOND COMING

Author: Walker Percy (1916-   )
Publisher: Farrar, Straus and Giroux (New York). 360 pp. $12.95
Type of work: Novel
Time: The present
Locale: Linwood, North Carolina

A comedy that asks some basic questions about modern culture

> *Principal characters:*
> WILLISTON BIBB BARRETT, the protagonist
> ALLISON HUNNICUTT HUGER, the young woman who is rebuilding
> her life

In this, his fifth novel, Walker Percy again explores the concerns which pervade his earlier books, concerns which readers recognize with surprise and delight as their own unarticulated questions: Why do we feel so devalued at four o'clock in the afternoon? Why is life not worth living except in the face of crisis or imminent death? Why do we love war better than peace, illness better than health? Are we creatures of free will, or aggregates of chemical reactions? Why can we abide neither believers nor unbelievers, and what has God to do with all of this?

Engrossing and refreshing on its many levels, *The Second Coming* stands among the best of contemporary literature. As do his other novels, except perhaps *Lancelot*, this work exhibits Percy's shrewd sense of comedy, descriptive skill, poignant concern for those who suffer, unshakable deference to human dignity, and extensive theological and philosophical learning.

The protagonist is once again Williston Bibb Barrett, who was the young "engineer" of Percy's second novel, *The Last Gentleman*. Now middle-aged, he still has the courteous and amiable ways of the well-born Southerner, is still attractive and likable, if somewhat remote. In the intervening years, he has had a successful Wall Street law practice and has been married to a "good cheerful forthright Northern Episcopal Christian" wife, inheriting her millions upon her recent death. He has taken early retirement in Linwood, North Carolina, a pleasant mountain resort not far from Asheville, and spends his time playing golf and looking after his late wife's philanthropies.

Despite the prospect of spending many comfortable years in prosperity and quiet civilized pastimes, Will is suffering from the symptoms of a disorder. He develops a golf slice. He falls down, usually on the golf course. He has delusions that all the Jews are leaving North Carolina. He begins to remember episodes from his past with such clarity that he is transported in time and place. He remembers everything. He becomes preoccupied with death, and with suicide.

His problem, as Will diagnoses it, is that "a person nowadays is two percent of himself." He asks whether it is possible for people to miss their lives in the same way as one misses a plane. He sees the times as demented and farcical:

> The Jews are gone, the blacks are leaving, and where are we? deep in the woods, socking
> little balls around the mountains, rattling ice in Tanqueray, riding $35,000 German cars,
> watching Billy Graham and the Steelers and M*A*S*H on 45-inch Jap TV.

Will's recognition of his state of death-in-life is not shared by those around him, although with the clarity of vision brought on by his disorder, he sees that they too are beside themselves. Jack Curl, his late wife's confessor and the chaplain of the nursing home her money has built, professes himself less interested in the signs of the apocalypse than in "opening a serious dialogue with our Catholic and Jewish friends." Jack wears a jumpsuit, dressed as God's handyman, but is afraid to talk about faith. What he offers Will, instead, is an ecumenical retreat, where he is to be "double-teamed with a Roman Catholic priest from Brooklyn, a real character," where the food is first class but "the important thing's it's a weekend with God. That's the bottom line." Will's grown daughter Leslie, a dissatisfied girl with a permanent frown, is a born-again Christian intent on writing her own wedding liturgy, the readings to come from the Bible and *The Prophet*. She has no use for anything that gets in the way of a personal encounter with Jesus Christ, and moves with her new husband into a love-and-faith community. Will's former girl friend, Katherine Vaught, Kitty of *The Last Gentleman*, has grown from an innocent Alabama girl dressed in cotton skirts into a bold, lusty too-tan lady golfer with a whisky voice and a loud bigoted husband. To her, Will's fear-and-trembling is "Tension! That's the enemy. . . . You know what I do? Stretch out and tell my toes to relax, then my knees—they do it!"

Those around him who are not beside themselves, nevertheless, hold no answers for Will. His whole marriage with his late wife Marion was a "communication breakdown." Marion, with her Episcopalian orthodoxy and sense of obligation, grew fat and crippled after the marriage, and gave herself to a life of service:

> She took to a wheelchair, ate more than ever, did more good works. She spent herself
> for the poor and old and wretched of North Carolina. She was one of the good triumphant
> Yankees who helped out the poor old South. In and out of meetings flew her wheelchair,
> her arms burly as a laborer's. Fueled by holy energy, money, and brisk good cheer, she
> spun past slack-jawed Southerners, fed the hungry, clothed the naked, paid the workers
> in her mills a living wage, the very lintheads her piratical Yankee father had despoiled
> and gotten rich on: a mystery.

Will's sharpened memory and his preoccupation with death lead him into conversations with the memory of his father, a Faulknerian figure, whom he addresses as "old mole." Recognizing that his father's suicide was intended to be as large a gesture as all his father's deeds, and that Will's own lukewarm life was lived to escape that largeness, he rages:

And I was never so glad of anything as I was to get away from your doom and your death-dealing and your great honor and great hunts and great hates. . . , yes, your great allegiance swearing and your old stories of great deeds . . . and under it all the death-dealing which nearly killed me and did you.

In a series of flashbacks, Will pieces together every moment of a hunting trip he, as a boy of twelve, took with his father. The trip left both man and boy injured of shotgun blasts, and when Will finally remembers what happened that day, and what his father was trying to teach him, he knows that the hunt was the only event that ever happened to him in his life. "Everything else that happened afterward was a non-event."

Will is freed by his recognition that he was meant to die on that hunt, and vows that his suicide will not be wasted—not simply "an exit, a getting up and going out"—as his father's was. He plans his own version of the Pascalian wager, an experiment to settle once and for all the question of God's existence. Will descends into Lost Cove cave demanding, like Jacob in the Old Testament, that God reveal himself and bless him; if God will not give him a sign, he will die.

Having seen the abyss, Will looks for the bridge in a sign from God. Perhaps he finds it. Days later, delirious and ill, he tries to crawl out of the cave and crashes through the roof of a greenhouse that has become home to Allison Hunnicut Huger. Allie, Kitty Vaught's twenty-year-old daughter and a diagnosed schizophrenic, has escaped from the mental institution where her parents have put her and tried to keep her since she came into a large inheritance. With repeated electroshock treatments, her memory has been buzzed away. Slim, pretty Allie, whose bonds to society have been erased along with her memory, is rebuilding the fundamentals of her life. Having written herself a memorandum before the electroshock treatment she took shortly before her escape, she has followed its directions to remember her name, change out of her hospital clothes, "locate and take possession of a house." Finding only the greenhouse left standing in the woods next to the ruins of her house, Allie has, by carefully mastering the physical principles of block-and-tackle, repaired and heated it, making it ready for winter. Language is more difficult. She practices declarative sentences, then requests. She watches how others act, and takes a few tentative steps toward imitation.

Allie nurses Will back to health. They begin to rely on each other, as each needs what the other can give. He falls down, she is a hoister. She remembers nothing, he remembers everything. He translates her peculiar language to the world, and fills the loneliness of the late afternoons. In as delicate and poignant a love story as can be drawn, they fall in love. Their union is threatened when Allie is almost returned to the mental institution, and Will is almost committed to a nursing home, his disorder finally having been diagnosed as "Hausmann's syndrome," a pH imbalance characterized by "wahnsinnige Sehnsucht"—inappropriate longings. Despite these obstacles, Will and Allie reunite and decide to marry and have children. Will arranges to take up the practice of law again.

Although Allie is by no means simply a vehicle for Percy's ideas, through this character he explores theories of language and of signs which he earlier treated in his scholarly essays. Before *The Moviegoer* was published in 1961, Percy had established himself as a serious and provocative writer on psychiatry, language phenomenology, and semiotics. (In 1975 he published a collection of these essays in *The Message in the Bottle*.) Allie, the clean slate, allows Percy to consider the relationship between language and power ("Give me the words," she tells Will, so she will know how to ask for the tools she needs to repair and heat the greenhouse); between love and learning; between the literal meaning of words and the intended meaning supplied by unstated agreement ("She took words seriously to mean more or less what they said, but other people seemed to use words as signals in another code they had agreed upon"). Allie's lack of knowledge discloses the network of signals upon which people rely to communicate. Worrying that she will run straight into people as she walks down the street, she notices that "oncoming people seemed to know without looking at her exactly when to veer slightly and miss her." This is a "trick" she thinks, an "exchange of signals which she must learn."

Allie is the most unique and delightful character Percy has created, because she is naïvely virtuous in her forced new innocence, but principally because of her language. Sounding like a "wolf child who had learned to speak from old Victrola records," she communicates in metaphors that are striking in their aptness. "Are you still climbing on your anger?" she asks Will, having just encountered him in the woods holding his golf club like a shotgun. Later, having discovered that she loves Will and that Will loves her, she tells him that they have become one, "but not in the sappy way of saying." "What way, then?" "One plus one equals one and oh boy almond joy."

Allie's strange language and Will's improbable disorder and odd quest become credible because Percy is scrupulously attentive to the details that cement the story into time and place. His characters wear Jaymar Sansabelt slacks, wear Shalimar perfume; he can describe the *clunk* of real gold bracelets; draw a picture of a Mercedes 450 SEL 6.9 liter sedan and green Winchester Super-X shotgun shells. The longer descriptive passages reveal a lyrical quality which detracts not at all from the clear image. Describing an 1899 stove that Allie is hoisting out of the ruins of the house on her estate, Percy says:

> What a stove! It was a castle of a stove, a rambling palace of a stove, a cathedral of a stove, with spires and turrets and battlements. A good six feet high and eight feet wide, it was made of heavily nickeled iron castings bolted together. . . . Panels of porcelain enamel, turquoise blue for the oven doors and the four warming closets, little balconies jutting out head-high, snowy white for the splashback, were fused to heavy cast iron

between frames of nickel. Bolted on one side was a nickel-iron box lined with heavy copper and fitted with a spigot. A water reservoir!

That Percy is among the best of the contemporary novelists is evidenced by the fact that *The Second Coming* will appeal to such a diverse audience, among them those looking for a funny, touching, engrossing story; those fascinated with the modern South; those eager for a documentary of contemporary life among the *hautebourgeoisie*; and those to whom any important question is, at bottom, a theological question. While every reader may quarrel with something Percy has to say, as his themes and treatment are provocative and invite response, this last group of readers may have the most serious quarrel. These readers form something of a discipleship. They believe, as young Will Barrett believed of the brilliant and dissipated Dr. Sutter Vaught in *The Last Gentleman*, that having posed the questions, Percy might also have some of the answers. Perhaps he has told what he knows here; if so, it is not completely satisfying.

Percy frames the questions of how one is to remedy alienation and how one is to find God in this world by sending Will Barrett, "like some crackpot preacher in California," into Lost Cove cave, to demand that God reveal himself. A question of Old Testament proportions deserves a theologically balanced answer. It is questionable whether a middle-aged man's love affair with a young damaged girl suffices. Percy has created a variety of well-drawn female characters, but has never, in his novels, described a mature intimate relationship between man and woman. Allie's youth and her disabilities leave in doubt the significance of Will's love for her. After all, Will has been married before, to a damaged woman who needed him, held a job before, been a father before. By entering this life for a second time, albeit with a heart filled with the joy of infatuation, Will appears only to numb his old sense of rage and longing, to defer its reappearance.

This resolution may itself be valid, of course, as a recognition that modern man is permitted only the questions, but not the answers. Or, Will may have come to accept Jack Curl's answer, that God is to be found in other people. Neither of these quite appears to be Percy's answer. Much too late in the book, in an episode unconnected to the story line, Will talks to a worn-out old Catholic missionary priest. Will asks him, "Do you believe that Christ will come again and that in fact there are certain unmistakable signs of his coming in these very times?" The old man cannot answer. "What do you want of me?" he asks. All Will knows, the reader is told as the book ends, is that he wants both Allie and the Lord, and that he must and will have them both.

The transcendental direction taken by the novel's final passages is too naked. Percy might, of course, cry foul to the criticism, tell his followers he is no oracle, or that their Old Testament longings are not timely, and tell them to look at Will Barrett for an image of themselves. On the other hand, it is fair enough to ask: why continue making the question so big if the answer is so little?

Angelika Kuehn

SELECTED POEMS

Author: Mark Strand (1934-   )
Publisher: Atheneum (New York). 152 pp. $6.95
Type of work: Poetry

An analysis of self, perception, and being from a solipsist's viewpoint

Mark Strand's poems have a dark climate; the speaker in them often feels cut off and threatened, and keeps himself going by minutely observing his condition. Because he is "rattled. . . / With spooks," he hopes "That nothing, nothing will happen"—that is, that he will be unharmed and die at the same time ("Sleeping with One Eye Open"). The world in which he feels this way is composed of objects that mean nothing beyond themselves and is where death seems lush on the one hand ("The Last Bus") and the last solipsism on the other ("Elegy for My Father").

To expose the anatomy of isolation seems to have been Strand's task as a poet from his first volume in 1964 to the present. As a solipsist of sorts, he is concerned with the nature of self. His old, familiar self makes him nauseous and nostalgic by going away ("The Man in the Mirror"), but even though he acknowledges this by ridding himself of attachments, the opposite is also true: "I change and I am the same. / I empty myself of my life and my life remains" ("The Remains"). He is stuck with the self-life he did not choose and cannot exchange ("My Life by Somebody Else"); he is still his mother's child ("Not Dying"), even if the self that was cannot—and cannot help trying to—define the present ("The Late Hour"). The best part of this self is a memory that one enjoys ("Pot Roast") and a primordial source to which one belongs ("Where Are the Waters of Childhood?"). The paralysis caused by the slippery self is the fear that it will leave and also stay and the understanding that it has "no place to go, no reason to remain" ("Coming to This").

In its relations with others, what does the self do? It either refuses to move into others' illusions about it ("The Way It Is"), or it becomes intimate with others through lies and violence ("Courtship"). This brings up the theme of behavior in Strand's poems. The self acts according to this dictum: " 'You shall live by inflicting pain. / You shall forgive' " ("The Mailman"). That is, behavior is a paradox if the self behind it is. In "Eating Poetry," Strand describes the act of poetry: since it is a breaking out of himself at the same time as it is a breaking into himself to fulfill himself, it is violent, animal-like, especially toward the other, in this case a librarian, "I snarl and bark at her." Another irony here is that the self comes to a primitive, unthinking life by performing a dreamlike and thinking act. If sadism lurks in this kind of behavior, so does masochism. Strand says in "The Accident," "A train runs over me," and in "The Dirty Hand" (an adaptation from Carlos Drummond de Andrade), "My hand is dirty, / I must cut it off."

The nature of seeing and of the mind is an important aspect of the nature of self. Strand says in "The Whole Story" that one cannot trust what one thinks he sees. His companion in the poem might not be on the train with him, and he himself might have lied about a fire he said he saw. We do not like the person who seems to be watching us, but we are that person without knowing it ("The Tunnel"). Those who dream about us do not see us let alone feel what we are going through in their dream ("The Kite"). "Nothing will tell you / where you are," Strand states in "Black Maps," which means an observer cannot see and his location cannot help him to. Not until "White," a more recent poem, does Strand's outlook on seeing improve: ". . . out of my waking / the circle of light widens. . . / . . . All things are one."

As for the mind or knowing, we cannot know why our lives deteriorate or if our acts are what we think they are ("The Man in the Tree"). At best all we can know is what it feels like to "keep going" ("Lines for Winter"), and when it comes to thinking, the best we can do is think about this endurance, not about why we cannot figure out what our purpose is ("For Jessica, My Daughter").

Dreaming is a kind of involuntary thinking that Strand is not depressed by; it can be lush as in "What to Think Of," where the poet's mind makes image upon image of beauty and power, or as in "Eating Poetry," where imagination changes a dull place into a savage and vital one. In fact, Strand suggests, if "you step out of your dress" (meaning, perhaps, your mental defenses), the power in the world—dark as it is—will reach you.

What is life itself, then, to a solipsist who yearns and feels nullified at the same time? It carries people toward as it carries them away from each other ("The Marriage"). It urges us to preserve it at its outset ("The Babies"), and to stay alive no matter what, to put "One foot in front of the other" ("The Hill"), to "open the door and walk in" ("Seven Poems"). It is a losing and a keeping: "if the body is a coffin it is also a closet of breath," Strand says in "Breath," just as he calls his dying a living and a story about it in "My Death." Again he brings up the tension in life when he says, "Everyone who has sold himself wants to buy himself back" ("The Way It Is"), and when he says that from wanting comes failure, from failure creation, and from creation zero. Life wants and does not want "to be born" ("My Son"); it wants to go away and to stay where it is ("Nights in Hackett's Cove"); it loves what it gets but cannot keep it ("Leopardi").

Poetry itself makes Strand feel happy and primitive, and although he says silly things about it like "If a man lives with two poems, / he shall be unfaithful to one" ("The New Poetry Handbook"), he uses storytelling as a serious image for life. Fiction means the made-up, the elusive. In dealing with people, Strand wants to "invent an ending that comes out right" ("Tomorrow"), although he also says "the book of our lives is empty" ("The Book of Our Lives"). In the same poem, fiction is a fitting trope for his solipsism. In one of the "chapters" of his life, he sees himself doing what he is—reading the chapter—and this freezes him. When someone says our lives are not simply a story, Strand points to the part in the story where this is said, and so puts an end to the argument. Then he quotes what the story says in the end: *"They are the book and they are / nothing else."* In "Exiles," readers are reduced to "voices" telling a story about themselves, and wanting to go back to its beginning. Finally, the story about the story is the poem itself, which exists for only a "moment," even if that moment "shines" in the dark ("The Garden").

Strand's view of self and life explains why there is so much irony and there are so many puns in his poetry. After all, if life is slippery, so are the poems which talk about it. "The Accident" is ironic because Strand has not really been run over by a train, which makes the strenuous effort to help him in the poem ironic, too. "The Untelling" is ironic because the real event it is about took place first in the mind of the teller who saw it without knowing what it meant, then in his memory (which distorts his original point of view), and finally the event is the poem which is the circular attempt to tell itself right. In "Sleeping with One Eye Open," "nothing" is a pun meaning safety and oblivion at the same time. When the mole in "The Dress" is "extending the length of his darkness," the image means tunnel, life, death and unknowing. When Strand sets up the sophism "More is less. / I long for more" ("The One Song"), the last "more" means "less" and "more" than what the statement restricts him to. In "I praise the moon for suffering men," suffering is so placed that it is an adjective that goes with "men" and a verb that goes with "moon," in which case it means "put up with."

Since modern European and South American poetry have influenced his work, Strand's imagery is mostly sinister, and since life is such a crisis for him, his imagery is basic. The moon appears in many of his poems. It is often a sign of brutality and dreams. Various kinds of black and white are staples among his images, as are enclosures—especially houses (often outdoors is used as a kind of enclosure). Sometimes his images are lush: ". . . tons and tons of morpho butterflies" ("What to Think Of"). Sometimes they are grotesque and funny: "Their teeth / poke through their gums / like tombstones" ("The Babies"). Sometimes they are surprising and memorable: ". . . the misfortunes come—/. . . their wooden wings bruising the air" ("The Room"); ". . . I dance out of the burning house of my head" ("The Dance"); "tomorrow's dust flares into breath" ("The Coming of Light").

Strand matches his basic, intimate, stripped down themes with spare sentences, mostly in the present tense. Their simple syntax seems the key to the cadences in his poems, although he does juggle the weights of vowels and consonants for sonic effect, as in this: "The muffled crack and drum / Of distant thunder / Blunders against our ears" ("The Kite"). Also, the progress of an action often controls his line-breaks, as in this: "He sneaks in the backdoor, / tiptoes through the kitchen, / the living room, the hall, / climbs the stairs and enters / the bedroom" ("Poem"). Elsewhere, the ends and beginnings of lines are used to highlight key words. For example: "It is all in the mind, you say, and has / nothing to do with happiness. The coming of cold ("So You Say"). "Nothing" and "cold" here are emphasized by their position, with "nothing" unexpectedly cut off from the "has" it goes with, and the "cold" the last word in the line.

For someone as caught up in his poems with those aspects of existence which undercut, repel, and sicken it, Strand has some amazing dedications. Many of them are to influential or well-known poets. Here the reader finds Donald Justice, Greg Orr, Howard Moss, Elizabeth Bishop, and Robert Penn Warren. For a spirit as exiled as Strand's seems to be, these high-ranking chums are strange and make one wonder if Strand's poems are a special sort of game he is playing with his colleagues. "White," the most hopeful poem in the book, is dedicated to the famous critic Harold Bloom and has a title and a movement close to A. R. Ammons' work, which Bloom has singled out for praise and detailed treatment.

Along with this odd if occasional name-dropping, there is a stance in Strand's poems which sometimes weakens their sense of crisis or makes it seem false. While the poems seem to be trying to sound childlike, they often sound facetious or display a cruel wit, as though the speaker in them were saying that if he is unsure of himself to begin with, then what business do the characters in them have being there or do readers have in spying on him. Perhaps this tone comes from Strand's solipsism: if to be means shadows and silence, how solid or inevitable can poems about it be? This implicit contradiction may annoy Strand, and since he wants to write poetry and does, he may use it as a form of revenge on himself for bothering with it and on his characters and readers for coming too close to him.

Mark McCloskey

SETTING THE WORLD ON FIRE

Author: Angus Wilson (Frank Johnstone, 1913-   )
Publisher: The Viking Press (New York). 296 pp. $12.95
Type of work: Novel
Time: 1948-1969
Locale: London and environs

A social comedy which portrays through the eyes of one aristocratic British family the changes which have overtaken English society since 1900, and a philosophical exploration of the moral and intellectual conflict between classicism and romanticism, conservatism and liberalism

> *Principal characters:*
> PIERS MOSSON (VAN), a young intellectual member of an ancient British family
> TOM MOSSON (PRATT), his brother
> GREAT GRANDFATHER MOSSON, the great grandfather of Piers and Tom and owner of Tothill House
> LADY MOSSON (JACKIE), his widowed daughter-in-law and an American heiress
> ROSEMARY MOSSON (MA), widow of Jerry Mosson, mother of Piers and Tom
> SIR HUBERT MOSSON (BART), heir to Great Grandfather, elder son of Lady Mosson, and a middleaged bachelor and banker
> MARINA LUZZI, Italian heiress and Hubert Mosson's fiancée

The tension between order and chaos often forms the basis of art. This tension is the theme underlying Angus Wilson's novel *Setting the World on Fire*. This story of two gifted and sensitive brothers during the decades since World War II explores with subtlety and grace this conflict which has inspired so much literature since the ancient Greeks.

This conflict represents the eternal struggle between the classical and the romantic, between the politically conservative and the politically liberal. The conflict also positions the importance of tradition, roots, family, and cultural history against the need for fresh air, change, and new blood. Stability is necessary if a civilization is to rise and flourish and produce a culture worth passing on to succeeding generations. Too much stability, however, may also be stifling and crushing to the very forces which are necessary to nurture the creative individuals who produce the culture upon which the civilization relies.

Perhaps there can be no resolution to this conflict, but it has been intriguing thinkers since the days of Pericles. Friedrich Nietzsche and other modern writers have been obsessed by the potential violence underlying this philosophical (and often moral) dichotomy. In *Setting the World on Fire*, Angus Wilson uses the structure of social comedy to analyze this conflict as it appears in twentieth century Britain. Perhaps some of the examples which appear in the novel are representative only of British society, but beyond these strictly social conventions lie some basic truths which have meaning for all civilized human beings.

In many of his novels over the last several decades, Wilson has turned his attention to the apparently universal desire for power. Taken to the extreme, this quest can lead to a Hitler or a Napoleon, but in everyday terms, this quest can be witnessed in relationships in the business world, in marriages, in scholarly or artistic worlds, in families, and in romantic liaisons. In one sense, this quest for power can be seen as part of the desire for order in the world, but it can become perverted when the desire swells into a blind quest for "my order" as opposed to anybody else's order. With wit and sharpness, and often with tenderness and understanding, Wilson has painted this lust for power, in its many sizes and forms, in books such as *Anglo-Saxon Attitudes* and *The Old Men at the Zoo*. With *Setting the World on Fire*, he shows how the power can almost imperceptibly change hands, as the structure of a society evolves. The change may be so gradual and so subtle that even the people who have held the power may not realize that they have lost it. Then, suddenly, the order that they knew and cherished, the order which guaranteed their power, has vanished, and they see only chaos, not realizing that a new order has evolved, an order which has left them behind.

England, for many years the ruler of an empire "upon which the sun never set," has, like Phaëthon, fallen from the sky. The image of the sun falling from the sky dominates this book, as it dominates the vast hall in the great London manor house of Tothill. As Richard II saw himself as a "blushing discontented sun" forced from the sky, so modern England grumbles and complains about its lost glory—or, in some cases, simply closes its eyes and refuses to acknowledge that it no longer is riding the chariot of empire across the heavens. Great Grandfather Mosson and Lady Mosson, his daughter-in-law, are two individuals who conveniently have refused to recognize that the world has changed, and that they no longer are the sun around which everything else revolves. They are able to be so blind because they have the insulation of a great fortune and a splendid estate which supports a rich history of its own. The newer generations, however, do not have the protection of money and position and are forced to stand on the very real earth and look for practical paths which they can follow. They can only wish to steal Apollo's chariot and ride across the sky, as Phaëthon forever seems to be doing on the ceiling of the great hall at Tothill House.

"Down, down I come, like glistering Phaëthon," cries Richard, when he is dethroned, and down fall the mighty and the complacent as the social structure which supported them vanishes. Only by transfusions of new blood can they expect to survive. At turn of the century, American money in the form of an American heiress saved the Tothill-Mosson world of privilege and position, just as generations before, the Mosson money saved the Tothill position. The most recent transfusion comes from an Italian heiress who brings money from her industrial family in Turin to reinforce the fading line. Yet, can injections of new money save a civilization, or will the influence of the *nouveau riche* inevitably coarsen and alter the old ways? Will the values which are being protected necessarily be changed—for better or for worse— by bringing these new influences into the fold? Might order be threatened more by these subtle changes than by the more violent changes threatening from outside? Angus Wilson poses the questions and explores them, but he does not draw clear-cut conclusions. He deliberately refuses easy answers, preferring to show the possibilities and let the reader discover the truth for himself.

One person's tragedy can be another's victory. A new production of the French opera *Phaëthon* written by one of the composers of the court of Louis XV, in the great baroque hall designed by Vanbrugh (who also designed Blenheim Palace, home of the Duke of Marlborough and the Churchills) is used by Wilson to demonstrate this simple truth. As Richard's tragedy was the beginning of Henry IV's triumph, so the collapse of one society in modern Britain may signal the rise of another. The references to Jimmy Porter (the hero of John Osborne's *Look Back in Anger*, the play which signaled the beginning of a new cultural wave in England), the Angry Young Men, and the entire post-World War II generation are used to highlight a conflict which Wilson assumes underlies the action of the novel. While on the surface, the story appears to be chiefly about the conflicts within one upper-class British family, the struggle Wilson is writing about is much more basic and reaches deeply into the fabric of British society. While some individuals may be shedding tears over Phaëthon's fall, others are glad that he has fallen, and they do not care who may have been burned as a result.

The histories of the Mossons and Tothills contain in miniature the national history of Britain. The various family members constantly refer to the historians or librarians who work to put the family "papers" in order. They are well aware that their family chronicle is a cultural and social—and economic— history of England, and if they are arrogant, they feel that they have a right to be. They assume that everybody else must be as fascinated by their history as they are. Like royalty, they take their privileges for granted and cannot understand when others are not willing to assume their natural superiority.

The great mansion of Tothill House is a living character in this rich and complex novel. Architecture is made by human beings, but in turn it has an influence upon human beings. The house itself represents the great conflict between order and chaos, classicism and romanticism. Designed and built by two different architects, embracing two different philosophical and architectural points of view, the great manor house is proof that harmony can result from this struggle, that the diversity and richness which results from the fusion of the two points of view can contribute to the richness and flourishing of a civilization. Unfortunately, this perfect union is seldom achieved.

As each generation intends to "set the world on fire" with its glory (here, it is Piers and Tom, the young grandsons, who intend to overwhelm the world with their gifts), so the representatives of each point of view, classic or romantic, conservative or liberal, bourgeois or artistic, intend to set the world on fire. These ambitions may be considered as vulgar by some people, but they are one of the realities of life and provide much of the impetus which keeps society moving. Further, the previous generation, even while it is being replaced by the new generation, often cannot help but feel proud of the generation which it has brought into the world. The struggle is not unlike that which was portrayed in ancient Greek tragedy: the sons destroying their fathers in order to build a new civilization upon their graves. Yet, even as the victory is theirs, so, too, is the punishment.

The Oedipal conflict is very real in this novel, as the women, Lady Mosson and Rosemary Mosson, connive and plot to keep the power in their hands. They are accustomed to power, accustomed to ruling from behind the scenes through their men, but they also are skilled and ruthless in their own techniques of using the power their position provides. This power can be as blatant as that of an employer toward an employee, and of a member of the aristocracy toward the middle or lower classes, or as subtle as that of a matriarch toward the younger members of her family.

Hubert Mosson sees order as the only salvation of mankind, and likens Phaëthon to Hitler. He believes that it is inevitable that such fools who try to usurp power from those to whom it naturally should belong (as Phaëton took the chariot from Apollo, Hitler took power from the established government, and as the upstart lower classes are trying to take power from the Mossons and their class) should come to a bad end. This must happen because such individuals upset the natural balance of nature and society and create chaos, from which only destruction and ill fortune can result. (Wilson's implied commentary on Hubert's point of view is seen in the fact that Hubert also is a secret sado-masochist, who eventually dies as a result of his imprudent, excessive sexual games.) Nevertheless, to Hubert, the balanced classical proportions of the Pratt section of Tothill House are reassuring, while the flamboyant baroque section of the house, the great Vanbrugh hall with its ceiling painting of Phaëthon, represents the dangers of disorder and excess.

The two brothers, Piers and Tom, known as Van (after Vanbrugh) and Pratt, are fascinated by the two aspects of their ancestral home and are caught up at an early age in the struggle between the classical and the romantic, order and disorder. Because they are of a new generation, however, they do not see the issues so starkly; to them, there can be no black and white, pure and simple, as there is to their elders. Their lives are a continuation of the search for truth and beauty, but they are capable of seeing truth and beauty in *both* the classical and the baroque, the old and the new, the status quo and change.

Memory plays an important function in this novel, both as a vehicle and as a theme in itself. Memory can transform experience into art. The act of remembering defines reality, transforms it, and sets perimeters around it. By necessity, selective memory takes the unguarded experience, shapes it, and changes it, making it into art. When the memories are part of the national experience, as so many of the memories of the Tothill-Mosson clan are, the transformation becomes part of the national epic, a continuing saga of a race and a people. The smallest personal events become symbolic for the national experience, and the small themes represent the larger ones; out of the particular emerges the universal.

Wilson utilizes in *Setting the World on Fire* his often skillful technique of the interior monologue, particularly when dealing with the brothers in their youth. Symbols are important to Wilson, and he uses them both to highlight character and to underline the meaning beyond character. At the same time, his gift for the telling phrase and biting description shines in this novel quite as brilliantly as in his previous fiction. This is a very British novel, and the often satirical dialogue represents that of a particular set of upper-class Britons. While American readers may not catch every nuance or class distinction Wilson has portrayed here, the crispness and sharpness of the exchanges remains effective and revealing. This is the novel of a master at satiric social comedy, and the work of a man who cares deeply about his characters, his land and its heritage, and the human race and its destiny.

Bruce D. Reeves

SHAYS' REBELLION
The Making of an Agrarian Insurrection

Author: David P. Szatmary (1951-   )
Publisher: University of Massachusetts Press (Amherst). 184 pp. $14.00
Type of work: History
Time: 1786-1787
Locale: Massachusetts

A study of the insurrection of yeoman farmers in Massachusetts known as Shays' Rebellion which focuses on the causes and consequences of the violent protest

> *Principal personages:*
> DANIEL SHAYS, captain in the Revolutionary War and a leader in Shays' Rebellion
> BENJAMIN LINCOLN, a merchant-speculator who became commander of the government troops in Massachusetts
> JAMES BOWDOIN, Governor of Massachusetts

David P. Szatmary, Visiting Assistant Professor in the history department at the University of Arizona, has written a fascinating study of Shays' Rebellion. This uprising of yeoman farmers in Massachusetts in 1786-1787 is one of the most intriguing incidents in our history, and the causes and impact of the rebellion continue to interest historians and political scientists. It is easy to dramatize Shays' Rebellion and make villains and heroes of the participants. In most of the books of the last century, the farmers were the villains, and the merchants, lawyers, and professional and government officials were the heroes. In the years after Professor Charles A. Beard's *Economic Interpretation of the Constitution of the United States* in 1913, the roles were reversed with the commercial, professional class seen as securing its own gain by ruthlessly crushing the farmers who had a legitimate demand for economic relief. The thesis of this book is that the insurrection was a result of a conflict between cultures; the subsistence farmers represented the traditional lifestyle, and the merchant capitalists the commercial way of life. In order to sustain this characterization of the conflict, evidence is needed that the farmers preferred their way of life and were fighting to preserve it.

The evidence presented to support the position that the subsistence farmers desired to avoid being drawn into the money economy and commercial society is that they did not cultivate all their land and that they did not plant the crops which could most readily be sold on the market. A few individual farmers are selected, and detailed information is given concerning the numbers of acres planted in each crop; the number of animals raised along with the pork, beef, and vegetables a family needed; and the amount of land that was left uncultivated. Szatmary seizes upon the percentage of uncultivated land to show that the farmers could have produced surplus for the market if they chose, and their decision not to represented their choice of a subsistence traditional way of life. This is a total misunderstanding of the problems faced by farmers without machinery, hired labor, slaves, and oxen rather than horses for work animals. They were cultivating all the land they could. Although a more mature man might have several sons to help him for a few years, he also had more family members to feed, clothe, and shelter. In one instance, Szatmary quotes a farmer who seemed unable to understand why a farmer who had three hundred acres needed to destroy wood and clear land any faster than he could make use of it. Instead of proving that he wanted to remain a subsistence farmer, this illustrates the limits to the amount of land a man could cultivate.

As further proof that these were subsistence farmers by choice, questions are raised about their failure to experiment with new crops and to continue to plant corn rather than flax, which was more marketable. Again the answer is to be found in the marginal nature of their existence. Farmers could not afford to experiment or to risk a crop failure, which would deprive their family of the fundamental necessities of life. The argument that they were subsistence farmers because they wanted to maintain this traditional pattern of life and avoid being drawn into a commercial society is not convincing. Although the failure to sustain the argument is critical to the thesis that Shays' Rebellion was a conflict between a traditional way of life and a commercial society, it in no way detracts from the pleasure of the book. The detailed information drawn from records, diaries, and other primary sources about the life of farmers in western Massachusetts affords a rare view of life in the late eighteenth century.

Unlike the characterization of the conflict as one between two cultures, the discussion of the economic conditions in Massachusetts in 1786-1787 and the description of the economic problems of the new nation generally are consistent with those commonly accepted. The merchants along the seaboard began to require the retail merchants in the western part of the state to pay their debts, and they in turn demanded the farmers pay their debts. The merchants were calling in their debts because they were hurt by the general depression that followed the war. Moreover, they were especially hard hit because the British cut off their trade with the West Indies and created restrictions and burdens on their trade with Britain. The demand to be paid in hard money created an impossible situation for the farmers who had little or no hard money and had, in the past, been allowed to pay their debts in produce.

The economic pressures on the farmers in Massachusetts were particularly great not only because trading patterns of New England were more disrupted than elsewhere in the new nation, but also because the policies regarding taxes and repayment of state debt were harsher. While some states were content to pay only the interest on their debts until the economy recovered, the policy in Massachusetts was to press for full payment of the debt, requiring an increase in taxes. As if that were not enough, the state tax was not fair and placed a larger portion of its burden on land. In addition to this, the state policy was a deflationary one, which reduced the available money. In contrast, some states followed an inflationary policy, which alleviated the burden somewhat. Not surprisingly, the farmers were aware of the different policies followed in other states and therefore knew their situation was unusually difficult. The grievances of the farmers were real.

These farmers had participated in the Revolution, which gave them an independent nation, and they had a strong feeling about the responsibility of government to answer the needs of its citizens. Since their grievances were real and they knew state legislatures could take action to improve their situation, they first turned to the legislature to provide them relief. The self-assurance and self-confidence of these farmers is vividly portrayed. They knew how to express their desires to the legislature. They prepared petitions, and, although their theoretical understanding of the problems and solutions might have been limited, they had had experience with paper money during the war, had used surplus produce to pay debts, and knew the taxes fell unfairly upon land. Accordingly, they petitioned for tender laws, for an inflationary money policy, and for changes in taxes. The petitions came from towns in western Massachusetts, but they had also organized at the county level during the Revolution with their committees of correspondence; so, county conventions were also utilized to convey their demands to the legislature.

The reader feels their shock and frustration when the legislature adjourned in July, 1786, without passing laws to ease their burden. There is also dismay that they sacrificed so much to create a government which now appeared as insensitive to their needs as the King, if not more so. These, however, were not men to take these injustices passively. They had paid too much to become independent farmers to acquiesce in the loss of their farm animals or their land through court actions instigated by their creditors. When the courts began to take land and animals to settle debts and when farmers were sent to jail because they were unable to pay their debts, the yeoman farmers, who had fought for their rights before, took matters into their own hands and forcefully prevented the court from sitting.

Although events in Massachusetts moved from peaceful petitioning to forceful obstructions of some courts and ultimately to armed rebellion with the attempt on the arsenal at Springfield, the farmers were reacting to circumstances and not following any plan. The responses made by state officials were critical, and there were a number of reasons for the failure to grant relief to the farmers. The merchants opposed the issuance of paper money because they did not see a large market for their products since the farmers were largely self-sufficient. The paper money would simply mean they would profit less from the goods they had already sold the farmers without stimulating any new market. In addition, Governor James Bowdoin and some legislators held securities which they hoped the Confederation or the state would refund in specie, and they did not want to risk having these refunded in paper money. Another factor in the unresponsiveness of the legislature to the demands of the western farmers was the fact that fewer of their representatives attended the sessions, and their pleas to move the capital to a more central location went unheeded. Nor did the legislators have any model in nearby legislatures. Although New Hampshire and Vermont made a few concessions to the farmers, their response was not fundamentally different, and the legislators viewed the paper money policy in Rhode Island as a disaster.

Thus, it is not surprising that the fall session of the legislature not only rejected policies which the farmers had been urging but also passed a Riot Act and suspended the write of habeas corpus. Furthermore, an act providing for the arrest of any person suspected of being unfriendly to the government was passed, and, on November 16, a bill was passed forbidding the spreading of false reports. The only concession made to the farmers was an Act of Indemnity which nevertheless provided that the person could still be sued, presumably for debts. Concurrently with these actions, the legislature and Governor worked to get military force to use against the farmers. First, they called up the militia, which refused to fight. Then they got the Continental Congress to vote for an army, which never materialized because the states refused to pay. Finally, they created a state military force supported by contributions from merchants, professionals, and lawyers in the eastern part of the state. The state forces made raids upon the Shaysites, and although some farmers still hoped the government would release prisoners and suspend the courts until after an election, by the end of the year, the conflict was moving toward outright rebellion.

Since state officials refused to grant concessions to the farmers, the character of their actions changed in late 1786. Although as early as 1782 there was an incident of farmers forcefully interfering with a court, the actions against courts now took on a more organized form. Most of the men had served in the Revolution, knew how to recruit, and had some military training. Although the disturbance in Massachusetts is referred to as Shays' Rebellion, Daniel Shays was just one of many Revolutionary captains who took part. Altogether several thousand of the so-called Regulators were involved in all of New England, but most engagements against the courts consisted of only a few hundred men. Now, however, the actions were better planned and better executed with the men moving in military form. Yet, the intent was to prevent the courts from taking action until the legislature provided paper money, tender acts, and modifications in the tax laws.

The repressive acts of the legislature together with the raids against the Shaysites convinced the farmers the government was tyrannical. They attacked the federal arsenal in Springfield on January 25, 1787, but were defeated by state troops. The Shaysites made another unsuccessful stand at

Persham on February 4, when they were overwhelmed by troops led by General Benjamin Lincoln. This ended the rebellion. Some Shaysites were able to mount a few raids afterward, but they are correctly characterized as social banditry. Ironically, the legislature passed a one-year tender act in June of 1787, and trade improved by 1788.

It is clear the Shaysites wanted the legislature to adopt policies that would give them relief from the hardships of the economic depression; it is equally clear that the merchants desired and implemented a different policy. It is not convincing that the farmers desired the policy in order to perpetuate a subsistence farming culture. When the conflict evolved into rebellion, it is noteworthy that each saw the other as destroying property rights and abusing the prerogatives of government. The merchants saw the interference with the courts as an unacceptable attack upon government, and the farmers viewed the court actions against their farms as unwarranted and the repressive acts of the legislatures as tyrannical. The conflict was over proper policies and the role of government. The value of the book is the extraordinarily high quality of research and prose which provides a moving and realistic story of Shays' Rebellion. Undoubtedly, the rebellion stimulated states to send delegates to the Constitutional Convention, and some provisions of the Constitution were intended to prevent such rebellions.

Doris F. Pierce

THE SIRIAN EXPERIMENTS
The Report of Ambien II, of the Five

Author: Doris Lessing (1919-   )
Publisher: Alfred A. Knopf (New York). 288 pp. $11.95
Type of work: Novel
Time: From the age of the dinosaurs to roughly the present
Locale: The earth, called either Rohanda or Shikasta

A report by Ambien II, a Sirian scientist, on the experimental stations which she oversees

> Principal characters:
> AMBIEN II, a scientist from the planetary system of Sirius
> KLORATHY AND NASAR, Canopeans

The Sirian Experiments is the third novel in the series bearing the general title *Canopus in Argos: Archives*, in which Doris Lessing uses the forms of fantasy and science fiction to explain the nature of good and evil, the presence of good and evil on the planet earth and in the characters of men, and to try to understand the collective human intelligence that prompts people to react in certain ways to certain stimuli.

There will be at least four novels in this series, perhaps more. The first was *Shikasta* (1979), the story of an emissary from Canopus named Johar, who viewed human history from prehistoric times to about fifty years into our future. Shikasta, as the earth is called, is seen through his journals and reports, as well as through the official history of the Canopean rulers who have sent settlers to earth. The second in the series, *The Marriages Between Zones Three, Four, and Five*, is not about these extraterrestrial rulers, but about the settlers themselves, who demonstrate in the form of a fable not only how they react to their unseen rulers but also how they receive goodness from one another, especially through the relationship of marriage. In *The Sirian Experiments*, third in the series, Lessing returns to the overview of the aliens, this time through the eyes of the Sirian scientist, Ambien II, who resembles in many ways the Canopean Johar.

Ambien is a capable woman. Why the Sirians are male and female is a good question, for they are effectively immortal, dying only rarely from disease or accident—for example, one of Ambien's friends is struck by a meteor. Usually, however, Sirians live forever, although aging over the long span does necessitate occasional repair. As an immortal, the Sirian can undertake long-range projects, such as the nurturing of the evolution of a planetary culture. Ambien is engaged in this sort of project, and the reports that she sends back to her planet (which is unnamed) reflect her personality: she is businesslike, and competent even in details like the piloting of the spacecraft she uses.

In the novel, the earth (which the Sirians call Rohanda and the Canopeans, Shikasta) has been used as a sort of experimental farm by the two galactic empires. The planet is still in the process of formation at the beginning of the story, and there is a long period of cooling and radiation in which different species of animals are placed on the planet to check their suitability as inhabitants. After a catastrophe which causes the death of the dinosaurs, the Canopeans and the Sirians try experiments with various races of pygmys, giants, apes, and some hominids. Canopus places its settlers in various regions on the continents of the northern hemisphere, and leaves them there with only a passing scientist every eon or so to mark their progress. Sirius has taken the southern hemisphere, and like its Canopean partners, allows the natives to set a civilization of sorts in motion.

Since the stock for these experiments originated on many different planets, mutations and adaptations occur after they have been transported to earth, none of them, it seems, for the good. Many of the races that had enjoyed lifespans of eight or nine hundred years find that they are living much shorter lives, and as a result become sullen and difficult to handle. Ambien correctly interprets this change as the disappointment of the settlers in discovering that they will live short, brutish lives, dying at the end of their struggles.

The novel incorporates legend in dealing with its philosophical themes: Ambien visits Adalantaland (Atlantus), and meets the beautiful and gentle queen of the island kingdom. Ambien is pleased with the people, whom she finds to be attractive, intelligent, and law-abiding. As she is flying over the island in her space bubble, however, she feels a sudden chill in the air, and experiences a moment of darkness to the sound of a hissing roar. The whole planet has shifted on its axis, and, in the sudden motion, the island is swallowed up in a vortex. The continents, which had lain close to one another, are whirled apart, into the positions that they now occupy.

Ambien notes the changes that the shift of the axis will cause (as John Milton does under similar circumstances in *Paradise Lost*): from now on, Shikasta will have seasons, replacing the constant year-round temperatures that its different regions had enjoyed; the planet will have a slightly longer year; and the polar caps will expand to form great layers of ice. The seas will become shallower, and many of the animals on earth will not survive the temperature changes.

Subsequent visits to Shikasta are equally nerve-wracking to Ambien. On a visit to the city of Koshi, she is mistaken for a whore, because she walks among the inhabitants in her uniform instead of in the ugly all-enveloping black cloak worn by native women in the city. She is rescued from a mob by a man, Klorathy, who takes pity on her and takes her to his apartments to explain the danger she is in. When Ambien concludes that Klorathy is not a native but a Canopean sent to survey the situation in the city, she reveals her identity. Klorathy takes her to another Canopean, Nasar, who is somehow identical to Klorathy (one Canopean is like another, he says). At this point the villains are introduced.

Nasar tells Ambien that the people of Koshi are so uncivilized because agents of Shammat, a planet of the star Puttiora, are in the town sowing discontent among its citizens. Nasar complains that he has been on earth for twenty-five thousand years, watching its settlement by the Canopeans and Sirians, and now he must watch all his fine work be destroyed by the Puttiorans. The Puttiorans, who had been up to the same mischief in *Shikasta*, are thoroughly nasty: they are cold and greasy, and smell bad.

Worse than their physical repulsiveness is the Puttioran habit of ruining the people among whom they settle. Ambien is taken as a prisoner to the house of a woman, Elylé, where for the first time she sees seduction when Nasar nearly succumbs to the charms of the corrupted beauty. Ambien recognizes the influence of the Puttiorans in the easy sexuality of Elylé and in her attempts to rob Ambien of her clothes and jewelry.

Ambien escapes, however, and ages pass during which she works on many planets, finally returning to Shikasta to the city of Grakconkranpatl on the "isolated southern continent." The inhabitants indulge in human sacrifice, and the unlucky Ambien is captured as she tries to make a grand entrance into the city in her white uniform. She immediately sees her mistake in not wearing something more regal. She is sentenced to be sacrificed, but here, as in Koshi, she has a savior, this time in the person of an Indian slave, Rhodia. The slave not only helps Ambien to escape, but also gives her own life to accomplish it. Ambien comes to realize that Rhodia, Nasar, and Klorathy are all the same person in different bodies, Ambien's Canopean guardian angel.

Ambien learns that the strength of Canopus lies in the kindness of its people and in their willingness to sacrifice themselves for others. She comes to think that her own planet, Sirius, is somewhat remiss in its duty to others, and she does not hesitate to take her own people to task when they do not measure up to the Canopeans.

During the passage of the years, the Puttiorans become more powerful on earth. Their chief representative, Tafta, a huge, cruel man, appears from time to time as despot, tyrant, and finally, by the end of the novel, as a scientist, leading the stupid Shikastans to their doom. The manifestations of the Puttioran presence include the sighting of their spaceships, which are mistaken for dragons and other mysterious flying objects. From time to time, the Puttiorans kidnap an earthling and take him or her to the zoo they have established on the moon, or to their planet as slaves for the gentry.

Meanwhile, the three alien empires establish observation posts on the moon to monitor conditions on earth. Those of Canopus and Sirius are content merely to observe, but the people of Puttiora rape the moon of its minerals and leave the satellite with its familiar cratered surface. From the Sirian station, Ambien is horrified to see the savagery and brutality of earth. Hordes of barbarians range across the planet conquering and killing. For a closer look, Ambien visits a kingdom high on the slopes of the Great Mountains, and becomes part of the personality of its queen, Sha'zvin. In the person of the Queen, she leads the people in resistance against the besieging barbarians. Ambien-Sha'zvin, on the advice of a character very much like Nasar-Klorathy, resists to the last, and is finally killed by the invaders.

Fleeing from the Queen's body back to the safety of the moon, Ambien is reunited with Nasar, who reveals to her the main problem of the planet— the white race, who even as they watch, is running wild, warring, killing, and destroying. The watchers fear that the acquisitiveness, pride, and savagery of the whites will eventually destroy the whole planet. The creed of Shammat has become their creed: kill, destroy, and enslave.

Heartsick from what she has witnessed, Ambien is recalled to Sirius and chastised, not for failing to stop the corruptions of the Puttiorans, but for associating with Nasar-Klorathy. Ambien begins to understand the weakness of her own planet—their pride. The Sirians believe so strongly in the rightness of their ways that they view Canopeans as inferior, but Ambien has noted the superiority of the Canopeans in every respect.

Ambien decides to use the ancient medium of a book to reveal the problems both of the Shikastans and the Sirians, and to use that same book to warn Shikasta of the malevolent power in their midst. Because she refuses to give up the idea of the book, her superiors send her into exile on the isolated although pleasant planet 13 of the Sirian Empire. She leaves only after confirming that Tafta, the Shammat agent, is still on Shikasta, now in his charming and smiling scientist's body, working to make sure the inhabitants of earth never realize the danger which faces them.

Lessing has stated that the series cannot be understood until the whole has appeared, but *The Sirian Experiments*, despite its ambitious themes, seems skewed on two points. First is the question of freedom of the will: if man is under the power of alien intruders, whose is the responsibility for the evil actions that result? The second point is the exclusive assignment of that responsibility to the white race. History records conquerors and tyrants in all shades; cruelty is not the exclusive characteristic of any particular race, but of human beings in general. If humans are the "murderous half-apes" the author describes, then all, not just some, need to work to erase the bit of Shammat in us all.

Walter E. Meyers

SO LONG, SEE YOU TOMORROW

Author: William Maxwell (1908-   )
Publisher: Alfred A. Knopf (New York). 135 pp. $7.95
Type of work: Novel
Time: The early 1920's
Locale: Chicago and Lincoln, Illinois

A combination of memoir and fiction which deals with the loss of innocence and considers the importance of finding a balance between bearing the pain and yet remaining sensitive

> *Principal characters:*
> THE AUTHOR, whose mother dies when he is ten years old
> CLETUS SMITH, a farm boy the author knows briefly
> CLARENCE SMITH, Cletus' father who commits a murder-suicide
> FERN SMITH, Clarence's restless wife
> LLOYD WILSON, a neighbor of the Smiths who falls in love with Fern

A memoir, a reckoning of an old regret, William Maxwell's first novel in eighteen years is both. This work originally appeared in *The New Yorker* and, in the style of that journal's fiction, evokes sharp recognition of the small domestic tragedies to which we are all heir.

Two stories are told here: one, an account of Maxwell as a boy of ten reacting to the death of his mother; the other, a fictionalized attempt to reach out to a boyhood acquaintance and make amends for a slight. The two threads become interwoven in the fictionalized account of a murder-suicide.

The author's perceptions color his characters' in an open way; thus, the reader shares his need to "rearrange things to make them acceptable." Friendship is held almost sacred, aloneness and loneliness are confronted, and limitations not only of others but of the self as well are recognized. In reaching out to the real/imaginary Cletus Smith, he hopes to resolve some of these conflicts.

All that is concretely known about Cletus and the tragedy of his family comes from photostatic copies of eight issues of the 1922 Lincoln, Illinois, *Courier-Herald*, court records of a divorce and a murder, and a coroner's inquest. These are pieced together with a mixture of truth and fiction to create a story of a sensitive farm boy forced by the circumstances of his singularity and youth to accept an untenable burden of deceit and murder.

This nightmare imitates the tensions generated by the sudden and unexpected death of Maxwell's mother. He, too, must accept and live with profound loss. The boy walks the floor with his disconsolate and oblivious father, an arm around the grieving man's waist, hoping to share some solace, find some reconcilement. An older brother with whom he shares a bedroom is detached from him also. Each grieves alone, and the boy is left to bear the unbearable in solitude:

Between the way things used to be and the way they were now was a void that couldn't
be crossed. . . . The idea that kept recurring to me . . . was that I had inadvertently
walked through a door that I shouldn't have gone through and couldn't get back to the
place I hadn't meant to leave.

This is a link to meeting Cletus on the scaffolding of a half-finished house.
The rudimentary doorways and open walls create an easy access which is
almost magical. There is a sympathy in the joining of two troubled boys—
but only in retrospect. Cletus is almost like an imaginary playmate and,
therefore, an extension of the narrator. The real and the fiction become a
fretwork on which to hang absolution.

A murder-suicide committed by Cletus' father removes the playmates from
each other permanently with only a chance meeting in Chicago a year and
a half later: "The meeting in the corridor . . . I keep reliving in my mind, as
if I were going through a series of reincarnations that end up each time in the
same failure." The boys recognize each other, but not a word is spoken by
either. Maxwell the adolescent and adult forever after feels guilty that he did
not offer a word or gesture of recognition, consolation. The boy who has
been acutely sensitive to slights toward himself has slighted another. This
moment exists as the regret which must be reconciled through fiction. The
author becomes storyteller giving speech to the inarticulate, crossing the void
at last.

Lincoln, Illinois, in the early 1920's is a farming community. In town live
the landowners and out of town their tenants, the farmers. These hardworking, austere, plain-speaking men and women shy away from the small-town
familiarity and rely on one another instead. The sound of a gasoline engine
sputtering and dying somewhere off in the fields can be heard, and farmers
removed from one another by many acres listen for it to start again.

The farmhouse of Lloyd Wilson lies an eighth of a mile closer to town than
that of Clarence Smith, and, if need be, one will leave his own work to help
the other: "Wrenches and pliers pass back and forth between them with as
much familiarity as if they owned their four hands in common." Newspaper
photographs of the two men printed after the tragedy show they even look
alike.

Outwardly there are no signs of conflict in these two families. The boy,
Cletus, hears things, however—his mother crying at night through the thin
walls, angry voices rising through the ventilator from the room below his
bedroom. This companionless boy, a good boy, tries to shut the discord out
by dreaming of a motorcycle he saw in the Sears, Roebuck catalog and by
helping his father with the chores. When he cannot concentrate on his homework, the teacher does not scold him for she "knows he is a gentle boy and
tries hard."

Dissent is beginning to take shape in the Wilson household, too, as Lloyd
tries to disguise his loss of passion for his wife. He wonders if all new expe-

riences are over for him, for he feels he has done everything there is to do already. Although each instinctively knows that the other has problems, the men respect the dignity of silence on personal matters.

The problems are joined quite unexpectedly, however, when Lloyd falls in love with Clarence's wife, Fern. He feels suddenly pulled into a situation over which he has no control. His manner toward the Smiths becomes remote and unnatural as he tries to control his feelings. In his imagination he guiltily tells Clarence he should not trust him because "all my life I've been a mystery to myself." From this point the tragedy unfolds slowly, inevitably—the characters are helpless to turn things back. What is done cannot be undone. Lloyd confesses his love to Fern, and she, a woman with "a look of sadness about her who perhaps expects more of life than is reasonable," reciprocates. Lloyd mourns for the loss of his best friend as though Clarence had been lost in an accident.

The lovers, only disguised now as neighbors, catch Cletus staring at them, seeing them as strangers. The innocence of the boy is being steadily eroded by the actions of the adults. Blamelessness and simplicity ironically create a burden on the heart of the innocent when confronted with deceit and faithlessness. There is no precedent for understanding why the sins of parents must be passed on to their children.

Fern's guilty conscience makes her suspect that Clarence knows. He, too, however, is an innocent, a man who gives the impression of being defenseless because he sees life as predictable, views promises as binding, and naïvely expects loyalty in return for loyalty. When she accuses him of deceitfully hiding his knowledge of the affair, "it was as if a hole opened suddenly at their feet and they fell into it."

Now events move in slow motion. A year passes. Lloyd and Fern are determined to see each other; Clarence hopes the affair will wear itself out. Fern deliberately flaunts her disobedience and what was once whispered behind closed doors now is shouted from the top of the stairs. Cletus still rides his Christmas bike down the dusty road after school, and his dog still runs to greet him, but the farmhouse he enters is marked by his mother's inattention and his father's sad whistling. Marie Wilson moves into town, finally defeated by her husband's alienation. Lloyd, aware that with a word she would stay, announces instead, "I have never before in my life been happy, and I will not give it up."

Clarence, whose behavior has been increasingly characterized by passionate violence toward his wife, visits a minister who recommends that Fern seek counsel. Instead, she takes Cletus and his younger brother Wayne and moves in with her aunt in a small, dilapidated house across from the fairgrounds. Her lawyer warns Clarence that he is not to harass her or his boys. Cletus, alone and lonely, worried about his father, is lured by the sounds of a house being built and wanders off to investigate.

In the courtroom, the violence in her marriage is what Fern's lawyer advises her to emphasize. Clarence has cross-filed on grounds of infidelity, but his only witness, the hired hand, is discredited as a drunk. It is never brought out that Clarence Smith is "pierced to the heart by his wife's failure to love him." He loses everything: his wife, his family, his farm.

Lloyd Wilson is found murdered before sunrise one morning slumped against a partition sitting on a milking stool. One of his ears has been cut off with a razor and the murderer has carried it away. Fifteen days later, Clarence Smith's body, shot through the head, is found lying face down across the dredging bucket at the bottom of Deer Creek gravel pit, a still bloody razor in his coat pocket. Cletus is summoned by the sheriff to identify a shotgun found floating in the pit. The author notes:

> Between the time that Cletus and I climbed down from the scaffolding and went our separate ways and the moment when he was confronted with the broken gun in the sheriff's office, he must have crossed over the line into maturity.

Maxwell presents adversity, not only that of others but also his own, using a style that is conversational, surely "midwestern" in its informality. This adds to the sense of simple people meeting fate on nonpretentious terms, yet clichés become almost extraneous in their frequency: "the short end of the stick," "teacher will be sore at him," "talking her leg off,' the "widow had other strings to her bow," "there is a line you can't cross over," "he climbed on top of her," "let the cat out of the bag." There is even a dog that thinks in clichés, and this is a problem, too. Maxwell has asked the reader to imagine a dog for Cletus, since farms and farm boys typically have such, but it is difficult to accept a dog in the same terms of innocence as humans. The dog, tied to a tree and left on the deserted farm, is "trying not to worry. Trying to be good—trying to be especially good." Also, when Wilson's little boys put their arms around her, she "felt some better." She repeatedly runs away from her new master, Smith's successor on the farm, and is finally "put out" with chloroform at the vet's by a distraught Clarence. Fear and pity can be honestly elicited for Cletus, for Clarence, for Lloyd, but it borders on exaggeration to ask these same feelings for the dog, however domestic the tragedy.

Maxwell's "roundabout, futile way of making amends" acknowledges Cletus' struggles as greater than his own. Even for him the wounds were long in healing and fester occasionally. He only hopes that Cletus "with his arms outstretched, like an acrobat on a high wire, with no net to catch him if he falls," survived the dreadful series of events that Maxwell transiently shared. Thus, he can reach out now to the boy he passed in the halls of a high school long removed and say, "I understand," yet he will see the image of Cletus again tomorrow and only hope to believe that "what is done can be undone."

Kathleen Massey

A SOLDIER'S EMBRACE

Author: Nadine Gordimer (1923-   )
Publisher: The Viking Press (New York). 144 pp. $8.95
Type of work: Short stories
Time: Recent decades
Locale: South Africa

Thirteen short stories that emphasize emotions in individual isolation in conflict with intricate and complex relationships, personal, social, and political

Nadine Gordimer, born in 1923 near Johannesburg, South Africa's "golden city," has for thirty years been identified as a South African writer. Recognition in the United States of Gordimer's work began in 1952, when her first collection of short stories, *The Soft Voice of the Serpent,* was published in New York. Since that time, she has published eight novels and eight collections of short stories.

A Soldier's Embrace, thirteen short stories, consistently continues to develop the themes, style, and characterizations of the previous collections, but Gordimer's imaginative range, embracing a variety of situations and emotions, keeps the stories from seeming repetitive. Gustave Flaubert said, "One never tires of anything that is well written." Like many writers, Gordimer confesses to being an "unconscious eavesdropper," and fragments of realistic conversations combine with highly imaginative elements to form many of her stories. It is difficult to say whether any of the stories are autobiographical; Gordimer maintains a private personal life. If, however, she writes from a personal experience and she claims to absorb and use what she experiences, that experience may be years in the formative stage, gathering characters to it, suggesting a theme, eventually relating perhaps to a nonpersonal event that took place another time, another place. All these elements then emerge as a cohesive story.

Gordimer never left South Africa for short visits elsewhere until she was thirty. She lives there now, uses the political and social systems of that country as a basis for the structure of her stories and novels, and forms many of her characters out of the complex relations and situations of blacks and whites. Gordimer is South African, was educated partially in a convent, and her father was a well-to-do businessman. She is fully aware of the position of the white liberal in South Africa. She has a firm knowledge of the language, customs, habits, superstitions, ceremonies, and tribal rituals of the blacks. It is not necessary that the reader have Gordimer's knowledge of the country and its inhabitants. She gives the reader a sense of the landscape and the wasted beauty of the land, different parts of the cities and their various dwelling places and shops by descriptive passages that never impede the progression of the story; the reader almost subconsciously absorbs them.

The sequence of the stories in this collection is conducive to the reader's awareness of the political, social order of which Gordimer says, "society is the political situation." The first story, "A Soldier's Embrace," exhibits the changing political situation after the confrontation between the Colonial government and the black regime that comes to power in an unnamed African country. The central characters, a well-known white lawyer who has been sympathetic to the black cause and his wife, move through phases of comfortable coexistence to an uneasy separate existence and fear, and finally leave the country. The last story, "Oral History," reflects the changing political scene, the emphasis now on the effect upon a black tribe and its Judas-like chief.

Gordimer says that when she read Eudora Welty's stories of rural Mississippi, she realized that "no place looked at properly need be considered at the end of the world." South Africa may seem to be at the end of the world because of its isolated geographical, political, and social conditions, but by contrasting the isolation of the country and the isolation of character situation, Gordimer places a double emphasis on this dominant theme. Most of her stories are set in Johannesburg, a city of contrast, where rich and poor, black and white, sophisticated Europeans and tribal Africans live, work, and come into daily contact with one another. With a microscopically observant critical eye, Gordimer creates characters who are uneasy, conscience-stricken, sometimes politically conscious, cultivated men and women, sometimes from the poorer, uneducated class, but all searching, usually unsuccessfully, for a comfortable life in their particular situation. They attempt to transcend the politically controlled social situations, to come to terms with the ambiguities of a South African society, fundamentally out of joint, to shape individual identities and find relationships in which class and color are of little importance.

The failure of this endeavor is evident in the last line of "Town and Country, Part One": "The girl's mother was quoted, with photograph, in the Sunday papers: 'I won't let my daughter work as a servant for a white man again.'" Also in the last line of "Town and Country Lovers, Part Two": "Interviewed by the Sunday papers, who spelled her name in a variety of ways, the black girl, speaking in her own language, was quoted beneath her photograph: 'It was a thing of our childhood, we don't see each other any more.'"

Even though she is a major figure in the advancement of literature coming out of South Africa, Gordimer should not be classed as a regionalist. The ever-changing political climate of South Africa imposes a limit upon her writing, on the development of her characters, but if she were geographically located elsewhere, another limiting influence would have taken the place of politics and social interaction, for every writer is limited by something. Unlike Chinua Achebé, who is concerned with universal human communication across racial and cultural boundaries and who imposes his authorial views on his work, Gordimer is not a political writer. She is concerned with politics only in the way it imposes limitations, affects, and molds the lives of her characters. Never does she use character or situation in the stories to make a political point, rather the reader perceives the situation in South Africa through the characters' experience. The communal richness of the black population is never sentimentalized nor patronized, and sometimes, as in the first story of the collection, "A Soldier's Embrace," the white characters emerge pale, alienated. The significance of the political situation, the continuing war over apartheid, is never more than implicit in her stories. She differs from Doris Lessing, whose primary focus is the discriminatory practices of men against women, in her variety of subject matter and theme.

Some critics have compared Gordimer's stories to those of J. D. Salinger. Unlike Salinger's characters, however, who are excruciatingly important to him as people, Gordimer's characters are important only in the way they act as vehicles for theme. The main thrust of her stories is the individual emotion as theme, whether it be warranted or unwarranted fear; misplaced love; loyalty that disappears under pressure; suffering as a condition of life, accepted or ignored; or the chance missed.

Because of the deliberate concentration on theme, some critics have labeled Gordimer *coldly* objective; a phrase that reappears in describing her approach is "cool camera eye." Gordimer's stories, characteristically brief, often convey very complex relationships, and it is this studied objectivity that enables the reader to see Gordimer's characters with crystal clarity. They stand alone, starkly illuminated. The photographer does not intrude.

Gordimer delineates complex relationships: in "A Soldier's Embrace," the interaction between husband and wife; between the wife and a black and a white soldier celebrating peace; among husband, wife, and formerly exiled black friend, Chipande; and among husband, wife, Chipande, and Father Mulumbua, a black priest, fighting for his political survival. In "Siblings," she dramatizes the involvement between twin sisters and their two children, one a boy who follows a traditional life of home, school, and social activities, and the other a girl who leaves home, torments her mother by telling her she is a lesbian, enters the hospital periodically either because of using drugs or trying to commit suicide by slashing her wrists; and the very different involvement of the boy and girl themselves.

The natural use of dialogue, the deliberate, careful choice of words, the phrasing, and the author's precise manipulation of characters, produce in the reader an empathy with a particular character and evoke the desired emotion. The success of a Gordimer story depends on her device of indirection that communicates an emotion, an ingredient of experience, and her manipulative and developmental ability that move the reader toward implication, rather than on overt statements about the desires and motives of her characters. She employs devices of indirection extremely well. Sometimes, however, she shows a lack of confidence in her own ability by too often in the last few lines of a story overstating the point she has already made, thereby destroying the effect she has so consciously crafted. In "The Termitary," she sets up the obvious, but good metaphor of the mother as termite queen. Both are imprisoned by duty and responsibility. In the last line, as if fearing that the reader may not understand, she had the daughter-narrator say, "Now she is dead and although I suppose someone else lives in her house, the secret passages, the inner chamber in which she was our queen and our prisoner are sealed up, empty." Although this flaw is not a contrivance to set up her stories only for the ending, the reader, having encountered it in more than one story, is distracted and anticipates such as ending in other stories.

She consistently overworks the use of parenthesis, often giving unnecessary exposition. "Shops were being looted by the unemployed and loafers (there had always been a lot of unemployed hanging around for the picking of the town) who felt the new regime should entitle them to take what they dared not before." Removal of such interpolations would not affect the story adversely; or, if the comments are important to the story, they should not be parenthetical.

That Gordimer begins with a conceptualized image of the desired effect on the reader is clear in her choice of titles, which envision the story's main focus. She sometimes involves the reader immediately by setting a tone in the first few lines of a story. For example, "The Termitary" begins: "When you live in a small town far from the world you read about in municipal library books, the advent of repair men in the house is a festival." Her style is successfully determined by the point of view she chooses for each story. The use of the omniscient point of view in "A Soldier's Embrace," "Town and Country Lovers," and "Oral History" frees Gordimer to encompass numerous relations from many angles and give a broad view of the complexities of the involvements. In "Siblings," "A Mad One," and "A Hunting Accident," told in limited third person, the reader sees all the action through the eyes of one character only. The focus is narrowed further still in "A Lion on the Freeway," "For Dear Life," "You Name It," "The Termitary," and "The Need for Something Sweet," by her use of first-person narration. In "Time Did," the "I" speaks directly to another character: "I had been lying there close to you, resting on the shore of your body attained. At these times you seem to take on physical functions for me; yours is the effort that makes us breathe."

Within the controlled limits of Gordimer's point of view techniques, the development of physical and moral character occur simultaneously. The narrative style is sometimes interior monologue as in "You Name it"; interior monologue punctuated by exterior dialogue as in "Time Did"; straight-line narrative including the character's imagined scenes and confrontations as in "A Mad One"; and remembered conversations and happenings intruding on the current situation as in "A Soldier's Embrace," when the lawyer's wife keeps remembering being caught between two soldiers, one black, one white, in a parade and responding to their embrace by impulsively kissing each on the cheek, an act completely out of character for her. Conflict and contrast develop as patterns, controlled without confusion by Gordimer's point of view techniques, her style, and her various felicitous devices.

Symbolism exists in Gordimer's stories properly in relation to the context of the story. In "Siblings" it is the scars on the inside of Maxine's often slashed wrists that her cousin tries to avoid seeing; in "A Mad One," the telephone by which Leif's sister-in-law intrudes on his family life and which Elena unplugs; in "A Lion on the Freeway," the cage denying freedom; and in "You Name It," the written name of Arno Arkanius, first on the sand, then on the inside wall of a telephone booth.

That critics have compared Gordimer to Anton Chekhov, Katherine Mansfield, James Joyce, Guy de Maupassant, Joseph Conrad, and Stephen Crane appears to be a contradiction in itself, for where is the common link among these writers? Perhaps Gordimer uses isolated elements or techniques from all of them, but in saying that, one must acknowledge that she is also different. She is neither as cool as Chekhov, nor as consciously, deliberately perfect as Mansfield, her style is not as lush as Conrad's or Crane's, but sometimes her dead, like Joyce's refuse to lie down. Why must Nadine Gordimer be compared to anyone? Her works are certainly worthy of being read and enjoyed for their own distinctive characteristics and qualities.

Although Gordimer has been cited as a "link between white and black culture in South Africa" and as the white South African woman who gives the most complete vision of South Africa available, she says that "no white South African writer can penetrate the African consciousness. If there is to be a true South African culture there should have been an honest intermingling of black and white." She remains, at least in her short stories, committed to fundamentals, and in her chosen dwelling place, to "the infinite variety of effects apartheid has on men and women."

Peggy Bach

SOLDIERS OF THE NIGHT
The Story of the French Resistance

Author: David Schoenbrun (1915-   )
Publisher: E. P. Dutton (New York). Illustrated. 512 pp. $15.95
Type of work: History
Time: 1940-1944
Locale: Primarily France; London and North Africa

A fast-paced and colorful depiction of the French Resistance movement and how it helped to create the attitudes prevalent in France today

The legend of the French resistance to the German occupation of the country during World War II has often been close to providing *the* national myth for France in the postwar years. Only in the last decade has that myth come under close scrutiny, examination, and debunking. David Schoenbrun, a journalist, television correspondent, and lecturer, brings a passion for and close association with a number of the figures of the Resistance to this book. He is not writing to discredit, but rather he essentially glorifies the movement and its partisans. For those who seek a fast-paced version of this episode in human history, and who are willing to accept Schoenbrun's posture of advocacy and rather simplistic explanations of motivation, the book will surely satisfy.

To some readers acquainted with and attuned to historical writing and argumentation, Schoenbrun's over-reliance on source material gleaned from personal interviews will seem suspect. Schoenbrun knows personally a large number of the survivors of the Resistance—a fact that he will not let the reader forget. The focus of the book is frequently distorted by the inclusion of insignificant memorabilia and descriptive phrases, all of which appear to be a kind of historical name-dropping. The story of the Resistance (and the intertwined theme of collaboration) is a very complex and morally torturous one, and Schoenbrun might have better served his public had he attained a greater objectivity toward his subject.

Resistants of every stripe and color are to be found between the covers of *Soldiers of the Night*—from Communists to right-wing French patriots, from Marie-Madeleine Fourcade to Boris Vilde, from Charles de Gaulle to Duclos. No reader or commentator can fault Schoenbrun on his attempt at thoroughness, nor for his lack of imagination in moving back and forth from scene to scene and place to place trying to reconstruct a movement which was really dozens of movements, fraught with a variety of both personal and ideological factors.

Soldiers of the Night depicts a resistance movement which grew from many disparate elements, and which through the course of the war (and even into the years immediately following it) reflected the tensions, workings at cross-purposes, envy, and jealousy inherent in this fact. Schoenbrun merits high marks for attempting to cover the full range of resistance activities and attitudes, but his accounting for the emotional and psychological burdens of the tensions between the various resistance elements is questionable.

In accounting for the fall of France in 1940, Schoenbrun offers a straightforward and primarily anecdotal description of the atmosphere in Paris, hardly looking beneath the surface. He may here sell himself short by ignoring the tensions and discordances of French society in the late 1930's which clearly led to the debacle. In the long run, by failing to account in the very beginning for these problems, he later fails to tie to their proper historical antecedents the tensions which reemerged in France on the heels of its liberation.

In the first section of *Soldiers of the Night*, the chapter entitled "Birth of the Resistance" portrays the disparate personal elements and perceptions which fed the resistance. On balance, the old conservative patriots sensed the imminent failure of Henri Philippe Pétain to stand against Hitler, as did groups of young Catholics, Communists, and others without clear prior religious or political orientation. These were individuals acting spontaneously, and for the most part without organization or focus. With de Gaulle stripped of his military post and in exile in London by the third week of June, 1940, the stage was set for the two parallel developments: "the Resistance of the Interior" and "the Resistance of the Exterior," which would not, clearly, always develop with any real degree of synchronization to each other.

The relationships between the various resistance groups in France were complicated and convoluted. Additionally, the communications and coordinations between the various combat groups working to sabotage the German occupation from within and the bodies planning for France's liberation and her future from without were problematic.

Until 1943, the various resistance groups operating within France often acted with elements in the Vichy regime; even the French police proved either willingly ineffectual or looked the other way with regard to their activities. The tide turned swiftly, however, with the coming of a German crackdown. That crackdown was brought on by Germany's deteriorating military position generally, and specifically by tensions with the Vichy regime, such as those evoked when officers of the French fleet blew up nearly one hundred warships based at Toulon. Swiftly, the German occupiers in the North of France extended their presence into the previously "free" zone in the south. This turn of events meant increased pressures on and challenges to the elements of the Resistance operating in France. The response to those challenges was forthcoming. At the turn of the year, 1942-1943, communication between the various resistance groups was strong enough to permit coordination of a joint effort to confront the Germans and their French sympathizers. This occurred in the city of Montluçon, and it marked a decided shift in resistance activity.

In *Soldiers of the Night*, the struggle for power and dominance in the Resistance is sketched in France itself, as well as in London and in Algiers.

In France, Jean Moulin was instrumental in forging the basis of unified resistance activities, until his capture by Germans and his death. The gap caused by his death was filled by summer of 1943 by Claude Surreulles, a de Gaulle loyalist, who set himself to the creation of an independent French government. Across the channel in England and across the Mediterranean in North Africa the Gaullists and the Giraudists parried day after day for position, influence and leverage—not least of all with their benefactors, the Anglo-American Allies.

The central theme of Schoenbrun's book is that the experience of the Resistance traced in microcosm the future tensions and conflicts which have characterized French public life from the Liberation to the present. This the author outlines swiftly and perhaps a bit sketchily in his final chapter, entitled "Epilogue: Out of the Shadows." To a great extent the chapter is a balance sheet on the men and women who led the various elements of the resistance and their fates in postwar France. In particular, Schoenbrun clarifies the argument that France's skepticism and stand-offishness toward European unity was born in the particular struggle of the Resistance, and that the shared attempt to give rebirth to an independent France is much at the heart of this. This view corrects the notion that France's postwar posture is a product of a long-standing French pride, or even arrogance, about the superiority of its "civilization," or that this direction, although personified by de Gaulle, was simply a matter of his rather singular and insular perception.

Schoenbrun, certainly, can be given much credit for attempting to produce a single-volume work in English on the Resistance. For some readers, however, his journalistic style may seem inadequate to this challenge. Schoenbrun's ploy of reconstructing conversations from reminiscenses, trying all too self-consciously to imbue the book with a sense of immediacy as he does, is subject to criticism. So, too, is his losing the forest for the trees. The heroism of the Resistance is, perhaps, better treated as a subtopic to the major political, moral, and human dilemmas of the German occupation of much of Europe during World War II. Schoenbrun, alas, never does tell his reader exactly what it was that made France so vulnerable to the occupation or precisely how the myth of the resistance came in postwar years to be as powerful as it has proven. Had he done so, this work, which often reads like a mediocre spy novel, would have been a significant contribution to unraveling this complex experience in human history.

Paul Monaco

A SOUTHERN RENAISSANCE
The Cultural Awakening of the American South, 1930-1955

Author: Richard H. King (1942-   )
Publisher: Oxford University Press (New York). 350 pp. $15.95
Type of work: Literary history
Time: 1930-1955
Locale: The American South

A work which suggests a number of reasons for the fullness and impact of literary expression in the American South during the years from 1930 to 1955

Anyone who came of age in the contemporary South, and who is even remotely conscious of that anomaly, "being Southern," has probably grown up hearing and breathing many of the magic names: Will Percy, William Faulkner, Thomas Wolfe, James Agee, Lillian Smith, C. Vann Woodward, Howard Odum, Rupert Vance, John Crowe Ransom, Allen Tate, Robert Penn Warren, and certainly W. J. Cash. The writings of these people—even when they are cited by those who do not read them—provide the major ideas and images and the evocations of a region intensely, defensively, even morbidly conscious of itself and its problems. Each of these writers has created at least one classically definitive work on the Southern mystique; a work about which thoughtful Southerners will have heard, perhaps even read and studied. Among the fictionists, the definitive work might be Faulkner's *Go Down, Moses*; among the historians, it could be Woodward's *Origins of the New South*; among the sociologists, it might be Odum's *Southern Regions of the United States*; and among the journalist-observers, it must be Cash's *The Mind of the South*.

Published four decades ago, *The Mind of the South* remains *the* great referential touch-stone: a flawed, controversial, passionate, insightful document. Richard H. King, in his richly informed study, *A Southern Renaissance*, evaluates Cash's book as one of those unusual works which improves upon rereading. He describes it as exciting, audacious, and "compelling even when it cannot persuade." Those exact words might well be applied to King's own book. His study does continue to reward upon rereading. Many will find his approach at times audacious; yet, he is always provocative and informative. As a scholarly landmark, King's book will be—like Cash's—investigated, castigated, lauded, and used by students of Southern history and culture for years to come. The book has, for instance, thirty-eight pages of chapter notes which, unlike most footnotes, are as sprightly and informative· as the text. It is hard to read them without feeling an urge to dash off to the library to pursue further this or that reference. His sixteen-page index, too, is full, thorough, and very helpful.

Notably, *A Southern Renaissance* is more than a mere historical account. It is an important, analytical work on a difficult subject. Any geographic and culturally peculiar region is impossible to write about definitively. Thus, King, a Tennessee-born, University of North Carolina-trained cultural historian, takes meticulous care first to define the regional and temporal boundaries of his subject, and then to limit (in order to deepen) his specific citations. No one, of course, can write about "the South." King explores here what he calls the "progress in self-consciousness" of a select group of Southern writers and intellectuals who were active between 1930 and 1955. Within those seemingly stringent confines, he systematically and soundly presents an enormously stimulating and various body of ideas.

King finds useful Woodward's location of the origins of the Southern Renaissance as being 1929, the year which saw publication of both Wolfe's *Look Homeward, Angel* and Faulkner's *The Sound and the Fury*. He also agrees with Woodward's summation of the Renaissance as being a singular flowering of the literary arts. For purposes of his study, King has used 1955 as the year the main phase of this "well ran dry," as the South became preoccupied with cold war, civil rights—with "other voices, other rooms."

Not intended, as King makes clear, to be a complete intellectual or literary history of the Southern Renaissance, this study rather examines only the attempts of a few white Southern writers and intellectuals who came to terms with the problems of their history, their region, and their culture. Because he concentrates only on those writers who see "the South and its tradition as problematic," King excludes such minority writers as Richard Wright, Eudora Welty, Ralph Ellison, and Flannery O'Connor. Rightfully, he notes that a complete history of the Renaissance would "demand extensive treatment." His reasons—debatable from several points—for excluding certain writers are, nevertheless, interesting: black writers are not included because their great theme was "to escape the white South;" women, with the single exception of Lillian Smith, are not included because, despite the "considerable merits" of their works,". . . they were not concerned primarily with the larger cultural, racial, and political themes" on which King chooses to focus.

Dealing thus with a relatively brief, although vigorous, span of time and utilizing a strictly selected, although prodigiously productive, few people, King's study suggests and explores the profound psychological forces which gave this particular development of historical consciousness its singularity. It is at the psychological level of his careful preparations, his exclusions and definitions, that King's deepest interests and his real methods become apparent. They are controversial and exciting. Not a traditional historian, he is mainly interested in the "whys" of the "whats" and the "whens." An admitted theoretician, not a recorder, he is profoundly influenced by Freudian psychology.

King is a young scholar who speaks of being "immediately and permanently hooked" on a writer. He cites Jack Nicholson's performance in *Easy Rider*, as an example of a Southern "type." Typically, too, his strongest indictment of anyone seems to be that they are "morally obtuse." He defends psycho-history, as well, as an "unfairly maligned" subspecialty among his colleagues. His approach, its necessary density and allusiveness, and wide-ranging and challenging juxtapositions, unfortunately, will put many readers off. His readership will be made small not because he is hard to follow, but because he is someone with whom it is hard to keep pace. He draws lines of connection in challenging directions; he drives the reader to the dictionary, to seek new resources, and to review old ones. He is an impressively skillful thinker who has done his homework. Not only has he studied his history lessons, but he has also studied psychoanalytic theory and cultural philosophy. He has read the works of Karl Marx, Sigmund Freud, Max Weber, Émile Durkheim, Friedrich Nietzsche, and Friedrich Hegel. He has thought about relationships between all these forces and their various phenomena; and he has read closely and wisely the major Southern writers.

All this training, preparation, and erudition comes together informatively and brilliantly within King's structure. Granted, the study is a sharply restricted one, but this restriction is compensated for by functioning in a synecdochial fashion. King's systematically psychoanalytic probings of writers such as Percy, Faulkner, Cash, or Tate speak volumes about other Southerners not included in this book, especially when readers carefully transfer King's ideas to them and their works. So, while he makes no attempt to treat them all, King gets at the basic structures on which they all build. Describing his work as a form of "cultural anthropology," King investigates a regional culture's systems of symbol and image—its conscious articulations and hidden underpinnings—as those factors responded to historical change.

Necessarily, the idea of flux imbues this book. King early cites as a guiding insight Allen Tate's observation concerning reasons for the importance of Emily Dickinson's poetry. Tate suggested that, coming as she did when the New England Theocracy was breaking up and yet had not been quite "reduced" by Ralph Waldo Emerson to "genteel secularism," Dickinson had creatively reflected the "clash of powerful opposites." The cultural turmoil of her place and time had forced her into genius.

The American South between 1930 and 1955 was undeniably a hotbed of powerfully clashing opposites. The conditions would produce some geniuses. King ultimately proposes that this very tension—so sharply focused between such contradictory impulses as an anachronistically romantic tradition and the harshly emerging realities of the twentieth century—was what caused the passionately eloquent responses of Southern writers and intellectuals in what Woodward labelled a Southern Renaissance. Out of that complex turbulence came complex art.

King attempts to determine of what that art is composed and why it takes the forms that it does. With each writer whom he treats, his process is consistent. First he outlines, defines, and explores both the strengths and problems of the traditions, the rationales, the received attitudes, and the myths extant in their region as experienced by those Southerners who came of age during World War I. Then, he shows how inexorably those political, economic, racial, moral, religious, and philosophical "truths" were altered and how those people who had held to such "givens" as guides were moved to respond.

Employing Freud's theory of therapy (that is, the movement of human memory to place itself in context through the stages of "repetition," "recollection," and "working through"), King analyzes psychologically each writer. He reasons that such a normative model is useful to historians to gauge the power of any work which treats the past as thematic. The author mentions Faulkner's approach to fiction: it takes the reader back, then through experience, and finally out the other side—at which point, the reader can then see the way that the character (and the reader himself) came into the work, only at a different level. New, workable truths have been discovered. King admits, too, that Faulkner dominates his book, but since his work illustrates Freud's process so powerfully, the dominance is justified. In Freudian terms, Faulkner's body of work truly comes to grips with the complex questions of who the Southerner is, where he is, and why. King unabashedly admires Faulkner's ability to create metaphoric history as he depicts his fictive characters' struggles within cultural change, as they contrive to play the game, and, perhaps even more powerfully, when the old rules have been changed and new ones have not quite been formulated. Faulkner at his best is protean and organic. His characters progress even when they lose. Thus, King sees Faulkner more as historian than as fictionist.

Not all the written responses resulting from such "working through" are as admired by King. The Agrarians, for instance, closed doors through the process rather than opening them; they early touted the old game even when they themselves no longer played it.

Part of the fascination in analyzing such cultural clashes is the discovery of the resultant polarity of responses. The early Agrarians, such as Allen Tate, John Crowe Ransom, and Donald Davidson, would defend in their famous document *I'll Take My Stand*, the old virtues of the antebellum South, "a felicitous, harmonious balance of yeoman and planter." They would develop a siege mentality against the New South, and they would argue for the rejection of any integration into the modern (Northern) economy of industrial and financial capitalism. In contrast to this defensive stance, Lillian Smith's response to change in her home region would be to argue vehemently for full, rational, populist, moral involvement in the twentieth century, in the nation, and in the world.

Of the thirty or so writers whom he discusses, King provides the most informative and memorable sections on Allen Tate, W. J. Cash, Will Percy, and William Faulkner. The application of his theories to such figures as Lillian Smith, Thomas Wolfe, James Agee, and Robert Penn Warren are intriguing, challenging, and suggestive; but he works closest to his scholarly bone and is most obviously excited himself when he explores the peculiarly Southern struggles with paradoxes, conundrums, ambivalences, and self-divisions which result in the final strengths (although often melancholy and ironic) of Tate, Cash, Percy, and Faulkner.

Within the confines of *A Southern Renaissance*, King grapples with the spiritual and cultural forces which shaped, and were somewhat shaped by, these four enormously complex, talented, and thus representative, Southern writers. He shows how each struggled, personally and professionally, through the process of repetition, recollection, and working through. Finally, they all made "superb failures," to use Faulkner's evaluative term. They struggled valiantly, although sometimes misguidedly, against overpowering odds. Tate, for example, spent the first half of his life writing essays and poems defending a rationale of retention, a conservative, protestant faith which he would later work through to "progressing" beyond, finishing his career living in the North as a Roman Catholic. Cash equivocated much of his life, stewing inchoately in rebellious juices he was too gallantly restrained to express. Finally, having relieved himself of such genteel restrictions, he seared his beloved region with one great bitter spurt of words. He left the South and committed suicide in Mexico, a paranoid alcoholic. Percy, the landed, accomplished scion of a genuine planter, the "last gentleman," would suffer profoundly the loss of the sweet past, the loss of the fearfully unquestionable strength of the traditional Southern patriarch, and finally the loss of any sure sense of himself except as his father's son. Melancholic, self-labeled a failure, caught-out-of-time, he would finally adopt a family of orphaned boys, rear them and be the gentle, flexible father his beloved tradition had denied him. Finally, Faulkner, the great thinking slew-foot bear in the Southern wilderness, would come to terms with not only the loss of tradition, but also with the increasingly apparent hollowness of tradition itself. That difficult movement was compounded by the need, then, to confront the equal sterility of much of the contemporary replacements of that tradition. Thus, Faulkner's response to change is complexly layered: dark and honest.

These men, their lives and their works—their resolutions of the problems of who they had to be because of where and when they happened to be—form the core of King's thesis: the conditions most conducive to memorable artistic productivity reside in a transitional period between old and new traditions. It is a psychological no-man's land. The best art reflects the tensions in a society and culture on the verge of dissolution. The American South produced an inordinate number of self-conscious and productive participants in that period, which Tate once described as "a good age to write about but a hard one to live in." It is on the cutting edge of experience's blade that action—seminal, frightening—takes place. Before the blade there is air, potential; behind it there is blood, severance. A painful process anywhere, anytime, this change in the tradition-bound South is an exquisite example.

As controversial as his psychoanalytic approach may be, King's book is destined to last; it is important, accessible, and useful. Aside from his thorough, painstaking scholarship, King adds to his book's appeal through, his obvious excitement regarding the larger miracle that is human intelligence— man's superimposition of brain over experience. As focused on the American South from 1930 to 1955, his lively intelligence illuminates and raises, finally, affirmative possibilities not only about that specific locale and era, but also about all human places and times. His is a solidly informed, highly readable, and strangely moving work to which readers will return again and again, both for confirmation and for departure. In our time of so much pedestrian scholarship, one cannot wish for much more stimulation than *A Southern Renaissance* provides.

Thomas N. Walters

THE SOVIET TRIANGLE
Russia's Relations with China and the West in the 1980s

Author: Donald R. Shanor (1927-   )
Publisher: St. Martin's Press (New York). 296 pp. $13.95
Type of work: Current affairs
Time: The present
Locale: The United States, Russia, and China

This work is a suggestion for an American diplomatic strategy for a triangular balance of power with the Soviet Union and China

Donald R. Shanor, the Director of the International Division of the Columbia University Graduate School of Education, and a journalist, begins his discussion on foreign policy with the observation that a new triangular pattern is emerging in the world, a Sino-Soviet-American system that includes elements of both alliance and rivalry in the relations of the nations it encompasses. In the relationship which places the Soviet Union and its camp on one side, China and sometimes Japan on another, and the United States and Western Europe on the third, a change in attitude of one toward either or both of the others transforms the triangle.

Combining historical narrative and political analysis, Shanor traces the evolution of China's policies toward and relations with the Soviet Union, Japan, and the United States. He concludes disparity in power is the key to the emnity between Russia and China and all other reasons—ideological, territorial, and political are subordinate to it. Although his chapters on bilateral relations contain little new information, they effectively illustrate the differences in Peking's, Russia's, and the United States's approach to each of the other's power and effectively emphasize the origins of the present sharply exacerbated quarrel China has with the Russians.

Shanor covers a wide field in his comparative analysis, perhaps too wide. Not only does he concentrate on Russia, China, and America and Western Europe and their impact on future world relations, but he also analyzes two aspects of détente policy: arms control and trade, and he focuses on the Strategic Arms Limitation Treaty (SALT II), human rights, the reunification of East and West Germany, Eurocommunism, the protection of spheres of influence, and the effect of the Pope on the politics of Eastern Europe. He argues his case with assurance, frequently quoting others in support of his contentions. He does not, however, identify all of his sources, which leaves his reader questioning the validity of some of the points he wishes to make.

He states that China, in spite of its long-standing animosity toward the United States over Taiwan and a number of other issues, has momentarily put aside differences in the face of the Soviet threat to its border. It is the author's contention that because of the complicated nature of the contemporary world, it cannot be assumed that the movement of China from the

Soviet to the American orbit will be permanent; therefore, the new triangle can serve only as an indicator of political behavior, not as a stable pattern of organization of any new block arrangement.

China, at the moment, cannot be considered a power rival, militarily, of either the United States or the Soviet Union, although diplomatically China's role could become one of importance. According to Shanor, the Soviets view China as their gravest problem in foreign policy and a costly one domestically when the border army and backup missile system is counted.

If the Chinese continue to develop nuclear weapons with the capacity to deliver them, at least in Asia, global power distribution could be altered. For the moment, however, Chinese interests seemingly are regional as opposed to American interests which are global. China's unique status allows her to exercise some independence against actions of Russia or the United States; however, this does not translate into military or economic power. Since China is responsible for no one else's security, aside from North Korea's, it is incumbent upon the United States to see that China does not move from her present position away from the Soviets. Playing the China card (a term the author claims originated in Moscow) is perceived wholly as a matter of intention. Shanor insists the Soviet's perception of the United States's intentions must be the ruling factor in determining how America plays its China card.

After the Soviet invasion of Afghanistan it was felt in Washington that a "complementary" defense could be established or expanded between the United States and China. Shanor lauds such a move as a demonstration to the Soviets that real cooperation is possible between the United States and a Communist country, but he cautions that if the triangle is to work it is not enough to transfer relationships from the Russians to the Chinese. The United States might wish to move China into a position of détente formerly occupied by the Russians but this may not be entirely wise. Such a move could leave the West with no leverage with the Russians. There would be nothing to embargo, suspend, or chill as a deterrent to future invasions. He asserts that this would make the world an even more unstable place.

The Soviet movement into Afghanistan in the closing days of the decade of the 1970's and the retaliatory measures taken by the United States in the opening days of the 1980's altered the triangle somewhat but, according to Shanor, did not basically change it. Russia's justification for the invasion was based on fear of encirclement. It was presumed, so states a Russian official whom Shanor never identifies, China and the United States would profit from the unrest in the Islamic world and would hit at the U.S.S.R. through turbulent Afghanistan.

The invasion of Afghanistan, Shanor claims, provided President Carter with the excuse he was looking for to withdraw from ratification in the Senate SALT II—a move the Russians had anticipated. They believed the consequences of a successful Muslim defiance of Communist rule in Afghanistan to be far more serious a threat to their domestic stability in the Muslim republics than the threat of no new SALT treaty. Some Americans were glad to have the Treaty withdrawn because it was felt the Russians were unreliable partners in arms control. Other factors also entered into the decision. National anger was at a peak over the holding of the fifty hostages in Iran, perceived as a sign of loss of the United States's power and prestige in the world. Although it had nothing at all to do with SALT, or, as far as was known, with the Russians, the hostage crisis posed a dilemma for Carter, who was seeking reelection.

Shortly after the invasion of Afghanistan, the President enunciated a new foreign policy position when he warned in his State of the Union address that "an attempt by any outside force to gain control of the Persian Gulf region will be regarded as an assault of the vital interests of the United States of America and such an assault will be repelled by any means necessary, including military force." A number of retaliatory moves were instituted by him including an effort to organize a worldwide boycott of the 1980 Olympics, a momentary suspension of American grain exports to the Soviet Union and a cancellation of other trade and cultural agreements entered into during the period of détente.

One of the main arguments presented by Shanor is that détente between the two biggest Communist countries and the West is not only worthwhile and achievable but also a practical way of reducing worldwide tensions. As a peace strategy and diplomatic doctrine détente was designed to create, in the words of Henry Kissinger, "a vested interest in cooperation and restraint, an environment in which competitors can regulate and restrain their differences and ultimately move from competition to cooperation." Shanor maintains that the Russians were able to accept the label of détente and then define the concept so narrowly as to exclude almost all elements of good relations leaving only the barest exclusion of bad ones. Two interrelated political ties affected the Soviet's desire for détente. One was the growing tension between the Soviet Union and China, the other was the desirability of reducing the threat of war and consequently the cost of armaments.

Détente became the official policy of both the United States and the Soviet Union in January, 1969, when Nixon assumed office. The acceptance by Americans of the policy was based on the hope that a relaxing of tensions could result in the development of economic, political, and strategic ties beneficial to both nations. If the two could be bound in a common goal, it might be possible for a lessening of incentives for conflict or war. Soviet global aspirations would be mollified, supposedly, because Soviet peace and prosperity would depend on the continuation of peaceful links with the United States. Because the United States and the Soviet Union are bound to differ in power perceptions and objectives, the "linkage" doctrine is naïve. Contraperceptions were in evidence when the Russians complained that Americans had broken the spirit of détente and included in their list of perceived infractions the fact that the United States tied increased trade to performance of human rights; made deals with China; and strengthened NATO. The United States's reply to these allegations was that all actions were consistent with the prerogatives of sovereign states and were in response to actions taken by the Soviet Union.

The United States in turn believed that after agreeing to détente, the Russians embarked on a massive arms buildup; set expeditionary forces to Angola, Ethiopia, and South Yamen; tried a coup in Portugal; cracked down on dissidents and American correspondents; plunged Southeast Asia into a new series of wars and devastation through its Vietnamese allies; and then turned on its own neutral neighbor, Afghanistan.

Differences in viewpoint are also markedly visible in the area of human rights. For Americans, inalienable rights are assumed to be part of the natural order of mankind's social arrangement, a philosophy foreign to the Soviet view. For the Soviets, rights are more or less reluctant concessions of the State. When the Carter Administration instituted a worldwide campaign in behalf of human rights and sharply attacked the Soviet Union's human rights policies, the Administration apparently was devising a cause around which America's foreign policy might be built. It was thought that the Soviet desire to acquire high technology goods from the United States could be used as leverage to obtain American foreign policy objectives in the human rights field.

Shanor raises the moral questions of whether the United States has any right to be concerned with the issues that are not within the limits of direct Soviet-American relations and whether it would not have been better to lose human rights at Geneva or Helsinki in the interests of better relations between the two great powers. He argues, convincingly, that relations should not be based on the interference in the internal affairs of countries, but should be directed in a positive way toward cooperation. He then counters this with: Human rights questions transcend national bounderies not only because Western nations say they do, but also because the Soviet Union, in signing the Helsinki agreements as well as previous international documents, concurs.

As Shanor explains it, the Soviet Union agreed to the Helsinki accord and to uncomfortable concessions because it wanted something else of Helsinki and had, in fact, pushed for the conference in the first place in order to achieve it. What they wanted and got was recognition of their hegemony in Eastern Europe. It never was the Russian's intention that the Helsinki conference should become a forum for negotiating international human rights. Shanor attributes the Soviet success to the negotiating skills and commitment of several anonymous diplomats who spent more than two years at the Geneva conference tables preparing the Final Act for signature at the Helsinki Summit. He faults the United States for not ratifying some of these same documents, claiming that failure to do so considerably weakened United States human rights arguments.

In reference to détente, Shanor believes that both the Soviet and American leadership were careful not to pronounce its death sentence or announce the rebirth of the Cold War in the angry exchanges that followed Afghanistan, but because Afghanistan did occur and the more recent Libyan seizure of Chad, Americans believe that the Soviet Union and its surrogates are heavily involved in stoking conflict with arms and troops. There will be a great temptation to close the door on the Russians and open it to the Peoples Republic of China for the expansion of economic détente. Should this happen and trade agreements reached between China and the United States be expanded in the 1980's at the expense of the Soviets, their magnitude could transform significantly the world's economic, political, and military relationships and have a profound effect on the world's balance of power arrangement. Whether world peace and prosperity would follow such a move poses a serious problem for the future.

It may well be that the United States stands on the threshold of a whole new epoch in Chinese and Russian relations which will require an even more intensive examination of antecedents, especially those pertinent to the emerging Sino-Soviet-American triangle. If Shanor's book, written for the general public, does anything, it makes the reader keenly aware of the significance of the impending change. The book's lack of documentation, however, seriously weakens what might have been an outstanding narrative.

Anita Bowser

SPEAKING OF LITERATURE AND SOCIETY

Author: Lionel Trilling (1905-1975)
Edited by Diana Trilling
Publisher: Harcourt Brace Jovanovich (New York). 429 pp. $17.95
Type of work: Essays

A miscellany of reviews, critical essays, and lectures, edited by the author's wife, Diana Trilling, who also contributed a brief memoir

Speaking of Literature and Society is the twelfth and last volume in the Uniform Edition of the Works of Lionel Trilling. This posthumous volume, edited by Diana Trilling, collects some fifty-eight pieces written between 1924 and 1968. Book reviews predominate; there are also a few critical essays, lectures, introductions, and the like. The volume concludes with Diana Trilling's fine memoir, "Lionel Trilling: A Jew at Columbia."

Occasional pieces such as these—especially the reviews, which make up the bulk of the volume—undergo metamorphosis over the years. They are read today, if at all, not for their ostensible subjects but for what they tell about the development of Trilling's thought. Interest has shifted from the book reviewed to the reviewer.

Reading these pieces which span more than forty years, one is struck by Trilling's consistent virtues: humane intelligence, erudition leavened by common sense, ability to learn from opposing points of view. These qualities—conspicuously absent from much contemporary criticism—are more impressive than any change in perspective which can be traced through the forty-odd years. One comes to this volume already knowing that Trilling became, in his late years, increasingly skeptical toward the claims of Modernism, which he had in the past so vigorously argued. In a review of Fyodor Dostoevski's short novels ("A Comedy of Evil," 1961), there is a passage worth quoting at length, because it sets out with great clarity the intellectual and spiritual conflict which informs *Beyond Culture* and indeed all of Trilling's major work in the 1960's and the 1970's:

> It is eighty years since Dostoyevsky died, and in that time his appalling perceptions have been made into the common coin of modern literature. Any number of writers of the *avant garde*, from Henry Miller and Samuel Beckett down, have appropriated some part of his vision and have been understood and approved by *Mademoiselle, Harper's Bazaar,* and *Esquire*. But at the time Dostoyevsky wrote, before his *epigoni* were born, his subversion of traditional morality and religion was not a *chic* but a revelation, and the more because it affirmed as much as it subverted, because it made the spiritual life—we might almost say the personal life—what it had not been for a long time, an adventure.

There was no "solution" to the conflict set out here. As the 1960's progressed, Trilling had ever more reason to remark the strange supermarket nihilism, yet he never denied the genuinely liberating force of Modernism. Holding opposing truths in tension, he was characteristically honest, ready to admit perplexity.

A retrospective collection of occasional essays offers no great surprises, no striking new angles of approach, but there are modest insights to be gained. Particularly interesting in this volume is Trilling's recurring affirmation of the value of *pride*. More often than not, "pride" is a pejorative term, but Trilling often speaks with frank admiration of the "strong pride" of a confident person. Trilling's admiration for pride is another evidence of his realism and fundamental common sense. Pride implies conflict and competition, which many advocates of self-realization do not want to admit into their universe. One of the brilliant reviews in this collection is Trilling's criticism of Karen Horney ("The Progressive Psyche," 1942), whose sentimental vision he contrasts with the psychology of Sigmund Freud, who presents man with "the terrible truth of his own nature."

Indeed, Trilling's concept of healthy pride is the keynote of his reviews of Ernest Jones's three volumes on the life of Freud ("The Formative Years," 1953; "The Years of Maturity," 1955; "Last Years of a Titan," 1957). These reviews, in which Trilling considers the life of his acknowledged master, bring him to a real eloquence. Freud's pride, he says, was "the secret of his moral being. He had the passionate egoism, the intense pride that we call Titanic. . . . His own egoism led him to recognize and respect the egoism of others." The same note is sounded in essays on Leon Trotsky ("his pride is, I think, his chief claim upon our sympathy"), James Joyce (in which Joyce is likened to Freud), and others.

Given this emphasis on pride, it is particularly interesting to read in Diana Trilling's memoir about "the single most decisive move" of Trilling's life: fired by the English department at Columbia University in 1936, he confronted the faculty members whom he knew best—and with a most uncharacteristic aggressiveness—he "told them that they were getting rid of a person who would one day bring great distinction to their department; they would not easily find another as good." He was right, of course, but "for the rest of his life," Diana Trilling says, "he would recur to this deeply uncharacteristic moment," speculating on what had caused it and why it worked—because it did work, and having said that he was that good, he became that good. A "miracle," his wife calls it, his confusions over his dissertation "seemed overnight to vanish," and soon it was his first book, *Matthew Arnold*, which would later be reissued in the Uniform Edition of the Works of Lionel Trilling.

John Wilson

THE STATE OF IRELAND

Author: Benedict Kiely (1919-   )
Introduction by Thomas Flanagan
Publisher: David R. Godine, Publisher (Boston). 389 pp. $14.95
Type of work: Short stories and novellas

A richly varied collection which honorably continues the great Irish comic tradition

Benedict Kiely's *The State of Ireland* collects, the book itself says, "A Novella and Seventeen Stories." The copywriters must plead guilty to denting the truth for a phrase's sake, since one of the "Seventeen Stories," the brilliant "Down Then by Derry," is thirty-eight pages long and most certainly a novella. *The State of Ireland* is beautifully bound and illustrated, another fine job of bookmaking from David Godine, and readers should also be grateful for the long and excellent introduction by Thomas Flanagan.

Benedict Kiely is known in America chiefly for his short stories which have appeared in *The New Yorker*, but his output is much more extensive, as Flanagan informs the reader: "eleven novels, three volumes of short stories, and four books of social and literary history." Much of that work was done while Kiely supported himself as a journalist: one of the most appealing qualities of his fiction, which the reader senses immediately, is his professional confidence, the confidence of a man who has made his living by the pen (and the typewriter) without writing trash.

The stories collected in *The State of Ireland* are accessible, charming, resonant—no guidebooks required. Kiely possesses a sharp wit and a gentle sense of humor, a sharp ear for speech, and a well-stocked literary memory, always ready to supply an unobtrusive line from William Wordsworth or John Webster, William Shakespeare or William Butler Yeats. His themes are simple and timeless. It is no surprise, then, that most reviews of *The State of Ireland* have been pervaded by nostalgia for a mythical Golden Age of narrative: Kiely, "the master storyteller," "the Irish storyteller," in the great oral tradition.

It is perfectly true that the qualities which distinguish Kiely's book from so much current fiction—not least, his humane spirit—are self-evident, so that a critic might easily be reduced merely to summarizing story after story, concluding: "read this book." If, however, *The State of Ireland* is, first, simply a book to read and savor, it is also an artifact, made by a craftsman, and it is also, as a development of a particular form, a small episode in the history of consciousness: a small, evolutionary episode. Perhaps this approach to Kiely's work is validated by the conclusion to Vivian Mercier's *The Irish Comic Tradition*, in which Mercier lists "four priceless gifts" which, he believes, the "Irish background" offered writers in this century:

contact with a living folklore and thus with myth; contact with a living folk speech; a traditional sense of the professional, almost sacred prestige of poetry and learning; a traditional sense of the supreme importance of technique to a writer, coupled with the realization that technique must be learnt, by imitation, study, and practice.

A modest consideration of Kiely's technique is, therefore, no decadent French import; it is as Irish as peat and malt whiskey.

Kiely as "The Storyteller" is a good place to start. Walter Benjamin, in his celebrated essay of that title, invested "the storyteller" with mythical dimensions even as he was proclaiming his inaccessibility: "He has already become something remote from us and something that is getting even more distant." To call a contemporary writer such as Kiely a "master storyteller" is also to evoke nostalgia for something that is lost. Now on the one hand, it is perfectly appropriate to call Kiely a "master storyteller," just as it is appropriate to cite the peculiarly Irish oral tradition as a source of his art. Yet, on the other hand, this approach to Kiely is quite misleading, for his stories are quite distant from the "straightforward" narratives which the name "storyteller" suggests, and if he is indebted to an oral tradition—as James Joyce and Flann O'Brien were also—he is above all a highly *literary* writer.

Even Kiely's most "straightforward" stories are far more complex and multilayered than "the storyteller's" narratives. Here the reader can see, reflected in the evolution of the short-story form, the general movement of human consciousness to an ever-greater self-awareness. Erich Kahler has described *The Inward Turn of Narrative*, the turn from external adventures—voyages and the like—to "internal" events. Kahler was primarily interested in this opposition between "outer" and "inner" content, but it is also possible to study the inward turn in terms of plot construction. The reader can, for example, compare Kiely's use of the "story-within-a-story" with the practice of many of his predecessors.

The story-within-a-story is a favorite device of the "traditional storyteller" (to use, for convenience, an unsupportable generalization). Very often the device works in the following way: the story begins with a "frame," perhaps a group of travelers meeting in an inn; soon a pretext is established to begin the "real" story, which is narrated continuously until its climax; then there is a return to the frame.

Compare this with Kiely's technique in the story called "The Heroes in the Dark House." This story begins and ends with framing scenes, but the climax of the story—insofar as it has a climax—is *in* the frames. In fact, one might say that the story begins with its climax, in the first sentence: "They were gone in the morning, the old man said." The old man, Arthur Broderick, has collected folktales for years. His "nine-times rejected manuscript" has finally been accepted by the United States Army, who will publish it for the troops to promote their understanding of Ireland while they are quartered there awaiting the Normandy invasion. Before he can finish a few explanatory notes, however, perhaps he could never really finish, the troops are gone, without warning, in a single night.

The old man is talking to a young scholar who, despite his youth and relative lack of knowledge, has been able to find a publisher for a book on folklore which duplicates, as far as it goes, Broderick's painstaking researches. They are talking in the old man's house over an oak table which, in 1798, was the top of a bellows which the Irish rebels used to forge pikes. The framing scenes establish a connection between the heroes in the folktales, the heroic rebels in 1798, and the young heroes setting out for the beaches of France. The first sentence of the story is a "climax" in two ways. It signals Mr. Broderick's final disappointment that his manuscript will never be published but as he tells the young scholar about the army's departure, he uses the language of the heroic tales he has made his own, so that their departure is beautiful, a confirmation that the heroes still live.

Given more space, this contrast in plot-construction could be studied more fully. There is another important difference, however, between Kiely's handling of the story-within-a-story and that of the traditional storyteller. Generally when Kiely uses stories-within-stories, as he does habitually, he is also reflecting on the use or meaning of storytelling itself. This is quite evident in "The Heroes in the Dark House," but it is implicit in many other stories as well. This "self-reflexive" quality is foreign to the traditional storyteller.

What is the point of all this fuss over labels? Does it really matter whether Kiely is called a "storyteller" or not? Yes, it does, because the myth referred to earlier of a Golden Age of narrative (good old storytelling) is surprisingly persistent. For purposes of discussion, Kiely has been contrasted with an over-simplified and in fact nonexistent "traditional storyteller." The conventions of art will always exist. Yet, there is no denying that the short story has evolved into an increasingly self-conscious form, and it is worth pointing out how far Kiely is from a storyteller whose story can be easily followed as one sits, listening to him talk, in the pub or around the campfire—how far he is even from *Dubliners*.

The complexity—yet such graceful complexity—of Kiely's multi-layered narratives is deepest and richest in the novella, "Down Then by Derry." It begins with a crazily circumstantial comic sentence (very much like the opening of Flann O'Brien's *The Third Policeman*) and ends with poignant lines from a ballad. There is more than technical virtuosity behind the range of language and emotion: here, against the fanatics who refuse to see, who cling to their hate and their one small truth, readers have the writer's greatest gift, a sense of the wholeness of life in all its comedy, its sadness, and its beauty:

> So he thought the rest of it: Oh, do you see yon high high building? And do you see yon castle fine? And do you see yon ship on the ocean? They'll all be thine if thou wilt be mine.

John Wilson

THE STORIES OF RAY BRADBURY

Author: Ray Bradbury (1920-   )
Publisher: Alfred A. Knopf (New York). 884 pp. $17.95
Type of work: Short stories

A hundred short stories spanning the career of one of America's masters of nostalgia

In an introduction to this collected edition of one hundred of his favorite stories, Ray Bradbury describes himself as like the man in the Irish police report—drunk and in charge of a bicycle. In his case, however, he says, he has been drunk with life and constantly moving through it with a mixture of terror and exhilaration. He discusses his work as the result of a childhood stuffed with images from science fiction, circuses, sideshows, and motion pictures, and how the people he has met and the places he has seen since childhood became additional raw material for turning into the finished products of his art. The Middle West, California, Mexico, and Ireland all appear in these stories, sometimes transmuted into the locales of fantasy.

The Stories of Ray Bradbury, at almost nine hundred pages, is far from a collection of all his work in the form, but the selection printed here from the beginning of his writing in the mid-1940's to the late 1960's includes many of his best-known and enjoyed tales and allows an appreciation not only of the career of a single writer but also enables the reader to draw some conclusions about the writing of fiction in the decades shortly after World War II.

A little research into the original places of publication of these stories shows how much harder it is to succeed at the writing of short stories today than it was thirty-five years ago. Then the newsstands were filled with a variety of vehicles from pulps to slicks, all of which printed fiction and most of which have disappeared. Bradbury built his reputation in now-vanished magazines such as *Weird Tales, Dime Mystery, Collier's, Planet Stories, American Mercury, Charm*, and others, all now gone. Even today's *Saturday Evening Post* went out of publication for a while, and its reappearance brought back only a pale copy of the magazine that used to be the summit of the fiction writer's hopes. Yet, these magazines were the market place for short fiction in the United States; when they departed, there were that many fewer places for a writer to learn the craft, and that much less incentive for a writer to work at less than novel length.

The collection also shows a curious fact about Bradbury's reputation: it explains why his name is most likely to be thought of when someone who does not like science fiction thinks of the genre: Bradbury's work was frequently displayed in the mass-circulation magazines such as *Saturday Evening Post, McCall's, Collier's*, and *Playboy*, but he published relatively little in the specialized science-fiction outlets. Bradbury's writing, sometimes criticized for sentimentality, filled the need of another market, too: much of it was first published in magazines such as *Mademoiselle, Charm*, and *Seventeen*.

A purist might object to the selection of stories on the grounds that some, but not all of, for example, *The Martian Chronicles* are here. The connecting thread of narrative in *The Martian Chronicles*, however, is so thin that little is lost by reprinting only some of its stories. Many of Bradbury's best short stories are included, and, as the collection shows, his strengths are best displayed in this form. From what may be his strongest collection, *The Illustrated Man*, are reprinted the stories "No Particular Night or Morning," "The Veldt," and "The Long Rain." From the above-mentioned *The Martian Chronicles* come "There Will Come Soft Rains" and "Mars Is Heaven," and, as stories representative of Bradbury's work, it is hard to fault this choice. "There Will Come Soft Rains" is the often-anthologized *tour de force* about an automated house that has survived a nuclear war. It is a story without human characters in which the robot mechanisms of the house show a maniacal perseverance in their tasks, although the reason for their existence is gone. "Mars Is Heaven" makes science fiction out of the transplantation of turn-of-the-century Illinois to Mars, where the familiar faces and buildings greet an American expedition to that planet. The sentiment for a vanished America is there, science fiction is there, and a characteristic macabre touch enters at the end, as the purpose of the town becomes clear to the captain of the expedition.

Bradbury has frequently expressed his admiration for Edgar Allan Poe, and there are few better continuers of the tradition of atmospheric horror than Bradbury. In his hands, however, the tale of terror takes on a different look, because whereas Poe often worked to make the familiar seem strange, Bradbury often does exactly the reverse, humanizing and domesticating the monstrous. The story "Homecoming" is perhaps the best example of this process. It is indeed the story of a homecoming, complete with nostalgia and family tradition and the renewal of ties. The family that gathers, however, includes vampires, witches, and werewolves. The stranger, the outcast, in the family is Timothy, the only one normal by our standards, who keenly feels his deviance from what is usual in his small society. Among them all, only he is mortal. "Uncle Einar" and "The Traveler" also deal with the Elliott family of "Homecoming."

The atmosphere of horror remains, although the supernatural disappears, from one of Bradbury's most famous stories, "The Next in Line." The story is set in the Mexican town of Guanajuato, and its chilling center describes a visit to the catacombs of that city, where the mummified dead produce an obsessive fear in the American woman who is touring the country with her husband. As events conspire to keep the couple in Guanajuato, the fear that she will die there and be left to shrivel in the dry tunnels overwhelms her. The story is as terrifying as anything Poe ever wrote, and the terror is produced entirely through the use of atmosphere: not a ghost appears, nor is one needed. In a coincidental comment about what generates emotion in a story, a picture book was published in 1979 joining the text of "The Next in Line" to photographs of the actual mummies of Guanajuato. Somehow the real thing was not as fearsome as the story, showing that the imagination is the best set decorator.

Bradbury's forte is fantasy, an ability that comes through even in those stories closest to genre-standard science fiction. In "Dark They Were, and Golden-Eyed," a human restaurateur on Mars meets the Martians themselves, and the figures of that dwindling race would be familiar to any fourteenth century balladeer: whatever they may be called, the Martians are the inhabitants of Fairyland, and their world is that third alternative to Heaven and Hell, the timeless world of enchantment. That fantasy is always very close to the surface in Bradbury's stories, and often familiar, often homely, when it does appear. When a ghost does show up in one of the tales, it is likely to be the ghost of old Aunt Tildy, as in "There Was an Old Woman."

In many of the stories, the fantasy results from the intrusion of the strange into everyday affairs. The idea of a setting on Mars may seem exotic, but as in "Dark They Were, and Golden-Eyed" or in "The Off Season," when the human character runs a hot-dog stand, much of the exotic disappears. The setting of "The Fire Balloons" is again Mars, but it is a Mars of human settlements, the familiar boom town of the American West re-created on another planet. The priests of the story face exactly the same situations they would have encountered in the California of two hundred years ago. The thrust of fantasy into the story, however, is again the appearance of the Martians, and the question of what kinds of sin are possible to creatures of nearly pure spirit becomes the central concern of Father Peregrine.

The reverse of this process, the unexpected advent of the ordinary into the strange, produces, oddly enough, exactly the same effect. It once again domesticates the bizarre, and puts it in human dimensions. In the science-fiction vein, an example of this reversal of atmosphere occurs in "The Long Rain." In that story, the crew of a spaceship has been wrecked and stranded on Venus, a world of eternal rain. They are making their way toward the Sun Dome, one of a number of rescue stations established on the planet for precisely such eventualities. In a setting in which one can drown simply by tipping his head back, in which one can go insane from the endless drumming of the rain, where fungi and vegetation spring up in minutes, the intrusion of the ordinary is in the form of the desires of the characters: what they yearn for is hot chocolate with marshmallow, dry towels, and sandwiches of chicken, tomato, and onion.

In the genre of fantasy, there is the process in the story "The April Witch." Here Cecy, one of the Elliotts of "Homecoming" and "The Traveler," wants, with the coming of April, to be in love, an oddly human desire for one of her kind. Her spirit enters the body of an ordinary girl for bathing, powdering, and dressing in preparation for one night at a dance. Cecy, whose body has never left the room in the Elliott house where she lies forever sleeping, cherishes the memory of that night.

Not all of Bradbury's fantasy comes in the form of character or setting. Sometimes it takes the form of usual people in usual places, who find themselves in the course of their everyday affairs doing unusual things. One such story with a Mexican setting is "The Wonderful Ice Cream Suit," the story of five poor Mexicans of identical size who collectively buy a white summer suit. They take turns, each wearing the suit for one night, and four are happy—their dreams are fulfilled—until the turn comes for the fifth member, notoriously slovenly in his habits. They adventure through the evening, protecting the suit from harm until, as the result of a traffic accident one of them realizes that the intrusion of the fantastic has not been the power of the suit, but the joy which lay in their minds, and that the fantasy has been within themselves all along, only released by the suit.

As "The Wonderful Ice Cream Suit" shows, Bradbury is skillful in the handling of humor, and perhaps finally, the sense of humor is the magical power lying within us to bring our fantasy to life. Some people are richer than others in this respect—their humor lying closer to the surface—or are fortunate enough to live in a society that fosters and encourages the play of fantasy. One such society is the contemporary Ireland of "The Anthem Sprinters," a story that takes its name from the habit of some of the Irish film audiences of dashing from the theater in the few seconds between the conclusion of the film and the playing of the national anthem. This situation, however, is only the beginning of the story, as the telling of the custom leads to a contest between two of the best of the sprinters as team captains, with the American narrator taking part. Yet, the narrator finds, as the film ends and he runs to the lobby, that the magic of the film has released the fantasy inside the Irish teams, and he returns to the theater to find them sitting there, captured by the final song, with tears streaming down their faces.

Bradbury's stories, be they set in Mexico or in Illinois or in Ireland or even on Mars, are the intrusion of the magic that can release the fantasy within the readers; and this collection of his best work contains many stories that do precisely that.

Walter E. Meyers

SUBLIMINAL POLITICS
Myths & Mythmakers in America

Authors: Dan Nimmo (1933-   ) and James E. Combs
Publisher: Prentice-Hall (Englewood Cliffs, New Jersey). 256 pp. $10.95; paperback $4.95
Type of work: Political science
Time: Primarily the present
Locale: The United States

An examination of American political culture and its relationship to mythical assumptions about the past and the present

Dan Nimmo and James E. Combs are professors of political science at the University of Tennessee and Valparaiso University respectively. Professor Nimmo, in particular, has written previously with an eye toward various manifestations of the American political culture regarding voting behavior and political communications. *Subliminal Politics* is essentially a continuation of Nimmo's chosen emphasis and, as is common with this type of inquiry, the work frequently departs from a purely political vein and delves into sociological arenas.

Political culture is an open ended field of study and different analysts will offer varying definitions. For the most part, the field attempts to consider public attitudes and beliefs as they relate to both political behavior and expectations. Nimmo and Combs have set as their target the role and nature of myth and mythmaking in American political culture, and their success in addressing this issue may depend more on how one views the nature of political culture than on the quality of the work itself. It should also be noted that Nimmo and Combs did not intend this book to be an exposé. There is no attempt to present a revisionist history of American political figures, institutions, or events. Rather, the authors attempt to analyze the role myth and mythmaking play in American political culture, both past and present.

The opening chapter of *Subliminal Politics* lays the foundation of the authors' approach by carefully tracing the nature of myth itself. A variety of scholarly viewpoints are examined including those of the philosophers Ernst Cassirer and George Herbert Mead. Although the emphasis is understandably limited to myth in a political context, the authors strive to clarify the roles myth plays in relation to reality. Clearly, Nimmo and Combs believe that myth is much more than a form of fantasy largely because it interacts with human understanding; and, because the past can only be approached from the perspective of the present, myth frequently serves as a framework for rationalizing and categorizing events and personalities that may otherwise prove difficult to place within the context of current circumstances. Given the complexities of present-day life which defy thorough understanding, the reduction of the past to an assortment of comforting myths helps to create a kind of established vantage point to facilitate understanding. Disorder, whether past or present, undermines what psychologists refer to as cognitive consonance and here myth and mythmaking perform a valuable role in bringing a viable perspective to both the individual and the society as a whole.

In particular, Nimmo and Combs present political myths in four broad categories: "Master Myths," broadly based societal assumptions; "Myths of Us and Them," stressing group distinctions; "Heroic Myths," personalities reduced to the status of legendary heroes and villains; and "Pseudo-Myths," the use of mythmaking for current, and somewhat temporary, political ends. Subsequent chapters, however, do not categorically address each of these types but rather loosely use the labels.

Because myth is so commonly associated with legends of the past, Nimmo and Combs devote the second chapter exclusively to American political history up to the point of Abraham Lincoln and the Civil War period. Limiting their survey to the mid-nineteenth century is in keeping with what the authors call the "Foundation Myth"; that is, Americans' perspectives on the nation's formative years. In sequence, Nimmo and Combs look at the American Revolution, the Critical Period (largely the Articles of Confederation era), the Constitutional Convention, the Early Republic (roughly the first half of the nineteenth century), and the Civil War. As a means of emphasizing the point that the past is viewed from the perspective of the present, these historical periods are given a brief historiographical overview which traces the manner in which mythmaking has served to describe the events. Again, it is Nimmo and Combs's contention that mythmaking is furthered by historians' tendencies to apply contemporary modes of understanding to personalities and activities of the past. As such, one encounters a "patriotic version" which contributes to the heroic image of the Founding Fathers, a "realist version" in which vested interests (particularly of an economic sort) guided policy, and a "technician's version" whereby pluralistic wants and needs engaged in a well defined struggle for influence within the framework of the system.

The reduction of various modes of historical inquiry to the realm of myth in Chapter Two offers the first evidence that Nimmo and Combs intend to broaden their appreciation of myth from what might be casually assumed. Since historical writing and investigation cannot translate a total appreciation of the period under analysis, Nimmo and Combs are essentially labeling history in general as mythmaking. In theory, even the most strenuous objectivity and the application of a wide variety of cause-and-effect techniques will fail to convey adequately the complex realities of the past. The result, then, is that mythmaking will forever be the curse of historical inquiry which can, at best, provide an imperfect version of previous times.

Having established such an approach, Nimmo and Combs devote the following four chapters to mythmaking of a more contemporary sort in American political life. If a genuine understanding of history is virtually impossible, acquiring a true knowledge of the present is no less hazardous. Here Nimmo and Combs delve into the "Pseudo-Myth" category which is regularly used to justify current actions, viewpoints, and even personalities and institutions. The American institutions of the presidency, congress, and the United States Supreme Court are all viewed as operating within the parameters of the political culture's mythical estimate of their expected roles; an estimate which contributes substantially to their image and authority. The crucial ingredient in "Pseudo-Mythmaking" is the notion that current actions are inexorably tied to established myths from and about the past. The mythical past becomes, in a sense, reusable or, as Nimmo and Combs state it, "the constant restatement of myth is a political present's way of using the past by placing present actions and actors in the historical legacy of earlier myths."

Beyond this, however, the authors expand their vision of myth and mythmaking to the idea of future trends. Here Nimmo and Combs essentially equate the future with the past as locations that cannot be fully understood from the present. All discussion of trends, therefore, becomes mythmaking which, like historical studies, is incapable of complete truth and knowledge.

Yet society as well as individuals living in the present require a strong measure of consonance to validate existence and to justify behavior. In order for opinions to be formed, decisions made, and policies adopted a more or less rational perspective must be attained. According to Nimmo and Combs's viewpoint, such a position is virtually unattainable since history offers only a formulaic vision of the past; the future is beyond certainty; and the present is too diverse, complex, and ill-defined for either an individual or a society to fully grasp.

The solution, as outlined in chapters four, five, and six, is left in the hands of political "flacks," popular entertainment mediums, and the power of the press. In each instance, the political culture is augmented and guided by assorted impressions of reality which are extensively colored by mythmaking. Political "flacks" become, for Nimmo and Combs, a collection of image-builders who, through lavish use of the media and related advertising modes, strive to create a public level of understanding of some current personality, idea, or event. In a similar manner, political mythmaking is furthered by television, movies, and even sporting events in that the viewer is encouraged to form some impression or identity linkage with what is being portrayed. The fact that the intended myth is not always accepted by the public in its expected fashion is, for Nimmo and Combs, a subtle form of indictment toward this type of mythmaking.

The much discussed power of the mass media, and particularly the press, is an additional source of mythmaking to the authors. Because the news media focuses upon daily noteworthy occurences, reality is blown out of context and mythmaking is elevated. The style of presentation and the content of the news reported become mere capsule images of the present, while the established status, image, and frequency of news reporting serves to identify the press as a direct link to knowledge.

Interestingly, Nimmo and Combs label their own profession of political science as an example of mythical knowledge. Like most forms of study which have struggled to become sciences through the application of logical methodologies and the elevation of mathematics to a state of deism, political science rests upon what Nimmo and Combs believe to be a myth. While political science is certainly the target here, the authors call into question the entire nature of scientific knowledge because it is based on the assumption that existence can be understood given the appropriate techniques. As methodologies are presented and accepted, myths that some facet of activity can be understood are also established. The result is a building block of myths assumed to be scientific knowledge and therefore beyond dispute.

In many respects, *Subliminal Politics* summarizes itself in the opening pages of the first chapter when the authors ask, "What, after all, do we really know?" Nimmo and Combs's elaboration on this question is a closer description of *Subliminal Politics* than an in-depth examination of the role of myths in American political culture. Regrettably, it is only in the final chapter that the authors deal directly with the idea of an American "Master Myth." This concept, which Nimmo and Combs refer to as the "American Monomyth," is described by the authors as "a recurring plot, that of a community threatened by evil but redeemed through heroic acts." This appreciation of the American saga is probably the single most potent statement in the entire book and it is disconcerting to see that it is only casually addressed in a few brief and concluding pages. It is here that a study of myth in American political culture could very well have proven to be of much greater value and insight.

One is left with the impression that Nimmo and Combs were themselves unsure as to what, if any, conclusions they should draw for the reader. In closing, the authors recommend that uncertainty ought to become accepted to a far greater degree than is currently the case. Inquiry into uncertainty would appear to be their recommendation, although it remains a curious message of advice coming on the heels of a book which systematically reduces all forms of knowledge acquisition to the level of myth and mythmaking.

Terry Alan Baney

SUN YAT-SEN
Reluctant Revolutionary

Author: Harold Z. Schiffrin (1922-   )
Publisher: Little, Brown and Company (Boston). 290 pp. $10.95
Type of work: Biography
Time: 1866-1925
Locale: China

A biography of Sun Yat-sen, covering his life from early childhood until his death in 1925

Principal personages:
SUN YAT-SEN, provisional president of the new Chinese Republic, founder and head of the Kuomintang
CHIANG KAI-SHEK, head of the Whampoa military academy and Kuomintang leader
HUANG HSING, deputy leader of the Chinese Alliance
SOONG CH'ING-LING, Sun's second wife
SUNG CHIAO-JEN, Chairman of the Kuomintang executive committee
YÜAN SHIH-K'AI, President of the Chinese Republic, 1912-1916

The status of Sun Yat-sen as the "Father of the Chinese Revolution" makes him unquestionably a figure of great historical importance. Indeed, both Chinas assiduously cultivate his legend. What kind of a man was he? Harold Z. Schiffrin's lucidly written biography endeavors to present the real Sun by dissipating the mystical aura that has surrounded him. Schiffrin, a specialist in Chinese history at Hebrew University in Jerusalem and Academic Director of the Harry S Truman Research Institute for the Advancement of Peace, draws from an extensive amount of scholarly research, including his own earlier *Sun Yat-sen and the Origin of the Chinese Revolution* (1968). In general, it is a balanced coverage of Sun's life, as well as an excellent summary of the tortuous revolutionary period. This makes the work a highly useful introductory history of modern China for the layperson.

It has been said that Sun's greatness lies in what he symbolized, rather than in what he actually achieved. His life and work symbolized China's quest for national resurgence. His success as a revolutionary leader however, may be subject to varying assessments. Schiffrin writes that Sun was endowed with such requisite qualities of personality as audacity, optimism, resilience, and self-confidence. He seemed to lack, however, that exceptional measure of abilities to make him truly equal to his great task. According to Schiffrin, Sun was only a reluctant revolutionary who did not possess the ruthlessness that marks a true revolutionary. Born of a typical peasant family in the Kwangtung province, he was exposed to Western influences early in life. A commercially successful older brother in Honolulu made it possible for him to attend a school run by the Church of England and, later, an American school in Hawaii. His brother summarily ordered the teenaged Sun home, however, when he expressed the intent to convert to Christianity. Sun was deeply attracted to things Western. Yet, the nationalist legacy of the Taiping uprising, conveyed to him earlier by a favorite teacher at his village school, also had a strong influence on him.

Sun continued his education in Hong Kong, while the Sino-French hostilities of 1883-1885 made him more fully aware of the grave problems burdening his country. It was at this time that the young Sun sensed the deep gulf between the patriotic, belligerent lower classes and the helpless, lethargic ruling class. Strangely, during this time of growing interest in politics and involvement in China's national resurgence, Sun formally embraced the Christian faith, thereby greatly angering his brother. Was it a demonstration of personal independence? With the help of Westerners, including an American businessman, he was able to attend a medical school in Hong Kong. Unfortunately, upon his graduation in 1892, he discovered that his diploma was not acceptable to Hong Kong authorities, and that he would not be allowed to practice medicine in the colony. Thus reduced to the status of an herbalist, Sun moved to Canton to open a practice. It seems he became more and more disillusioned about a medical career, however, turning his energies instead toward politics.

Sun drafted far-ranging reform proposals and tried to interest leading statesmen of the Manchu Dynasty in them. These efforts were to no avail, and he soon abandoned in frustration his pursuit of official patronage. Sun felt ignored and slighted by the establishment because of his lowly social background. Schiffrin suggests that this was what led to his vow to overthrow it. Together with a small circle of associates he formed the Society to Restore China's Prosperity. Appeals for financial support went out to overseas Chinese, particularly those on Hawaii, where his brother strongly approved of his nationalist endeavors.

China's humiliating defeat at the hands of Japan in 1895 had a potent catalytic effect on the pace and direction of modern Chinese history, according to Schiffrin. In its aftermath, Sun launched his first conspiracy. He strenuously courted the support of the imperialist powers, especially Britain's, by catering to their aspirations and prejudices. His conspiracy failed, as would several others later. He had, however, drawn attention and support. The Chinese government put a price on his head. Consequently, Sun went to Japan, where he enjoyed the hospitality of a number of influential persons. He was tireless in his efforts to mobilize support and raise funds. He toured the United States and then went to London, hoping to persuade the British government to assume "benevolent neutrality." His efforts on the diplomatic front were less than successful. Moreover, he was subjected to a somewhat bizarre and frightening experience. He was kidnaped and detained in the Chinese legation. Only the last-minute intercession of friends saved him from being returned to China and certain execution. As it turned out, the whole affair was to Sun's advantage, for he became a press sensation and was thrust into the international limelight.

In Schiffrin's depiction, Sun displayed some of the characteristics of the "confidence man." Indeed, his style was a bit puzzling, if not dismaying, in its blatant opportunism and posturing. On the one hand, he humbly petitioned the imperialist powers for help, while, on the other, he energetically advocated the pan-Asian cause against European exploitation. Although mere tactics in an effort to activate all possible levers to achieve his goals for China, his credibility came to be questioned in both camps. Nevertheless, his ceaseless activities, including a brief association with the Filipino liberation effort, clearly projected Sun as the dominant figure in opposition to the Manchu Dynasty.

The Boxer Uprising at the turn of the century presented fresh opportunities for Sun's group. This fanatic antiforeign outburst ultimately led the regime to declare war on all imperialist powers with ports and spheres of influence in China. Far from reducing foreign encroachments, however, this conflict left China, even more than before, a subject nation. In turn, this condition intensified nationalistic and revolutionary aspirations. Sun's organization was forced into premature action, however, in the Waichow uprising, and he failed for a second time. Apparently undaunted, Sun traveled extensively abroad, seeking support in such places as San Francisco, New York City, and London. In Brussels, he wooed the Socialist International. Functioning without a solid home base was difficult and discouraging. His old base of operations in Japan was denied him, for he was no longer welcome there after the Japanese victory over Russia in 1905. Despite the odds against him, Sun still succeeded in merging several oppositionist groups to form the Chinese Alliance. His control over this political organization, however, was tenuous.

There was much groping for a political program that could unite the Chinese masses, whose bitterness was deep and whose potential for self-sacrificing struggle was great. The eventual Program of the Revolution, however, largely ignored the severe agrarian injustices. The Alliance made some headway in Canton, primarily through the efforts of Sun's deputy Huang Hsing. Several more uncoordinate uprisings were staged in the years 1907 and 1908. Although unsuccessful, they mattered as demonstrations of popular support for Sun's republican cause. As for Sun, he viewed money as the key to success. While the pace of revolutionary activities in China quickened, he intensified his quest for funds abroad. As Schiffrin describes it, a kind of chain reaction had been touched off, particularly by the actions of the Railway Protection League against the foreign railway construction. When at last the revolution was proclaimed in December 1911, Sun was only its nominal leader. In fact, he was in Denver at the time. Several northern generals had jumped on the republican bandwagon, and the imperial family gave up. Sun, who had been made the provisional president of the new Chinese Republic, deferred in a statesmanlike gesture to the powerful military leader Yüan Shih-k'ai. Thus, following the abdication of the child emperor on February 12, 1912, Yüan was elected president in Nanking.

For Sun, then, it was a bittersweet victory. Yielding to Yüan made possible the peaceful settlement. Yet, the revolution remained incomplete. The Dynasty was merely replaced by the militarists, and the old bureaucratic elite was able to hold on. The subsequent period of rampant warlordism, according to Schiffrin, wrecked both republicanism and traditional gentry power. Meanwhile, in August, 1912, the Kuomintang, the new nationalist party, was formed, with Sun as its head. Sun strove hard to keep the revolutionary dream alive, as the regime under Yüan deteriorated into a military dictatorship. Sun's young associate Sung Chiao-jen, chairing the Kuomintang executive committee, was assassinated by henchmen of the Yüan regime. In the face of terrorism and chaos, Sun's efforts concentrated more directly on ridding the country of Yüan. He lived and worked in Shanghai, which was beyond the reach of the government in Peking throughout the divided and unstable warlord rule which followed Yüan's death. During this difficult and problematic time he was helped immensely by his new wife, the beautiful Soong Ch'ing-ling.

The Paris Peace Conference of 1919 let China down, and when the Japanese were allowed to take over previously German Shantung, the nationalist outcry was great. The May Fourth Movement was born, as students proved their mettle as organizers and propagandists for Sun. Ironically, the absence of effective central government during the period of warlordism from 1916 to 1928 allowed a flourishing of public opinion and intellectual discourse. The ordinary people, however, were worse off than under the Manchu Dynasty. Sun now agitated for the assumption of direct political control. He had himself elected "extraordinary president" of the Chinese Republic in 1921 and formed a countergovernment in Canton. Failing in his pleadings to obtain recognition from Western powers, as well as in his military expedition to unify the country, he was forced to abandon Canton. Back in Shanghai in 1922, Sun appeared ready to deal with anyone. The Kuomintang entered into an alliance with the small Chinese Communist Party. Also, the uniform Western rejection had pushed Sun toward the Soviet Union. Indeed, when Sun was able to reestablish himself in Canton, the Soviet Union was willing to support him. In addition to some financial and military support, the Soviets sent Sun an intriguing and highly capable adviser named Michael Borodin. Among other important actions, Borodin saw to the reorganization of the Kuomintang along the lines of the Soviet model. The party's platform was rewritten to oppose more specifically imperialists, warlords, and the privileged classes. Sun's three principles of socialism, nationalism, and democracy, however, were retained. There can be no doubt that Borodin helped transform the

Kuomintang into a much more effective political organization.

The party's military strength was built up under Chiang Kai-shek, Sun's loyal associate and the head of the newly created Whampoa military academy. It was Chiang who was to succeed in unifying the country under the Kuomintang, if only for a brief period. At the age of fifty-eight, Sun died of cancer on March 12, 1925. He had struggled on behalf of his revolutionary cause for nearly forty years. His resilience and his faith in the future of his country were amazing. The mandate he left was a powerful one; but his capacity for national leadership was never fully tested. As Schiffrin notes, this is probably why Sun so easily became a legend. His notion that by an act of will the Chinese could leap from backwardness to modernity was embraced by Mao Tse-tung, and his scheme for using foreign capital to build socialism is being attempted by the current leaders of China.

Only the symbolic Sun Yat-sen has endured, and his memory is celebrated in both the Peoples Republic and in Taiwan. Possibly one day he will be, as Schiffrin thoughtfully concludes, the unifying symbol for the two political entities. In this work Schiffrin has managed to capture some of the drama of the life of a very human revolutionary. It is the best biography of Sun Yat-sen available in the English language.

Manfred Grote

SURE SIGNS
New and Selected Poems

Author: Ted Kooser (1939-   )
Publisher: University of Pittsburgh Press (Pittsburgh, Pennsylvania). 93 pp. $9.95; paperback $4.50
Type of work: Poetry

A substantial collection by a poet of the American Midwest

The American Midwest has been a place artists and writers have often wanted to escape. Archibald Higbie, the artist in Edgar Lee Masters' *Spoon River Anthology*, loathed Spoon River because there was no culture there. In flight from his ordinary background, Higbie went to Rome and to Paris, to "breathe the air that the masters breathed." He never succeeded, however, in rooting Spoon River out of his soul and his work, exhibited in Europe, only confused people. "Sometimes the face looks like Apollo's, / At others it has a trace of Lincoln's."

The commonplace life Archibald Higbie, the failed artist, tried unsuccessfully to escape is the material of Ted Kooser's poetry. His previous collections, *Official Entry Blank, A Local Habitation and a Name, Not Coming to Be Barked At*, and now *Sure Signs*, steadily reveal life in the American Midwest, as it is now and as it has been in the recent past, within the memories of his father and grandfather.

Kooser's Midwest is a world of small towns and rural disintegration, of abandoned farmhouses, country cemeteries, churches converted into barns, and farm couples who have retired to "Houses at the Edge of Town." It is a world of the old, the isolated and impaired, of emptiness, enigma, of life lived off to the side or in corners, as his titles imply: "Old Soldiers Home," "Living Near the Rehabilitation Home," "The Very Old," "In the Corners of Fields."

Kooser's world is one in which things and people are forever being abandoned, left behind: ladders behind garages, a "white dish broken over the road." It is a world of loss and bereavement, of galoshes in a closet "collapsing with grief." The poem "Advice" interprets this world of loss:

> We will always be
> leaving our loves like old stoves
> in abandoned apartments.
> Early in life
> there are signals of how it will be—
> we throw up the window one spring
> and the window weights break from their ropes
> and fall deep in the wall.

"The Old Woman" (she could be Archibald Higbie's mother) suggests much of the sense of isolation, abandonment, and bitterness found in these poems:

> The old woman, asleep on her back,
> pulls up her knees and gives birth
> to an empty house. She kicks off
> the quilt and sheet and rakes her shift
> up over her hips, showing her sex
> to the photos of children
> arranged on the opposite wall
> who, years before, turned their
> moonlit faces away.

Kooser, an underwriter in an insurance company in Lincoln, Nebraska, turns his face toward his place and people. Unlike Archibald Higbie, he escapes into the life of the Midwest to make the dull and everyday, the drab and the bleak shine as if by magic in his poems. In so doing, he illustrates how one can still discover America through literature. "The land was ours before we were the land's," Robert Frost wrote in "The Gift Outright," condensing into a memorable line the notion that, unlike European countries, the United States was a nation, a political entity, before it was a land and people. The land, and life on the land, was "unstoried, artless, unenhanced." American literature, however, in region after region, has transformed forbidding physical terrain, bereft of history, memory, and tradition—mere locality—into place, a word which assumes human involvement and participation, a locality deeply felt and experienced. Kooser's poems contribute to this ongoing discovery of America. They call to mind T. S. Eliot's observation, in "Little Gidding," that the last part of the earth we discover is that which we have known from the beginning; that the goal of our exploration is to "arrive where we started / and know the place for the first time."

Kooser's poems are explorations and arrivals that transform locality into place. The landscape and objects on it assume the features and qualities of people, while people come to resemble the landscape. In "Self-Portrait at Thirty-Nine" the speaker's face, observed in a barber shop mirror, resembles the Midwestern rural landscape: "There's a grin lost somewhere / in the folds of the face, with a fence / of old teeth, broken and leaning. . . ." Conversely, the "Snow Fence" seems to be a trapper or prospector—or perhaps a farm animal—as it "takes the cold trail / north; no meat / on its ribs, / but neither has it / much to carry." In "A Drive in the Country," snowdrifts on the roadside "lie in the grass like old men / asleep in their coats." It is trees that resemble old men in "Walking Beside a Creek": ". . . the trees, their coats / thrown open like drunken men, / the lifeblood thudding / in their tight, wet boots." In "So This Is Nebraska," barns are "those dear old ladies . . . / their little windows / dulled by cataracts of hay and cobwebs." An abandoned truck appears to be a farmer resting from labor: ". . . top-deep in hollyhocks, pollen and bees, / a pickup kicks its fenders off / and settles back to read the clouds."

The wind in "In an Old Apple Orchard" is an old man who has "gone off /
late in the day / toward the town, and comes back / slow in the morning, /
reeling with bees." In "Late September," ladders behind garages, by hay-
stacks and barns are "tough old / day laborers, seasoned and wheezy, / drunk
on the weather, / sleeping outside with the crickets." Cedars in a country
cemetery are "stringy and tough as maiden aunts, / taking the little gusts of
wind / in their aprons like sheaves of wheat."

Sometimes through telling detail that achieves a surrealistic effect, Kooser
renders the essence of life on the plains of Nebraska, Kansas, Minnesota, the
Dakotas. In "Late Nights in Minnesota," he shows

> . . . a bulb burning cold in the jail,
> and high in one house,
> a five-battery flashlight
> pulling an old woman downstairs to the toilet
> among the red eyes of her cats.

(The poem does for the Midwest what Wallace Stevens' (who also combined
the worlds of insurance and poetry) "Disillusionment of Ten O'Clock" does
for New England. Compare Stevens'

> The houses are haunted
> by white night-gowns.
>
> Only, here and there, an old sailor,
> drunk and asleep in his boots,
> Catches tigers
> In red weather.)

The abandoned pickup in "So This Is Nebraska" suggests the feeling of the
place: ". . . you feel like letting / your tires go flat, like letting mice / build
a nest in your muffler, like being / no more than a truck in the weeds." "A
Hot Night in Wheat Country" condenses history, culture, and tradition in a
view from an open upstairs window: "a great white plain stretches away—/
the naked Methodists / lying on top of their bedding. / The moon covers her
eyes with a cloud." In "A Place in Kansas" a ship's anchor incised over the
door of an abandoned stone house in a wheatfield suggests something mysterious, enigmatic: "There was no one to ask / what the anchor was doing in
Kansas, / no water for miles. / Not a single white sail of meaning / broke the
horizon. . . . It's like that in Kansas, forever."

Two things detract from the pleasure of these poems. Titles are unnecessarily repeated in the first lines of several poems. One reads, for instance,
"At the Bus Stop Next to the Funeral Home," and then reads the title again
as the first line. Similar repetitions occur in "After My Grandmother's
Funeral," "The Very Old," "The Blind Always Come as Such a Surprise,"

and "There Is Always a Little Wind."

Repetition of another kind also calls attention to itself. Many of the poems seem to be versions of one another, as is the case with "A Widow" and "The Widow Lester," or with "In a Country Cemetery in Iowa" and "There Is Always a Little Wind." Sometimes one has the feeling that two poems might be parts of a longer poem ("Sitting All Evening Alone in the Kitchen," "Highway 30"). Certain poems might better have been presented as parts of a sequence ("An Empty Place," "Shooting a Farmhouse," "North of Alliance," "Grandfather," "Abandoned Farmhouse").

These repetitions, however, are minor matters detracting only slightly from the reader's enjoyment. The lucid accessibility of these poems makes it evident that in all really important ways, Kooser cares for the reader, whom he imagines in the opening poem. His ideal reader is a beautiful woman who, forced to choose between having her raincoat cleaned and buying his poems, decides to have the coat cleaned! One thinks of Marianne Moore's "Poetry": ". . . there are things that are important beyond all this fiddle." Yet, Kooser's poems meet the difficult criterion Moore lays down in subsequent lines: ". . . one discovers . . . after all, a place for the genuine."

Sure Signs belongs with Edgar Lee Masters' *Spoon River Anthology*, the poems of Frost and William Carlos Williams, with Jesse Stuart's *Man with a Bull-Tongue Plow* and Millen Brand's *Local Lives*—poems dealing not with America the abstraction but with what is really there. *Sure Signs* belongs to that body of poetry which reveals the continental United States as contiguous geographical areas and overlapping cultural regions with histories, traditions, and memories that render political boundaries such as states relatively insignificant.

Jim W. Miller

THE TALE BEARERS
Literary Essays

Author: V. S. Pritchett (1900-   )
Publisher: Random House (New York). 223 pp. $10.00
Type of work: Essays

Twenty-three essays that critique books by or about selected authors, with emphasis on twentieth century Britons and Americans

In protest to Romanticism's doctrine of self-expression, New Criticism stormed American literary critics in the 1930's. Books abundant with symbols and literary allusions like James Joyce's *Ulysses* helped lead such scholars as R. P. Blackmur and Cleanth Brooks to separate literature from other types of discourse such as philosophy and science in search of the intrinsic meaning and thus the intrinsic value of any given poem or novel. Although never blanketly accepted, New Criticism has most recently been attacked by deconstructionists such as Jacques Derrida in France and Paul de Man in the United States who insist that literature is composed of an arbitrary sequence of words which bears no necessary relation to the writer's situation or intent. Scholars deconstruct literature by discerning the full range of possible interpretations, any one of which a reader might accept validly. Despite the appeal of the debate, neither New Criticism nor deconstruction, both of which find support in scholarly journals as well as even *The New York Times Book Review*, has enlisted such prolific critics as V. S. Pritchett who view the academic debate with disdain.

Although Pritchett usually treats his subjects with kindness and even generosity, he occasionally snipes at academic critics in his latest book, *The Tale Bearers*. During a discussion of Max Beerbohm, Pritchett says, "I feared what would happen to Max if he was put through the American academic mangle. There seems to be a convention that this machine must begin by stunning its victim with the obvious. . . ." In an essay on E. F. Benson, he muses,

> I have often thought that professors of English Lit. should take time off from the central glooms of genius and consider these lesser entertainers who are deeply suggestive; but perhaps it is as well that the Academy winces at the idea for we would hate to see our fun damped down by explication.

Yet, in *The Myth Makers*, last year's companion anthology, he decried "the present academic habit of turning literary criticism into technology."

Pritchett's literary accomplishments provide the powder for his rock and salt shots at academic literary criticism. *The Tale Bearers* is the eighty-one-year-old's thirty-second book and his seventh volume of literary criticism. It follows five novels—of which *Mr. Beluncle* is his most celebrated, ten short-story collections, two biographies, two autobiographies, and six travel books, including *The Spanish Temper*, a model for that genre. Pritchett, who was knighted a few years ago for his literary accomplishments, abstains only from writing poetry and essays on poetry and poets' lives, largely perhaps because poetry criticism has become an enterprise of academicians.

Although he is vocal, Pritchett counters the academics chiefly by example. He is concerned with the nuances of a writer's personality and the social milieu that helped to fashion it. He is capable of precise and complex scrutiny of style, and he will exercise this capability from time to time, but he usually analyzes a writer by digging for the wellsprings of personality and watching for the ways that they will surface in the writer's works. Often this search for the sources of personality becomes a modified Freudian analysis: Pritchett writes about Henry James the hermaphrodite (James is not alone), and he classifies imagination into pre- and post-puberty. The themes of childhood and adolescence recur prominently. Pritchett does not emphasize the psychological at the expense of the social, though, so he offers the reader an effort at balance.

"E. M. Forster: A Private Voice" is indicative of Pritchett's method of explication. Among his nineteen books, including *Where Angels Fear to Tread*, *A Room with a View* and *Howards End*, Forster is best known for *A Passage to India*, his last novel (though *Maurice* was published much later), which he wrote when he was forty-five years old. Moral courage and sharp observation of character mark Forster's novels, Pritchett says, mainly because of the Victorian middle class into which he was born, his overbearing mother, and his slow actualization of his homosexuality.

The essay on Forster reads like a modified short story (Pritchett ranks high as a short-story writer). The essay, understandably, begins with setting. Forster was the only child of a family rooted in the more liberal (and wealthy) strain of philanthropical Puritans, comfortable Anglo-Irish clerics, poor teachers who had prior connections with trade and even coarse country cousins (in particular one "huntin' and shootin' uncle" who wanted to make a man out of him). By 1879, when Forster was born, his family had become securely middle class, and snobbish at that. Shortly thereafter, his father died of consumption, and the baby, who was also suspected of being frail, was spoiled and protected by his mother, his grandmother, and a host of aunts, one of whom endowed the infant with enough money to keep him independent for life. Forster grew up effeminate and precocious.

Pritchett also emphasizes Forster's mother, and for good reason. When she died, her sixty-six-year-old son had spent most of his life living with her. They were all but married, the result of which was an astonishing bondage. Largely because his mother forbade the discussion of sex, Forster did not know how sexual intercourse took place until he was thirty and had written three successful novels on love and marriage. Later, when he had begun to pursue homosexual relationships, he and his mother agreed that he could spend two nights per week without her in London. He did, but on those two nights he always sent a postcard to her. Forster tied the knot but never cut the cord.

Forster began to realize that he could love no woman but his mother when he was studying at Kings College, Cambridge. At that time also, he began to submit to his homosexual temperament. After he was graduated and began to travel, he had affairs with a poor tram conductor in Egypt, a court baker in India, and a number of men in the Cockney section of London. Although no more than a sexual novice at the time, Forster wrote *Maurice*, a novel about homosexuality, but English law prevented it from being published.

Although Forster succeeded as a novelist, he did not publish one during the last forty-six years of his life. Pritchett guesses that *A Passage to India* was Forster's last novel because he was bored with the fare of marriage and heterosexual love. Furthermore, Forster's financial independence kept him from *having* to write novels, and his conscience prodded him to write essays on a number of social and political issues.

Such illustration provides as good a means as any of discussing Pritchett's approach. He belongs to no school, but rather numbers among a few independent men of letters capable of articulating breadth as well as depth. Pritchett once said that the literary critic's job was to "get an essence, show his wit and his hand, and make his decisive effect with alacrity in fewer than 2,000 scrupulous words." Blending biography, criticism, summary, and excerpt with his own viewpoint, Pritchett does exactly that.

The format of the present volume resembles that of *The Myth Makers*, a collection of nineteen essays on non-English language Continental and Latin American prose writers. In *The Tale Bearers*, Pritchett reviews works by or about Max Beerbohm, E. F. Benson, Rider Haggard, Rudyard Kipling, Joseph Conrad, T. E. Lawrence, E. M. Forster, Graham Greene, Evelyn Waugh, Angus Wilson, and Henry Green (English); Henry James, Edmund Wilson, Saul Bellow, Mary McCarthy, and Flannery O'Connor (Americans); Samuel Pepys, Jonathan Swift, Richard Burton, and Frederick Rolfe ("characters"); and Lady Murasaki, Ruth Prawer Jhabvala, and Flann O'Brien ("exotics"). These twenty-three essays were published formerly in *The New Statesman*, *The New Yorker*, and *The New York Review of Books*. Indeed, the rather loose connection between the writers—although Lady Murasaki's *The Tale of Genji* (eleventh century) is the only one not originally written in English—is due to the fact that these were the subjects that came to Pritchett for review.

Pritchett is a literary critic in the highest sense of the word. His concern is to understand rather than complain, and he does so with an engaging style. About Evelyn Waugh's snobbery, for instance, Pritchett quips, "To object to his snobbery is as futile as objecting to cricket, for every summer the damn game comes round again whether you like it or not." Pritchett writes with detail, metaphor and lucid, short sentences; he writes gracefully and to the point. Because these essays were as often as not occasioned by biographies, Pritchett gives the reader a feeling for a body of scholarship as well as the writer. If genius is marked by "an incessant activity of mind," as he has said, then undoubtedly he ranks among the brightest.

The flaws in *The Tale Bearers* are, at worst, minor. Pritchett sometimes appears to be too kind, as when he calls Edmund Wilson's plainness "democratic, in the sense that this distinguished man will not for long allow one phrase to be better than another." In a few essays, such as the one on Conrad, he quotes excessively. Also, he calls Henry James a Bostonian; James, of course, was a New Yorker. Pritchett's essays are engaging and instructive nevertheless, a credit to literary criticism and the world of letters at large.

John P. Ferré

TALLEY'S FOLLY

Author: Lanford Wilson (1937-   )
Publisher: Farrar, Straus and Giroux (New York). 60 pp. $9.95; paperback $4.95
Type of work: Drama
Time: The evening of July 4, 1944
Locale: An old boathouse on a farm near Lebanon, Missouri

An amusing, moving play about the wooing of a mid-Western spinster by a middle-aged Jewish accountant

> *Principal characters:*
> MATT FRIEDMAN, a forty-two-year-old Jewish accountant
> SALLY TALLEY, a thirty-one-year-old spinster

The best way to discuss Lanford Wilson's trilogy of plays about the Talley clan would probably be to ignore their order of production/publication and treat them as a single unified family chronicle, beginning with *A Tale Told* (as yet unpublished), which explores the family traumas and crises at the end of World War II, then *Talley's Folly* (produced, 1979; published, 1980), the romance between the family oddball, Sally, and her middle-aged Jewish suitor, and finally *5th of July* (produced, 1978; published, 1979), which jumps ahead thirty-three years to dramatize the plight of the Talleys born after World War II, illusioned in the 1960's, and disillusioned in the 1970's. At the same time, however, each play is a separate, powerful whole that can be appreciated on its own terms. This is especially true of *Talley's Folly*, the most commercially successful of the three, indeed, of Lanford Wilson's entire career.

Since the production of his first play, *The Madness of Lady Bright* in 1964, Wilson has been one of the most consistently stimulating, provocative, and—although clearly influenced by Anton Chekhov and Tennessee Williams among others—original of contemporary American playwrights. In plotting, characterization, and dialogue, he seems to be an "old-fashioned" realist, in attitude and awareness a thorough contemporary, and in theatrical approach, an experimenter.

Despite the color and variety in his work, however, all of the plays utilize one of three structural approaches. A few, primarily the domestic conflict plays such as *Lemon Sky*, *5th of July*, and *The Mound Builders*, are conventionally realistic in organization. A small number of intimately related characters come into conflict over a single problem or cluster of problems, most often based on shifting family relationships. Another set of dramas, which might be called the "ensemble plays"—*Balm in Gilead*, *The Hot l Baltimore*, *The Rimers of Eldritch*—are put together much more elaborately. In these plays, an extremely large cast more or less splits into a series of character clusters, each with their own mini-plays to act out in the context of the whole. The rhythm and movement of these plays is controlled by juxtaposing the various groups against each other and fluidly moving between them, while gradually building an overall sense of meaning and direction until the whole finally jells. Then, at the other extreme, are the small, tightly focused plays, where everything is narrowed and intensified into a confrontation between two vital, troubled characters. Examples of this approach are his brilliant early one-act plays *The Madness of Lady Bright* and *Home Free*, his provocative, flawed full-length work *The Gingham Dog*, and, of course, *Talley's Folly*.

Talley's Folly is the story of an unlikely affair between two individuals who seem to have little in common beyond the fact that they are both outsiders. Matt Friedman, a forty-two-year-old-Jewish accountant, enters and talks directly to the audience. He introduces himself, gives a tour of the set, an old Victorian-styled boathouse on the Talley farm, verbally establishes mood and atmosphere, and sketches in the social and personal background of the play.

The boathouse setting provides the play with both its title and its atmosphere. "Talley's Folly" is the name given the boathouse when Sally Talley's Uncle Everett "Whistler" Talley first built it in 1870. The character of the old oddball Uncle remains in the background of the play as referent and model against whom the narrow, rigid, conformist, "successful" Talleys of the mid-1940's are measured. The ornate boathouse "constructed of louvers, and lattice and geegaws" gives the play an otherworldly, sentimental, nineteenth centuryish feeling. This atmosphere is enhanced by sentimental music in the background coming from the Fourth of July celebrations in the park on the other side of the small lake. This music, Friedman says, sets the tone of the play: "this should be a waltz one-two-three, one-two-three a no-holds-barred romantic story."

After Matt goes through his introductions twice (once quickly "for the latecomers"), Sally appears. She is irritated by Matt's persistence, as well as by the behavior of her own family back on the hill (the subject of the last play, *A Tale Told*). Matt represents a possibility in her life that she had rejected—or thinks that she had rejected—yet her attraction to him is clear and the overall shape and direction of the play is evident from its first moments. Matt will gradually break down Sally's resistance until she gives up, admits she loves him, and agrees to go off with him. In the process, we get to know and like these two individuals, and also, finally, to learn their secrets: why has this middle-aged Jewish man, apparently without any previous attachments, suddenly decided to woo aggressively a thirty-one-year-old Midwestern WASP spinster? Why has Sally Talley, a moderately attractive, socially prominent young woman, remained unmarried and almost ostracized by her family? And what exactly is her relationship to that family?

The course of their previous romance is never really given in any detail. One year previously, Matt and Sally had had an intense one-week relationship (he calls it "an affair," she denies it). How they met and why they separated so abruptly are never explained. Since that week he has pursued her by mail, without response, and in person with a visit to the hospital where she works (she hid from him in the kitchen). This Fourth of July evening visit to the Talley farm represents his last chance and, when we meet him, it has not gone well. Brother Buddy Talley has driven him off with a shotgun, sister-in-law Olive has called the police, and his car—he says—is out of gas. When Sally appears, it is to get rid of him or perhaps rescue him, but not to renew their romance.

The play moves much like a boxing match in dialogue. He asserts, questions, pokes holes in her answers; she denies, evades, rebukes, threatens constantly to leave, asks questions of her own, and exposes his vulnerabilities. Approximately the first half of this long one-act play focusses on the breaking down of Sally's deceptive resistance, until she is at last willing to deal honestly with the situation. The second half of the play is devoted to digging out the answers to the hidden personal questions that are keeping them apart.

The combat is delightful. Both Matt and Sally are intelligent, witty people and their repartee is lively, stimulating, and humorous. Matt is a natural comic and mimic; Sally is an excellent straightman. Wilson's adroit skill in using details and props fleshes out the early moments of the play. It is an old cast-off pair of ice skates that Matt uses to break down Sally's initial resistance. Once they are "skating together" on the wooden floor of the old boathouse, it is only a matter of time before Sally gives in to Matt.

The lightness of the early dialogue gradually darkens as the couple get closer to admitting their "secrets." The final revelations, however, turn out to be less startling than anticipated. Matt, a Jew displaced by World War II, has no nationality or racial identity and, therefore, has turned his back on the world. He focusses this feeling in his decision to refuse to father any children into such a world. Sally's secret is, due to a TB infection contracted (innocently) during her high school years, that she can bear no children—a fact that accounts for her standing in the family clan; they had wanted her to marry the business partner and her illness messed up the "merger." Thus, in the end, Matt and Sally turn out to be ideally suited.

Yet Wilson makes it clear that these hidden factors were not the primary difficulties in their relationship. The real problems lie in the nature of human communication and the fear of being hurt. Midway in the play, Matt underscores this theme by repeating a conversation he had earlier:

> He said people are eggs. Said we had to be careful not to bang up against each other too hard. Crack our shells, never be any use again. Said we were eggs. Individuals.

Matt, however, has an answer to that analogy.

> What good is an egg? Gotta be hatched or boiled or beat up into something like a lot of other eggs. Then you're cookin'. I told him he ought not to be too afraid of gettin' his yolk broke.

Matt has waited until he was middle-aged before seeking love, because his traumatic childhood experiences had left him emotionally crippled and withdrawn. Meeting Sally, he suddenly realized that to be completely human he would have to make himself vulnerable and risk further emotional damage. He then succeeds in passing that insight on to Sally. She at last comes to understand that her fear of their relationship was actually rooted in her fear of being hurt—but that the alternative would be a lifetime of emotional sterility. Only marriage to Matt will enable her to break loose both from the suffocating atmosphere of the Talley family circle and from her own inhibitions and fears to develop fully her human potential. That the marriage does, in fact, do this for her is proven when she reappears thirty-three years later in *5th of July* as a resourceful, compassionate, feisty widow.

Wilson has frequently been compared to Tennessee Williams, an identification acknowledged by both playwrights (they collaborated on "The Migrants," a CBS-*Playhouse 90* script; Wilson wrote the libretto for the operatic version of *Summer and Smoke*). Both playwrights tend to focus on marginal, alienated individuals, those rejected, cast off, or broken by society and "life" (Williams perhaps more so than Wilson). Both are "realistic" playwrights whose theatrical techniques skirt the edges of "expressionism" and "surrealism." Both are "poets" in the theater who write highly charged, intensely lyrical dialogue. And both stress themes of loneliness, noncommunication, frustrated love, and loss of meaning in a crass, materialistic world. These similarities can very clearly be seen by a comparison between *Talley's Folly* and Williams' first play, *The Glass Menagerie*.

Matt Friedman's "introduction" to the audience/reader resembles that made by Tom Wingfield in *The Glass Menagerie*. They both describe the setting, give historical and personal background, and set the mood and tone of their respective plays. Perhaps the most important thing they do, however, is express the playwrights' own attitudes toward the action of the play. To Tom Wingfield it is a "sentimental" "memory" play that blunts the harsh realities of life. Matt Friedman considers his play a "romance," but suggests that that does not make it any less true. Both plays are about spinsters who encounter vital men who offer them a chance (at least psychologically) to escape their barren presents and bleak futures. Yet, Williams' Laura Wingfield is ultimately disappointed and will, we are given to understand, be destroyed by a world too harsh for her delicate sensibilities. Sally Talley, however, is no Laura Wingfield. With Wilson's approval, she escapes her sterile life and is able to find a new, happy one with her "gentleman caller."

Perhaps even more revealing are the two absent characters who hover in the backgrounds of the two plays, the "Father" in *The Glass Menagerie* and "Uncle Whistler" in *Talley's Folly*. The Williams Father "was a telephone man who fell in love with long distance" and deserted his family, as Tom, the son, is about to do. Unable to deal with the world he lived in, the Father ran away from it. On the other hand, Uncle Whistler stayed put, kept his integrity, built his crazy structures despite community mockery, reared a huge family, and was "happy." Integrity and happiness are real possibilities for Wilson, never more than vain, sentimental hopes for Williams. Wilson's characters are tougher, stronger, less self-pitying, and more energetic. The world he pictures is, like Williams', crude, dark, and chaotic; but decency and love can survive in it and even, for some especially courageous and tenacious individuals, they can flourish.

All of which is not to fall into the facile generalization that Wilson is the superior playwright because he is more "positive" than Williams. Even at his best, Wilson's plays never attain the emotional intensity or theatrical power of Williams' greatest dramas, nor has he created any individual characters as memorable as Amanda Wingfield, Blanche DuBois, Stanley Kowalski, or Hannah Jelkes. In 1980, however, the Wilson version of the world seems more real, more deep, and more satisfying than that posited by any other current American playwright. For all of its virtuosity and power, *Talley's Folly* is not Wilson's best play—"bigger" plays like *The Rimers of Eldritch*, *The Hot l Baltimore*, *The Mound Builders*, and *5th of July* have more depth and resonance—but it is a marvelous crystalization of Lanford Wilson's insight into the modern world and his compassion for those who live in it.

Keith Neilson

THE THIRTIES
From the Notebooks and Diaries of the Period

Author: Edmund Wilson (1895-1972)
Edited, with an Introduction, by Leon Edel (1907-   )
Publisher: Farrar, Straus and Giroux (New York). 753 pp. $17.50
Type of work: Journals and diaries
Time: The 1930's
Locale: The United States and the Soviet Union

In this collection of notebooks and journals from the 1930's, skillfully edited by Leon Edel, Edmund Wilson provides not only useful information about the social and literary history of that decade but also about his own intellectual growth

Leon Edel's most recent edition of Edmund Wilson's scattered journals and diaries brings forward the work he began with *The Twenties* (1975). For a reader unfamiliar with that volume, this *caveat* must apply: *The Thirties* is by no means a comprehensive, integrated social or literary history of the decade; instead, the book comprises a selection of Wilson's unpublished notebooks, some of them quite spontaneous and idiosyncratic and others fairly "literary," but none of them polished for publication. This is not to say that Wilson set low store by the manuscripts. He had always intended, according to Edel, that the journals might be edited as "trade" books but not as scholarly editions. To Edel, the writer's diaries are "the notebooks of a chronicler, a way of tidying the mind for his craft of criticism: no meditations, no prayers, no invocation to the muse, no polished mirrors."

Nevertheless, the journals in loose chronological order form a generally unified picture of the decade. Much of the unity derives explicitly from the historical circumstances. From 1929, when Wall Street was shaken by the stock market crash, until 1939, when in Europe the guns of August signaled the start of World War II, America suffered the great upheaval of depression. *The Thirties* chronicles, from an impressionistic and frankly Leftist viewpoint, the suffering of a nation during hard times. Compared to other impressionistic social histories of the decade, most notably Frederick Lewis Allen's *Since Yesterday* (1939), Wilson's journals are more subjective, far less comprehensive and reliable in terms of scholarship, and less acutely selective of meaningful data. Wilson's reportage, however, often makes up in vigor for its lapses in depth. With unsentimental curiosity, he recorded for his own benefit precisely what he saw, felt, and understood. His observations provide focused, often memorable impressions of the decade marked, as always with this writer, by vividness, intelligence, and lucidity.

Wilson's journals are unified, moreover, by the pattern of his life. *The Thirties* was a decade of intense, productive work. In 1931, he published his classic study of the Symbolist Movement in early twentieth century European literature, *Axel's Castle*; and in 1940, as the culmination of his researches into the history of twentieth century Marxist-Leninism in the Soviet Union, he completed *To the Finland Station*, portions of which he had published late in the 1930's. These two major works represent important polarities in Wilson's interests, from a study of literary aestheticism to one of the history of socialism. Why did he change so dramatically the subject of his writing? As he witnessed the crushing weight of depression upon Americans in many walks of life, he determined to investigate the economic forces molding society. In 1929 and 1932, he visited scenes of labor strife and recorded in separate journals accounts of the suffering of workers in Michigan, Kentucky, and West Virginia. In 1935, thanks to a Guggenheim Fellowship, he traveled to the Soviet Union to test on the basis of actual experiences his theories of socialism. As a result of his various travels—through the coal mines of impoverished Kentucky, the auto plants of Detroit, the grim scenes of Leningrad, Moscow, and Odessa—he brought to his economic studies an unusually thorough knowledge of practical human experience. For most of the decade Wilson was free to pursue these researches. Until 1939, he was a freelance journalist, not tied to academic assignments but sustained to work through the modest sale of his books and magazine pieces or by his inherited income. During the summers of 1930 and 1936, he resided comfortably at Provincetown, and periodically throughout the 1930's, he had time to travel for pleasure, noting in his journals significant features of the landscape or particulars that would strike him.   /

From yet another dimension the decade presented a special unity for Wilson—the shape of his emotional life. In 1930, he married his second wife, Margaret Canby, in Washington D.C. She was apparently a lively, affectionate woman of generous instincts, not particularly an intellectual partner but one who suited a side of Wilson's gregarious nature. As a couple, the Wilsons enjoyed parties, travel, and—in defiance of Prohibition—heavy drinking. Margaret's sudden tragic death in 1932 (she accidentally fell from a flight of stairs and fractured her skull) shattered Wilson's complacent existence. Frequently throughout the rest of the decade he was to think with regret about his wife, and to suffer recurrent nightmares. For Wilson the imprint of her death marked the 1930's with a tragic stamp, not to diminish until 1938 with his marriage to Mary McCarthy (for which episode, unfortunately, Edel has no journal).

A single long piece, "The Death of Margaret," is the most sustained, touching, and—from a literary point of view—excellent journal of the volume. In this thirty-four page section which Edel correctly calls a monologue, Wilson pours out in agony his frustrated love, his sexual fantasies, his dreams, his crudest and noblest passions centering upon Margaret. The author evidently intended the journal for eventual publication, because he had typed and partly edited the copy before his death. Surely he recognized in the writing a Joycean splash of language, partly stream-of-consciousness, and in its subject a powerful confession of the spirit. For what emerges, more than a eulogy for the dead wife, is a self-portrait of the stricken writer, a man whose emotions are rigidly contained by his critical intelligence, by a certain coldness and austerity. In retrospect, he cannot forgive himself for failing to show love—or perhaps even to feel warmth—for the live Margaret, whom he now adores dead. Perhaps the most poignant line in the journal is his laconic: "After she was dead, I loved her."

Wilson was to take other lovers. With rare candor he describes his affairs with several mistresses, all of whom appear to have been married women estranged from their husbands or divorcées. If he had other casual romances, he keeps the confidence to himself. His longtime affairs seem to have been animated mostly by sexual passion or habits of affectionate friendship, not love. Among these women (whose real identities Edel has masked) are "Anna," "K," and most notably "D," the original for Imogen Loomis in Wilson's fascinating—and for his time, shocking—story "The Princess with the Golden Hair." Rereading these anecdotes of sexual intrigue, one feels more a sense of sadness than titillation. Wilson was not a warm-hearted or adventurous lover, even with Margaret; rather, he examined love with the same cool critical eye that he was to turn upon literature or politics. In the play of sexuality, he could clearly observe his own and his partners' amusing games and, as a spectator, could stand apart and judge the performance of the participants.

With the same austere critical eye he measured both the obscure and the famous people whom he encountered. Among many distinguished literary acquaintances whose lives at some point touched his during the 1930's are Louise Bogan, Malcolm Cowley, e. e. cummings, John Dos Passos, F. Scott Fitzgerald, Ernest Hemingway, Dorothy Parker, Paul Rosenfeld, and Nathanael West. In addition, he knew many political pundits, mostly of the Left, ranging from Harold Laski and Rex Tugwell to William Z. Foster. Perhaps the most disappointing aspect of the journals is Wilson's failure to detail memorable pictures of these people. Some he knew well and affectionately, like cummings; others, like Dos Passos, deeply impressed his thinking even though they were not close friends. In general, however, Wilson treats these personages only in relation to the immediate circumstances of his own life, rarely furnishing for them literary "portraits." Unlike other famous writers of journals—André Gide, Arnold Bennett, Anaïs Nin, to mention a few conspicuous examples—Wilson avoids set descriptions of places as well as of people and seldom provides passages of philosophical rumination. Compared to Henry James, who often worked out in his literary journals vexing problems of characterization, plot, or theme for his fiction, Wilson usually passes over in his notebooks questions of the writer's craft. His journals, consequently, concern only indirectly his line of thinking or the stages of argument that occupied his attention during the years of his research for *To the Finland*

Station. These artistic and critical concerns must have been internalized. Instead, his journals provide direct comment on the immediate actions of his life, the places he visited, the people whose lives touched his.

To be sure, Wilson offers many tidbits for the student either of literature or social history. Most of his comments on famous writers are anecdotal, some not greatly elevated above the level of gossip. For example, he records for his own delectation an apocryphal story that Scott Fitzgerald worried about the small size of his penis. This piece of trivia he credited to John Peale Bishop, who in turn picked it up from Ernest Hemingway, certainly not an objective source of information on his rival Fitzgerald. Hemingway, according to Wilson, proved to be the hero of this tale, for he urged upon Scott the importance of looking at his penis in the mirror, to discover its true size. In another anecdote, zestfully (and uncritically) recorded as a judgment of Dos Passos, Fitzgerald supposedly was "never really drunk but used the pretense of drunkenness as a screen to retire behind." Wilson enjoys mentioning these crumbs of gossip, perhaps to refresh his memory when discussing authors at cocktail parties; but one must note that, in his published criticism, he refrains from using such mean comments. For a true understanding of Wilson's balanced judgment on Fitzgerald, for example, the reader should better turn to the critic's essays.

In the journals Wilson's judgments on political figures are similarly incomplete or, in some cases, distorted. He never quite seems to take the measure of Franklin Roosevelt. Possibly he could not accept in Roosevelt's patrician background sound credentials for the role he advanced as liberal. Wilson cavils at "Roosevelt's unsatisfactory way of emphasizing his sentences, fairyish or as if there weren't real conviction behind them—in spite of his clearness and neatness. . . ." At this point Wilson catches himself and reflects that regular radio announcers do "the same thing." It is typical of Wilson to reconsider many of his own impressions, particularly those that on first reading appear harsh. For example, during the 1930's Wilson relished including in his journals gossipy, sometimes nasty comments that he had overheard about Jews. Judged by the social attitudes of his class, his remarks are not seriously malicious, although they are certainly unworthy of his character. When the writer's uncle, however, repeats in his presence certain anti-Semitic jokes— jokes that he might himself have passed on at some previous time—he is suddenly alert to their mischief: "Uncle Win was becoming imbued with Fascist ideas." Countering the effects of superficial judgments, Wilson's fine, sane intelligence continually reviewed ideas that he had casually accepted without challenge, or reconsidered with sharper penetration his observations of people. The great test for his prejudices was his visit to the Soviet Union in 1935. Prepared to discover in that land a socialist paradise, or at least a society better regulated than capitalist America, he watched intently, took notes, made shrewd judgments. "One reason they treat each other so well on streetcars," he wryly observes, "is that they can be fined for hooliganism, if they don't."

Perhaps this quality of intellectual integrity—of seeing clearly, dispassionately, responsibly—is most valuable in Wilson's journals. His patiently accumulated data, generally sound for the time, are no longer significant as social history; and his literary material, although interesting to the specialist, scarcely ever comes up to the standards of his published criticism. Instead, *The Thirties* is worth reading for reasons that Wilson would probably have considered superficial: because of the light that the notebooks throw upon the author. For the journals are a pleasure to read, are entertaining both for their substance and style. They allow the reader to see with Wilson's eyes—that is, with clarity, precision, directness—and to understand with a portion of his trained intelligence. From *The Thirties*, one not only relives impressions of a troubled decade; one also senses the spirit of a rational and good man.

Leslie Mittleman

THOMAS CARDINAL WOLSEY

Author: Nancy Lenz Harvey (1935-   )
Publisher: Macmillan Publishing Company (New York). 232 pp. $19.95
Type of work: Biography
Time: 1472-1530
Locale: England

Another biography of King Henry VIII's lord chancellor which unconvincingly attempts to portray a more personal side of the cardinal

> *Principal personages:*
> THOMAS CARDINAL WOLSEY, lord chancellor of England under King Henry VIII
> KING HENRY VIII, King of England, 1509-1547
> THOMAS II (HOWARD), THIRD DUKE OF NORFOLK, the King's adviser and implacable foe to Wolsey
> CHARLES BRANDON, DUKE OF SUFFOLK, another enemy of Wolsey

Although he is vastly overshadowed in importance by the two towering figures of Henry VIII and Thomas More with whom he was chiefly involved, Thomas Cardinal Wolsey has received much attention from biographers from his time when his gentleman-usher George Cavendish wrote one of the first modern English biographies, down to the present age. Every generation, it seems, attempts to reinterpret the far-reaching events of the King's "secret matter" of his divorce from Catherine of Aragon, and the key person originally involved, the son of an Ipswich butcher, was Thomas Cardinal Wolsey.

Through his logical and efficient mind and considerable organizational skills, Wolsey worked his way up through various ecclesiastical offices to become the leading prelate of England, a candidate for the papacy, and lord chancellor of England, second in power only to the king. From this position of eminence he had virtually unlimited powers, and he personally conducted most of the realm's important affairs including arranging for the minutiae of provisioning English troops in their overseas campaigns. Unfortunately for him, the cost of such power was also high, for while King Henry VIII received the benefits of his talents, Wolsey was held personally responsible by the nobility and the public for the negative aspects of such things as the various taxes levied to carry out the King's foreign wars. As with all great men, Wolsey acquired important enemies on the way to power. Two of them, Thomas II (Howard), third Duke of Norfolk, and Charles Brandon, Duke of Suffolk, were to hound him until, in 1529, they succeeded in having him indicted for his abuse of legatine authority. The real reason for his fall, of course, was his failure to resolve the matter of Henry VIII's divorce.

Cardinal Wolsey is still an intriguing and elusive enigma after more than four hundred years. On the one hand, he sincerely attempted to achieve reforms within the church prior to the suppression of the monasteries (a fact not emphasized in the present biography), and in fact, the Cardinal was also responsible for the money derived from that suppression which went to set up Cardinal College, usually considered merely another of his attempts at self-aggrandizement. He was also instrumental in devising the first graduated tax in history. Yet, he is remembered today for his amassing of great personal wealth such as Hampton Court with its sumptuous art collection, and his pride in achievement exemplified in his extensive retinue, for which his stables alone housed more than one hundred horses.

In this brief biography by Nancy Lenz Harvey, the author attempts to evaluate and interpret the Cardinal's actions, motivations, and mental state based upon the inconclusive records of the times. Without adding any new factual information, the author attempts to delve into the psychological well-springs of Cardinal Wolsey. One clue to his actions which she attempts to establish is presented in the opening description of the Cardinal suffering from constipation. Harvey suggests this was a lifelong torment of the Cardinal which he interpreted as the "wages of sin." It is true that the cardinal suffered from the usual illnesses common to the people of the day, and Harvey takes pains to point out these illnesses at every opportunity. For example, she even includes one of the more frivolous charges brought against him when the Great Seal was taken from him, that of knowingly coming in contact with the King when he was suffering from the pox. Simply by emphasizing all these maladies suffered during the course of a long and eventful life invests them with an importance perhaps unwarranted in an age of poor sanitation, nutrition habits, and medical knowledge.

Without indicating why, Harvey dates Wolsey's birth on March 24, 1472-1473 (the year depends on whether one refers to the old style or new style calendar); yet, other biographers trace his birth to the year 1471, a year in which the plague was ravaging England. Also, she fails to point out the effects of the plague on the lower classes, especially on someone like Wolsey's father, a butcher by trade. According to some accounts, there were three sheep for each human being in England because of the plague, a ratio which brought new wealth to the lower classes. Although Thomas's father, Robert Wolsey, had frequently been in trouble with the authorities as a newcomer to Ipswich, by the time Thomas was growing up, his father was a landowner and prospering nicely. None of this is alluded to by Harvey; instead, she says of Thomas's youth: "He chose his friends conveniently and sparingly. As he watched those students about him, he knew that the boy in them would hold them back, while the man in him reached out, took knowledge, and gained power." This is pure conjecture based upon the selection of those details which conveniently fit the hindsight gained from the man's later life. His father's relative affluence would seem to mitigate such early extreme ambitions. That the biographer presents no evidence to corroborate her theory of his early opportunism is bad enough, but that she omits any detail about the conditions of life faced by the common people forces the reader to accept her judgment without suggesting the possibility of any opinion to the contrary.

This overweening ambition born of deprivation felt by a member of the lower class is presented as a second motivating force behind the cardinal. Yet, in a later section of the book, Harvey voices her disagreement with almost all previous biographers in her analysis of Wolsey's coveting of the papacy. She says, "In Wolsey's mind, the papal crown was mere tissue to the strengthened fabric of his cardinalate." She states as evidence of this lack of regard that the position would not yield significant additional wealth, and that he had never liked to travel and had never been to Rome. To a man proud of glorying in his achievements such motives are questionable. The political maneuvering toward gaining the papacy for Wolsey, she attributes to the King: "While attentive to the details of massive endeavor in the name of his king, Wolsey never launched a campaign for his own advantage." As a biographer, Harvey is entitled to her opinion, but the references she cites are inconclusive and unsatisfactory in convincing the more informed reader. All evidence of the man's intentions must, of necessity, be circumstantial, but worse than the inconclusiveness of her argument is her omission of evidence cited by other biographers in defense of their opinions of his ambition in this realm. Her failure to indicate that this is a controversial point is also annoying.

Another area of omission in this biography is the lack of adequate background material supplied for the reader. It is always a problem of the biographer to determine how much information the reader has of the period in general and of the specific details relating to the particular individual in question. Without an understanding of the times one is unable to evaluate properly a man of those times. One case in point is that of Wolsey's relationship with Jane Larke, which resulted in the birth of two children. Harvey simply reports that the cardinal took a mistress for whom he later found a husband and supplied a dowry. By omitting mention of the common practice of "noncanonical marriage" and the fact that the celibacy of priests had not been completely accepted in England at the time, she makes Wolsey appear to be hypocritical and a bad clergyman. To understand Wolsey's actions more fully, one must take into consideration that a system of regular fines had been instituted to forgive the breach of celibacy vows and these fines accounted for some of the church's regular revenues. In addition, according to Charles W. Ferguson, author of the definitive biography of Wolsey, *Naked to Mine Enemies*, the cardinal's views on marriage and celibacy were openly and vehemently aired, and he was responsible for a Parliamentary Act which relieved several Chancery priests from vows of celibacy. If Harvey wishes to dispute this interpretation, that is her prerogative; however, she has the obligation of presenting evidence and of refuting that evidence marshaled by previous biographers. In the present case, she does not even mention Ferguson's book.

The footnotes indicated that Harvey relies mainly on primary sources as well she should; yet, her handling of the material frequently leaves much to be desired. Many times when she offers her interpretation of an event, her citation simply refers to a letter or another nebulous document which certainly presents factual information but does not account for the judgment made. Again, there are times when she quotes at great length on matters of little importance which could more aptly be summarized. For example, two pages are devoted to extracts from the letter of the Venetian ambassador concerning the French invasion of Italy in 1515. If this were a full scale biography or if that campaign were more crucial to an understanding of the cardinal, perhaps such detailing would be justified. This quotation device would be more effective if Harvey had used it in making some of her crucial judgments on Wolsey's motivations.

Another evident scholarly deficiency is in the author's treatment of earlier biographers. Her notes indicate a familiarity with all the important works, but as indicated above, she fails to clarify where she disagrees with commonly accepted opinions. Most seriously, although she cites most of the earlier biographers at least once, she never cites Ferguson, the most recent, and in many scholars' opinion, the definitive biographer. Harvey's book offers a totally different picture of Wolsey, and for the person familiar with Ferguson's account, a very unconvincing account. If her purpose were to refute currently held opinions, she should forthrightly attack the leading proponent of that opinion rather than pretend he does not exist. It is possible that the depiction of Wolsey contained in this book could be more accurate than that of previous biographies, but the evidence presented is sparse and unconvincing.

The brevity of *Thomas Cardinal Wolsey* may make it attractive to a reader interested in a superficial survey of Wolsey's life, but its oversimplification, its lack of background material, and its variance with previous biographies makes it less than reliable for the layperson. Despite its many footnotes, the book is also unsatisfactory for the scholar.

Roger A. Geimer

THUNDER ON THE RIGHT
The "New Right" and the Politics of Resentment

Author: Alan Crawford (1953-   )
Publisher: Pantheon Books (New York). 381 pp. $13.95
Type of work: Current affairs
Time: The 1960's to the present
Locale: The United States

The author discusses the New Right movement, its tactics, its goals, and its future, contrasting it with the "Old-Guard," conservative faction based in the Northeastern United States

> *Principal personages:*
> RICHARD VIGUERIE, a right-wing politician who compiles accurate "target" mailing lists
> HOWARD JARVIS, best known as the foremost proponent of the "Proposition Thirteen" bill in California
> STANTON EVANS, a Southern conservative, editor of the *Indianapolis News*, chairman of the American Conservative Union, and an ardent defender of the New Right faith
> WILLIAM F. BUCKLEY, JR., a witty, erudite member of the "Old-Guard" with the ability to make liberal friends
> THE REVEREND JERRY FALWELL, a New Right minister and founder of the Moral Majority, Inc.

Alan Crawford's *Thunder on the Right: The "New Right" and the Politics of Resentment* serves notice to liberal and moderate Americans that the New Right movement grows stronger in numbers and power with each passing election. Yet, it also argues that the movement may fragment because of its continual impossible demands upon its spokespersons.

Crawford pictures himself as an American journalist of conservative persuasion who is disturbed by what he sees as the growth of a monster: the so-called New Right movement. His message is threefold: first, the New Right's beliefs are a menace to fundamental constitutional guarantees such as free speech and the separation of church and state; second, the New Right is very much on the offensive, gathering adherents through efficient organization and planning; and, third, it may never be the political power broker it would like to be because New Conservatives find it hard to follow their own leaders.

As Crawford notes, the United States, almost from its inception, has had strong political parties representing divergent points of view: one advocating a powerful centralized government with considerable control over citizens' behavior and another wanting a tightly reined, relatively weak government, allowing the states considerable powers to create legislation. Until recently, Crawford argues, conservative leaders have served America well by challenging the assumptions of liberals and moderates and thus diluting their influence. Crawford also believes that, until recently, conservatives were gentlemen of the old school—the so-called Eastern Establishment, persons best represented by pundit and gadfly William F. Buckley, Jr., whose *National Review* enunciates traditional conservative positions. As the author sees it, however, millions of conservative middle Americans living in the South and Midwest have never felt comfortable with Eastern Establishmentarians as leaders, since they are considered out of touch with ordinary people and their problems.

The ranks of New Rightists are filled not by the rich and well connected but rather by middle-American small businessmen, farmers, and ranchers, those without old wealth or Ivy League ties to fall back upon. This newer strain of conservatives finds the older one "lackluster" in response to the perceived threat from the left and center as well as suspect because of the Old Guard penchant for learned argument and reasoned policymaking. If Buckley is the hero of the Old Guard (and it is very possible that he is such a thing), then Joseph McCarthy, the Communist-hunting extremist of the 1950's, is the hero of the newer faction.

At base, the New Rightists see themselves as possessing the *machismo* lacking in old-line right-wingers. Their heroes, Crawford states, are those tied to the myth of the old West: John Wayne and his band of cowboys fighting off the redskins or shooting "bad guys" who threaten virtuous settlers. The old right-wingers picture themselves as John Waynes fighting those who would destroy the simple codes of Western life. By speaking the language of *machismo*, such New Rightists as the Reverend Jerry Falwell, a television minister from Virginia, and Phillip Crane, a former Illinois presidential contender, reach their carefully targeted audience, telling it what it wants to hear.

According to Crawford, the "tough guy" message enunciated by the leaders of the New Right is invariably the same: namely, that America has fallen on terrible days and is rotten through and through because of liberal permissiveness and atheism. To them, America is a helpless giant (to borrow Richard Nixon's phrase), a captive of the liberal establishment and those conservatives who are "soft" on liberalism. Behind the feeling of helplessness is real fear.

Fear takes different forms. First, there is the fear of the United States becoming another Great Britain mired in the slough of welfare and dying industries, perfect prey for Russia and her Communist allies. To Crawford, many Americans from lower-middle- and lower-class backgrounds are genuinely alarmed about Russian power to the extent that they feel communism to be winning the ideological war with capitalism. To these people, such programs as welfare, school busing, socialized medicine, and other liberal inventions are slowly sapping the strength of the free enterprise system by taking care of those who should be taking care of themselves.

Second is the fear of American helplessness in an actual war with Russia. The United States, they believe, is fast becoming a second rate nation because of the pernicious influence of liberal presidents and congresses lacking the nerve to bolster sufficiently our defense budgets. Counter to this image is the one they hope America will again project: that of a Herculean America led by the only real leaders left in the country, the true believers of the New Right.

Third is the fear of America abdicating her traditionally assumed role of moral arbiter for the world because of the same liberal thinking that led her to be behind the Soviet Union in the missile race. To document their case for American decline, the conservative spokespersons turn their attention to a host of issues. Phyllis Schlafly, an Illinois housewife and anti-Equal Rights Amendment (ERA) crusader, sees the proponents of the ERA as termites eating away the foundations of the American family by destroying the traditional roles of men and women. Anita Bryant, former entertainer and housewife, finds that homosexuals have too many rights and too easy access to America's impressionable young. The Reverend Falwell, on the other hand, decries the preoccupation of Americans with sex and drugs.

To them, America is in incredibly deep trouble today. They see her as mocked by third-rate countries, betrayed by leftists from within, lectured by left-leaning allies who fear Russian guns more than American displeasure, rotted from within by drugs and depravity, and ever more threatened by nuclear annihilation.

In the view of the New Right, no president since Herbert Hoover has been an adequate leader. One president after another—Franklin D. Roosevelt, Harry S Truman, Dwight Eisenhower, John F. Kennedy, Lyndon Johnson, and even Richard Nixon—has failed the nation he served by pandering to leftist liberals. So also has one congress after another passed bills which strengthened the hand of the Federal bureaucracy against that of the individual and the constituent states of the union. The Supreme Court too has brought dishonor upon itself time and again by striking down everything from school prayer to segregation. Thus, the members of the New Right see themselves as persons betrayed, and they are angry about it.

Until quite recently, such anger would go undirected for the most part because of the lack of communication between persons sharing the New Right vision. Single issue groups of the New Rightist bent did not want to "waste" energy meeting with other single issue groups, preferring instead to go it alone.

According to the author, however, the fragmentation of the New Right ended when Richard Viguerie of suburban Virginia began making lists of like-minded New Right-wingers and circulating them in order to stir interest in issues and candidates. In 1975, Viguerie, along with New Right leader Howard Phillips, coordinated the campaign to unify various protest groups under the banner of the Conservative Caucus. Viguerie and Phillips met frequently in Washington, D.C., with the leaders of New Right causes and hammered out a strategy which would "take control of the culture."

Among the groups Viguerie and Phillips brought together were several having a large following including the Committee for Responsible Youth Politics, the American Security Council, the National Right to Work Committee, and the Heritage Foundation (among many others). Viguerie was soon able to use the membership lists of such organizations to create this master list of New Rightists. From his Falls Church, Virginia, offices, he became a direct mail specialist, targeting a vast market for conservative fund raisers.

During the 1970's, Viguerie put together a staff of three hundred persons and sent out nearly one hundred million pieces of mail a year from three hundred mailing lists containing the names of twenty-five million Americans. According to the author, Viguerie's twin computers operate twenty-four hours a day and printers and tape units create vast numbers of letters. In addition to his direct mailing, Viguerie publishes *The New Right Report* as well as the monthly *Conservative Digest*, but neither of these has had the impact his mailings have had over the past few years.

As a matter of fact, it was Viguerie's mailings and subsequent fund raising that Crawford believes helped turn the tide against notable liberal legislators in recent elections, particularly in the last one in which a host of liberal senators and congressmen were tossed out of office by voters seeking conservative directions in government. By doubly alarming his already alarmed audience about the "evils" foisted on the American people by leftist politicians, Viguerie was able to generate enormous amounts of money for his New Right cause. He gave the "silent majority" a roaring voice.

Appealing in a neopopulist way to the forgotten Americans of the small towns and cities, Viguerie and others who learned his organizing methods struck real paydirt. He said what they wanted to say: that the individual still counted for something, that Big Brother in Washington should be destroyed before it was too late, that liberalism only leads to societal decay.

Yet, despite New Right victories in recent years, Crawford relates, Reaganites and ex-Goldwaterites find that the real thrill of victory simply is not there. In one of his most telling passages, Crawford explains that the ideal New Right candidate is ideologically pure and does not bargain with liberals even to the slightest degree. Therein lies the dilemma, for once a New Right candidate is elected to office, he or she begins wielding power and in order to wield power effectively, he or she must, upon occasion at least, compromise with moderates and liberals. Yet, according to the harsh dictates of the New Conservatives, compromise automatically means weakness on the part of the compromiser and weakness of resolve cannot be tolerated. In short, it is nearly impossible for New Rightists to have leaders, because leaders cannot remain "pure in spirit" and still hope to govern.

Thus, as Senator Goldwater has discovered and as President Reagan is discovering, being a New Right hero is a tough assignment. Such concern for purity being a hallmark of the New Right is part of the reason both Old Guard conservatives and liberals find it so disconcerting.

Crawford concludes his book with a stern warning for those who oppose New Rightists and their programs, saying, "Nothing less [than liberty] is at stake, as the American Right moves from a traditional conservative defense of representative government against the onslaughts of direct democracy into a celebration of government by rabble-rousing, by adding machine, by majorities of the moment."

With *Thunder on the Right*, Crawford has not only defined his enemy, but he has also sounded the battle cry and started the war. For the reader who would grasp the realities of today's clash of ideologies, this book is, without question, indispensable.

John D. Raymer

TIME OF DESECRATION

Author: Alberto Moravia (1907-   )
Translated from the Italian by Angus Davidson
Publisher: Farrar, Straus and Giroux (New York). 376 pp. $12.95
Type of work: Novel
Time: The present
Locale: Rome, Italy

A political novel which is a kind of morality play for our time, in which a group of characters act out, in their sexual exploits, the lessons to be learned from the basic tenets of prevailing political ideologies and systems

> *Principal characters:*
> DESIDERIA, a young woman of Rome
> VIOLA, her mother
> TIBERI, a respected antique dealer and manager of Viola's business affairs, also her lover
> EROSTRATO, a young Sicilian, who becomes Viola's lover and secretary
> QUINTO, a comrade from Milan, leader of the group to which Erostrato belongs

Alberto Moravia, whose first novel, *The Time of Indifference* (*Gli indifferenti*) written when he was eighteen years old, has now completed what he says is his last novel. Called *Time of Desecration* by the translator, Angus Davidson, the novel was published in Italy in 1978 under the title *La Vita Interiore*.

The new novel, like many of Moravia's others, is set in Rome and is a description of the prevailing social and political state of Italy today. It, also, like many of his other novels, uses two women, mother and daughter, and their relationship as the base of the allegory.

At the time of the telling of the story, the daughter, Desideria, is a beautiful young woman. Her story begins, however, when at the age of twelve, as a lonely and unattractive child, she ate and masturbated obsessively, because, as she says, she was fat. Viola, her adoptive mother is passionately involved in maintaining a façade of respectability, although she is involved with Tiberi, her business manager, in a series of affairs with her daughter's young governesses. Identified as American and just as passionate concerning her wealth and position, Viola is the symbol for capitalism. Erostrato, a young man who also is Viola's lover, lives on "an existential see-saw." At one time Fascist, then Communist, he is also a pious Christian, who is drawn into the occult. Paid by the police as an informer, he is, in addition, a revolutionist. The shifts in his beliefs from one extreme to another present no difficulty for him. He is an opportunist and profits materially from all of his alliances.

Desideria, at the age of twelve and while going to her mother's room for the key to the refrigerator, accidentally witnesses her mother, her governess, and Tiberi in a sexual scene. Infuriated, Viola, with puritanical hypocrisy, attacks Desideria for her gluttony, telling Desideria for the first time that she is the child of a prostitute, who had been willing to sell her baby. The child is almost destroyed by her mother's cruelty. The trauma leaves Desideria with a great hatred for her mother and a compelling desire for revenge. At the same time, food becomes revolting to her and she stops eating, soon growing into a beautiful young woman. Because Desideria is so attractive, Viola's behavior becomes indulgent and seductive. At this point, a "Voice," which only Desideria hears, takes over her life and attempts to control and direct her, first in symbolic acts of transgression and desecration against class, property, money, marriage, and religion. Later, as Desideria grows older, the Voice takes her deep into Marxist rhetoric and finally into open revolt. Desideria welcomes the Voice. Its presence gives her identity. Fear of the Voice, however, leads her into almost total compliance with it; and when the Voice directs her to use her beauty to entrap and destroy Viola, Desideria complies up to the point of actually accepting Viola as a lover. The Voice grows increasingly strident and demanding, but Desideria, in spite of Viola's gross behavior, retains a daughter's love for mother and, although it alternates with a savage hatred, the bond is there and it prevents the Voice from taking absolute control over the daughter. Her revolutionary acts are symbolic ones until, through Erostrato, Desideria meets Quinto and, directed by the Voice, she is led into real violence and pointlessly kills both Quinto and Tiberi.

In spite of the Voice and in spite of the struggle waged by Desideria, however, Viola and Erostrato do survive. As in all political struggles, decisive victories are not possible; Moravia points out, and by the same analogy, that all political systems are corrupting and exploitative forces from which there is no escape.

In the novel Moravia explores a political system which has become perverted and irrational in its attempts to destroy the middle class and its power and institutions. Individuals become instruments of a dehumanizing power. Desideria is as a nation under seige from the forces of both the left and the right. She retains her virginity, despite the efforts of Viola and her two lovers, Tiberi and Erostrato, until she is raped at gunpoint by Quinto, the proletarian leader of a revolutionary group. He is her first contact with a real member of the proletarian force, and she despises and fears him. She kills him not because of the rape but because of her perception that he refuses to accept her as an equal participant in the group, just as she kills Tiberi when he proposes marriage to her, which she perceives as a bondage from which there will be no escape.

Yet, the novel is more than simple allegory. To Viola, Desideria, and Erostrato, Moravia has added human dimensions. There is between the three of them a bond of caring—of simple human love. Desideria, after she has struck Viola across the face, is devastated; she tells the interrogator: "A mother's cheek is not like other cheeks." Erostrato, who says he longs for the revolution when all rich people like Viola will cease to exist, has moments of compassion and pity. He hopes that Viola will escape with her jewels and gold, and after that the revolution will become perfect, new, and beautiful. There are even rare moments when Viola herself speaks with an honesty and openness that bring her into focus as a person who has suffered and is suffering pain and anguish over the emptiness and futility of her life. She may be crying for basically selfish reasons, as Erostrato tells Desideria, but the tears are real. Exploitative of each other, nevertheless, between Erostrato and Desideria there are moments of concern and kindness. She is sensitive to and perceptive of his needs. Once, for example, after she tells him that he wants to retrogress into prenatal nothingness, she notices that he does not understand what she is saying and moreover that he feels inferior because he does not understand, so she attempts an explanation that is acceptable to him rather than harmful to his pride. Although the two are never completely honest with each other, there are moments of frankness, and Desideria never tells Erostrato about the Voice because she thinks it would give her undue authority over him.

Despite the fact that Desideria is controlled by the Voice, she is by no means irrational. Characterized not only as intelligent but studious as well, she is capable of appraising situation after situation into which the Voice leads her, and, increasingly, she is able to resist its orders. Gradually, she achieves a sense of self-possession, and she realizes that she is neither an honest girl to whom her mother's lesbian advances would be incomprehensible nor the cunning revolutionary that the Voice would like her to be. At one point, she dismisses the Voice, saying that she does not intend to listen to any more rubbish. She declares herself to be no more than a simple bourgeois girl who does not get along with her mother. She will move out, she thinks, and get her own flat as a solution to her problem. The reaction of the Voice to this solution, however, is immediate and violent. Desideria is plunged into a painful, convulsive fit which lasts through the night. It is enough to destroy her resistance, and she agrees to go along with the planned intrigue: she is to make love with Viola and Erostrato in order to kidnap Viola and hold her for ransom.

The novel takes the form of a question and answer session between an interrogator who is designated by the pronoun "I," and Desideria. In a foreword to the novel, Moravia identifies the "I" with himself as author and Desideria with a "character" in the novel, the questions and answers having taken place over the seven-year period Moravia was writing the novel. In answering the interrogator's questions, Desideria seems to create herself; and this is also a point that Moravia makes in the Foreword. Nevertheless, as one goes deeper into the novel, it becomes apparent that the questions of the author determine the answers of the character. Thus, the author becomes in a very real sense a character in the novel involved in a much more subtle plot than is apparent at surface level, one in which the author by writing and the reader by reading participate. The interrogator, by shaping responses to his own questions, takes over Desideria's life and controls her thoughts and actions in exactly the same way that is attributed to the Voice, which is characterized as omniscient. She is the author's instrument in the same way that she is the instrument of the Voice. The reality of the novel thus becomes voice; moreover, the structure of the novel insists on the identification of author's voice, interrogator's voice, and the Voice. The question one must ask, then, is whose interior life is being developed? Character's or author's? In the novel Moravia shows himself at the time of and in the act of creation. Does he mean to suggest that in his use of human needs and the weaknesses of flesh, in his exploration of sex in all its variations for purposes of political allegory, that he has engaged in desecration? The novel appears to conclude on that idea. Desideria has killed Quinto, as the Voice has ordered her to. Then the Voice urges her to take the pistol and kill her mother and Erostrato. At this point, she refuses to obey the Voice, and, at the same time, she refuses to continue to answer the questions of the interrogator. Her story is not finished, the interrogator says. He wants to know from her what happened; he wants to know the conclusion. Life has no conclusion, she tells him, what matters is not her story but herself. The interrogator knows enough, she argues, to make others understand who she is. He persists, however, arguing that what she has to tell him of the conclusion might give him more insight into her personality. She tells him good bye. He responds by pleading with her to continue, to finish. She replies by recalling Hiroshima and the imprint of a human body on a plaster wall: the body that made the imprint had been devoured and thus annihilated by the explosion. In the same way the author's imagination has consumed Desideria, so that she exists only in his writing, "as an imprint, as a somebody."

Although the characters act with passion, the tone of the novel is entirely dispassionate; and what finally emerge are disembodied voices, imprints on pages, as an author—who in his lifetime is highly praised and recognized worldwide—at the end of his career questions his techniques and purposes. The effect is powerful; the stand courageous.

Mary Rohrberger

TO KEEP OUR HONOR CLEAN

Author: Edwin McDowell (1935-   )
Publisher: The Vanguard Press (New York). 313 pp. $10.95
Type of work: Novel
Time: 1952
Locale: Parris Island, South Carolina

The story of the basic training of a group of Marine recruits at Parris Island during the Korean War

> *Principal characters:*
> THOMAS DUTTON, a recruit from whose perspective much of the novel is narrated
> TECHNICAL SERGEANT FLOYD KRUPE, the senior drill instructor who promotes and condones the physical and psychological abuse of the recruits
> CORPORAL CHRISTOPHER SANDERS, the assistant drill instructor who protests the brutality of the other instructors
> SERGEANT BENNETT AND SERGEANT PEPPER, drill instructors
> ROBERT BEGAY,
> JONATHAN GABRIEL,
> JAMES GILLIAN, AND
> STANLEY TEW, recruits in training with Dutton
> SUSAN BREWER, a widow who falls in love with Sanders

This novel is prefaced by two quotations, one from the *Marines' Hymn* and the other from William Shakespeare's *Measure for Measure*. The title of the novel has its source in the Hymn—"First to fight for right and freedom,/ and to keep our honor clean,/ We are proud to claim the title,/ of United States Marine." From Shakespeare comes the commentary on the fantastic tricks played by proud men dressed in "a little brief authority," the tricks that make the angels weep. These literary references indicate something about the subject of the novel, the fatal flaw that consistently has appeared in Western man's character from the time at least of the Genesis story—the devastating sin of pride.

As the *Marines' Hymn* proclaims, the Marine is proud precisely because his horor is clean and he fights for right and freedom. Meanwhile, the angels mourn the folly of man. In the first few paragraphs of the novel, the treatment that Edwin McDowell will give to this familiar theme of pride and punishment becomes apparent. The recruits on the bus headed for Parris Island "realized for the first time the finality of their decision to join the Marines." Once they pass through the gates, there is no escape. Their irrevocable choice to become Marines—or, in other words, to make themselves proud—leads them into a miasma of brutality and perverted patriotism.

Thus, the fictional reality of the novel presents an ideal context for exploring the complex ontological question of sin and its relationship to suffering, the theological mystery that is one of the bases of the Judeo-Christian heritage. As McDowell creates his narrative of what really happens at the infamous Parris Island training camp, he has the opportunity to deal with a myth central to Western cultural tradition. A group of men have chosen to become Marines, to groom themselves to be the best, the most patriotic, the elite of fighting men. They enter basic training and subsequently are subjected to irrational, savage brutality and humiliation at the hands of their drill instructors.

As in every experience for which there is no rational explanation or justification, mythic interpretations of the world offer solace to the sufferer. The Marine recruit, who has believed himself capable of being superior, suffers Prometheus-like for his pride, and survives to become part of that elite group only if he is able to endure the senseless punishment that he has brought down on himself.

The fictional world created by McDowell is replete with possibilities for a profound exploration of man's nature. Unfortunately, he ignores these possibilities and develops instead a narrative that turns out to be primarily a journalistic account of the techniques used by the Marines to convert normal young men into soldiers capable of killing before they are killed. This is partly the result of too much attention to the actions of his characters and too little development of their personalities. The reader knows what they do, but very little about what they really are.

Although this novel is the story of a large number of characters, the four most important form a representative group. Floyd Krupe is the senior drill instructor, a typical example of the tough, dedicated teacher of weak, untrained, young recruits. Thomas Dutton is the would-be soldier, characterized by the idealism and dedication of youth. Christopher Sanders is the hero, the assistant drill instructor disturbed by injustice and disillusioned by his inability to right the wrongs of the world. Susan Brewer is the young woman victimized by the Korean conflict, a war widow with a child, who falls in love with yet another man destined for the battlefield, Corporal Sanders.

Each of these characters is faced with a conflict in the course of the novel. Dutton, who has joined the Marines because his best friend died as a Marine in Korea, finds that the brutal training period has inured him to the injustices of the world. It has changed him from a considerate, naïve young man into a potentially violent soldier. Sanders learns a great deal about the suspension of ethical values in the face of the realities of war. Susan Brewer learns to accept the fact of her husband's death and to feel love for another man. Krupe is the unyielding character, quoting Friedrich Nietzsche on courage and cowardice, demanding strict obedience and submission of his troops, and ignoring the mistreatment meted out by the assistant drill instructors. Krupe's insistence on the institutionalized values of the military is in part a compensation for the fact that his brother became a collaborator with the enemy after his capture in North Korea.

The predicament of these four characters has possibilities for an interesting novel, but McDowell misses almost every opportunity to develop the conflicts of Dutton, Sanders, Brewer, and Krupe. There are many confrontations— Dutton facing Krupe the villain and Sanders the hero, Brewer agonizing over her involvement with Sanders, Sanders and Krupe arguing about brutality— but none of this is very effective, and almost none of it seems authentic. These are stock characters in very predictable situations. They say and do precisely what the reader expects them to say and do. As there are no surprises, there is no tension followed by relief, and nothing to hold the reader's interest except the extensive details about the training received by a Marine recruit at Parris Island in 1952.

The novel seems to be not a novel at all, but an unsuccessful attempt at fictionalizing a real-life experience. It is primarily journalistic rather than novelistic. This distinction, of course, has nothing to do with whether Parris Island really exists in the world of the actual reader's experience, or whether the author is a Marine sergeant "trained at Parris Island," as the dust jacket indicates. Rather, the distinction between journalism and fiction depends on the reality that exists outside the novel, of which the narrative is a partial account. If that reality is the one in which the actual reader exists, the novel is surely bound to be unconvincing. If, however, that reality is a self-sufficient, integral fictional world, the novel will have the potential at least of being an "authentic" account of a "real" experience. Whether the fictional reality of which the narrator speaks seems authentic depends on the complex interaction of the narrator and his material, on his basic assumptions about the reality portrayed in the novel.

One of the problems in McDowell's novel is the lack of a clearly defined narrative voice. The narrator is omniscient, but his omniscience is unconvincing and irritating. Frequently, he narrates the thoughts and motivations of several different characters in a single paragraph without ever justifying his ability to do so. Even more distracting are his occasional judgmental attitude and his proclivity to analyze motivations rather than let the characters reveal through their words and actions the reasons for what they say and do. When the narrator says about Sanders, making love with Susan, that "for a brief moment he thought about Linda and about the possibility of holding back, but by then he was no longer capable of making a choice," he makes a confusing, erratic shift from Sander's awareness of his own experience to the narrator's superior knowledge of the character's actions. In like manner, the narrator's presentation of the boxing match in Chapter 14 lacks control. "But Leslie Potter lost on a technical knockout when the referee wisely halted the fight to prevent him from being cut up worse by his opponent, an unspectacular fighter whom Sanders was certain would have presented little difficulty for Tew or Dutton." In the context of a single sentence, he gives a factual account of the fight, renders qualitative judgments—wisely, unspectacular—

and then shifts to Sander's evaluation of a character whose name is not even mentioned.

This narrator never has a clear conception of what he is doing. The result is a maze of minor characters who lack any distinct identity, and even of major personages who all sound the same. Taken out of context, much of the dialogue could not be identified as delivered by Sanders, or Krupe, or Dutton, or even Susan Brewer. The language is awkward, unconvincing, and seldom interesting.

McDowell does attempt some interesting narrative techniques. There are flashbacks, a shift in point of view from Dutton to Sanders, and a symmetry in the first and last chapters. None of this, however, is successful. The novel remains what it always seems to be—thinly disguised journalism. Because there is not enough development of the characters as individuals to make them believable, the narrator's omniscience seems false. If he really is all-knowing, why does the reader not know these people? Why does the reader not even care when James Gillian is wrongly accused of being a homosexual, or when Jonathan Gabriel commits suicide to avoid repeating his basic training? Why are there no rewarding insights into the meaning of this unjust, brutal experience at Parris Island? War is hell. Man is good, or evil, or both. Brutality may lead to salvation. The end justifies the means. Man suffers for hs sin of pride. The possibilities are legion, and that is the reason that *To Keep Our Honor Clean* is such a disappointing novel.

This novel turns out to be a sort of diary of a training camp experience, and that simply is not of much interest. The fictional reality portrayed by an effective novel provides a vicarious experience for the reader, an experience that, while fictional, seems authentic. McDowell's novel does not do that. Rather, it leaves the reader with the impression that he has read an account of someone else's life without understanding what it is like to have lived that kind of life.

Gilbert Smith

TO THE MARIANAS
War in the Central Pacific: 1944

Author: Edwin P. Hoyt (1923-   )
Publisher: Van Nostrand Reinhold Company (New York). 292 pp. $12.95
Type of work: Military history
Time: December, 1943-August, 1944
Locale: Central Pacific

A military history of the American amphibious campaigns to capture the Marshall and Mariana Islands in World War II

> *Principal personages:*
> REAR ADMIRAL MARC MITSCHER, United States Navy
> ADMIRAL CHESTER W. NIMITZ, Commander in Chief of the United States Pacific Fleet
> VICE ADMIRAL JISABURO OZAWA, Commander of the Japanese Imperial Navy
> LIEUTENANT GENERAL YOSHITSUGO SAITO, Commander of the Japanese forces on Saipan
> MAJOR GENERAL HOLLAND M. SMITH, United States Marines
> BRIGADIER GENERAL RALPH SMITH, United States Army
> ADMIRAL RAYMOND SPRUANCE, United States Navy

Edwin P. Hoyt continues his military history of the Pacific War in this sequel to his *Storm over the Gilberts*, which described the invasion of Tarawa and Betio. His present study can be divided into three sections: the invasions of Kwajalein, Eniwetok, and the other islands of the Marshalls which provided an advanced base for invasion of the Marianas group; the carrier battles during the Marianas invasion; and the struggle to capture Saipan, Tinian and Guam. This secured the Marianas as a base for long-range B-29 attacks on the Japanese homeland.

The struggle to capture what sometimes amounted to only a few square miles of coral atoll was essential to a grand strategy that had evolved by 1943. Because most American resources were being stockpiled in Europe in anticipation of D-Day, the Pacific had secondary priority. General MacArthur wanted to push from the south through Indonesia to the Philippines, but his campaigns of 1942 in New Guinea and the Solomons were slow. Therefore, it was decided that the major American offensive would strike directly across the Pacific to the Marshall Islands and then to the Marianas, to penetrate the Japanese "Inner Empire."

Since Micronesia had hundreds of islands in a three million square mile area, Admiral Chester W. Nimitz, Commander in Chief of the Pacific Fleet, decided to take only essential islands and ports which could serve as unsinkable carriers and protect the advancing American naval forces from the air. The costly Marine invasion of Tarawa showed the campaign would be difficult, and it made clear the need for better training and tactics for amphibious landings in the Marshalls. Kwajalein was to be the first target.

By 1943, the Japanese navy had already lost seven hundred planes in the Solomons. The Navy had to protect the far-flung empire in the Pacific, but the Japanese army insisted on keeping half of all aircraft production. The Navy was thus forced to redefine a defensive line from New Guinea to Truk and up to the Marianas. This meant the Marshalls would not be seriously defended. The local garrisons were expected to fight to the death without hope of further help.

On January 29, 1943, Rear Admiral Mitscher sent four carrier task groups to destroy Japanese air bases in the Marshalls. The new F6F Hellcat fighter was heavily armored, and proved to be superior to the unarmored zeros that rose to meet them. Japanese air power was quickly destroyed. The first major objective was the island of Roi-Namur to the north of Kwajalein. Using new vessels for amphibious landings, the Landing Ship Tank (LST) with a bow which could be lowered to disgorge Landing Vehicles Tank (LVT), marines took the island with few casualties. Their landing was preceded by point-blank naval bombardment and aerial attack. Most of the 3,700 Japanese troops were killed or shell-shocked by the bombardment. Hoyt concludes that the relative ease of the operation was due to effective bombardment.

The next objective was several small islands near Kwajalein. They were to provide a supply and artillery base for assault on Kwajalein itself. This too was successful and artillery was landed. Although it was only three miles long, Kwajalein received seven thousand naval shells and twenty-nine thousand rounds of artillery before invasion on February 1. The surviving Japanese still put up a stiff resistance, retreating into networks of tunnels. Every foot of ground was contested before the atoll was finally won on February 6. Of the five thousand Japanese defenders, only seventy-nine survived.

The next target was Eniwetok atoll, with the second largest lagoon in the Marshalls. As a preliminary, a carrier-based attack was mounted against Japanese ships and planes on Truk, 670 miles to the southwest. Although the main Japanese fleet had already abandoned Truk for the Palaus one thousand miles west, carrier bombers dropped four hundred tons of bombs on ships and ninety-four tons on airfields, sinking 200,000 tons of Japanese shipping.

Meanwhile the three thousand Japanese on Eniwetok prepared for the attack they knew was coming. As before, heavy bombardment preceded the landings of marines on February 19, but once ashore the opposition on the beach was fierce. The Japanese established fields of fire from concealed positions on high grounds. Spiderwebs (elaborate connected tunnels) allowed Japanese snipers to appear behind advancing American troops, and these had to be eliminated one by one with tanks, demolition, and flamethrowers.

By early 1944, the new B-29 Superfortress was operational and its range made Saipan in the Marianas the next logical invasion point in the Central Pacific campaign. It would also provide an advance submarine base. Mac-Arthur argued once again for a southern approach, but success in the Marshalls caused the Joint Chiefs of Staff, on March 12, to decide on an attack on the Marianas. Meanwhile, the Japanese Navy High Command decided that their one hope was to engage the Pacific Fleet and try for a great victory. Remaining Japanese naval forces were reorganized and fuel conserved for the coming showdown. Unfortunately for Japan, attrition had decimated the ranks of skilled pilots, and the replacements of 1944 had only a few hours solo flying time and almost no combat training. In May, 1944, the fuel crisis was so acute that all training flights were suspended.

On the American side, Admiral Spruance assembled the largest force to date in the Pacific: 535 ships carrying 127,500 men were prepared for the invasion of Saipan, Tinian, and Guam. The Marianas posed a more difficult military objective than the Gilberts and Marshalls, for they were not sandy coral atolls, but rugged mountaintops rising out of the Pacific. The major objective, Saipan, was thirteen miles long and five miles wide, but only the west coast offered a suitable invasion route. Because of the greater size of the island, preliminary bombardment was not as effective as in the Marshall landings.

The thirty thousand Japanese defenders on Saipan were led by Lieutenant General Yoshitsugo Saito. Although he received few supplies, Saito had prepared an in-depth defense. His best troops were dug in along the beaches, backed by tanks and reserve troops where the mountains rose sharply. There was a second defensive line among the caves and ravines. Saito issued his order: "Destroy the enemy on the beach."

On June 16, following a naval barrage, the first wave of LVT's and nearly seventy amph-tracs landed in the face of heavy fire. Once on the beach, the marines secured a beachhead under artillery and mortar fire, some units suffering up to thirty-five percent casualties. About two thousand marines were casualties on the difficult first day on Saipan, and that night Japanese troops and tanks staged a counter attack to drive them back. This attack was repulsed, and, on June 17, the marines and army troops moved farther inland against stiff resistance.

Gradually the beachhead was extended until the southern tip of Saipan was secured by June 20. The Japanese, however, still held two-thirds of the rugged island—ideal terrain for their defensive tactics. The marines could not make a clean sweep; small Japanese units had to be routed cave by cave.

Hoyt relates that service rivalry began to appear as the army moved much slower than the marines, since the army was unwilling to accept many casualties. This split resulted in a command change on June 24. The Army Twenty-Seventh Division was a National Guard unit with, according to Hoyt, weak leadership. General Ralph Smith was relieved of duty after complaints were made by the Marine General Holland Smith. This incident led to greater interservice rivalry.

Despite enormous losses and a hopeless situation, Japanese resistance did not falter on Saipan, with each soldier determined to cause as many American deaths as possible. Not until July 9 was Saipan finally "secure," and on that day thousands of Japanese soldiers and civilians on the northern tip of the island jumped to their death off Marpi Point. General Saito had committed seppuku in a cave on July 6. For this strategic island, the United States had nearly seventeen thousand casualties, including four thousand dead. Japanese losses were twenty-four thousand. It was a costly but important victory: five months later a hundred B-29's took off from Saipan to begin the saturation bombing of Japan.

While the struggle for Saipan was being waged on land, a major naval engagement occurred on the sea. Admiral Ozawa commanded the remnants of Japan's once powerful fleet, and when news of the American invasion of Saipan came on June 15, he was ordered to proceed to the Marianas. He had nine carriers but only 430 planes, while Admiral Spruance had fifteen carriers and one thousand planes. Spruance, whom Hoyt contends was overly conservative in joining battle, waited for Ozawa to launch the first strike.

At dawn on June 19, Ozawa was within striking range, and he launched the Japanese attack from his carriers as well as the base on Guam. The American carriers, warned by radar, were able to launch all their fighter planes before the Japanese gained the advantage of surprise. The majority of the first Japanese strike force was shot down by the superior American F6F Hellcats. Meanwhile, the American submarine *Albacore* radioed the location of the Japanese fleet and then successfully torpedoed Ozawa's flagship, the carrier *Taiho*. At noon another submarine, the *Cavalla*, torpedoed the carrier *Shokaku*. The *Shokaku* had served since Pearl Harbor but it went down that afternoon, followed by the *Taiho*. The air battle, later called the Great Marianas Turkey Shoot, was a disaster for the Japanese carrier force. Only a third of the 370 Japanese planes returned, and fifty more based on Guam were destroyed.

At dawn on June 20, American carrier-based aircraft again struck Japanese planes on Guam and effectively ended Japanese air power in the Marianas. The remnants of Ozawa's fleet steamed rapidly north toward Okinawa. By the time he was spotted by United States search planes, Ozawa was three hundred miles away. Despite the lateness of the day and the distance, Admiral Mitscher launched 131 bombers and eighty-eight fighters in pursuit. They managed to sink one carrier and damage three others. Japanese naval power never recovered. The airplane recovery was at night, however, and many of the American planes ran out of fuel on the way back: 100 out of 216 were lost.

Hoyt notes that the invasions of Tinian and Guam were anticlimactic since Saipan was the main objective. Tinian was only three miles south of Saipan and posed a threat to the American position there. Tinian had nine thousand defenders, but they were greatly reduced by one of the most sustained bombardments of the Pacific War. Both naval guns and artillery based on Saipan shelled the island every day from June 13, reducing defenses to rubble. On July 19, a new weapon was introduced: napalm.

The invasion of Tinian began July 24 and by the first week in August organized resistance ended. As on other captured Pacific Islands, however, isolated units and individuals holed up waiting to ambush. More than five hundred Japanese were killed in the next five months.

Guam presented a similar pattern of futile but dangerous resistance. It was the largest island north of the equator between Hawaii and the Philippines. Partly for that reason, it had been kept as an American possession from 1898 to 1941, and as the first American territory to be recaptured from the Japanese, it was an important symbol. The Japanese had about nineteen thousand sailors and soldiers on Guam in July, 1944. Systematic bombardment began on July 8 and the invasion force of thirty-seven thousand marines and nineteen thousand soldiers landed on July 21, encountering entrenched Japanese troops. After four days of exhausting fighting, the Japanese launched an abortive major counterattack. Not until August 10 was the island cleared of organized resistance, but about ten thousand Japanese were still hiding in the jungle. Most of these were gradually killed or starved, although a few remained long after the war.

Hoyt sees the battle for the Marianas as a pivotal point in the overall Pacific strategy. In the summer of 1944, MacArthur finally convinced President Roosevelt of the political advantages of retaking the Philippines, using the Central Pacific forces to support the southern route. The difficult fighting for Saipan and Guam showed that the Japanese would continue to resist. Pockets of resistance, while strategically unimportant, would be expensive to eradicate.

Hoyt has written a number of military histories and has had a long career as a journalist. His writing style shows his background: it is clear, concise, and effective. Too many military studies are encumbered with the purple prose of heroism or take the other extreme and read like the battle manual style of official histories. Hoyt shows his skill by stressing clarity and understatement. Rather than detract from the truly epic qualities of the Central Pacific land, sea, and air operations, his approach enhances understanding and appreciation of the difficulties faced by both Americans and Japanese. His sources are mostly from the American point of view but he does not neglect the Japanese perspective; nor does he leave out the tactical and technological weaknesses of the Japanese defenders. The command structure is analyzed and interservice rivalry is considered. While little new material is uncovered or reinterpretations offered, the book is a very readable account of an important phase of the war in the Pacific.

Richard Rice

THE TRANSIT OF VENUS

Author: Shirley Hazzard (1931-   )
Publisher: The Viking Press (New York). 337 pp. $11.95
Type of work: Novel
Time: 1930's-1970's
Locale: Primarily London and New York City

A tightly constructed, ironically narrated love story which places intelligent characters in an international setting

> Principal characters:
> CAROLINE (CARO) BELL, an Australian employee of the British government
> EDMUND (TED) TICE, a British astronomer, in love with Caroline
> PAUL IVORY, a British playwright and Caroline's lover
> ADAM VAIL, an American, Caroline's husband
> GRACE THRALE, Caroline's sister
> CHRISTIAN THRALE, Grace's husband
> DORA BELL, half-sister to Caroline and Grace

Shirley Hazzard has had considerable international experience. She has worked for British Intelligence in Hong Kong, for the British High Commissioner's Office in Wellington, New Zealand, and for the United Nations in New York and Italy. In addition to three previous novels and a collection of stories, she has written a book about the U.N., called *Defeat of an Ideal*. In Hazzard's most recent novel, *The Transit of Venus*, characters move easily about the globe; the novel's settings include Australia, South America, Portugal, and Sweden, as well as England and America, and each character is carefully located in a cultural and historical milieu, as well as a personal one. Hazzard's global perspective, however, extends beyond such matters, to the realm of metaphor and point of view. Often in this novel, she seems to have placed herself on some neighboring planet in order to observe the earth and its inhabitants through a telescope. From this remote vantage point, she views human history—from the prehistoric observatory at Avebury to the destruction at Hiroshima—as it impinges on the morality and behavior of her central characters, Caroline Bell and Edmund Tice.

Ted Tice is, by profession, an astronomer, and Hazzard draws her novel's governing mataphor from an astronomical phenomenon, the transit of Venus, in order to reveal "the cosmic power of love." In addition to its ordinary meaning of "passage" or "change," "transit" has an astronomical definition: like an eclipse, a transit involves the temporary alignment of three celestial bodies. The planet Venus passes between the earth and the sun twice a century, the two transits occurring eight years apart. It is this meaning which suggests the terms used by Hazzard to name the second and fourth parts of her novel. "The Contacts" are the phases of an eclipse and "The Culmination" is the short period of totality. "Transit" can also refer to the use of a telescope to survey an astronomical phenomenon; thus, in Hazzard's novel, Venus is not only making a transit, but also being observed as she does so. The precise moment of transit is, of course, transitory; at the novel's end the reader sees, as if through the telescope of history, a pair of lovers who are "like amorous figures from mythology," marking a moment when human love defies time. About the brevity of the transit, Caroline Bell notes, "'The years of preparation. And then, from one hour to the next, all over.'" Caro's apparently innocent remark occurs in a dinner conversation with Ted Tice, a conversation during which Ted also tells her about an eighteenth century astronomer whose efforts to observe the transit of Venus were defeated by bad weather. Ted admires that astronomer: "'His story has such nobility you can scarcely call it unsuccessful.'" As the novel unfolds, one learns of Ted's own nobility and of his devoted scrutiny of Caroline, whom he clearly sees and deeply loves.

Appropriately enough for an astronomer, Ted is most remarkable for the clarity of his vision, despite a childhood injury which has left one eye noticeably flawed. Of working class origins, he is a highly respected scientist who is certain to achieve international eminence. Even as a young man, he has definite ideas about where telescopes should be located for the greatest possible visibility; more important, he appears to be able to see into people and their relationships—to see, even, into the future. His way of looking gives him enormous moral authority, and the clarity of his insight and foresight is contrasted with distortions in the vision of others, particularly Caroline. Caro is a physically strong woman, highly intelligent, darkly beautiful. She moves "with consequence as if existence were not trivial," and she honors above all things knowledge, heroism, and excellence. As a young woman, the reader is told, Caro has already become "impatient of the prime discrepancy— between man as he might be, and as he was. She would impose her crude belief—that there could be heroism, excellence—on herself and others, until they, or she, gave in." Caroline also believes herself to be in the process of acquiring knowledge, which she views as "stately, pale, pure as the Acropolis." Hers is, however, a knowledge of abstractions, a knowledge arising from reading and speculation rather than from the emotional complexity of experience. When she tells her lover that "'Someone you know well might surprise you with an action that was monstrous, or noble,'" she speaks without seeing either the monstrosity or the nobility of those closest to her. Caro's moral vision is flawed, as the reader is reminded when, in middle age, she visits an ophthalmologist who prescribes glasses. "'You were always the one, weren't you, who could read the name on the boat, or the announcement on the billboard?'" he asks her. "'You could decipher the fine print. Well, things catch up with you. Nature doesn't like exceptions.'" As Hazzard works out this metaphor of vision, the reader can lay Caro's moral blindness beside the intense clarity of Ted's astronomer's eye, and so discern a pattern that is essential to the novel's meaning.

It would be misleading, however, to suggest that the interconnected astronomical and visual metaphors are obtrusive or even prominent. In fact, they are completely submerged in the narrative, which holds the reader because Hazzard's characters and their relationships are so compelling. Caroline, despite her natural affinity for Ted Tice and despite his devotion to her, loves Paul Ivory, a talented playwright whose good looks and good luck make him, in several senses, a star. Like Ted, Paul will leave his mark; indeed, both are "marked men, and symbolically opposed . . . it seemed that one of them must lose if the other were to win." Paul and Ted are similar in another way: both have consciously decided to defy the social order, but their defiance takes contrasting forms, as do their motives. Paul is fascinated by the possibilities for risk which arise from the concealment of an immoral act, not revealed until the novel's conclusion. Ted, on the other hand, decides when he visits Hiroshima at the end of the war that the "colossal scale of evil could only be matched or countered by some solitary flicker of intense and private humanity." As the plot develops, the contrasting moralities of these two men are manifested in their behavior toward each other and toward Caroline. While Ted admires Caro's strength and respects her sexual reticence, Paul is sarcastic, condescending, and manipulative. After he takes Caro's virginity, he is surprised at the depth of his feeling for her: "It had not occurred to Paul that Caro's influence might increase with her submission. Or that she would remain intelligent." The triangular relationships among these three characters are complicated still further by Caro's eventual marriage to Adam Vail, an American hero who brings her temporary security and contentment.

Although a summary of these relationships makes the plot of the novel sound hackneyed, Hazzard's treatment of her material is deft, intelligent, powerful. She handles Caro, Ted, Paul, and Adam with ironic seriousness and less significant characters with a lighter touch that borders on the satirical. Caro's brother-in-law, Christian Thrale, is a middle-level British bureaucrat whose self-satisfaction invites puncturing, and Hazzard is always ready to puncture. Another knowing treatment is that of Caro's neurotic half-sister, Dora, who is constantly threatening suicide: "I CAN ALWAYS DIE," Dora says, and the narrator adds, "as if this were a solution to which she might repeatedly resort." Commenting on Dora's "privileges of victimization," the novelist describes her "longing to be assigned some task so that she could resent it," and characterizes Dora's hysterical memory of her happy childhood as "Tranquillity recollected in emotion." Hazzard's sense of irony encompasses scene as well as character, as when Caro's sister, Grace Thrale, tells Ted that Caro is to be married. The scene takes place in the rug department of Harrods: "Grace was getting to an end of details and would soon be starkly left with a man's anguish. A salesman brushed by, with a customer. 'We have it in celadon or kumquat. Or can order in mandarin.'" Similarly, at the introduction of Paul Ivory, Hazzard explains that when he "walked in espadrilles on the paths and passages of Peverel, the sound inaugurated, softly, the modern era."

Throughout *The Transit of Venus*, Hazzard's word play astonishes and delights. Her instinct for the rich possibilities inherent in cliché and small talk produces many felicities; for example, a pretty female secretary taking minutes at a meeting of stodgy male bureaucrats is "China in the bull shop." As Hazzard portrays Caro, she is capable of savagely ironic verbal sallies: "At the party, Paul Ivory had said to Caro, 'My brother has run off with a little shopgirl.' And Caro in reply: 'I too have been a shopgirl. We are not necessarily diminutive.'" When Christian Thrale says that his aging mother "would be better off in a home," Caro answers, "'She has a home. You mean an institution.'" Hazzard's pleasure in the pun is also evident. Shortly after Caro's sister, Grace, has been contemplating her "mortification," she has a conversation with her hairdresser, who "took her head between his hands, under a light, as if it were a skull. . . . Alas, poor Grace. After a while he said, 'It is not a case for dyeing. . . . You are not ready to dye.'" Another verbal ploy of which Hazzard is master is the aphorism. Her lapidary observations work best when they are metaphorical, as when she comments on the person who repeatedly threatens suicide: "To the utterer, the threat is an addition that requires increasing dosage. Bystanders, on the other hand, are slowly immunized." Only occasionally does this stylistic virtuosity flag. There are minor lapses into alliterative abstractions that are difficult to penetrate and that do not seem functional; for example, Caro in New York "observed freakishness, fads, and obscure forms of endurance; as well as flagrant forms of self-assertion and conformity." Such lapses are, however, the exception. On the whole Hazzard writes, with precision and wit, an enviably elegant prose. Her style commands and rewards the reader's most energetic attention.

Hazzard's plot and point of view, as well, require that one attend to each bit of narrative and dialogue, since apparently insignificant details can and usually do foreshadow or explain some subsequent or prior event. The most important events of the plot occur before the novel begins and after it ends, but Hazzard manipulates chronology so that these "offstage" occurrences gain tremendous emotional impact. The point of view is omniscient; the narrator reveals in the second chapter that Ted Tice will "take his own life," but "not for many years," creating an illusion of knowledge and thus establishing a parallel between the reader and Caroline, both of whom must learn to see more clearly in order to comprehend "the helplessness of all humanity to foretell or shield themselves from chaos." The density and economy of the novel are such that irony piles upon irony, creating a tightly constructed momentum; the reader begins to feel, with Caro, "'the terrible ignorance, looking back.'" For this reason, one should either commit to a sustained reading or resolve to go through the book more than once.

The stylistic brilliance of *The Transit of Venus* awesomely, movingly illuminates the human effort to live in a world governed by temporality. From a perspective that is at once intimate and remote, Hazzard examines the difficulty of goodness, the necessity of love, and the intransigent fact of death, all the while acknowledging the chaotic complexity of the events and forces that shape the individual. At one point in the novel, a minor character backs away from a cocktail party and observes it with a curious detachment not unlike Hazzard's own:

> . . . these impressions passed in ritual rather than confusion: the simultaneous preoccupation of girls with love and dresses, the men with their assertions great and small, the women all submission or dominion; an imbalance of hope and memory, a savage tangle of history. These welling together in a flow of time that only some godlike grammar—some unknown, aoristic tense—might describe and reconcile.

While Shirley Hazzard's "grammar" in this novel is not precisely godlike, her ability to see into and magnify the recesses of human motivation makes *The Transit of Venus* a work of intense power and extraordinary beauty, like the familiar earth seen from the moon.

Carolyn Wilkerson Bell

TRANSPORTS AND DISGRACES

Author: Robert Henson (1921-   )
Publisher: University of Illinois Press (Urbana). 126 pp. $10.00; paperback $3.95
Type of work: Short stories

A collection of five short stories that reconsiders historical or legendary events by introducing the voices and actions of the very human characters involved

The title of Robert Henson's collection of short stories, *Transports and Disgraces*, is taken from a poem by Emily Dickinson:

> The Past is such a curious Creature
> To look her in the Face
> A Transport may receipt us
> Or a Disgrace—
> Unarmed if any meet her
> I charge him fly
> Her faded Ammunition
> Might yet reply.

Enchantment or infamy, to which of these ends do Henson's chosen characters come true? History is often related in terms of facts and figures, names and dates, or it is obscured by the twistings and turnings of the path that legend takes. Here, however, that which is most often taken as truth assumes a different aspect, and those who seemed the underdogs show a surprising new face.

The first story illustrates the scheme delightfully. "Billie Loses her Job" throws new light on the legend of John Dillinger, Public Enemy Number One, an American hero. The protagonist is Evelyn "Billie" Frechette, hailed by the press as the only woman Johnny ever loved. She is, strictly speaking, a gun moll, but Henson creates depth beneath the surface and gives Billie a story to tell about life with Dillinger that is uniquely her own.

Imprisoned for nearly two years for harboring a criminal, Billie is persuaded to join a traveling carnival after her release to exalt the legend of the Indiana farm boy who made good. Henson, who follows the facts which can be gleaned from the newspapers of the day and various books written about Dillinger, fictionally teams her with Dillinger's father who is on the same circuit. They are constantly at odds because the man his father remembers is not the man Billie recalls. In fact, Billie recalls very little that pleases Mr. Dillinger or the expectant audience. She confuses her favorite song "Home on the Range" as his favorite; bread and gravy, her best-liked meal, is mistaken as his—but the audience is not to be fooled. "She ain't Billie Frechette . . ." they mumble to one another, and by the end of the run she is being heckled.

Billie, clearly not stupid, simply refuses to be anything other than herself, and that person is quite clear minded. Her alliance with Dillinger spanned a year, and although she cannot recall how many scars he had, she surely does reveal some details which vilify the legend, but she does this passively, unconsciously self-assured. Billie is not bent on destroying the legend; she merely does not want to become a part of it.

Another story which deals with the myths surrounding infamous historical figures is "Lizzie Borden in the P. M." This selection was an O. Henry prize story in 1974. Again, the main character is not the one traditionally portrayed. Lizzie's older sister Emma, a colorless, retiring old maid, is the storyteller, and her tale is a chilling one.

Henson's technique here is to call on historical events and consider them from Emma's sharp minded point of view. The saga of Lizzie Borden is viewed by historians from one extreme to the other. There is much opinionated wrangling about whether she was guilty of hacking her father and stepmother to death or not. Henson's opinion, voiced through Emma, is that she was quite mad, one of those cool psychotics who live among us and possess a charisma that is disarming. Emma, however, is not to be fooled. She has lived with Lizzie too long and has seen too many inconsistencies. After Lizzie's acquittal, they live in the same house for twelve years, and during this time Emma becomes increasingly convinced of her sister's craziness and probable guilt.

Drawing from the transcripts of the trial, Henson has Emma recall a series of events that quite logically lead to Lizzie's culpability: vying with her step-mother for her father's attention (she insists that Mr. Borden wear her high school ring on the little finger of his left hand where it clashes noticeably with his wedding ring); her extreme agitation when she learns that he has purchased a house in his wife's name without telling his daughters of his intentions (she now refuses to speak to either of them or to dine with them); showing the police exactly where a daylight robber has entered the house (the only items stolen were those belonging to Mrs. Borden, both daughters and the maid were home when the robbery took place, and Lizzie has to be sent to her room for she "could not stop talking and interfering"); placing a lock on *her* side of a bedroom door adjoining the bedroom of her parents (*after* her father has placed one on his side, not entirely convinced of Lizzie's innocence in the robbery), and, finally, her questionable behavior the day of the murder and during the few days following (she claims to have been in the barn eating a pear when her father was murdered, but her heavy blue silk dress shows no signs of dust from the loft or of the blood that had seeped onto the floor from her father's body which she was the first to discover).

After her acquittal, records show that she and Emma moved "up the hill" to a large home. Henson allows that this was only Lizzie's idea, and Emma, of course, corroborates this. Not only does Lizzie, carrying at all times now a black fan which had become a part of her costume during the trial, have the house named "Maplecroft," to be carved on the doorstep, but she also changes her name to Lisbeth. She carefully prepares a scrapbook of the trial for Mr. Moody, the assistant prosecuting attorney, with police photos of the two bodies carefully arranged at the beginning. It is inscribed on the flyleaf: "For Mr. William Moody, as a memento of an interesting occasion."

Emma, quite understandably, becomes increasingly agitated. One day, while she and her only friend, Miss Jubb, are visiting in her room, Lizzie returns from a shopping trip and presents the two women with the fruits of her excursion: two porcelain paintings. Miss Jubb is delighted, but, unfortunately, breaks hers when later, in her own home, she attempts to hang it. Returning to the store of its purchase to have it repaired, she learns that two porcelains had been stolen on the day of Lizzie's shopping trip. This incident is recorded as actually having happened, and again Lizzie Borden is not held responsible.

Tired of being pulled into games with her sister and convinced of her unsoundness of mind, Emma steals away one night never to return or see Lizzie again. She hears rumors over the ensuing years of her sister's strange behavior—buying a black limousine and being driven about every day looking neither to the right nor the left, purchasing all the copies of a book about the trial and secreting them away intending to distribute them to anyone with enough nerve to ask for one—and the news of her death and her burial at night with no ceremony, the casket escorted by black pallbearers dressed in black seems to give the finishing touch to the life of this utterly eccentric woman.

Throughout, the sane, reasonable, balanced voice of Emma is contrasted with the whimsical and irregular one of Lizzie to create a story that is particularly satisfying to read.

The protagonist in "The Upper and Lower Millstone" is a woman intrigued by Power as was Billie in the first story. Rahab, the beautiful harlot of Jericho, is acutely aware of her position as one who is swept along by events that are entirely out of her hands. Unlike Billie, however, she possesses an instinct for intrigue, revenge, and survival which allows her to become actively involved, at least, in the chaos she sees around her.

This story, another O. Henry award winner, focuses on the biblical tale of Joshua and the Battle of Jericho. Rahab's unique function is to cut through the rhetoric of imagery and expose the strategy and foresightedness of the Hebrew forces.

Rahab is at first called a harlot because it is convenient for the incompetent, brigand king of Jericho to label her thus; she later selectively sells her favors because it is practical to do so. One night she harbors two Hebrew spies who promise her immunity if she agrees to secret them. She is disappointed in their riddling way of speaking about forces of good and evil, but helps them escape the city. When the warriors of Joshua appear, forty thousand strong, marching in complete silence, only trumpets blasting as they move in ordered procession around the walls of the terrified city, Rahab admires their organ-ization and discipline. She is, therefore, not dismayed to be taken with them when the city is stormed. It is not long, unfortunately, before she discovers that they, too, worship idols and create tales that obscure the great leadership of Joshua. Instead of recognizing that Joshua had defeated Jericho by cun-ningly demoralizing the city, versions of the tale spring up that tell of heaped up waters, walls struck flat, and an angel taking charge the night before. Rahab is disgusted. Even Joshua himself attributes the success of the campaign to the power of the Lord. She almost wishes the walls of Jericho would rise again, for "between that tyranny and this demagoguery, what was there to choose?"

She incurs Joshua's wrath by her outspoken ways, but is saved unexpectedly by Solomon who straightforwardly explains the need for inspiration in a campaign that is far from its completion: "These are less heroic times than formerly. . . . The Jordan isn't the Red Sea. . . . At least he's clear on the point that he doesn't talk to the Lord face to face, as Moses did. . . ."

Henson's version of the Battle of Jericho is refreshing, unexpected, and this sense of novelty extends to the last two stories. In "Lykaon," readers learn that the Trojan War was caused by a disagreement over a tax on ships. Helen, however, wishes to introduce a more "idealistic" element into the story, so she suggests to Lykaon, the last surviving son of Priam, now a slave performing as a bard, that he alter the story in the normal fashion of poetic embroidery. Lykaon, still a prince although in servant garments, has already balked at lionizing Achilles and refuses to honor Helen's wishes. She has him killed but has already taken the first step toward creating a legend herself by informing Menelaus that she had been seduced in Troy.

"The Education of Michael Wigglesworth" submits that that formidable Puritan was a free-thinker who, although loyal and righteous, challenged the dogma of the first generation of goodmen in New England. The inevitable influx of common men is greatly feared by the settlers because "they formed a churning demoniac underside that continually challenged downward-seeping righteousness with upward-thrusting corruption." Michael is a young man whose questioning, alert mind does not automatically see evil in every unto-ward work or deed. That he grew up to write "Day of Doom" deliberately in ballad form to appeal to the masses indicates a sympathy and understanding that is historically obscured by the Puritans' much touted reputation for fire and brimstone.

All the stories in this collection deal with characters and events that are to one degree or another common knowledge. It is a challenge to separate fact from carefully constructed fiction for Henson's careful "historical" research is impressive. It is, however, the human element that gives these five mar-velous tales their ring of authenticity.

Kathleen Massey

THE TRAVELER'S TREE
New and Selected Poems

Author: William Jay Smith (1918-   )
Publisher: Persea Books (New York). 167 pp. $13.95
Type of work: Poetry

This, the first full-length collection of Smith's poems since 1970, reconfirms his unique-ness among living poets and the enduring excellence of the work he has done over the past thirty-five years

William Jay Smith's poems are notably different from any others written in our time. As Richard Wilbur notes on the dustjacket, he is "one of the very few contemporary poets who cannot be confused with anybody else and who stands alone in a laudable way." This selection of his poems, arranged with great care and intelligence, provides not only great pleasure, but also ways of speculating on the development of his distinctive voice.

The book is divided into two parts, each broken down into titled subsec-tions. The first part contains poems more recent than *The Tin Can* (1966), including ten translations of recent vintage; the second part contains judicious selections from *Poems* (1947), *Celebration at Dark* (1950), *Poems 1947-1957*, and *The Tin Can*. In a discussion of this kind, it makes sense to start with the second part, tracing what one can toward an apprehension of those qualities which make Smith's poetry what it is.

The eleven poems from Smith's first book are all short—the longest is twenty lines—and characterized by certain neoclassical qualities: deftly mas-tered traditional forms, avoidance of overt intrusion of "personality," pre-cision, and grace. If that were the end of the description, it would suffice for the poems of several people whose work began to appear shortly after World War II. Smith's widely praised "lightness of touch," however, is deceptive, even in a few of these early poems. Beneath the bright surfaces there is a strong undercurrent of darkness, sometimes expressed in images which par-take simultaneously of "dream" and "reality," so that what is presented has a new and startling dreamlike quality, although it does not surrender its ability to persuade the reader that this is the way things are.

"The Barber," for example, consists of eight lines which seem to begin in a real enough world of haircuts; but even here there are certain oddities:

> The barber who arrives to cut my hair
> Looks at his implements, and then at me.
> The world is a looking glass in which I see
> A toadstool in the shape of a barber chair.

The use of the word "arrives" in the first line raises questions which cannot be answered with complete confidence; but it undercuts some usual expec-tations. There is something hesitant in the whole scene, as if both the speaker and the barber were mildly surprised at the situation. The end of the poem fulfills these expectations:

> The years are asleep. A fly crawls on the edge
> Of a broken cup, a fan in the corner whines.
> The barber's hands move over me like vines
> In a dream as long as hair can ever grow.

As the speaker's world slows down toward stasis and the dream takes over, the poem itself abandons the pattern it had set for itself, letting go of the rhyme between the first and fourth lines of each quatrain. The result is that the poem does not "snap shut like a box," but opens onward, propelling the reader into reverie. It is all done with unobtrusive deftness; but it is nevertheless accomplished.

In *Celebration at Dark* and *Poems 1947-1957*, there becomes apparent in Smith's poetry a new tone, achieved by a delicate combination of light-verse rhythms with images which are often dark, surreal, or frightening, as in these two stanzas, the third and the seventh, from "Galileo Galilei":

> Apple trees are bent and breaking,
> And the heat is not the sun's;
> And the Minotaur is waking,
> And the streets are cattle runs.
>
> * * *
>
> Galileo Galilei
> Comes to knock and knock again
> At a small secluded doorway
> In the ordinary brain.

This is so far from the flatness of much contemporary poetry that less competent poets will think it too old-fashioned; but by combining images of devastation with the rhythms of someone like Edward Lear, Smith found a haunting and memorable voice in which to speak to his own time. Some of his most famous poems—"Mr. Smith," "The Ten," "American Primitive"—operate according to this principle, which is by no means to say that the principle can be mastered by any and every poet, for, although it is composed partly of recognizable techniques, one of the essential ingredients is the vision that can make, as in "The Ten," a nightmare out of a casual newspaper statement that Madame Henri Bonnet is one of the ten best-dressed women of a given year. It is unjust to quote only the first stanza of a poem, but here that will be enough to illustrate the kinds of connections Smith's vision enables him to make:

> Mme. Bonnet is one of the best-dressed ten;
> But what of the slovenly six, the hungry five,

> The solemn three who plague all men alive,
> The twittering two who appear every now and again?

Until the early 1960's, this was the kind of poetry which came most readily to mind at the mention of Smith's name. In *The Tin Can*, there were several more poems which fulfilled the expectations of spooky deftness. Here Smith has selected five of those: "The Lovers," "Dachsunds," "Pidgin Pinch," "Quail in Autumn," and "The Idiot Below the El," perhaps one of Smith's finest short poems in this mode. What made this volume genuinely remarkable, however—a contender for the National Book Award—was not only that Smith continued to improve on what had become his established mode; but it was also that he had developed a way of working with extremely long lines, typographically suggestive of Walt Whitman but rhythmically still Smith's own. The expansive lines, unrhymed, provided room for a more leisurely pace, without sacrifice of intensity. Perhaps the most nearly flawless of these poems is "Morels," an account of finding, preparing, and eating

> These mushrooms of the gods, resembling human organs
> uprooted, rooted only on the air,
>
> Looking like lungs wrenched from the human body, lungs
> reversed, not breathing internally
>
> But being the externalization of breath itself, these
> spicy, twisted cones,
>
> These perforated brown-white asparagus tips—these morels, smell-
> ing of wet graham crackers mixed with maple leaves . . . .

At the time these poems appeared, practitioners such as Allen Ginsberg had conditioned readers to expect certain qualities of looseness, even windiness, in poems that look this way on the page. "Morels," which is a single sentence always under control, demonstrates that in the hands of someone accomplished in the exacting traditional forms, a sacrifice of rhyme and meter need not be accompanied by a sacrifice of economy. The four other poems in this section which are cast in long lines tend toward a more ambitious scope and vision, culminating in the final poem, "The Tin Can," which takes its title from a Japanese expression, as explained in the epigraph: "When someone gets off by himself to concentrate, they say, 'He has gone into the tin can.'"

This poem is among the very few successful modern poems which are overtly concerned with the search for the right words under the always difficult circumstances of trying to write. It avoids the self-indulgence of most such poems in the same way that Smith has always avoided it: there is a speaker in the poem who calls himself "I," but readers are never asked to endure any embarrassing self-revelations; the poet withdraws behind the brilliant images suggestive of loneliness, fear, lust, ambition, and, finally, of the hope that comes with a recollection of playing in a dump near a cannery, festooned with bright ribbons of tin. This image might provide the impetus needed to leave behind "the raging women, and the sickening mould of money, rust, and rubble."

The new poems in the first half of this book are arranged so as to present first a few more poems in this style, notably "Fishing for Albacore" and "What Train Will Come?," both of which appeared in *New and Selected Poems* (1970), and both of which expand the poet's vision toward an inclusion of violence and devastation. "Fishing for Albacore" delicately balances the excitement and comradeship of a father and son on an offshore fishing expedition against the blood and chaos of a successful catch; "What Train Will Come?" explores the human urge to violence which results in the hopelessness and blight of urban civilization. This latter poem also introduces a new technical advance, in that it combines long lines in each "stanza" with the refrain. Rhyming extremely long lines is a risky business, but Smith carries it off handsomely.

The next three poems, also in the long-line style, are on the surface poems of travel—"At Delphi," "Venice in the Fog," and "Journey to the Dead Sea"—and as such are successful evocations of remote places. They are, however, also poems of discovery—of self, or knowledge of love.

With the title poem and those which follow it in the first part of the book, Smith introduces yet another stylistic development. "The Traveler's Tree" and "The Tall Poets" are both cast in what may be the most difficult of forms: by the most basic of definitions, they might be called free verse, but occasional lines and sets of lines will be rhymed and metered, although there is no readily discernible pattern for the occurrence of either rhyme or meter. This style can be used for humorous effects, as other poets including W. H. Auden have demonstrated; but to maintain a somber tone in such a style is extremely difficult, because the appearance of rhyme must seem inevitable, rather than coming as a humorous surprise. "The Traveler's Tree" takes its point of departure from a paragraph by Thomas H. Everett, author of *Living Trees of the World*, in which is described a palmlike tree, shaped like a fan, in the hollow bases of whose leaf stalks travelers could find water. The poem itself is an imaginary journey through remembered scenes to various exotic landscapes, culminating beside a small dark house beside which grows one of these trees:

> And breaking off that branch, you will break off your dream
> and be again a boy in a small boat
> drinking from a paddle
> the transparent water of a mountain stream.
>
> Then cross the threshold and enter the dark house.
> You will be welcome. I will be waiting. I will be there.

A demonstration, almost a parable, of the power of the imagination, this poem is clear evidence that Smith continues to range fruitfully over the variety of verse forms at his disposal, as temperament and vision are altered by time and circumstance.

"The Tall Poets" might look at first like a tossed-off satirical bagatelle, a snatch at the opportunity provided by the sailing of the tall ships up the Hudson on July 4, 1976. In part, it seems a complaint against whatever fates have conspired to keep the speaker, a poet who is called William, out of the front rank of contemporary poets. Yet, it is more than either of these things, although it partakes of those ingredients. The fact is that William Jay Smith's place in contemporary poetry is secure enough; this poem is a satire on the tendency to verify this by a look at the list of his prizes, rather than by a look at his poems. It is outrageously funny in its portrayal of the flat stuff that often passes for the best poetry of modern time; but it is also hilarious on the subject of Smith and his appearance and his difficult struggles with the writing of poetry.

There has not been space here to dwell at length on the purely humorous poems which Smith has made a permanent part of today's literature, or on his continuing mastery of short poems in traditional forms. The emphasis has been on the shifts his work has taken over the years, because, as this fine book demonstrates, Smith's boldest explorations have most often resulted in beautiful, important poems. That these explorations have often taken the form of translations from other languages is splendidly but briefly indicated in this collection; in ten recent translations from Hungarian, Serbo-Croatian, and Russian, he reminds readers that he is one of the best verse translators now living, and that he knows how to let his own powerfully distinctive style yield to the styles of his originals.

Henry Taylor

TRUMAN'S CRISES
A Political Biography of Harry S. Truman

Author: Harold F. Gosnell (1896-   )
Publisher: Greenwood Press (Westport, Connecticut). 656 pp. $35.00
Type of work: Political biography
Time: 1884-1953

A biography of Harry S Truman which analyzes and assesses his political leadership and career

> Principal personages:
> HARRY S TRUMAN, thirty-third President of the United States, 1945-1953
> BESS TRUMAN, his wife
> GEORGE C. MARSHALL and
> DEAN G. ACHESON, Truman's secretaries of state

In the last decade, Harry S Truman has become something of a folk hero to many Americans. Richard Nixon's pretentious and less than forthright style made Truman seem more beloved, because Nixon appeared to be such a contrast to the image the Missourian projected. The affection and respect which most Americans now display toward the thirty-third president is in stark contrast to the disapproval directed at the embattled and discredited Truman who turned over his office to Dwight D. Eisenhower in 1953. Remarkably, this transformation has occurred despite the absence of a definitive Truman biography. The public's perception of Truman has been powerfully influenced by dramatic presentations and television programs based largely on such biased sources as the former president's own memoirs and his version of history as recounted in Merle Miller's *Plain Speaking*.

The popular view of the events of 1945-1953 is quite different from the interpretations made by those revisionist historians who hold that the United States was largely responsible for the onset of the Cold War with Russia. These specialized studies, however, were written largely for the scholarly community and are little known to the general public. Only recently has much of the essential documentary material necessary for a definitive evaluation of Truman been made available. Robert Donovan's *Conflict and Crisis* included much of these data, but that book only deals with Truman's first administration. Harold Gosnell's *Truman's Crises* is the first complete scholarly account of Truman's entire political career.

Gosnell is particularly well qualified to write a political biography of Harry Truman. Long respected as one of the founders of modern American political science and a major scholar, he brings to his work the background and skill necessary to evaluate Truman's political career in scientific as well as human terms. He also profits, in a practical sense, from his personal involvement in the Truman Administration. After many years as a professor of political science, Gosnell joined the federal government in 1940 and stayed for a decade. He was working in the Bureau of the Budget when Truman became president, and after the war he served in the State Department. Through much of the twenty years he worked on *Truman's Crises*, he maintained personal contact with the former president and interviewed many of the key figures of his administration. He thus writes with a first-hand knowledge of many of the events he recounts.

The Truman that emerges from this study is earthy, fun-loving, optimistic, out-going, and conscientious. In many ways he is also inept. Most of his failures Gosnell traces to his lack of background and training and such personal characteristics as excessive loyalty to friends, partisanship, cockiness, and inconsistency. Essentially, however, the biographer is sympathetic and concludes by rating Truman as one of the nation's "near great" presidents.

This massive biography does not slight Truman's prepresidential years. More than a third of the volume is devoted to his rise from the son of a Missouri horse trader and farmer to Vice-President of the United States. Gosnell traces his boyhood, the influence of his family, and his search for a career. In 1922, when Truman was thirty-eight years old, he entered politics by running for a county administrative post. It is here that the author's expertise as a political scientist become evident. Gosnell's first book, in 1924, dealt with machine politics in New York state. Thus, he is very much at home in his analysis of the Kansas City Pendergast machine in which Truman became a cog. Gosnell believes that anyone going into politics in Jackson County during the 1920's had to deal with the fact that underworld influences were strong and that corrupt businessmen and corrupt politicians were in league with one another. That Truman could survive and prosper in such an environment while developing the reputation for honesty he maintained throughout his eighteen-year political career is a fascinating story in itself. It was Boss Pendergast's decision to make Truman his candidate for the United States Senate in 1934 which made possible his eventual elevation to the White House. During his first term he suffered the derision of his colleagues as the "senator for Pendergast," but he developed a quiet competence while delivering a consistent New Deal vote.

In 1940, he faced a major crisis when he ran for reelection because President Franklin D. Roosevelt threw his support to Truman's opponent in the Democratic primary. By dogged determination and skillful campaigning he won the renomination, however, and rode to victory on Roosevelt's coattails in the general election. His reelection tended to rid him of the Pendergast machine contamination and he felt vindicated by the results. Returning to the Senate with renewed confidence, he received a choice assignment as the chairman of a special committee to investigate the war effort. The committee developed a reputation for integrity and competence which elevated its chairman to the status of a national figure. When the Democrats sought a compromise candidate for the vice-presidency in 1944, Truman was, in many ways, a logical choice. He, however, had found the life of a United States Senator very congenial so he resisted efforts to nominate him until pressured indirectly by Roosevelt to accept.

Gosnell has given readers an encyclopedic account of the Truman Administration which is also rich in interpretation. Understandably, the first administration gets proportionately more attention than the second because of the momentous nature of the events which crowded the early years. The new president learned his job amidst the problems of ending the war, demobilization and reconversion, and the beginnings of the Cold War. Although Roosevelt left his successor few plans for the postwar period, concluding the war was the least difficult because of the momentum that had developed. Demobilization and reconversion efforts were handled rather badly, but Gosnell absolves Truman of much of the blame. He correctly points out that Americans expect too much from their presidents because in many ways their powers are very limited. He admits that Truman made some bad decisions but attributes these to acting too quickly or trying to placate both conservative and liberal advisors. The latter made him appear to be indecisive and inconsistent.

Revisionist historians have held Truman responsible for much of the development of the Cold War with Russia. They have criticized his too literal interpretation of the Yalta agreements and his unnecessarily abrasive attitude toward Russia. Gosnell, however, applauds Truman's leadership "in standing up to Stalin and Molotov on the reparations issue" and only criticizes his inability to see through Stalin's dissembling ways. Throughout the book he commends Truman's attempts to contain Soviet expansion and implies that it did not go far enough. Generally, however, Gosnell seems less sure of himself when dealing with the administration's foreign policies. For example, he contents himself with merely describing such far-reaching developments as the Truman Doctrine, the Marshall Plan, and the establishment of NATO. He firmly rejects the views of the revisionists and holds Secretaries of State George Marshall and Dean Acheson responsible for any errors that were made. By implication he also concedes that Truman was dominated by these two men.

The author directs his strongest criticism at the administration's Far Eastern policies and the handling of the Korean War. He is in accord with the basic decision to oppose the North Korean invasion but finds fault with Truman's refusal to increase defense expenditures in the 1947-1950 period, the too heavy reliance on the atomic bomb to restrain Russian adventurism, the refusal to extend the Truman Doctrine to Asia, and the invasion of North Korea. In spite of these mistakes, he found the president courageous in firing MacArthur and avoiding an expansion of the Korean conflict into a world war. Although Gosnell is generally supportive of Truman's hard-line policy toward the

Soviets, he does concede that a less rigid stance might have led to more fruitful negotiations.

In his concluding chapter, Gosnell reviews the major decisions that faced Truman during his presidency and passes judgment on his performance. Although he awards him higher marks for his foreign policy than for his domestic achievements, he gives him an "A" for effort. Historians critical of Truman and even some of his friends have accused him of recommending domestic programs that he knew Congress would not pass simply to attract the votes of the electorate. Gosnell, however, argues that Truman really believed in the measures he urged on Congress and that his purpose was to save the New Deal from Republican encroachments and agitation for future action. His lack of success is attributed to the hostile congressional majorities made up of Republicans and Southern Democrats that he faced rather than any lack of conviction or effort on his part.

In at least one area, Gosnell overstates the case for Truman. He credits him with administrative skills and foresight which led to the expansion of the president's institutionalized staff in the executive office. Actually, Truman opposed the establishment of both the National Security Council and the Council of Economic Advisors and only accepted them out of political necessity. He never did learn to use them effectively.

In many respects, Gosnell has written a case study on political leadership as well as a biography. Harry Truman is certainly the central character but the book is rich in its examination of the political forces at work during his governmental career. As a political scientist the author perceptively describes and analyzes voting patterns, machine politics, congressional operations, and the leadership role of the President. It is truly a "political biography."

Truman's Crises is a valuable addition to the study of the postwar president. As the first comprehensive, thoroughly researched biography of the man, it fills an obvious void. It is also an interpretative work, but since it is based so largely on published sources it offers little new information or original insights. One cannot assume that it will become the definitive biography because it does not tap the recently opened files in the Truman Library. It is likely, however, to serve as the most complete one volume account for many years.

Alfred D. Sander

THE TWYBORN AFFAIR

Author: Patrick White (1912-   )
Publisher: The Viking Press (New York). 432 pp. $14.95
Type of work: Novel
Time: 1912-1940
Locale: France, Australia, and England

The story of a bisexual Australian man, Eudoxia-Eddie-Eadith, who struggles with his sexual identity in the atmosphere of the French Riviera before World War I, Australia between wars, and London on the eve of World War II

> *Principal characters:*
> EUDOXIA VATATZES/EDDIE TWYBORN/EADITH TRIST, the main character of the novel, in three different roles: a young woman on the Riviera, a young man in Australia, and a middle-aged woman in London
> EADIE TWYBORN, his mother
> JOAN GOLSON, his mother's lesbian lover, who falls in love with Eudoxia on the Riviera
> CURLY GOLSON, her husband
> ANGELOS VATATZES, Eudoxia's lover and supposed husband
> MARCIA LUSHINGTON, Eddie's mistress in Australia
> PEGGY TYRRELL, the cook on the ranch in Australia
> DON PROWSE, the manager of the ranch
> ADA POTTER, the housekeeper of Eadith's brothel in London
> RODERICK GRAVENOR, a distant cousin who falls in love with Eadith
> URSULA "BABY" UNTERMEYER, Roderick's sister, who frequents the brothel out of curiosity
> PHILIP THRING, Roderick's nephew

The Twyborn Affair is the tenth novel by Patrick White, the Australian writer who was awarded the 1973 Nobel Prize for Literature. It is an elegant, refined exploration of a very complex theme, the sexual identity of a man who prefers to live as a woman. The history of Eddie Twyborn is primarily the story of his struggle to guard the secret of his dual existence. His evasive maneuvers are motivated not by a feeling of shame, but by his conviction that discovery would make it impossible for him to relate to those he finds attractive.

In each of the novel's three sections, the protagonist plays a different role. On the French Riviera, he is Eudoxia, the lover of an elderly Greek gentleman, Angelos Vatatzes. In Australia, he is himself, Eddie Twyborn struggling to be a man among men on a sheep ranch. In London, he is Eadith Trist, the aging madam of a house of prostitution.

Although it is clear that the novel is Eddie's story, the existence of two other characters dominates this narrative of tormented deception. Eadie Twyborn, Eddie's mother, is seldom seen but always oppressive in her absence. Joan Golson, Eadie Twyborn's lesbian lover, is the link between Eddie and many of the other characters and the stimulus for almost everything that Eddie does in his attempts to escape detection. Riding through the countryside on the Riviera, Joan sees Eudoxia and Angelos walking arm in arm. Later, she observes them playing the piano through the window of their cottage. After she elicits an invitation to tea, Eudoxia's fear of discovery motivates him to flee to another village, where Angelos dies of a heart attack. Years later, after Eddie has spent the war in the trenches and then gone to Australia to visit his parents, Joan Golson comes for a visit. Eddie flees to the south of Australia to work on a sheep ranch run by a friend of his father. Joan Golson again comes to visit, but Eddie disappears. On the eve of World War II, Eadith, the madam of prostitutes, encounters Joan on a street in London. He learns of the whereabouts of his mother in the same city, which discovery leads to the climactic scene of their reunion on a park bench outside a church. Eadie Twyborn, who always wanted a daughter, asks this "woman" dressed in her elegant, worn finery, whether he might be her son, and is relieved to hear that he is her daughter, Eadith. The last moment of the novel portrays Eddie, in the clothes of a man and the makeup of the madam, dying beside a soldier on a street in London, his hand blown off by a bomb. As the city turns to flames, Eadie sits in her hotel room transfixed amid a fantasy of waiting for her daughter in an Australian garden, while the bulbul bird sings and turns its face to the sun.

This story of a man's search for sexual identity is curious in many ways. Not until that final scene is it clear that it has been a struggle to gain his mother's acceptance and love, to be the daughter that he should have been. Throughout the novel, the vacillating sexuality of almost all the people around Eddie creates a web of intricate relationships. Joan Golson, married to a man but in love with Eadie Twyborn, lusts after Eudoxia, the beautiful woman who is really a man, and writes Eadie letters about the "delicious creature" that they both should pursue. Angelos Vatatzes, Eudoxia's "husband," fears that Curly Golson has come to take her away from him. Eadie's friend Marcia Lushington becomes Eddie's mistress while her husband exhibits a fatherly interest in Eddie that verges on incest. Don Prowse, the tough, masculine ranch manager, engages Eddie in a series of subtle seduction scenes, finally rapes him, then cries for forgiveness and willingly submits to rape as Eddie takes his revenge. Roderick Gravenor, in love with Eadith Trist, confesses to her that he is "different" as he almost succeeds in seducing her. His nephew, Philip Thring, refuses the advances of the prostitutes, but finally loses his virginity with Eadith, the madam queen in full drag.

The final scene of the novel is a perfect culmination to this history of indeterminate sexuality. Eadith trades her finery for Eddie's clothes and turns the brothel over to Ada Potter. Going through the streets of London in search of his mother, he sees in a mirror that he is still wearing the makeup of Eadith the madam. In this grotesque state of ambivalent sexuality, he dies alongside the soldier who shouts, "something happening at last, eh?" just before the bomb hits.

Although the theme of the novel and the plot developments are potentially lurid and sensationalistic, Patrick White maintains an attitude of tasteful elegance. He accomplishes this remarkable feat through a skillful control of the narrative voice and through his invention of a fictional reality dominated by an atmosphere of upper-class gentility. This is a world of dainty tea cakes, perfumed face powder, aromatic cigars, leather armchairs, and the graceful choreography of well-rehearsed social interaction. Behind the delicate sensibility of this polite British society lurks an obsession with sensuality, seldom expressed except in evasive, circuitous terms.

The omniscient narrator of *The Twyborn Affair* has access to the thoughts of all these characters. In fact, the portrayal of this reality is developed primarily through the perceptions of the characters themselves. What the characters perceive reveals much about their values, and furthers the exploration of the novel's intricate relationships. Joan Golson the Australian is intimidated by Lady Tewkes with her "rings growing out of the bone itself," by the mercilessly polite, arrogant English with their unflinching eyelids and noncommittal smiles when faced with what is "regrettably colonial." After her meeting with Eudoxia and the "last delicious spasm" of a glance into her eyes, Joan Golson churns away on her bed in the Grand Hotel Splendide at S. Mayeul "amongst the scum and knotted tresses of dreams."

Through this technique of portraying reality in terms of each character's perception, the narrator is able to create a story of perverted passions, told in the proper, fastidious language suitable to the social refinement of the participants in these events. Their dreams, however, reveal the sordid depths, the scum and knotted tresses of their emotions.

The consummate skill of Patrick White as a novelist is evident in the parallel that he creates between the story that his narrator tells and the techniques of telling it. Through the first third of the novel, there is no clear indication of whose story this is. The perspective shifts from Joan and Curly Golson to Eudoxia and Angelos Vatatzes, and back again, with frequent references to Eadie Twyborn. Until the beginning of Part Two, there is no suggestion that Eudoxia is really a man. Thus, one of the most powerful scenes of the first part, in retrospect, becomes ironic and overwhelming in its significance. On the Riviera, Monsieur Pelletier watches a figure in the distance, poised nude on a rock, preparing to swim. He becomes aroused by the equivocal nature of the scene, as he is unable to determine from a distance whether it is a man or a woman. As he masturbates, consumed by the mystery of the swimmer, the scene becomes a metaphor of his entire life experience. It is also a metaphor of the experience of the swimmer, Eudoxia Vatatzes. This episode sets the indeterminate sexuality of the protagonist long before the reader suspects the truth about Eudoxia, or even before there is any indication that this novel is not the story of Eadie Twyborn, as it seems it will be.

The technique of this scene is the key to White's success in creating a polished portrayal of distorted, disturbed sexuality. The narrator always presents this reality in terms of the characters' observations of it, and those observations are always perceptions based on the characters' own experience. Monsieur Pelletier's interpretation of the swimming scene reflects his experience, condensed in one moment, which in turn explains the predicament of Eudoxia-Eddie-Eadith. By the end of the novel, the narrator has revealed an intricate reality made up of the complex sexual responses to Eddie Twyborn of many characters, some of whom do not even know one another. The narrator observes that Monsieur Pelletier and Mrs. Golson had not met at any point, and that "it was only in the figure now clambering down over rocks, that the two might have agreed to converge."

The Twyborn Affair is a remarkable exploration of a maze of complicated relationships, at the center of which are Eadie and Eddie Twyborn: Eadie, a mother in love with her son as if he were her daughter, and Eddie, the object of his mother's lesbian lover's desire and the lover of his mother's best friend. While this plot material has the potential of being quite tasteless, it is transformed into a fascinating analysis of authentic human experience. The key to White's artistry in this novel is the emphasis on each character's rather obsessive observance of his surrounding. Whether it be Eddie concentrating on Don Prowse's nipples wreathed by a "generous golden fell," or Eadith rubbing gravy from her bronze tunic as if "all the stains of her life were concentrated in this greasy emblem," the minute details of fleeting reality are dissected and implanted in the accumulated experience of the characters.

Through this concentration on the characters' perception and studied evaluation of details, the novelist effectively exploits the characteristic of fiction that has contributed most to its universal appeal, its voyeuristic quality. The ideal reader of fiction—that imagined audience addressed by the fictional narrator—is forced into the position of voyeur and made to observe the reality of the novel with an intensity seldom achieved in the real-life experience of the actual reader. The authenticity of the fictional reality depends to a great extent on the novelist's ability to evoke that intense observation of experience. Patrick White has created an extraordinary example of novelistic art in *The Twyborn Affair* through a concentrated analysis of the complexities of human sexuality.

Gilbert Smith

UNDER THE FIFTH SUN
A Novel of Pancho Villa

Author: Earl Shorris (1936-   )
Publisher: Delacorte Press (New York). 622 pp. $14.95
Type of work: Novel
Time: 1878-1923
Locale: Mexico

An epic novel about the life of Pancho Villa and his role in the Mexican Revolution

Principal characters:
TLAMATINI POPOCA, the Indian narrator of the novel
DOROTEO ARANGO, the Mexican child who, as a man, takes the name Francisco Villa and becomes a leader of the Revolution
MICAELA ARANGO, his mother
MARTINA ARANGO, his sister, raped by the wealthy landlord
LIVIANA APRISCO, Villa's wife
ABRAHAM GONZALEZ, the governor of Chihuahua and close friend of Villa
GILDARDO MAGAÑA, a follower of Zapata who teaches Villa to read during his imprisonment in Tlaltelolco
LUIS AGUIRRE BENAVIDES ("Luisito"), Villa's personal secretary
FRANCISCO MADERO, president of the provisional government established after the fall of Porfirio Díaz in 1911
IGNACIO PARRA,
TOMÁS URBINA,
JOSÉ SOLÍS,
FELIPE ANGELES, AND
ELEUTERIO SOTO, revolutionaries who fight with Villa's forces
VICTORIANO HUERTA,
VENUSTIANO CARRANZA,
PASCUAL OROZCO,
ÁLVARO OBREGÓN, AND
EMILIANO ZAPATA, leading participants in the Revolution in various parts of Mexico

The subtitle of *Under the Fifth Sun*—"A Novel of Pancho Villa"—indicates that this is historical fiction. Because fiction is a portrayal of an imaginary, invented reality, and written history is a narrative of the reality known to the reader as his own, the historical novel presents enormous problems to the artist who creates it and to the critic who seeks a responsible method of dealing with it. In Earl Shorris' epic portrayal of the life of Pancho Villa, the problem is more complicated than in many historical novels. *Under the Fifth Sun* is a detailed recounting of Villa's career as the bandit turned Revolutionary General, and the details are historically accurate. Almost all the characters are "real," and what they do is what they actually did, according to the most reliable contemporary accounts of the Revolution. Although there is no acknowledgment of sources in the novel, it is likely that Shorris relied consistently on the *Memoirs of Pancho Villa*, a compilation and elaboration of Villa's personal archives by the Mexican novelist Martín Luis Guzmán, author of *The Eagle and the Serpent* and intimate friend of Villa. Guzmán's work, which is itself a kind of novelization of Villa's autobiography, reads like an authentic memoir. Shorris takes the form further into the realm of fiction by transforming it into an account told by someone else, but he does not let his fictional mode interfere with the authenticity of his history.

The novel by Earl Shorris is primarily history only in the sense that most of the events narrated are either historically true or else based on traditions so generally accepted that they are included in many respectable history books as probable. Yet, the novel is a novel, and as such, it portrays an imaginary world created by an artist. Shorris is a skilled writer who is able to transform a multitude of historical facts into the kind of intimate, integral experience that fiction provides. He accomplishes this transformation through his choice of narrative perspective.

The narrator of *Under the Fifth Sun* is Tlamatini Popoca, a descendant of the Aztecs, who describes himself as "smoke and flowers, night and wind, keeper of the tonalpohualli, reader of the tonalamatl, and thinker of inquiries." He is the last of his kind, "the only defiance that remained." The narrator does not explain his comment about defiance, but it becomes clear throughout the novel. It is a defiance of the modern world, the scientific world that has taken the place of the ancient one in which truth is to be found in the signs of the natural world. Death, like all events, is a predestined confluence of place and time. Four times the world has been destroyed: "after the flood, men were changed into fish; after the fire, men became birds; after the wind, men became donkeys; and when the world was the place of giants, the jaguars came and ate them." The last world is the present, the Fifth Sun, which will be destroyed in earthquake and fire.

This is the concept of existence proclaimed by the narrator of this panoramic account of the Mexican Revolution. Even though the narrative is a series of events which one might call "historical," the novel is not simply a report, rather the fictional world created here consists of but one thing: the telling of the events. Because the experience of the storytelling itself is fiction, and the narrator is imagined, the history of Pancho Villa becomes a fictional reality quite like that of any novel. That reality, of course, has its parallel in reality, but it is a fiction, regardless of the authenticity or accuracy of the events portrayed.

This transformation of reality to fiction is the process through which the novel may be considered true, even though it is in fact an imaginary, invented story. This novel is a serious attempt to deal with the question of historical truth, and because of that, Shorris has created the story of Villa's life as a narrative of Mexican history told by an Indian sage. The narrator Popoca is omniscient, although never obtrusively so. Throughout the narrative, he interprets the events in terms of Aztec mythology and legend. The attitude of the narrative always seems to be that things occur as they will occur, because of that inevitable confluence of time and space. The narrator only foresees and interprets what must occur.

This concept of the world is very appropriate to the reality portrayed in *Under the Fifth Sun*. There is little indication that Villa has any grasp of political realities, a fact borne out by Guzmán's version of Villa's memoirs. Rather, his rise from common bandit to charismatic Revolutionary general seems to be preordained. It is never at all clear why he succeeds, why he becomes the leader that he does. While this would be a serious flaw in another novel about Villa, in this one it creates a successful blend of history and mythic interpretation. The unexplained inevitability of the events reflects the narrator's interpretation of the world.

Shorris uses as one of the epigraphs of his novel the well-known quotation from Octavio Paz' *The Labyrinth of Solitude* about machismo as "power, the will without reins and without a set course." Social life in Mexico, according to Paz, is interpreted as a combat between the strong and the servile, the aggressive, insensitive macho and his victim. In this novel, Villa is portrayed as the ideal macho and even the narrator fails to understand the irony of that portrayal in the context of a mythic world view that proclaims the inevitability of the events. This irony, which is Shorris' most admirable accomplishment, explains the dedication of the novel: "For Tony, as if lies could be lessons." The things men do and the reasons they do them are lies. Truth is to be found elsewhere.

The novel creates a society dominated by the concept of a struggle for power on every level. The brutality of the strong against the weak, the horrible suffering endured by both the revolutionary soldiers and the civilians, the widespread evil generated by war, all these details are narrated as if they were the inevitable consequences of living. Through it all, Villa moves on as if he were driven by "the will without reins and without a set course." His dealings with women are much the same. Liviana Aprisco, his strong-willed wife, is merely the woman he comes home to when everything else is done. His other two wives, whom he weds while still married to Liviana, are only brief pastimes for him. At no point does he allow himself to be vulnerable with a wife, or a lover, or a prostitute, for more than a brief moment.

This portrayal of Villa as the macho creates another of the ironies of the novel. In the last moments of the narrative, Villa encounters Socorro Riendo, a woman who was once his lover but betrayed him to the authorities. He again has sexual intercourse with her, and then is assassinated in the street as he is leaving her home. Popoca, the narrator, who came down from the mountains to see Villa because he realized that the "year of the consideration of endings" had arrived, fails to warn him. Rather than "counting the days," Popoca allows himself to be seduced by an obscene woman, the "marigold woman," who then in the morning light appears deformed and drives him away with hideous laughter. For Villa, Liviana had been his "luminous wife, this woman of marigolds and roses."

The mythic version of Pancho Villa's life, told by the Aztec wise man, develops an interpretation of the Mexican cultural heritage which coincides with Paz' analysis in *The Labyrinth of Solitude*. All Mexican women are descendants of the weeping mother, La Malinche, the mistress of Cortez. They are raped, dishonored, made subservient, yet they are powerful and will persevere. In Villa's childhood home, "time is a circle turned by an old woman who lives in the secret shade of a cool white house in Canatlán." It is only when Villa gives up his revolutionary activities and becomes a wealthy land-lord that he dies, betrayed by a woman, a daughter of La Malinche, with whom he allowed himself to be vulnerable.

Through his development of the ironies of Villa's machismo, ironies that fulfill the prophecy inherent in the narrator's mythic interpretation of the world, Shorris creates a serious portrayal of an enigmatic hero. His novel is successful primarily because the interpretive function of the narrative is unobtrusive and subtle. The novel is a detailed, extensive portrayal of the evil of a war in which atrocities are considered necessary to achieve an end that is good. The treatment of that contemporary theme is balanced by the narrator's context of the myths of the ancient, native culture of Mexico.

Gilbert Smith

UNDER THE SIGN OF SATURN

Author: Susan Sontag (1933-   )
Publisher: Farrar, Straus and Giroux (New York). 204 pp. $10.95
Type of work: Essays

A collection of essays, most of which first appeared in The New York Review of Books, *on film and the arts*

Once the darling of the avant-grade in the 1960's in two influential collections of essays, *Against Interpretation* and *Styles of Radical Will*, Susan Sontag in this recent collection tempers her views now that the advance guard has become the main column. Although her heroes here are still the Marxists and structuralists and her villains are the Fascists and Reactionaries, she is less the outspoken champion now than she was twenty years ago. Moreover, although still cryptically quotable, the essays here are not as controversial as when she called for an erotics rather than a hermeneutics of art in "Against Interpretation" or when she termed sexuality one of the "demonic forces in human consciousness" in "The Pornographic Imagination." Furthermore, one will not find here essays that will have as much influence on the critical establishment as her earlier "Notes on Camp" or "The Aesthetics of Silence."

These new essays are occasional pieces; some, such as the articles on Paul Goodman and Roland Barthes, are so slight as to be personal tributes only. The longest piece, "Approaching Artaud," is a reprint of the Introduction Sontag wrote for a collection of Artaud's selected writings which she edited for Farrar, Straus and Giroux. There is also an essay on Leni Riefenstahl's propaganda films for Adolf Hitler (which she does not like) and an essay on Hans-Jürgen Syberberg's *Hitler, a Film from Germany* (which she likes a great deal). Pieces on Elias Canetti and Walter Benjamin round out the collection.

The essay on Benjamin provides both the title and the keynote for Sontag's collection. "I came into the world under the sign of Saturn," says Benjamin, "the star of the slowest revolution, the planet of detours and delays." As usual, Sontag writes about intellectuals she likes, which also happen to be those most like her. Like Artaud, Barthes, Canetti, and Benjamin, Sontag is marked by the saturnine temperament—a temperament which Sontag says is characterized by the self-conscious relation to the self, seeing the "self as text." It is a temperament, Sontag adds, which is the most apt one for intellectuals. Sontag says that other major characteristics of such a temperament are blundering (from seeing too many possibilities) and stubbornness (because of the longing to be superior). Like other structuralist intellectuals who share this sign of Saturn, Benjamin takes as his theme the attempt to spatialize the world, to understand reality through topography. Benjamin's works are filled with the metaphors of maps and labyrinths. "His goal," says Sontag, "is to be a competent street-map reader who knows how to stray." Other characteristics of Benjamin, which Sontag seems to share with Barthes, Canetti, and

Syberberg, are the perception of learning and thinking as forms of collecting. As Benjamin says, the most praiseworthy method of collecting books is by writing them. Sontag, author of nine books, surely agrees.

Like Benjamin, Canetti is also an incurable thinker and writer. In fact, says Sontag, Canetti is a type of intellectual often found in the essays of Benjamin—the reclusive scholar devoted to building a library in his head, living in a "desperate attempt to think about everything." Like Sontag herself, Canetti is the "eternal student, someone who has no subject or rather, whose subject is everything," like a scholar in a story by Jorge Borges. The natural mode for the saturnine melancholic, says Sontag, is allegory; the natural limit is the essay form; the natural need is to be alone, to get work done; the natural style is total immersion. Anyone who has read Sontag's collections, especially the thematically linked essays in her collections *Illness as Metaphor* and *On Photography* will readily recognize these characteristics as Sontag's own. Her perception of the symbolic significance of both illness and photography and her effort to make symbolic maps of these areas (which is different from them as actual territories) link her with the European freelance intellectuals she writes about.

Roland Barthes, the most significant literary intellectual of the French structuralist movement similarly loves, as does Sontag, classifying, mapping, and perceiving the symbolic significance of a wide variety of activities and artifacts. Sontag admires him for his love of the perverse, for his being what she calls a disciplined "appetitive writer." All his works are an "immensely complex enterprise of self-description"; and almost everything he read he wrote about, says Sontag. Calling Barthes a "voluptuary of the mind," who, along with Paul Valéry, gives being an aesthete a good name," Sontag similarly defines herself, or at least what she wishes for herself.

In an essay that takes up almost one third of the collection, Sontag presents Antonin Artaud as an example of the modern disestablished artist who refuses to be morally useful to the community, who, on the contrary, seems concerned to transform the community itself into the transcendent realm of art. In his efforts to close the gap between art and life in such experiments as the theater of cruelty, the magical theater, and the theater of the flesh, Artaud saw all art as theatrical and was bent on theatricalizing life itself; and the first step toward such a goal is toward the theatricalizing of the self. Modern literature, says Sontag, projects the "romantic conception of writing as a medium in which a singular personality heroically exposes itself." Trying to link art and consciousness leads inevitably to the kind of metaliterary considerations that Sontag has found appealing since she termed her first collection of essays "metacriticism." Sontag says that Artaud's poetics is one in which "art is the compendium of consciousness, the reflection by consciousness on itself, and the empty space in which consciousness takes its perilous leap of self-transcendence."

The most predominant theme for Artaud is the link between suffering and writing, a theme in which he treats his mind as if it were a "kind of body." Sontag says Artaud's gift is for "a kind of physiological phenomenology of his unending desolation." Artaud's need to transcend body through body led him to alchemy, the tarot, the cabala, astrology, and other esoteric systems. In fact, says Sontag, in the 1920's Artaud had almost every taste that became prominent in the counterculture of the 1960's. As a result Sontag believes that Artaud is one of those esoteric thinkers, like Marquis de Sade and Charles Reich, who have become classics because they have not been read, because in some intrinsic way they are unreadable. "For anyone who reads Artaud through," says Sontag, "he remains fiercely out of reach, an unassimilable voice and presence."

Sontag also admires Syberberg's seven-hour film in four parts, *Hitler, a Film from Germany*, for his self-reflexive view and his extreme antirealism. For Syberberg, history is unrepeatable and ungraspable except indirectly— "adventures in the head . . . staged in the theater of the mind," says Sontag. It is not surprising that Sontag would admire one of the film's central conceits—that Hitler, who never visited the front, viewed the war every night through newsreels and was therefore a kind of filmmaker intent on making *Germany, a Film by Hitler*. Sontag calls Syberberg's film the most ambitious symbolist film of the twentieth century, a ghostly phantasmagoric film haunted by its models (Méliès and Eisenstein) and its antimodels (Riefenstahl and Hollywood). Calling Syberberg the greatest Wagnerian since Thomas Mann, she claims that here he realizes Wagner's great ideal of the invisible stage. For Sontag, the film is a "meta-spectacle" that creates Hitler as a phantom presence in modern culture. A pastiche work in the model of James Joyce, the film deserves the kind of ideal viewer that Joyce desired for his novels— one who could devote his life to it.

Perhaps the best-known essay in the collection is the one entitled "Fascinating Fascism," a combination of one long piece on Leni Riefenstahl, which is the most polemical in the book, and a short essay on a paperback picture book entitled *SS Regalia*, which Sontag rightly terms pornographic. Primarily, the essay is Sontag's effort to cancel out the attempted purification of Riefenstahl's reputation in 1974 after the publication of a book of photographs by her entitled *The Last of the Nuba*. Both the influence of the feminist movement and the new focus of the avant-garde on the beautiful have resulted, says Sontag, in efforts to whitewash Riefenstahl of her involvement in Nazi propaganda, especially in her most famous film, *The Triumph of the Will* (1935). Sontag spends much of her essay pointing out the factual misinformation in the Introduction to the photographs of Nuba natives. She also argues with Riefenstahl's insistence in the 1950's that *The Triumph of the Will* was history when she denied that it was propaganda, calling it instead cinema verité. Sontag quite easily squashes such a claim by noting the transformation of reality which Riefenstahl engineers in the film.

In her 1965 interview in Cashiers due Cinéma, Riefenstahl also claimed (in response to an interviewer's suggestion that what both her films *The Triumph of the Will* and *Olympia* share is a "certain idea of form") that her primary concern was with beauty, a care for composition, an aspiration to form, that she called something very German. "Whatever is purely realistic, slice-of-life, which is average, quotidian, doesn't interest me." The publication of *The Last of the Nuba* then confirmed for Riefenstahl partisans, says Sontag, that "she was always a beauty freak rather than a horrid propagandist." To combat this idea, Sontag spends the rest of the essay laboriously showing the relationship between the photographs of the Nuba tribesmen and the techniques used by Riefenstahl in her propagandistic films.

Such an effort seems more laborious than perhaps the task merits. Sontag is able to cite only one critic, Jonas Mekas in *The Village Voice*, who praises Riefenstahl's focus on beauty and form while ignoring her role as the creator of the single most important Nazi propaganda instrument. For whatever reason, it is a task that Sontag performs with a great deal of effort and commitment. In so doing, Sontag places herself in somewhat of a contradictory position with regard to the artists she praises in the rest of the book. Granted, it would be unthinkable for such a socially committed thinker as Sontag to praise Riefenstahl; however, it seems difficult for such a passionate aesthetic thinker as Sontag (who praises form, pattern, and schematizing in Artaud, Benjamin, Barthes, and Canetti), to scorn what she calls Riefenstahl's Fascist aesthetic in *The Triumph of Will*. Especially since, according to Sontag, it can be seen in such works as Walt Disney's *Fantasia*, Busby Berkeley's *The Gang's All Here*, and Stanley Kubrick's *2001*—an aesthetic that is characterized by the rendering of movement in rigid patterns and by the transformation of the masses into design and form.

For Sontag to praise Syberberg for his eschewal of actuality and for his preference for Wagnerian patterns and then to scorn Riefenstahl for her eschewal of the "purely realistic, slice-of-life, which is average, quotidian" seems contradictory. The only reason Sontag can really offer for her preference for the formal system-making of Barthes and Canetti and her vigorous attack on Riefenstahl for the same formalizing of experience is to cite the uses to which their work has been put. Although it is just as possible for some groups to use the plays of Artaud for propaganda as it is to use the films of Riefenstahl, Artaud did not create purposely for propaganda, and of course Artaud was not used to justify the Nazi war machine and the unspeakable atrocities that rolled under it. This kind of a judgment; however, is a moral, not an aesthetic judgment; therefore, it is somewhat surprising to have such a thoroughgoing aesthete as Sontag take this approach.

Although one can grant with Sontag that the attempted purification of Riefenstahl indicates a Fascist longing of which one should be aware, surely

Sontag must be aware that the very formalists and structuralists which she so much admires and praises lend themselves to the same kind of characteristics which she claims are typical of the Fascist aesthetic. It is precisely such films as *Fantasia, 2001*, and *The Gangs All Here* that are most susceptible to the kind of systematic structural deconstruction that Barthes has mastered. It may be that those critics who have attempted to redeem Riefenstahl are precisely those who have been reared on the avant-garde milk of Susan Sontag's teaching.

Charles May

THE UNITED STATES AND THE CARIBBEAN
1900-1970

Author: Lester D. Langley (1940-   )
Publisher: The University of Georgia Press (Athens). 332 pp. $22.00
Type of work: History
Time: 1900-1970
Locale: The United States and the countries of the Caribbean and of Central America

The story of United States relations with the countries of the Caribbean area, from the years of Theodore Roosevelt to the time of Lyndon B. Johnson

> *Principal personages:*
> THEODORE ROOSEVELT, twenty-sixth President of the United States, 1901-1909
> WILLIAM HOWARD TAFT, twenty-seventh President of the United States, 1909-1913
> WOODROW WILSON, twenty-eighth President of the United States, 1913-1921
> FRANKLIN DELANO ROOSEVELT, thirty-second President of the United States, 1933-1945
> JOHN FITZGERALD KENNEDY, thirty-fifth President of the United States, 1961-1963
> LYNDON BAINES JOHNSON, thirty-sixth President of the United States, 1963-1969
> RAFAEL TRUJILLO Y MOLINA, Dictator of the Dominican Republic, 1930-1961
> ANASTASIO SOMOZA, Dictator of Nicaragua, 1936-1956, and founder of the Somoza dynasty
> FULGENCIO BATISTA Y ZALDIVAR, leading Cuban political figure after 1933 and President of Cuba, 1940-1944 and 1952-1959
> FIDEL CASTRO, Dictator of Cuba, 1959 to the present

In 1979, and again in 1980, the Caribbean area was wracked by unrest. A revolution overthrew the Somoza dynasty in Nicaragua; a bloody civil war erupted in El Salvador; and a long-running guerrilla insurgency in Guatemala threatened to grow even worse. This renewed turmoil spurred talk among many Americans about the possibility that the United States might be forced to intervene militarily to prevent the countries in the area from being taken over by Fidel Castro's Communist regime in Cuba. If such American armed intervention ever does take place, it will certainly not be greeted with unalloyed enthusiasm by America's non-Communist neighbors to the South. For history has taught many of them to be wary of a country whose history, they believe, is marred by imperialism and colonialism.

This is the message that can clearly be inferred from Lester D. Langley's new book, *The United States and the Caribbean, 1900-1970.* Langley, a Professor of History at the University of Georgia, has previously written about the United States drive for supremacy in the Caribbean from 1776 to 1904. In his new work, he continues that story, carrying it up to the present day.

This book contains little that is new or original in its interpretations; it does, however, give a good, brief survey of American policy in this region. Although awkwardly written at times, *The United States and the Caribbean, 1900-1970* does provide some badly needed historical perspective on our current troubles in the Caribbean and Central America.

Langley's definition of the Caribbean area is, as it must be, a somewhat arbitrary one. Panama, Nicaragua, and Guatemala are included within the area, as are Cuba, Haiti, the Dominican Republic, and the Commonwealth of Puerto Rico. Mexico, however, is not included; and Colombia is discussed only briefly, in connection with American acquisition of the Panama Canal Zone. Venezuela appears only briefly as the stimulus to President Theodore Roosevelt's enunciation of the Roosevelt Corollary to the Monroe Doctrine. Yet, Venezuela does have a Caribbean coastline; the activities of American oil corporations played a major role in its development; and it is today one of the leading members of the Organization of Petroleum Exporting Countries (OPEC). There is also relatively little in Langley's book about the countries of the English-speaking Caribbean: the Bahamas, Jamaica, or even the American dependency of the Virgin Islands.

The United States, Langley shows, achieved hegemony in the region as the result of the Spanish-American War of 1898, in which Spain was expelled from her last island possessions in the New World, Cuba and Puerto Rico. Langley divides American policy into three main phases: (1) the Protectorate era, lasting from about 1900 to 1921, during which the United States Federal government intervened at will in the affairs of the region; (2) the interwar era, from 1921 to 1945, during which the United States shifted from a reliance on armed force in dealing with the Caribbean states toward the use of subtler means of carrying out its policies in the area; and (3) the Cold War era, lasting from 1945 to 1970, which witnessed the first real break in the traditional American hegemony over the region: the appearance of the Communist regime of Fidel Castro in Cuba.

The book is organized in a traditional sequential narrative fashion. Each chapter deals with American policy toward several countries of the area within the same chronological period. To follow the thread of the narrative about any one country, therefore, the reader must wind his way through the labyrinth of successive chapters. The strict adherence to the chronological approach sometimes makes the work rather dull and textbookish. There are provocative interpretations found at the beginning and the end of each of the three sections of the book; one would only wish for more such interpretive material.

In the first section, Langley shows how, following the defeat of Spain, the United States, guided by the same sense of national mission that animated British imperialists, established an empire of her own. With the exception of Puerto Rico, this empire would consist, not of colonies, but of "small politically unstable republics with fragile economies."

It was, Langley implies, President Theodore Roosevelt who first began the practice of interfering in the affairs of nominally independent Caribbean countries. Through subterfuge and guile, Roosevelt encouraged a Panamanian revolt against Colombia, paving the way for both American acquisition of the Panama Canal Zone and the building of the Panama Canal. When the newly independent Republic of Cuba fell into political chaos, Roosevelt also intervened forcefully there, setting up a military government which supplanted native rule for three years (1906-1909).

Langley is, however, not quite as harsh in his judgment of Theodore Roosevelt as some other American historians have been. The author does not believe that the Roosevelt Corollary to the Monroe Doctrine, establishing fiscal solvency as the basis for a state's right to freedom from foreign intervention, was really meant as a pretext for the establishment of American protectorates over independent Latin American republics. Roosevelt's establishment of a customs receivership in the debt-plagued Dominican Republic, Langley argues, was meant simply to "stave off calamity and allow the Republic to repay its European creditors." Thus, the author contends, the man of the Big Stick was actually much more cautious about intervention than were his two immediate successors, William Howard Taft and Woodrow Wilson.

President Taft is said by many historians to have attempted, as part of his new policy of Dollar Diplomacy, to manipulate the internal politics of Caribbean states with the aid of the big New York City banks. Although Langley does agree that Taft was an interventionist, he demonstrates that his policy was, in the end, forced to rely more on bullets than on dollars. In 1909, Taft and his Secretary of State, Philander Knox, aided and abetted a successful revolt against the outspokenly nationalistic dictator of Nicaragua, Jose Santos Zelaya. In 1912, Taft had the Marines sent to Nicaragua to help put down a revolt against Adolfo Diaz, the pro-American politician who had become President of that country in 1911.

It was, Langley makes clear, under Woodrow Wilson, who was President from 1913 to 1921, that American interference in the politics of its Caribbean neighbors reached its height. In July, 1915, Wilson had the Marines sent to Haiti, and in May, 1916, he had them sent to the Dominican Republic. The United States then proceeded to subject both these countries to a prolonged occupation, under which, despite their nominal sovereignty, they were deprived of all rights to self-government. Wilson was determined to impose American notions of political order and economic progress on the politically unstable nations of the Caribbean.

After Wilson had left office, Americans began to reevaluate their Caribbean policies. The occupation regimes in Haiti and the Dominican Republic, marked by brutality, atrocities, and the high expenses of suppressing native rebels, provoked dissent within the United States among perceptive members of the political, journalistic, and intellectual elites. Partly as a result of such criticism, aired in the United States Senate, the United States government withdrew its forces from the Dominican Republic in 1924; ten years later, the last Marine would leave Haiti as well. During the years 1926 to 1933, there was renewed armed intervention in the strife-torn republic of Nicaragua, where United States Marines became locked in a frustrating combat with the intrepid guerrilla warrior Augusto Cesar Sandino. Its high cost and ultimate futility offered further proof to American policymakers that such reliance on force was no longer effective in protecting American interests. The time was ripe for a new policy, that of the Good Neighbor.

This policy first publicly enunciated in 1933, was largely the handiwork of that professional diplomat, Sumner Welles. It did not, the author insists, mean a renunciation of American hegemony in the region; instead, it merely meant that new methods would be used to maintain that hegemony. Throughout the 1930's, Langley argues, Secretary of State Cordell Hull continued to try to maintain continued American economic domination over the Caribbean republics by pressuring them into signing favorable trade agreements. In the case of Cuba, the author contends, Hull was especially successful in doing this. Although the Good Neighbor policy implied the renunciation of armed intervention in the affairs of the sovereign states of the Caribbean area, it did not, Langley makes clear, imply the renunciation of subtler and more covert means of interference in their internal affairs. Instead of relying on the Marines to protect American interests against local nationalists, the United States now came to rely on the native strongman dictators who sprang up in the region: Rafael Trujillo y Molina of the Dominican Republic, Anastasio Somoza of Nicaragua, and Fulgencio Batista y Zaldivar of Cuba.

To what extent was the United States government responsible for the rise to power of these three dictators in the 1930's? Langley insists that, although the United States "accommodated and even praised" the dictatorship of Rafael Trujillo, it did not "create" it. Trujillo rose to power on his own, making adroit use of the American-created national police force in order to do so. The author points out that Nicaraguan dictator Anastasio Somoza himself believed that his assassination in 1934 of his archrival, the popular anti-American guerrilla leader Augusto Sandino, had the blessing of the American Ambassador in Managua, and that later Latin American critics of the United States have shared this belief. Langley does not, however, come to any definite conclusions of his own regarding American responsibility for Somoza's rise to power. The author does, however, strongly suggest that two successive American Ambassadors to Cuba, Sumner Welles and Jefferson Caffrey, played a crucial role in encouraging young Sergeant Fulgencio Batista to seize the reins of power in 1933-1934. Batista owed his success during those politically troubled years, Langley argues, to his "unmatched ability to discern American desires in Cuba." Batista offered something other Cuban political figures either could not or would not provide: political stability and a favorable climate for American investments.

Although the Roosevelt Administration accommodated itself to those Caribbean dictators who were pro-American, it became more and more frightened by the threat to the Western Hemisphere posed by European dictators. The more the United States became drawn into the struggle against Adolf Hitler's Germany, the more Roosevelt's State Department pressured the Caribbean republics to make their own contribution to the Allied cause. Guatemalan dictator Jorge Ubico's admiration for the Spain of Francisco Franco, and Panamanian leader Arnulfo Arias' reluctance to grant military bases to the United States, led a worried Secretary of State Hull to regard both leaders as Fascists. In the end, however, all of the Caribbean republics (including Panama, after Arias' ouster by a revolt in 1941) cooperated fully with the American war effort. The sudden cutoff of foreign markets and sources of supply brought about by World War II, Langley points out, wreaked great hardship on the Caribbean republics, increasing still further their traditional economic dependence on the United States.

Soon after World War II, the United States became involved in a new global conflict: the Cold War with Russia. During the first fifteen years after World War II, Langley makes clear, the United States government exerted considerable pressure on the Caribbean republics to line up behind her in the Cold War, but paid almost no attention whatsoever to the pressing economic needs of the region. When, in 1954, a reformist regime in Guatemala, led by Jacobo Arbenz Guzman, seemed to be shifting from the American to the Russian orbit, President Dwight David Eisenhower and Secretary of State John Foster Dulles, working through the Central Intelligence Agency, aided and abetted a successful military revolt against the Guatemalan leader. It was during these Cold War years that there occurred the first successful challenge to United States hegemony in the region in the twentieth century: the formation of the pro-Soviet regime of Fidel Castro in Cuba.

Earl E. T. Smith, who served as Ambassador to Cuba during the last few years of the Batista regime, has argued that it was the presence of liberal Castro sympathizers in the United States State Department that made the triumph of Castro over Batista possible. Langley disagrees with this position. Instead, he espouses the interpretation of the American historian of Latin America, Ramón Eduardo Ruíz, holding that it was Cuba's fragile social structure, and not anything that Washington did or did not do, that made the Batista regime so vulnerable to Castro's armed assault in 1956-1958.

From 1959 onward, hostility between the United States and the new Castro regime grew steadily worse. Langley tells the story of how, in the first year of the presidency of John Fitzgerald Kennedy, in April, 1961, an invasion of Cuba by anti-Castro refugees, armed and equipped by the Central Intelligence Agency, met with disastrous failure at the Bay of Pigs. He also recounts the story of President Kennedy's masterful handling of the Cuban Missile Crisis of October, 1962, in which the young President succeeded in forcing the withdrawal of Soviet missiles from that island. By the beginning of 1963, Langley makes clear, Cuba had been completely incorporated into the Soviet bloc.

It was the shock of Cuba's defection, Langley believes, which moved Kennedy's successor, President Lyndon B. Johnson, to intervene in the Dominican Republic. After the assassination of Trujillo in May, 1961, that small Caribbean republic underwent a prolonged period of political instability. In the autumn of 1963, the newly elected Dominican President, Juan Bosch, a one-time anti-Trujillo exile suspected by the American ambassador of being politically naïve and excessively tolerant of communism, was overthrown in a military coup. On April 24, 1965, a pro-Bosch military rebellion broke out; when the anti-Bosch faction appealed for American help, Johnson ordered the landing of the United States Marines. Langley bitterly deplores this decision of an American President, "obsessed with Communism," to prevent the return to power of a man who the author believes was the best hope for Dominican democracy at that time.

By 1970, Langley argues, the efforts of the United States to prevent a second Cuba had shown themselves incapable of preventing the steady erosion of American hegemony in the Caribbean; the decade to come would see a continuation of this trend. Thus, in 1976, President Omar Torrijos Herrera of Panama was able to extract new, and more favorable, Panama Canal treaties from the United States. America's island possession of Puerto Rico, the author contends, was witnessing a "striking resurgence" of the pro-independence movement after many years in which economic growth had seemingly made the island content with the halfway house of Commonwealth status. Although he does mention the harsh Latin American reaction to the Dominican intervention as one cause of America's loss of influence in the Caribbean, Langley fails to mention the blow to American self-confidence dealt by the failure of another act of military intervention; the long and costly war with Vietnam.

Langley's book contains nothing that would surprise scholars in the field of United States-Latin American relations; its interpretations of recent events, however, might well be somewhat surprising to the nonspecialist reader. Cuban anti-Americanism, the lay reader will be surprised to learn, is by no means merely an invention of the Castroite Communists. Resentment against the Colossus of the North, fueled by all-too-frequent Yankee meddling in Cuban politics, had long existed in that country even prior to Castro's takeover in 1959. Similarly, the chief cause of the recent decline of American power in the Caribbean, Langley argues, is not simply the activity of some worldwide Communist conspiracy; rather, it is the traditional North American contempt for the peoples of the Caribbean.

Although Langley is highly critical of United States policy toward the

Caribbean republics, he does try, in most cases, to be fair. He attempts to steer a middle course between flag-waving chauvinism, on the one hand, and strident anti-Americanism, on the other. He shows that, Marxian analysis notwithstanding, trade did not always follow the flag: Cuba did experience, from 1900 onward, the intrusion of American capital, but other Caribbean countries subject to American political influence did not. While pointing out that the American occupation of Haiti and the Dominican Republic did not set either country on the road to democracy, he does praise the achievements of the American occupiers in the realms of road-building and public health. The Caribbean peoples' attitudes toward the United States, the author notes, have been quite ambivalent. Although the policies of the United States might be condemned, "the American lifestyle is very much admired."

Although Langley promises, in the preface, to tell the reader about American involvement in "the political, economic, and cultural lives" of the Caribbean countries, his narrative does tend to concentrate on political events. Some discussion of the patterns of immigration to the United States from Cuba, Haiti, and the Dominican Republic, and of the role of Cuban exiles in the economies of the United States and Puerto Rico since 1959, would have been useful. The United States is said to have "disparaged" the culture of the Caribbean peoples, but this generalization is substantiated only in the sketchiest fashion. Woodrow Wilson is said to have been a "Protestant missionary" who was "bent on reforming" the Catholic societies of the Caribbean. Yet the author says nothing at all about the activities of American Protestant missionaries in the island republic of Cuba during the years 1898 to 1958. Langley even ignores one of the most glaring examples of the aping of Yankee customs in the Caribbean: the adoption by Cubans of baseball as their national sport.

Langley's book is based partly on secondary sources written by himself and other scholars, partly on his own long years of acquaintance with the primary sources. The secondary sources include both works of the traditional American nationalist school of historiography and the contributions of the newer Revisionist school, with its sharp critique of American foreign policy in the area. The number of scholarly works of either type diminishes greatly as events recent in time, and still controversial in nature, are discussed. The primary sources used include published books and articles written by contemporary diplomats, soldiers, journalists, and travelers, individuals who either participated in the events described or observed them at first hand. Since Dana Gardner Munro was a State Department official during the 1920's, his well-known histories of United States-Caribbean relations, consulted frequently by the author, span the boundary between primary source and secondary source. No archival sources are directly cited or listed, although such sources probably form the basis of most of the scholarly books and articles to which Langley referred.

Langley's book contains a good number of aids to the reader. *The United States and the Caribbean* includes two maps of the countries of Central America and the Caribbean; these are of great help to the individual whose knowledge of the geography of the region is sketchy. The excellent annotated bibliography not only tells the general reader what work has already been done on various special topics, but also points out to the scholar areas where further research is needed. Unfortunately, the footnotes are placed at the back of the book making it inconvenient for the reader to consult them.

Paul D. Mageli

VATICAN DIPLOMACY AND THE JEWS
DURING THE HOLOCAUST, 1939-1943

Author: John F. Morley (1938-   )
Publisher: KTAV Publishing House (New York). 327 pp. $20.00
Type of work: History
Time: 1939-1943
Locale: Europe

A history of Vatican Diplomacy and the Jews from 1939 to 1943, focusing on a country-by-country description of the activities of the Vatican diplomats relative to the Jews

> *Principal personages:*
> POPE PIUS XII, Pope during World War II
> LUIGI CARDINAL MAGLIONE, Vatican Secretary of State during World War II

John F. Morley's *Vatican Diplomacy and the Jews During the Holocaust, 1939-1943*, will undoubtedly remain for some time into the future the definitive description of Vatican activities regarding the Jews and the Holocaust. The volume is well conceived, meticulous in its research, and thorough in its analyses. Basing his study on approximately four thousand documents recording diplomatic exchanges between the Vatican Secretariat of State and its diplomats in Europe from 1939 to 1943, instructions and orders from the Vatican, accounts from papal nuncios of their experiences and observations, and the memoranda both of papal emissaries and of outside parties, this volume is an accurate portrayal of the role played by the Vatican in the Holocaust.

The author's study of these and other sources was designed to reveal how the Vatican and its emissaries responded to Nazi persecution and destruction of the Jews from the outset of the papacy of Pius XII to the time in 1943 when published records ceased to be available and most of Europe's Jews had already been murdered. During this period, the Vatican Secretariat of State had diplomatic emissaries or apostolic delegates in Berlin, Vichy, Berne, Rome, Bucharest, Zagreb, Bratislava, Budapest, Ankara, London, and Washington. In addition to studying and analyzing Vatican response to the plight of the Jews in these countries (except for England and the United States), the Morley book also studies the situation in Croatia and Poland. The book is a country-by-country description and analysis of Vatican response.

The Vatican records, according to Morley, confirm, corroborate, and elaborate documents already available in such archives as Yad Vashem in Jerusalem, the Centre de Documentation Juive Contemporaire in Paris, the Institute for Jewish Affairs in London, the World Jewish Congress in New York City, the Public Record Office in London, and the Myron Taylor archives of the Roosevelt Library in Hyde Park, New York, and in many secondary sources from various major library collections in the United States as well as

La Civilta Cattolica library in Rome. Relying on such a wealth of documentary evidence, Morley investigated "whether Vatican diplomatic effort, in fact, was directed toward the rights of the Church and its members, as well as being oriented toward the needs of non-Catholics, specifically Jews." These were the two criteria which the Vatican claimed as the foundations of its World War II diplomacy.

The first of these criteria was clearly a responsibility of diplomacy because survival of the Church depends upon maintenance of the rights of the Church and its members. The second of the criteria was part of the historic and publicly proclaimed role of the Holy See as the guardian of universal morality and humanitarianism. Since this has over the years and during the period 1939 to 1943 been a self-proclaimed foundation of Vatican diplomacy and policy, failure to adhere to such a criterion while at the same time claiming to manifest this criterion would be damning.

In order to determine Vatican diplomacy and policy relating to these criteria, Morley provided a country-by-country chronological description of the stages of the Holocaust and the role taken by first, the papal nuncios; second, the Secretary of State, Luigi Cardinal Maglione; and, third, the Pope regarding each of these stages. The stages that the Jews underwent included racial legislation to isolate and pauperize, deportation to ghettos and death camps, and final destruction. In addition to testing the success or failure of the Vatican in adhering to the criteria on which World War II diplomacy was based, Morley explored other interesting issues, such as the reactions of Church officials to each stage of treatment of Jews, causal factors to explain the action or lack of action in behalf of Jews, and whether or not there was a Vatican attitude toward the Jews. The Morley book has been very carefully constructed, the criteria for Vatican diplomacy have been meticulously laid out, the questions asked of the evidence have been appropriately posed, and the evidence has been accurately presented. Altogether, Morley's effort is admirable. If there is any problem it is one of repetition of two different types. Morley summarizes each chapter with a section of "Conclusions" that is generally repetitious of the chapter that preceded it. Based on this repetition, Morley draws his conclusions for each chapter. It is possible that some of this repetition could be eliminated, although this is a minor problem.

A first illustration of the Vatican's response to persecution of the Jews may be discerned in the Vatican's actions in regard to a request of the German Catholic hierarchy in 1939 to petition the government of Brazil to extend visas to three thousand Catholic Jews facing German persecution. Although the visas were eventually granted, the whole issue was beset with so many problems and issues that Brazil suspended the program in 1940 and ended it in 1941. Several conclusions must be made about the Vatican as it involved itself in the Brazilian visa project. It is clear that the Vatican was only concerned about baptized Jews or members of the Church and not about Jews in general. Moreover, diplomacy alone was employed in the visa project and became an end in itself, ignoring the genuine suffering of people. Certainly, the Vatican refused to do anything to disturb the status quo. Finally, the visa project was ever after recalled by the Vatican as an illustration of how much the Vatican had done for the Jews.

The situation in Rumania was most interesting where Archbishop Andrea Cassulo was the papal nuncio in Bucharest. Cassulo was very active in pursuit of the rights of baptized Jews. He viewed the suffering of the Jews, in fact, as inspired by divine plan to increase the number of baptisms. For this reason, he was not concerned about anti-Semitic legislation. As the Jews of Bukovina and Bessarabia, after much privation, were deported to Transnistria in 1941, the nuncio reluctantly protested only in behalf of converted Jews and in mid-1942 refused to intervene in behalf of Jews. In the fall of 1942, however, in response to requests of Jewish leaders, he did protest the treatment of Rumanian Jews, visiting Transnistria in the spring of 1943. Eventually Cassulo gained a significant reputation among Jews for his willingness to intervene in behalf of Jews.

Morley characterized Vatican diplomacy in France from 1939 to 1943 as "ambivalent." While French bishops protested deportations of French Jews to death camps beginning in July, 1942, there is no evidence that any such protest came from the papal nuncio, Archbishop Valerio Valeri. In fact, lack of protest and continued diplomatic relations between the Holy See and France were viewed by the French bishops as support of the policies of Marshal Pétan. Altogether "Valeri wrote nothing and said little to defend the Jews of France."

Following Adolf Hitler's dismemberment of Czechoslovakia, Slovakia's papal nuncio was Archbishop Saverio Ritter, located in Bratislava. Ritter was soon replaced by Monsignor Giuseppe Burzio, Vatican chargé d'affaires to Bratislava. One persistent problem that the Church constantly protested against from 1939 to 1942 were Slovakia's racial laws. It is clear, however, that the Church did not object to the maltreatment of Jews, but rather to infringement on the rights of Catholics "of Jewish origin." This was made clear in a letter to the Slovakian government by Vatican Secretary of State Maglione on November 12, 1941. The Holy See also protested deportations of Jews beginning in the spring of 1942. Three-fourths of all Slovakian Jews were deported. A significant aspect of this protest was that the Slovakian government did not make special provision for the rights of baptized Jews. The Church also protested Slovakian Jewish girls being forced into prostitution for German soldiers. A year later, in the spring of 1943, the Church again protested the deportation of remaining Jews because by this time the Vatican fully understood that deportation meant death and, most importantly, because a substantial proportion of those to be deported in 1943 were baptized Jews. The first diplomatic protest of the Vatican to deportation was of no avail, while the second only delayed the process to 1944. The Holy See did not consider any means other than those diplomatic protests to stop deportation from the heavily Catholic nation of Slovakia. Morley insisted that diplomacy failed because of Vatican "indifference" to deportation and limitation of diplomacy to "strictly Catholic interests."

In Germany, papal diplomacy was in the hands of the nuncio, Archbishop Cesare Orsenigo. Orsenigo frequently intereceded with German officials on matters relating to the Church and its personnel. The Holy See, however, requested Orsenigo's exertion in behalf of the Jews only once during the war years and that exertion involved a request for information about deported French Jews. Morley characterized Orsenigo's efforts in behalf of the Jews as reflecting "lassitude and indifference." As difficult as was Orsenigo's position in Nazi Germany, however, even more important than his own indifference regarding the Jews as the position of the Vatican Secretariat of State which evidently had "no concern for the Jews."

The German invasion of Poland eventually left that nation with no papal representation, save Archbishop Orsenigo, who tried to tend to the interests of Poland's Catholic population. Orsenigo's efforts in behalf of Poland were severely limited by his location and by the refusal of the Germans to allow official papal observers in Poland. "The Vatican said and did nothing on behalf of the Jews of Poland." Moreover, "Pope Pius XII said little and did nothing on behalf of Polish Catholics." Given the nature of the tragedy that befell Polish Jews and non-Jews alike at the hands of the Nazis, there can be no explanation or justification for the indifference of the Church to the suffering people of Poland during the war years.

It was not until July, 1941, that the Vatican was able to send a representative to Croatia. He was an abbot, Giuseppe Ramiro Marcone, who became an apostolic visitor. So favorably did Marcone comport himself in Croatia that he was eventually given by the government all of the honors of a papal nuncio and became dean of the Croatian diplomatic corps. Strictly speaking, Marcone was not a diplomat in the view of the Vatican. His diplomatic authority was *de facto* and his extensive contacts with Croatian leaders were nonofficial. Yet, he exerted more authority than did many papal nuncios. On several occasions, Marcone intervened with the government in behalf of the Jews of Croatia. This was encouraged by the Vatican. While the government of Croatia was urged to be humane, it was not condemned for its anti-Semitic policies or its efforts at deportation. Marcone "saw spiritual benefits" from the conversion of Jews under the pressure of the Holocaust. He supported Catholic rights among the converted. It is difficult to discern much merit in this position, especially since Marcone reported to the Vatican that by July, 1942, two million Jews had already been killed and that the Jews of Croatia could expect to be dealt with in a similar way. In the view of Morley, the popular Marcone could have done much to aid the Jews of Croatia, but chose not to exert himself beyond a minimal effort.

As in other countries, the major concern of the Vatican with the government of Italy involved the racial laws. The Vatican repeatedly attempted to change these to remove restrictions on baptized Jews. Also as in other countries, the Vatican was not concerned about restrictions on nonbaptized Jews. The Vatican was effective and successful in behalf of Jews, both baptized and non-baptized restricted to camps around Italy. Deportations were discouraged by the Vatican and the Vatican allowed the lodging of many Jews in Catholic religious institutions in Rome. The Vatican did nothing, however, to prevent deportation of about a thousand Jews from the Roman ghetto. The tragedy here is that practically on the home territory of the Vatican, and while claiming a uniquely spiritual and moral stature for their diplomacy, in this case of the deportation of Italian Jews to a certain death, the Vatican "concurred by their silence." It is clear, therefore, that the response of the Vatican to the plight of Jews in Italy was better by degrees than it had been in the other countries of Europe, but not really significantly different in kind. Formal acquiescence with deportation and Nazi objectives remained characteristic of Vatican posture.

Based on Morley's analysis of *Vatican Diplomacy and the Jews During the Holocaust, 1939-1943*, several conclusions are noteworthy. It is clear that the papal nuncios were not concerned about the sufferings of the Jews in the period. If, on a few occasions, actions were taken to aid Jews, those actions were directed at individuals. Only in regard to racial laws was there a consistent response by the Vatican and its nuncios. Here the concern was with converted Jews, regarded as a part of the Church. The Vatican's unchanging response to Hitler's racial policies was a religious view that denied race as religiously significant, but never went beyond the Catholic religion to support a genuinely humanitarian ethic in the preservation of Jewish or Protestant lives. This was the reason that the papal nuncios did not exert themselves much in behalf of the Jews. While actively defending the rights of the Church, "By a lack of total response to the Jews in their hour of greatest need, the nuncios failed to live up to the high calling that they proclaimed for themselves." Their responses to the plight of the Jews were weak, sporadic, indifferent, inadequate, reluctant, and lacking conviction. This response was both expected and counted upon by the Nazis throughout Europe, especially in the deportations in Italy where something substantive could have been done by the Vatican, but was not.

These views of the papal nuncios must be extended to the Secretary of State, Luigi Cardinal Maglione, for Maglione directed papal diplomacy during the years of World War II. It is clear from analyses of Vatican diplomatic communications that Maglione directed Vatican efforts to defend Church rights throughout Europe. He, like the nuncios, opposed racial legislation not on general grounds, but only because they restricted the rights of baptized

Jews. Thus, anti-Jewish legislation was not objectionable as long as it did not interfere with the Church's rights. Maglione was also not much concerned about deportation of the Jews, about their sufferings in ghettos, concentration camps and death camps, and about their destruction at the hands of the Nazis. Almost more than any other agency or government, the Vatican, through its religious and diplomatic network, knew what was happening to the Jews, and yet Maglione responded to pleas for helping the Jews in the way he instructed his nuncios to respond—namely, "that the Vatican had done, was doing, and would continue to do all possible for the Jews." This proposition, in the view of John Morley, "must be unequivocally denied."

Finally, it is important to note that the policies of the Secretary of State and the nuncios originate with the Pope. Pope Pius XII provided direction for Maglione and the nuncios. The Pope decided the diplomatic posture of the Vatican and its agents. The only justification for the conduct of Vatican diplomacy was Pope Pius XII's desire to maintain relations with Nazi Germany and other nations of Europe. In order to maintain relations, the Pope, the Secretary of State, and the nuncios all abandoned humanitarian concern for the suffering and deaths of both Christians and Jews in the Holocaust. By concentrating exclusively on maintaining diplomacy, Pope Pius XII, the Secretary of State, and the nuncios failed the Jews, failed Christians, and failed the Catholic Church's claim to universal humanitarianism and spirituality. John F. Morley's splendid book provides ample documentation of these conclusions. His is a brutally honest book that obviously has required much courage to write. In the never-never land of "what might have been," one can only wish that the Vatican had maintained the spirituality to act differently and that such a tragic volume had been unnecessary.

Saul Lerner

THE VIEW FROM 80

Author: Malcolm Cowley (1898-   )
Publisher: The Viking Press (New York). 74 pp. $6.95
Type of work: Essay

An extended essay in which a master critic and observer presents his view of life after age eighty

This book is for everyone. Malcolm Cowley has, in his own words, entered "the country of age" and declared it "different from what you supposed it to be." His essay is a "report, submitted as a road map and guide to some of the principal monuments." Ninety-eight percent of the American population is under eighty years of age, and everyone can certainly profit from the wise, warm, and witty insights Cowley offers to those who will someday be old. The two percent of the population who are more than eighty years old finally have an experienced spokesman to explain what being old is really like, for, as he points out, a person who is merely in the sixties or seventies is not yet fully informed. They still, he says, "have the illusion of being middle-aged." Cowley's subject is *life*, and everyone needs to know more about that. He tells us what aging and old age mean and how to seek out the pleasures and tolerate the pains in the country of the old.

Cowley is unusually well qualified to appraise the patterns of a culture and offer measured judgments about large, important subjects. He is the premiere critic for understanding and articulating the events and ideas and personalities that dominated a major literary generation of twentieth century American literature: the "lost generation" that included not only Cowley himself but also Ernest Hemingway, F. Scott Fitzgerald, Thomas Wolfe, Stephen Crane, William Faulkner, e. e. cummings, John Dos Passos, Thornton Wilder, and more than 350 others, who lived mainly in the left bank area of Paris during the 1920's. He told about them in two books. *Exile's Return* (1934) established the idea that his generation, formed by the expatriate life and the experiences of war, differed significantly from previous generations of American writers. In part, they differed in that they came to believe an unexpressed idea that theirs was the generation that would change the world for the better in this new century. In *A Second Flowering: Works and Days of the Lost Generation* (1973), Cowley continued his finding of patterns, this time exploring the long careers of the major writers of the lost generation and finding that some of the most extraordinary writers of his generation "lacked the capacity for growth after middle age that has marked some of the truly great writers." He also found that Faulkner may be the only one to remain a "world figure" in literature. Pronouncing such judgments became a career for Cowley, and his work is among the most respected criticism of the 1920's as a reward for its excellence in clarity and perception.

The View from 80 benefits from Cowley's special gift of writing with grace and simple eloquence. Typically, his books are part memoirs and part history. They are, in other words, created out of his own experience and reading, without relying much on other sources. Luckily, his books do not suffer from ideological biases or axe grinding. When they contain parts that are weak, the weakness derives from Cowley's own lack of experience with the writer he discusses. The experience, however, on which he does report is wide ranging and without peer. He demonstrates his value twice in two recent books, *—And I Worked at the Writer's Trade* (1978) and *The Dream of the Golden Mountains: Remembering the 1930s* (1980). In the first, he recalls his work as writer and editor and even offers a theory of literary generations in a chapter dealing with Hemingway. In the latter, Cowley provides a fascinating memoir of the cultural and social climate during the Depression and New Deal. While he participated in Communist-front writers' organizations, he did not join the Party. He is particularly good at detailing the consciousness of the middle class and professions and at explaining how the sense of decay of capitalism and, indeed, of American culture gave rise to a vision that was religious in its intensity. As the young became involved in this new vision, they could dream of "the golden mountains," of merging with the workers, suffering their hardships, and being born again.

Those were the years when he was young. He lived life fully. He was not merely a writer, editor, and lecturer. he was a visiting professor at several leading colleges and universities; he helped organize the first American Writers Congress in 1935; he was associate editor for short periods of time for *Broom, Cessation*, and *New Republic* (1929-1944); he translated numerous books from the French; and he edited numerous works, most notably *The Portable Faulkner* (1946), which, more than any other factor, is credited with reviving Faulkner's work for the reading public and paving the way for him to publish more, to receive the Nobel Prize, and to become one of America's most prominent authors. From 1956 to 1959 and from 1962 to 1965, he was President of the National Institute of Arts and Letters. He also published three books of poetry—*Blue Juniata* (1929), *The Dry Season* (1941), and *Blue Juniata: Collected Poems* (1968). He is a man whose experience and accomplishments, one being to live past eighty, entitle him to educate others about what it is like to be old and to offer octogenarians some sage advice.

The View from 80 continues to offer anecdotes and appraisals of patterns that Cowley has established as his style. For example, he tells when an individual realizes he or she is old—the signs are subtle. He recalls the near-collision he had several years ago in a parking lot. When the irate driver of the other car saw him, he immediately cooled down and said, "Why, you're an old man." Then there was the time a young woman got up and offered him her seat on a crowded bus. While he declined her offer, he accepted a similar offer the next year, "though with a sense of having diminished myself." So how do we start growing old? "We start by growing old in other people's eyes, then slowly we come to share their judgment." With this pronouncement is the implication that the casual judgment is more harsh than anger or outright condemnation, and this view characterizes a strong part of the book: that of challenging old-age stereotypes.

What are the signs of growing old, of entering the "country of age"? The body sends some messages on occasion. For example, "You are old" when the bones ache, when more little bottles of medicine crowd the medicine cabinet, when year by year the feet seem farther from the hands, or when a man "can't stand on one leg and has trouble pulling on his pants." More sadly, a person becomes old when "a pretty girl passes him in the street and he doesn't turn his head." Or, when everything takes longer, such as shaving, dressing, and the like—but when time passes quickly." Also, when it becomes harder for the aging person "to bear in mind two things at once." The old person "feels as strong as ever when he is sitting back in a comfortable chair." There the person ruminates, dreams, remembers. The moment he rises to do something such as go hunting, however, as he did ten or twenty years ago, the body sends its messages.

What can one do in this situation, having become one of only two percent— or 4,842,000 persons—of the octogenarians? The greatest temptation is "simply giving up." Society even aids the old to think less of themselves, to think of giving up, by making them "feel that they no longer have a function in the community. Their families don't ask them for advice, don't really listen when they speak, don't call on them for efforts." As Cowley points out for the readers benefit, the aging person, even before eighty, may undergo another identity crisis like that of adolescence. What one does is to deal with age by vigorous living, by a sense of purpose, accompanied by some work outlet— just as it is essential in earlier life.

Perhaps, although Cowley does not say this explicitly, if we "look at ourselves with a sense of humor, we can adapt to the limitations of age." Besides "giving up," Cowley explains the vices—"new vices"—of age and some less widely known "new compensations." Among the vices of age are "avarice, untidiness, and vanity, which last takes the form of a craving to be loved or simply admired." Some people hoard money, perhaps to take "comfort in watching it accumulate while other powers are dwindling away." Is the untidiness resulting from accumulating junk derived from the feeling that "everything once useful, including their own bodies, should be preserved"? If the elderly person, in order to avoid the vice of untidiness becomes excessively neat, is that not also some milder vice? Are these efforts to avoid a sense of purpose, some useful work outlet or project? While Cowley does not say so explicitly, he finds these vices dismaying and recommends guarding against them.

Vanity as a vice deserves special attention, for apparently those who enter the country of the old often yearn for recognition of what one has been: a beauty queen, an athlete, a scholar, a leader, a soldier. Creams, powders, and dyes come into use. Photographs of younger versions of the old adorn the living room; and then there is the seeking of honors and "the innocent boast" at parties. "Attentions which seem trivial and conventional are marks of honor—the morning call, being sought after, having people rise for you. . . ." As Cicero observed, "What pleasures of the body can be compared to the prerogatives of influence?" Cowley does, however, point out the pleasures of the body and the mind that older persons can look forward to. Vanity can be avoided.

Pleasures include such nonstereotyped activities as simply sitting still "with a delicious feeling of indolence that was seldom attained in earlier years." The older person at such moments "has become a part of nature." The future does not exist for such a person; he is outside the battle. Meals, too, serve as "climactic moments of the day," and sleep "has become a definite pleasure, not the mere interruption it once had become." Those in nursing homes may be "busiest when their hands are still." The stream of "persons, images, phrases, and familiar tunes" play in their minds, combining their past with their present. They may "conduct silent dialogues with a vanished friend . . . often more rewarding than spoken conversations." These pleasures require inner resources, and for those lacking these, he comes back to find a project, a sense of purpose—not to give up.

Cowley does not exhibit any false hopes about aging, nor does he indulge in self-pity. Everyone wants to know the chances for living past eighty, so he cites the Census Bureau reports of 1978 that states that white males have a life expectancy of 6.7 years if they reach the age of eighty, white females 8.6 years, and black females 11.0 years. His considered opinion is that "without grave diseases or crippling accidents or inherited defects, and with a careful diet, the normal human life span might be about 90 years—a little more for women, a little less for men." He notices that artists, if they survive their early life, live "longer productive lives" than those in other callings. Apparently, what they do stirs the blood, and that is essential to long life. Fiction writers apparently live too "hypertensively in their imaginations," and they tend not to last long. Musicians, scientists, mathematicians, and philosophers seem long-enduring. Lawyers last long too, often by becoming judges. Cowley concludes from these observations that "a general rule might be that persons called upon to give sage advice—unless they are doctors—live longer than persons who act on that advice."

The question that obsesses Cowley is what to do with the years the Census Bureau "grudgingly allowed" the aged. He worries about the ones who let themselves be isolated in retirement communities or nursing homes—"often too soon"—"where they are left without an occupation to dignify their lives." He notes that the work force "won't take you back" and that "older persons are our great unutilized source of labor." "A growing weakness of American society is that it regards the old as consumers but not producers." Even that is an error, as he notes, for the retired enjoy an average income far below the national median—so they make poor consumers. He cites numerous examples of those who have found in their neighborhoods a niche of their own, "their work." "But at 80, what shall it be?"

He turns to books for guidance, yet, very few offer any personal experience. He finds that the few available writings were produced by men and women in their fifties or early sixties, "a time when most of them wanted to paint a bright prospect of their years to come." He recommends Alex Comfort's *A Good Age* as full of sound advice. Comfort agrees with Cowley: "What the retired need," he says, ". . . isn't leisure, it's occupation." Cowley thinks, however, that Comfort may be too tenderhearted about the prospects for long-continuing sexual energy. He regards Simone de Beauvoir's *The Coming of Age* as stressing the grim picture of age without giving attention to the compensations of old age. He recommends her book for its many fascinating anecdotes, which is not damning with faint praise.

At a time of life when social horizons narrow—old friends vanish and new ones are hard to find, entertaining visitors and making visits become problematic—the older person "is drawn back into himself." In this situation, Cowley offers a kind of wisdom from which at least ninety-eight percent of us can profit:

> Those who have led rich lives are rewarded by having richer memories. Those who have loved are more likely to be loved in return. In spite of accidents and ingratitude, those who have served others are a little more likely to be served.

Those who are selfish and heartless now "will suffer from the heartlessness of others, if they live long enough." The basic fears haunt many of the old— "declining into simplified versions of themselves" is one. If they once were habitually dissatisfied, "they become whiners and scolds." "If they were habitually kind, in age, they become, like Emerson, the image of benignity." Or they may fear becoming helpless, "the fear of being as dependent as a young child, while not being loved as a child is loved." Then there is the thought of death, often "less a fear than a stimulus to more intense living." The "'flaming thunderbolt' of imminent death sometimes rouses older persons to extraordinary efforts." He ought to know, for Cowley himself has shaped a life in his old age that is the envy of many a young man or woman at the peak of a career.

Each person, Cowley pronounces, must discover his own purpose. "Every old person needs a work project if he wants to keep himself more alive." The project "should be big enough to demand his best efforts, yet not so big as to dishearten him and let him fall back into apathy." he suggests that a *new* project calls upon "aspects of the personality that were formerly neglected and hence may release a new store of energy." Then there are those who take to painting or to speculating in Wall Street or to counseling or to caring for gardens. Whatever it is, he wonders whether we can all be artists, "each in his own fashion." The one project that tempts Cowley is "trying to find a shape or pattern in our lives." While our lives may seem random and "a monotonous series of incidents," "each of them has a plot." Cowley himself has set a lifetime series of good examples, from his first book in 1934 to this most recent one. First, one must untangle materials and memories and then arrange the stories in sequence. The result, as Cowley has found, "might lead to an absolutely candid book of memoirs." The old have "nothing to lose by telling the truth." The pursuit is fascinating and may "help us to possess our own identities." Perhaps, he says, we can say "I was and am *this*." Cowley himself has felt that he wasted his twenties by not writing the books of which he was capable. He has changed that pattern for the better and for the benefit of all.

Gary L. Harmon

THE VIKING WORLD

Author: James Graham-Campbell
With special sections by Sean McGrail, R. I. Page, and Christine Fell
Publisher: Ticknor & Fields (New Haven, Connecticut). Illustrated. 220 pp. $25.00
Type of work: History and archaeology
Time: The ninth to eleventh centuries
Locale: Europe, the North Sea, the North Atlantic, and North America

The history and culture of the Scandinavian people in the early Middle Ages of Europe, summarizing the findings of current archaeological and historial research in shipbuilding, exploration, trade, artwork, and literature

> *Principal personages:*
> GORM THE OLD, King of Denmark (died c. 950)
> HARALD BLUETOOTH, King of Denmark and Norway (died 986)
> EIRIK THE RED, discoverer and settler in Greenland, c. 985
> LEIF ERIKKSON, discoverer of "Vinland," c. 1000
> CNUT SVEINSSON (CANUTE THE GREAT), King of Denmark, Norway, and England, 1016-1035
> HARALD HARDRADA (HARD-RULER), King of Norway (died 1066)

The Anglo-Saxon Chronicle records that in the year A.D. 793, "ravaging of the heathen men miserably destroyed God's church at Lindisfarne through plunder and slaughter." Those heathen men were probably Norwegian Vikings who had crossed the North Sea to raid the Lindisfarne monastery. With that attack the age of the Vikings had commenced.

In the old Scandinavian language the word "viking" (or more accurately, "vikingr") meant pirate or raider. The word still conjures up a picture of hordes of ruthless barbarians descending on peaceful monasteries and coastal towns, bringing terror and destruction. "Stinging hornets," "fearful wolves," "wrathful, foreign, purely pagan people," are some of the epithets that Christian chroniclers of the early Middle Ages used to describe the Vikings. For well over two centuries, the Northmen massacred, burned, plundered, and enslaved the communities and people of Western Europe, leaving a permanent memory of havoc and horror. Furthermore, there is little doubt that the Vikings themselves delighted in their own bloodthirstiness: in the words of a tenth century Icelandic poet, "I've been with sword and spear slippery with bright blood where the kites wheeled. And how well we Vikings clashed! Red flames ate up men's roofs, raging we killed and killed; and skewered bodies sprawled sleepy in town gate-ways."

The attack on the Lindisfarne monastery was a hit-and-run affair, as were subsequent raids on other monasteries and towns on the east coast of England and Scotland in the next few years. Then, in the early ninth century, the Norwegian Vikings were joined by other pirates from Denmark, and the attacks on the British Isles became more frequent and were carried out by larger numbers. In the mid-ninth century, the Vikings began no longer to raid and return home but to establish permanent bases along the coasts of England and Scotland where they would spend the winter and prepare for new raids further inland in the following spring. According to the Anglo-Saxon Chronicle, in the year 865 "a great heathen army came to England and took up its winter quarters in East Anglia." In the following year that army moved to capture the English town of York, and within a few years had seized control of most of eastern England from York to London. The Vikings had come to settle and stay.

To the west, Norwegian and Danish Vikings commenced their raids on the east coast of Ireland in the mid-ninth century and soon, as in eastern England, they had established winter bases. One of these bases, called "Dubh-Linn," would, in time, become the chief settlement of the Scandinavians in Ireland, and the place from where they launched new raids up the rivers and along the coasts of Ireland.

The Viking attacks upon the continent of Europe also commenced in the mid-ninth century. As a monk of the Frankish monastery of Nourmoutier would write in the 860's, "the number of ships grows: the endless stream of Vikings never ceases . . . the Vikings plunder all in their path . . . Rouen is laid waste, plundered and burned: Paris, Beauvais, Meaux taken, Melun's strong fortress leveled to the ground. . . ."

Unable to drive the Vikings off, the local rulers of England and Frankland tried to bribe the raiders to leave the Christian communities in peace. The bribes were at first only one-time payoffs, but that seemed to have whetted the Viking appetite for more; so, they became regular periodic payments, known as the Dangeld. From contemporary French records, one learns that some thirteen Dangeld payments were made by the French kings in the ninth and tenth centuries, and that they totaled some seven hundred pounds of gold and more than forty-three thousand pounds of silver.

The causes or reasons for the aggressive irruptions of the Scandinavian Vikings in the ninth, tenth, and eleventh centuries can only be guessed. Certainly the search for wealth must have been a primary motivation. Pressures of increased population in the Scandinavian homelands apparently drove many to seek new land for settlement and stimulated what the Vikings called "landtaking": the seizure of additional territories. Also, it appears that strife among the warrior aristocracy in the Scandinavian kingdoms led many to become pirates and conquerors of distant lands.

More important, however, was the development of the famous Viking longships in the eighth century, which both stimulated and made possible the swift and successful raids from the Shannon to the Seine and from the Rhine to the Rhone over the next two hundred years. One of the longest chapters of *The Viking World* is therefore devoted to a detailed explanation of the construction of the longships and other Scandinavian vessels. Shipbuilding methods are explained, and drawings of typical ships are presented, based on recent and on-going archaeological discoveries in Scandinavian burial sites. It has been determined that the Vikings built ships of several different types, depending on whether they were to be used for raiding or trading. The longships were those built for speed. They were long and slender (approximately sixty feet by eight feet) with a very shallow draft which enabled them to make landings directly on beaches. They were primarily propelled by oars, but carried a short mast and square sail to be used when possible. Modern reconstructions of the longships have attained speeds of seven knots and more under oars. The Vikings themselves did the rowing and the navigation. They steered by the stars, the angle of the ocean swells, and the prevailing winds and landmarks. Using these beautifully designed, strongly built, and skillfully navigated ships, the Vikings would become the most accomplished seafarers of the North for some three hundred years.

Because the Viking raids were such dramatic, terrifying events, the contemporary chronicles rarely mention the equally important peaceful trading activities of the Northmen. Probably more of the Scandinavians, however, were engaged in the production and shipping of trade goods than ever engaged in piracy and plundering, and recent archaeological discoveries show that many more larger, slower trading vessels were built in the Viking Age than the longships. The Norwegians and the Danes appear to have continued to prefer piracy to commerce, but the Swedes, who were penetrating eastern Europe, went more often as merchants than as raiders. Scandinavian merchants traded furs, timber, jewelry, foodstuffs, and, most of all, slaves, for the precious metals and luxury goods of Eastern and Western Europe, and in so doing went deeply into Russia, the Byzantine Empire in the east, and the Islamic lands in the east and west.

In the year 980, a man called Eirik the Red was "after some killings," forced to flee from his home in southern Norway. He went to the Norwegian colony on Iceland from which, after "some more killings," he was banished. He and some of his followers sailed westward until they discovered Greenland and settled there. The settlements in Greenland flourished from the tenth to the twelfth centuries, and then went into a decline. By circa 1500, because of a combination of changing climatic conditions, diseases, and the decline in trade, the Scandinavians were forced to abandon the Greenland colony.

Around 985, Bjarni Herjolfson, another Viking leader, and his crew were sailing for Greenland when they became lost in a heavy fog and were blown off course by strong winds. After many days, they sighted a flat, wooded land which was not Greenland—it was probably the coast of North America. Bjarni Herjolfson did not attempt to hold that new land, but sailed back to Scandinavia. Not long after that, however, Leif the Lucky, the son of Eirik the Red, set out with the intention of finding that western land. It appears that Leif made his first landfall on the coast of Labrador, then journeyed southwesterly to a place that Leif called "Vinland." Modern scholars have speculated and investigated to try to determine the precise location of Vinland. In the year 1965, a map which purported to show Vinland as sketched by a Viking was produced in the United States. That map, however, has been rejected by experts as a forgery. Archaeologists have determined that there was a Norse settlement established in northern Newfoundland, but that it was the elusive Vinland cannot be affirmed with certainty. Nevertheless, by the eleventh century, there were Scandinavian settlements all across the northern hemisphere, from Newfoundland to Novgorod in Russia, from Greenland to Normandy.

Our knowledge of the Vikings comes from several sources: excavations of some of their towns and trading centers; studies of their graves, especially the royal graves; their surviving poetry; and runic inscriptions. Among the towns and other sites that have been excavated are Trondheim and Kaupang in Norway, Lund in Sweden, York in England, Dublin in Ireland, and most recently (1979), the headquarters of Danish kings at Hedeby in what is now Schleswig in northern Germany. These excavations and the other sources reveal that the Scandinavian society in the Viking Age was aristocratic in structure. At the top were kings or princes who ruled over lesser chieftains called "jarls." The jarls, in turn, headed the warrior bands which were drawn from the freemen of their localities. The freeman (called "karler") made up the largest group of the Scandinavian society. Some of them were Viking pirates and raiders, but most were farmers, hunters, trappers, fishermen, and artisans. There were also numerous slaves (called "proell") who had few, if any, rights and were regarded with scorn by the freemen.

Throughout Scandinavia, in the homelands and in the colonies, the rule of the kings was limited by periodic public assemblies of freemen. Each assembly was called a "Thing." In those Things the customary law was administered, new legislation formulated, and a new king or prince elected when necessary. Kingship generally was hereditary within a royal family, but the succession from father to son was not assured in every case. Any prospective new king had to be approved by the freemen meeting at the various Things within the kingdom.

One of the earliest of the kings of Denmark in the Viking Age was called Gorm the Old. Much of what is known about Gorm the Old is now regarded as myth and legend, but it appears that for some two decades he held the kingdom of Denmark together, raised a family memorial stone, and sired a line of powerful kings.

Gorm's son and successor was Harald Bluetooth who extended his authority over both Denmark and Norway, and permitted Christian missionaries to convert his subjects. Still more prominent was Harald Bluetooth's grandson, Cnut Sveinsson (also known as Canute the Great). Cnut was king of Denmark, Norway, and England, and his supremacy over Sweden was also acknowledged so that he "came nearer than anybody to establishing a real North Sea empire." The conversion of the Scandinavians to Christianity continued under Cnut, while artistic and literary influences from England and the Continent were steadily changing the culture of the Northmen. Those influneces continued even after the death of Cnut in 1035 and the collapse of his personal empire.

Probably the most memorable of the Norwegian kings was Harald Hardrada. He was half brother to the sainted King Olaf—one of the first Christian martyrs among the Norwegians. On the death of Olaf, Harald fled to Constantinople where he joined the famous Varangian Guard, those Scandinavian mercenaries who defended the eastern Christian emperors. In 1046, Harald returned to Norway and shortly after was able to gain rule over the whole kingdom. He sought to add Denmark to his Norwegian kingdom, but he failed. Harald then turned against England by invading Yorkshire in 1066. From the south, the English king Harold rode to meet Hardrada at Stamford Bridge. Harald Hardarda was defeated and killed. It may be said that with that event the Viking Age ended.

There is in *The Viking World* a rather extensive chapter on Viking art, especially the ornamental wood carvings. Another chapter considers the Scandinavian runes and runic writing. It is not known when or where the runic alphabet originated, but by the Viking Age a runic alphabet of sixteen characters was in use. The runes were used for many purposes: memorials, boundary markers, ownership marks, and magic formulae. They were inscribed on stone, or metal, or even painted. Rune-inscribed stones have been found all over Scandinavia, in England and Ireland, and even as far away as Constantinople where, on a marble ledge in the church of Hagia Sophia, some proper names in runic have been carved. No runic inscriptions have ever been found in America. A few years ago, there appeared the Kensington stone which purportedly was a runic writing left by a group of Swedes and Norwegians in Minnesota in 1362. Investigation has shown the Kensington stone to be a fraud.

The latter chapters of *The Viking World* deal with Viking poets ("skalds") and their poetry and with a brief consideration of early Norse religion. Here some of the stories of Odin and Thor, Freya and the Valkyries, and Valholl, the home of gods and heroes, are explained. By the tenth century, the worship of the old gods was passing among the Northmen, supplanted by the Christian religion. As early as 986, Harald Bluetooth asserted that he had made the Danes Christians and built a stone church at Jelling, Denmark, to mark the new dispensation. Iceland was converted to Christianity by circa 1000; England, Ireland, and Normandy were all Christian by then as well. The book concludes with a description of the building of early Christian churches in Scandinavia as examples of the triumph of that faith in the lands of the Vikings.

The authors of *The Viking World* have done a first-rate job in summarizing the essence of the culture and character of the Vikings. The narrative is clearly written, the photographs are abundant and appropriate, the maps and illustrative drawings are well done. In all, this is an excellent introduction to a subject which continues to fascinate many readers.

James W. Pringle

WALLACE STEVENS
A Celebration

Editors: Frank Doggett and Robert Buttel
Publisher: Princeton University Press (Princeton, New Jersey). 361 pp. $22.50
Type of work: Essays

Honoring the centennial of Stevens' birth, this volume presents a variety of biographical and critical essays by many of Stevens' best-known critics

Whether Wallace Stevens should be considered America's foremost twentieth century poet remains open to critical conjecture, the kind of deliberation that affects the average person not one whit. Undeniably, his work looms large, precursor with whom any serious later poet must contend if, as Harold Bloom would assert, that later poet is to claim supremacy in our poetic affections. Certainly his work presents the complexity, subtlety, and originality one expects from a great poet whose vision encompasses the philosophical concerns of the age. Undoubtedly, Stevens' versatility and craftsmanship with language remain unparalleled among modern poets. Together, these qualities gain Stevens high esteem among students of poetry, although they impress most people not at all.

As a matter of fact, what most impresses people even aware of the name Wallace Stevens is that he was a somewhat unpoetic figure for a poet, being a businessman-lawyer for an insurance company. Such incongruity disturbs expectations, calls to question the system of values usually associated with poets, and makes one wonder about the sincerity of the poetry. The poetry, furthermore, seems too complicated, beyond average comprehension, and generally inaccessible given the degree of effort the average person will expend to read a poem, much less understand it. In sum, then, Wallace Stevens raises a great many questions about the notion of what a poet is.

He does this even for students who admire his work and try to come to terms with it. They ask how the creator of works such as *Harmonium* could possibly spend his days in the mundane chores of the insurance business, how he could hold in mind simultaneously legal matters, financial matters, and the sublime matters of art and imagination. Drawn into the beauties of wordplay and intricate rhythms, they question from whence came the inspiration—not the insurance business, they assume. Their questioning has not been eased to any great degree by Stevens, who seemed to make a real effort to separate his public poetic life from his private personal and business lives. At only a few points in the great body of Stevens' work does any sense of the poet as personage come through in any but shadowy images. In fact, more often than not, the reader will find himself mislead by suggestions of who the poet is. Stevens wanted this; perhaps it would be more accurate to say he needed to create the false images to preseve himself. Students, of course, are left shaking their heads in wonder at the seeming conflict.

Wallace Stevens: A Celebration should disabuse and educate those literary purists who persist in the romantic notions of what constitutes a poet, for here, the reader has a collection that does more than enough to explain why Wallace Stevens was who he was. Combining biography and literary criticism, the volume reveals the poet's many sides. Wilson Taylor states the matter aptly when he says, "Stevens was truly a diamond of many facets." Continually the book shows the quotidian concerns that fill a life, even the life of a supremely talented poet whose primary passion was poetry and other literary achievements. Selected letters to Wilson Taylor, for instance, show Stevens dealing with the world in ways everyone must, as he orders boxes of prunes and apricots for the winter, sends payment for a book Taylor purchased for him, and laments problems with having a geneology drawn up by a woman who never did finish.

A biographical piece by Taylor describes Stevens' duties for the Hartford Accident and Indemnity Company as a surety lawyer. Taylor speaks of the relationships Stevens had with coworkers and subordinates, the witty and humane way that he handled daily life at the office. One gets the impression from these passages that the whole man was always present in every instance, pursuing a consistent course of action and essentially untroubled by what seems from the outside to be a bifurcation. As Taylor points out, Stevens' life as a corporate executive was only a means to an end, the end being a comfortable life for his family and the opportunity to write poetry without financial hardship's constant distraction. Taylor recalls that Stevens only rarely mentioned his poetry but that he found ample release for his wit within the demands of meetings, correspondence, and personal conversation. Socially, he loved business lunches and dined with a wide range of acquaintances, especially while in New York, where company business took him often.

Peter Brazeau informs the reader that Stevens enjoyed acting the role of man-about-town and took advantage of all the cultural amenities that New York offered: theaters, art exhibits, concerts, fine restaurants. Usually when in town for business, he dispatched the business as promptly as possible to leave ample time to embark on whatever cultural expedition he had in mind. He also greatly enjoyed the New York nightlife with its dancing and drinking entertainments. Another pastime was shopping, especially in out of the way shops and delicatessens where unique articles and pastries could be found.

Holly Stevens' biographical piece, "Holidays in Reality," presents yet another side of the poet's life, discussing vacations and excursions the Stevenses took to Maine, New York, Florida, and in Hartford itself. She remembers, for example, encounters with labor leader John L. Lewis and the poet Robert Frost at Casa Marina in Key West, where the Stevens family went fairly regularly. Once Holly went to an afternoon cocktail party with Frost, without her parents' knowledge and to Frost's delight that he had put one over on Stevens. Although she spent the party sipping ginger ale in a corner and merely observed the general revelry, Holly points out that her enjoyment derived from the occasion's novelty, because her parents seldom entertained at home. Her fond memories of the family outings support the contention that Stevens was a devoted family man and that the family was a close one filled with warmth. She closes her essay by giving an insight to the poet's life, an insight that fits perhaps the image readers should have of the poet at his leisure in the nearby city park, where he spent some time almost every day.

> It provided a perennial vacation at hand; where he could meet old friends, or make new ones; where he could revisit familiar spots but could always find something new; where ideas could come and breed and grow; where the poet could enjoy a needed solitude or bring his family. It was a place for "finding of a satisfaction, and may / Be of a man skating, . . . a woman / Combing. . . ."

Readers are bound to celebrate this volume's perspective, which humanizes the literary figure, for it makes plausible the poetry's creation, which seemed to be the product of an enigma. It does this while providing a range of critical essays and approaches representative of Stevens criticism. The effect is interesting, because the combination of biographical and literary examinations accentuates the multifaceted personality evident in the poetry. Stevens' poetic complexity and personal complexity, then, are paralleled, editors Frank Doggett and Robert Buttel having leavened the sometimes arcane literary criticism with personal observations by those close to the poet. Several previously unpublished manuscripts appear in the book also, to give the flavor of Stevens' creative process and the changes of mind that produced his art. Overall, the book succeeds in gathering together disparate elements to illuminate what was a shadowy figure.

To an extent, all the critical articles in *Wallace Stevens: A Celebration* assist this effort, although obviously some articles do a better job than others, the others couching their arguments in the pompous obscurity so prevalent among scholarly writings. "Particles of Order: The Unpublished *Adagia*" by A. Walton Litz takes a look at the notebooks Stevens compiled beginning in the early 1930's. Here Stevens recorded quotations and sayings he had encountered in his rather eclectic reading. Litz also examines Stevens' library, noting the heavy concentration on sagacious sayings. Readers learn, for example, that Stevens acquired more than thirty collections of aphorisms, proverbs, or pithy journal entries, and that these formed a substantial portion of his working library. Readers are shown connections between Stevens' own informal notebook collection of aphorisms and his poetry. The point is reinforced that "Stevens' poetry, from beginning to end, is filled with memorable aphorisms around which the tentative arguments revolve." Certainly, the fact that "the *Adagia* were the end result of a lifelong passion for aphoristic statements and gnomic utterances" makes them a valuable part of our knowledge of Stevens and his work.

In another dimension, several of the critical articles examine Stevens' poetics, the play of theory and technique that makes Stevens' work a densely fertile ground for investigation. That he brought to bear in his work the diverse intellectual currents available to the twentieth century mind, that he fashioned these currents into an intensely discursive poetry, and that he managed at the same time to delight in the sensual images and effects of language within the ponderous heaviness of philosophical discourse give his poetry first-class stature. Ultimately, of course, it is the diversity of effects that astonishes most Stevens' readers. The depth of intellectual pondering is only one characteristic. As Irvin Ehrenpreis points out, "Stevens' best poems are those that draw and hold us by their surface."

These surfaces glitter and truly deserve the critical attention given them in this volume and in all the volumes of criticism amassed over the years. Stevens' verbal dexterity never ceases to amaze poetry students, whether they applaud or abhor the poet's stance and tone of voice. His handling of ideas, the complexity of thought evident consistently throughout his work, challenges a response, but the necessary response must be a learned one, the result of more than a casual passage through a particular poem—in other words, more than the usual attention readers, young ones especially, give to poetry. Stevens' poems beg for a return engagement, a chance to open themselves to interpretation, precisely because their surfaces provide dense imagery, exotic locutions, and philosophical juxtapositions that startle and intrigue. They therefore also benefit from critical explication, the product of trained minds looking with experience and a breadth of understanding commensurate with the broad knowledge and vision of the poet.

Wallace Stevens: A Celebration, then, does two things well. It addresses the poetry with the scholarly apparatus necessary to lay bare Stevens' extraordinary art, to make accessible its implications and to make clear its significance to twentieth century poetic development. Moreover, this volume addresses the character of the poet which brings the reader a step, an important step, closer to understanding the mind and experience that produced such a fine body of work. Probably this is the book's greatest achievement, for the wealth of criticism available on Stevens has no appeal for the average reader, indeed ignores most readers' needs. The desire to know the man, however, to touch in some small way his experience, can be satisfied by the entertaining and informative biographical pieces offered here.

Gary B. Blank

WALT WHITMAN
A Life

Author: Justin Kaplan (1925-   )
Publisher: Simon and Schuster (New York). Illustrated. 429 pp. $13.95
Type of work: Literary biography
Time: 1819-1892
Locale: The United States, primarily New York and Washington, D. C.

An account of Whitman's poetry in the context of his life and times, this volume recounts Whitman's role in the tumultuous events of American history in the nineteenth century and his record of its complex coming-of-age in his Leaves of Grass

The United States has always had a peculiar love-hate relationship with its artists, one that grows out of one's complex and often contradictory national identity. If, on the one hand, one aspires to noble ideals of national life and destiny such as those recorded in the Declaration of Independence, bequeathed by the philosophers of the Enlightenment, one also espouses a boundless opportunism that has little time for the life of the mind. If people profess devotion to freedom and human dignity, the national experience has all too often brought out a narrowness and meanness of spirit that manifests itself in the crudest of provincialisms and jingoistic patriotism. Cities, in part, participate in the international life of culture and the arts, while small towns and rural areas, in part, revel in isolationism and suspicion of all that is foreign and different.

It is, perhaps, both ironic and appropriate that of all the great American artists Walt Whitman has received far more than his share of the consequences of so complex and contradictory a cultural mix. For Whitman was the poet of American exuberance, of American optimism, of the deeply ingrained sense that America represented a new chance for European humanity to live up to its great ideals. Whitman celebrated that America in his great epic poem *Song of Myself* and its attendant volume *Leaves of Grass*. In doing so, he drew on the great poetic models of national identity in the West—the classical epics of the Bible—but he transformed them into a form and a voice and a language distinctively American. As a result, those provincial nineteenth century American intellectuals, who looked to Europe for their sense of culture, could not grasp the value of his achievement. The audience of mass America, the common people whom Whitman celebrated in his work, could not respond either, for he asked of them a degree of self-awareness and self-celebration which they were incapable of achieving. Hence, he faced, with courage and self-confidence, the attacks of the prudish and the proverbial.

Ironically, the problem continues. Whitman did have his influence on twentieth century American poets, but only indirectly, through his influence on European writers whom Americans then copied. Canons of critical taste through much of the twentieth century had little use for Whitman's prose-like rhythms, his unabashed romantic love-affair with America, his seemingly uncontrolled rush of language. Yet, Whitman remains an authentically American poetic voice, perhaps before the 1930's the greatest poet America has produced. To get at the heart of the American character, readers must deal with him.

Justin Kaplan's biography is a significant step in that direction, and readers must be grateful for it. If it has a weakness, it is in its failure to deal critically with Whitman's poetry, but that is perhaps because there is as yet no critical language appropriate to it. Here, the poetry comes all too frequently as commentary on Whitman's life, rather than as the subject of revealing commentary. Instead, Kaplan provides perhaps the clearest and most revealing picture yet of Whitman the man in the context of his times. The reader sees him moving among the economic, social, and political turmoil that was to culminate in the Civil War. He is seen amidst the literary figures of his age— Ralph Waldo Emerson, Henry David Thoreau, James Russell Lowell, and the rest. He is seen in his own family situation—the economic and personal struggles, and Walt's role in attempting to meet them. What comes through is a vivid portrait of Whitman the man, in all his complexities and contradictions.

One point should be dealt with immediately—the question of Whitman's sexual orientation. Although Kaplan never states explicitly, what comes through his discussion of the evidence is that Whitman was probably homosexual in orientation, although never in practice. Whitman's comments about having children, used by many to argue for his heterosexual orientation, dissolve into conventional ways of saying that he had many people he felt paternal toward. The homoerotic passages in his poetry, as well as his many close friendships with men and his coolness toward women, make clear the direction of his sexual feelings. At the same time, however, the evidence used by many to argue that he was a practicing homosexual also dissolves into gossip, conjecture, and overreading of ambivalent passages. What Kaplan makes clear is that Whitman kept his sexual expression under tight reign, often at great personal cost.

What upset so many nineteenth century Americans was not Whitman's homosexuality, but his sexuality, his celebration of himself as a sexual being, and his celebration of all humanity as sexual. In the context of nineteenth century repression of that dimension of humanness, Whitman's avowal of sexuality as a natural part of human life was more than many could tolerate. The eroticism of his verse cost him at least one government job, and made distribution of his work often difficult to achieve. More than one publisher rejected his work on only those grounds, turning him down when Whitman refused to allow the eroticism to be cut from his work. In an epic confrontation which Kaplan dramatically describes, Whitman and Emerson spent the good part of a day wandering around Boston Common discussing the issue. Emerson, who, uniquely among American intellectuals, had praised the first edition of *Leaves of Grass*, urged Whitman to allow his work to be expurgated for the sake of getting it published. Whitman refused, and the relationship between the two men was never again so cordial.

Indeed, the central theme that comes through Kaplan's work is Whitman's abiding sense of confidence in himself and in his poetry. That sustained him through a long and often difficult life filled with economic uncertainty and little critical acclaim. Kaplan traces the history of that confidence through a series of vividly realized scenes similar to the one of Whitman and Emerson roaming Boston Common: Whitman meeting Thoreau in a small room of the Whitman home, Whitman among the literary figures of New York, Whitman tending the Civil War wounded, Whitman watching Abraham Lincoln in Washington and mourning his death, and so on. Each of these scenes reveals Kaplan's affection for his subject and gives readers striking images of "the good, grey poet" to take away.

The strength of this book, therefore, lies in its ability to evoke an image of nineteenth century America and Whitman as a man and poet within it. Kaplan clarifies Whitman's role as a poet of America while creating a vivid picture of his times. His story is a good one, and he tells it with vigor and energy.

John N. Wall, Jr.

WALTER LIPPMANN AND THE AMERICAN CENTURY

Author: Ronald Steel (1931-   )
Publisher: Little, Brown and Company (Boston). 669 pp. $19.95
Type of work: Biography
Time: The twentieth century
Locale: Primarily Washington, D. C., and New York City

A heavily documented study of Walter Lippmann, the greatest journalist of this century, a counselor of presidents and kings, whose later years were spent trying to bring an end to a divisive war

> *Principal personages:*
> WALTER LIPPMANN, a very important and widely known American journalist
> THEODORE ROOSEVELT, twenty-sixth President of the United States, 1901-1909, and a hero of Lippmann
> FRANKLIN DELANO ROOSEVELT, thirty-second President of the United States, 1933-1945, who was first lionized then later criticized by Lippmann
> LYNDON BAINES JOHNSON, thirty-sixth President of the United States, 1963-1969, who first attracted then repelled Lippmann

During the twentieth century, American journalism has come into its own. Its hallmarks are terseness, clarity, and economy of phrase, and its greatest practitioners have been called artists in their own right. The magnitude of the talent of journalists such as Walter Winchell and Stewart Alsop makes them far more than mere reporters of the world's important events: they are artists in their own right, interpreting the news of the day, and finding in it the seeds of future events. As true artists, they, like the best novelists, not only have the power to sway emotions and make readers dream dreams of a better world, but they also have, the great journalists, the power actually to effect the outcome of world events because their readers include the mighty few who wield real power. Ronald Steel, professor and an author of several books about politics and foreign affairs, has written what may be the definitive study of the finest of all American journalists: Walter Lippmann, the trusted confidant of many of the twentieth century's movers and shakers.

As with almost any life that has transcended the ordinary, Lippmann's is a study in agony and ecstasy, the agony often coming from his having been at loggerheads with presidents with whom he would rather be friends, or his having been betrayed by those whom he trusted. What inspired him most, on the other hand, was the acquiring of influence over the powerful leaders of the most powerful nations on either side of the "Iron Curtain." "Influence," as Steel says, "was Lippmann's stock in trade; was what made him a . . . public figure."

Influence came slowly but steadily as Lippmann gained readers and stature; and, since there were few writers who could coherently discuss complicated foreign and domestic affairs day after day, he could not help but be noticed.

The influence he acquired gave him substantial leverage with decisionmakers which, in turn, allowed him to help make decisions affecting millions. As Steel points out, however, it is impossible to ascertain exactly how many decisions were made because of what Lippmann wrote, for he possessed the intangible power of the pen rather than more discernible powers. What is known is that Lippmann was widely quoted—perhaps more so than any other journalist—in high circles and that presidents, prime ministers, and princes vied for his attention. Such people came to him because, Steel speculates, "they literally did not know what they ought to think about the issues of the day."

Lippmann was a Jew in a Gentile world, but he never seemed to feel out of place. In fact, it is pointed out, he adopted the viewpoints, habits, and speech patterns of white Anglo-Saxon Protestants and spurned anything that would mark him as Jewish. Lippmann was surprizingly uninterested in the idea of a Jewish homeland, even after hearing about the deathcamps of Adolf Hitler's Germany.

As a young man, Lippmann started his career in those relatively halcyon days prior to the bloodbath of World War I. That he began writing before the war explains his confidence in man's betterment and belief in progress, views that those who grew up with the Great War and its aftermath found impossible to hold. Throughout his career, he would be ever the optimist, believing that somehow right would triumph over might and good win over evil.

After the War ended in 1919, the Western world was completely changed. The complacent world view held by leaders of the nineteenth century was smashed on the battlefields of Ypres and the Somme. New ideologies came to the fore and people needed to know all about them. Bolshevism, socialism, and other "isms" demanded explanation. People wanted to know where events were leading, what would come next, and who would be doing the governing. Since man had revealed himself to be an unimaginably base and bloody minded creature in the Great War, all things were in doubt. Gone forever was the notion that mankind was perfectible. Now the question was, "Is the human race going to destroy itself with the terrible weapons it has created?" Luckily for those who asked such questions, Lippmann had come on the scene.

Until the advent of television news in the early 1950's, persons in need of advice and direction turned to newspapers like the New York *World* featuring great columnists such as Lippmann. Lippmann's wry, analytical columns had a devoted following. Readers were particularly impressed by his detachment from the events he discussed; and yet, he was far from a distant observer of the political arena.

Steel stresses the point that Lippmann was both a man of thought and a man of action. It did not matter which president was in power—Franklin D.

Roosevelt, Harry S Truman, John F. Kennedy, or whomever—Lippmann tried to get as close as possible to him. He eagerly sought invitations to the White House, and, depending upon who was in office, he often was extended the invitation. When he went to the White House, he went to give those in power the benefit of his advice. He wanted them to turn his advice into policy and, many times, they did. Additionally, he wrote speeches for political candidates such as Al Smith and John W. Davis and served as unoffical adviser to Kennedy in the early days of his presidency.

Like any other politician, Lippmann wanted to wield power, but unlike other politicians, he did not want to run for office (although at one time his name came up for discussion). His behind-the-scenes lobbying sometimes backfired, leaving him alienated from those at the seat of power. Among those whom he offended were Franklin D. Roosevelt, Harry Truman, and Lyndon Johnson. Basically, he liked Roosevelt, although he quarreled with many of his programs, but he distinctly disliked Truman and Johnson, both of whom he blasted on several occasions.

His marvelously complete education at London, Carlsbad, Germany, and St. Moritz, Switzerland, as well as later study at Harvard splendidly equipped him to communicate with those in power positions. Hand in hand with a superb conversational ability went a corresponding talent for vivid written expression.

Whether writing for the *World*, *The New York Herald Tribune*, *The New Republic*, or *Newsweek*, Lippmann was always airing his most deeply held beliefs. Of Russia, he would say that because of the Western powers belligerence toward that nation at Yalta, it was forced to drop the "Iron Curtain" on Eastern Europe in 1945. He believed in a balance of power between the United States and her Soviet adversary, which would insure the peace of the world. Too many weapons held by one side could intimidate the other side and drive it to war.

He detested the Truman Doctrine and other doctrines like it which seemed to "Open the door to unlimited intervention" on the part of the United States. He correspondingly advocated the abolition of sweeping global policies, choosing to substitute in their place more particularized doctrines aimed at limited regions such as the Mideast or Southern Africa. By limiting the scope of American policy, a president would be able to avoid overextending United States military forces.

Furthermore, he advocated using American troops only when the occasion called for them; that is, when some nation vital to the West was being taken over by Communists. To Lippmann, the Republic of South Vietnam was not a nation vital to American or Western European interests. Yet early, he sensed that President Kennedy wanted to prove something in Vietnam, wanted to do what the defeated French were unable to do: destroy the Communist threat from the North. In agony, Lippmann spent his last years watching three presidents allow American troops to become victims of a war which was neither important to American interests nor winnable. He was especially distraught over Johnson's refusal to listen to his advice about getting the United States out of Vietnam.

What he felt America needed most in the dark days of the Vietnam conflict was a leader like his supreme hero, General Charles de Gaulle of France, a man who was a living symbol for his country. Thoroughly disillusioned with the run of American presidents since Roosevelt's death in 1945, Lippmann longed for someone who had the almost supernatural aura of de Gaulle, a real leader who would inspire his people to build a truly great society. Lippmann, unfortunately, died in 1974, the year of Watergate, one of the lowest points in American history. The man who longed for a leader of lofty stature last saw in the presidency Richard Nixon, one of the most flawed of presidents.

Ideologically, Lippmann began his career as a liberal who often called himself a "radical," then gradually, he became more conservative. At the end of his life, he could best be described as a liberal on foreign affairs and a moderate on domestic ones. Writing for *Newsweek*, he would always manage to find some sunbeams coming through the clouds. As upset as he became over the state of his nation, Lippmann never really doubted the decency and good sense of the American people, and he conveyed that confidence to his readers.

John D. Raymer

WAR WITHIN AND WITHOUT
Diaries and Letters of Anne Morrow Lindbergh, 1939-1944

Author: Anne Morrow Lindbergh (1906-   )
Publisher: Harcourt Brace Jovanovich (New York). 471 pp. $14.95
Type of work: Diaries and letters
Time: 1939-1944
Locale: New Jersey; Long Island; Martha's Vineyard; Bloomfield Hills, Michigan; and Connecticut

The self-portrait of a famous but intensely private woman, tracing her involvement in the American isolationist movement as well as her struggles as an emerging writer and young mother in a country for which she felt both disaffection and attachment

Principal personages:
ANNE MORROW LINDBERGH
CHARLES A. LINDBERGH, her husband
CONSTANCE CUTTER MORROW MORGAN, her sister
ELIZABETH CUTTER MORROW, her mother

Anne Morrow Lindbergh, renowned a generation ago as the wife of Charles Lindbergh and mother of the fated kidnaped baby, is now beginning to take her own place in American letters. With the publication in the past nine years of five volumes of her letters and diaries, the remarkable inner self of Anne Morrow Lindbergh has gained expression.

Although she has been a writer of essays and novels for five decades, Lindbergh has not enjoyed much critical recognition. For its symbolic meditations on the role of the modern woman, *Gift from the Sea* (1955) has enjoyed the most popularity and acclaim. Her occasional and travel pieces, essays in defense of her prewar isolationist position, her two novels and one book of poetry have received little attention. *War Within and Without: Diaries and Letters of Anne Morrow Lindbergh, 1939-1944* completes an autobiographical series which covers the period from Lindbergh's adolescence and college days at Smith College through her marriage and childbearing years to the end of World War II. *Bring Me a Unicorn* (1922-1928), published in 1971, describes her education, ending with her meeting Charles Lindbergh in Mexico, where her father was ambassador. *Hour of Gold, Hour of Lead* (1929-1932), published in 1973, recounts her sudden fame as Lindbergh's fiancée, their marriage, and the flights (for which she was navigator) opening up transworld air routes. The second half of that volume covers the senseless kidnaping and her grief in its aftermath; the book ends with the miracle of birth, that of her second son. *Locked Rooms and Open Doors* (1933-1935), appearing in 1974, covers her return to flying, the family's struggle with publicity, and the attempt to lead a normal, secure life. The volume ends with the voyage to England to begin a four-year sojourn as voluntary expatriots. *The Flower and the Nettle* (1936-1939), published 1976, chronicles the years in England and France, the beginning of her publishing career, the Lindbergh's involvement in diplomatic circles abroad, and the birth of another son, Land.

War Within and Without concerns her return to America, her involvement with the prewar isolationist movement, her frequent relocations, her writing difficulties, and the birth of two more children during World War II. Much more of this volume is composed of diary entries, thus giving an intensely introspective and private view. The earliest volumes were mostly letters written to family members and close friends; with the publicity hounds at her door, she censored her own communications, and so the material is not fully revealing. Her earlier volumes were full of tales of flying and descriptions from exotic cultures—northern Siberia, Alaska, or China—where she and Charles were the first white faces ever seen, coming out of the air in a tiny seaplane. In the early 1930's, she had gained a certain notoriety as her husband's flight partner. She had flown cross-country when seven months pregnant, donned the heavy boots and regalia of the flying suit, and accepted the physical rigors of primitive aviation. In this volume, that robust life has disappeared; now she is domestic and only semi-public; there is little physicality (beyond giving birth) to her existence. She almost seems another person. She completely supports Charles' public life, helps him with his speeches, attends and gives receptions, but stays in the background, filling her life with writing, children, decorating, and gardening—and seems not at all frustrated except when she is unable to keep up with her writing.

In her Introduction to *War Within and Without*, Lindbergh glosses the prewar period with its "great debate" over United States involvement in World War II. This era—from about 1938 to 1941—is, claims Lindbergh, almost totally lost from history as most people have forgotten the passion with which many Americans, most of them *not* pacifists, argued for an isolationist position. The Lindberghs returned from Europe committed, like many intellectuals, to that stance. Charles was later to become heavily involved in the America First movement, an organization devoted to keeping the United States out of the war, urging a negotiated peace, and protecting representative government. The issue of the undeclared war has plagued every president from Roosevelt forward; Korea, Vietnam, and El Salvador show the continued relevance of the debate.

The isolationist movement brought together a strange mix of people—Quakers, other pacifists, American Legionnaires, labor organizers, and right-wingers of various sorts. Some of Lindbergh's most perspicacious writing in this volume comes in her descriptions of various leaders of the movement. She tellingly notes that the socialist leader Norman Thomas becomes "inflamed about 'Humanity' but not about men as individuals, only as workers, as sufferers, as classes. He does not really love *men*, only 'Mankind.'"

Her own public involvement was minimal (she never officially joined "America First"), but she supported her husband throughout and wrote several important essays on the subject. *The Wave of the Future* (1940) gave the moral argument for isolationism; the book's proceeds went to the Quakers, the group she most admired. Near the end of 1941, she did disagree with Charles's allegation that the Jews were one of the groups pressuring the United States toward war. She correctly foresaw that he would be crucified by public opinion and called anti-Semitic, Fascist, and Nazi. After Pearl Harbor, of course, the movement became anachronistic, and Charles Lindbergh immediately issued a statement calling for the complete support of the war effort. He himself became an adviser to the bomber factory at Willow Run, Michigan, and later tested planes in the Pacific.

Anne's own position during this period was colored by her self-identification as a European-American. Quizzical and ambivalent toward Americans, she felt more at home with Europeans. A visit to the National Gallery was refreshing because it felt like Europe again. In her diary entries about the war's progress, she always wonders how the various European nationalities are reacting. A good example of her ambivalence is her attitude toward the Food for Europe program begun after the fall of France. Many felt that this program would only enhance the German position; starving Belgians or Frenchmen, they reasoned, would hamper the German military. Lindbergh, with her sympathy for the individual, could not countenance a view in which the end justified the means.

While many of Anne Morrow Lindbergh's letters and diary entries are concerned with the isolationist controversy, the bulk of the work is devoted to the persistent conflict between her dual professions: wife-mother-homemaker and writer. Lindbergh went to Smith College during an era of expanding educational opportunities for women. Her mother, in fact, as a member of the Board of Trustees, became an interim president of the college in the 1930's; her great theme in life was "education for women." Women of Anne's generation and class came to expect education—not so much as a passport to a career but as a necessary prelude to marriage and motherhood. For two generations following, American women were to be frustrated by the curious message they received: "Get an education, but stay at home and run your household; use your education for your children and your husband; do not put career aspirations ahead of the other demands of your life."

Anne Morrow Lindbergh perfectly reflects this attitude. She considers her writing her "work" and is sustained in this by her husband and her circumstances (the household employed a secretary, a nanny, and a cook, often a housekeeper and a gardener as well). At every location she had a "room of her own" for her writing: a tent on Martha's Vineyard, a barn on Long Island, a trailer in Michigan. Only on Wednesdays did she assume the care of her children. She was plagued, however, by guilt feelings; she went through periods of depression, feelings of inadequacy about both writings and parenting, writer's block, ambivalence about having another child. She says that, ironically, when she ceases writing and becomes a full-time mother, she feels no frustration: it is the transition that is so difficult, the interruption. Yet, the following week she can write, "I want to stop being good housekeeper. . . . I want to go back again to being a *bad* housekeeper and a *good* writer." Lindbergh is most perceptive as she writes about the Superwoman trap— wanting to do everything well and knowing that it is impossible.

Still, the work (writing) provided the greatest satisfaction though, and cost her the most. Significantly, the volume contains (according to the index) sixty-two entries on writing. In many ways, the book is comparable to other writers' diaries, those of Virginia Woolf, for example, or Anaïs Nin. Lindbergh chronicles the frustrations and joys of writing and rewriting, of the excitement of working *well* when all the "little and great bits" come together, of giving up everything to write—"children, people, Christmas." She knows all too well that "[writing] can *never* be taken lightly, never. Its cost is always in your lifeblood." The writing, however, will continue because it serves so vital a purpose:

> One writes to think, to pray, to analyze. One writes to clear one's mind, to dissipate one's fears, to face one's doubts, to look at one's mistakes—in order to retrieve them. One writes to capture and crystallize one's joy, but also to analyze and disperse one's gloom.

Surely, there is no better statement of the process and importance of writing.

The French flyer and writer Antoine de Saint-Exupéry became a friend in 1939. Lindbergh was ecstatic when he visited her home, for here at last was a creative, professional relationship. She felt she was finally being taken seriously as a writer in her own right. Her warm feelings for Saint-Exupéry continued, although she was not to see him again (he was killed in 1944); she often mused on their differing attitudes toward the war and how they would relate were they to meet again.

Although she often recounts the trials of motherhood and her own feelings of maternal inadequacy; no clear picture of her four children emerges. Occasionally, there is a description that "captures" the child, but for the most part the book is about self and marriage. She does detail the birth of Scott in 1942, when during labor she used a photograph of an Indian mask to focus her mind and her breathing, refusing "the gas" continually offered, understanding that losing consciousness would rob her of her strength as well as her awareness. Finally, she was persuaded to use anaesthesia and dreamed vividly during the brief minutes of unconsciousness. "Natural" childbirth was very unusual at this period, and Lindbergh shows herself to be ahead of her time.

She was completely devoted to her relationship with Charles. Incomplete without him, she lived a waiting game while he was away. She seems to have had few friends of her own and relied on her family a great deal. Their marriage was perhaps best symbolized by their nightly walk. Of it, she wrote:

"One shares, and one walks openly, quiet and serene, letting the outside world and the occasional thoughts of another walking beside one drift into one, and the two become merged, in a still pool of perception."

On the great question of whether to make much or little of the difference between men and women, Lindbergh emphasizes such differences and tries to build on the strengths implied in them. She persists in remaining subservient to her husband, but acknowledges the accompanying frustrations and their implications for her self-esteem. Lindbergh often discusses feminine identity, believing that women take pleasure at interior decorating while men would not want to take the effort, or that in a discussion women will worry more about the mix of people, exhibit greater sympathy for individuals, analyze less. Some of these generalizations are obviously socialized stereotypes, but they are typical of her generation.

Surprisingly, Lindbergh criticizes the writing of Virginia Woolf and Vita Sackville-West for having a "fungus quality," because they thought of themselves as writers first and "not ever" as wives or mothers. In her first volume, a younger Anne Morrow had ecstatically reviewed *Orlando* (Woolf's fantasy about sex differences), and elsewhere Lindbergh refers positively to other Woolf writings. In fact, Lindbergh's descriptive techniques are very similar to Woolf's. Particularly in a retrospective passage, an account will be built up with layers of sensory and time-eclipsing detail.

Very introspective, open and honest, Lindbergh understands the perpetual conflict between "seeing and being, between vision and action, between mortality and eternity." The writer, she claims, must always stand in the middle of that conflict. Working with one's hands is a way of managing the conflict, and Lindbergh often used flower arranging to assuage writer's block. In "doing flowers," one can quickly produce a vivid, "real," aesthetic object—the activity counteracts the intense frustrations associated with writing. Lindbergh's involvement with sculpture at the Cranbrook Academy in Michigan had essentially the same motive.

In form and method, *War Within and Without* is a peculiar species of autobiography. It is not written from a later point in time, nor is it written with a particular purpose or theme. The writing is all to the moment, and then edited forty years later. Its continuities are those which were natural to Lindbergh's life in the years covered by the book. Here, however, an impasse is reached: the reader has no way of knowing how much is omitted from particular letters or entries. Lindbergh says that she edited only to exclude repetition, but can she be believed? One example may illustrate the problem. The endpapers reproduce a letter from Anne to Charles, June 13, 1942, which appears in the text in an extremely reduced version omitting discussion of the children's illness and Anne's love of cutting roses as a means of restoration of her equilibrium. This material is not repetitive. How much else, one wonders, has been omitted? Far from merely shortening the book, Lindbergh is, one suspects, creating and shaping the impression she wants the reader to gain of her younger self.

There is another matter about the writing, one illustrating Lindbergh's great narrative skill. Many diary entries are quite long—up to six or eight printed pages for one day. The entry is written as if in the present, not letting the reader know the outcome of the event—as in the lost puppy incident of November 23, 1941, or better, the entry for Monday, December 8, 1941. That entry begins by recounting the events and feelings of the week before, with no mention of Pearl Harbor; then she tells of Sunday's activities, and finally recounts the details of where she was and her feelings when she heard the radio announcement. The result of this technique is to make the book often read like a novel and not like a diary.

The volume has an excellent index which includes not only the usual names and places (with which this book is full), but also ideas, concepts, and themes as well. There are entries on death, on fears for her children, on feelings of pressure, on marriage, on motherhood, on women, on writing. Such a device makes the book useful as raw material for social history of the period, as well as for the still-to-be-written definitive biography of both Charles and Anne.

Since the public events, especially about the War, are always interspersed with Lindbergh's own intimate reflections about herself, her family, or nature, this book is more pleasurable than a straight history. On a Wednesday (her day to care for the children), she will say, "The hardest part of taking care of children is not physical but mental. One cannot *think through* one clear thought with them around"; and the next paragraph will begin, "The Germans are 12 miles from Paris."

As a description of the joys and frustrations of being a writer, mother, wife, thinker, citizen, this volume is unsurpassed. As the culmination of the earlier volumes of an interesting form of autobiography, the book rounds out a picture of upper-class young American womanhood in the second, third, and fourth decades of this century. Not yet forty at the end of this work, Anne Morrow Lindbergh still has more than thirty years of life to chronicle. One wonders what form that autobiography will take.

Margaret McFadden

THE WAR WITHOUT A NAME
France in Algeria, 1954-1962

Author: John E. Talbott (1940-   )
Publisher: Alfred A. Knopf (New York). 305 pp. $12.95
Type of work: History
Time: 1954-1962
Locale: France and Algeria

The story of France's last colonial war and its effect on French politics

Principal personages:
PIERRE MENDES FRANCE, Premier of France, May, 1954-February, 1955
GUY MOLLET, Premier of France, January, 1956-May, 1957
JACQUES MASSU, French military officer and victor over Algerian rebels in Battle of Algiers (1957)
CHARLES DE GAULLE, French national hero of World War II and President of France, 1958-1969
JEAN-PAUL SARTRE, philosopher and opponent of Algerian War
JEAN-JACQUES SERVAN-SCHREIBER, magazine editor and critic of French Army methods during the Algerian War
RAOUL SALAN, French military officer and conspirator against de Gaulle
MAURICE CHALLE, French military officer and conspirator against de Gaulle
FERHAT ABBAS, Algerian nationalist leader and President of the rebel government, 1956-1961
BENYOUSSEF BEN KHEDDA, President of Algerian rebel Provisional Government after 1961 and signatory of the peace agreement of March 18, 1962

In the late 1960's and early 1970's, the Vietnam War divided the American people and shook American politics to its foundations, forcing one American President, Lyndon B. Johnson, out of office. The bitter controversy that accompanied the war has left a searing memory in the minds of all Americans who were alive and politically aware at the time. Yet, the experience of divisive dissent in the wake of war is by no means unique to America. Between 1954 and 1962, equally great bitterness was created in the domestic politics of a European country, France, by another so-called dirty war: the losing battle to keep Algeria, French. It is this subject that John Talbott, a Professor of French History at the University of Santa Barbara, treats in his new book, *The War Without a Name.*

Talbott has produced a narrative of almost unacademic crispness and readability, one that will be of great value to the general reader whose knowledge of both Algerian and French history is rather vague. Aside from its insightful observations on public opinion in metropolitan France during the course of the war, however, it offers little that is new to the specialist. The spareness of the narrative is, to some extent, achieved at the expense of vividness and detail. The issues of loyalty to conscience versus loyalty to the state, and of government attitudes toward the right of dissent in time of war, are pursued at the expense of other equally interesting aspects of this particular historical episode. Talbott's work supplements, but does not supplant, the other recent work on the war: *A Savage War of Peace*, by Alistair Horne.

The outbreak of violence on November 1, 1954, throughout the remote areas of eastern Algeria, took most Frenchmen by surprise. In Chapter One, Talbott gives the reader the historical background of the Algerian War. Colonial Algeria, he explains, was sharply divided between a relatively privileged European settler minority, on the one hand, and the Muslim majority, on the other. The author shows how, for more than two decades, the appeals of Muslim moderates like Ferhat Abbas for peaceful, gradual reform had met with repeated evasions and rebuffs, until a small band of young nationalists, most of them veterans of the French Army, finally decided that European settler domination could be overthrown only by armed rebellion against France. The impression is given that armed rebellion was more or less inevitable: relatively little effort is spent on examining those occasions when judicious introduction of reforms might have enabled moderates among both Muslims and settlers to resolve peacefully the differences between the two communities.

The second chapter traces the gradual military buildup of French forces in Algeria. It demonstrates how the reformist Radical Premier of France, Pierre Mendes France, who had recently ended French military involvement in Indochina and who had been moving toward conciliating native nationalists in Morocco and Tunisia, nevertheless felt compelled to order measures taken to repress the Algerian insurrection. Hardline sentiment was so strong that even François Mitterand, then the youthful Interior Minister and a later kingpin of leftist politics, declared: "Algeria is France."

Before being voted out of office by the French National Assembly, on February 5, 1955, Mendes France had appointed Jacques Soustelle governor-general of Algeria. While determined to defeat the rebels militarily, Soustelle, like many other Frenchmen, also believed that improving the Algerian Muslims' economic position would hasten victory by depriving the rebels of mass support. The author compares this French belief to the American conviction that improving South Vietnamese living standards would eradicate the revolutionary nationalism of the Vietnamese Communists.

Under Mendes France's successor as Premier, Edgar Faure, the steady military buildup continued. Between January and December, 1955, the total number of French troops in Algeria was increased from seventy-five thousand to one hundred eighty thousand. Yet France was not officially at war: she was engaged in what the government termed "operations for the maintenance of order."

In the third chapter, the author shows how, at the beginning of 1956, the newly elected Socialist Premier, Guy Mollet, despite his campaign promises to seek a peaceful solution in Algeria, actually strengthened the French commitment to military victory. After being greeted, upon his visit to Algiers on February 6, 1956, by a European settler riot, Mollet hastily withdrew the nomination of the aging Arabophile, General Georges Catroux, as successor to the departing Soustelle. Instead, he chose the hard-line Socialist, Robert Lacoste. By the end of 1956, Mollet had increased the number of French troops in Algeria to more than four hundred thousand men. Calling to mind once again America's bitter experience in Vietnam, Talbott compares Mollet to Lyndon Johnson, and compares the Special Powers Law of March 16, 1956, overwhelmingly approved by the National Assembly, to the Gulf of Tonkin Resolution passed by the United States Senate in 1964. The Special Powers Law granted the executive virtually unlimited powers to suspend individual rights, if necessary, in order to deal with the rebellion. Talbott doubts that the February settler riot was, in itself, sufficient to change Mollet's policy from conciliation to repression. He suggests that fear of being accused of abandoning the settlers might have induced Mollet to keep sending troops even if the riot had never occurred.

To Talbott, Mollet's precise motives for escalating the war are less important than the fact that he decided to do so, and was able to do it with so little danger of political retribution, either in the Chamber of Deputies or at the bar of French public opinion. Despite some timid dissent in the Socialist ranks over the war, Mollet's Cabinet was the longest-lived in the history of the Fourth Republic; it endured from January, 1956, until May, 1957. When it finally was overthrown, however, the act was not due to opposition to Mollet's Algerian policy, but rather to discontent over his proposal for a tax increase.

It was not that there was any lack of atrocities to spur antiwar feeling at home. After an American ultimatum had halted the joint Anglo-French expedition against Egypt, in November, 1956, a shamed French Army worked more zealously than ever to regain its honor by crushing the Algerian rebels. The French government decided to send the elite corps, the paratroopers, to the city of Algiers itself. Throughout 1957, the tough and energetic World War II resistance hero Jacques Massu, commander of the paratroopers, relied on the most brutal methods possible to break the back of the rebel underground in Algiers. Suspects were frequently tortured in order to obtain information; once arrested, many of them disappeared completely.

Yet, in Chapters Five and Eight, and in scattered passages throughout the book, the author makes clear just how weak the principled opposition to the Algerian War was, as compared with the potency of the antiwar movement in the America of 1965-1973. The philosopher Jean-Paul Sartre, in the periodical *Temps Modernes*, did, it is true, condemn the war as immoral and call for a victory of the rebellious Algerian Muslims of the *Front Liberation*

Nationale (FLN). There was also a French pro-rebel activist, François Jeanson, who succeeded in organizing the secret transport of weapons to the rebels; some of the members were put on trial in September, 1960. The number who carried opposition to the war that far, however, was small.

Besides such extremist forms of opposition to the war, there was also a more moderate variety of dissent. The distinguished literary critic Pierre-Henri Simon, in his essay *Contre la Torture* (1957), exposed Army interrogation tactics, as did the small group of dedicated left-wing Catholics who wrote for the periodical *Esprit*. Jean-Jacques Servan-Schreiber, editor of the magazine *L'Express*, likewise strongly condemned torture, although he balanced his condemnation by making it clear that he favored a continued French presence in Algeria. The reaction of Paris intellectuals against the mysterious disappearance, in 1957, of Maurice Audin, a mathematics professor suspected of aiding the rebels, showed that the war had by no means snuffed out public concern for human rights.

Yet somehow, all these little streams of dissent never coalesced to form a mighty river of widespread opposition to the war. Antiwar sentiment, at least in its most vocal expression, remained restricted to university professors, secondary schoolteachers, journalists, writers, students, artists, and other intellectual types: it found no resonance among the broad masses. The leading organization on the French Left, the French Communist Party, never took an unequivocal antiwar position during the years of the Fourth Republic; and even under the Fifth Republic, it followed, rather than led, public opinion. The Fourth Republic was overthrown, and the Fifth Republic seriously threatened, not by extremist advocates of peace with the Muslim rebels at any price, but by die-hard defenders of *Algerie Française*. Why was the French experience so different from the American one?

Talbott does offer some tentative answers. The average Frenchman, it is clear, was never exposed to the antiwar viewpoint as long, or as intensively, as the Americans would be in the late 1960's. Under both the Fourth and Fifth Republics, any attempt at journalistic muckraking incurred the risk, under the Special Powers Act, of police seizure of the entire issue of the offending magazine or newspaper. The threat of financial loss could not stifle dissent completely, but it could induce an editor to think twice before printing an article that assailed too sharply either the war or the Army's conduct of the war. Almost all book publishers, fearful of government reprisals, refused to print antiwar books until near the war's end: the only exception was a small, courageous publishing house, *Editions De Minuit*. Since the radio and television network of France was under government ownership and control, antiwar dissent could not reach the French people through these media. Talbott points out that, in any case, the majority of Frenchmen, during the period 1954-1962, did not own television sets. The Algerian conflict, unlike the American involvement in Vietnam, never became a "living-room war," in which citizens were exposed night after night to the horrors of a far-off battlefield.

Even among those metropolitan Frenchmen most directly affected by the war, dissent almost never took an extreme form. Every young French male subject to the draft and most draftees were, by the end of 1956, subject to being sent to Algeria. The government did not recognize any conscientious objector status. Yet the rate of draft evasion and desertion was, Talbott contends, astonishingly low compared with the American experience during the Vietnam conflict. He sees several reasons for this fact.

First of all, the conscripts' service in Algeria was not especially risky. The active chasing of guerrillas was performed by elite paratroop units, composed of volunteers: draftees, on the other hand, were generally assigned to guard both public and private property and the main lines of communication. Of all the draftees sent to Algeria, only a relatively small percentage ever saw combat: of these only a small percentage were killed or injured.

Furthermore, there was little support from the wider French society for the idea of draft resistance. The French Communists never supported the notion of draft resistance at any time during the course of the war: they were too intent on trying to re-create an alliance with the Socialists, thereby breaking out of their political isolation, to be willing to take such a risk. It was in order to obtain such an alliance that they had voted, like the other parties, for the Special Powers Law of 1956. Even the moderate critics of the war, men who had led the outcry against torture, strongly deplored all appeals for desertion, draft evasion, or assistance to the FLN. For most soldiers, and for most other Frenchmen as well, the emotional bonds of loyalty to the nation were simply too strong to permit them to do such things.

Talbott's discussion of the other side of dissent, that of the diehards who demanded continued French rule at any price, is less thorough and also less original than his examination of left-wing antiwar dissent. The author does tell the story of both the May, 1958, revolt, which brought about the fall of the Fourth Republic and the return of World War II Resistance hero Charles de Gaulle to power, and the abortive putsch of April, 1961, led by General Maurice Challe, against a President de Gaulle who was determined to grant self-determination to Algeria. He does not, however, give a sufficient explanation for the difference in result between the two years.

In May, 1958, the appointment to the Premiership of Pierre Pflimlin, a man who had merely declared his willingness to talk with the Muslim rebels, provoked the open defiance of governmental authority by both the French military officers in Algiers and the European settlers. The Fourth Republic was able to bring this insubordination to an end only by calling General de Gaulle back to power. In April, 1961, de Gaulle, who had publicly stated that self-determination for Algeria was his goal, was able, by the force of his eloquence on nationwide radio and television, to break the back of a second revolt by French military officers in Algeria. General Raoul Salan, a ringleader of the attempted putsch who had helped bring de Gaulle back to power in 1958, now went underground to help organize the Secret Army Organization (OAS), a gang of militant young settlers and renegade officers dedicated to preventing Algerian independence by force. General Maurice Challe, the leader of the putsch, surrendered and accepted punishment. Pflimlin fell, de Gaulle survived.

Talbott suggests several reasons for the failure of the 1961 putsch attempt. Basing his conclusion partly on an interview with an organizer of draftees' resistance, Talbott concludes that spontaneous acts of sabotage by conscripts in Algeria did play a role in bringing the putsch to a screeching halt. Whether it was de Gaulle's powerful appeal, heard on countless soldiers' transistor radios, that inspired this resistance, or whether it had sprung up even before the speech of April 24th, is a question which the author raises without coming to a final conclusion of his own. More important than the draftees' resistance in stopping the putsch, the author contends, was the lack of enthusiasm for the revolt in the officer corps itself: most of the officers were "fence-sitters" rather than *Algerie Française* diehards.

Yet, why were so many officers timid, legalistic fence sitters in 1961, and enthusiastic putschists in 1958? The author mentions that General Jacques Massu, when approached by disaffected colonels in early 1961, refused their request that he lead a revolt against de Gaulle. Yet Massu, the hero of the Battle of Algiers, was the darling of the European settlers: it was his dismissal from his command in January, 1960, for having allegedly expressed doubts about de Gaulle's Algerian policy to a German newspaperman, which had provoked the first incident of settler rioting against de Gaulle in Algiers. Talbott does not attempt to explain why Massu, who had been a major figure in the revolt against the Fourth Republic in May, 1958, did not join the conspiracy against de Gaulle in 1961. Perhaps his abstention from the conspiracy can be attributed to an unshakable personal loyalty to de Gaulle, a loyalty forged by the bitter years of participation in the Resistance during World War II, when the officer corps had been sharply divided between Gaullists and Vichyites.

It seems probable that it was the presence of fervent Gaullists as conspiratorial wire-pullers behind the 1958 revolt that might have made the difference between 1958 and 1961. These men exploited the issue of French Algeria in order to win settler and military support for their chief's return to power. Jacques Soustelle, who had spent considerable time in Algeria as governor-general and had become converted to the settler viewpoint, did, it is true, turn against de Gaulle over Algeria after 1958. Yet most of the Gaullists, men such as Michel Debre and Jacques Chaban-Delmas, were willing to stick by the General even when his Algerian policy changed. Their loyalty was personal, not ideological. Perhaps it was the absence of this crew of intrepid Gaullist plotters, with their superb organizational skills, that doomed the

April, 1961, putsch to failure. Such a thesis however, is not examined at all by Talbott. There should be more biographical material on both Jacques Massu and the leading civilian Gaullists, in order to make their actions in 1958 and 1961 more comprehensible.

In the final chapter, the author gives the reader the story of the final phase of the Algerian War, lasting from April, 1961, to March, 1962: the wearisome negotiations between the French government and the Muslim rebels of the FLN; the replacement of the onetime moderate Ferhat Abbas as head of the FLN by the more radical Benyoussef Ben Khedda; the violent, and ultimately futile, attempts of the OAS to sabotage the peace process; and the achievement, on March 18, 1962, of a cease-fire agreement, bringing independence to Algeria at last. Talbott does not condemn de Gaulle for having been willing to risk, for the sake of an agreement with the Muslim rebels, the sacrifice of the interests of the very European settlers who had helped him return to power. Instead, he regards de Gaulle's decision to quit Algeria not only as the only one that was realistic, but also as the only one consistent with his broader ideas concerning France and her future. For, to de Gaulle, France's future greatness lay in Europe, not in North Africa; the Algerian embroglio was a tragic entanglement in a dying colonial past, one he wished France to be rid of so she might get on with her continuing task of internal economic renovation.

The person interested in the problem of dissent in time of war, and of government attitudes toward individual rights in time of war, will find Talbott's book quite satisfying. It is, however, less than satisfying to the reader who is interested in the problem of the breakdown of democracy and how it can be avoided. Nor will it satisfy the person who is interested in recent African history, the history of decolonization, or the study of comparative race and ethnic relations.

In the final chapter, Talbott seems to accept the notion that the panicky exodus of the vast majority of the European settlers to France, in the months after the cease-fire agreement, was more or less inevitable. The sense of inevitability is strengthened by Talbott's habit of treating the settlers as a faceless, extremist mass, with no nuances of opinion among them. True, most of the settlers were diehard opponents of reform; but there were at least a few advocates of settler-Muslim reconciliation among the settlers, although such individuals became increasingly powerless after 1958.

One such settler liberal was Jacques Chevallier, the Mayor of Algiers. Prior to the outbreak of rebellion in 1954, and even for some time thereafter, he strove for an improvement of Muslim economic conditions and for at least some attempt to remedy Muslim grievances. Chevallier is mentioned at least a few times in Horne's massive book on the war; he is not mentioned at all in Talbott's book. It is possible that the settlers became as extremist as they did, thereby depriving Chevallier of all influence, because they were prodded and manipulated by military men and by mainland politicians, who were using them for their own purposes; but this possibility is not at all discussed by Talbott. The dilemma of the liberal in times of ethnic polarization, which still exists in various parts of the globe from Northern Ireland to South Africa, is a theme which is by no means fully explored in *The War Without a Name*.

Talbott's sources are contemporary books and periodicals, both French and American, plus recent scholarly articles on the subject, both those written by Talbott himself during the past five years and those written by other scholars. He also makes use of memoir and autobiographical literature in the French language, both by French writers and by Algerian Muslims. Although the Parisian press is cited fairly often, he cites the European settler press only once, to demonstrate settler acclaim for the paratroopers in 1957; he does not probe any more deeply into settler opinion. Talbott has relied partially on interviews to write the article on which his discussion of the Maurice Audin affair is based. He has also relied on interviews for other scattered pieces of information mentioned in the book. It is unfortunate, however, that he never interviewed any Gaullists, former military officers, or onetime influential figures in the European settler community of Algeria: doing so might have shed some light on dark corners of his narrative.

There are relatively few aids to the reader. There is a map of Algeria near the front of the book, but there are no photographic illustrations of any of the men who played major roles in the events of the war. The bibliography is a simple listing of sources, rather than a critical assessment of the existing literature. The footnotes are placed at the end of the book, making it inconvenient for the reader to consult them.

Paul D. Mageli

THE WAYWARD AND THE SEEKING
A Collection of Writings by Jean Toomer

Author: Jean Toomer (1894-1967)
Edited, with an Introduction, by Darwin T. Turner
Publisher: Howard University Press (Washington, D.C.). 450 pp. $14.95
Type of work: Autobiography, short fiction, drama, and poetry
Time: The 1890's-1920's
Locale: Washington, D.C. and New York

A posthumous collection of writings by Jean Toomer which traces his life through the publication of Cane, *followed by selected representative creative work*

Principal personages:
EUGENE (JEAN) TOOMER, a writer
NATHAN TOOMER, his father
NINA PINCHBACK TOOMER, his mother
P. B. S. PINCHBACK, her father, one-time Acting Governor of Louisiana
NINA HETHORN PINCHBACK, his wife
WALDO FRANK, a New York writer and Jean Toomer's friend

In 1923, Jean Toomer published his first book, *Cane*, a collection of poetry, sketches in poetic prose, and several more traditional short stories, which contrasted the lives of rural blacks in Georgia and urban blacks in the North. Toomer called it "a swan-song" of "the folk-spirit" which would soon "die on the modern desert."

Influential writers of the day, black and white, from Waldo Frank and Sherwood Anderson to W. E. B. DuBois and William Stanley Braithwaite, praised it and looked ahead to another book by this fresh and immensely talented voice. There was to be no other, although Toomer's voice was far from silent.

This current volume, *The Wayward and the Seeking*, has been assembled by Afro-American literature critic and anthologist Darwin T. Turner to rectify and to explain that situation. It is divided into five sections ("Autobiographical Selections," "Fiction," "Poetry," "Drama," and "Aphorisms and Maxims") and fills in the hitherto sketchy outline of his work previously available.

Several of these pieces were published in Toomer's lifetime in major literary periodicals or anthologies, and several have been discussed in recent scholarship, but it is good to have them collected in one place, even though this collection is far from complete. Toomer's work includes several more places and pieces of fiction of varying length, many other poems, and several purely philosophical works, as well as more extended autobiographies.

It is the autobiographical material here included which is one of the book's key values. Editor Turner has made selections from several autobiographies or autobiographical fragments Toomer wrote over the years and has arranged them to present a clear, consecutive narrative, primarily of Toomer's boyhood and young manhood, culminating in the publication of *Cane* when he was almost twenty-nine. Interspersed are relevant excerpts from his essay "On Being an American," in which Toomer discusses his attitudes toward race and personhood. Later years are not dealt with, since Turner suggests that Toomer's major concern during those years was his spiritual development rather than anything directly associated with his life as a writer.

It is regrettable that Toomer was unable to publish a full-length autobiography during his lifetime, for these selections reveal a superbly sensitive and rational mind and spirit of which America can never have enough. Written in a lucid style, often with passion, often with a faintly ironic view of himself and his experience, they have significance beyond his own life because of their many valuable insights, not the least of which is their view of life in turn-of-the-century Washington for a family of mixed blood.

Eugene's boyhood was spent in what would be considered a white middle-class neighborhood. Racial heritage seems not to have been a concern in the family or the community. Indeed, the Toomer-Pinchback racial background was somewhat uncertain. All Toomer says he knew for sure is that his grandfather, P. B. S. Pinchback, announced that he had Negro blood when he was running for public office in Reconstruction Louisiana. He became Lieutenant Governor and Acting Governor, and helped to enact legislation favorable to blacks. Toomer, however, remained unsure to what extent Pinchback actually believed he had Negro blood.

With the vividness of a fiction writer, Toomer portrays his grandfather as a domineering Southern politico who remained in Washington with his family, enjoying the companionship of various political cronies, even though he lost his newly-won seat in the United States Senate when it was contested. Also well-drawn are the portraits of the rest of the family: a meek but strongly loving grandmother, ever sensitive to young Eugene's mental-emotional state; a couple of uncles at various times, moving between not especially successful business and marital ventures; and finally a mother, with an independent spirit and yet bound to the home of her parents because of a dissolved marriage. Eugene's father Nathan, like the two home-returning sons of grandfather Pinchback, did not measure up to the high notions of worldly success Pinchback harbored for his family, and he abandoned his wife before Eugene was born.

Toomer offers a fascinating view of middle-class boyhood at the turn of the century, describing his games, with a perceptive interpretation of the meaning of "fun," his friendships, and his discovery of sex. His comments on sex are quite straightforward, and still relevant, as he criticizes the failures of an older generation to explain sex to their children.

He spent three years in New York with his mother and her new husband, but when she died, he returned to Washington with his grandparents. These high school years found Toomer in a neighborhood midway between the white and black worlds. He terms this colored community an aristocracy, composed of people with mixed racial background who possessed positions of authority and respect as well as financial stability, and again he emphasizes that race was not an issue.

After high school, Toomer embarked upon an extended period of higher education. He tried agriculture at the University of Wisconsin, physical culture in Chicago, history and sociology in New York, never completing a course of study but gaining new fields of interest through extensive readings in literature, politics (of the socialist bent), psychology, and sociology, until he was fully prepared for a place in the intellectual ferment of the teens and twenties. As his mind kept expanding, so did his experience, as he rejected the notion of success according to the standards of the world and of his grandfather, to whose home he would perpetually return during these "wandering years," as Turner calls them. He worked as a gym instructor, store manager, librarian, even a Ford salesman, as he gradually realized that he wanted to focus his efforts strictly upon writing. So, he returned to his aging grandparents' home in Washington, taking care of them while having a place to live and to write. He had a welcome three-month vacation from his nursing duties when he was offered a stint as substitute principal of a school in a small town in Georgia. Thus, he was introduced to a new world, which moved him so strongly that upon his return he was able to re-create it in the sketches, poetry, and often autobiographical stories of *Cane*.

Despite its acclaim by the literary elite of the day, *Cane* sold fewer than a thousand copies until it was reissued in 1969. Yet, even now it is among the least-known and least-read masterpieces in American literature, perhaps because then, as now, it was perceived as Toomer insisted he did not want it perceived or presented: chiefly as the work of a black writer rather than as primarily a work of art.

It is fortunate that the growing interest in Afro-American literature during the past fifteen years has brought *Cane* into the curriculum, and yet it remains largely segregated in Afro-American literature classes, rather than being read side by side, except for occasionally excerpted pieces in American literature anthologies, with Toomer's major contemporaries such as Sherwood Anderson, Theodore Dreiser, Robert Frost, and Sinclair Lewis, all of whom Toomer read avidly, or even such innovative giants as Ernest Hemingway, William Faulkner, and Gertrude Stein. Thus, its appeal has been narrowed in a way in which Toomer would not approve.

He deplored the misunderstanding of his writing owing to its categorization as black literature. The circle in which he moved was largely white, and with Caucasian features, his racial makeup was not discernible. It was not, however, that he refused to identify himself with black blood; in fact his autobiography affirms its assets. Rather, being composed of a mixture of strains, he considered himself as embodying a new race, the American, which he looks forward to in his autobiography and his poem "The Blue Meridian." He lived not so much as a black man passing as white, but as a person whose race was of no consequence, often to the surprise and even disbelief of a late-twentieth century reader, who may criticize him for his refusal to involve himself in the racial struggles of his day.

He felt that identification with only the black or the white race would deny part of his full identity, and the quest for wholeness of the human being was his constant theme throughout life. This quest led him to become a disciple of George Gurdjieff, described briefly in the final section of the autobiographical selections. Gurdjieff's philosophy of the harmony of all aspects of the human self coincided with Toomer's beliefs; but unfortunately, Toomer's increasing involvement in philosophic concerns weakened his art, as evidenced in much of this book.

The two long plays here included, for example, lack rounded characters, consistently natural and believable dialogue, and true dramatic tension and shape. The first two ingredients are not necessary in an Expressionistic drama such as *The Sacred Factory*, which depicts symbolically a frustrated woman's struggle toward greater self-fulfillment than her husband believes is good for her. Here, Toomer fittingly uses a chorus to voice the characters' thoughts and to express the social forces acting upon them; other of the dramatic devices here might be effective on stage, although the dramatic structure is weak.

Natalie Mann, however, is a much more realistic play, but burdened with stilted dialogue and cardboard characters, although the intention is noble and, like *The Sacred Factory*, remarkably feminist, dealing with the character's move toward independence of being and thought, away from reliance upon family, society, and even the liberating force of her lover (an idealization of Toomer himself), whom Toomer has to kill with operatic inexplicability before Natalie can be completely free. Despite its weaknesses as drama, *Natalie Mann* is worth reading for its insight into upper-middle-class black society and social outcasts in the 1920's.

Toomer's poetry, at least as represented by the twelve poems here selected from Toomer's unpublished collection whose title gives this book its name, similarly shows awkward handling of form—surprisingly so, for *Cane* had proven him a poet in the play of sound, imagery, rhythm, and repetition in the prose sketches as well as in those pieces more traditionally presented as poems. Much of this later poetry is quite prosaic, relying upon abstractions, with rhythm either mechanical or absent. One prose poem, "Sing Yes!," fails to earn the exalted affirmation it insists upon because of the total lack of anything concrete, visual or sensual. Toomer labors to use the parallel constructions of Walt Whitman, whose work he greatly admired; yet, it is Whitman's weakest qualities of vague generalizing and insistent didacticism that Toomer seems most to have acquired.

There is one poem more fully realized than the others, however, and artistically more satisfying, if not wholly so: "The Blue Meridian," previously published in the Langston Hughes-Arna Bontemps anthology, *The Poetry of the Negro, 1746-1970*, as well as in two earlier versions during Toomer's lifetime. While retaining the same flaws of overuse of abstractions and some infelicitous shifts in levels of diction ("The Big Light, / Let the Big Light in! / O thou, Radiant Incorporeal . . ."), the poem does manage to achieve a unified philosophic point about America's future, much in the style and method of *The Bridge* of Hart Crane, also associated with the Waldo Frank circle of 1920's writers. Toomer's poetic language is not as compressed as Crane's, being occasionally flat. He has a genuine poetic idea, however, told with fine choice of metaphor and symbol, juxtaposition of contrasting voices, styles, and vocabularies as in *The Waste Land*, concrete images (although not as fully developed as Crane's or T. S. Eliot's), and skilled development of thought through the repetition of several refrains with significant variation.

The poem is Toomer's dream of a new American—and by extension, human—race that will transcend contemporary materialism and racial categories, to achieve "the joining of men to men / And man to God," fusing the great European, African, and red races into a moving whole.

Turner's most irritating editorial decision is the use of twenty-five pages for selected "Aphorisms and Maxims" from Toomer's revision of a book he privately published in 1931 called *Essentials*. These are, Turner says, "arranged on pages according to his original intention," but Toomer's original intentions are hardly met in the extracting of only parts of several different sections of his long manuscript, so it seems a bit foolish to have many of these pages nearly blank with only one or two sentences at the top. Some of these statements are insightful on human nature and human values, but none is worded so succinctly or makes such original revelations that it merits so much empty page space for the reader's further pondering.

The fiction section, especially "Withered Skin of Berries," offers by far the most memorable, indeed haunting, writing in the collection. This story is not only impressive and beautiful in its style and language, but it is also superbly developed in plot and theme, more extensively in fact than the bulk of the sketches and stories in *Cane*. Turner unfortunately gives no specific information on the story's date (1930) or composition, and only by omission suggests that it was not published before, although "why" is an inevitable question to ask, since it is fully on a par with most of the pieces in *Cane* and deals with important concerns on several levels.

Vera is a light-skinned typist in Washington, and a virgin who teases the men that desire her. The story presents her encounters with three men, two black, one white, focusing on her obsession with one Dave Teyy, a black poet who becomes a godlike ideal for her, with the richest sense of life and of the full expression of body and spirit (although the other two men, both friends of Dave, do not lack sensitivity to nature).

Associated with Vera's sexual and spiritual conflict is a social conflict which has remarkable resonance when viewed in conjunction with the facts of Toomer's own life. Vera, although regarded as white by everyone in her office (including Carl, the white man who seeks to date and eventually marry her), is actually black in all other aspects of her life. This partial denial of her race is a further example of her denial of her full being (Toomer's persistent thematic concern). Her choice between toying with the white man Carl and fully involving herself with the black man Dave is complicated by Carl's own prejudice against "niggers" and her office mates' malicious discovery of another young black woman who was "passing."

This story is definitely a valuable addition to the Toomer legacy and to American literature as a whole, dealing honestly with some major human issues with brilliant artistry as Toomer interweaves point of view to present Vera as seen by a perceptive narrator, by the men in her life, and by herself. Leit-motifs of language and imagery, including prose poems of skillful and absorbing repetition and variation, are manipulated masterfully in a Wagnerian way, with the story's poetic prologue paragraph repeated at the end with vastly illuminated meaning.

The second piece of fiction, "Winter on Earth," consists of several fragments of varying length depicting the icy isolation of a Chicago winter, juxtaposed with Toomer's mythic creation of an island utopia, White Island, prehistoric rather than futuristic, on which life is lived in harmony with nature and other human beings. The White Island segment ends abruptly, however, and seems uncompleted, although it was earlier published in the *Second American Caravan* (1928) along with an expanded version of the rest of the piece.

"Mr. Costyve Duditch" is similar to the other two pieces of fiction only in its playing with different points of view to provide varied perspectives. It disappoints, however, because Toomer seems unsure whether his purpose is merely to sketch a character, to provide a Joycean epiphany, or to explore questions of mortality and permanence. It concerns a perennial traveler (race unspecified) who courts recognition but fears attention focused on himself rather than on his travels. His blunt talk on death at an otherwise superficial tea party throws a damper on the event and ironically shifts emphasis to himself as an individual. Thematically, it is certainly interesting. It and "Winter on Earth," in their previously published versions, have been analyzed by Brian Joseph Benson and Mabel Mayle Dillard in their *Jean Toomer* (1980).

Darwin Turner reports that editors did not wish to publish his selection of six Toomer stories (including these three) for fear that "the quality and content might damage Toomer's reputation." One could see such an objection being made to the poetry and plays included, but it is difficult to see how anyone could object to "Withered Skin of Berries" at least, a story that Joyce or Lawrence could be proud to claim, and as strong an argument for a positive assertion of black identity as might be written today.

Scott Giantvalley

THE WESTERN ALLIANCE
European-American Relations Since 1945

Author: Alfred Grosser (1925-   )
Translated from the German by Michael Shaw
Publisher: Continuum (New York). 375 pp. $19.50
Type of work: Political science
Time: 1945-1977
Locale: Western Europe and North America

An analysis of the changing relationships among the principal partners of the Western Alliance—the United States, France, Germany, and England during the years since the close of World War II

Principal personages:
KONRAD ADENAUER, Chancellor of West Germany, 1949-1963
CHARLES DE GAULLE, President of France, 1959-1969
JOHN F. KENNEDY, thirty-fifth President of the United States, 1961-1963
JEAN MONNET, father of European Unity

Alfred Grosser has written a very interesting, if uneven, history of the Western Alliance from the uncertain days following World War II to 1977. The aftermath of great wars is always a time of instability since the balance of power has been altered in unpredictable ways. Sometimes the situation is clear enough and the actors astute enough that a firm peace can be established, as was the case in 1815 at the Congress of Vienna. Other times, though, the variables are so confusing and the participants so swept along by currents of opinion which have their own momentum that solid relationships cannot be established. Such was the case with the Treaty of Versailles, which Marshal Foch described as "a twenty years truce." Surely in 1945, very few would have anticipated the *de facto* settlement which emerged following Germany's second bid at European hegemony. Yet, by virtue of the creation of the Western Alliance, one of the most enduring periods of peace and prosperity has occurred. No one can doubt that as long as the Western nations hold together in pursuit of common goals, security will be maintained. As Grosser makes abundantly plain, however, the Alliance is riven by rivalry, mistrust, and separate national interests.

The events leading up to the formation of the North Atlantic Treaty Organization (NATO) in 1949 are well known, and Grosser does not dwell on them. The interpretation of these events is still being debated, but Grosser basically believes that NATO was a necessary response to Soviet expansionism which was desired by the Europeans as much or more so than by the Americans. This admission is not easy for Grosser to make, for he is as influenced by French anti-Americanism, one of the major themes of his book, as those in charge of French policy, whom he criticizes from time to time. For a French anti-American to admit that the Alliance is necessary and in the interests of

Western Europe is difficult for it takes the sting out of the contention that the Alliance is only a cover for America's imperialistic ambitions in Europe.

The heart of Grosser's book does not lie in the East-West confrontation, but in an examination of the relations among the partners in the Alliance. The emphasis on these various partners, as Grosser explains in his introduction, is not evenly distributed. The countries he knows best are France and Germany. England is a bit of an enigma to him; the United States is approached more as a myth than a reality; Italy, Belgium, the Netherlands, and the others are only dealt with as they play an important role. Primarily, *The Western Alliance* is a description of French and West German relations with each other and with the, to them, strange country across the Atlantic to whom their destiny is tied. Here, too, a qualification should be made. Professor Grosser discusses the activity of the major politicians and opinion makers, along with an occasional public opinion poll, but makes little attempt to relate policy to underlying social structures or a thorough analysis of popular beliefs. While such information is obviously necessary, the author does have more than enough to do portraying the behavior of the important political actors of the Western countries during a period lasting more than thirty years.

From Grosser's point of view, the dynamic of the Alliance has developed around three major themes: the French and German attitude toward the United States; the ongoing attempt to create a united European political unit; and interacting within this framework, the various events which have stimulated change—primarily economic developments and policy toward the Third World.

During the period from 1945 to 1950, England still enjoyed the prestige of its heroic struggle against Nazism and continued the special relationship it had formed with the United States during the war. Although lacking the means to implement American policy, English leaders were brought into American policymaking and in this role continued to play a major part in world events. Anglo-Saxon foreign policy during these years was directed toward strengthening Western Europe, and Grosser generally gives America high marks for its generous Marshall Plan aid. He also deemphasizes Central Intelligence Agency (CIA) involvement in European politics and believes rather that American attempts to encourage moderate democratic groups in France and Italy were carried out by legitimate, aboveboard means, using economic incentives and direct, high-level contacts.

The success of the Marshall Plan, however, produced a new dilemma, for by bringing Western Europe back to an economic par with the United States, a situation evolved in which the Europeans now wanted political equality. The tensions around these new demands, which have not been resolved, provide the main focus of the book.

England, whose economic progress in the 1950's and 1960's did not equal that of France and Germany, and who found it increasingly difficult to maintain the special relationship with the United States, retreated more and more into an isolationist position. This retreat left France and West Germany as the principal European powers. Each of these two countries has acted according to such different sets of assumptions, however, that unified action has been very difficult to achieve. This lack of unity has meant that, despite all the sound and fury, the United States remains the dominant partner in the Alliance.

France is saddled with a past and a self-image that make it hard to adjust to its contemporary position in the world. For three hundred years, from the Thirty Years War to 1940, France was either the leading or one of the leading powers in Europe. Furthermore, during these three hundred years, France developed a way of life, familiar to all visitors, making it feel it had achieved the ultimate in civilized living. The bloodletting of World War I, the defeat in 1940, and the rise of the Soviet Union and the United States have meant that France can no longer defend itself or intervene on a global level in a determinant manner. Yet, the French have been unable to relinquish either their attachment to the nation-state or their self-conception as a world power. The result has been both an obstructionist attitude toward the United States and an unwillingness to pursue European unity at the political level. As Grosser points out, this attitude, personified by General Charles de Gaulle, has always stopped short of the brink, and France remains a member of the Alliance and a participant in the European community.

Germany's position is, if anything, even more difficult. West Germany labors under three burdens. The first is the burden of the Nazi past, which means that Germany's acceptance in the international community is still insecure. The second burden is Germany's division into two separate states, while the third is West Germany's geographic position as the western country most exposed to Soviet aggression. The fact is that the foremost domestic goal, the reunification of the two Germanys, conflicts with the necessity to ward off the Soviet threat, which demands embedding West Germany more and more deeply into the Western Alliance and accentuating the division of Europe.

These three burdens have determined that Germany's foreign policy is very different from France's. After World War II, the Germans discovered that the return to international legitimacy lay with cooperation with the United States, for the Americans were far less hostile than the French and even the English, who had both suffered a good deal more at the hands of Germany. Thus, good relations with the United States have always been in the interests of West Germany. Second, the Germans recognize their dependence on NATO much more clearly than do the French, again accentuating the need for strong ties with Washington. West German foreign policy has consistently placed its relations with the United States as its dominant concern.

The German economic miracle, however, has complicated this configuration. By 1970, the German economy was out-performing the American, with the mark far stronger than the dollar, resulting for the first time in serious differences of opinion in Bonn and Washington. German economic strength also meant that, almost unwillingly, the Germans were being thrust more and more into the center of world events, because so much depended on how they managed their economic resources. Germany is slowly becoming independent of the United States, with the odd by-product that France, ever wary of its neighbor across the Rhine, is now beginning to value Washington more as a counterbalance to German strength.

These two national foreign policies were reflected in the third great movement Grosser describes—European unification. Interestingly enough, the prime force behind European unification has been extragovernmental, led by the Frenchman Jean Monnet. Attempted first on an economic basis in the 1950's—and supported by the United States—France, Germany, Italy, Belgium, the Netherlands, and Luxembourg came together in the European Coal and Steel Community, and then, in 1957, in the Common Market. Shortly thereafter, de Gaulle returned to power with his desire to assert France's independence. At first, de Gaulle viewed the Common Market as a possible vehicle which he could use, on the condition that Germany would accept French leadership. The Germans, however, continued to view Washington as the principal ally, sabotaging de Gaulle's vision. Attempts in the early 1960's to establish supranational political institutions foundered. While Britain, Ireland, and Denmark have now been admitted to the Common Market, Grosser believes that the European countries have drawn ever further from the establishment of a supranational political unit. He continues to believe, however, that unity is the only path Europeans can take to regain the political influence to which their economic strength and culture entitle them.

With the dwindling hope of a united Europe, the Alliance is now a union of independent countries, and the accelerating squabbles over various national interests threaten to jeopardize its strength and common purpose. Economic problems are the source of many quarrels, especially now that inflation, high interest rates, balance of trade deficits, and unemployment grow ominous. Generally, everyone wants a currency structure which favors their own exports, inflation producing stimulation to take place in another's territory and a tariff system which subsidizes one's own products. There are no easy solutions, and the situation has been complicated by the rapid increase in oil prices which places heavy pressure on the weaker economies. The growing importance of the Middle East has meant foreign policy differences toward this vital area as everyone scrambles to ensure their own supplies. These sections make for sorry reading, but these same disputes exist within individual countries as well.

Policy toward the Third World has been characterized mostly by a tendency to take advantage of the difficulties of the others. Thus, the United States criticized England and France for their Suez invasion, without reinterpreting its own policy in Panama. John F. Kennedy denounced the French war in Algeria and then sent military advisers to Vietnam. The French, in turn, were only too glad to champion the underdog in that struggle.

Military strategy toward the Soviet Union has also been uneven, with an unwillingness to make the financial commitment necessary to build up conventional forces in Europe capable of stopping a Russian attack. The Western Alliance is in some disarray, yet for the foreseeable future, common political and economic systems among the North Atlantic countries and fear of the Russian model will keep together the organization which has done the most to create a stable world order in the years since World War II.

Stuart Van Dyke, Jr.

THE WHITE LANTERN

Author: Evan S. Connell (1924-   )
Publisher: Holt, Rinehart and Winston (New York). 286 pp. $11.95
Type of work: Essays

A collection of popular essays about discovery and quest, whether the search be geographical, literary, or scientific

The White Lantern does not pretend to be a serious, scholarly work, and for this reason the good humor and wit with which it is written do not seem to be out of place. The book could be taken to be a "tertiary" source because, in most cases Evan S. Connell has not referred to the primary sources at all. A perusal of the book's bibliography reveals essentially a list of secondary sources. For example, in his chapter on the scientific revolution of the sixteenth and seventeenth centuries, he refers to Arthur Koestler and the Marqués de Santillana, but not directly to works by Nicolaus Copernicus, Galileo Galilei, or Isaac Newton. Such a synthesis as Connell has produced is eminently readable but one should not take the work as gospel. In fact, there is an inherent danger in this type of writing—the potential for the introducion of error and misrepresentation.

The White Lantern contains several such mistakes. The book is in error when it states that chimpanzees do not eat baboons. Jane von Lawick-Goodall, in her continuing studies of chimpanzees, observed their hunting behavior in which they chase down, kill, and consume baby baboons. An unintentional misrepresentation is to be found in the chapter on the scientific revolution: one gets the impression from reading Connell that the planet Pluto was discovered not long after the discovery of the planet Neptune (1846), when in fact Pluto was not discovered until 1930 when American Clyde Tombaugh sighted it. Also, it would not have been possible for the Russians to have retaliated against a move by the United States with a nuclear bomb in 1947 for the very simple reason that the Russians did not have the bomb until 1949 and were incapable of intercontinental delivery until the mid-1950's.

On the positive side, the book is very well written as one should expect from a novelist with a number of works to his credit (including a collection of essays of the same sort as in *The White Lantern—A Long Desire*). The story of the early seventeenth century Swedish King Gustav's dreadnought is a masterpiece of literary reconstruction of events. The King had ordered the construction of a very large ship which had unseaworthiness inherent in its design. Because the King was involved, however, no one wished to gain his displeasure by pointing out this fact. Naturally, the ship went down on her maiden voyage in full view of the watchers on the shore. An inquest was held to fix blame but eventually it simply petered out. In a couple of generations all memory of the event was lost. Connell reconstructs the events of the day the ship went down. The chapter has a purpose—that of revealing human folly—and he draws parallels with Watergate and the My Lai massacre. "And why was nobody guilty? Because everybody was following orders."

The book's title chapter illustrates the contrast of personality types in geographical quest, in this case, for the South Pole. It is true that much has been written concerning this, and one approaches one more rendering with some anticipation of boredom: one will be pleasantly surprised. The retelling is fresh, and additional detail has been textured into the background of the piece which makes it a pleasure to read. The centerpiece is the contrast between personalities and, therefore, between the approaches of Amundsen, the first to arrive at the Pole, and of Scott whom one would characterize as "mystic poet, not an explorer." There is quite a contrast between the Norwegian Amundsen and the Englishman Scott. Amundsen got to the Pole first in his race with Scott because of planning and detailed preparation. He had even quantified, as far as was possible, the stages of the journey when the sleds would have certain weights and had even worked out to the day when sled dogs would be slaughtered for food. On January 25, 1912, the return of the expedition to its base camp marked the exact date which Amundsen had set in Norway two years before. Amundsen, as Connell notes, viewed "bad luck" as bad planning. Poor Scott, on the other hand, relied upon luck, and this is why he and his companions died on the journey.

Connell, in order to demonstrate the inhospitable nature of the Antarctic environment, lists some of the organisms that are found there—penguins, obviously, and a few spiders, lichens, and grasses—and some that are not. There are no indigenous humans, no land animals, no birds except the penguin, and no trees. One should not, however, shrug off the tenacity of the biosphere too lightly. There are algae that grow *inside* quartz rocks and which quite merrily photosynthesize their lives away; and, too, one-celled organisms live in the snow in some places in Antarctica. They, when crushed by a boot heel, turn the snow red. (The phrase "white lantern," is derived from astronauts' descriptions of the Antarctic from outer space.)

Connell has great fun in his chapter on the deciphering of lost languages. Perhaps in no other area of human experience has there been produced so much pseudoscientific nonsense. Further, from the pseudoscience (for it feeds on itself) have been generated many harebrained quests. The mid-sixteenth century priest Diego de Landa mistakenly thought he had discovered the basis of the Mayan language. (He must be added to the roster of infamy as the destroyer of most Maya writings in his religious zeal.) It was left for a later cleric, nineteenth century French abbé Brasseur de Bourbourg, to find in de Landa's Mayan alphabet the lost continent of Mu. Mu is a mythical Pacific Ocean sunken counterpart to Atlantis. Such geographical mania is a recrudescent phenomenon, and it seems that each generaiton has its Ignatius Donnellys wasting time, energy, and treasure searching for Atlantis, Mu, and the

918	*Magill's Literary Annual 1981*

hollow earth. Fortunately, each generation has its debunkers as well; Connell is such. The chapter on languages is further illustration of human folly and shows, further, that not even the very intelligent are immune from browsing in pseudoscientific pastures. As Connell remarks of Brasseur de Bourbourg, "the fact that he was intelligent makes him all the more preposterous." Could it be otherwise even in our times of high technology? With the enormous explosion of knowledge and information, it is difficult to keep up with one's own field and nearly impossible to keep up with what is going on elsewhere. There are prominent examples in our times of bright scientists making foolish pronouncements in fields other than their own. The chapter also contains an engaging account of the legitimate searchers after the meanings hidden in dead languages. The account of Rawlinson propped on a ledge three hundred feet above the ground copying ancient Persian inscriptions is indeed, as Connell says, enough to give one vertigo just thinking about it.

No book about quest in modern and contemporary times could be complete without the evolution story. This story, like that of the scientific revolution, has been told many times. Again, however, Connell's retelling does not produce ennui. This chapter ("Olduvai & All That") is the first in the book, and the wry humor in it is a presentient of more to come. He deals with Archbishop Ussher's calculation of the date of creation, the problem of the size of the ark, and the various evolutionary jokes and hoaxes which have been perpetrated. The Piltdown hoax is dealt with as well, but one will find a fresher account of that in Stephen Jay Gould's book *The Panda's Thumb*.

Most amusing, perhaps, is the story of the Cardiff giant. This hoax had its improbable origin in an argument between Hull, an iconoclastic cigar manufacturer, and a preacher named Turk. The quarrel was concerned with the question of giants on the earth. The Bible had said that there were, and the reverend was a literalist fundamentalist. Hull had a large stone sculptured to represent a fossilized giant. It was then arranged that the giant would be "found" at Cardiff, New York. Hull's relish over the hoax is reconstructed by Connell. Hull eventually exposed the giant as his hoax. What did Turk do when it was revealed that he had been duped? "Did he pray? Did he forgive? Did he foam at the mouth? Furthermore, one can't help wondering if the experience taught him anything. Probably not. Fundamentalists are so fundamental."

Connell takes occasion to remark on the science and religion relationship. There is first the attack on the part of the scientist who is armed with some "impertinent fact" to be soon followed by the theological counterattack in the attempt to preserve dogma as fixed and unchanging. Connell comes down on the side of science. Yet, he apparently regards (and correctly) the science-religion controversy as unending. That he is right in this can easily be verified by looking at the contemporary legislation in a number of states requiring equal time for "scientific" creationism and evolution. (Dorothy Nelkin has recreated the recent history of this trend in her *The Science Textbook Controversies & the Politics of Equal Time.*)

Connell throughout *The White Lantern* repeatedly jabs at human folly, and pseudoscience is of that species. He refers, for example, to the "gods-from-other-worlds hucksters." The most recent reference in his bibliography which deals with pseudoscience, however, is the twenty-five-year-old book of Martin Gardner, *Fads and Fallacies*. There has been a great deal written about the phenomenon of pseudoscience since the appearance of Gardner's book. Journals have been inaugurated to study it. Philosophers of science are seriously considering how one can distinguish between real science and pseudoscience. There *are* some recognizable features of pseudoscientific argumentation. Two of the most prominent are the circular argument and the argument from ignorance. The first consists of assuming what it is that one wishes to "prove" and then tailoring the "evidence" accordingly. The second consists of saying, essentially, "You can't prove it isn't so." The argument from ignorance proves nothing; it is, in fact, an attempt to avoid the labor of proving (as is also the argument from analogy, another part of the pseudoscientific stock-in-trade). Connell's book is not deficient in not mentioning these forms of pseudoscientific argumentation, for he has illustrated them with examples.

Connell has a gift for the *bon mot*, and one cannot refrain from mentioning some of them. Some examples are found in the evolution controversy, "the Scopes trial, that little masterpiece of idiocy . . ."; spoofing of creationism, "the clouds split with a blinding flash, a huge Anglo-Saxon finger pointed down . . ." and "One does not expect high logic on the battlefield or at the conference table." One could speculate that Connell's humor perhaps has roots in a deeper feeling that he has concerning the human condition. There are Toynbean echoes in his account of the fall of the static ancient Indian culture of Harappa and Mohenjo-Daro to Sanskrit invaders. "Their civilization may have already been disintegrating, which usually is the case when a nation succumbs to an invader. There is evidence of this in the cheap construction of later buildings, in subdivisions, and so forth—things we ourselves are familiar with." It is not self-evidently true that this is a deterministic law of history; nor does the parallel necessarily apply to "things we ourselves are familiar with." It is true that *sometimes* the past can be a guide to the future. The Spanish-American philosopher Santayana remarked that those who could not remember the past were doomed to repeat it. It is possible, however, to have too slavish a devotion to the past. Modern society is *structurally* very different from ancient societies of the Near and Middle East and Asia. At the very least, we have high technology and they did not. Other substantial differences would not be difficult to find.

In sum, *The White Lantern* is an uneven book, but the balance sheet will show much more on the positive side. Some factual errors have been noted, and the jumping about from century to century can at times be a little irritating. By and large, however, Connell's distillations are well and wittily written.

Robert L. Hoffman

WHITNEY FATHER, WHITNEY HEIRESS

Author: W. A. Swanberg (1907-   )
Publisher: Charles Scribner's Sons (New York). 518 pp. $17.50
Type of work: Biography
Time: 1860's to 1925
Locale: The United States, Europe, Russia, and China

A study of a wealthy entrepreneur and his daughter, replete with details of conspicuous consumption but with little insight into the persons involved

Principal personages:
> GROVER CLEVELAND, twenty-second and twenty-fourth President of the United States, 1885-1889 and 1893-1897
> HERBERT CROLY, first Editor of *The New Republic*
> J. P. MORGAN, wealthy banker
> FLORA PAYNE, W. C. Whitney's first wife and Dorothy Payne Whitney's mother
> WILLARD DICKERMAN STRAIGHT, Dorothy Payne Whitney's first husband
> DOROTHY PAYNE WHITNEY, daughter of Flora and W. C. Whitney
> WILLIAM COLLINS WHITNEY, entrepreneur and Dorothy's father

What W. A. Swanberg's biography of William C. Whitney—the first half of *Whitney Father, Whitney Heiress*—is all about can be summarized by Swanberg's own comment. "The great fortunes being made in this virtually taxless boom era often required the rich to think anxiously about how to spend enough money to keep from stumbling over it." His is the story of the "robber barons" of the nineteenth century, of Rockefeller and Morgan and the Vanderbilts and Astors. As Swanberg says, great fortunes were made, and great fortunes were spent, often in an unstated but obvious competition to see who could build a larger house or throw a more elaborate party or give more diamonds as wedding presents.

William Collins Whitney was born in moderate circumstances in 1841, married wealthy Flora Payne, survived her and a second wife, and left $22,906,222 at his death in 1904. (In today's terms, the dollar figures given here should be multiplied by about ten; thus Whitney's estate was worth approximately $220 million.) In terms of superfluous, ostentatious consumption, however, Whitney was an also-ran. Certainly, while Flora was alive, the Whitneys threw lavish party after lavish party, but not as lavish or as foolish as some. For example, in 1883, one branch of the Vanderbilts built a house for $2,900,000 in an effort to force recognition of them by Mrs. Astor. A Vanderbilt daughter was provided with a titled European for a husband, the cost to the family was almost $10 million, and both the daughter and her husband hated each other.

Only in one area did Whitney seem to excel. He owned "more land in the states of New York and Massachusetts than anyone except the commonwealths themselves. It took thirteen miles of fence to enclose his Massachusetts property." Others obviously made more money—Whitney's brother-in-law left an estate of $178,893,655—built larger and more expensive houses, controlled more corporations, probably watered more stock (although there is question here), and controlled more political deals than did Whitney. He was involved in all these areas, of course, but was not number one in any of them.

Swanberg is not a muckraker, he is not out to bring focus upon Whitney's shady dealings. When Swanberg discusses Whitney's monopoly of public transportation in New York City, he says that "even if he entered the traction field with the intention of building an efficient and useful transportation system, somewhere along the line he threw the switch that wheeled him off into wholesale stockjobbery." That indictment, however, is qualified by the author's statement that everything Whitney did was legal; in fact, lawyers, especially Elihu Root, must bear some of the guilt. "Unfortunately a lawyer who advises a client as to how he can stay within the law in conducting business that is manifestly unfair and disastrous to the public was then and still is within his rights." So who is more guilty, Whitney or his lawyer? Swanberg does not say.

Apparently Whitney did have two positive accomplishments. While serving as Secretary of the Navy during Grover Cleveland's first term, Whitney found the fleet in terrible shape, including some ships with guns which could not fire straight ahead. He changed all that and, thereby, must receive recognition "for pioneering the revolution in American naval power." In addition, he was one of the founders of the Metropolitan Opera Company.

None of the negative or positive aspects mentioned above receives much detailing in the book, most of which is spent in giving details of parties and houses and letters from William to Flora. Why then devote one half the book to William C. Whitney? Does he deserve this kind of attention? No, finally, he does not. His is a somewhat interesting life, but not an intriguing or influential one, especially in comparison to others.

Even though the first half of the book can be faulted, at least it is about William C. Whitney, the announced subject. In all honesty, however, the second half—supposedly about William and Flora's last child, Dorothy Payne Whitney—is more about Dorothy's first husband, Willard Straight, than it is about Dorothy, the "Whitney Heiress" half of the title.

Dorothy was born in 1887 and married Straight in 1911. Chapter One of Book Two concerns Dorothy's life between the time of William's death and her meeting of Willard. The next chapter is about his background. The remaining five chapters tell of Dorothy and Willard together, until his death in 1918. Most of the details concern Willard's activities—in business and in the Army—and Dorothy's reactions to his activities; only in passing does the reader discover much about her activities.

That is a shame, for she might well have been an interesting subject, certainly more interesting than Willard. In an age when the woman's role was restricted to home and drudgery for the poor and home, parties, and European tours for the wealthy, Dorothy was apparently an exception. In addition to her expected activities, she enrolled in "a course in political economy at Columbia . . . saved used clothing for the poor . . . helped at the Henry Street Settlement . . . cheered Nazimova in *A Doll's House*." She also cofounded *The New Republic*—and supported it for more than thirty-eight years with contributions of $3,700,000—and was one of the founders of the New School for Social Research. When she married again, she went to Devon, England, where she and her husband founded the liberal, progressive, coeducational Dartington School. The last forty years, fully one-half of Dorothy's life, are briefly summarized in an eight-page epilogue.

While Book One contains numerous details of society life, Book Two is filled with letters from Willard to Dorothy and Dorothy to Willard. Occasionally Swanberg mentions a meeting with the staff of *The New Republic* to discuss policy and editorial positions. These discussions with Dorothy's involvement would have made more lively reading than most of the letters from Willard, expecially those containing his frustrations that others would receive a field promotion in World War I, while he would not, and thus he would not be equal to them in postwar business or social life.

The suspicion is that the records of the editorial discussions at the journal or the philosophical give-and-take surrounding the establishment of the New School do not exist, while the letters and the newspaper accounts of housing costs and party gowns do. Because these records exist, however, does not mean a book should be written about them.

John C. Carlisle

WILDERNESS OF MIRRORS

Author: David C. Martin
Publisher: Harper & Row Publishers (New York). Illustrated. 236 pp. $12.50
Type of work: History
Time: 1941-1978
Locale: Washington, D.C.; Berlin, Moscow, London, and Paris

The story of the secret war between the Central Intelligence Agency (CIA) and the Soviet security agency (KGB), told through a chronicle of the careers of two key agents

> *Principal personages:*
> JAMES JESUS ANGLETON, CIA chief of counterintelligence
> WILLIAM KING HARVEY, CIA base chief in Berlin, special operations officer
> RICHARD MCGARRAH HELMS, Director of the CIA, 1966-1973
> WILLIAM EGAN COLBY, Director of the CIA, 1973-1976
> HAROLD "KIM" PHILBY, a high British intelligence officer and double agent for the KGB
> ANATOLI GOLITSIN, a well-placed KGB agent defecting to the CIA

Ever since the revelations of widespread domestic spying by the Central Intelligence Agency (CIA) and the subsequent Congressional investigations of CIA activities, numerous intriguing accounts of the twilight world of intelligence have appeared. David C. Martin, a journalist with the Washington bureau of *Newsweek*, presents a fascinating and highly readable addition to this list.

Martin focuses on the contrasting personalities and careers of two high American CIA officials and is thereby able to project vividly to the reader some of the intensity and bitterness of the struggle between American and Soviet Intelligence. These two individuals, James Jesus Angleton and William King Harvey, are seen by the author as personifying this struggle which has been raging since the end of World War II. They were celebrated as heroes and condemned as villains. Whatever one's judgment may be, however, they were certainly highly unusual, interesting, and enigmatic men. As has been suggested by others, they could have been straight out of a story by John Le Carré or Ian Fleming. Likewise, many of the events described seem stranger than fiction.

The brilliant Angleton—a "strange genius," master of deception, Ivy League intellectual, orchid grower, and expert fly fisherman—headed the counterintelligence activities. The blustery Harvey—"hard-drinking and gun-toting," "America's James Bond," former Federal Bureau of Investigation (FBI) agent and Midwestern lawyer—spearheaded some of the CIA's important clandestine operations and unmasked the infamous double agent Harold "Kim" Philby. The story begins in a Washington hotel room, where a Samuel Ginsberg was found dead. Ginsberg was actually General Walter Krivitsky, the former chief of Soviet military intelligence in Western Europe. Was it really a suicide or, in fact, an execution? The author raises the question as he comments on the change of the American perception of Soviet espionage from an "almost touching" complacency to acute concern shortly after World War II.

When the CIA was created to replace the defunct Office of Strategic Services, the core of its agents devoted itself to counter the Soviet security agency (KGB). These agents were drawn into a bewildering world of intrigue, which Angleton was to refer to later as the "wilderness of mirrors." Angleton and Harvey played major roles in the secret war; they were also intense competitors. Most obviously, they were a study in contrast. Angleton came to the CIA with extensive experience in the Office of Strategic Services and a background that included tutoring in counterintelligence by Kim Philby, the double agent unmasked by Harvey. That perhaps was the real reason why Angleton held such a grudge against Harvey. Martin surmises that Angleton was attempting to atone for his failure to detect Philby by spending the rest of his professional career in counterespionage. Harvey had made it to the top in the FBI's counterespionage unit, when a minor infraction of the stringent rules imposed by its director J. Edgar Hoover forced his resignation. He was welcomed in the Office of Special Operations of the newly created CIA and henceforth harbored a strong hostility toward the FBI.

The atmosphere in the agency was charged by the growing awareness of the extensiveness of Soviet operations. The CIA was coming into its own and developed effective countermeasures. Among the most successful was the cracking of the Soviet code, which led to the discovery and conviction of such spies as the Rosenbergs and Klaus Fuchs. Harvey was sent to the Berlin post, the front line of the secret war between the CIA and the KGB. According to Martin, he was well suited for this assignment. Harvey was the "point man," while Angleton was the "paper man." In Washington, Angleton developed an elaborate project which, by the mid-1950's, not only violated the longstanding American concepts of fair play, but the law as well. It was a massive mail opening scheme, involving practically all letters from the Soviet Union coming over the Port of New York. The operation generated a huge watch list of some two million names of American citizens, including many rather notable individuals. In hindsight, it all seems such a terrible waste of effort. Even then the CIA's inspector general found it to be of little value; and some top-level policymakers wondered whether such blatant imitation of Soviet tactics might not be self-defeating.

Indeed, far more promising was the utilization of scientific and technological know-how. Carl Nelson of the communications office had developed a system which could detect the "echoes" of the clear text message which came along with the enciphered text of Soviet wire communications. Thus, wiretapped Soviet lines could be "read" by the CIA. Following successful application of this invention in Vienna, authorization for the construction of a tunnel in

Berlin was given, in order to tap into lines linking Soviet headquarters in East Germany with Moscow. This was the famous Operation Gold, with Harvey in charge. The tunnel was in operation for nearly a year and celebrated as a triumph, giving Harvey special recognition as America's top spy. The consternation and frustration were great, and the near paranoia about KGB plots is understandable when it became known that the secret of the tunnel had been blown from the start by a Soviet "mole" within the British intelligence agency named George Blake.

No one was more suspicious than Angleton. Several possibly lucrative defectors were suspected to be provocation agents. One important exception was Anatoli Golitsin, who was accepted as bona fide by Angleton. Golitsin raised the specter of a high-placed KGB agent inside the CIA, leading to Angleton's single-minded and all-consuming search. Certainly, the revelations of the high-level penetration of the British counterintelligence unit (MI 5) by Soviet "moles" were shattering and must have heightened Angleton's acute concern about similar possibilities in the CIA. Angleton may also have known about the additional revelations made public only in 1979 and 1981 and not mentioned by Martin. These pertain to Anthony Blunt, who had confessed as far back as 1964 to spying for the KGB while with MI 5. The treason of this well-known art historian became public when the parliament withdrew his knighthood in 1979. Even more devastating were the charges recently made in public against the deceased former head of MI 5, Sir Roger Hollis.

Thus, a degree of paranoia may at least be understandable. In the sphere of clandestine operations the CIA endured severe setbacks as well. It had to accept the blame for the Bay of Pigs fiasco in 1961. President John F. Kennedy, humiliated and angered, ordered a shake-up of the agency. The failure stiffened the President's resolve to get rid of Castro, and he continued to rely on the CIA to do the job. These developments led to Harvey's assignment to develop a scheme to assassinate the Cuban leader. This operation, known as "Mongoose," was apparently doomed from the start. As head of the task force Harvey came into direct contact with Robert Kennedy, whom he resented for his "amateurish meddling." Kennedy, in turn, was infuriated by certain of Harvey's measures and effectively ended the latter's usefulness. Director Richard Helms saw no alternative but to remove Harvey from the scene by sending him to Rome as station chief.

The plot against Castro failed; but, as cruel fate would have it, President Kennedy fell victim to an assassin's bullet. Was the KGB involved in the Kennedy assassination? Was it a retaliatory act? Martin raises these questions. A defected Soviet agent by the name of Nosenko turned over information suggesting that the KGB found Lee Harvey Oswald undesirable. Nosenko's credibility as the only witness of Oswald's Russian experience, however, was questioned. Angleton was under the spell of Golitsin, who implicated Nosenko as a disinformation agent. It could never be established whether he was a "plant" sent to cover up the KGB's complicity in the Kennedy murder. The CIA eventually rehabilitated and resettled Nosenko, but his testimony was excised from the Warren Commission's final report.

Angleton's single-minded concentration on the "mole" hunt had a terribly debilitating effect. In fact, the fear of KGB penetration was more devastating than the possible damage that a real Soviet agent could have caused. Martin's account entails the possibility that Angleton was acting on deliberately conflicting evidence introduced by several Soviet defectors, intensifying his belief in a "mole" that had penetrated to the heart of the CIA. Espionage operations against the Soviet Union had come to a halt. The careers of several outstanding officers were damaged beyond repair, because Golitsin had made them suspect in Angleton's eyes. Relations with friendly intelligence services were endangered. The ultimate absurdity of it all was when Angleton himself came under suspicion. William Colby, propelled into the directorship in 1974, was highly irritated by Angleton's ultraconspiratorial turn of mind. When he learned that Angleton had told the French intelligence chief that the CIA station chief in Paris was a Soviet agent, Colby had had enough. The opportunity to ask for Angleton's resignation came when the scandal over the CIA's spying activities on antiwar protesters broke into the open. The subsequent "orgy" of investigations threatened an unprecedented revelation of CIA secrets. Angleton became a media cult figure. Harvey, who meanwhile had been forced into retirement, was briefly brought back from obscurity. He died of heart failure in 1976 at age sixty. The secret war goes on, however, and there are no winners or losers, only victims.

Martin poses many troubling questions. The most serious, of course, is whether the Soviets skillfully engineered this debacle or whether the CIA was doing this to itself. Martin does not really come to grips with this issue. His fascinating story is pieced together from fragmentary information. The primary sources are countless interviews with retired intelligence officers, including many, many hours with Angleton; but no documentation whatsoever is given. Martin also relies on released documents, the public record, and an undoubtedly substantial amount of other previously published material. The necessity of keeping his primary sources confidential may be conceded to the author, but he might have cited the other material. This certainly would have enhanced the book's utility for serious students of the American intelligence establishment.

Manfred Grote

WILL
The Autobiography of G. Gordon Liddy

Author: G. Gordon Liddy (1930-   )
Publisher: Dell/St. Martin's Press (New York). 374 pp. $13.95
Type of work: Autobiography
Time: 1932 to the present
Locale: The Northeastern and Middle Western United States

*The sometimes harrowing, many times amusing, and always fascinating account of
an "underground man" who surfaced to tell his tale of political espionage, betrayal,
and triumph over enemies*

> *Principal personages:*
> G. GORDON LIDDY, the most famous of the convicted Watergate
>   burglars
> J. EDGAR HOOVER, the dictatorial director of the Federal Bureau
>   of Investigation, 1924-1972
> JOHN DEAN, special adviser to President Nixon who divulged all he
>   knew about the Watergate break-in and cover-up
> RICHARD M. NIXON, thirty-seventh President of the United States,
>   1969-1974, who was implicated in the Watergate cover-up
> JOHN MITCHELL, Attorney General of the United States during the
>   Nixon years
> JOHN EHRLICHMAN and
> ROBERT HALDEMAN, assistants to President Nixon, both convicted
>   for their participation in Watergate

G. Gordon Liddy is a fascinating character and his autobiography, *Will*,
reinforces his reputation as a colorful man whose quest for the limits of his
courage catapulted him into celebrity. Few readers of *Will* would deny Liddy's
implicit premise that he, through sheer determination, managed to alter the
course of American history and many readers have discovered that Liddy,
despite his eccentricities, is an intelligent man who tells a good story.

    The reader quickly discovers that Liddy's life had far more to it than simply
an involvement in the Watergate break-in at National Democratic Headquarters in Washington. In fact, the Watergate episode, although showcased,
often takes a back seat to even more unusual escapades. It is difficult to
believe, and this is the only trouble with the work, that he did half the things
he says.

    Early in life, Liddy learned some hard lessons, many of which he taught
himself. As a young man reared in Hoboken, New Jersey, in the 1930's, he
was cursed by terrifying feelings of inadequacy brought on by his fear of
various things, from the roar made by the dirigible *Akron* as it flew over his
home to the fluttering of small moths at night in his bedroom. "Soon," confesses Liddy, "my every waking moment was ruled by that over-riding emotion: fear."

    His fears grew geometrically, each new one greatly heightening his hysteria.

(Some fears, such as that of the "moth-millers" casting shadows on his wall, seem absurd, while others, such as fear of pain and fire, do not.) Eventually, he became obsessed by a fear of God, fueled by nightmarish tales told to him by priests and nuns at Hoboken's SS Peter and Paul Church, stories about how God became furious with small boys who failed to make the proper sign of the cross. Moreover, he was informed that prayers must be said nightly for all deceased family members so that their souls would not feel the torments of Purgatory. God's omnipotence, compared with young Liddy's vulnerability and awkwardness, made Him seem more the ogre than the Father. The priests and nuns made Him out to be cruel rather than compassionate, demanding rather than forgiving.

Appalled by his paralyzing fear of all sorts of phenomena, Liddy constantly tried to make himself brave by testing his will rather than stewing in his own cowardice. "Will," it soon becomes apparent, is Liddy's byword and his supreme god. In fact, in his estimation, to be stoical in the face of life's terrors is to exercise will power which in turn allows one to feel pride rather than shame, to be in control rather than controlled, to deny all feelings of submission and weakness.

Liddy's belief in will has been alluded to many times since he became famous for participating in Watergate, and he has been called many things because of his unbending attitude toward those who wish to obtain vital information about the Watergate break-in from him, from Fascist, to dunce, to criminal, to lunatic. Yet, in press accounts, there is evidence of a sneaking admiration for Liddy's sense of self and dedication to abstract principle.

As the guilty and fear-ridden child in Hoboken, Liddy decided to do something about his "spinelessness" and, in so doing, rid himself of self-loathing and regain his health. His mother's tales of American Indians bravely enduring physical torture without showing signs of suffering and of runner Glen Cunningham overcoming the handicap of badly burned legs and becoming a champion runner inspired Liddy, who came to believe that if these people could find self-respect, so could he.

Liddy was to continually test himself in order to achieve his goal of self-mastery. His accounts of these tests are numbered among the highlights of his life story. For one test, he focused on his dread of rats by chasing an enormous wharf rat, cornering it, and yelling loudly at it, forcing it to run into the water. Much later in life, he was once again to encounter and deal with the rat fear, this time not only chasing and cornering a large rat, but also eating it. (Such demonstrations of "will," of course, can also be taken as signs of mental disorder.)

The best explanation for why Liddy refused to cooperate with those investigating Watergate is an understanding of this behavior as part of a continuum. Certainly Liddy is consistent, the fearful child who pushes away feelings of anxiety by showing will power giving way to the paranoid adult who deals with "soft" feelings by becoming rigid and self-contained.

If one believes what Liddy says (and at times it is very hard to do so), his obsession with will greatly helped him. It enabled him, for example, to be calm when faced by angry locals in a small town in Indiana during his stint as Federal Bureau of Investigation (FBI) officer and to use force whenever it was necessary to fight.

His obsession also gives rise to his reputation as a Fascist devoted to Nazi regalia, oaths, and rituals. This reputation, however, is not entirely undeserved, for, despite his talk about identifying with the victims of Nazi persecution, Liddy seems remarkably fascinated by both Adolf Hitler's power and Heinrich Himmler's exploits. It seems safe to say that, whether he knows it or not, Liddy does have a Fascist streak.

He admits, for example, that being brought up in a German area of Hoboken helped form his outlook on the world; he was, by his own admission, taken with symbols of Nazi brute power such as the airship *Hindenberg*, Hitler's Nuremberg rallies, and the chilling songs about "fatherland" and "blood and steel." Liddy identifies with both victim and victimizer, although the greater of the two identifications is with the former, not the latter. Yet, it is curious that he goes to such lengths to establish his reputation as a friend of the downtrodden Jews.

Just as Liddy classifies entire nations by the will of its people—or lack thereof—he also classifies individuals he encounters. Among his heroes is former FBI Director J. Edgar Hoover and, true to form, what he most admires is Hoover's incredible will to command and overcome obstacles. Attorney General John Mitchell of the Richard Nixon White House is also singled out by Liddy as an exemplar of manliness and courage under fire as is Nixon himself. To Nixon, Liddy gave his all, preferring to go to prison rather than tell what he knew about the Watergate burglary. Perhaps it is to his credit that Liddy remained quiet, never divulging information to anyone, although his stubbornness may be another indication of some mad inner rigidity rather than a token of a noble nature.

Because he hates weakness, Liddy despises those who equivocate to prosecutors just as he hates quitters, cowards, and liars. At the pinnacle of Liddy's dishonor roll is John Dean, the young lawyer who served as President Nixon's special adviser before Watergate ended his career. Dean "squealed" on his friends and coworkers in the Nixon White House and, despite the fact that he too went to jail for his part in Watergate, Dean is considered by Liddy to be the lowest of the low.

Ever since he was a young man, Liddy prided himself on his unquestioning duty to and admiration for authority figures. His youthful fear of God and his enthusiastic saluting of the flag were one and the same: demonstrations of a love of powerful things by a man who once felt completely powerless. One does not have to be a psychologist to see an emergent pattern.

Will has taken many reviewers by surprise. Expecting low comedy and little else from this pompous, strutting Watergate burglar, they have found pathos and drama in Liddy's story despite themselves. Liddy has led an interesting life filled with adventure. Long before the Watergate incident, Liddy was chasing desperadoes in Gary, Indiana, and rats in Hoboken, swearing blood oaths and confounding enemies with his incredible will, getting in and out of trouble, and learning CIA dirty tricks.

Although few readers would exchange lives with Liddy, he has a certain rough charm—even charisma—which makes him stand out from the crowd. It is difficult not to like Liddy, for despite his heroic posturing and preening, one detects the sad, scared little boy in him. His life story is riveting reading because he is at once fool and man of insight, bully boy and protector, clown and dignified stoic. Like all interesting persons, he is difficult to identify absolutely.

No doubt *Will* has been so popular with readers because its writer is a "character." Yet, without denying his eccentric nature, it is fairer to say that Liddy, while surely no saint or great intellect, is a genuinely engaging fellow. He has done what few people have either the capacity or will to do: namely, to live in accordance with inner principles.

His book is a classic of the most minor order, but a classic nevertheless, the testament of one strangely possessed man whose belief in will helped bring an American presidency to its end.

John D. Raymer

WILLIAM FAULKNER
His Life and Work

Author: David Minter (1935-   )
Publisher: The Johns Hopkins University Press (Baltimore, Maryland). 325 pp. $16.95
Type of work: Literary biography
Time: 1897-1962
Locale: The United States, primarily Mississippi, New Orleans, New York, and Hollywood

A study of Faulkner's writings in the context of his life, this work finds deep affinities and reciprocities between the settings and issues of Faulkner's biography and the characters and themes of his fiction

William Faulkner's art is replete with paradox at every level. He is at once America's greatest regional artist and its greatest national artist. His major work is grounded deeper than most in a specific region—the South—and reflects its historic experience of isolation, exploitation, racism, defeat, poverty, and their consequences for the human spirit, or sense of self. At the same time, and precisely because of the narrowness of William Faulkner's focus on this peculiar region, his work explores more deeply than most what appear increasingly to be the essential qualities of the American experience. For what characterizes the Southern experience is, finally, what characterizes the American experience—the isolation from cultural roots, the exploitation of the land, the racist assault on Indians and on other settlers not of WASP backgrounds, the defeat at the hands of the wilderness or the economy, the essential emotional and economic poverty of the majority of Americans. What characterizes Southerners is, perhaps, the fact that their great defeat came earlier than it did for the rest of the nation; forced to live with shattered dreams, with the national guilt over slavery, with grinding poverty, at least some Southerners came to find in narrative, in the telling of stories, at least a way to endure if not to understand their history and their character.

Such were Faulkner's roots. In his chronicles of his "little postage stamp of earth," the fictional world of Yoknapatawpha County, Mississippi, Faulkner created in the Compsons and the Sartorises images of the failed Southern planter aristocracy, and in the Snopses images of the new American humanity. In the one, readers see the exhaustion of European culture in the new world as it sought to duplicate itself but had to rely on slave labor to tear space for itself out of the wilderness. In the other, readers find the new American, amoral, individualistic, acquisitive, willing to sacrifice everything to make another step up the ladder toward its definition of success. In all these families there is hardly a success story, a true hero in any traditional sense; Faulkner's theme is, finally, the nature of failure, the nature of human limitations. The only moments of "success" are those small victories of compassion and love and caring which at least leaven the time. All there is to hold on to in

Faulkner's world is the telling of stories, the very use of language to narrate, the struggle through narrative to find meaning, that in ways necessarily imprecise and unclear give history and context and the ability to go on with life.

Although David Minter's work does not evoke this larger context for Faulkner's writing, it does explore more deeply than any other recent study the complex network of interactions between Faulkner's life and personality and his fictional world. Unlike Joseph Blotner's recent two-volume *Faulkner* (1974), which relates in elaborate and lengthy detail all the events of Faulkner's life, Minter's *William Faulkner* notes only the events relevant, in his view, to a coherent and complex and finally very satisfying overview of Faulkner's literary career. Blotner's work is, as Minter points out, "a storehouse of facts," but little more. What makes Minter's work so distinctive and important is his ability to make a whole piece out of the facts, a myth about Faulkner that, finally, has the ring of authenticity to it. He does not slight the complexity of the man or the work; in the final analysis, he creates a Faulkner who is plausibly the author of his fiction, a considerable achievement in literary biography.

Minter's Faulkner is no saint; his was a "flawed life." Deeply desirous of tenderness and affection, he was prevented by a profound shyness and a sense of aristocratic reserve from asking for the love he desperately needed. This sense of inner conflict, so profoundly Southern in its simultaneous capacity for great feeling and need for protection in social convention, Minter finds manifest in the great novels. For they display the drive to love, to self-revelation, as well as the fear of exposure and the compulsion to self-protection. In a Thomas Sutpen, hero of *Absalom, Absalom!* for example, the drive toward family and prosperity contains its own self-destructive seeds, so that his child by one woman winds up destroying his child by another. In a Quentin Compson, the inability to love and be loved for himself turns into a passion for his sister that can only lead to suicide.

Indeed, Minter's Faulkner is a man who finds in artistic expression the distancing from his past and his inner world that enabled him to be honest and personal within it. By transforming life into art, which is assertively "not-life," Faulkner was able to reveal himself with an honesty he was incapable of in real life. Trapped in a marriage that must never have been more than superficially satisfying, coming from a region profoundly suspicious of the life of the mind and of art, growing up in a social milieu that valued superficial displays of emotion as well as rigid social distinctions, Faulkner found in art the possibilities of displacement and disguise that finally enabled him to express himself profoundly and personally.

Minter's view of Faulkner's life falls into three loose divisions. The early period, in which Faulkner wrote poetry and his early novels *Soldiers' Pay* and *Mosquitoes*, is characterized by an increasing sense of literary and artistic vocation and the discovery in prose of a medium of expression suited to the man's gifts and temperament. The middle period, the age of the great novels *The Sound and the Fury, Absalom, Absalom!,* and *Go Down, Moses,* is characterized by the discovery of the ability to use his region's inheritance of the love of language and narrative, its complex narrative skills to conceal as well as reveal, to create profoundly moving and magnificent works of art. The final period, loosely that from the end of World War II to Faulkner's death in 1962, is one of increasing difficulty in writing, of trying to write a novel— *A Fable*—of ideas and abstractions rather than one of particularities, a task unsuited to his gifts.

One of Minter's strengths is his placing Faulkner's works in the context of his struggle to create art as well as to make a living. Except toward the end of his life, Faulkner always faced financial difficulties. A number of his works, as well as his stints in Hollywood as a script writer, were done explicitly to make money. As Faulkner aged, he felt an increasing conflict between the desire to create art and the demands of his bank account; with a sense of ebbing energy, he experienced increasing frustration, which resulted in an increasing difficulty to write even the kinds of books he wanted to write. Clearly, the bouts of drinking, the almost pathetic affairs with younger women, the reckless episodes of horseback riding that Minter describes in Faulkner's later years bespeak a self-destructiveness, a sense of the loss of the power to create as well as a loss of people and possibilities dear to him. Nevertheless, Minter suggests that Faulkner's last novel—*The Reivers*—was a kind of culmination, a last exploration of his great themes and methods, so that Minter can conclude that Faulkner died after having completed the project he set out to do. His death was, therefore, not tragic, but an ending that had to come, and he knew had to come, but was delayed until after his life's work was complete.

Inevitably, in any critical study, there are omissions, or, at least, any reviewer will wish for more discussion of certain points. Here, what seems to be underemphasized is Faulkner's role as a great experimenter in fiction, one of that generation of American writers, including Gertrude Stein, Ernest Hemingway, and Sherwood Anderson, who transformed our images of what was possible and permissible in fiction, and along the way created an American literature that ranked, for the first time, with writing anywhere in the world. Minter does note Faulkner's friendship with Anderson in New Orleans, but he does not delve into where Faulkner might have learned to take the liberties with the conventional novel form that are so dramatically a part of his great works. This, however, is only a small reservation, for what Minter does give the reader is a version of Faulkner that is satisfying and convincing, and will repay careful attention.

John N. Wall, Jr.

WINDROSE
Poems 1929-1979

Author: Brewster Ghiselin (1903-   )
Publisher: University of Utah Press (Salt Lake City). 238 pp. $25.00
Type of work: Poetry

Not quite a definitive Collected Poems, this volume includes the best work of an important poet, and gives promise of more fine work to come

This extremely handsome book, produced with the taste and care which have come to characterize the publications of the University of Utah Press, brings together most of the work in Brewster Ghiselin's four earlier collections, and adds to them twenty-four new poems. Specifically, it contains most of the poems, now carefully rearranged, from *Against the Circle* (1946) and *The Nets* (1955); all but a few poems (in Italian) from *Country of the Minotaur* (1970), and all the poems printed in a handsome limited edition, *Light* (1978). The new poems, arranged in two groups, "Waters" and "Shapes, Vanishings," reveal a finely honed sensibility not yet content with the dazzling successes of earlier work.

Over the past fifty years, American poetry seems to have become increasingly preoccupied with the personal, manifested as confession or subjective vision. What this means, or whether it is good or bad, is not pertinent here; it is noted because in such a context, Ghiselin's poems are rather startling for the vastness of their scope, and for the reticence of those few poems which seem to arise from the poet's close involvements with other people. Ghiselin's subject is most often the place of man in nature—nature in the broadest sense, as when a particle physicist says, "In theory, quarks exist in nature." Such an utterance takes readers some way from the Nature of British verse or landscape painting; and Ghiselin's poems, too, are far from that world, encompassing the ocean, the western desert and mountains, the moon, stars, and comets, as well as man, that salesman of real estate, that installer of streetlamps.

Ghiselin's explorations of seascape and desertscape often lead him to a kind of large statement rare in the poetry of today. It is earned, in these poems, by a close attention to observed details—the precise shape of a rock or a bird's head, for example—and an attention to the sound of words which sometimes becomes excessively fastidious. Ghiselin has thought long and productively about the motions and sensations of the human vocal apparatus, and writes many lines and phrases consciously designed to produce specific movements of the tongue and throat which, the reader finds when he executes them, have often a surprising appropriateness to the moment of the poem in which they occur.

In his search for precision and memorable statement, however, Ghiselin does not forget that ceaseless change is integral to his subject; and so a certain fluidity is felt even in his most definitive-sounding lines. He produces nothing unfinished—far from it—but he manages to avoid giving the impression that he wants his words carved in stone. His poems are always on the move.

It is perhaps this quality of movement that enables Ghiselin to work with stories and characters from classical mythology. Such material has become unfashionable, mostly for sound reasons; Robert Bly's statement, that a classical reference means instant death for the poem in which it occurs, is perhaps intemporate, but Bly has reason to be impatient: such material weighed heavily on most of the worst poetry of the 1950's. Ghiselin invokes, however, only those myths which have life for him, and which he has the skill to make live; and so in his hands they still speak to our condition. As he says in the title poem of his third book, "Only because a man is here/This is the country of the minotaur."

Most of the aforementioned qualities and tendencies are evident in the first poem in this book, "The Vision of Adam." This, at about 150 lines, is by a hundred lines the longest poem in either of Ghiselin's first two books; not until *Country of the Minotaur* would he again approach the long meditation. Adam—not literally the first man, but a man with the Namer's name—at the edge of the ocean, ponders his place in the tension between wind and wave, land and sea, wondering how to satisfy his desire for something like truth. At last he enters the ocean, near sundown, and in the darkness, feels the power of life in the sea, and achieves a recognition of the kind of vision he has sought. It is curiously unvisionary:

> "There is no need of image, for him who can hide himself perfectly
> Under the shield of darkness," he thought, "and with naked hands
> Touch the live God, unbewildered by the mind's light,
> Prismatic through concept, coloring the world.
> I need always in me the Power without shining or darkness
> Flowing from the fountains that nourish
> Serpent and bird, ocean, and sun and moon, and the strong earth.
> These babblings are truth and falsehood mingled.
> No man tells the truth."

The conclusion of the poem acknowledges the human ability to possess secrets for which there is no language, but which are available to almost anyone with good eyesight: the sun, the sea, the loveliness of vultures in flight. The poem describes no hallucinatory vision, but the more difficult realization that may come with the hard-won recognition of things as they are. Most of the short poems that comprise the rest of *Against the Circle* and *The Nets* are devoted to achieving such recognition.

An interesting example of Ghiselin's attention and precision is "Watercolor by Paul Nash: 'Folly Landscape, Creech, Dorset,' " which falls in to that subgenre of poems about paintings. This poem manages to transcend the pitfalls of the genre, too many examples of which tend to recall the proverb about the relative value of words and pictures. "Watercolor" becomes a poem about something else, departing almost immediately from a literalist look at the picture; the opening lines describe a "folly," one of those odd stone structures built on the English countryside by eccentric gentlemen:

> Piercing a length of wall a child could circle
> In three breaths running, three great doorways gaze
> Through stonework paled by blisters of high cloud

Presumably, the running child is not depicted in the painting. Readers see the child, however, and are led on to see an imagined landscape informed by a poem, rather than a report on a picture. The odd structures on the hills are "solitude/And absence, voices in an enormous hall"; the arches have no function, provide no shelter, but make of themselves a "Threshhold leading from the wind into the wind." "Watercolor" is a poem of only a dozen lines, but it moves quickly and majestically from the child to the gigantic absence at the end.

Similarly, "Rattlesnake" begins as a first-person speaker encounters a snake; the pronoun "I" appears four times in nine short lines. When the speaker kills the snake, however, a general withdrawal of life from the landscape seems to occur:

> I crushed him deep in dust,
> And heard the loud seethe of life
> In the dead beads of the tail
> Fade, as wind fades
> From the wild grain of the hill.

The shift from "I" and "him" to "beads," "tail," "wind," and "hill" is absolute by the last line; it emphasizes, as do many of Ghiselin's poems, that the human notion of permanence is subject to revision among the hard but mutable mountains.

The one-sided nature of the human interaction with the nonhuman world is treated ironically in another short poem form *Against the Circle*, "The Indifferent Mountains":

> They stare above me, hard and bleak and strange
> After a thousand days as when I came,
> Looking beyond me, aware of one another,
> Mountains like faces in a foreign street.
> They have not seen my youth.

The next several lines speculate on various romantic recollections of childhood, and on what difference it would have made if the mountains could have seen those moments. If they had, "They could not look with a mask-hollow stare./They would remember as the southwind does."

One goes back to that last line from time to time, to see whether the southwind actually remembers anything or not. The mountains, however, have not seen anything, ever; if the speaker had spent his childhood among them, instead of the brief period of a thousand days, they might seem less removed from his world; but as Ghiselin says again and again, theirs is an old world into which man has lately come.

This is the predominant approach to nonhuman nature throughout these poems. The theme achieves its finest expression in several poems from *Country of the Minotaur*, which, as Ghiselin says in the Preface to this volume,

> stands as first printed, except for the omission of the final section, poems written in Italian, accompanied by literal translations. These, no longer in the place of conclusion, seemed likely to impede passage of most readers to the poems of the fourth book, *Light*.

In fact, Ghiselin has made one slight change which he does not mention: he gives the title "Triptych" to the third and central section of the book, thereby making explicit what seemed likely even when "Sea," "The Wheel," and "Aphrodite of the Return" were preceded only by a blank page bearing the numerae III.

"Sea" is, at some 260 lines, Ghiselin's longest poem; it may also be his finest. Divided into eleven sections, the white space between them providing room for movement and reverberation, "Sea" is a vast lyrical meditation on the sea as source and repository of life, and on the permanent cycle of change. A central tension in the poem is introduced early in the poem:

> But all are issue of the dust. The clear
> Water here in my hand is full of dust,
> Dissolvings of life and death: powder of fire
> And sea-born earth returned to the using sea.

The dust that gathers from the unmaking of mountains is perhaps a surprising choice for a central image in a poem called "Sea." Ghiselin's vision, however, is inclusive, his attention unwavering, and the constant interaction between water and dust becomes a stunning portrayal of the movement inherent in apparent stillness:

> Beautiful to us therefore the winds' violence,
> The lifted modulations of the dust,
> The dry hills that are called everlasting
> Vague in the veils of their mortality.

A statement of such scope and finality of tone is hard to follow, even in a long poem; Ghiselin's tactic is to focus on something smaller in Section VII:

a skull rolling in the shallows. He gives it speech, and it sighs its desire for life, even amidst pain and filth: "Now I am a clicking system of reminders." Yet, the section concludes with the recognition that the skull's words are those of the speaker of the poem, "detained by dreams."

The concluding sections of this poem return to the cycle of change, and to the exhilarating impossibility of finding words for it, and end with a knowledge of "something past belief," "The changes of the water and the dust,/And silence under every syllable."

"The Wheel" is sharper in tone, more critical of human tendencies to make things which outrun human power. The wheel is man-made:

> The dark of my theme
> Gathers on the street corners—names no day. . . .
> The repetitions of the wheel ascend
> All high places, fill up with honey light
> At evening the target towers.

This poem reminds the reader that he is part of the changing earth. The only animal cursed with knowledge of the extinction of species, yet humans fail to imagine, at least constructively, their own extinction.

The "Triptych" ends with a much shorter poem than either of the first two. Although it is only forty-two lines, "Aphrodite of the Return" achieves largeness of scope, and its "place of conclusion" in the sequence, by means of a shifting and wide ranging consciousness in its speaker, who moves from direct observation to statement and back again with an almost bewildering swiftness. The speaker visualizes Aphrodite on the waves, in the person of the woman he loves, and sees the possibility of love as a force like other natural forces, which may have power enough to redeem us, as dolphins "[stitch] the sea, sheltering only in their act,/As a running needle clothes itself in the garment."

Light and the new poems in *Windrose* seem to be of a piece, interestingly different in some ways from what has preceded them. There is more variety of tone in these poems; touches of humor, satirical and otherwise, mellow the whole assortment. "Let There Be Light" and "And There Was Light" are concerned with the installation of streetlamps in the speaker's neighborhood—not a subject that one would have expected to see in Ghiselin's work. The first poem notes the way light has of lifting or dulling one's sense of fear, and the way humans have of unwittingly plotting their own destruction. The second poem finds the neighborhood protected by "Four Thousand Lumen Mercury Vapor Ornamental Luminaires," but the extravagance of the satire in that line gives way to a moving conclusion:

> But I, in our endless light,
> Whirl like a bird blown down
> With its boughs in a blast of sparks

> To fly from fire at the heart
> Of a dark forest.

True, in his most recent poems, Ghiselin continues to be at his best observing waves, birds, mountains, and other entities beyond the human scale of things. "Song at San Carlos Bay," for example, is among his very best poems. In these recent poems, however, it is good to see a willingness to go at something a little slighter now and then, something a little less vast in vision and implication. It is also good to see a desire to widen the boundaries of print by typographical experiments with word placement and white space. Others have made similar experiments, to be sure; but that Ghiselin continues in his seventies to expand his technical resources as well as his receptiveness to various subjects, is among the signs that one of America's very finest poets is not ready to call this his last collection.

Henry Taylor

THE WOMAN WHO LIVED IN A PROLOGUE

Author: Nina Schneider (1913-   )
Publisher: Houghton Mifflin Company (Boston). 479 pp. $13.95
Type of work: Novel
Time: 1900 to about 1973
Locale: New York and New Hampshire

Ariadne Assair Arkady writes her life story, spanning the first three quarters of this century, in order to reach an understanding of who she is in distinction from all the roles she has had to play, among them, daughter, wife, mother, lover, and grandmother

> *Principal characters:*
> ARIADNE ASSAIR ARKADY, the narrator-protagonist, who in her
> seventies writes her story
> ADAM ARKADY, her husband, a computer expert, publicly proud
> of her but privately cold
> PAUL DONANT, her jealous lover and an artist
> JEREMY STAROBIN, M. D., her doctor and confidant
> ABSALOM, her eldest, a schizophrenic and runaway
> ARIEL, her daughter, a successful artist and mother
> AARON, her son, killed in action
> BENJAMIN, her son, in the family computer business

Now, when so many women's novels about women follow a predictable pattern—proper marriage and children, disenchantment, a raised consciousness, departure from home, discovery of a new self—Nina Schneider's *The Woman Who Lived in a Prologue* has significant and refreshing differences. To a point she follows the formula: there is the marriage, there are the children, there is disenchantment. Here the similarity stops. One difference is that Ariadne, the narrator and protagonist, remains wife and devoted mother. The real distinction, however, is that Ariadne's quest is not for liberation from what she has experienced in her roles as daughter, wife, mother, lover, but for an understanding of that life, with its vicissitudes, its moments of glory, its hours of pain, its days of humdrum activity.

In the course of the novel, this central character quotes from Virginia Woolf certain lines that one might imagine challenged Schneider to create this compelling book: "A painstaking woman who wishes to treat life as she finds it, and to give voice to some of the perplexities of her sex, in plain English, has no chance at all." Ariadne's *is* a story, painstakingly told, of life as she has found it, and her perplexities are its substance. If many of these perplexities remain unresolved or ambiguously resolved, this is not for lack of effort on her part: it is expressly to assess her life, to understand its winding course, to seek order in its seeming chaos, that she writes.

Her impulse to write her story dates back, as she recalls, to her twenty-ninth year, when by chance she found in a *New York Times Book Review* these words: "In each of us there exists one novel." An efficient housewife, a notable hostess, and four times a mother then, Ariadne looked into herself and, ironically, found nothing for a book: "A novel in me? There wasn't enough for a Mother's Day postcard." This is ironic since literature—as will be shown later—gives her, life-long, her main points of reference for her own experience. As her life has progressed and become more complex, she has made several false starts on her book; but only in her seventies, the present time of the novel, is she able to devote herself to the task, free now of the old demands and obligations.

When she begins this search for herself, Ariadne ponders:

> My problem is, I've been pottering about with my egg basket for so many years that I have a suspicion I have become the actions I've scratched out. Chicken! And what does an old hen, one that's done with laying, have to talk about except eggs lost in cabbage patches, chicks, mash, and the pecking order?

Her urgency, however, is to discover the answer to "Where do *I* begin?" so she can "chart my existence from then." Nor is she ready to accept what the actuarial charts tell her; however old, she yet wakes "every morning to the sensation that my real life is waiting, immanent."

Her aim is to find out who she is, whether there is order to be found in her personal chaos, what her relations really have been with the people in her life, where and why she has failed to connect, what if any have been her successes. The result is a portrait of a fully credible woman who, from the perspective of wisdom earned through her vicissitudes, discerns her past as she could not while immersed in its events.

From her account of her earlier years, Ariadne's life on the surface has been conventional and calm, troubled only by common hardships and sorrows: the struggle of a young couple through the Depression, the deaths of a war hero son, her parents and other relatives, the disappearance of her eldest child, Absalom. Otherwise, most people's perception of her would be that of a woman well married, a marvelously efficient Jewish housewife, mother and helpmate. By contrast, the character whom the reader comes to know has suffered through the abortion of her first baby at her unemployed husband Adam's insistence; an immediate second pregnancy and Adam's subsequent disaffection; a total loss of self-esteem; a tormenting although exhilarating love affair with Paul, an artist and Lothario, that ends with another pregnancy, a second abortion and the consequent loss of her dear friend Dr. Starobin's sympathy; wracking self-questioning about her guilt in relation to Absalom's disappearance; and the problem of dealing with her daughter Ariel's first-born, a Down's syndrome baby.

In large part, the tension between these public and private selves shapes the consciousness that is Ariadne as she writes her book. Much of her effort is devoted to trying to understand how these disparate parts of her life can be said to make up a whole and integral person. Old now, she can see how inchoate, how innocent, how ignorant, have been her motives and impulses and drives. She can wonder how much of her has been governed by choice, how much by chance, how much by pressures which she had no means to combat.

There are many directions in which one could go in discussing Schneider's novel. For example, is it, like many first novels, autobiographical? There seems no occasion to think so. Apparently, Schneider and her heroine have in common chiefly their being immigrants from Europe, their knowledge of Jewish life, their early attraction to Sir Thomas Malory and their life-long love of poetry. Very unlike Ariadne, Nina Schneider is a magna cum laude graduate of Brooklyn College, twice married, mother of two, prolific author (with her second husband) of juvenile books on scientific and technical subjects with titles such as *Let's Find Out About Electricity* and *How Your Body Works*, contributor of poems to several journals, and university teacher. Further, although Ariadne has died before her book is published, one is able to hope that *The Woman Who Lived in a Prologue* is not the "one novel" that Schneider will find in herself.

Then there is the matter of narrative technique. Probably the most important device shaping the novel is its point of view. Schneider's art seems artless to the extent that the reader never questions whether this is "really" the protagonist's work being read. Ariadne writes in first person almost entirely, the several exceptions being when, to distance herself from a humiliating scene, she adopts the third person. As becomes clear in the first pages, Ariadne as narrator is a woman of wit, intelligence, high literacy and high verbal ability.

In this character, Schneider has created a very conscious artist, one who divides her novel into three books and fifteen chapters, in addition to a Prologue and an Epilogue, each of these having titles and epigraphs that serve to tie together her only roughly chronological account of the memories that she relives as vividly as the days during which she writes. The titles and epigraphs are—to adopt the required "willing suspension of disbelief"—not Schneider's addition but Ariadne's; the character is indeed her own autobiographer, and she has chosen her epigraphs as carefully as T. S. Eliot did his, to give direction to her reader.

The fact that contrary to her cousin Jessica's advice she rejects the idea of writing a novel with a conventional beginning, middle, and end seems to indicate Ariadne's awareness that life cannot be so tidily charted. Yet, she persists in her struggle to find order:

In the fictional world, incidents are supposed to add up to a right course, a revelation. But these tableaux I see behind me—an event here, an event there—float apart as I study them. Scenes invade and impinge on scenes, impervious to order. . . . In after-touching memory I try to formulate patterns; I want every gesture, every incident to fall into place as a part of becoming.

As these words indicate, the narrative line is complex. A scene from Ariadne's seventies may lead her to one from her childhood or early married years; or she may pause within a recalled episode to meditate upon a thought that has just occurred. In these meditations as much as in her actions, Ariadne reveals the depth of her passion for life. For instance, thinking of her paratrooper son's death in World War II, she writes of the absurdity of wars:

> If not for those Utopian grandiosities that spring up fully armed, dragon's teeth sown in the service of arrogant doctrine, Aaron [would be alive]. . . . I, a matriarch, say take the world away from men and give it to mothers for a while. It needs to be washed, put to sleep, so the bloody mouths, the trashed limbs, the shredded nerves may heal. Give the damn thing back to us who salvage coffee tins, preserve unripe tomatoes, conserve orange peel, as ants carry off eggs because they are eggs. Stop the fighting. . . . Put down your explosives. Everybody, into bed for a nap.

That Ariadne determines to write a novel after finding the quotation from the book review hints at the importance of literature to her. It is, in fact, integral both to her way of perceiving experience and to her prose style. For instance, one of her earliest-loved books was Malory's *Morte d'Arthur*, where Lancelot the Misfit, driven mad by love, not devout Arthur, enchanted her; much later, these two knights give her metaphors for describing her ardent but tormented and tormenting lover Paul and her proper but cold husband Adam. Throughout her narrative she alludes—often without quotation marks, often in close paraphrase—to *Tristram Shandy*, to William Shakespeare (*Romeo and Juliet* encourages her dreams of romantic love; Othello's rages become Paul's), and to lines from a wide range of poets, among them Christina Rossetti, Robert Browning, Gerard Manley Hopkins, Andrew Marvell, the Bible, William Butler Yeats, John Donne, and particularly, T. S. Eliot.

She first encounters Eliot in high school through "The Love Song of J. Alfred Prufrock"; subsequently, she absorbs his major poems to the extent that his phrases are part of her everyday life, giving her means of expression and giving both herself and her reader a reference point, a further context, for understanding her feelings. Thus, "Prufrock" furnishes her with lines she paraphrases in dealing with her hurt at her children's rebellion: "I have learned them all already, learned them all," "I too have wept and prayed." *The Waste Land* supplies words for her dismay at Adam's failure as a lover with lines from the neurotic bedroom scene in "A Game of Chess": "Speak to me. Why do you never speak to me?" (By contrast, words from Donne's arrogant love poems echo through her account of her affair with Paul: "'I wonder by my troth what thou and I did till we lov'd'" and, indirectly quoted, "For God's sake let me love.") Then *Four Quartets* is alluded to in lines such as "It was not, to say it again, what one had expected," and "the intolerable shirt of flame," as is "Marina" ("Woodthrush calling through the fog" when Ariadne contemplates the distance between herself and her daughter).

Permeated as her mind is by literature, however, the woman as she writes can admit that her reading has sometimes failed her and that some of her perplexities have been caused by illusions gained from books: "I was the best-read girl in the class but I hadn't figured out how Tess of the D'Urbervilles *and* Hester Prynne got pregnant if they didn't want to. Or how, if they had wanted to," and "Nothing in literature has allowed an Ariadne to grow up and become the bereaved Jocasta or the wailing Niobe."

Besides matters of technique, there are many other potentially fruitful points worthy of consideration in Ariadne's narrative: her growing understanding of her husband, Adam; her long friendship with Dr. Jeremy Starobin; her relations with Ariel, her one child whom she believes to be fulfilled in that she is both a successful artist and a successful mother. Or, one might focus on the after-effects of a teenage crush on a lifeguard, the "Irish cupid" whose fumbling efforts at lovemaking are recalled repeatedly; or, on the fine portraits of Ariadne's old-world relatives; or, on the use of natural imagery and the significance of her garden; or even, on the theme of the viability of old art forms for the next generations.

To select only one further aspect of the novel for comment, then, is to do an injustice to the richness of Schneider's work. Because language is a writer's tool, however, perhaps it is fitting to center briefly on that topic here.

Language is of natural interest to Ariadne, for she herself has a way with words that at times invests even painful memories with a certain wit, and that always reflects her concern for language as a medium of communication that is too easily abused. Remembering her first abortion, how she was in physical and emotional pain and Adam was withdrawn and cold, old Ariadne can give even such a scene a fillip with a phrase that does not deny the pain but that reflects her present perspective on it: "So there we were, Adam and I, with my physiology and his humiliation and only one bed." She can describe her reaction to Adam in their bed by saying, "I get the disappointed feeling one has when the bath water runs cold, and my mind wanders to whether I've added cat food to my shopping list." Her pleasure in and command of words is always evident; she plays computer-language games with her grandchildren, winning "wows" for her "'the heart cannot thump for joy at discovering the precisions encased in a capacitor,'" and she reports with evident satisfaction that these youngsters say she looks "like a cross between a silent screen star and the dean of St. Paul's." Empty social conversation, on the other hand, is given a satiric slash: Ariadne's son Benjamin leaves his wife when he discerns her as a nonperson whose dialogue is limited to "'Fabulous . . . gourmet . . . finalize . . . sort of . . . love it . . . kinna . . . I mean . . . the vibes just turn me off. . . .'"

When the reader reluctantly reaches the end of the novel, the question naturally arises: Who, then, is Ariadne? Readers have seen that to the teenage lifeguard, she is Miss Goody Two-Shoes; to herself, a coward, as fearful of acting as her husband is of feeling; to Dr. Starobin, a child-woman who should have known that his love for her was not simply Platonic; to her husband, "little mother" even after he learns of her affair with Paul; to Paul, "'the best lay of my life'" but probably deceitful; to her daughter, a nagger but a dependable source of help; to her granddaughter, Dinah, a "'sexy old lady'" whose clothes she borrows. Finally, to the reader, she is a person of strength, charm, integrity, passion, honesty—a whole being. Her real qualities appear forcefully in two episodes narrated as the novel nears its end. Decisively and in defiance of both conventional morality and the law, she twice acts to enable her offspring to have their own lives: in her forties she does an outrageous deed that frees her daughter Ariel to become a fulfilled woman; and now, in her seventies, she turns her back on her beloved garden, dresses her grandson Daniel as her chauffeur and, so that he can avoid the Vietnam War, moves with him to Canada, where she completes her book.

Ariadne does not die within her narrative, obviously; but her death is recorded in the list of characters that precedes her Prologue. Perhaps readers are to assume that her grandson has added this list and published the manuscript. In any case, the Epilogue, with its bleak winter setting in an alien place, brings the story to a moving close. Even without the record of her death date, the reader infers that she is nearing her end, for she writes of physical signs that all is not well with her. Her spirit is high, however; no matter what perplexities life has brought her, she is ready for more. Harking back to an earlier thought, that human lives, unlike those of trees, are too short for learning to live fully, she closes her book with a kind of prayer:

> Let me begin again.
> Give me time. Not chicken time. I need sequoia time. My past has been a Prologue.
> I'm not ready to be an Epilogue.

The reader necessarily sees these closing words in relation to the title, *The Woman Who Lived in a Prologue.* For Ariadne's years, seen by her as bringing her only to the beginning of wisdom, a prologue to life, have on the contrary been full, full of the human experiences of love, of disappointment, of despair, of grief, of exultation. And what can the reader desire for this woman but that her last days be serene; as she has said earlier, *Romeo and Juliet* is now behind her and she is ready to read *King Lear.*

Margaret Raynal

WOMEN ON LOVE
Eight Centuries of Feminine Writing

Author: Evelyne Sullerot
Translated from the French by Helen R. Lane
Publisher: Doubleday & Company (Garden City, New York). 334 pp. $12.95
Type of work: Essays and writings

A study of changing feminine attitudes toward love from the twelfth to the twentieth century, with selections from the writings of 158 French women

Women on Love has its genesis in a traumatic childhood experience, author Evelyne Sullerot's first—and only—reading of the tale of Griselda, the all-suffering patient wife who was persecuted unspeakably by her husband and yet never ceased to love and obey him. The story so horrified the ten-year-old girl that she fainted on the spot. Her sympathetic mother assured her that not all love was like that, that men made up such stories for each other to compensate for their fear of being unloved, and she told her young daughter another story, this one by a woman, the Comtesse d'Aulnoy, about a prince who was transformed into a bluebird and paid nightly visits to the windowsill of his beloved to converse with her.

Thus, even as a child Sullerot was convinced that men and women experienced love in quite different ways, and as she studied treatises on the subject later in her life, she became increasingly disturbed at the one-sided view being given. She notes that Denis de Rougemont's well-known *Love in the Western World*, which she discusses at some length in her opening chapter, might more accurately be entitled *Masculine Love in the Western World*, for in it woman figures as object, as guide or obstacle on man's path to salvation, but never as a separate being with a quest of her own. *Women on Love* is Sullerot's attempt to redress the balance by allowing women to speak in their own voice of the joys and the pains they have experienced through love during the eight hundred years from the Middle Ages to the present. The writers quoted are all French, but the sentiments expressed are, Sullerot feels, representative.

The book is composed of four separate but integrally linked elements: a series of essays exploring the historical, sociological, philosophical, and literary aspects of love in each period; an anthology of writings by women, consisting of selections from a few words to a page or two in length; drawings, etchings, and engravings contemporary with the writings; and short biographical sketches of all the writers represented except those living in the twentieth century. While the introductory essays are in some ways of the greatest interest, the selections from the writings are clearly intended by the author to be the center of the book. The passages were chosen, she explains, for their intrinsic beauty, the sincerity of feeling displayed, and their representativeness of the styles and attitudes of each era.

To encourage readers to respond spontaneously and open-mindedly to each piece, she has identified her excerpts only by number, in the hope that a poignant letter from an unknown will receive the same attention and appreciation as a passage from George Sand or Simone de Beauvoir. The numbers refer the reader to the biographical sketches at the end of the book, or, in the case of twentieth century writers, simply to a name. There is, therefore, no way to tell except from the context whether one is reading from a work of fiction, a letter, a journal, or a poem. Perhaps genre and even the question of whether sentiments are "real" or fictitious are irrelevant in a work in which the intent of the author is to convey the variety of ways in which women have reacted to love. It would have been useful, however, to have a brief appendix giving the source of each passage to enable readers to pursue in more detail selections of special interest to them.

Sullerot freely acknowledges that the subject of love does not lend itself to neat chronological surveys of changing trends and progressive steps toward an ideal. What she tries to do in both her introductions to each chapter and in the passages quoted is to bring out the major characteristics of each era, while taking into account countervailing forces and individuals whose experiences are atypical. She begins her analysis with a description of the *fin amor* of the Middle Ages—what English-speaking scholars have generally referred to as courtly love. In the writing of the twelfth through the fifteenth centuries, woman is most often spoken of as queen or master meting out rewards to her adoring, deserving knight. It is the woman who sets the terms and tone of a relationship from the earliest stages of courtship into a sexual liaison; the man's role is to please her in every way possible.

In the Renaissance, sentiments of this kind linger in literary imagery, but there is a greater diversity in the experiences of women, with men exercising greater dominance and even, at times, brutality. The sixteenth century also saw the beginnings of a tension between sensuality and chastity, a conflict that would continue to be significant in succeeding eras. In the next century, women were again striving for control over men in the salons of the *precieuses*. Popular fairy tales such as "Beauty and the Beast," in the version of Madame Leprince de Beaumont, capture their vision of themselves as civilizing forces and givers of life to the men they love. Unlike the medieval ladies, however, they did not wield power in sexual relationships; they made much of "modesty," fearing that they would be entirely dominated by any man to whom they yielded.

The eighteenth century, Sullerot notes, brought tenderness into women's experience of love and the beginning of a new view of marriage as a relationship in which mutual affection was possible, if not common. In this era, the feelings of young girls came to the forefront for the first time; some of the most attractive passages in this chapter come from the journal of a schoolgirl, Helene Massalska.

With the advent of Romanticism at the beginning of the nineteenth century, tenderness gave way to the grand passion, and countless women wrote of all-consuming, ecstatic relationships in which they submitted themselves totally to the men they adored. Love was seen as a kind of demonic force against which they were powerless, or a religious experience that transported them beyond themselves. With these heights of feeling came equally great depths, and many selections reflect anguish and despair.

Sullerot observes that it would be impossible for her to distance herself from her own century enough to isolate its major attributes, but she does discuss several characteristics she has observed. At the beginning of this period, there was a wave of lesbian writing, a reaction, she suggests, against the self-immolation of the Romantic era. She also quotes a number of pantheistic outpourings that couch sexual awakening in the vocabulary of nature worship, most notably in the work of Anna-Élisabeth de Noailles, a writer she finds unjustly neglected. The second half of the century has brought the glorification of the "couple," two people creating a life together, as well as the advent of "anonymous intimacy," which has produced a good deal of writing about sexual gratification completely removed from emotional experience.

A rapid survey of Sullerot's book would lead to the conclusion that for most women love is extramarital (a review of the biographical sketches reveals very few wives writing to or about their husbands but many mistresses addressing their lovers), painful more often than joyful, all-encompassing, and frequently obsessive. Sullerot points out the narcissism in much of the writing she quotes. Women seem far more concerned with their own feelings than with the individual who has evoked them, and they are more likely to speak of their own beauty than of the physical attributes of the men they love, except in very recent years.

Women, or at least the women quoted here, seem in the words of Madame de Staël to "have no existence apart from love. The story of their life begins and ends with love." Falling in love brings them to life, and the breaking of a relationship is like death. They often seem to have no identity except that conferred on them by their lovers, a characteristic Sullerot finds disturbing and ultimately damaging. She attributes this obsessive single-mindedness to women's confinement to the realms of sentiment and domesticity; most of them had no other outlets for their feelings or their talents. The results could be destructive to both men and women. Sullerot speaks of women feeding upon, paralyzing, and devouring the men with whom they are associated and themselves being reduced to worthless husks if they are deserted, as they are with distressing frequency according to the biographies.

Any book dealing with women and love must focus at least briefly on the institution of marriage, and Sullerot dramatically illustrates the changing attitudes toward it. Early writings describe young girls unwillingly bound to repulsive old men; a medieval husband who locks his wife in a tower to ensure the legitimacy of his heirs; a Renaissance monster who makes his wife dress in black, shave her head, and drink from the skull of her murdered lover. Later passages show wives writing to gentler, more compatible spouses with whom they voluntarily share imprisonment and even death during the Revolution. The letters of Madame de La Fayette, wife of the popular general familiar to all students of American history, gave particularly moving insights into these sentiments. In general, however, even during the past two centuries the writers whom Sullerot quotes find more to attack than praise in matrimony. It is seen as enslaving by the followers of Comte de Saint-Simon and Charles Fourier in the nineteenth century, as a barrier to communication by Simone de Beauvoir. Somewhat surprisingly, however, Sullerot suggests that now, when people seek sexual satisfaction without emotional relationships, marriage may be the one thing that can ensure the survival of love in the sense in which she discusses it in this book.

Women on Love certainly proves the author's major premise, that woman's experience of love is not the same as man's. It demonstrates equally clearly that there is great diversity of experience among women. The passages quoted range from the passionate outcries of Héloïse to Abélard, to the pantheistic sensuousness of Anna-Élisabeth de Noailles, poetry, to the whimsical allegorical guide to courtship of Madeleine de Scudéry, to the blunt, matter-of-fact account of being raped recorded by Céleste Mogador, a dance hall hostess and minor novelist of the nineteenth century. The book is not, and does not claim to be, representative of all women in all places; for instance, an anthology that included work by English and American women would, as Sullerot points out, have to deal with the Puritan tradition that has never been important in France. She also recognizes that many women have not articulated their feelings—the poor, the illiterate, the happily married—her studies may give disproportionate emphasis to those who have suffered most and therefore felt the greatest need to express their feelings.

With these limitations in mind readers should find much to please them in this book. The introductory essays are detailed and thought-provoking, even when they do not come to easily comprehended conclusions. The voices of the more than 150 women whose words are quoted are still moving in Helen R. Lane's lucid translation. One loses, inevitably, the stylistic differences that would be obvious in French, but the selections nevertheless provide a tantalizing introduction to the work of many fine writers, both well-known and obscure, and the illustrations show changing attitudes toward love that need no translation. This is not a book for one sitting—the joys and pains of love, however effectively expressed, begin to blur after a chapter or two—but it offers much pleasure to anyone who wishes to savor it a few pages at a time.

Elizabeth Johnston Lipscomb

MAGILL'S
LITERARY ANNUAL

1981

CUMULATIVE AUTHOR INDEX
1977-1981

I

II

III

V

VI

VII

IX

XI

XII